"The Seek" June 20th 1975

Byron,
Best wishes for
the future we wish
all that will miss you.

Margaret Afford Baxter
(forget not that pragmatism
is above all the pursuit
form of thought)

Javier F. Vi____
"KEEP THE FAITH"

Julie Baldwin

Margaret Henahan

Natalie Thomson

Hans-Jürgen Richter

Good luck
wherever you be
Maggie Williams

Rob Brook

Tracey Holland

All the best —
Deana Fowler

Good luck always!
Lorna White

Wishing you lots of pleasure
centre stimulation,

Tom Lupriak

Tom Lockwood

THE
GREAT BOOK
OF WINE

CREATED AND PRODUCED
BY
EDITA LAUSANNE

THE GREAT BOOK OF WINE

Galahad Books • New York

Originally published in Switzerland by Edita Lausanne

First English Printing by World—1970

© Copyright 1969, 1970 by Edita Lausanne

Library of Congress Catalog Card Number: 74-80064

ISBN 0-88365-252-8

PRINTED IN SWITZERLAND

CONTENTS

FOREWORD 9

WINE AND CIVILIZATION

HISTORICAL OUTLINE 12
by Géo-H. Blanc, member of the Confrérie des Vignerons, Vevey, Switzerland

THE VINE SPECIES 16
by Géo-H. Blanc

VINES, WINE AND WORK 21
by Géo-H. Blanc

WINE AND THE ARTS 31
by Walter Tobler, vinegrower and specialist in folk art

THE GREAT WINE REGIONS OF THE WORLD

INTRODUCTION: THE VINE CONQUERS THE WORLD 40

THE WINES OF BURGUNDY 43
by Pierre Forgeot, delegate of the guild of merchants of fine wines of Burgundy

THE WINES OF THE RHÔNE 87
THE SWISS WINES OF THE RHÔNE VALLEY 90
by Philippe Cherix, member of the Confrérie du Guillon, Lutry, Switzerland
THE WINES OF SAVOY AND THE FRENCH JURA 96
by Joseph Jobé
THE WINES OF THE CÔTES DU RHÔNE, THE CÔTES DE PROVENCE, OF LANGUEDOC AND ROUSSILLON 97
by Jean Bertin-Roulleau, journalist and gastronome

THE WINES OF THE LOIRE 113
by Alexandre Fresneau, technical adviser to the I.N.A.O., Tours, France

THE WINES OF BORDEAUX 129
by Gaston Marchou, member of the Connétablie de Guyenne, Bordeaux

THE WINES OF SPAIN 171
by Eladio Asensio Villa, president of the International Office of Vine and Wine, Paris

THE WINES OF PORTUGAL 193
by Suzanne Chantal dos Santos, Portugal House, Paris

THE WINES OF ITALY 217
by Giovanni Dalmasso, president of the Italian Academy of Wine and Vine, Sienna

THE WINES OF THE RHINE 243

THE WINES OF THE UPPER RHINE AND NEUCHÂTEL 246
by Joseph Jobé

THE WINES OF ALSACE. 250
by Joseph Dreyer, member of the Confrérie Saint-Etienne, Colmar, France

THE WINES OF GERMANY. 253
by Helmut Arntz, president of the Society of the History of Wine, Germany

THE WINES OF CENTRAL EUROPE, THE BALKANS, THE SOVIET UNION 285
by Joseph Jobé and Boris Pogrmilović, editor-in-chief of *Poljoprivrednogvjesnika*, Zagreb, Yugoslavia

THE WINES OF THE EASTERN MEDITERRANEAN 297
by Joseph Jobé

THE WINES OF AFRICA

NORTH AFRICA 305
by Denis Bouvier

SOUTH AFRICA 310
by Kenneth Maxwell, Stellenbosch Farmers' Winery, South Africa

THE WINES OF NORTH AMERICA 321
by Robert Thompson, Wine Institute, San Francisco

THE WINES OF SOUTH AMERICA 335
by Denis Bouvier

THE WINES OF AUSTRALIA AND NEW ZEALAND 341
by John Stanford, Australian Wine Advisory Service, Sidney

VINTAGE CHART 344

THE WINES OF CHAMPAGNE 345
by Jean Arnaboldi, editor of the magazine *Bien vivre*, and Joseph Jobé

THE WAYS OF WINE AND MAN

WINE AND HEALTH: A DOCTOR'S GUIDE 368
by Gérard Debuigne, doctor and biologist

YOUR OWN CELLAR 375
by Bernard Grenouilleau, president of the Compagnie des Courtiers-Gourmets Piqueurs de Vin of the city of Paris

FOR DRINKING 385
by Pierre Andrieu, laureate of the International Wine Office, Paris, Grand Prix of the Confrérie des Chevaliers du Tastevin, Nuits-Saint-Georges

WINE AND FOOD 403
by Flavien Monod, gastronome

LIST OF COLOUR MAPS 413

CREDITS AND ACKNOWLEDGEMENTS 414

INDEX OF WINES 416

FOREWORD

The fact that millions of human beings have from earliest times regarded wine as a noble drink is due to an unusual sequence of events. When a comparison is made with other crafts and customs that have not survived the rough passage of history, the story of wine is remarkable. Without such a fortuitous succession of events, neither vine nor wine would ever have become so widely and so highly esteemed throughout the world.

In the beginning, the only grape capable of producing a pleasant-tasting drink grew wild all over the Middle Eastern countries. It was precisely here that men first began to cultivate the soil, select plants, and live in organized communities. Had the vine been just an ordinary plant, it would probably have shared the same fate as the Middle Eastern and Egyptian civilizations. It was the wine that saved the vine. This subtle beverage was found to possess extraordinary virtues; the intoxication it produced was attributed to divine powers. Consequently, the vine was held to be a gift from the heavens and wine a drink associated with the worship of the gods and the celebration of those favourites of the gods: heroes, poets and artists. Men offered wine in homage to the deity; in their turn, through wine, the gods endowed men with strength, inspiration and a liberating sense of well-being. Wine was at that time as much appreciated as it was rare.

Carried on the tide of the expansion of the Roman Empire, the vine spread and flourished far beyond the boundaries of its native land. Leather bottles, amphoras and butts, all filled with wine, found their way back to Rome from the heart of Gaul, Germania, Africa and the Iberian Peninsula. This wide-flung empire finally crumbled before the onslaught of the Barbarians, who knew nothing of wine, but the art of viniculture had been already handed on and the succeeding chapter in wine's history ensured not only its survival but its spectacular revival. Indeed, since the evening when Jesus Christ shared the bread and wine of the Lord's Supper with his disciples, wine has been an indispensable part in the cult of the new religion which was destined to spread throughout the world. Wherever Christianity was adopted, men endeavoured to cultivate vines and, either by indigenous production or importation, to obtain wine. Monks, bishops and missionaries promoted and encouraged viticulture. Nor were the nobility by any means indifferent to the prestige of a drink so closely associated with holy rites and one, moreover, that promoted gaiety and enthusiasm. Wine became their chosen drink for ceremonial occasions and victory celebrations.

Through the centuries, wine became more popular, and more democratic too. Industrial revolutions, social changes, the gradual breakdown of class barriers and the increasing economic power of the bourgeoisie were all responsible for this development. The luxury of a private cellar was no longer the prerogative of lords spiritual or temporal. Improvements in vine cultivation and vinification methods helped further this new turn of events.

As its religious symbolism and associations have evolved, so wine has developed an almost mystical reputation in everyday life. It endows every occasion with a special significance, whether a family gathering, lover's tryst or merely when friends meet. At the present time, we have the good fortune to enjoy the welcome traditions bequeathed to us. We must understand and appreciate this gift of the gods before we, too, pass it on.

What is the best way to cultivate a palate for wine? How and when should different wines be served? What are the finer points of wine? The answers to these and many other questions will be found in this book which provides a comprehensive range of information to put you at your ease whenever conversation turns to vine and wine. And never forget that you do not really taste a wine unless you look at it, nose it and talk about it.

Joseph Jobé

The names of wines are printed in small capitals and the species of vine in italics. British weights and measures are used throughout. The publishers have selected the illustrations in this book without being influenced in any way by commercial or publicity considerations. The same holds true for the some 6,500 wines in the lists.

WINE
AND CIVILIZATION

HISTORICAL OUTLINE

"And Noah began to be an husbandman, and he planted a vineyard: and he drank of the wine, and was drunken." This is the first biblical mention of that illustrious plant to which Old and New Testaments continually allude in countless allegories, parables, symbolic references and stories.

The history of the vine in actual fact, however, goes back much farther. From the very earliest times, it is linked with that of Eastern mythology and particularly with the legend of Dionysus which spread from Asia to Egypt, through Thrace and the Mediterranean lands.

The worship of Dionysus, or Bacchus, by his initiates went far beyond mere veneration for the creator and patron of the vine. In the earliest Orphic concept, Dionysus was considered a supreme deity. Soon, however, his character was defined more sharply: the cult of Dionysus developed into the celebration of vine and wine. In Athens, it furnished occasions for large-scale festivities, called the Dionysia, with processions, carousing and plays. In Rome, one day every year was dedicated to Bacchus. As for the Bacchanalia, in which more limited numbers indulged, they probably originated in Egypt. Thence they spread to Greece and finally to Rome where they degenerated into outrageous displays of debauchery and disorder. The public authorities at last banned the Bacchanalia, not without stormy arguments, in 186 B.C.

Thus wine, quite literally, had its own god. As a result, it enjoyed an almost sacred reputation, was featured in many religious ceremonies and pagan rituals even before the dawn of Christianity, and continued to play a prominent part in biblical writings. It is hardly surprising, therefore, that wine has inspired a wealth of pictorial representation, a symbolism of real documentary value. An Assyrian bas-relief shows two figures drinking against a setting of vine branches and grapes, while an Egyptian tomb decoration accurately depicts the order of viticultural tasks, the grape harvest and the cellar work in the presence of the scribe responsible for keeping the books. Writing tablets uncovered in Carthage, Tunis and Morocco supply us with similar information, and innumerable other relics and traces, whether buried underground or on the sea bed, are constantly coming to light. All these discoveries swell the already great volume of records with which museums, palaces, ancient temples, cathedrals, monasteries and castles are so plentifully stocked, so that archaeological remains alone could provide virtually all the information necessary to trace the history of wine cultivation back to remotest antiquity.

Wine occupies a regal place in the literature of every age. Centuries before Christ, Homer refers to the most famous vineyards in ancient Greece. He gives details concerning cellaring and drinking customs. Innume-

Almost always trained upwards, the Egyptian vine, claimed by Diodorus, the Greek historian, to have been imported by the god Osiris, served to embellish gardens. At this period, no royal or princely domain nor temple was without its vine-arbour and, accordingly, its wine.

The vine was also cultivated from a very early date in the basin of Mesopotamia and is frequently featured in Assyrian decoration during the time of the Sargonides. In this bas-relief from the seventh century B.C., King Assurbanipal enjoys a cup of wine under a vine-bower.

rable poets throughout the centuries have drawn on wine for their inspiration and some of them, notably Virgil, have made a valuable contribution to its history. On the other hand, accurate and comprehensive information can also be found in treatises on agriculture such as the *De re rustica* by Columella, a Latin agronomist born in Cadiz during the first century. He describes all the viticultural practices which are still applied today, such as tilling, planting, fertilizing, propagation by cuttings, grafting, layering, dressing, as well as winemaking.

Thanks to the works of such writers as the poet Hesiod, the historians Herodotus and Xenophon and the geographer Strabo, we know exactly where the vineyards were located in ancient times. In Asia, they flourished on the shores of the Persian Gulf, in Babylonia, in Assyria, on the shores of the Caspian, the Black Sea and the Aegean, in Syria and Phoenicia. Palestine, the homeland of the legendary Canaan grape, possessed a whole range of renowned wines. These wines were produced from plants that were selected and cultivated with the utmost care and in accordance with the methods prescribed by Hebrew law.

Flourishing in Egypt and Asia, the cultivation of the vine reached the heights of glory in Europe. It gained a foothold in Greece, particularly in those islands with the evocative names of Lemnos, Lesbos, Chios, Samos, Kos, Tenos and Naxos. On the latter the magnificent ruins of a huge portico, the last remains of the temple of Dionysus, still rise majestically above the sea. The chain of vineyards stretches on through Rhodes, Crete

Cythera, Leucadia and Corcyra. Suspended, as it were, between the two azure seas, these vines yielded wines which were shipped to the Mediterranean cities, chiefly to Rome, where good Greek wines, sometimes fetching exorbitant prices, long enjoyed unrivalled prestige. Meanwhile, the Italian vintage wines of Mamertine, Falernian and many others soon began to acquire comparable esteem. These were left to age for ten, twenty, thirty years, and sometimes even longer.

Great wine-drinkers as they were, the imbibing of the ancients frequently developed into inveterate drunkenness. The example was set at the highest social levels. The imperial orgies of Nero, Caracalla and Tiberius, to mention only a few, have remained famous. It was solely due to their bacchic exploits that many individuals won favour with Tiberius or other emperors and were thus invested with important offices. In Rome, for a very long time, women were forbidden to drink wine, yet certain Egyptian bas-reliefs depict women of high society clearly in a state of inebriation.

So it seems that drunkenness was not unknown in ancient times, but there were also those enlightened drinkers who knew how to appreciate, respect and to recognize wine as one of the finest gifts of nature and the gods. Wine was and remains one of the basic elements, even one of the motivating forces, of Mediterranean civilizations.

Reaching Gaul in the wake of the Roman armies, viticulture spread up the banks of the Rhône as far as Lyons, swept beyond to Burgundy, and on to the Rhine which it also reached via Helvetia. (Wine was known

This Greek jug, called an *oinochoe*, was used in the second half of the sixth century B.C. The only ornamentation on the black ground is a narrow red strip with the inscription "Lysias made me".

The Greeks used this striking high-handled jug, which was called a *cyathos*, to draw wine from the mixing-bowls and pour it into the drinkers' cups.

already in these regions. As soon as they had tasted it, the Gauls, the Cimbri and the Germans had began to import it in large quantities.) At the same time, travelling along the banks of the Garonne, the vine reached Bordeaux. In the third century it occupied the same areas in Europe as it does today, including the districts around the Danube, thanks to the Emperor Probus who willingly converted his legionaries into vinegrowers when there was no fighting to be done.

But Rome suffered the repercussions of this expansion. The overproduction of Italian vintages and the competition of wines from the Empire resulted in falling prices. The slump led the Emperor Domitian to order vines to be pulled up in some regions, particularly those that produced only mediocre wines. Such measures were not dissimilar to those put into practice much later, in the Middle Ages and even in modern times. For the same reason there developed laws, regulations and prohibitions regarding winemaking, trading and shipping, and even the economics of viticulture itself. Cato the Elder is known to have calculated the depreciation over a certain period of his slaves, who were to him no more than the machines of his time.

In spite of these crises and hazards, viticulture prospered, reaping the benefit of the Pax Romana, nor was it unduly affected by the fall of the Roman Empire and the disturbed period that ensued. The Church had taken affairs in hand. The bishop, master of the city, was its vinegrower and cellarman. Not only must enough wine be produced for Holy Communion but also to pay homage to the monarchs and high-ranking dignitaries who broke their journeys at the town. Most important of all, there were the episcopal funds to be kept supplied. This secular viticulture, flourishing throughout the Middle Ages, ran parallel to another branch of viticulture practised by the monks, with the abbeys serving as hostelries. Situated on the main highways, they welcomed men of power—who, in their turn, showed their generosity—as well as the poor and pilgrims. Both monks and travellers appreciated wine.

Kings, dukes and feudal lords were not long in following the example set by the monks and the Princes of the Church. Vines bordered the castle as they did the monastery. Wine retained all its former prestige.

With the growth of the bourgeoisie, many of the vineyards around the towns passed into the hands of rich citizens. The wine trade benefited from an ever increasing clientele in northern countries, particularly Holland, Flanders and England, to which there flowed a steady stream of ports, Madeiras, sherries and certain Mediterranean wines, wines from Bordeaux and Burgundy and, later, from Champagne. Bordeaux belonged to England from the twelfth to the fifteenth century and quite a number of Lord Mayors of London

In ancient times, the wine jugs used in Mediterranean countries assumed a great variety of shapes. This Etruscan *olpe* with its round mouth and high handle is reminiscent of the Greek jug *oinochoe*.

This Roman amphora, fashioned in a lustrous polychrome glaze, bears testimony to the great progress achieved in the workmanship and styling of wine vessels by the time of Alexander the Great.

were natives of Bordeaux. Flanders, however, recognized the Duke of Burgundy as its sovereign lord.

A great deal of wine was drunk in the countries to the north. In fact, their inhabitants proved far more intemperate than the natives of winegrowing countries, where the taster of ancient times, like his counterpart today, preserved an almost sacerdotal sobriety.

In 1579, the Dutch acquired independence and began concentrating all their efforts on commerce. They boasted a large and superlatively well organized navy, warehouses and stores. Systematically they applied themselves to a study of the market and succeeded in creating demand and controlling consumption. At the time of Louis XIV, they were buying vast quantities of "small" wines which they proceeded to blend, adulterate and resell at a large profit, openly defying the wine-exporting countries where the integrity of the vintages was scrupulously observed and where the wine trade was subjected to the close surveillance of the guilds and the authorities. It was also the Dutch who, initially for purely lucrative purposes, instigated the production and heavy consumption of spirits.

From the early Middle Ages, especially in France but also in Italy and the regions bordering on the Rhine, viticulture and the wine business played an important part in the extensive development of the communities, the sovereign granting various rights, franchises and privileges to the wineproducers and hence to the municipal authorities. This explains why the pages of the history of wine are often turned by political events. For instance, among the leaders of the Paris uprising in July 1789, when the Bastille was destroyed, were certain wine merchants who hoped to capitalize on the riots and bring about the abolition of the very unpopular taxes levied on wines imported into the capital.

As early as the Renaissance, the map of European vineyards corresponded very closely to that of today. Colonization and the spread of Christianity brought viticulture to countries overseas, such as Latin-America, Mexico, California, South Africa; or gave it new impetus, as in Algeria. There, as in all other Moslem countries, viticulture had been curbed by the teachings of the Koran which forbade the use of alcohol. Nonetheless, twelve centuries after Mohammed Algeria was among the leading wineproducing countries.

Among the many vicissitudes in the history of the vine and wine, the cryptogamic diseases and the parasites brought from America in the middle of the last century were the most deadly. But man's ingenuity and perseverance invariably found a way to overcome all such calamities. During the nineteenth century, winemaking methods were greatly improved, and today they have reached an almost scientific degree of perfection. In this age of space flights and nuclear science, wine has retained all its former prestige. Closely linked with the origin of our civilization, it represents one of its proudest and most pacific achievements. Wine is still the most gracious and the noblest drink of all.

THE VINE SPECIES

"Plant your vineyard from good stock." The old French adage proclaims a fundamental truth and underscores the all-important part played by the species of vine in determining the success of the end result, whether this be the wine glinting in our glass, the unfermented grape juice faithfully echoing the original flavour of the fruit, or the ripe young cluster of grapes decorating the dining-table.

The knowledge of the countless varieties of vine, their distant origins, their types, and their history linked to the history of civilization itself, is a many-sided science, embracing botany, biology, anthropological geography, and even paleontology. The layman, however, has barely ever heard such words as *Merlot*, *Gamay* or *Riesling*. Little does he care if the northern vineyards are descended from wild vines, as some specialists would have us believe, or if these vineyards were planted with vines brought from southern climes by those migrating north. The true wine-lover, on the other hand, is well informed in such matters.

Among the species yielding red wine that are cultivated in France, he will award the palm to the *Pinot Noir* from Burgundy, the *Gamay* from Beaujolais, the *Cabernet-Sauvignon* from Bordeaux, and the *Grenache* which thrives along the banks of the Rhône, in Provence, Languedoc and Roussillon. He will also award honourable mentions to the *Malbec* and the *Merlot*, grapes which are often blended with *Cabernet*, as well as to *Cinsaut*, *Mourvèdre*, *Carignan*, *Savagnin* from the Jura, the *Black Muscat* from Frontignan, the Savoyard *Mondeuse* and the *Tannat* cultivated in the Hautes-Pyrénées.

The range of white grapes is equally wide. There is the *Chardonnay*, responsible for the excellence of the wines from Champagne and the vintage wines from Burgundy, the *Sauvignon Blanc* and *Chenin* which produce the wines from the Loire and Anjou, *Semillon* from the famous vineyards in the Gironde, *Muscadet*, *Clairette*, the *White Muscats* and, finally, the *Chasselas* with which most of the vineyards in the French-speaking cantons of Switzerland are planted.

All these species of grape yield a great variety of different wines, alternately full-bodied, fruity, robust or rich, but this is not the place to start a glossary of the subtle and innumerable nuances so readily distinguished by the professional palate.

Several French grape species have been introduced into other wineproducing countries, such as Spain, Italy, Russia and California, whilst the *Sylvaner*, *Riesling* and *Traminer* which yield the Rhine and Moselle wines can also be found as far afield as Hungary and Czechoslovakia, and notably in Alsace and Switzerland.

In Italy, a variety of *White Muscat* yields the Asti. *Barbera* originates in Piedmont, *Nerello* in Sicily. *Soave* prospers from Verona to the Adriatic. Spanish sherry, Portuguese port and Madeira also have their own species of grape while California, a large wineproducer, has adopted the wines from this hemisphere.

Sometimes a wineproducer will content himself with one particular species of grape; but then again, after due consideration, he may decide to combine two or more different varieties. Thus, the wine from Médoc owes its scent and spiciness to the *Cabernet*, its well-balanced richness to the *Merlot*. Similarly, the grape species *Grenache*, *Mourvèdre*, *Syrah* and *Clairette* blend their different virtues and temperaments in the opulent Châteauneuf-du-Pape, the leading Côtes du Rhône.

Apart from the vines cultivated for wine grapes, there are all those that yield dessert grapes: the French *Gros-Vert* and *Chasselas*, the Italian *Regina* and *Ignea*, the Spanish *Almeria* and *Malaga*, the *Rish Baba* from Persia, the *Emperor* from California, and many more besides, without forgetting the widely cultivated *Zante* and *Muscat* and other varieties whose grapes are usually dried and eaten in the form of raisins.

This brief summary has only skimmed the surface of a major chapter in the study and lore of wine. Albeit rudimentary, its aim has been to evoke the wondrous riches and diversity of this complex and universally famous plant which seems truly to have been, together with corn, one of the earliest and most ancient products of cultivation.

The botanist Linné conferred the name of *vitis vinifera* on the vine which provides us with both dessert grapes and wine grapes. Its origin can be traced back to the Tertiary period, some forty-five million years ago. Today, several thousand species of this plant are known to man.

16

Dessiné d'après Nature par Spaëtte de Fontainve.

17

The *Chardonnay* (below) is also called *Pinot Blanc Chardonnay*. Widely grown in Champagne and particularly in the famous "Côte des Blancs" region, this grape endows Champagne with all its piquant freshness and delicacy, and also accounts for the fame of the great white wines of Burgundy. Californian winegrowers use it to produce a light, white table wine.

For a long time, the *Pinot Blanc* (above) was confused with the *Chardonnay* (above right). *Pinot Blanc* is found in Burgundy, Champagne, Alsace and in Germany, where it is known by the name of *Weissburgunder*. It is also grown in Hungary, Yugoslavia and California. This is one of the great species.

The *Harslevelü* (lime leaf) is of Hungarian origin and has never left its native soil. Blended with another grape, the *Furmint*, it produces the famous Tokay wine which, incidentally, has no connection with the *Tokay* from Alsace, a wine made from the *Pinot Gris*.

18

The *Grenache* appears to have originated in Spain where it is known as *Garnacha* or *Alicantina*. After having been somewhat spurned, it has now acquired great popularity on both sides of the eastern Pyrenees and as far as the lower Rhône valley.

The *Yellow Riesling* of the Moselle (below, right), a selected grape, gives wines of this region freshness and attractive sharpness. Other *Riesling* selections are cultivated in Alsace, Austria, Bulgaria, Switzerland, Yugoslavia, South Africa and California.

The *Pinot Noir* (below) probably originated in Burgundy. One of the great varieties, it is found in regions having the same climate as its native province. Its German name is *Blauburgunder*. The juice of the *Pinot Noir* is colourless and it is the colouring matter in the grape skins which, during fermentation in the vat, brings to the wine the brilliant ruby hue so extolled by the poets.

The *Riesling* (above) is pre-eminently a species originating on the banks of the Rhine and the Moselle, but it adapts perfectly to various other regions. The *Riesling* from Rheingau has its own very positive character and should on no account be confused with the *Riesling Italico* which is produced from another species of grape and thus yields an altogether different type of wine.

The *Chenin Noir* (opposite, left) was the original vine of Anjou. A hardy and fertile species when young, it yields a delicate, clear wine of a fine red colour. Its cultivation is confined exclusively to the valley of the Loire.

19

VINES, WINE AND WORK

My grandfather was a vinegrower. I remember seeing him using the sulphur spray which was carried on one's back and worked by means of a pump. In those days he wore an old straw hat, old jacket, old trousers and ancient laced boots, all tinged with the blue of the Bordeaux mixture which also stained his moustache and his heavy eyebrows. I remember, too, the wine harvests. In those days, they used to press the grapes, in the vineyards, into containers which were then emptied into a large barrel securely fixed on to a cart. It was quite a long journey to the wine-press. There, in the open, waited an enormous vat. The barrel was rolled on to two stout planks and spewed the grapes into the vat whose contents were subsequently transferred to the wine-press.

The wine-press was worked by an enormous wooden beam called a yoke. At one end there was a rope whose other end was wound round a second vertical beam, turned on its own axis by means of meshed cogs and driven by a crank which was operated by hand. All night long, the creaking of the beams, the groaning of the stretched ropes and the metallic rhythm of the ratchets could be heard, while the must, in its natural state, free from additives and rich in its own yeasts, trickled through pipes into the cellar. And two or three days later the fanstastic work of the fermentation began.

This is not ancient history; it happened less than fifty years ago. Yet in those days, men still seemed to take real pleasure in performing these humble and manual tasks, in practising this craft which perpetuated the time-honoured traditions to which the vinegrower was profoundly attached but which, frequently, were very localized and accepted as routine. Then, too, almost everything depended on the efforts and the skill of man, that highly developed, intelligent machine, that very inexpensive source of power.

Today, my grandfather's vines are cultivated in much the same way as they were fifty years ago. They still occupy terraces laid out on steep slopes, are still planted in relatively close rows. This is the custom in nearly all northern vineyards planted on the sides of hills. Elsewhere, in the plains, where the vine can spread out at its ease and where it is encouraged to stretch to medium or full height, machines have long since made their appearance. Subsoil ploughs break up the ground and turn it over, work that can also be carried out with explosives.

Tractors now clatter along between the well-spaced rows, pulling machines behind them that clean the soil and lay the second dressing. Lightening the labours of today's vinegrower are improved sprays, usually machine-driven, atomizers and other accessories, sometimes airborne on airplanes or helicopters, which spread insecticides, fungicides and other substances.

If the cultivator of vines in the days of yore could be compared to a foot-soldier, he now belongs to the ranks of a motorized army of far greater efficiency. As for the production of wine, it has increasingly become the business of oenologists, scientifically trained, who spend much of their time bent over test-tubes, microscopes and other equipment, converting the mysteries of wine into chemical formulae. However, they do not disdain the vinicultural experience handed down through countless generations nor neglect visits to the cellars to inspect the wine in its own habitat, tasting it critically, guiding its progress and nurturing it to maturity as has been done from time immemorial.

Indeed, even if methods have been modernized and the vinegrower, in order to secure his livelihood, has resorted to technical advances and to rationalization of work, the responsible tasks involved in the cultivation of vines and production of wines have remained basically and essentially the same.

Naturally, practices may vary, depending on the region, climate and species of grape. But, by and large, the vinegrower in France performs the same tasks and goes through very much the same motions as his counterpart in Bessarabia or California, experiencing the same hopes and anxieties, the same satisfactions and disappointments. Dependent on his vines he is, himself, subject to the eternal rhythm of the seasons. While today machines have taken over so many viticultural and vinicultural processes, there are still many tasks, such as dressing the vines, that still require, and will always require, the experience and unique manual dexterity of men.

The new year for the vines begins in November when, the grapes all gathered in, the vinegrower thoroughly sluices and scrubs his wine-press, utensils, appliances, vats and casks, not forgetting to use the sulphured wick to prevent mildew. The last leaves drop away from the vine stems after a final glorious display of rich autumnal colours: every shade of gold and yellow in the case of the white grape plants, the resplendent spec-

This illuminated design from the fifteenth century, taken from the *Livre des profits champêtres* by Pierre de Crescens, illustrates the stages in vine cultivation during the Middle Ages: hoeing, weeding, training plants on trellises, grape-gathering, pressing by foot and broaching the cask.

trum of crimsons and purples for those which bear the black grape. Thus stripped of its working apparel, the vine obtains to all outward appearances a brief respite.

But if the vine may sleep, the vinegrower can take no rest. This is the time of year when, not so very long ago, the women and children pulled out the vine-props, laying them in orderly groups of six, well spread out between the rows of vines. Today, it is increasingly the practice to leave the vine-props in position as metal vine stakes have long since come into use. Moreover, vines trained into the shape of a goblet, the stem supported by a central prop, seem gradually to be ceding ground to vines trained on wire.

Under the obliging sun of an Indian summer, earth that has gradually slipped downhill is transported by the vinegrower back to the top of his sloping vineyard. This arduous task was performed with the aid of a basket harnessed on the back in times gone by, so that after a few years of this work the same man could truthfully claim to have carried the entire vineyard on his

back. Nowadays, this burden and other heavy work has been taken over by power-driven machines, whose sputtering fills the air. But first of all, the digging had had to be done, trenches to be made at the base of the vines all along the walls. And if the walls had shown signs of wear or damage, the vinegrower had to take up his trowel and perform a mason's work, repairing and repointing. "Mortar of winter, mortar of iron", so runs an old French saying.

Earth to carry uphill, walls to reinforce are jobs to be done in terraced vineyards spread over the hillsides and not in vineyards on the plains. However, whether on the hills or plains, autumn is the time for tilling and ridging, worked by ploughs which lift and turn over the earth all along between the rows. The old vine-plants must also be grubbed out and their gnarled, blackened and twisted stumps sometimes feed their owner's fire.

Naturally, all this time, down in the cellar, the new wine requires care and constant attention. At ground level, the vinegrower takes shelter from the cold and inclement weather, repairs his tools, puts his equipment in order, cuts new vine-props, sharpening them into points and impregnating them with tar or sulphur. It is also in winter that he prepares the straw used for tying the vine shoots, although this is being replaced more by metal or plastic fasteners.

Once Christmas is past, time rushes by. At the end of January, with the days stretching out, the vinegrower feels a compulsive urge to take up his pruning shears. "If we would drink," runs an old French proverb, "we must dress the vine before St. Gregory's day", St. Gregory's day falling on March 12th.

Dressing the vine necessitates long experience and the greatest care. The olant must be trained and the root stock kept to a reasonable size. Most important of all, production must be controlled, next year's fruit

VIGNERON

Vinegrowers of every age were strenuous workers.   In 1351, the King of France required that they perform "their day's work loyally, from sunrise to sunset", which left little time for drinking the product.

growing on the young shoots that sprout from last year's vine stock. Therefore, these root stocks must be judiciously dressed and, following the example of Janus, the god whose two faces looked in opposite directions and who gave his name to the year's first month, the future judged while paying due consideration to the past.

The vinegrower knows that an overly sturdy vine stock yields fewer fruit than one of less strength that produces a generous quantity but runs the risk of becoming spent. He also knows that the young shoots farthest from the stock bear the most. All his knowledge is behind the apparently casual wielding of his pruning shears. Every cut displays experience and foresight, guiding the development of each branch. If he cuts short, leaving only two or three buds, he wishes to husband the vine stock and not force it to an immoderate yield. If he cuts long, leaving three or four buds to a branch, he aims at a more plentiful harvest. It is up to the vinegrower to decide whether the vine is capable of such output. A wise master, he decides nothing without due consideration and as a result the vine, originally a highly fertile plant, is made to comply obediently with the prescribed directions. These directions vary according to region, species of grape, soil and climate whether the vine must have low, medium or tall growths, single stem, lattice-work or "goblet" shaped branches. Dressing vines may be a highly specialized technique but it is also an art and involves a kind of complicity between the man and the plant.

When winter is over, the dressed shoots weep, each horn bearing its glittering pearl. The buds, still muffled in their fleecy down, are ready to open. The vinegrower experiences his first qualms. At any moment, the frost can cut down the young shoots. If this happens, the vines will have to be faithfully tended throughout the year without hope of a satisfactory yield. In northern vineyards, this threat hangs over the vinegrower's head until the end of April, and sometimes even into May the beginning of which month is notorious for its treacherous weather.

Before dressing, the vinegrower has been attending to grafting, essential since the arrival of the phylloxera, a minute plant louse which found its way to Europe from America in the middle of the last century. This terrible little creature attacked the roots and wrought the most appalling havoc; it would have brought about the annihilation of European vineyards had not the appropriate remedy been found and applied. It was discovered that the roots of the American vines were immune to phylloxera and so now almost every European vine is grafted on to an American root. When this has been done the vinegrower lays out the grafts in boxes full of damp sawdust, which are then stacked in some overheated place. In May, they will be planted in nurseries. Since this job requires considerable care and skill, the vinegrower sometimes prefers to entrust it to the nurseryman.

With winter well and truly behind, and a warm haze rising in the morning sun, the first small flowers venture timidly along the foot of the wall while machines resume their humming and all nature begins to stir. The spring ploughings leave behind a clean and tidy vineyard, a joy to behold with its tautened and refurbished wires stretching out as far as eye can see, or with its vine props standing to attention like the pikes of a vast army of footsoldiers drawn in battle array. The soil, as yet innocent of weeds, conceals the ploughed-in manure, unless dried manure or mineral fertilizers have been spread, which is increasingly the practice.

From now until the end of summer, unless the vinegrower relies entirely on weed-killers, the motorized hoe will regularly travel between the rows of vines, replacing men who, not long since, still raked away the weeds with pathetic doggedness from spring to autumn. Each vinegrower's descendants emancipate themselves more and more from this drudgery, acquiring machines that do the job just as well and much more quickly.

In the spring, the grafts in the nursery must be lifted, their roots trimmed and paraffin wax applied. They are then put in sand in a cool place, to prevent them shooting before they are planted in their permanent vineyard. It is also in the spring, as soon as the buds open, that the vinegrower begins the treatments against parasites, insects and cryptogams. This battle with disease continues without respite until a few weeks before the grape harvest.

The red spider is first on the scene, followed shortly afterwards by the first batch of caterpillars and the first fluttering swarms of dancing butterflies. The mushrooms and other fungi are not far behind. The drama has begun, and the vinegrower is all too grimly

This miniature from the *Tacuinum sanitatis*, a medical book translated from the Arabic in the fourteenth century, portrays in the most natural and unaffected manner grape-picking as it was carried out during that time in Italy. Worthy of note is the grape-treading, a primitive method of pressing now abandoned; and the use of composite crops, still widely practised in some parts of Italy even to this day.

commonly known as vine-worms, ravage the leaves or bunches of grapes before, during and after flowering.

The fungoid growths are equally destructive. The oidium's fibres spread over leaves and branches, their sinister suckers infiltrating everywhere. Mildew is the enemy of leaf, branch and grape, which it withers, darkens and dries out. Black rot, also from America, and the fungi causing white rot or excoriose, which sets in after hail, are allies of those fungi causing root rot and a grey rot, a disease of the grape; and finally there is apoplexy, the ultimate and fatal phenomenon of a stock disease. These pests could claim their right to exist as being granted by the Creator but, if allowed to proliferate, they could quickly put an end to the cultivation of the vine.

The vinegrower, once again enlisting the aid of the scientist, relies on his laboratory to produce all kinds of washes and powders for spraying and on the technologist to devise all manner of machines from the humble bellows and the old hand-operated spray, carried on the back, to self-propelled sulphurators, powered diffusers and atomizers. The arsenal includes flowers of sulphur, liquid sulphur, copper sulphate, lime, carbonate of soda, acids, perchlorides, oxides, hydrates, dioxides, arsenic and nicotine. Finally, there are multi-purpose concentrated products called synthetic fungicides, each combining several remedies to simplify the vinegrower's work. All these chemicals are administered to the vines, with the same care and foresight as a mother tends her child, in order to ensure their satisfactory growth and development.

familiar with the plot and the leading players with their outlandish names, although he is never sure about what will happen in the last act.

Among the animal parasites, of which the phylloxera is the most deadly, there is a large cast of coleoptera. The larva of the leaf-hopper devour the undersides of leaves. The common vinegrub is also dubbed "the writer" because it busies itself cutting out fine strips on the leaves, resembling writing, while its larva attack the vine roots. The leaf-roller, which rolls up the leaves into cigar shape, inside which its grubs snugly nest, joins with weevils of various kinds to complete this unwelcome throng.

The pyralis, the two annual generations of cochylis or vine-moth, the four generations of leaf-roller moths or endemis are very attractive fly-by-nights, waking at dusk or dancing in the moonlight, but their caterpillars,

The artists of the Middle Ages, who were so fond of depicting the various crafts, have bequeathed us faithful pictorial representations in richly illustrated prayer books. The cooper's art was not forgotten. Here are vat-makers, jug-makers, shook-makers, and hogshead binders busy before the approaching wine harvest. After chamfering and turning over the staves, they fit and bind them together with wooden hoops.

Great precision, perseverance and endless patience are required. There can be no clock-watching when the work is pressing; during these long summer days the time for sleep is all too short. Arduous work indeed, spurred on by the hope of due rewards, but also accompanied by the philosophical acceptance of possible frustration. Then, patience and hope give way to resignation which is neither weakness nor despair but courageous wisdom, for the vinegrower can always hope for better fortune next year, as the same vine lives on through many years, good, bad or indifferent.

The battle against parasites, launched in the spring, is waged alongside the other viticultural tasks, particularly those concerned with the leaves. Called "thinning out" in certain regions, this is the first dressing carried out on the young shoots at the time the dry branches are pruned. First of all, as soon as the vine has flowered, the leaves are thinned out and the unwanted buds cut away. The shoots appearing at the foot of the vine and others which do not contribute to the growth of the plant, sprouting elsewhere than on the dressed branches—all such parasite growth is removed. This delicate task, requiring almost specialist skill, prepares for and facilitates the next winter's dressing. The strength of each plant is taken into account. Carried out early in the season in vineyards to the south, this operation is left until later in those regions subject to frost. But the vine will not wait so this work must be done quickly and perhaps extra labour employed.

Next the tips of the herbaceous shoots are removed, thus controlling future growth. Later and up until August, new toppings or clippings are carried out, although the usefulness of this practice seems questionable. Completing this stage of the work the vine shoots are attached to their props or guide-wires with straw or raffia ties, or rings.

For ten to fifteen days or more the buds in each cluster flower one by one and an exquisite perfume floats over the vineyard, reminiscent of mignonette or incense. Sunny, warm weather gives the vines the chance to blossom and set quickly and in the best conditions. Rain and cold retard the flowering and hamper fertilization. Under these conditions, the pollen may be washed away or the crop may fail because of degenerative phenomena or even by excessive vigour of the plant.

If everything goes according to plan, the buds come out well, the plant has flowers in good weather, there is no loss of pollen and all the parasites are eradicated.

The year's labours are rewarded. This scene from the mid-fifteenth century comes from the prayer book which belonged to the Duchess of Burgundy. The seasonal grape pickers, hired in market-places, are paid in cash or in kind by the owner of the vines. It has been a good harvest and everybody, well content, goes off to the wine-press, which is the property of the local lord of the manor or of the local council.

CRIEUR DE VIN . 1586.

Sworn public officials, the wine criers were commissioned to promote the sale of wine on behalf of the inn-
keepers.   Jug and glass in hand, they vaunted their wares round the streets or outside the inns. Patron-
ized by the King of France, their guild grew to great power in the thirteenth and fourteenth centuries.

This ink and wash sketch by Leonar Bramer of Delft, entitled "Halt before the Inn", deftly portrays a pastoral scene of the seventeenth century. The wine shop of those days was often no more than a casually converted farmhouse where, in summer months, passers-by stopped for a few refreshing moments. A barrel serves as a table. Who cares? Life is for living, there is music and companionship and the wine is cool.

The small, hard grapes that the young bunch proudly held out towards the sun now droop towards the ground. Gradually, they become translucent. They are beginning to ripen. About this time, the shoots begin to turn brown and lignify. The owner walks round his vines, carrying brush and pot of paint, marking the stocks from which, in a few months time, he will take grafts for future nurseries.

While the vine, now ripening, passes through its third phase, the vinegrower can at last obtain a brief respite. However, right up to harvest time, a danger hangs over his head. One sudden shower of hail may crash down with a storm, despite all the artillery the vinegrowers can muster in the shape of rockets that explode into the very heart of the clouds—the result is ruthless destruction of leaves, shoots and bunches of grapes.

Whatever the summer may have been, there comes at last a time when in the wide autumnal skies vast, wheeling flocks of starlings appear, avid for the ripe grapes, only momentarily frightened off by the firecrackers exploded by alert vintners among the vines. High time now for the harvest!

First comes a thorough clean-up of all the implements to be used, which are subsequently left to dry in the sun. As soon as the grapes are ripe, the pickers spread out across the vines. The grapes are heaped in crates and loaded on lorries which are quickly driven to the press. Bearing little resemblance to a wine-press of my grandfathers' day on its stone pedestal, with its beam and huge vertical screw, the modern version is a horizontal cylinder into which the harvested grapes are poured after first being crushed in another machine. In fact, especially in large enterprises such as the wine co-operatives, the press has become a kind of small factory where everything is carried out faster, more reliably and where there is very much less manual work than in the past. Knobs and levers are pressed to bring electric, hydraulic and pneumatic forces into play.

In some enterprises, the red grapes are no longer vatted, the process which gives the wine its colour. This operation, extending over several days, necessitates considerable equipment which obviously takes up far more space than the cylinder where the grapes are simply heated to achieve the same result.

29

This progress and these new methods have in no way altered or detracted from the extraordinary phenomenon of fermentation which the ancients attributed to some superhuman spirit and whose mystery was at last explained by Louis Pasteur.

The yeasts responsible for fermentation are present on the grapes, carried by the winds and insects—supplied, in fact, by nature. But once again that dispenser of the good as well as the bad has been tamed and harnessed to suit man's requirements. Careful observation, selection and judicious training have resulted finally in the production of fine, good yeasts, free from such bacterial maladies as the *tourne*, acescence and other vine diseases. Strong, healthy, honest yeasts prevent sluggish, incomplete fermentation. They are incorporated in the must after being rendered aseptic.

When fermentation is finally complete, the yeasts have finished their work and fall to the bottom of the vat where they form the wine lees. After depositing its lees, the young and troubled milky new wine, saturated with carbonic gas, will clear of its own accord, but usually man lends a helping hand. Clarifying the wine, by adding gelatine-based products, white of egg or separated milk which draw the lees and other impurities down to the bottom of the vat is a long-established craft, now replaced by the more efficient and less hazardous filtering process which also rids the wine of any doubtful germs it may still contain. Among these are the germs which, needing air, proliferate on the surface: the bacteria of acescence which can change the wine into vinegar, and the surface fungoid growths which spread a thin, whitish film over the wine, reducing its alcoholic strength and value.

To avoid such dangers, the cellarman shields his wine from contact with the air by filling his vats right up to the top, or by burning a sulphured wick to use up any oxygen left in the empty space over the liquid.

Even more dangerous are the germs breeding in the depths of the wine and not requiring air. The *tourne* readily attacks badly fermented wine, making it extremely unpalatable, while the dreaded grease disease makes the wine ropy, oily and insipid. Red wines, poor in tannin and acids, are vulnerable to another disease that turns them bitter.

So much for the bacteria. But there are still various chemical actions to contend with. Brown casse yellows and sweetens new wines and gives them an artificial taste of age. Black casse gives the wine an unpleasant, leaden colour while white casse makes it cloudy and milky. Again, the wine may acquire musty, earthy smells and stagnant, mouldy tangs, reminiscent of iron or bad egg: these are nearly always the result of faults or negligence, carelessly picked grapes, badly maintained vats or cellars, and are seldom met with in the cellar of the conscientious and enlightened vinegrower.

Such mishaps and diseases can generally be prevented by ensuring the utmost cleanliness from the grape harvest to the time of bottling. A good cellarman should also keep his eye on the thermometer. Wine appreciates warmth while it is coming up to its second fermentation, during which it loses its excess acidity, but it needs cool surroundings to clarify itself. Unless these conditions are fulfilled, the wine becomes capricious and unpredictable. In actual fact, the producer could confine himself to certain essential tasks: thorough preparation of his casks, the judicious management of yeats, careful cellaring and the intelligent use of the sulphurated wick; ensuring that his vats are constantly full; heating, cooling and airing the cellars when the wine demands it and, finally, filtering and decanting at the right moment. Given these and good weather, and if the wine contains the correct elements in the right proportions, all should be well.

However, within the limits of statutory regulations, which clearly stipulate that wine is pure, fermented grape juice, oenology prescribes various methods to remedy various deficiencies, defects or lack of balance, to accelerate or retard various vinicultural processes.

The vinegrower's cellar is a hallowed place, jealously guarded, secret and reserved for the initiated who form a kind of fraternity. Highest in rank is the wine-taster. Often the diplomatic envoy from some customer, he takes his responsibilities seriously. On other occasions, he may be just a favoured guest. At all times, he is an artist, endowed with enviable physical attributes, the first being excellent sight in order to detect anything that may dim or cloud the crystal transparency of the wine. His nose is a finely-tuned instrument, capable of capturing and analysing every nuance of the bouquet. His taste buds are particularly acute. Having examined and critically sniffed the wine, he rolls it round his mouth, chops it up and down against his palate, rests it on his tongue and contemplates, allowing his senses to appeal to his memory. And at last he lets the noble liquid slip gently down inside him, feels the warm glow, savours its strength and flavour and then, and only then, pronounces judgement.

This elaborate ritual in honour of the wine is perfectly understandable. When the glass is raised in the cellar, the wine gleams as though it held captive the fugitive summer long past, bequeathing us some of its lingering light and splendour. At this moment, the vinegrower reaps the full recompense for his efforts. He now finds justification for the pride that never leaves him throughout the long seasons and his entire working life which he has dedicated to this hard and unremitting task, constantly renewing his confidence in nature and his faith in what the future holds in store.

WINE AND THE ARTS

Throughout the viticultural regions of Europe, vine and wine have always provided sources of inspiration for popular art. For centuries, craftsmen have embellished all kinds of workaday articles which play a part in the making and selling of wine, ranging from the wine-press itself to the sign above the tavern. In the Middle Ages, popular art reflected, above all, the vision of a profoundly religious man with a keen sense of symbolism. Christ was frequently represented on or around the wine-press. The wine-press itself is an allegory of Christ's sufferings and a symbol of the prophecy of Isaiah (lxiii,3): "Alone I have trodden at the wine-press and no man from among the peoples was with me. I have trampled them in my wrath, I have crushed them in my fury; their blood has spattered my apparel and all my raiment is stained withal."

All through the Middle Ages the Bible, which mentions vine and wine in more than two hundred passages, proved a virtually inexhaustible source of inspiration.

One of the most frequently used themes was that of Joshua and Caleb. The two scouts sent by Moses to explore Palestine brought back a gigantic bunch of Canaan grapes, a sign of the anticipated plenty of the Promised Land. The vine symbolized Christ and life eternal; hence the bunch of grapes held by Jesus, Mary and various saints always alludes to the sacrifice of Christ and the Last Supper. In medieval art, the shape of the vine, symbol of God's people in the Bible, was often borrowed to represent Christ's genealogical tree. Down the centuries, vinegrowers naïvely entrusted the destiny of their vines to popular saints. As rough weather, parasites and disease have always menaced the vine, it is not surprising that when a saint performed a miracle that favoured the vines or the wine he was quickly adopted as protector of the vineyard. In Switzerland, for instance, St. Othmar and St. Theodule were both credited with increasing the quantity of wine during bad harvests; hence they were accorded, as

Billhook in hand, St. Vernier patronizes the vineyards of the Rhine and Burgundy. St. Vincent, attired in deacon's vestments, is also a patron of Burgundy wine. St. Urban, the thirteenth-century Pope, protected Alsace and many German wineproducing regions from hail.

Joshua and Caleb, sent to Canaan to reconnoitre the country, discovered grapes which grew to an unbelievable size. They hoisted one of the giant bunches on to a pole and carried it back together.

a symbol, a small wine cask. St Vernier was always depicted as a vinegrower and was worshipped in the Rhineland, in Burgundy and the Auvergne. The martyrology of the French Church has this to say about St. Urban: "His patronage in the sight of God often protected the vines from bad weather and destruction. More than once, by his prayers, he drove away the rains, scattered the winds, preserved the vines from storms which threatened: it is because of this that vinegrowers invoke his aid against the vagaries of inclement weather and he is always portrayed with a bunch of grapes." This particular St. Urban was Bishop of Langres. His rôle seems to have been confused with that of his namesake, the more famous Pope Urban, so much so that today it is the celebrated Pope who is recognized as the patron saint of vinegrowers. Many saints became protectors of vineyards simply because their feast-days happened to fall during the flowering of the vine or the ripening of the grapes. As for St. Vincent, very popular throughout Burgundy, he was probably adopted by vinegrowers as a result of a play on the French words *sent le vin*, in other words, *Vincent*. An old saying, still quoted in Santenay, maintains that any vinegrower not keeping St. Vincent's day will have his buttocks eaten by ants while he is having tea. St. Vincent is generally shown as a deacon, holding a palm leaf and a bunch of grapes.

From the sixteenth century onwards, almanacs and record books began to appear, containing symbols of the months as well as pictures of the vinegrower's principal tasks, weeding, dressing the vines, harvesting or making wine casks. These printed pictures brought themes hitherto only found in the prestigious prayer books owned by the great feudal lords within reach of a much wider audience.

Again from the same period, and taking into account the increasing skill of contemporary craftsmen, various articles and guild emblems connected with viticulture proliferated. Local customs began to spring up. In addition to their round-topped chests and guild flags, the vinegrowers, like the coopers, had their own domestic figurines. A favourite subject was the vintager, bowed under the weight of the narrow wooden tub full of grapes on his back. In German-speaking countries these figurines were known as *Buttenmännchen* and were often very attractively worked in wood or metal, gracing the table at social gatherings.

Even today at the carnival that marks the end of the grape harvests in Lower Austria, very unusual types of decorative emblems, peculiar to the region, can still be seen in the traditional processions. These are either wheels made from plaited straw, indicating that the vinegrower is selling his new wine on the spot, or painted wooden suns, drawing attention to the fact that the vineyard is being looked after by guardians. Another interesting local custom is the parading of the "vineyard goat", a frame of wood with a carved goat's head, laden with fruit and generally considered as the symbol of fertility. At the end of the festival, it is either sold at auction or presented to the mayor.

In all wineproducing districts, the architecture of the vinegrower's house is a compromise between work requirements and economic necessity. Naturally, the style varies from one region to another, and according to the social and financial status of the individual, but it is always noticeably different from the farmhouses and other country dwellings. The byre and the barn lose ground to the preponderance of vinegrowing over other kinds of cultivation. The cellar, forming the very foundation of the entire building, not only influences the appearance of the house but often indicates the financial circumstances of the owners by its decoration, borrowed from town residences. Sometimes its wide, arched door is the main ornamental feature of the façade. Whatever kind of building it may be, brick or stone, its cellar is always constructed in a similar way. It is made as deep and thick as possible and usually from natural stone. Symbolic grapes and vine-shoots often decorate the doors, beams and even the implements. The same decorative motifs are also seen on crucifixes, particularly at the boundaries of vineyards.

The armorial bearings of many families and municipalities depict the vinegrower's work, with pruning-knife and wine-press in evidence as well as the ubiquitous bunch of grapes and twining vines. More than any other activities, the tasks involved in making wine, storing it, carrying and distributing it have encouraged the development of popular art. Everyday articles, traditional in kind and shape, are favourite subjects for decoration. The wooden wine-press is often richly decorated, as it is part of the patrimony, handed down from one generation to the next. Wine casks as well may have their own decoration. Valuable family possessions, these enormous wooden barrels were carved with the names of the vinegrower and his wife for whom they were built, with armorial bearings, monograms and even, like a house, the year of construction, and were often inaugurated at a wedding.

The front of these sometimes richly carved tuns is particularly characteristic of viticultural art. No doubt these casks, containing special wines from the large vineyards belonging to religious communities or princes, were first carved and ornamented in the wine cellars of monasteries and castles. The great chapters like those of Speyer or Würzburg exercised widespread influence throughout southern Germany, and this custom of decorating the huge casks was revived in the cellars of Austrian monasteries in the baroque period. Clearly, it was the monks who set the fashion for embellishing casks with pictures of saints or the patriarch Noah, considered as the father of viticulture. Occasionally, the abbeys engaged their own wood-carvers, but the work was more usually entrusted to the coopers themselves. During the eighteenth century and into the early part of the nineteenth, a cooper would spend countless, devoted hours carving and painting religious motifs, such as the patron saints of the guild. In the course of the nineteenth century, traditional designs were gradually superseded by simpler or more down-to-earth imagery, carvings of family names or portrayals of everyday scenes. The large casks, fitted with a trap-door through which a lad could clamber to clean the inside, were particularly well suited to carvings, even on the door itself. Now usually a plain piece of wood, this door was often carved in a very special manner in times gone by. The designs frequently featured fishes, naiads, tritons and other legendary creatures, symbolizing the great volume of liquid contained within the barrel. The richest collections of carved tuns are probably those now in the Wine Museum at Speyer, in the Palatinate, at the Julius Hospice in Würzburg in Bavaria, and in the Wine Museums of Beaune in Burgundy and of Kreme in Lower Austria.

Considering their size, so far above average, these giant casks represent significant monuments to the craftsmen of those days. They were constructed as much for the supply of some stronghold as to nourish the vanity of some great personage. Their real function, however, was usually to combine the different wines contributed as tithes into one blend so that all the officials entitled to perquisites in the form of wine received the same quality, thereby eliminating all grounds for complaint.

Most of these giant casks of the baroque period have now disappeared. Among the most richly decorated that of Königstein in Saxony should be mentioned. It was built for King Augustus the Strong. Other notable examples were the second Heidelberg tun, built in 1664 for the Grand Elector Charles-Louis of the Palatinate, and that of Ludwigsburg, built between the years 1717-20 for the Duke Eberhard Louis of Württemberg. The master-cooper Michael Werner of Landau in the Palatinate constructed the first Heidelberg tun for Jean Casimir in 1589; as a result he became famous and was given orders for similar casks from many other potentates. In old engravings, Werner and his helpmates can be seen at work on these enormous casks, proving that even in those days such an undertaking was considered an extraordinary feat and worthy of wide renown. One of these mammoth casks, with

Little figures in painted wood, the *Büttenmännchen* were characteristic of popular Germanic art and were often used for decorations at social gatherings.

This delicate sign in wrought iron once graced the "Cep" inn at a town called Chur, in the Swiss canton of the Grisons.

Even the bung-hole of a cask provides an excuse for adding an amusing design in carved wood.

This "goat" was a symbol of fertility. Carved in wood and laden with grapes it formerly played a leading rôle in the processions at the wine festivals that ended the grape harvests in Lower Austria.

The elaborate fronts of many casks have now taken their places in collections. On this tun, which is dated for 1880, the carved decoration is still strictly traditional.

STRANGERS RESORT

J. CARTER

The New World also had its inn signs in the last century. Some were very simple, representing merely a symbolic object such as a bunch of grapes, a bottle or a drinking glass. Others, like this one, are genuine pictorial descriptions of life in days gone by. Errors in perspective were held to be of little consequence, as long as the subject was reasonably well-proportioned and the colours bright enough to attract attention. The wine, served in decanters and prominently displayed, seems to have been in plentiful supply at the "Strangers' Resort". Although vineyards already existed at this time in the New World, much wine was imported from Europe and, when good, was both scarce and expensive.

a capacity of nearly 53,000 gallons, can be seen to this day by visitors to the cellars of Heidelberg Castle.

Along with the big casks, the coopers produced small barrels for a great variety of purposes. One might be used by the vinegrower to carry his daily ration of wine when he was going to spend all day working in the vines. Another might be presented to the abbot at the time of his election. Still another would be used, year after year, to hold the Midwinter wine. This was a new wine, blessed on December 27th on the occasion of the festival of St. John the Apostle and devoutly treasured, to be drunk only on rare occasions, at a wedding, for instance, or before setting out on a long journey, being credited with beneficial virtues.

Amusing little casks, enabling three different wines to be drawn off by working a disc, are further examples of the coopers' art. They were very much in keeping with the spirit of the baroque age when games and tricks of every kind were much in vogue. After decades of apparent neglect, this craft is now being revived in various regions, notably in Lower Austria, and seems

to be in great demand by publicans, wine merchants and affluent private individuals. Created purely for decoration, these casks come almost exclusively from vinegrowing regions: the South Tyrol, Lower Austria, the banks of the Rhine and the Moselle.

The cultivation of the vine and wine gave rise to a multitude of smaller receptacles. Almost until the end of the eighteenth century, the bottle as a means of preserving wine was still unknown in German-speaking territories. The wine was stored in casks in the cellar, simply drawn off into jugs and then poured into glasses or goblets. The bottle, a French innovation, only appeared in these regions towards the end of the eighteenth century and only with the introduction of sparkling wines. Flasks which slipped easily into the pocket or into saddlebags were used to carry wine when travelling and these first flat, pouch-shaped bottles began to make their appearance around 1820, together with the wood or leather cases which were designed to hold them. This shape of bottle can still be found today in the typical flasks of Franconia called *Bocksbeutel*.

35

To the left and right are two *Heurigen Kränze*, wheels of plaited straw. Following an edict by Empress Maria Theresa, Austrian vinegrowers have hung these wheels over their doors to show passers-by that there is new wine in their cellar. In the centre is one of the wooden suns which, rising above the vineyards of Wachau, warned that they were guarded against trespassers and helped to frighten away unwelcome birds.

Other longer bottles, also flat and generally fluted, were designed to be carried on the person. All had screw stoppers in pewter or, in the case of gentlemen of rank, even in silver or gold. Humbler versions in wood, earthenware or even fashioned from gourds and used by farm workers, have also been discovered. Many such receptacles, fitted with a strap, were intended for carrying to work in the fields. Whenever possible, they were left in a spring or stream to keep the wine cool. They might be decorated with proverbial inscriptions, simultaneously bacchic and biblical, such as "Wine gladdens the heart of he who drinks in moderation, but it is harmful to the man who drinks too much", or "What is life without wine?" Innumerable small potteries turned out various types of pitchers, usually with handles, decorated with vine leaves, coats-of-arms and bacchic quotations while elsewhere pewter flagons were popular drinking vessels.

The tavern signs in small towns and in the countryside can also be considered as picturesque and characteristic examples of contemporary art. Those carved in wood have become extremely rare today. Magnificent specimens of hanging signs with their decorative supporting brackets testify to the high standard of wrought-iron work achieved in the eighteenth century. Depicting the vine and a bunch of grapes, as well as a variety of other motifs, these are for the most part the work of long-forgotten village craftsmen.

Our age is one of unceasing change. Like so many other crafts and professions, those associated closely or remotely with vines or wine have developed rapidly over the last few decades. Everywhere, glass or synthetic materials have replaced wood while implements and recipients whose design seemed to have attained near-perfection are rapidly disappearing from the scene of the cultivation of the vine and are taking their places in museums and auction rooms.

The same tasks engendered the same types of implements all over Europe, but each region endowed them with its own characteristic style. The cooper, the basket-worker and the maker of edged tools all worked to order and to local requirements. In one district, the grape-baskets borne on the back and the harvesting panniers might be made in wicker and, in another, wood. They might be round and deep in one province, oval and shallow in the next. Methods of cultivation, harvesting and wine-making influenced the shape and design of every article. Notwithstanding the fact that their ultimate purpose was the same, they differed from vineyard to vineyard in the same way that their owners differed. Vinegrowers they all may be, but distinguished one from the other by their traditions and working habits. Today, all these tools and implements form part of a common heritage and bear witness to a highly productive art that can be admired in museums devoted to the vine and to wine.

Active promoters of the European vineyards in the Middle Ages, the monks often boasted famous cellars, the forerunners of our inns and public houses. The casks were broached and the wine, mercifully not reserved exclusively for divine service, was drunk on the premises.

THE GREAT
WINE REGIONS OF
THE WORLD

THE VINE
CONQUERS THE WORLD

The great botanical family of Ampelidaceae, to which the vine belongs, is very widely represented in all cultivated regions of the world. All plants belonging to the genus *vitis* bear grapes but out of the forty-odd known species only one, the European *vitis vinifera*, produces the edible grapes used to make wine. *Vitis labrusca*, a species of American origin, is sometimes cultivated for wine but produces poor results. *Vitis vinifera* thrives only within the temperate zones of the two hemispheres, between latitudes 50 and 30 degrees North and 30 and 40 degrees South. This vine does not stand up well to excessive heat or rigorous cold, nor does it tolerate overly abundant rains or severe drought. Furthermore, it is difficult to make wine when the ambient temperature is above 15° C. (about 60° F.).

A rapid look at history shows that the regions where *vitis vinifera* has developed are also the regions where various civilizations reached the peak of their development. This is scarcely surprising, for of all plants which have been improved and transformed by the genius of man, the vine—even more than wheat or rice—is a silent witness to his patience and his untiring work over many generations.

The original or autochtonous vineyards were in the Caucasus (Georgia and Armenia), on the isles of the Aegean Sea and in Egypt. It was these that gave birth to the present-day vineyards. Other natural vineyards in China, Japan, and the eastern and central parts of North America, did not benefit from conditions suitable for their development and they have remained more or less in an embryonic state. But starting out from the Eurasian regions, *vitis vinifera* spread widely, for many and very different reasons.

Some of the vineyards owe their existence to the brutal facts of military conquest: a good many French vineyards began to appear as the Roman legions established themselves in the country. Sometimes it was the political supremacy or ideology which sufficed to propagate the vine cultures—this was the case with the Greek vineyards when, at the dawn of modern history, Continental Greece was under the influence of the Aegean powers. Nearer home, colonial conquests have resulted in the vine being transplanted to Australia, New Zealand, South Africa and South America.

The missionary zeal of the Christians has often been reflected in a vine culture derived from their liturgical needs for altar wine: thus it was that the Spanish, after the Islamic interlude in the Iberian Peninsula, reintroduced the cultivation of the vine and the use of wine in southern Spain. Similarly, the first vines in California were planted by Franciscan missionaries. Elsewhere, it was the victims of religious persecution who spread a type of culture with which they were closely connected, as in South Africa, where the first vinegrowers, well versed in their calling, were the French Protestants who emigrated there after the Repeal of the Edict of Nantes in 1685. Some of the vineyards of southern Russia were created, at the end

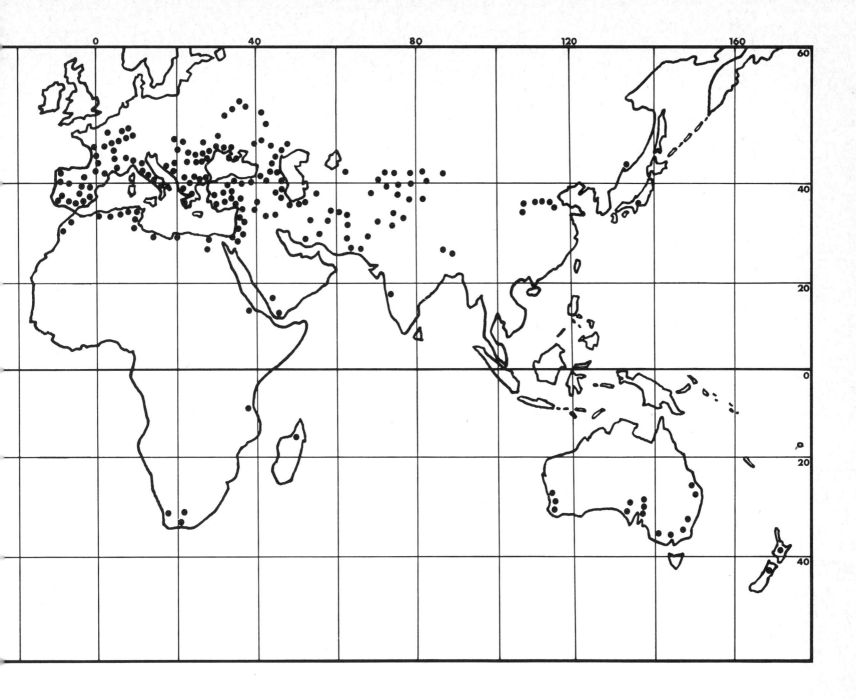

of the nineteenth century, by the snobbery of an aristocracy which wanted to produce on its own estates wines to which it then gave such famous names as Sauternes or Vougeot. Now Russia is the fifth largest wineproducer in Europe.

The expansion or reduction of the viticultural areas depended also—as is increasingly the case today—on economic fluctuations. In Brazil, following a slump in coffee, plantation owners did not hesitate to lease out part of their lands to vinegrowers of Italian origin. And before the First World War, in the former Austro-Hungarian Empire the areas cultivated to vines varied in direct relation to the economic and political situation of the various parts of the Empire.

The present state of the viticultural regions of the world is therefore the result of very numerous factors, which in turn depend on many facets of human activities. It is for this reason that the vineyards of the world vary to a marked degree within the climatic limits that are suitable for them.

The *Office International de la Vigne et du Vin* (O.I.V.) (International Office of Vine and Wine) in Paris has been collecting, studying and publishing, for the best part of half a century now, all the information possible on the vine and on wine in the world. The office functions as a centre of co-ordination and also of scientific, technological, economic and legal information for most of the viticultural countries.

THE WINES
OF BURGUNDY

PIERRE FORGEOT

The Bible relates that the vine was created on the third day with the other plants (Genesis i. 2). But how long did it take to reach Burgundy after Noah and his Ark came to rest on Mount Ararat? No written evidence can possibly tell us. It is generally thought that, long before the Christian era, there were vines, albeit wild, growing in the present Burgundy wine area in the middle of eastern France, north of the Côtes du Rhône region and south-west of Champagne and Alsace. It was only through a slow process of change, doubtless beginning about the third century B.C. and advancing as their skill in the art grew, that our ancestors were able to improve the quality of the grape. Roman rule lasted five centuries and was vital to the development of the vineyards of Burgundy. Many of the Roman legionaries came from the wineproducing areas of Italy, and they brought to the Eduans—as the inhabitants of this region of Gaul were then known—their experience in the cultivation of the vine and in winemaking.

With the clearing of suitable vineyard land and the planting of better selected vine-stock in the first century A.D., it became possible to expand the vineyards and begin to produce the types of wines best suited to the province. The results were spectacular. By the fourth century, Numene was able to report: "The wines of this region are the subject of foreigners' admiration." Somewhat later, in 570, Gregory of Tours proclaimed: "There is no liquor preferable to the wine of these vineyards—it is a noble Falernian." About the year 456, the Burgundians proper arrived

on the scene. They may rightly be called a migrant people, having apparently left the distant plains of Asia several millennia before the Christian era. By about 900 B.C., they had reached what is now called Norway and spread through Sweden, Germany and Switzerland before replacing the Romans in the fifth century in south-eastern Gaul, where they created their vast kingdom. In 534 the Burgundians were defeated by the Franks, but though their passage was brief, they had none the less imprinted their personality on the character, habits and customs of the region, and they gave their name to the province.

During this period and through the Middle Ages, Christianity became firmly established. Large religious estates were created through endowments made to churches, convents, abbeys and other institutions, rivalling and soon surpassing those of princes. This state of affairs continued until the French Revolution secularized religious orders and divided their land.

Burgundy was not spared the various disasters of the Middle Ages—invasions (Arab, Norman etc.), civil wars, pillaging, famines, plagues. In his history of Beaune, Rossignol writes: "The archives contain but a few vague words which bear witness to that universal desolation." It is not difficult to imagine that the cultivation of the vine made little progress in those times. Its rise began only in the tenth century with the creation of two monastic orders that were to exert an immense influence on the whole of Europe. The monks cleared the ground, replanted vine-stock and did much for the vineyards of Burgundy, putting them on

43

the road to becoming what they are today. The research carried out first at the Abbey of Cluny and later at Cîteaux led to methods of cultivation and winemaking that, by and large, were the same as those we now employ. The spiritual and physical expanse of these two abbeys was immense—was not one of the abbots, St. Mayeul, called in his own lifetime "the prince of monastic religion and the arbiter of kings"? Cluny possessed two thousand dependencies and Cîteaux more than three thousand. In other words, their power was an important factor in the spreading growth both of Burgundy wines and of their fame.

In fact, the quality of Burgundy wines was even the cause of serious diplomatic incidents! Petrarch tells us: "The cardinals [then in Avignon] no longer wish to return to Rome, since there are no Burgundy wines in Italy. Our prelates believe that their lives will not be happy without this liquor—for them, wine is the fifth element." For his part, Pope Urban V said: "I am little concerned to see again those transalpine lands where there is no Beaune wine."

These were the fourteenth and fifteenth centuries, auspicious times for Burgundy, both because of the monastic orders of which we have just spoken and because of the growth of the court of the Grand Dukes of the West, as the dukes of Burgundy then preferred to be called—Philip the Bold, John the Fearless, Philip the Good and Charles the Bold. For over a century, from 1364 to 1477, these four dukes, "the immediate lords of the best wines in Christendom", raised their duchy to such heights of power as to intimidate the kings of France and the princes of Europe. At the death of Charles the Bold, their power extended beyond the duchy of Burgundy (Dijon, Beaune, Mâcon) to the county of Burgundy (Besançon) and across a large part of Holland, Belgium, Luxemburg, Alsace and the counties of Nevers, Artois and Picardie. They cared much for their wines and gifts of them were greatly esteemed, as this letter from Pope Innocent VII testifies: "My son . . . Greetings. . . . This Beaune wine that you have sent Us has a good and agreeable taste. It is quite pleasing to Our palate and constitution. We have made almost regular use of it as a curative during Our recent illness. Therefore, We call upon your Lordship and request that you send Us more as soon as the possibility arises. We shall be very pleased to receive it and your Lordship will thus be doing Us a very great favour."

Cultivation of the vineyards gradually became more democratic as first the bourgeoisie and then the peasant vintager received greater freedom. The vines were no longer the exclusive property of the nobility and the clergy; the latter, in fact, frequently indulged in such excesses that decent folk were obliged to react. The

competence of the monks in the subject of wine and their taste for the beverage caused many a ribald comment. As they said at the time:

Boire en Templier, c'est boire à plein gosier,
Boire en Cordelier, c'est vider le cellier.

To drink like a Templar is to drink heartily,
To drink like a Franciscan is to empty the cellar.

The vineyards were finally and totally democratized in the eighteenth century by the French Revolution. The sale of the property of the clergy and the nobility divided up their immense estates and initiated the process of fragmentation, which subsequently increased through successive splits caused, in particular, by inheritances. This fragmentation characterizes the vineyards of Burgundy even today—quite unlike the large estates of Bordeaux. There are twice as many vinegrowers in Burgundy as in Bordeaux, in a cultivated area one-third the size, and very few vineyards are wholly owned by a single person. Moreover, towards the end of the last century, the whole area was nearly lost to the notorious pest, phylloxera, an insect from America which attacked the roots and killed off the vine-stock. The whole industry was facing collapse, for no practical and effective remedy could be discovered. In the end, the only way to save the vineyards was to graft old vine-stocks on to American phylloxera-resistant stock. This cure did not affect the quality of the product; quite the contrary, it made possible the creation of improved varieties, better suited to the consumers' requirements.

There are certain conditions that must be fulfilled if a really fine wine is to be produced—and we shall only be discussing fine wines here. To the old saying: "The finest gesture a person can make is to fill his neighbour's glass", folk-wisdom will immediately add: "Tell me what you drink and I'll tell you who you are." It being understood, of course, that, as M. de Borose remarked: "good things are made for good people; otherwise we should be obliged to believe that God created them for bad people . . . which is unthinkable !"

Five specific factors must coincide if a Burgundy is to be able to develop its best qualities:

THE SOIL. Vines are not planted just anywhere but generally on the slopes of hills. The soil on flat country is too rich; the grape absorbs too much water and the wine is diluted. On hilltops the soil is poor; the vine does not grow properly, the grape does not take in all the elements it requires and the wine is incomplete.

In the words of Gaston Roupnel: "Before wine can even be conceived, its chosen soil must be very old and its cradle a tomb replete with the ashes of years and the dust of centuries." One is often surprised to

44

Created in about 1150 by the Bernardine monks of Cîteaux, the Clos-Vougeot estate very soon became a model vineyard. It has quite accurately been called the navel of Burgundy. Despite the many vicissitudes of its early history, it grew steadily until the fourteenth century. Its 128 acres are today divided among 60 different owners.

see in this land of great growths so many different names side by side but, nevertheless, possessing significant differences in quality. The mystery of the extremely complex composition of the soil affecting the final result is mentioned by Maurice Constantin-Weyer in his book *L'âme du vin* ("The Soul of Wine"): "A secret alchemy works upon even the least of the soil's riches to produce an elixir beyond compare."

THE VINE. To plant a "hybrid" on the slope of a hill is a little like bandaging a wooden leg. The great wines of Burgundy demand two types of vine-stock: for red wines, the *Pinot*—the finer the grape the better the result—the juice of which is colourless and very sweet; for white wines, the *Chardonnay* grape is used, to which the same applies.

There are two main secondary types that go with the two "greats". One is the *Gamay*, a red grape with white juice which produces the remarkable wines of the granite soil of the Beaujolais. As two writers of the region have commented: in order to savour their excellence to the full "you would need a *corniole* [gullet] as long as a swan's to make the pleasure last longer". The other is the *Aligoté*, a white grape, very old, which gives one single wine, the BOURGOGNE ALIGOTÉ.

THE CARE OF THE VINE. Tilling, pruning, looking after the vines, pest control—all these are decisive factors in the proper cultivation of the vine and the production of healthy, promising grapes. The work is done throughout the year, thus justifying an ancient saying: "The vine grows in the vintner's shadow."

The vintage itself is also part of the "care of the vine", for to gather the grapes at the correct stage of ripeness is vital and the date, always chosen with great care, is very important.

Of course, many imponderables can upset the patient vintner's work. Spring frosts, around the beginning of May, may occur in any year, resulting in the loss of up to three-quarters of the crop. *Coulure* (premature dropping of the fruit) is feared when rain or cold in June inhibit fecundation. Hail is a formidable danger to the vine; where it falls, all or most of the crop may be destroyed. The final unforseeable factor beyond man's control is the proper sequence of rain and sun. To produce a great vintage, rain is needed at the right times, and sun is needed in large amounts especially in the two months before harvesting.

VINIFICATION. It is often said that the rules of hygiene are like unattractive women—nobody follows them. To which strong-minded people add without hesitation the following maxim: "Lean heavily on your principles—they'll always give way in the end." Neither of these maxims can be applied to winemaking, especially since Burgundy adopted the shorter vinification method in 1938 in order to produce more flexible wines which matured much earlier while still maintaining their former high standards. And this is where the splitting up of vineyards mentioned above is regrettable, since strict rules have to be followed and the vintner often finds it difficult to keep up with the progress made and adopt the new methods.

STORAGE AND TREATMENT. The French word *elevage*, which loosely translated means "upbringing", is much misunderstood when applied to the winegrowing profession. It has been remarkably well explained by two nineteenth-century authors, Danguy and Aubertin: "Once made, red wine must, through constant and unceasing care, be brought to the point at which it possesses all the necessary qualities for it to be tasted with pleasure." In 1885, Dr Lavalle wrote: "Precisely because of all its perfection, the wine of Burgundy demands intelligent care and, like those splendid

The Burgundy wine area, of which just under half lies in the Beaujolais, consists of 105,000 acres unevenly scattered among four departments. Only the Chablis region in the north between the Yonne and the Armançon seems to hold itself aloof from the natural continuity provided for these glorious vineyards by the river Saône. The other regions on its right bank form an almost continuous belt between Dijon and Villefranche. The Côte de Nuits from Fixin to Corgoloin and the Côte de Beaune from Ladoix-Serrigny to Santanay have shared the benefits of the prestige gained by their vineyards with the whole of Burgundy. The vineyards of Mercurey, more widely scattered than the rest, provide a link with the compact southern group of the Mâconnais and the Beaujolais, linked to the Burgundy area by many geographical and commercial bonds.

flowers that must be painstakingly cultivated for several years before they will open their marvellous blooms, full of brightness and perfume, it requires a knowing hand to lead it skilfully and patiently to the point at which it is worthy to be offered to a man of taste."

In Burgundy, it is the buyer-shipper who, over the last few centuries, has lovingly prepared the necessary sanctuaries: cellars vaulted or built so as to maintain a relatively even temperature. The fact is that the vintner, once again because of the fragmentation of property, and the small number of large estates, quite frequently confines himself to the growing side, and his job ends as soon as the wine is made. Furthermore the investment is considerable—a large amount of space, installations (always interesting to visit), capital to build up large stocks of bottles and barrels for the ageing period and sufficient qualified personnel are all necessary. Finally, a sales organization must be set up in France and abroad to dispose of the product. These are circumstances that have made the Burgundian wine shippers, though few in number, very important people. There are two hundred of them, to be found mainly in the large wine centres.

France accounts for about 50 per cent of the buyers of the great wines of Burgundy. They are distributed through three types of buyers—wholesalers from outside the Burgundy area who sell them in their own particular markets and also to a significant number of retailers; hotel, restaurant and café owners, and individual wine merchants; and private individuals, who buy in barrels or assortments of bottles.

In 1967, exports went to 138 different countries throughout the world—11,844,300 gallons of wines with an *appellation contrôlée*, produced in Burgundy. For several years, Burgundy has ranked first among all the production areas of French *appellation contrôlée* wines by value and by volume of wines sold outside France. Quite an achievement, as the official statistics will show. For, again in 1967, Burgundy produced 12.5 per cent of all French wines entitled to an A.O.C. label

(A.O.C. = Appellation d'Origine Contrôlée = Registered Designation of Origin), while its exports accounted for 39.4 per cent of French A.O.C. wines exported (excluding Champagne and sparkling wines). To be precise, exports were 8,250,640 gallons of wines in casks and 3,593,220 gallons in bottles. These figures do not include non-A.O.C. (but labelled) wines crossing the frontier since the customs statistics do not go into sufficient detail. But here too, Burgundy is at the head of the list by a wide margin.

Exports of bottled wines are limited by higher selling prices, due to the special processes involved, to customs duties and the considerable costs of transport. Even so, the United States buys only bottled wines. Canada's imports are 90 per cent bottled and other countries are yearly increasing their import percentages in this category.

Among the chief importers of A.O.C. Burgundy wines in terms of volume, Switzerland ranks first. Though a small country in terms of population, it is closely linked to the province and absorbs over one-third of its exports. Next comes the United States, which now takes 14 per cent of Burgundy's foreign sales and, in terms of value is becoming its biggest customer (25 per cent of the total). For, besides from the ordinary wines, Americans are buying fine and great wines, but solely in the bottle. West Germany's position is uncertain because of its present regulations. With the opening of the frontiers, this market, taking 13.4 per cent at present, may be completely transformed. Next comes Belgium, traditionally a lover of Burgundy wines, with 12.3 per cent. Great Britain follows next with very little concern as to A.O.C.s; Britons still tend to drink wine *à la tasse*, i.e. by the glass. Imports are, as in the past, piecemeal, and therefore frequently consist of "labelled wines" lacking an A.O.C. but meeting the desired quality requirements. Further principal importers of A.O.C. Burgundy wines are Sweden, Canada, Denmark, the Netherlands and Italy, where sales are increasing rapidly.

THE WINE AREAS

Over the centuries the kingdom, duchy or province of Burgundy has been like a balloon, swelling and shrinking as circumstances dictated. Its frontiers were always vague, varying hugely around a central kernel consisting of a few hundred square miles centring on the cities of Beaune and Dijon. The only definite and undisputable characteristic of Burgundy is that it has always been a crossroads, a fact that throughout

its history has brought more trouble than benefits.

No feature in its geographical shape is sufficiently precise for us to be able to describe its shape. Only in the east did the Saône River clearly mark part of the boundary between the duchy (Beaune-Dijon) and the county of Burgundy (Besançon), that is between the present Haute Bourgogne and the Franche-Comté. The very nature of the terrain confirms these differences—the plain of the Saône, the vineyard slopes, the forests of the mountainous Morvan and of the Châtillonnais, a maze of fields, meadows and different crops. The twentieth century has not improved matters much, even though the division of France into departments, often arbitrarily welded together, should have given Burgundy, along with the soul which it has always had, at least a clearly defined territory. But no—and this is true of a number of other French provinces—according to the various civil, military and religious authorities there is not one Burgundy, but several, the land they cover differing quite inexplicably.

When the need arose to define the Burgundy wine area, the official attempt to do so was frankly an innovation. Ignoring history and thankfully taking into account more realistic and practical considerations, the Civil Tribunal of Dijon, in a decree dated April 29th, 1930, defined the production areas authorized to use the title Burgundy as follows,: "Local, consistent and time-honoured usage, has it that the Burgundy wine area is exclusively composed of the Côte-d'Or, Yonne and Saône-et-Loire departments, plus the Villefranche-sur-Saône *arrondissement* in the Rhône department."

The Villefranche-sur-Saône district, or to call it by its better-known name, the Beaujolais, has never been politically a part of Burgundy at any time in its history. As the writer, A. Julien said in 1816: "There is cause for astonishment in my joining the Beaujolais and Burgundy, since the first is part of the Rhône department. But my intention is to present and group together wines of the same type, and the wines of the Beaujolais have very little in common with those of the Lyonnais."

It is, therefore, solely on the basis of its geographical situation, the nature of its wines and its commercial traditions that this great wine area has been adopted as an integral part of the Burgundy area. There have never been any complaints about it.

Turning to the north, we find, just above the Beaujolais, the vineyards of the Mâconnais in Saône-et-Loire, quite close to the hills and a little away from the Route Nationale 6 in the south of the department, which narrows towards the north. There it meets the Mercurey region, which lies mainly on the hillside and is sometimes called the Côte Chalonnaise, a comparison with the famous wine areas farther north.

Next we enter the Côte-d'Or and follow Route Nationale 74, a triumphal procession of all the most glorious names in Burgundy. It is a narrow belt of vines, about 200 to 900 yards wide and 30 miles long; the first part is called the Côte de Beaune and the other the Côte de Nuits, after which we reach the administrative capital, Dijon. Finally, right at the top of the map, in the Yonne, we find a small patch of 7,000 acres of vines mainly around the village of Chablis.

We shall return to discuss in greater detail the structure of these various regions of the Burgundy wine area as officially defined by the law.

DESIGNATIONS OF ORIGIN

Someone once wrote: "Good wine warms the heart, revives the brain and overhauls the machinery." It should come as no surprise to learn that a beverage with such powers has been strictly controlled since the very earliest times.

We must return to the beginning of the fifteenth century to find a document which, by its very tone, bears a certain similarity to our modern designations of origin. It is the edict of Charles VI, in February 1415, which states that: "the wines of Burgundy shall be those that are produced above the Pont de Sens, whether in the region of Auxerrois or in that of Beaulne". It further divided the wines of Burgundy into two categories—Basse-Bourgogne (Lower Burgundy) for parishes from the Pont de Sens to Cravant, including, in particular, the Auxerrois; and Haute-Bourgogne (Upper Burgundy), which was sub-divided into four regions: the Beaunois, the Mâconnais, the Tournus and the Dijonnais, in that order. The king seems to have had good advisers, since the divisions he established have been respected to this day.

Over two hundred years later, we come to the repression of fraud. On April 27th, 1622, Louis XIII prohibited, with suitable penalties, the sale, "as Burgundies, of wines of the Lyonnais and the Beaujolais".

For many years to come, the *tastevin*, or sampling cup, was to be the sole judge in disputes. "Beaune wine" was, for a very long time, the name given to all the fine wines of the Côte-d'Or and "Auxerre wine" to the wines (then mainly red) of the Yonne.

However, a basic law was enacted on August 1st, 1905 to repress "fraud or attempted fraud as regards the nature, quality, type, origin and denomination of the product". This was supported by the law of May 6th, 1919 which defined the designations and production areas, and the decree-law of July 30th, 1935 which dealt with designations of origin and established the A.O.C. system.

Thus were defined the areas in each wineproducing commune that, according to ancient custom, were entitled to call their produce quality wine, *ceteris paribus*. Thus we now have A.O.C.s bearing the names of the villages of Fleurie, Pouilly-Fuissé, Meursault, Beaune, Nuits, Chablis, etc.

This region, in fact, is made up of small-holdings, called *climats*, the names of which often refer back to quite ancient title deeds. According to local, consistent and time-honoured usage, a number of these *climats* have been selected in an official document as being most likely to produce the best wines. They are, generally speaking, halfway up the hillside and are called the *Premiers Crus* (First Growths). On labels, price lists and bills, the name of the *climat* or vineyard always comes after the name of the village, as in the cases of BEAUNE-GRÈVES, MEURSAULT-CHARMES, POMMARD-RUGIENS, NUITS-VAUCRAINS, CHAMBOLLE-MUSIGNY AMOUREUSES, etc.

Then, from these First Growths, the law has selected what used to be called *têtes de cuvée* (best of the vintage), which really had to be the best of the best. These are now called the *Grands Crus* (Great Growths) whose names stand out alone on labels and in documents. For example—CHAMBERTIN, MONTRACHET, CLOS VOUGEOT, CORTON, CORTON-CHARLEMAGNE, etc.

Within any commune that is not so selected, wines may be produced but they are entitled only to a more general designation—and then under certain conditions, e.g. BOURGOGNE, BOURGOGNE ALIGOTE, BOURGOGNE-PASSE-TOUT-GRAINS and BOURGOGNE GRAND ORDINAIRE, or a regional designation such as BEAUJOLAIS, MACON, PETIT CHABLIS.

Furthermore, as we have already noted above, the types of vine-stock upon which the right to an A.O.C. depends are also strictly controlled.

Since it is quite difficult to assess quality officially, one way around the problem was thought to be the supervision of two factors—the yield per hectare and the level of alcohol in the wine. The first of these may have a direct bearing on the quality. Nevertheless, it is all quite relative and frequently, if all the necessary conditions have been fulfilled throughout the year, quantity and quality may not be incompatible. This is why the law allows the yield (in the villages of the Côte-d'Or, for example, it is 35 hectolitres per hectare i.e. about 300 gallons per acre) to vary from year to year, according to the quantity and quality of the crop. The procedure is, of course, very complicated and is determined by a decree from the Minister of Agriculture.

The degree of alcohol specified is, in each case, a minimum level and an indifferent standard at that. As Georges Duhamel said during a chapter of the Brotherhood of the Knights of the Tastevin: "Though

alcohol is the vital spirit of wine, it is certainly not its soul." Nobody would dream of buying a great Burgundy wine on the basis of its alcoholic content, as though it were a table wine.

This quite complicated procedure is but a small beginning, since the movement of wine in France is not unrestricted, but governed by a whole series of legal documents as well as all the decrees on wine production. For example, every year before the harvest, the vintner must declare all the wine he possesses. After the harvest, he must declare the amount produced in every one of his vineyards. These two statements are kept by the appropriate services of the indirect taxation authority. If the wine leaves the wineproducer's cellars, whether for sale or as a gift, it must be accompanied by an official document, the excise papers delivered by the above-mentioned authority. Its function is to "release" from bond wines destined for bars, hotels, restaurants, retailers, middlemen and private persons, where the duties must be paid at the outset. If the wine is for a wholesaler or exporter, these papers act as a sort of permit for payment of duties to be deferred in the case of wholesalers or not to be levied at all in the case of exporters.

It is, therefore, easy to check on remaining stocks, which is done by the indirect taxation authority twice a year and also by the fraud and quality control brigade, which may make spot checks at any time.

Further explanation is needed of a number of well known Burgundy A.O.C.s which are difficult to find on any wine map. For example—CÔTE DE BEAUNE-VILLAGES. The fact is that the A.O.C. given by law may, in some cases, be changed, but always downwards. This is called *déclasser* (to downgrade) a wine.

It is often a voluntary process, generally to meet commercial requirements. Thus the wines of many little-known villages are sometimes hard to sell under their own names and are, therefore, downgraded to a more regional A.O.C.—CÔTE DE BEAUNE-VILLAGES or BOURGOGNE, for example. Or a shipper who has created a trade name puts it under a simple regional A.O.C., the highest common denominator of all the wines sold under the name.

Downgrading may, of course, also be compulsory. For example, two or several wines from different A.O.C.s may, for one reason or other, be mixed. In principle, the resulting wine may not use either or any of the original A.O.C.s, but must use one common to them all. Thus, the blending of a CHAMBERTIN with a CHARMES-CHAMBERTIN gives a plain GEVREY-CHAMBERTIN; a BEAUNE and an ALOXE-CORTON gives an ordinary BOURGOGNE. Downgrading is also compulsory if the grower exceeds the allotted maximum yield of any particular A.O.C.

49

BOUCHARD PÈRE & FILS

CHAMBERTIN

1959

APPELLATION CHAMBERTIN CONTROLÉE

MIS EN BOUTEILLES PAR

BOUCHARD PÈRE & FILS, NÉGOCIANTS A BEAUNE (COTE-D'OR)

4
1
3
2

5

CHAMBERTIN

1. Chambertin – the name of the wine. This simple title should never be confused with the A.O.C. Gevrey-Chambertin (see opposite page). Chambertin is one of the Great Growths of the commune of Gevrey-Chambertin. – 2. The compulsory inclusion of the A.O.C. ensures that the wine is from the 33 acres of the Chambertin *climat* and no other. – 3. The vintage. The fact that it is on the label and not on the neck band is an additional guarantee of authenticity. – 4. The name of the shipper, compulsory in the case of A.O.C. wines. – 5. Bottled by the shipper – anc

BOUCHARD PÈRE & FILS

CHAMBERTIN

1961

CLOS DE BÈZE

APPELLATION CHAMBERTIN CONTROLÉE

MIS EN BOUTEILLES PAR

BOUCHARD PÈRE & FILS, NEGOCIANTS A BEAUNE (COTE-D'OR)

4
1
3
1a
2

5

CHAMBERTIN - CLOS DE BÈZE

1. Chambertin – the name of the wine. At first glance, no difference between this label and the above. One thing, then, is certain – it is a Chambertin and therefore a great wine. – 1a. Clos de Bèze provides an additional clue. This *climat* is also a Great Growth of the commune of Gevrey-Chambertin (see map on page 84). However, although a Chambertin-Clos de Bèze may be called Chambertin, the reverse is not possible. On some labels, the Clos de Bèze comes immediately below Chambertin in the same type-face. – 2. The compulsory inclusion of the A.O.C. has Chambertin alone; it could equally mention Chambertin-Clos de Bèze. – 3. 4. 5. As above.

BOUCHARD PÈRE & FILS

CHARMES-CHAMBERTIN

1959

APPELLATION CHARMES-CHAMBERTIN CONTROLÉE

MIS EN BOUTEILLES PAR

BOUCHARD PÈRE & FILS, NÉGOCIANTS A BEAUNE (COTE-D'OR)

4
1
3
2

5

CHARMES-CHAMBERTIN

1. Charmes-Chambertin – the name of the wine. In this case, a different name comes before the word Chambertin. It is not the name of the commune but of the *climat* (see map on page 84). Such a label designates a Great Growth, albeit of lesser repute than the two above. Similar labels are used by other *climats*: Chapelle-Chambertin, Griotte-Chambertin, Latricières-Chambertin, Mazis-Chambertin and Ruchottes-Chambertin. All these are Great Growths from the commune of Gevrey-Chambertin. – 2. The A.O.C. may not mention Chambertin alone but must by law cover both – Charmes-Chambertin. – 3. 4. 5. As above.

GEVREY-CHAMBERTIN "LES CAZETIERS"

1. Gevrey-Chambertin – the name of the wine. Here we have the name of the commune; it is therefore not a great wine but a village A.O.C. – 1a. Under the village A.O.C. comes the *climat* concerned – "Les Cazetiers". Since this name is in the list of First Growths (see page 76), the full title, "Gevrey-Chambertin Les Cazetiers" indicates a First Growth from Gevrey-Chambertin. That is to say, a wine whose precise geographical origin guarantees its quality. The name of the vineyard must be mentioned on the label in letters no higher or wider than those of the A.O.C. of the commune. – 2. Note that the A.O.C. mentions Gevrey-Chambertin; it might also have been in full – "Gevrey-Chambertin Les Cazetiers". – 3. 4. 5. As above.

GEVREY-CHAMBERTIN

1. Gevrey-Chambertin – the name of the wine. This label bears only the village A.O.C. It is, therefore, a wine from somewhere in the commune of Gevrey-Chambertin other than a vineyard producing Great or First Growths, except where the latter may have been downgraded to Gevrey-Chambertin. – 2. The A.O.C. guarantees that the wine is exclusively from the commune of Gevrey-Chambertin. This is not necessarily a guarantee of quality. – 3. The vintage. – 4. 5. More than in the previous cases, the name of the shipper is the real guarantee of quality. By clearly indicating his name, the shipper stakes his reputation.

BOURGOGNE (BURGUNDY)

1. 1a. Bourgogne – the generic name and "La Vignée", a trade name. This label is very different from the previous ones, firstly because it does not bear the name Chambertin or Gevrey-Chambertin. The generic classification as Burgundy means that the wine is from different places in Burgundy. It may even be Gevrey-Chambertin alone. The shipper is not satisfied with the generic description alone and has added his trade name "La Vignée". This means he attaches great importance to the quality of this wine. – 2. The Burgundy A.O.C. only means that the wine was made in Burgundy. In judging its quality, the trade name and the name of the shipper will be decisive factors. – 3. Bottling by the shipper himself also indicates that he attaches a great deal of importance to the quality of the wine. N.B. – It will be seen that the vintage is not mentioned on the label. In this case, it will be on the neck of the bottle or there may be no vintage indicated at all.

COMTE DE M. DE LUPÉ   VICOMTE F DE CHOLET

VOLNAY

APPELLATION CONTROLÉE

LUPÉ-CHOLET

LUPÉ-CHOLET & C°

Négociants à Nuits-Saint-Georges (Côte-d'Or) France

IMP. G. PARIS à NUITS St GEORGES

Joseph Drouhin

Beaune

APPELLATION BEAUNE CONTROLÉE

Clos des Mouches

RÉCOLTE DU DOMAINE

MONOPOLE DE VENTE

JOSEPH DROUHIN

A BEAUNE, COTE-D'OR, AUX CELLIERS DES
ROIS DE FRANCE ET DES DUCS DE BOURGOGNE

SOCIÉTÉ CIVILE DU DOMAINE DE LA ROMANÉE-CONTI
PROPRIÉTAIRE A VOSNE-ROMANÉE (COTE-D'OR)

GRANDS ÉCHÉZEAUX

APPELLATION . GRANDS ÉCHÉZEAUX . CONTROLÉE

15.766 Bouteilles Récoltées

Nᵒ   L'ASSOCIÉ-GÉRANT

ANNÉE 1962   *H. de Villaine*

Mise en bouteille au domaine

FILIBER à NUITS

VOLNAY
1. Volnay – the A.O.C. This is a village growth in the Côte de Beaune. A simple A.O.C. guaranteeing quality. – 2. In such cases, the name of the shipper is decisive in any *a priori* judgement of quality.

BEAUNE CLOS DES MOUCHES
1. Beaune – the A.O.C. – 2. The name of the vineyard is "Clos des Mouches". Since it is written in larger typeface than the A.O.C., it must be a First Growth. If it were not, the type-face of the name of the vineyard would have to be no more than half the height and width of that of the A.O.C. – 3. The name of the shipper. His sales monopoly *(monopole de vente)* should be taken as a guarantee of authenticity and quality.

GRANDS ÉCHÉZEAUX
1. Grands Echézeaux – the name of the wine, immediately followed by the A.O.C. At first sight, we see it is not a village A.O.C. It is probably a Great Growth. The connoisseur will then identify it as one of the seven Great Growths of the commune of Vosne-Romanée. – 2. The indication of how many bottles were made and the individual bottle number leave no room for doubt; we have ample proof that this is a very great wine, nicely confirmed by the date of the vintage. – 3. The name of the proprietor is enough to convince even the most cautious. – 4. That it is estate-bottled is a logical conclusion from the fact that the number of bottles made has already been mentioned.

MERCUREY

1. Mercurey – the A.O.C. This is not a great growth or a village A.O.C. but that of a region following the Côte de Beaune (see page 78). Mercurey wines are not unlike the Côte de Beaune wines. – 2. In the case of communal or regional A.O.C.s, the good name of the shipper is the guarantee of quality.

BROUILLY

1. Brouilly – the A.O.C. Only a Beaujolais fan would know that this is a First Growth Beaujolais, for the word Beaujolais is not on the label. Thus *a minimum knowledge* of the wines of this region is required to tell what wine a Brouilly is. The same type of label is used for the following names: Chénas, Chiroubles, Côte de Brouilly, Fleurie, Juliénas, Morgon, Moulin-à-Vent and Saint-Amour. – 2. Bottling by the shipper is an additional guarantee of authenticity.

BEAUJOLAIS

1. Beaujolais – the A.O.C. This is a regional name. A clear distinction should be made between Beaujolais, Beaujolais Supérieur and Beaujolais-Village, which are three quite separate A.O.C.s. The first is the most common. – 2. The shipper's name here is very important, for there are as many types of Beaujolais as there are producers.

THE CHABLIS REGION

Let us now study the regions of Burgundy in detail, starting in the north and finishing far to the south.

The vines of Chablis go far back in time. They were first widely grown under the Roman occupation. Their home is in the department of Yonne, which takes its name from the river passing through it on its way to Montereau, where it meets the Seine.

The capital of the department is Auxerre, known in the ancient chronicles as Autissiodurum, Autricidurum and Alciodurum, and later Auceure or Aucerre. It is a very ancient town which already existed in the time of the Celts and flourished in Roman times. It was by then a "city"—*civitas Autissiodorum*—and gave its name to a vast region stretching as far as the Loire —the *Pagus Autissodorensis*. Although St. Pilgrim first christianized the inhabitants in the third century, the sixth bishop of the region, St. Germain, who owned vineyards there, contributed equally to the spread of the faith. His youth was eventful and his public life dubious until he was appointed to this important post. At that time he changed suddenly and completely; his conduct became exemplary and he well deserved his eventual canonization. All the while, he carefully tended his extensive vineyards, and though he could not enjoy his wines himself, he unstintingly offered them to his guests who, as an ancient writer records, greatly appreciated them. Together with St. Martin, he was one of the most popular saints.

The wines of the region were then known as the wines of Auxerre. They were red wines and kept their name until the eighteenth century. Meanwhile the wines of Chablis were gaining a reputation of their own. This came through a long-established monastery, founded in 510 by St. Sigismund, and subsequently through a junior branch at the Abbey of Cîteaux, at Pontigny, built in 1114, which created a *clos* (vineyard) like the Clos de Vougeot. Benefiting, as we have seen, from the reputation of the parent branch, it is not surprising that the quality of the wines it produced became known throughout Europe. The vine spread across the whole region and by the twelfth century "the number of presses had to be increased considerably", as the Abbot Leneuf tells us.

It is true that these vineyards had one great advantage; while land transport was difficult because of the vehicles used and the bad condition of the roads, to say nothing of the robbers, brigands and other unsavoury characters so popular at the time, the two waterways of the Yonne and the Saône enabled the wines to reach Paris easily. The capital had "French" wines—that is local wines from the Ile de France—but the better wines were supplied by Auxerre. This enabled production to increase so that by the nineteenth century it was the largest in Burgundy. In 1788, 79,487 acres were under vines; by 1866, 93,235 acres were planted and in 1888, when the phylloxera struck, 100,323 acres were producing wine. The bourgeois and the nobility of Paris also contributed: they liked, as they do today, to have a country residence and vineyards in the region. In 1527, there were an estimated 700 or so. By the end of the sixteenth century, Olivier de Serres could write: "One sees the great towns vacated by presidents, councillors, bourgeois and other notables, who retire to their rustic farms for the wines, preferring to take so much trouble to drink well rather than to drink badly and avoid the discomforts of their rustic seats."

The development of the vineyards was abruptly halted by the invasion of phylloxera at the close of the nineteenth century. At the same time, its once so favourable situation was changed for the worse by progress. The birth of the railways opened up new areas to modern transportation. The completion of the Paris-Marseilles line made it possible to ship the wines of the Midi easily to Paris. The vines of the south grew in better conditions and, in particular, were not threatened by frost. Yields were higher and prices lower in spite of transport costs. The winegrowers of the Yonne, faced with this competition and defeated by the ravages of phylloxera, did not believe expensive restocking to be worthwhile. Almost the only area to be restocked was the Chablis, where the great white wines were grown. That is why, in 1967, the official figures for the Yonne were: 8,542 harvest declarations for 6,973 acres under cultivation—consisting of 3,931 acres for ordinary wine (for everyday consumption) and 3,042 acres for A.O.C. wines; the average production of the latter is 770,000 gallons of which 5 per cent is red.

Chablis is a small town that has preserved many facets of the past. It was once a fortified town but the Porte Noël is almost the last vestige of those times. The town is almost exactly halfway between Auxerre (Route Nationale 6) and Tonnerre (Route Nationale 5) and is divided by the river Serein, which is a tributary of the Yonne.

The importance of the Serein is that it has cut a valley at an altitude of about 450 feet through low hills (the average height of which is 900 feet) on which the Chablis vines grow.

On the right hand bank of the Serein, facing Chablis, grow the vines that produce the great wines sold under the name of Chablis Grand Cru, followed sometimes by the name of the vineyard. There are seven of these vineyards: Les Blanchots, exactly opposite the town near the road going up to Fyé: then, to the north, Les Clos, Valmur, Grenouilles, Vaudésir, Les Preuses and Bougros. Altogether, these Great Growths produce an average of 18,150 gallons a year on about 112 acres.

Other wines produced are the Chablis Premier Cru, in scattered vineyards on both sides of the river. The main vineyards entitled to this A.O.C. are on the right bank—with Mont de Milieu and Montée de Tonnerre to the south of the Great Growths and to the north Fourchaume, with Vaucoupin in the commune of Chichée. On the left bank, we find such names as Forêts, Montmains, Vaillons, Mélinots, Côtes de Lechet, Beauroy and others, and in Chichée, Vaugirard and Vosgros. The average yield of this designation is 148,500 gallons from 680 acres.

The third A.O.C. is Chablis, used by various vineyards in the region, still on the same hills as mentioned above. The average production is 141,900 gallons on about 766 acres.

The fourth A.O.C. of the region is Petit Chablis, a name given to white wines grown in a larger area but on quite scattered vines. The average is 68,200 gallons on 300 acres.

If we add all these figures together we have an average production of 376,750 gallons; as against the 770,000 gallons mentioned above. The difference is made up by more general types grown throughout the region—Bourgogne (red or white), Bourgogne Grand Ordinaire (red or white), Bourgogne Aligoté (white). The same occurs in the other wineproducing communes, especially those of the Côte d'Or.

In sum, the least and the most one can say about the white wines of Chablis is that this name is synonymous, throughout the world, with dry white wine, positive proof of their great fame.

In 1759, Canon Gaudin wrote to Madame d'Epinay: "My Chablis wine has body to it. Its fragrance caresses the throat and leaves a delicate aftertaste of mushrooms." Under the Restoration, the Chevalier de Piis, presiding over an epicurean dinner, sang its praises thus:

> Qui pourra mettre en oubli
> Le limpide et sec CHABLIS
> Qui joint à tant d'autres titres,
> L'art de faire aimer les huîtres?

> Who could ever forget
> The clear and dry CHABLIS
> Which adds to its many virtues
> That of inducing a love for oysters?

In the nineteenth century a wine expert called Jules Guyot passed the following judgement: "The wines of Chablis occupy one of the front ranks of the white wines of France. Spirited without the spirit being felt, they have body, subtlety and a delightful fragrance. They are, above all, outstanding for their cleanness and digestibility as well as the stimulating, warming and clear effect on the intellect. Despite their justly deserved reputation of long standing, their real value is, for me, far higher than their fame."

It is scarcely necessary to add further praise after the passages quoted above. Since the last century the white wines of the Chablis region of Burgundy have been irreproachable. It delights all winelovers when drunk with fish and seafoods during the first part of a well-planned meal.

THE CÔTE DE NUITS

We now leave the region of Chablis and turn west. After 22 miles of many different landscapes, in which there are but a few insignificant vineyards, we reach the Côte d'Or and the administrative capital of Burgundy, Dijon. It is a town with many interesting monuments, such as the former palace of the dukes of Burgundy, La Chartreuse de Champmol, the cathedral of St. Benigne, the churches of St. Michael and Our Lady, old buildings, a magnificent fine arts museum etc., but little to do with the great wines of Burgundy. However, there are large manufacturers of liqueurs —including Crème de Cassis, the famous blackcurrant liqueur and such specialities of the town as mustard and gingerbread. In the past there were many vineyards around Dijon which formed the "Côte Dijonnaise". But first phylloxera and then the growth of the town itself gradually wiped them out.

Dijon was once reputed for its vins de garde (wines worth laying down) that took some little time to "settle down" but that aged well and could be kept for many years. Since the short vinification process has been used, these wines are, like all Burgundies, ready earlier. They develop all their qualities much sooner but must also be drunk much sooner.

In order to visit the Côte de Nuits and the Côte de Beaune, we must head due south along Route Nationale 74 which will take us into Saône-et-Loire and on the way show us all the most famous growths of Upper

Burgundy. This road is about 720 feet above sea level and to the right of Dijon we can see the small hills that overlook the plain from between 450 and 900 feet. Their summits are almost always denuded or covered with Austrian black pine. On their slopes grow the vines that produce the A.O.C. wines, the Route Nationale almost forming their farthest limit. In the plain that continues to the Saône and the Jura grow scattered vineyards producing a number of ordinary wines but not sufficient to supply the needs of the department. Before beginning our visit of the Côte de Nuits, let us look at a few figures. In all the Côte d'Or there are 14,000 acres of vineyards producing an average 4,500,000 gallons of A.O.C. wines and 6,000 acres producing about 3,300,000 gallons of ordinary wines. All these wines are made by 13,000 vintners—which once again goes to show how far the land has been split up and the disadvantages this brings.

THE COMMUNE OF CHENÔVE

This is the first of the winemaking villages to come into view, at the foot of a hill 2 ½ miles from Dijon. Here can be visited the great vineyard of the dukes of Burgundy, which contains two magnificent thirteenth-century presses, one of which, used mainly for white wine, was in use until 1926. The names CLOS-DU-ROI and CLOS-DU-CHAPITRE recall their ancient masters. The A.O.C. wines are sold under regional A.O.C.s.

THE COMMUNE OF MARSANNAY-LA-CÔTE

Two miles farther on, south of Chenôve, lies this commune, famous for its rosé wines. They have become its speciality, since rosé wines are rare in Burgundy where the preference is for great red or white wines, unless catastrophic weather conditions have wiped them out—fortunately a rare occurrence. Rosé wines, obtained by crushing red grapes without vatting them, can only be sold under a regional A.O.C.—BOURGOGNE, for example, followed in the case of Marsannay by the name of the commune.

THE COMMUNE OF FIXIN

This village gives us our first A.O.C. bearing the local name—Fixin. It is an ancient village and was once attached to the abbey of Bèze. Apart from its wines, it is also famous for a statue by the sculptor Rude, *The Awakening of Napoleon*, set up in a park in 1847 by Noisot, the commander of the grenadier guards.

The vineyards of Fixin cover 316 acres. Under this A.O.C. about 50,000 gallons of red wine are made. However, other wine is sold under the more general A.O.C.—CÔTE DE NUITS-VILLAGES and other regional A.O.C.s. In the nineteenth century, the wine experts Danguey and Aubertin wrote as follows about the wines of Fixin: "These wines have a spirit, colour and bouquet that develops with age, as well as a great ability to keep a long time." We might mention in passing the classed First Growths of the commune: LA PERRIÈRE, named after a formerly famous quarry, the CLOS-DU-CHAPITRE, near the old buildings of the Chapter of Langres, LES ARVELETS, the name of which derives from *arbelaie* (place where maples grow), AUX CHEUSOTS, today called the CLOS-NAPOLÉON, LES MEIX-BAS and finally LES HERVELETS.

THE COMMUNE OF BROCHON

This village, about half a mile to the south of Fixin, was famous in former times as the home of Dijon's tragic poet, Prosper Jolyot de Crébillon (1674-1762). It now produces wines of which the best are sold as GEVREY-CHAMBERTIN and others as CÔTE-DE-NUITS-VILLAGES or as regional A.O.C.s. The area under cultivation is 116 acres. Some inexpensive wines are also produced from the *Gamay*, but are not exported.

THE COMMUNE OF GEVREY-CHAMBERTIN

Quite nearby, some eight miles from Dijon, lies the very important wine village of Gevrey, which by royal decree added the name of its best vineyard, Chambertin, to its own in 1847. In the Rue Haute the ruins of a castle belonging to the abbots of Cluny can still be seen. There are a great many vineyards producing a range of very great red wines. Let us consider first of all the Great Growths of which the following first two are the most famous.

CHAMBERTIN-CLOS-DE-BÈZE owes its name to the monks of the abbey of Bèze, who owned this land from the seventh century, through an endowment made by

The imposing château of the Clos-Vougeot lies in the hearth of the famous vineyard. Built in 1551 by the forty-eighth abbot of Cîteaux, Dom Jean Loisir, it was confiscated by the decree of February 13th, 1790, passed through many hands, lay uninhabited for a long time, and was finally rejuvenated in 1944 when it was taken over by the illustrious brotherhood of the Knights of the Tastevin of Burgundy.

Amalgaire, the Duke of Lower Burgundy. The area under cultivation is 37 acres and the average yield of this designation 7,722 gallons.

Immediately next to it lies the vineyard of CHAMBERTIN, named after a vinegrower named Bertin who originally owned land adjacent to that of the monks of Bèze, on which he planted the same wine-stock and produced an excellent wine. It became known locally as the *champ du Bertin* (Bertin's field), and has since become one of the most celebrated wines of Burgundy. Its area is 32 acres and it produces an average of 6,600 gallons. Gaston Roupnel said of this wine: "It blends grace with vigour. It joins firmness to delicacy and subtlety. All these contrary qualities produce in it an admirable synthesis of unique generosity and absolute virtue. It is in itself as great a Burgundy as it is possible to have."

CHARMES-CHAMBERTIN. Part of this vineyard was formerly called Mazoyères-Chambertin. Charmes apparently comes from *chaume* meaning "fallow land". Area—78 acres: Average yield—17,600 gallons.

CHAPELLE-CHAMBERTIN. This vineyard once held a chapel dedicated to Our Lady, built in 1155 and razed to the ground in the time of the French Revolution. Area—13 acres: Average yield—3,200 gallons.

GRIOTTE-CHAMBERTIN. This name signifies either a place planted with cherries (*griottes*), or an area of rock called, in the local dialect, *criot*. Area—13 ½ acres: Average yield—1,540 gallons.

LATRICIÈRES-CHAMBERTIN. Area—17 acres: Average yield—3,520 gallons.

MAZIS-CHAMBERTIN. Area—31 acres: Average yield 4,620 gallons.

RUCHOTTES-CHAMBERTIN. Area—8 acres: Average yield—1,672 gallons.

The difference in quality among these Great Growths is slight. Gaston Roupnel said of these wines, which all add the name Chambertin to their own: "Nothing is more appropriate than this ancient usage. Between Chambertin on one hand and Latricières and Charmes on the other hand, the difference lies in a toning down of vigour and robustness, often compensated for in good years by a more clearly tangible delicateness that is more sensitive, more mature."

Apart from these Great Growths, there are about 171,600 gallons of great red wines entitled to the A.O.C. GEVREY-CHAMBERTIN. Many vineyards are classified as First Growths. These, too, were praised by Gaston Roupnel, who valued highly "these firm, ruddy wines, of full and flavoured body".

This village, 2½ miles away from Gevrey-Chambertin, followed somewhat tardily the fashion of the Côte and in 1927 added to its own name that of one of the most famous vineyards. It was, perhaps, commercially a mistake, since Morey is easier to pronounce in every language and therefore a better market prospect.

Its remarkable wines, though relatively little known, were sold as Chambolle-Musigny or Gevrey-Chambertin before the law on A.O.C.s was passed. Nevertheless, among its vineyards are four Great Growths (red), of which the Burgundy expert Dr Ramain said in the last century that they were "powerful nectars, full-bodied, sappy, with their own special savour and a strong fragrance of strawberries or violets". These Great Growths are four in number, although most of one of them, the vineyard of LES BONNES-MARES, lies in Chambolle-Musigny and will therefore be dealt with under the next heading.

CLOS-SAINT-DENIS. This name was given because the vineyard once belonged to the abbey of St. Denis of Vergy, founded in 1623 by the archdeacon of Autun near Nuits-Saint-Georges. Area—16 acres: Average yield—3,366 gallons.

CLOS-DE-LA-ROCHE is the near neighbour of the Great Growths of Gevrey-Chambertin. Area—38 acres: Average yield—7,172 gallons.

CLOS-DE-TART. This once belonged to the Bernadine nuns of the convent of Our Lady of Tart, which received it in 1260 from the Chevalier Etienne Dojon. During the Revolution it was sold for 68,000 pounds. Area—18 acres: Average yield—3,300 gallons.

Apart from these Great Growths, about 40,000 gallons of MOREY-SAINT-DENIS (including First Growths) are produced, almost all red, of which Danguy and Aubertin gave the following appreciation: "A fine colour, a bouquet developing with age, full-bodied and winy."

THE COMMUNE OF CHAMBOLLE-MUSIGNY

About a mile and a quarter to the south, quite far away from Route Nationale 74 and some three miles from Gevrey-Chambertin, huddled in a coomb, we find the tiny village of Chambolle-Musigny. The name of its most famous vineyard, Musigny, was added to it in 1878. Dr Lavalle, the nineteenth-century writer on Burgundy wines, wrote: "Many people are of the opinion that this commune produces the most delicate wines of the Côte de Nuits". There are two great wines:

MUSIGNY. "The wine of silk and lace, the supreme delicateness of which knows no violence but can veil its vigour", as Gaston Roupnel put it. The name of the vineyard is very ancient; it is already found in an Act of 1110. It produces a few gallons of white wine —quite exceptional in this area and for a Great Growth—about 180 on the average, as against 6,500 for red in a total area of 26 acres.

LES BONNES-MARES. As we have seen, this vineyard lies partly in Morey-Saint-Denis (4½ acres) and partly in Chambolle (34 acres). Its name recalls perhaps the *Maires*, the goddesses who protected the harvests in many ancient nations, or possibly the word *marer*, to plough. An average of 8,580 gallons is produced here.

Apart from these two Great Growths, Chambolle-Musigny has First Growths entitled to the village A.O.C. Danguy and Aubertin said about them: "They have a fine delicate bouquet and several wine experts have said they are the finest, most perfumed and most delicate in the Côte de Nuits. They are extremely winy, beautifully coloured and pungent." Area—427 acres: Average yield under the CHAMBOLLE-MUSIGNY A.O.C. (including First Growths) is 92,664 gallons. The following are some of the First Growth vineyards: LES AMOUREUSES, LES CHARMES, LES CRAS, LES BORNIQUES, LES BAUDES, LES HAUTS-DOIX, DERRIÈRE-LA-GRANGE, LES FOUSSELOTTES, LES PLANTES, LES CHATELOTS, LES GRUENCHERS, AUX BEAUX-BRUNS and AUX COMBOTTES.

THE COMMUNE OF VOUGEOT

About half a mile from Chambolle, beside the Route Nationale, lies the smallest village in the Côte but certainly one of the best known throughout the world, especially since the brotherhood of the Knights of the Tastevin began inviting wine-lovers from every country to its "Chapters" held in the château on the property. Apart from these and official guests, representatives of the press, radio, television and cinema —the modern means of communications—are particularly fond of the place. It is not surprising that its name is on everybody's lips. The CLOS-DE-VOUGEOT is "a solemn and beautiful thing, powerful yet not overpowering", said Gaston Roupnel.

The property was first developed by the monks of Cîteaux, early in the twelfth century. There followed a patient task of regrouping, since, apart from endowments, several parcels of land had to be incorporated before it reached its present size of 124 acres.

At first, the monks built a modest chapel, a shelter for their presses and a cellar for their new wines. The wines, when ready, were taken to a safer refuge and better cellars in the Château of Gilly-les-Vougeot, a few miles away in the plain. During the Renaissance, in 1551, the 48th abbot, Dom Jean Loisir, had the château built. It remained the property of Cîteaux until the Revolution, when it was sold as a "national asset". Thus began the subdivisions that only stopped when 65 owners shared the vines and the Brotherhood owned the building.

The wine produced at the Clos-Vougeot, classified as a Great Growth, has always enjoyed the very best of reputations and even received military honours. Stendhal tells us how Colonel Bisson, while passing on his way to join the army on the Rhine, halted his troops and made them present arms before the Clos to the sound of bugles and drums. The Duke of Aumale apparently did the same.

An average of 28,600 gallons of wine with the A.O.C. CLOS-VOUGEOT or, to give it its modern form, CLOS-DE-VOUGEOT A.O.C., is produced yearly. Another nineteenth-century wine-lover, Dr Morelot, defined it as follows: "With ROMANÉE and CHAMBERTIN and a few others, it shares the first position among the wines of the Côte d'Or and even the whole of France."

The commune of Vougeot yields, from just over 30 acres, various other red wines entitled to the VOUGEOT A.O.C., but not to be confused with the Great Growth. The First Growth vineyards are: the CLOS-DE-LA-PERRIÈRE, LES CRAS, LES PETITS-VOUGEOTS and the CLOS-BLANC.

THE COMMUNE OF VOSNE-ROMANÉE

Courtépée wrote in the eighteenth century: "There are no common wines in Vosne." This little village, two miles from Vougeot, has no fewer than seven Great Growths, of which two are produced in the neighbouring commune of Flagey-Echézeaux but are legally linked with Vosne-Romanée.

The name ROMANÉE recalls ancient deeds and perhaps the beginnings of these vineyards during the Roman occupation.

Three different wines carry this name:

LA ROMANÉE. About 550 gallons produced from just over two acres of land.

ROMANÉE-CONTI. This vineyard became the property of the princes of Conti in 1760. So generously did they spread the fame of their "velvet and satin" wine, as Mgr. de Juigné described it, that their name became forever linked to the property. On 4 ½ acres, an average of 1,100 gallons (just over 6,500 bottles) are produced of this wine, which Ramain called "magnificent, with a penetrating bouquet of violets, mingling with a perfume of cherries, the colour of sparkling rubies and an extremely delicate softness". This vineyard was also the last to resist phylloxera. During the last war, however, the shortage of carbon disulphide led to the vine's destruction. New grafted vine-stock had to be planted and the first vintage took place in 1952.

ROMANÉE-SAINT-VIVANT, another vineyard to bear the Romanée name, harks back to the monastery of St. Vivant, founded at the beginning of the tenth century à few miles from Nuits-Saint-Georges (24 acres producing an average 3,650 gallons).

RICHEBOURG is a wine of which Camille Rodier once said: "This splendid growth with its incomparable velvetiness and wealth of bouquet is one of the most sumptuous of Burgundy." Part of its 20 acres belonged to the monks of Cîteaux before the Revolution. Average yield—5,300 gallons.

LA TACHE. With an area of 15 acres this vineyard produces an average 3,740 gallons.

LES GRANDS ECHÉZEAUX and LES ECHÉZEAUX. These vineyards, the south-east neighbours of the Clos-Vougeot, are in the commune of Flagey-Echézeaux. The first—Area 23 acres: Average yield 6,600 gallons. The second—76 acres and 12,100 gallons.

A final appreciation: "Burgundy has produced nothing better than this little corner, which epitomizes its enchantments and whose wines express the tender generosity of its spirit."

THE COMMUNES OF NUITS-SAINT-GEORGES AND PREMEAUX

Nuits-Saint-Georges (Saint-Georges, the name of its best vineyard, was added in 1892) is the little Burgundian village that gave its name to this part of the Côte. Little remains of its past except the church of St. Symphorien, founded in the thirteenth century. But it was here that the Brotherhood of the Knights of the Tastevin was founded by Georges Faiveley and Camille Rodier. The first chapter was held on November 16th, 1934 in the Caveau Nuiton. This soon became too small as success followed success, and today it is the Château of Clos-Vougeot, a more imposing structure, that shelters the hosts and guests at the numerous events organized by the Brotherhood.

Many important wine shippers are to be found at Nuits, together with firms specialized in the manufacture of sparkling Burgundy, of which more than one million bottles are made each year. In 1882, one of the shippers, a much travelled man and long a student of the wines of the region, had the idea of using the Champagne method. The result was a white, a rosé and a red sparkling wine, the latter of which is in particularly great demand in the Nordic countries, Great Britain, the United States and other English-speaking countries. There are also several liqueur manufacturers and two large fruit juice firms in Nuits-Saint-Georges. This all goes to make the town a thriving commercial centre. As Paul Cazin remarked: "The only thing you don't see in Nuits is water."

The two communes in the title of this section produce wines sold under the A.O.C.s of Nuits or Nuits-Saint-Georges (which is the same thing) on an area of 928 acres, averaging 171,600 gallons of red and 660 gallons of white wines.

Dr Lavalle once wrote: "Generally speaking, the wines of Nuits are less firm, less harsh than the wines of Gevrey and mature more quickly. They have more body and colour than those of Chambolle-Musigny."

Nuits has a civic hospice, founded in 1692. Through the centuries, endowments have led to its possessing considerable property solely in vineyards producing the First Growths of the town. Every year its wines are sold by public auction, usually the Sunday before Palm Sunday. There are fourteen vintages and in 1968, for example, 102 batches were sold in 37 lots.

THE COMMUNES OF PRISSEY, COMBLANCHIEN AND CORGOLOIN

A.O.C. Côte de Nuits-Villages

These three communes are the last of the Côte de Nuits. The last two are mainly famous for their large quarries which yield a stone which is easy to polish and used to cover floors. The wines are partly covered by the A.O.C. Côte de Nuits-Villages.

The wines sold under this A.O.C. do not come from all the villages of the Côte de Nuits, but solely from the following five: Brochon and Fixin, mentioned at the beginning of the chapter; Prissey, Comblanchien and Corgoloin. The more famous A.O.C.s—Gevrey-Chambertin, Morey-Saint-Denis, Chambolle-Musigny, Vosne-Romanée and Nuits-Saint-Georges may never be sold as Côte de Nuits-Villages. The average amount declared under the A.O.C. Côte de Nuits-Villages is 86,592 gallons, all being red wines.

We shall now leave the Côte de Nuits with its very great red wines. Recalling what we said at the beginning of this chapter, our advice is not to let them get too old. René Engel, that reputed wine expert and Grand Cardinal of the Brotherhood of the Knights of the Tastevin, is fond of saying: "Old wines are unfortunately not always the best. . . . To have very old wines in one's cellar is a little like having a centenarian grandmother in the family. She is proudly presented to the guests, but they must be apologized to in advance in case she has a dewdrop on the end of her nose or if she is only half awake."

THE CÔTE DE BEAUNE

The second part of the great vineyards of the Côte d'Or begins after the stone quarries of Comblanchien.

The wines here are more varied and though there is only one Great Growth, Corton, among the red wines, all the Great Growths in the white wines are in this area. It used to be said that all the wines of the Côte de Beaune were "early" wines (vins de primeur) as opposed to the "laying down" wines (vins de garde) of the Côte de Nuits. In other words, they could be enjoyed much younger. Today, however, all wines are ready sooner than in the past.

Let us then follow the south-westerly road that leads from Ladoix-Serrigny in the direction of Mâcon as far as Cheilly. Some names are not always well-known, but if one day the wine-lover can spare a few moments to make the acquaintance of these wines he will have some agreeable surprises. As Guy Faiveley, Grand Master of the Brotherhood of the Knights of the Tastevin, once remarked: "There are some wines that are poets, others that are prose-writers. There are those that are performers or lithe acrobats and others that are over-powering boxers."

THE COMMUNE OF LADOIX-SERRIGNY

This winegrowing commune produces red and white wines sold under various A.O.C.s including Corton. The area under vine is 335 acres. The reds are sold, apart from under the appellation Corton—which is the only red Great Growth of the Côte de Beaune—mostly as Côte de Beaune-Villages. There is an average yield of about 1,100 gallons of white wine and 26,400 gallons of red sold as Ladoix.

Aloxe is a pretty village on a small hillock. In 1862, the name of its most famous vineyard was added to it. Throughout the ages, it has been graced by the exalted. The Emperor Charlemagne owned many *ouvrées* (about one-ninth of an acre) of vineyards. The Emperor Otho was also an owner: he seems to have given his name to CORTON—the *curtis* ("estate" or "garden") *Othonis* ("of Otho"). The large abbeys, including Cîteaux, possessed land in this corner of Burgundy. Two Great Growths are produced here. CORTON was mentioned by Voltaire when writing to Gabriel le Bault, president of the Parliament of Burgundy: "The older I become, Sir, the more I value your kindness. Your excellent wine is becoming indispensable to me." Especially as he did not want to pay for it ! The dukes of Burgundy and later the kings of

Founded in 1443 by Nicolas Rolin, chancellor to Philip the Good, the Hôtel-Dieu in Beaune is an architectural jewel of Burgundy. Together with the Hospice de la Charité, it makes up the illustrious group of the "Hospices de Beaune". Their vineyards, increased throughout the centuries by endowments, now cover 130 acres. Every November the traditional sale of their wines takes place, the proceeds being used to maintain the institutions.

France owned 110 *ouvrées* (about 12 acres) of one of the vineyards in this A.O.C. It is still called *Le Clos du Roy*, "the king's vineyard". Corton produces about 52,800 gallons of red and 1,460 gallons of white wine. "The Cortons of good years are perfect wines, worthy of the most delicate gourmet's table," said Dr Lavalle.

The second Great Growth is Corton-Charlemagne, a white wine, the name obviously recalling the Emperor Charlemagne. He loved the region and made numerous gifts to the churches in the province, especially those of St. Vincent at Chalon-sur-Saône, Saulieu and other places. The annual yield averages 17,600 gallons, of which Camille Rodier said: "A white wine of great bearing, rich in alcohol, forceful, golden, sappy, smelling of cinnamon and tasting of gun flint."

Aloxe-Corton produces an average of 77,000 gallons sold under its name, 99 per cent of the yield being red. Dr Lavalle said of them in the last century: "They are the firmest and frankest wines of the Côte de Beaune."

THE COMMUNE OF PERNAND-VERGELESSES

Behind the Aloxe hillock, at the bottom of a coomb in a very pretty setting, the village of Pernand-Vergelesses produces part of the Corton and Corton-Charlemagne wines. As well as the Corton, red wines are sold under the village name or as Côte de Beaune-Villages. There are 3,256 gallons of white and 27,940 gallons of red wine produced on 353 acres. Danguy and Aubertin wrote: "These wines are a little firmer than those of Savigny: they have fire and strength and are worth laying down."

THE COMMUNE OF SAVIGNY-LÈS-BEAUNE

Away from the Côte and at the mouth of a deep valley lies this ancient village which, for a very long time, was the home of important wine shippers. In more recent times they have tended to pass over Savigny in favour of Beaune and Nuits, but this village is still quite busy, for its wines are famous. Under the Savigny A.O.C., 5,390 gallons of white and 125,400 gallons of red wines are produced. Camille Rodier said of them: "These perfumed, mellow, young and healthy wines are rich in bouquet."

THE COMMUNE OF CHOREY-LÈS-BEAUNE

Facing Savigny from the other side of Route Nationale 74 is Chorey-lès-Beaune. Its 300 or so acres produce 33,000 gallons of red wine sold under the village name or under the name of Côte de Beaune-Villages. In 1828, Dr Morelot wrote: "The good Chorey wines are used when the best quality wines are passing through a bad period. They improve them and make them agreeable to drink."

THE COMMUNE OF BEAUNE

Beaune, which has given its name to this part of the Côte since the Roman occupation, is the real capital of Burgundy. Its life is centred around the disposal of fine wines. Over sixty shippers use the numerous cellars which through the centuries were dug into its ramparts. Convents, churches and abbeys in the town and surrounding area have also used them to keep their wines well protected. Many lords have had the same idea, not to mention the militant religious orders.

The imposing bastions that rise from the ramparts and are visible from a great distance, have been and still are used to store the bottles and barrels in the deep shelter of their seven-yard thick walls. For this very reason, the shippers' installations are extremely interesting to visit, as the tourists know full well. Beaune is, therefore, an extremely ancient town still almost completely surrounded by walls which guard the many historical monuments—the Basilica of Our Lady, the ancient church of St. Nicolas, the palace of the dukes of Burgundy, which has been made into a wine museum that no enthusiast should miss, the belfrey, the old houses, etc., and towering above the rest, the *Hôtel-Dieu*, a marvel of the fifteenth century. It was founded in 1443 by Nicolas Rolin, then chancellor to Philip the Good, Duke of Burgundy, and his wife, Guigone de Salins, to aid the destitute. It has managed to continue its ancient role, a rare achievement. The "ladies of charity" still go from room to room caring for and comforting the sick, as they have done uninterruptedly for nearly five and a half centuries. Although the old hospital now has a modern neighbour, it has not suffered as a result. Its own life flourishes, as can be attested by the tens of thousands of tourists who visit it every year. Over the centuries, many donations have been made to the *Hôtel-Dieu* and the *Hospice de la Charité*, which are kept under joint management. Some

125 acres of vineyards have gradually accumulated to the estate of the Hospice de Beaune: in Corton-Charlemagne and Meursault for white wines and in Aloxe-Corton, Auxey-Duresses, Beaune, Corton, Monthelie, Pommard, Savigny and Volnay for red wines. The auctioning of the Hospice's wines on the third Sunday in November is renowned throughout the world as being "the world's greatest charity sale". And it is a fact that it enables the work of Nicolas Rolin to be continued year after year in support of the old and sick and the needy. In 1966, 752 casks brought to the estate 2,312,033 new French francs.

The vineyards of Beaune cover a large area: 1,329 acres are contained within the area allowed to sell wines under this designation. The average yield is 196,900 gallons, of which 95 per cent is red. Dr Lavalle, the famous wine expert of the last century,

whom we have already quoted, gave this appreciation of them: "I think that the great wines of Beaune are worthy of the greatest praise. The best vintages, in good years, reach a point at which they cannot be distinguished from the most outstanding wines, except by well-practised experts; and are more often than not they are sold at the highest prices. The second best vintages are the everyday wines of princes."

The vineyards of Beaune that give the best wines are: LES MARCONNETS, LES FÈVES, LES BRESSANDES, LES GRÈVES, LES TEURONS, LE CLOS-DES-MOUCHES, LE CLOS-DU-ROI, LES AVAUX, LES TOUSSAINTS, LES BOUCHEROTTES, LES VIGNES-FRANCHES, LES AIGROTS etc.: there are too many to mention them all.

A look around the cellars and a visit to the Hôtel-Dieu is the normal programme of more than 300,000 tourists who visit Beaune every year.

THE COMMUNE OF POMMARD

Who does not know the name of this village two miles south of Beaune? Nevertheless, to reach it you must leave Route Nationale 74 and take Route Nationale 73 towards Autun, passing through several miles of vineyards.

Pommard, a name easy to pronounce in any language, was for this very reason long a synonym for the wines of the Côte de Beaune. The law on A.O.C.s

restricted the use of its name to those wines produced on the 838 acres in the commune. Many wines from neighbouring villages were affected by this measure, since they lost a traditional and easy marketing channel. About 209,000 gallons of "firm, ruddy, frank and long-lasting wines", to quote Dr Morelot, are now produced under the POMMARD A.O.C. These wines were steady favourites of the great lords and abbeys.

THE COMMUNE OF VOLNAY

En dépit de Pommard et de Meursault,
C'est toujours Volnay le plus haut.

In spite of Pommard and Meursault,
It's still Volnay that's the highest.

This Burgundy saying does not refer to the relative qualities of the wines but to the geographical situations of these villages, with Volnay on top of the hill above its vineyards and Meursault and Pommard below.

On an area of 530 acres are produced an average of 135,850 gallons, all of red wine. The wines of Volnay are qualified by Camille Rodier as being "less ruddy than BEAUNE or Pommard, noted especially for their elegance, smooth taste, perfect balance and quite delicate bouquet. After MUSIGNY, they are the finest wines in all Burgundy." It should be noted that VOLNAY-CAILLERETS are produced in Meursault.

THE COMMUNE OF MONTHELIE

A mile and a half from Volnay, with its back to the Côte, this village is made picturesque by its ancient houses that rise like steps up the hill. Its vines grow on a little over 230 acres which produce an average 880 gal-

lons of white wine and 30,800 gallons of red. A technical advisor to the I.N.A.O. (National Institute for Designations of Origin) had expressed the opinion that these wines are not as well known as they ought to be.

THE COMMUNE OF AUXEY-DURESSES

At the foot of Monthelie, deep in a large valley, lies the little village of Auxey-Duresses. The area was much frequented by the Gauls, who built a camp on the mountain overlooking the countryside. On about 370 acres under the village name an average of 16,170 gallons of white wine and 30,800 gallons of red

are produced. The red wines are *forts gravains*, meaning not lacking in colour, body or bouquet. Pierre Léon Gauthier wrote: "On the vines of Duresses ripens a wine that was long sold under the VOLNAY and POMMARD labels—this was before A.O.C.s—without any detriment to the good name of those great wines."

63

THE COMMUNE OF SAINT-ROMAIN

At the foot of the magnificent cliffs that surround the valley of Auxey-Duresses the houses of Saint-Romain climb like stepping stones up the slope. The village once possessed a castle, the ruins of which are still to be seen. Now its 358 acres produce an average 10,780 gallons of white wine and 46,922 gallons of red under the village name. Roland Thévenin, poet and mayor of the village, sang its praises thus:

O SAINT-ROMAIN hardi, robuste et si fruité,
Nous aimons ta fraîcheur ainsi que ta finesse.

O SAINT-ROMAIN, forthright, robust and so fruity,
We love your freshness and delicacy.

THE COMMUNE OF MEURSAULT

We now return to the Côte, to the little town of Meursault which covers the entry to the valley leading to Auxerre. It was probably the first place occupied by the Romans when they penetrated this region. The vineyards of Meursault cover 1,030 acres and have always been famous for their white wines. For four miles the soil becomes quite unlike that of Beaune or Volnay, and the *Chardonnay* grape is king. There are some 9,200 gallons of red wine produced here but the 209,000 gallons of white wine are better known by far. Camille Rodier wrote: "MEURSAULT white wines have the following special characteristic—they are both dry and mellow, which is quite unusual. They are rich in alcohol, a beautiful golden green in colour, bright and clear, they keep well and have the frank taste of ripe grapes and a touch of hazelnut. They are among the most famous white wines of France."

Meursault is also famous for its *Paulée*, which takes up the last of the Three Glorious Days devoted to the wines of Burgundy. The *Paulée* was created in 1923 by Count Lafon and is the official dinner closing the vintage. It is given by the vineyard owners for all those who worked in the vintage with them. Nowadays, about four hundred persons attend this joyous banquet, which is not too official, since custom has it that everyone brings a bottle of his greatest and rarest wine to pass around the table—and that does not tend to dampen the celebrations!

THE COMMUNES OF PULIGNY-MONTRACHET AND CHASSAGNE-MONTRACHET

At the northern end of the Côte d'Or, in the commune of Gevrey-Chambertin and the neighbouring villages are the Very Great Growths of red wines. In the south, we find the Great Growths of white wines. Puligny-Montrachet, like the Côte de Meursault, produces almost nothing but white wines. There are five Great Growths in this region which we shall describe in descending order of merit.

MONTRACHET sits astride two communes: two-thirds in Puligny and one-third in Chassagne. Both added its name to theirs towards the end of the nineteenth century. In 1878, Bertall wrote: "this admirable white wine is the first among the white wines of Burgundy, as CHÂTEAU-YQUEM is the first among the white wines of Bordeaux. Let us not compare the two, say enthusiasts, let us merely say that they are both the first among the white wines of the world." This goes hand in hand with Dr Lavalle's comment in 1855: "The wine of Montrachet must be considered as one of those marvels whose perfection can only be appreciated by a small number of the elect." Only 20,000 or so bottles are produced annually on an area of 18 ½ acres. There is very little true Montrachet and the enthusiast must be careful not to confuse it with all the other wines that include the word Montrachet in their A.O.C.s.

CHEVALIER-MONTRACHET is geographically just above MONTRACHET and is about the same size. The wine can be drunk a little earlier than its neighbour, but it rarely attains the same perfection. It is, therefore, classified just below MONTRACHET. The average yield is 2,662 gallons or about 15,000 bottles.

BÂTARD-MONTRACHET grows on 29 acres just below Montrachet; the two are separated by a path. The vineyard sits astride Puligny and Chassagne and produces an average 6,710 gallons.

BIENVENUE-BÂTARD-MONTRACHET (Area—5 ½ acres, average yield—2,046 gallons) and CRIOTS-BÂTARD-MONTRACHET, situated in Chassagne, producing an average 880 gallons, are the last of the Great Growths of white wines.

The origin of these names is often debated. One story, which we summarize here although we cannot guarantee its authenticity, has it that during the Crusades, the governor of the castle of Montrachet had a son who departed for the Holy Land. Meanwhile, the old lord was bored at the castle and took to passing near the Clos des Pucelles, where the young maidens of the region disported themselves. The Devil tempted him and nine months later a blessed event took place. The Duke of Burgundy, who was not amused, decreed

64

The name Corton Charlemagne recalls the ownership of the Emperor, who once held many acres here. And Corton is a reminder of another Emperor—Otho, for the name is said to have come from *Cortis Othonis*—the garden of Otho.

The pretty village of Aloxe-Corton nestles on the slopes of a wooded hillock overlooking the road from Beaune to Dijon. The name Corton was added to the village name of Aloxe to honour the only red Great Growth of the Côte de Beaune.

Meursault stands at the entry of the valley leading to Auxerre,
and is, of course, famous for its delicious dry and mellow white
wines. It is also known for its *Paulée*, the vintage dinner.

that in the line of the Montrachets, the old lord was henceforth to be known as Montrachet the Elder, the Crusader as the Chevalier Montrachet and the child as the Bâtard Montrachet. The crusader was killed in battle so the bastard inherited and was welcomed at the castle with cries of "welcome to the bastard of Montrachet". But the lord, already an old man, could not bear to hear the baby crying and protested in patois: *a crio l'Bâtard* (the bastard is crying). When the castle was destroyed, these names were given to the vineyards in their memory.

Puligny-Montrachet produces 73,480 gallons of white and 5,830 gallons of red wine on nearly 580 acres under the village name. Camille Rodier says of them: "These fruity, distinguished and sweet-smelling white wines are related to the better MEURSAULTS." And, in fact, LES CAILLERETS, LES COMBETTES, LES PUCELLES, LES FOLATIÈRES, etc. are very distinguished wines.

Chassagne-Montrachet produces much more red wine than Puligny, averaging 924,000 gallons. These are among the best on the Côte. Camille Rodier had no hesitation in saying: "The red CHASSAGNES are undeniably like certain good vintages of the Côte de Nuits." There is also a good deal of white wine—53,900 gallons on average, resembling all the others produced on this part of the Côte, relatively dry and extremely subtle.

THE COMMUNE OF SAINT-AUBIN

Just behind Chassagne, towards Paris on Route Nationale 6, we cross this little winegrowing village whose area under vine is about 300 acres. Under its name, or more generally under the appellation CÔTE DE BEAUNE-VILLAGES, an average of 12,760 gallons of white and 19,140 gallons of red wine are produced. The hamlet of Gamay, where the vine of the same name was born, is part of Saint-Aubin.

THE COMMUNE OF SANTENAY

Santenay is the last winegrowing commune of the Côte d'Or. It has been inhabited since time immemorial and its grottoes contain many traces of their neolithic and iron-age inhabitants. Although a wine village, Santenay has distinguished itself further by possessing, of all things a mineral water spring! The villagers tend to avoid it, however, and leave it to the "city folk" to enjoy. The 939 acres under vine produce, under the SANTENAY label, an average 83,400 gallons of red and only 2,200 gallons of white wines. Minimum alcohol content for the red wines is 10.5º and for the white wines 11º. Dr Lavalle describes these wines as follows: "They are firm, mellow and always keep well. With age, they acquire a very delicate bouquet." The best are from the *climat* of Les Gravière, the only one in the commune with a *tête de cuvée* classification. Some wines are blended with those of other communes and sold under the A.O.C. CÔTE DE BEAUNE-VILLAGES.

THE COMMUNES OF CHEILLY, DEZIZE AND SAMPIGNY-LES-MARANGES

After the Côte d'Or, we enter Saône-et-Loire through these villages. As their vineyards are next to Santenay, they are included in the Côte de Beaune, but are sold either under their own names or under the A.O.C., CÔTE DE BEAUNE-VILLAGES. The area under vine is about 300 acres in Cheilly, 100 acres in Dezize and 150 acres in Sampigny-les-Maranges. Very little wine is declared under this appellation and the villages are producing an average of 4,500 gallons, 2,600 gallons and 2,500 gallons of red wine respectively.

THE CÔTE DE BEAUNE-VILLAGES A.O.C.

This is an A.O.C. that is used a great deal and that is well-known to consumers. The preceding tour of the Côte de Beaune villages reveals many names that are not familiar to the wine-buying public. The CÔTE DE BEAUNE-VILLAGES appellation allows these lesser known villages to come together under the same title, thus avoiding any difficulties they might otherwise have in selling their excellent wines. (They nevertheless retain the right to produce wines under their own names if they wish to do so.) CÔTE DE BEAUNE-VILLAGES always indicates a red wine, and comes from the villages or parts of the villages in the following list: Auxey-Duresses, Chassagne-Montrachet, Cheilly-lès-Maranges, Chorey-lès-Beaune, Côte de Beaune, Dezize-lès-Maranges, Ladoix-Serrigny, Meursault rouge, Meursault-Blagny, Monthelie, Pernand-Vergelesses, Puligny-Montrachet, St-Aubin, Sampigny-lès-Maranges, Santenay, Savigny.

THE REGION OF MERCUREY

We now leave the Côte d'Or for Saône-et-Loire, but, in a sense, we are still in the Côte de Beaune of which Mercurey is traditionally a continuation through its methods of cultivation and vinification, the character of its wines and its trading customs.

These vineyards were named the Côte Chalonnaise after the town of Chalon-sur-Saône, a busy trading centre in the first few centuries of our era since it was well situated for both land and river transport. At a later date, it became an important wine centre for the region, but this has gradually been eroded by industry, which is now master of the town.

We shall travel from north to south in dealing with the four A.O.C.s in the region—RULLY, MERCUREY, GIVRY and MONTAGNY.

RULLY. This is an ancient village, 14 miles from Beaune, near Chagny and Route Nationale 6. It dates back to Roman times. Its caves were even inhabited during the stone ages. It was originally on the hill, but the plague of 1347 forced the inhabitants to resettle farther down. The village still has a thirteenth-century feudal castle, which was altered in the fifteenth century.

The vineyards of the RULLY A.O.C. give 18,832 gallons of white wine and 5,170 gallons of red. This white wine is very individualistic, heady and perfumed and lending itself to the Champagne method. It was the original reason for the considerable trade in sparkling Burgundy wines which developed in this village.

MERCUREY. The wines permitted to use this A.O.C. are produced in a large vineyard situated within several communes. Mercurey is reminiscent of the Roman occupation through its very name; Saint-Martin-sous-Montagne is one of the many villages named after the most popular saint in Burgundy; and finally, across the Orboise River from Mercurey, there is Bourgneuf-Val-d'Or. These wines are in all respects similar to those of the Côte de Beaune. "They differ from the Santenays only by an imperceptible degree," said Claude Bonvin. A. Jullien wrote: "The red wines of Mercurey are distinguished by their perfume: they are honest and may be kept for a long time." The average yield is 220,000 gallons of reds and 15,000 of whites. The First Growths take the names of the five following vineyards: CLOS-DU-ROY, CLOS-VOYEN, CLOS-MARCILLY, CLOS-DES-FOURNEAUX, CLOS-DES-MONTAIGUS.

GIVRY. The ancient township of this name goes back to Gallo-Roman times. It produces, in its confines, the wines allowed to use this A.O.C. Once upon a time they were in great demand, but since the law on A.O.C.s, few enthusiasts have heard their name—a great pity. In the nineteenth century, A. Jullien said that the privileged growths of this commune were superior to those of Mercurey. Frank, strong and perfumed, they are the wines of connoisseurs. Nowadays, the average yield under the GIVRY name is 30,470 gallons of red wine and 4,840 gallons of white.

MONTAGNY. The wines sold under this A.O.C. come from the communes of Montagny, Buxy, Saint-Vallerin and Jully-les-Buxy, with a total area of 754 acres producing 51,150 gallons of white wine alone. It is said they "keep the mouth clean and the head clear".

THE MÂCONNAIS

This is the most important wine area of the Saône-et Loire, taking its name from its capital. Mâcon, "the queen of the Saône", is called thus because it lies beside a magnificent stretch of water, which makes it a metropolis for boat lovers as well. Known in Roman times as *Matisco in Aeduis*, the city was part of the Eduens, the same Gallic province as the future Côte d'Or. The town was important in Roman times. It possessed grain stores and a factory producing arrows and javelins "because the wood in the region was excellent for the purpose". At that time, it was built at the foot of the Roman Castrum, but gradually the city slipped down towards the Saône, especially after being devastated by the Barbarians in the fifth century and the Saracens in the eighth. It still possesses many Gothic and Renaissance remains, including a famous wooden house and various aristocratic residences of the eighteenth century.

The Mâconnais is, therefore, a very ancient region, with magnificent vineyards and remarkable Romanesque churches in many of its tiny villages. There were more vineyards before the phylloxera plague than today. In the north of the region, for example, lies Tournus, a very ancient town with the famous Romanesque church of St. Philibert and some very old houses. The vineyards surrounding it were mentioned by the poet Ausonus and were increased in size by the abbey of Cluney. It was even said that "Tournus produced a *Pinot* wine at the end of the sixteenth century as good as the most famous." However, there remain today but a few scattered vineyards producing mainly white wines. One must go down to the south of the Mâconnais to find a very important vineyard at the foot of a hill, where, according to Lamartine "the autumn grapes distill their balmy liqueur". Lamartine considered himself "a vintner rather than a poet" and his memory is kept all along the "Circuit Lamartinien", through Milly-Lamartine where he lived as a child, the château of Monceau, one of his favourite residences, and the château of Pierreclos, home of Marguerite, the Laurence of his *Jocelyn*. This area contains the various A.O.C.s we are about to look at.

POUILLY-FUISSÉ. The white wine sold under this A.O.C. is too well known throughout the world to need a lengthy description. It comes from the communes of Pouilly, Fuissé, Solutré, Vergisson and Chaintré. This region is easy to locate because of the two spurs of rock that stick up like saw teeth at Vergisson and Solutré. At the foot of the latter lies the prehistoric site after which the Solutrian epoch of paleology was named. A large number of human skeletons and the bones of thousands of horses have been found there. The view from the top of these rocks is magnificent, with vineyards surrounding them on all sides and stretching, to the east, as far as Mâcon and the Beaujolais on the horizon. POUILLY-FUISSÉ charms the eye before the palate. Its colour is golden shot with emerald: it is as vigorous as the greatest growths of Burgundy; its thoroughbred delicacy is perfumed with a particularly delightful bouquet. An average 462,000 gallons of this wine are produced.

POUILLY-VINZELLES and POUILLY-LOCHÉ. These two A.O.C.s, also applicable to white wines, are different from the previous ones. POUILLY-LOCHÉ may be called POUILLY-VINZELLES but not vice versa. The vineyards are near those of POUILLY-FUISSÉ and the quantity is very similar, but not much is produced under these two A.O.C.s—33,000 gallons of POUILLY-VINZELLES and only 11,000 of POUILLY-LOCHÉ.

MÂCON. The vineyards of the Mâconnais are too extensive to permit giving all the details of the various A.O.C.s. Some villages have been singled out and are allowed to append their names to the word Mâcon (these are white wines) or are allowed to sell their wines as MÂCON-VILLAGES.

The difference between MÂCON SUPÉRIEUR and MÂCON white wines is mainly a matter of yield per acre and minimum alcoholic strength. As for the red and rosé wines, usually made from the *Gamay* grape, some villages may append their names to Mâcon, but their wines may never be sold as MÂCON-VILLAGES, which is strictly for white wines. These Mâconnais wines hold an important position in the Burgundy wine selection. White wines that may be sold as MÂCON-VILLAGES or MÂCON SUPÉRIEUR are often sold as BOURGOGNE BLANC and have a worldwide reputation under this general A.O.C. The red wines, without claiming the qualities of the Côte d'Or wines, honourably fulfil their role as the vanguard of the fine wines of Burgundy. They are quite full-bodied and agreeably fruity early wines, to be drunk young but unlikely to turn vinagery even if kept for a long time.

THE BEAUJOLAIS

We are now in the south of Burgundy, in this great and beautiful vineyard of the Rhône department whose northern tip overlaps the Saône-et-Loire department.

The region gets its name from the château of Beaujeu, built in the middle of the ninth century and very important under the first family of the house of Beaujeu until 1265. One of the lords, Humbert III, built a new village in 1110 nearer the Saône, then the major artery of communications. He little realized that the new village, Villefranche, would gradually assume the position and influence of Beaujeu in the management of the affairs of the Beaujolais until, in 1532, it became the capital of the region.

The province, at first a buffer state between the Mâconnais and the Lyonnais, was later joined to the kingdom of France, where it remained until 1560. Then it fell into the hands of the Bourbon-Montpensiers and still later, in 1626, into the hands of the Orleans family.

The revolutions of 1789, 1830 and 1848 passed almost unnoticed in the Beaujolais, which throughout its existence has known events of greater local impact —invasions, pillages, famines and plagues. In 1790, the province was integrated into the newly created departments—first Rhône-Loire, then Rhône from November 1793 when Lyons, its capital, revolted against the Convention.

The present vineyards, 32 miles long and between seven and ten miles wide, have 37,065 acres of fine wines, reaching an altitude of over 1,600 feet towards the Monts-du-Beaujolais that crowd the western horizon. To the east, Route Nationale 6, following the Saône at several hundred yards distance, marks the far boundary of the vineyards. It is necessary for the traveller to leave the main road if he wants to further his acquaintance with this beautiful region. The vineyards of the Beaujolais were not always admired as they are today. Their history and development are quite unlike those of the other regions of Burgundy. Although some names are indubitably Roman in origin—Jullié, Juliénas, Romanèche, for example—the first document known to speak of vineyards, the Cartulary of St. Vincent, goes back to the end of the tenth century. The next is of a vineyard at Brulliez, now called Brouilly, mentioned in an endowment made in 1160. Another ancient document referring to the existence of vines tells of a canon of Lyon, Odon Rigaud, who, in 1282, gave his cathedral church a great bell called the "Rigaud" and a vine, the produce of which was to be kept for the persons who rang the bell. This is the origin of the expression, well known throughout Burgundy, "to drink by ringing the Rigaud" or "to drink like a bell-ringer".

The wines of Beaujolais were originally used to quench the thirst of Lyons. Even now there is still a saying that three rivers flow into the town—the Rhône, the Saône and the Beaujolais. They were very often in competition with the vintners of the Mâconnais, who had to pay extremely high duties before their produce was allowed into the town.

Furthermore, since the Beaujolais is not part of the duchy of Burgundy, its wines could not be sold there. An ordinance of 1446 stated that in Dijon "provisions may include the wines of Tournus, the Chalonnais and the Beaunois and this side of the mountains as far as Messigny, but not those of the lowlands such as the Lyonnais, the Viennois, Tournon and other places".

It was purely by chance that the wines of the Beaujolais, towards the seventeenth century, became known outside their own area. Some merchants from the Lorraine, while in Mâcon, tasted some wines unknown to them. They were taken to where they were produced and bought several cellars. The news was heard by two other shippers, this time from Paris, and business rapidly expanded between the Beaujolais and the French capital.

However, when it came to taking the wines to the north the means of transport were found to be all but non-existent. The opening of the Briare canal made it easier to reach Paris via the Monts-du-Beaujolais and the Loire—a very important event for the wines of the Mâconnais as well, since they also benefited.

After the royal edict of 1776, which at Turgot's instigation established unrestricted transport and trade of wines throughout the kingdom, the difficulties of transporting the wines of the Mâconnais and especially those of the Beaujolais diminished and the region really began its rapid development. During the nineteenth century, the Beaujolais became more and more a part of Burgundy and through its constant development the first among the Burgundian vineyards.

The region is traditionally divided into two halves, Lower and Upper Beaujolais, which are no more than geographical terms. Taken as a whole, they look like a great expanse of hills and dales descending from west to east, which offer every variety of exposure to the sun. The region is scattered with a great number of isolated vineyards, often featuring the very beautiful houses of the masters or small châteaux and their outhouses, the historical successors to the Roman *villae*. The tiny villages are also very scattered. The overall effect of the setting, the scattered villages and the variety of exposures of the soil is quite unusual and extremely pleasant.

Lower Burgundy begins about 12 miles from Lyons, just before Saint-Jean-des-Vignes, an evocative name. It continues to the north through the districts of Anse, the Bois-d'Oingt and Villefranche-sur-Saône. It includes very many villages and a beautiful landscape of vines, fields and woods, varying according to the altitude and exposure. It produces what is called *vins de comptoir*—over the counter wines sold in the bars of the Lyonnais to refresh the thirsty and tired citizens. They are doubtless less delicate and less complete than their northern neighbours, but then they are modest wines and lay no claims to perfection.

Upper Beaujolais consists of the districts of Belleville-sur-Saône and Beaujeu in the Rhône department, and La Chapelle-de-Guinchay canton to the south in the Saône-et-Loire. It would be very much worth the unhurried tourist's while to spend a few hours looking around the area. There are two well-signposted routes—the quick route, marked by red signposts which will take him from Villefranche to Crèches-sur-Saône, almost missing the hills but passing through all the "growths" of the Beaujolais; or the tourist route, mapped out in green, which is very much to be recommended. When you reach Beaujeu, you are well advised to leave it and take departmental road 136 up through spectacular scenery and remarkable views of the whole region. Then come down the Fût-d'Avenas Pass with its panoramic observation platform. On a clear day the view embraces a good deal of the Beaujolais and the Saône plain right up to the Jura and the Alps. We can guarantee that none who tries it will regret this detour, which enables the traveller to get a better idea of the size and variety of this district.

In the Upper and Lower Beaujolais, the wines are permitted to use three A.O.C.s—BEAUJOLAIS, BEAUJOLAIS-SUPÉRIEUR and BEAUJOLAIS-VILLAGES. There are, further, nine "growths". They are almost entirely red wines, since the 55,000 gallons of white Beaujolais amounts to 0.4 per cent of the total average yield and are, in fact, produced in vineyards that border on the white Mâcon area.

BEAUJOLAIS is the basic A.O.C. and the difference between it and BEAUJOLAIS-SUPÉRIEUR is the minimum alcoholic content which is a degree higher for the latter. The average yield for both A.O.C.s, 7,480,000 gallons, is as vast as is the area under production.

Victor Rendu wrote that: "The fine and almost fine Beaujolais wines are delicate, light and sappy. Though they are not so rich in bouquet as the great wines of Upper Burgundy, they do not lack fragrance. They are, in general, not deeply coloured; or, to be more accurate, they settle quickly and come rapidly to maturity. Precociousness is one of their main features."

Let us say, then, that the Beaujolais is a good unpretentious wine to be drunk with friends, their full glasses clinking merrily in the bar or wine cellar but always far from any formal occasion. It fosters sudden friendships because it is a wine that inspires those who appreciate its intrinsic qualities—friendliness, tenderness and generosity.

The wines that may use the A.O.C. BEAUJOLAIS-VILLAGES come from 28 wine communes in the Rhône department and eight in the Saône-et-Loire: Juliénas, Jullié, Emeringes, Chénas, Fleurie, Chiroubles, Lancié, Villié-Morgon, Lantigné, Beaujeu, Régnié, Durette, Cercié, Quincié, Saint-Lager, Odenas, Charentay, Saint-Etienne-la-Varenne, Vaux, Le Perréon, Saint-Etienne-des-Oullières, Rivolet, Arbuissonnas, Salles, Saint-Julien, Montmelas, Blacé and Denicé in the Rhône; and Leynes, Saint-Amour-Bellevue, La Chapelle-de-Guinchay, Romanèche, Pruzilly, Chânes, Saint-Vérand and Saint-Symphorien-d'Ancelles in the Saône-et-Loire. These wines may also be sold under their own names, often tacked on to the word BEAUJOLAIS.

From this list we should mention Vaux, not so much for its excellent wines as for the reputation it has gained through the second name given it by the writer Gabriel Chevalier—Clochemerle.

The average yield under this A.O.C. is 3,300,000 gallons. Louis Orizet, the poet of the region, wrote: "BEAUJOLAIS-VILLAGES, we love you because you are not quite great. If you were we would have to wait many months to drink you, which would be a pity.... A boon to the mistress of every household, a Beaujolais goes with all sauces.... It has that rare privilege for a red wine—to be drunk cool...." The late Georges Rozet, historiographer of the Brotherhood of the Knights of the Tastevin, wrote: "They do not overwhelm the drinker and their basic quality is their smoothness. They are soft, fruity, tasty, inviting, etc.... There is no end to the list of adjectives used to define them. I should like to see them placed in three columns like litanies, like the flowing epithets that poured once upon a time from the inexhaustible pen of the creator of Pantagruel."

BEAUJOLAIS-VILLAGES is an extremely agreeable wine and, at a modest price, will accompany any dish without disappointing. It will not be browbeaten by strong dishes and, in spite of everything, always manages to guard its own flavour intact. It need not be drunk by the thimbleful either. "Let me refill your glass" was the watchword of the inn-keepers of yore when they saw their customers' glasses rapidly emptying. One can do that with this wine and still abide by the rule of Burgundy: Drink well (never let a wine unworthy of you pass your lips) and to your own measure (never drink too much—it is inadvisable and nothing to be proud of).

Since we have to begin somewhere, let us begin our discussion of the nine "growths" of the Beaujolais from the southernmost of these—it would be too difficult to classify them by quality.

BROUILLY and CÔTE-DE-BROUILLY. At about the level of Belleville-sur-Saône, 5 miles towards the hills from this town, the Mont-Brouilly reaches up to an altitude of some 1,300 feet. On top is a chapel, built in 1857, which can be seen from anywhere in the region and is a place of pilgrimage for the winemakers. The wines using the BROUILLY A.O.C. are produced in six communes huddled around the hill. The average production is 792,000 gallons on about 2,000 acres of land. BROUILLY is typical of Beaujolais wines—halfway between the light wines and the Great Growths. It loses nothing by ageing.

CÔTE DE BROUILLY comes from vines that cling to the sides of the hill and cover about 500 acres. The average yield is 18,532 gallons.

The above two A.O.C.s are entirely different and should not be confused.

MORGON. A few miles to the north, the little hamlet of Morgon, with its narrow, winding streets, has given its name to the 1,360 acres of vineyards in the Villié-Morgon. It is a very sturdy wine which can be kept for a very long time. Average yield—616,000 gallons.

CHIROUBLES. The village bearing this name is much nearer the hills, and high up. Thanks to Pulliat, the writer on vines, it was the first to plant the grafted vine after the phylloxera plague.

The total area under the CHIROUBLES A.O.C. is about 3,000 acres, producing 209,000 gallons of a distinguished wine, halfway between MORGON and FLEURIE.

Continuing along the road beyond Chiroubles we reach, just before the Fût-d'Avenas Pass, the lookout point mentioned earlier, which offers a fine view of most of the Beaujolais and the Mâconnais.

FLEURIE. The name is aptly chosen for "the queen of Beaujolais", as this scented wine is called. A little more versatile than the rest, it is more delicate and finely perfumed. This commune, its name redolent of spring, lies near Romanèche-Thorins. Its slender clocktower looks down upon the many châteaux and masters' houses, some quite old, scattered around the countryside. The area under the FLEURIE A.O.C. is one of the largest in the Beaujolais, about 1,730 acres producing an average 517,000 gallons.

MOULIN-à-VENT. This growth, without doubt the best known and most sought after in the Beaujolais, is produced on part of the Chénas (Rhône) and on Romanèche-Thorins (Saône-et-Loire). There are about 1,730 acres of vineyards. Its name comes from an ancient windmill, the only one of its kind in the region, of which only the tower remains. A writer once stated that: "No one has ever contested the excellence of these vines. They are the realm of Bacchus, and Moulin-à-Vent and Thorins form the very heart of it. The soil is so precious to the vine that none is spared for the larger trees." The wine was formerly known as THORINS—Romanèche, the bearer of a Roman name, appended the name of its best vineyard to itself. The average yield is 484,000 gallons of fine, ruddy wine—full-bodied, firm and, after a few years, very much like some of the wines of the Côte d'Or.

CHÉNAS. Once again a vineyard straddling two communes, Chénas (Rhône) and La-Chapelle-de-Guinchay (Saône-et-Loire). It overlooks the Moulin-à-Vent vineyard, with its hillock that was formed, according to legend, by the giant Gargantua unloading his basket.

It is also said that the name of Chénas cames from the oak trees *(chênes)* that formerly covered the district and indeed most of the Beaujolais.

The area of this A.O.C. is 457 acres producing an average of 132,000 gallons of generous, perfumed wine.

JULIÉNAS. The wine that may use this A.O.C. is produced within the commune of Juliénas—named after Julius Caesar, it is said, as well as Jullié, Emeringes and Pruzilly, covering 1,310 acres. The first grapes of the Beaujolais are said to have ripened along the Roman

road, on vines planted in this soil which so resembles the one that Claudel described as: "dry and lumpy like curdled milk and full of tiny pebbles that retain the heat like firebricks so that the plump and sleepy grapes cook through on both sides". It gives 374,000 gallons of full, fruity, warm wine that matures well.

SAINT-AMOUR. We conclude our trip around the nine growths of the Beaujolais with this A.O.C. produced in the commune of the same name situated in the Saône-et-Loire. If this name did not exist, it would have to be invented—"holy love of the vine, holy love of the wine that flows for the holy love of mankind". This vineyard lies between Juliénas and Pouilly-Vinzelles, 8 miles south of Mâcon. Its vines now belong with the Beaujolais, though for a long time they were one of the gems of the Mâconnais. They used to belong to the Chapter of Saint-Vincent-de-Mâcon. Area approximately 530 acres and average yield 167,200 gallons of fresh, frank, agreeable wine.

Emile Vuillermoz said that these growths provided "all the chromatic scale, from the velvety notes of the delightful FLEURIE, though the more mysterious sounds of BROUILLY, the resonance of JULIÉNAS, the arpeggios of MOULIN-à-VENT, the frank impact of MORGON and the harmonies of CHÉNAS, to the clear sounds of SAINT-AMOUR and CHIROUBLES".

This ends our journey in this vast area that gives us Beaujolais, the wine that used to be drunk in all the taverns from "pots"—stone jugs painted blue. We have also reached the end of our pilgrimage around the different growths of Burgundy—CHABLIS, CÔTE DE NUITS, CÔTE DE BEAUNE, the regions of Mercurey and the Mâconnais. Henri Béraud's comment would apply to many of them: "This wine is not a *nouveau riche*. It remains and shall remain what it has always been. Its clear flow will bring us a little of the soul of the vintagers who have brought it into existence on their hillsides, a soul full of strength, wisdom and joviality."

LIFE IN BURGUNDY

It has been written of the Burgundians that they are "deep-thinking, even calculating, moderate like their country in all ways, active and energetic but loving logical order and reasoned practicality, greatly preferring life as it is and its material benefits, genial observers, formidable scoffers, often ingenious and witty".

We might add a few touches to this quite realistic portrait as regards their eating and drinking habits. And here everyone agrees with Clément Vautel: "There can be no lasting pleasure nor possible harmony in a house where the lunch is a failure and the dinner bankrupt."

How can one not enjoy good food when it is accompanied by "that divine juice that its lovers drink pure in the morning and unadulterated at night" and which, apart from all its other merits, "is pleasant to wives when their husbands have drunk it"?

But let us finish our portrait by remembering that Burgundy has been called, among other things, "a hospitable land". Why not? One need scarcely ask on seeing the pleasure on the faces of those returning from this region. Nor do they stint their numbers: Beaune, as already noted, has 300,000 visitors a year.

The daily round in Burgundy is quiet and unspectacular. The vintner's work requires a good deal of patience throughout the year and the cellarman remains always underground. From time to time, however, the calm surface breaks and the sound of laughter, songs and dances fills the air. Harvest time and the Vine and Wine Festival organized every September in Dijon by the Burgundian Committee are two such occasions.

Life in Burgundy is also punctuated by other events—we have already mentioned the sale of wines at the Hospices of Beaune, the oldest of the three known as *Les Trois Glorieuses*. In connection with this famous sale, which, let us recall, takes place on the third Sunday in November, there are various events in Beaune on the Saturday, such as the general exhibition of the wines of Burgundy and, in the evening, at the Château of the Clos-Vougeot, the "extraordinary" chapter of the Brotherhood of the Knights of the Tastevin. On Sunday, the exhibition continues and the wines of the Hospices of Beaune are sold. The day ends with a dinner by candlelight in one of the bastions of the town belonging to the Hospices. On Monday, the last day, there is the *Paulée* of Meursault, which is the traditional dinner marking the end of the vintage.

In all the regions of Burgundy that we have visited only briefly in this book, there are special celebrations attractive to follow and pleasant to participate in.

In the north, Chablis houses the Brotherhood of the Piliers Chablisiens (Pillars of Chablis), which holds its chapters in the wine-cellar of Vaucorbeil several times a year, usually on St. Vincent's day. This is the occasion for the exhibition and tasting of the wines of the Yonne and for the traditional event in the region —*le repas du cochon* ("the feast of the pig"). The singing and dancing of a chorus lends added charm to these candlelight banquets.

In Dijon, we have the Burgundian Committee which holds its rites in the magnificent thirteenth-century cellar of Clairvaux and organizes the Vine and Wine Festival. The rites are accompanied by folklore groups and recall the dubbing ceremonies of the Middle Ages. New distinctions are conferred in the Order of the Grand Dukes of the West, a reminder of the four great dukes of Burgundy.

Continuing south, we pass by the Clos-de-Vougeot, to greet the institution that is so much admired and copied everywhere—the Brotherhood of the Knights of the Tastevin—who were the first to establish contacts

Lifting his *tastevin*, the wine-taster prepares to pass judgement. This shallow cup, solid silver or silver-plated, has two sets of facets, with different reliefs to help the wine-taster in his examination.

Vintage time in Burgundy. Armed with their shears the vintagers (*layots* in the Burgundian patois) gather the grapes into their wicker baskets. The baskets are then carried on carts along the paths between the vines and their contents are emptied into large barrels for conveyance to the wine-press. Unlike in the Burgundy vineyards, planted to the *Pinot Noir*, in the Beaujolais the *Gamay* grape is used.

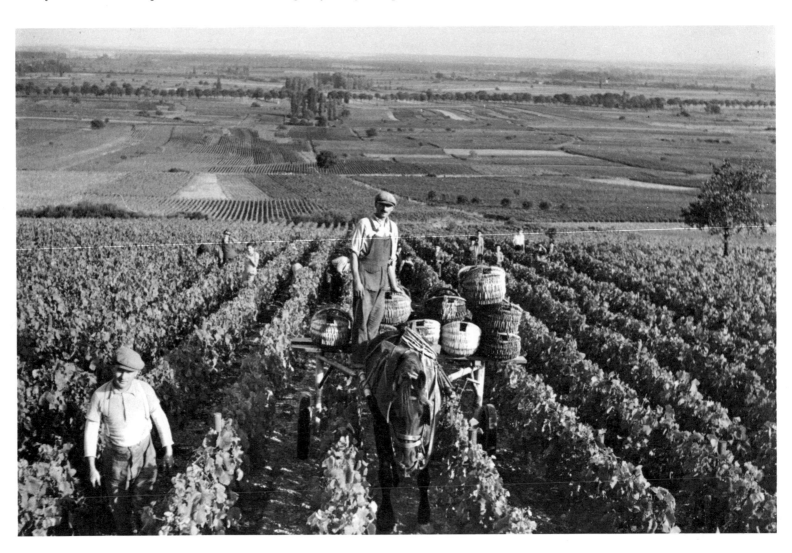

between wine-lovers and the wines of a province. "To invite someone is to assume responsibility for his well-being for as long as he is under your roof," said Brillat-Savarin, and this is the rule of the Brotherhood during its chapters. They have proved so successful that they have had to organize additional chapters, splendid banquets during which the sponsors instill their spirit of gaiety, humour and the wit that is the mark of companionable people. They are assisted by the Cadets of Burgundy, created by the Brotherhood, and they have attained the necessary skill in folklore throughout the years as well as the much more complex arts of music and diction.

Let us remember, in passing, the Saint-Vincent-Tournant, created by the Brotherhood, which brings together all the winegrowing communes of the Côte in a religious and secular ceremony for the feast of the patron saint of vintagers. There is also the *Taste-vinage*, at which good wines are selected for the wine-lover—this has become a famous ceremony. Any wineproducer or shipper wishing to participate must possess a given number of bottles of the same vintage. He then must send in samples—one to be tasted and the others for subsequent checks. In the cellar of the Château of the Clos-Vougeot, the specialists meet the press and, of course, consumer representatives. The

tasters are always very severe: between 30 and 35 per cent of the wines are rejected each year, not because they are bad, but because they do not attain the level of distinction required. These two events have been very successful and well attended from the start.

About 12 miles farther south, in the little village of Savigny-lès-Beaune, the *Cousinerie de Bourgogne* (Cousinhood of Burgundy) meets under the sign of hospitality that is legendary in the province. "Bottle on the table and heart in hand" is its guiding principle and "all gentlemen are cousins" is its motto.

The headquarters of the Brotherhood of the Vintagers of Saint-Vincent is in Mâcon, in the Saône-et-Loire. During its chapters, distinguished guests and wine-lovers, if their conduct in wine matters is irreproachable, are received as knights or officers. These chapters are enlivened by a choir which sings all the traditional songs of the region.

Finally there is the Brotherhood of the Companions of the Beaujolais, created in 1947 and now holding its own vattings at Lacenas, after being received into all the most important cellars in the Beaujolais. The Companions swear an oath of wine to promote the wines of the Beaujolais in every way and to love and assist other companions. He who breaks his oath is "for all time unworthy to drink with an honest man".

The Chapters of the Brotherhood of the Knights of the Tastevin are held regularly in the ancient cellar of the Château of Clos-Vougeot. When their "wine education" is complete, the new members of the Brotherhood are initiated by a ceremony that combines humour and the picturesque.

WINES OF BURGUNDY

CHABLIS • WHITE WINES

Regional appellation : Chablis, Petit Chablis.

Principal first growths

Chablis-Mont de Milieu, Chablis-Montée de Tonnerre, Chablis-Fourchaume, on the right bank of the Serein.
Chablis-Forêts, Chablis-Vaillons, Chablis-Mélinots, Chablis-Côte de Léchet, Chablis-Beauroy, on the left bank of the Serein.
Chablis-Vaucoupin, Chablis-Vaugros, Chablis-Vaugiraud, in the commune of Chichée.

Great growths

Chablis-Vaudésir, Chablis-Preuses, Chablis-Les Clos, Chablis-Grenouilles, Chablis-Bougros, Chablis-Valmur, Chablis-Blanchots.

CÔTE DE NUITS • RED WINES

Generic appellation :

a) Bourgogne ordinaire, Bourgogne grand ordinaire • b) Bourgogne Passe-tout-grains • c) Bourgogne, Bourgogne Marsannay, Bourgogne Hautes Côtes de Nuits • d) Vins fins de la Côte de Nuits or Côte de Nuits-Villages (Communes of Fixin, Brochon, Prissey, Comblanchien, Corgoloin).

Appellation of communes	Appellation of first-growth communes	Great growths	First great growths
Fixin (only red wine)	La Perrière, Les Hervelets, Les Meix-Bas, Aux-Cheusots, Le Clos du Chapitre, Les Arvelets.		
Gevrey-Chambertin (only red wine)	Les Véroilles, Village Saint-Jacques called "Le Clos Saint-Jacques", Aux Combottes, Bel-Air, Cazetiers, Combes-aux-Moines, Estournelles, Lavaut, Poissenot, Champeaux, Les Goulots, Issarts, Les Corbeaux, Les Gémeaux, Cherbaudes, La Perrière, Clos-Prieur (only upper part), le Fonteny, Champonnets, Au Closeau, Craipillot, Champitonnois called "Petite Chapelle", Ergots, Clos-du-Chapitre.	Charmes-Chambertin Chapelle-Chambertin Griotte-Chambertin Latricières-Chambertin Mazis-Chambertin Ruchottes-Chambertin	Chambertin Chambertin-Clos-de-Bèze
Morey-Saint-Denis (red wine and 1·6 % white wine)	Les Larrets or "Clos-des-Lambrays", Les Ruchots, Les Sorbés, Le Clos-Sorbés, Les Millandes, Le Clos-des-Ormes, Meix-Rentiers, Monts-Luisants, Les Bouchots, Clos Bussières, Aux Charmes, Les Charrières, Côte Rôtie, Calouères, Maison Brûlée, Chabiots, Les Mauchamps, Les Froichots, Les Fremières, Les Genévrières, Les Chaffots, Les Chenevery, La Riotte, Le Clos-Baulet, Les Gruenchers, Les Faconnières.	Clos-de-Tart Clos-St.-Denis Clos-de-la-Roche	Bonnes-Mares
Chambolle-Musigny (only red wine)	Les Bonnes-Mares, Les Amoureuses, Les Charmes, Les Cras, Les Borniques, Les Baudes, Les Plantes, Les Hauts Doix, Les Chatelots, Les Gruenchers, Les Groseilles, Les Fuées, Les Lavrottes, Derrière-la-Grange, Les Noirots, Les Sentiers, Les Fousselottes, Aux Beaux-Bruns, Les Combottes, Aux Combottes.		Musigny (2 % white wine)
Vougeot (only red wine)	Le Clos Blanc, Les Petits-Vougeot, Les Cras, Clos de la Perrière.		Clos-de-Vougeot
Vosne-Romanée (only red wine)	Aux Malconsorts, Les Beaux-Monts, Les Suchots, La Grand'Rue, Les Gaudichots, Aux Brûlées, Les Chaumes, Les Reignots, Le Clos des Réas, Les Petits-Monts.	Romanée Romanée-St-Vivant Grands-Echezeaux Echezeaux	Romanée-Conti Richebourg La Tâche
Nuits-Saint-Georges (red wine; 0·4 % white wine)	Les Saint-Georges, Les Vaucrains, Les Cailles, Les Porets, Les Pruliers, Les Hauts-Pruliers, Aux Murgers, La Richemonne, Les Chabœufs, La Perrière, La Roncière, Les Procès, Rue-de-Chaux, Aux Boudots, Aux Cras, Aux Chaignots, Aux Thorey, Aux Vignes-Rondes, Aux Bousselots, Les Poulettes, Aux Crots, Les Vallerots, Aux Champs-Perdrix, Perrière-Noblet, Aux Damodes, Les Argillats, En la Chaîne-Carteau, Aux Argilats, Clos de la Maréchale, Clos-Arlots, Clos des Argillières, Clos des Grandes Vignes, Clos des Corvées, Clos des Forêts, Les Didiers, Aux Perdrix, Les Corvées-Paget, Le Clos-Saint-Marc.		

CÔTE DE BEAUNE • RED WINES

Generic appellation :

a) Bourgogne ordinaire, Bourgogne grand ordinaire • *b)* Bourgogne Passe-tout-grains • *c)* Bourgogne • *d)* Côte de Beaune • *e)* Côte de Beaune-Villages

Appellation of communes	*Appellation of first-growth communes*	*Great growths*
Aloxe-Corton . . . . . . (1 % white wine)	Les Valozières, Les Chaillots, Les Meix, Les Fournières, Les Maréchaudes, En Pauland, Les Vercots, Les Guérets, La Maréchaude, La Toppe-au-Vert, La Coutière, Les Grandes-Lolières, Les Petites-Lolières, Basses-Mourettes.	Corton
Pernand-Vergelesses . . . (11 % white wine)	Ile-des-Vergelesses, Les Basses-Vergelesses, Creux-de-la-Net, Les Fichots, En Caradeux.	Corton
Savigny-lès-Beaune . . . (4 % white wine)	Aux Vergelesses, Aux Vergelesses dit Bataillière, Les Marconnets, La Dominode, Les Jarrons, Basses-Vergelesses, Les Lavières, Aux Gravains, Les Peuillets, Aux Guettes, Les Talmettes, Les Charnières, Aux Fourneaux, Aux Clous, Aux Serpentières, Les Narbantons, Les Hauts-Marconnets, Les Hauts-Jarrons, Redrescuts, Aux Guettes, Les Rouvrettes, Aux Grands-Liards, Aux Petits-Liards, Petits-Godeaux.	
Chorey-lès-Beaune . . .	Chorey-lès-Beaune.	
Beaune. . . . . (5 % white wine)	Les Marconnets, Les Fèves, Les Bressandes, Les Grèves, Les Teurons, Le Clos-des-Mouches, Champs-Pimont, Clos-du-Roi, Aux Coucherias, En l'Orme, En Genêt, Les Perrières, A l'Ecu, Les Cent-Vignes, Les Toussaints, Sur-les-Grèves, Aux Cras, Le Clos-de-la-Mousse, Les Chouacheux, Les Boucherottes, Les Vignes-Franches, Les Aigrots, Pertuisots, Tielandry ou Clos-Landry, Les Sisies, Les Avaux, Les Reversées, Le Bas-des-Teurons, Les Seurey, La Mignotte, Montée-Rouge, Les Montrevenots, Les Blanches-Fleurs, Les Epenottes.	
Pommard	Les Rugiens-Bas, Les Rugiens-Hauts, Les Epenots, Les Petits-Epenots, Clos-de-la-Commaraine, Clos-Blanc, Les Arvelets, Es-Charmots, Les Argillières, Les Pézerolles, Les Boucherottes, Les Sausilles, Les Croix-Noires, Les Chaponnières, Les Fremiers, Les Bertins, Les Garollières ou Jarollières, Les Poutures, Le Clos-Micot, La Refene, Clos-du-Verger, Derrière-Saint-Jean, La Platière, Les Chanlins-Bas, Les Combes-Dessus, La Chanière.	
Volnay	En Caillerets, Caillerets-Dessus, En Champans, En Chevret, Fremiets, Bousse-d'Or, La Barre or Clos-de-la-Barre, Le Clos-des-Chênes, Les Angles, Pointe-d'Angles, Les Mitans, En l'Ormeau, Taille-Pieds, En Verseuil, Carelle-sous-la-Chapelle, Ronceret, Carelle-Dessous, Robardelle, Les Lurets, Les Aussy, Les Brouillards, Le Clos-des-Ducs, Les Pitures-Dessus, Chanlin, Les Santenots, Les Petures, Village-de-Volnay.	
Monthélie . . . . . . (2.5 % white wine)	Sur Lavelle, Les Vignes-Rondes, le Meix-Bataille, Les Riottes, La Taupine, Le Clos-Gauthey, Le Château-Gaillard, Les Champs-Fulliot, Le Cas-Rougeot, Duresse.	
Auxey-Duresses . . . . . (32 % white wine)	Les Duresses, Les Bas-des-Duresses, Reugne, Reugne called La Chapelle, Les Grands-Champs, Climat-du-Val called Clos-du-Val, Les Ecusseaux, Les Bretterins called La Chapelle, Les Bretterins.	
Santenay . . . . (2 % white wine)	Les Gravières, Clos-de-Tavannes, La Comme, Beauregard, Le Passe-Temps, Beaurepaire, La Maladière.	
Cheilly, Dezize, Sampigny-lès-Maranges	Le Clos-des-Rois, La Boutière, Les Maranges, Les Plantes-de-Maranges.	
Chassagne-Montrachet . .	Clos-Saint-Jean, Morgeot, Morgeot called Abbaye-de-Morgeot, La Boudriotte, La Maltroie, Les Chenevottes, Les Champs-Gain, Grandes-Ruchottes, La Romanée, Les Brussolles, Les Vergers, Les Macherelles, En Cailleret.	
Other appellations . . . . *of communes*	Saint-Romain, Meursault-Blagny or Blagny, Puligny-Montrachet, Ladoix, Saint-Aubin.	
Saint-Aubin . . . . . . (4 % white wine)	La Chatenière, Les Murgers-des-Dents-de-Chien, En Remilly, Les Frionnes, Sur-le-Sentier-de-Clou, Sur Gamay, Les Combes, Champlot.	

CÔTE DE BEAUNE • WHITE WINES

Generic appellation: *a)* Bourgogne ordinaire, Bourgogne grand ordinaire • *b)* Bourgogne aligoté • *c)* Bourgogne • *d)* Côte de Beaune.

Appellation of communes	Appellation of first-growth communes	Great growths	First great growths
Aloxe-Corton		Corton-Charlemagne	
Pernand-Vergelesses		Corton-Charlemagne	
Chorey-lès-Beaune . . .	Chorey-lès-Beaune.		
Saint-Romain			
Meursault . . . . (4 % red wine)	Aux Perrières, Les Perrières-Dessus, Les Perrières-Dessous, Les Charmes-Dessus, Les Charmes-Dessous, Les Gene-vrières-Dessus, Les Genevrières-Dessous, Le Poruzot-Dessus, Le Poruzot-Dessous, Le Poruzot, Les Bouchères, Les Santenots-Blancs, Les Santenots-du-Milieu, Les Caillerets, Les Petures, Les Cras, La Goutte-d'Or, La Jennelotte, La Pièce-sous-le-Bois, Sous-le-Dos-d'Ane.		
Puligny-Montrachet . . . (6·4 % red wine)	Le Cailleret, Les Combettes, Les Pucelles, Les Folatières, Clavoillons, Le Champ-Canet, Les Chalumeaux, Les Referts, Sous-le-Puits, La Garenne, Hameau-de-Blagny.	Chevalier-Montrachet, Bâtard-Montrachet, Bienvenues-Bâtard-Montrachet, Criots-Bâtard-Montrachet.	Montrachet
Chassagne-Montrachet . .	Morgeot, Morgeot called Abbaye-de-Morgeot, La Boudriotte, La Maltroie, Clos-Saint-Jean, Les Chenevottes, Les Champs-Gain, Grandes-Ruchottes, La Romanée, Les Brussoles, Les Vergers, Les Macherelles, Chassagne or Cailleret.	Bâtard-Montrachet Criots-Bâtard-Montrachet	Montrachet
Other appellations . . . . of communes	Ladoix, Meursault-Blagny or Blagny, Saint-Aubin, Cheilly-Dezize-les-Maranges, Sampigny-lès-Maranges.		

MERCUREY REGION

Generic appellation : Bourgogne.

Appellation of communes	First growths
Mercurey (red 95 %) . .	Clos-du-Roy, Clos-Voyens or Les Voyens, Clos-Marcilly, Clos-des-Fourneaux, Clos-des-Montaigus.
Givry (red 87 %)	
Rully (white 80 %) . . .	Margotey, Grésigny, Vauvry, Mont-Palais, Meix-Caillet, Les Pierres, La Bressande, Champ-Clou, La Renarde, Pillot, Cloux, Raclot, Raboursay, Ecloseaux, Marissou, La Fosse, Chapitre, Préau, Moulesne.
Montagny (white) . . .	

MÂCONNAIS

Generic appellation : Bourgogne • Mâcon supérieur (red wine 37 % and white) • Mâcon-villages (white wine) • Mâcon (red wine 76 %) Pinot-Chardonnay-Mâcon (white wine).

Appellation of communes	Pouilly-Fuissé (white), Pouilly-Vinzelles (white), Pouilly-Loché (white).

BEAUJOLAIS

Generic appellation : *a)* Bourgogne ordinaire, Bourgogne grand ordinaire • *b)* Bourgogne Passe-tout-grains • *c)* Bourgogne aligoté *d)* Bourgogne • *e)* Beaujolais • *f)* Beaujolais supérieur • *g)* Beaujolais-Villages.

First growths . . . . . . (red wine)	Brouilly, Chenas, Chiroubles, Côte de Brouilly, Fleurie, Juliénas, Morgon, Moulin-à-vent, Saint-Amour.

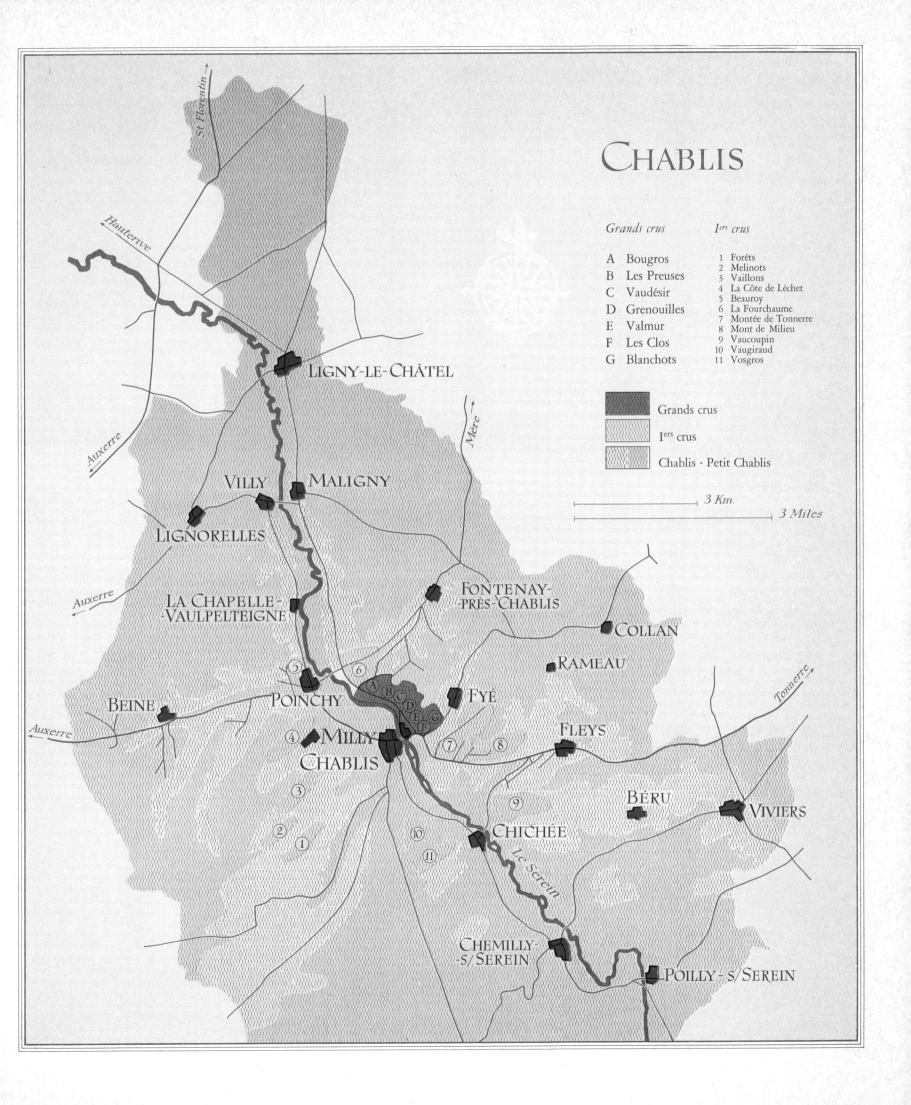

CHABLIS

Grands crus

A   Bougros
B   Les Preuses
C   Vaudésir
D   Grenouilles
E   Valmur
F   Les Clos
G   Blanchots

I^{ers} *crus*

1   Forêts
2   Melinots
3   Vaillons
4   La Côte de Léchet
5   Beauroy
6   La Fourchaume
7   Montée de Tonnerre
8   Mont de Milieu
9   Vaucoupin
10   Vaugiraud
11   Vosgros

Grands crus

I^{ers} crus

Chablis - Petit Chablis

3 Km.

3 Miles

St-Florentin

Hauterive

Auxerre

LIGNY-LE-CHÂTEL

Mère

VILLY   MALIGNY

LIGNORELLES

Auxerre

LA CHAPELLE-
-VAULPELTEIGNE

FONTENAY-
PRÈS-CHABLIS

COLLAN

RAMEAU

POINCHY

FYÉ

Tonnerre

BEINE

Auxerre

MILLY

CHABLIS

FLEYS

BÉRU   VIVIERS

CHICHÉE

Le Serein

CHEMILLY-
-S/SEREIN

POILLY - S/SEREIN

Grands crus

1 La Tache
2 Romanée
3 Romanée-Conti
4 Romanée-Saint-Vivant
5 Richebourg
6 Echezeaux
  Grands-Echezeaux   7 Clos-de-Vougeot

Appellations de commune   NUITS-SAINT-GEORGES   VOSNE-ROMANÉE   VOUGEOT

← Beaune

PREMEAUX

NUITS-
-SAINT-GEORGES

VOSNE - ROMANÉE

2 Km.

2 Miles

LA CÔTE DE NUITS

14 Mazoyères-Chambertin
15 Latricières-Chambertin
16 Charmes-Chambertin
17 Chambertin
18 Chambertin-Clos-de-Bèze
10 Bonnes-Mares   19 Griotte-Chambertin
11 Clos-de-Tart   20 Chapelle-Chambertin
8 Musigny   12 Clos-Saint-Denis   21 Mazis-Chambertin
9 Bonnes-Mares   13 Clos-de-la-Roche   22 Ruchottes-Chambertin

CHAMBOLLE-MUSIGNY   MOREY-SAINT-DENIS   GEVREY-CHAMBERTIN   FIXIN

CHAMBOLLE-
-MUSIGNY

BROCHON FIXIN FIXEY

Château du
Clos-de-Vougeot

GEVREY-
-CHAMBERTIN

MOREY-
-ST. DENIS

LES BARAQUES

Dijon →

VOUGEOT

 Grands crus   I^ers crus   Appellations de commune

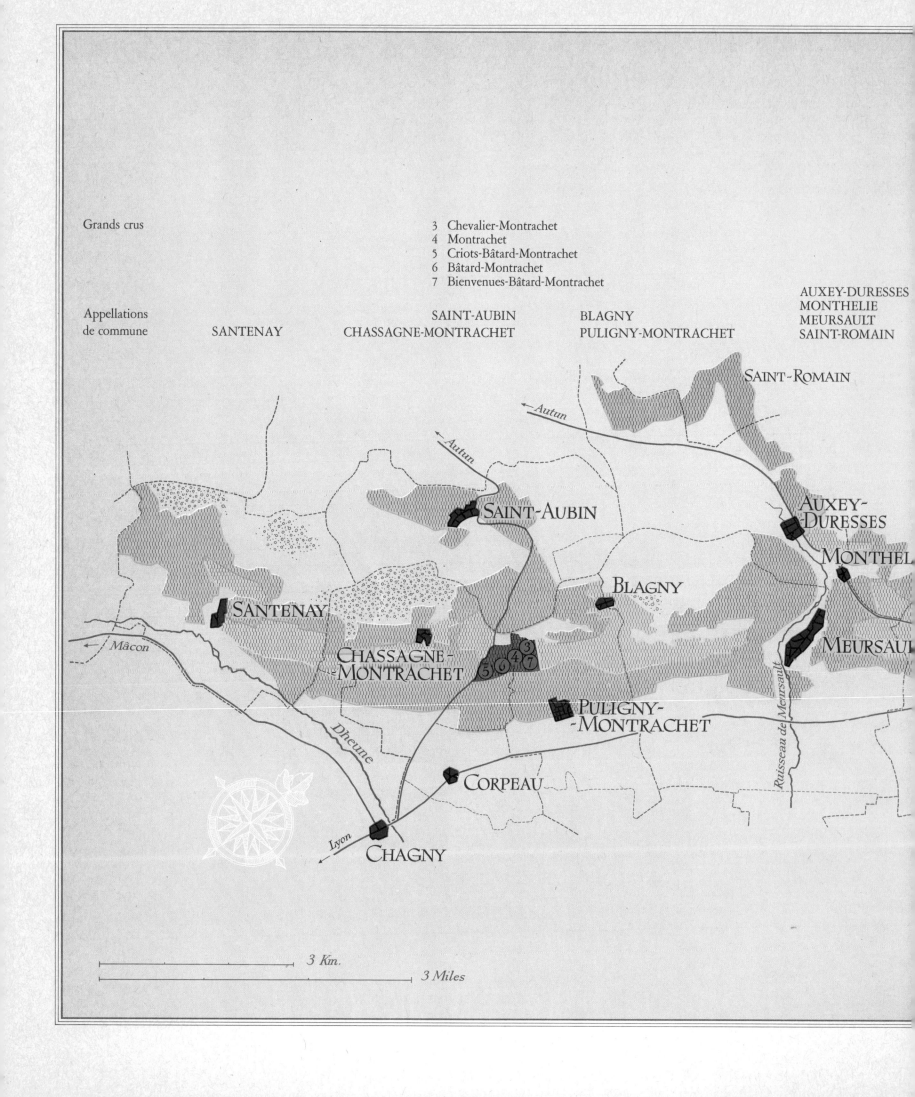

Grands crus

3 Chevalier-Montrachet
4 Montrachet
5 Criots-Bâtard-Montrachet
6 Bâtard-Montrachet
7 Bienvenues-Bâtard-Montrachet

Appellations
de commune

SANTENAY

SAINT-AUBIN
CHASSAGNE-MONTRACHET

BLAGNY
PULIGNY-MONTRACHET

AUXEY-DURESSES
MONTHELIE
MEURSAULT
SAINT-ROMAIN

SAINT-ROMAIN

← Autun

Autun

SAINT-AUBIN

AUXEY-
DURESSES

MONTHEL

BLAGNY

← Mâcon

CHASSAGNE-
MONTRACHET

3
5 6 4 7

MEURSAUL

SANTENAY

Ruisseau de Meursault

PULIGNY-
MONTRACHET

Dheune

CORPEAU

Lyon

CHAGNY

3 Km.

3 Miles

LA CÔTE DE BEAUNE

1   Corton (rouge - red)
2   Corton-Charlemagne (blanc - white)

PERNAND-VERGELESSES
SAVIGNY-LÈS-BEAUNE   ALOXE-CORTON
VOLNAY   POMMARD   BEAUNE   CHOREY-LÈS-BEAUNE   LADOIX

SAVIGNY-
-LÈS-BEAUNE

VOLNAY

POMMARD

PERNAND-
VERGELESSES

ALOXE-CORTON

LADOIX

BEAUNE

CHOREY-LÈS-BEAUNE

Grands crus   Iers crus   Appellations de commune

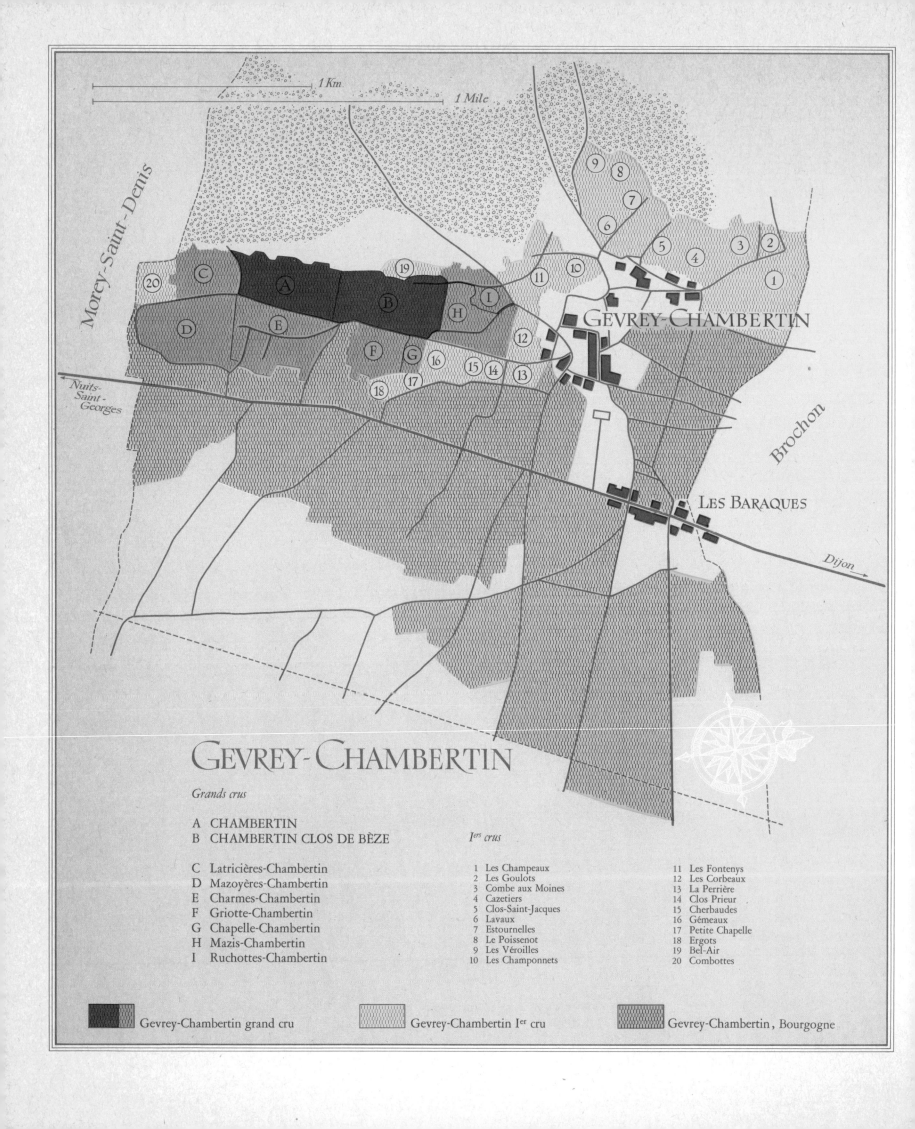

GEVREY-CHAMBERTIN

Grands crus

A CHAMBERTIN
B CHAMBERTIN CLOS DE BÈZE

C Latricières-Chambertin
D Mazoyères-Chambertin
E Charmes-Chambertin
F Griotte-Chambertin
G Chapelle-Chambertin
H Mazis-Chambertin
I Ruchottes-Chambertin

*I*ers *crus*

1 Les Champeaux
2 Les Goulots
3 Combe aux Moines
4 Cazetiers
5 Clos-Saint-Jacques
6 Lavaux
7 Estournelles
8 Le Poissenot
9 Les Véroilles
10 Les Champonnets

11 Les Fontenys
12 Les Corbeaux
13 La Perrière
14 Clos Prieur
15 Cherbaudes
16 Gémeaux
17 Petite Chapelle
18 Ergots
19 Bel-Air
20 Combottes

Gevrey-Chambertin grand cru   Gevrey-Chambertin Ier cru   Gevrey-Chambertin, Bourgogne

MERCUREY

Rully

Aluze

Chagny
Beaune

Tour
St.Hilaire

Fontaines

l'Orboise

Autun

MERCUREY

BOURGNEUF-
-VAL-D'OR

l'Orboise

R.N. 78

Châlons-s/Saône

St. Martin
/s-Montaigu

St Mard-
-de-Vaux

ST. MARTIN
S-MONTAIGU

St. Jean-de-Vaux

l'Oroise

Mellecey

1 Km.

1 Mile

MÂCONNAIS

Pierreclos

Pouilly-Fuissé
Pouilly-Loché
Pouilly-Vinzelles

VERS-LA-CROIX

VERGISSON

Prissé

CHANSERON

Davayé

SOLUTRÉ-
POUILLY

Chasselas

LE PLAN

Mâcon

FUISSÉ

Charnay-
les-Mâcon

Leynes

LOCHÉ

Mâcon

VINZELLES

CHAINTRE

MEZIAT

LES GALOPIÈRES

Chânes

LE BAS DE SAVY

Mâcon

Crèches-s/Saône

Varennes-
les-Mâcon

1 Km.

1 Mile

Le Beaujolais

LEYNES

PRUZILLY
St Vérand
CHANES

JULLIÉ
JULIÉNAS
St Amour-Bellevue

St Amour

EMERINGES
Juliénas
Chénas

CHÉNAS
Moulin à vent
La Chapelle de Guinchay

FLEURIE
St Symphorien d'Ancelles

LES ARDILLATS
Chiroubles
Fleurie
Romanèche - Thorins

CHIROUBLES

VILLIÉ-MORGON
LANCIÉ

BEAUJEU
Morgon

LANTIGNIÉ

RÉGNIÉ

DURETTE
CERCIÉ

QUINCIÉ
Côte
de Brouilly
St Lager
BELLEVILLE S/ SAÔNE

Brouilly

CHARENTAY

St Etienne-
La-Varenne
ODENAS

Le Perréon
St Etienne-
des - Oullières
St Georges de Reneins

VAUX-EN-
BEAUJOLAIS
ARBUISSONNAS

SALLES

St Cyr-
le-Chatoux
BLACÉ
St Julien

Chambost-
d'Allières
Montmelas-
St Sorlin

RIVOLET
DENICÉ

St Just-d'Avray
LACENAS
VILLEFRANCHE S/ SAÔNE

CHAMELET

LIERGUES
Limas

JARNIOUX

POMMIERS

Ville-
s. Jarnioux

Ternand
Pouilly-
Le-Monial

ANSE

LACHASSAGNE

St Clément-
s. Valsonne
Le Bois-d'Oingt
MARCY
LUCENAY

ALIX

CHESSY
CHARNAY

Les Olmes
CHAZAY

BULLY
Lyon

Mâcon

Chauffailles

Charolles

Roanne

Roanne
Tarare

Saône

5 Km.

5 Miles

THE WINES
OF THE RHÔNE

PHILIPPE CHERIX and JEAN BERTIN-ROULLEAU

In the course of history, some rivers have divided the land through which they flowed, while others, much more rarely, have united and held together the peoples of each bank. Few rivers have done this to such lasting effect and over such a long period as has the river Rhône. Since time immemorial, it would seem, Nature has drawn man's attention to this vast furrow of fertility so propitious to peaceful relations: and when the vine crept in, right behind the first Greek merchants and the Roman legions, it was at home from the beginning. For close on six hundred years, the plant lingered in the plains of the Lower Rhône, fruitful in what was then Gaul around Narbonne, reaching the town of Lyons only in the first century of our era. From there, part of the vine escaped up the river Saône to conquer Burgundy, and it is surely one of the Rhône's claims to glory that it thus facilitated this bewitching viticultural colonization. Savoy and the Pays Romand saw in their turn this wine of the Rhône, and the vine-shoots of Dionysus reached even farther—as far, indeed, as they could go, until the great Alps stopped them and they reached the river's very source.

What an astonishing destiny for that thin trickle of limpid-clear water that springs from the unending fountain-head of the Furka glacier! Jostled from all sides in the rocks, the infant river drops dizzily to where, some 1,640 feet lower at Vispertermimen (altitude 4,260 feet), the vine awaits. From here onwards to the sea, these plants will never leave the river's banks. In this rocky region, the vines must struggle for life under a sun that is often harsh: but the winegrower of the Valais canton, his face dried like parchment by the winds, the burning *fœhn* and the chilling *bise* in turn, is a hard and tenacious man. His task is a veritable gamble, yet the result is admirable: a range of wines, mostly whites and mostly dry, of which some are real works of art. The plants lie on the slopes in asymmetrical plots, giving the landscape a curiously mottled effect. Almost all the planting is on the river's right bank, facing the sun, or in the lateral valleys.

The river continues its flow down towards the plain, its waters more and more cloudy, swollen with the rivers feeding it from north and south.

Suddenly, at Martigny, the Rhône appears to change its mind. It forms a sharp right-hand turn and seems about to betray its southern destiny as it tries to return to a Germanic land. But then the plain opens wide and the river hurls itself forward: laden with mud and silt, it digs its bed deeply between the cantons of Vaud and Valais. The vines thin out on the left bank but spread profusely on the other.

The Rhône is still a great grey torrent full of fury when it meets Lake Leman. The soothing lake disciplines, warms and cleans the river in a series of operations that the eye does not even suspect: the Rhône seems to have disappeared completely. Yet it is but hidden, mysteriously, in the waves and the vine has not ceased to follow the river. It spreads in steeply terraced rows along the shores to Lausanne, the Lavaux region where begins that marvellous land of La Côte in which the living seems so easy. The plants, lined up neatly as though on shelves, give every sign of opulence.

Across the lake lies France. On the slopes of the Savoy mountains (Chablais and Faucigny), cultivation is much more sparse, and winters harsh. Here in this hard, tormented countryside, dominated by the forerunners of the mighty Alps, the vineyards produce a vigorous white wine: CRÉPY.

Farther west, the vineyards close up against each other between the lake and the Jura mountains. Geneva is not far away, where the lake is usually called Lake of Geneva. And the river, bursting at the very gates of Calvin's city out of the deep waters, can once again appear between its own banks and run, flirting, through the vineyards of the Mandement and the Upper-Savoy Genevois.

From Seyssel to Vienne, across the frontier now, in France, for about 110 miles the vineyards are scarce, and the Rhône, fortified with the waters of the Saône, rolls on towards Dauphiné, widening as it goes. The vine is not stubborn to the point of trying to grow in soils that do not suit it, but this momentary self-effacement of the Rhône vineyards is already preparing a special awakening. Only a few miles from Vienne, at Ampuis, where the vines are grown in little bow-like arches, with the plants tied together three-by-three, there is a cultivation of CÔTE RÔTIE. This is the threshold of an enormous vineyard stretching for almost 125 miles southward. The CÔTES DU RHÔNE, which include about one hundred varied communes, form two distinctly different agglomerates: one near Tournon, the other near Orange. The first is concentrated around HERMITAGE, while the second is around that illustrious CHÂTEAUNEUF so loved by the popes.

The whole of this very picturesque region has a wild, tormented surface, with marls, molasse and alluvial deposits forming stony slopes and high dry terraces where the red grape dominates. The river Rhône, here gorged with the waters of the Isère and the Drôme, has on occasion some formidable floods, but fortunately a hot sun makes haste to comfort the unfortunate vinegrower.

This is now the Pays de Vaucluse, that which formerly was the Comtat Venaissin: it is already part of the Provence, that region of extremes *par excellence*, where brutal rains and parching drought, cutting *mistral* wind and northern *tramontane* alternate with each other. Eternal Provence, with its perfume of plants and fruit, its heavy silence scarcely rippled by the chirping of the grasshoppers or the solid swearing of the winegrowers. The flavour of the western language pleases the Rhône and reminds it of other tongues of other folk of the vineyards: the roughness of the Valais and Savoy *patois*, the slowness of the accent of the Leman, the dry rhythm of the man from Lyons and then, from Valence on, the French that the people of Provence sing so well.

The Rhône, now become enormous, is preparing itself majestically to flow into the all-absorbing sea. But the vineyards along its banks will stop near Avignon. From there, taking full advantage of the wonderful richness of the southern soil, yet wishing to avoid the humid Camargue, the vines spread to east and west so that, from Saint-Raphaël to Perpignan, other vineyards are formed: those of the Côtes de Provence, Languedoc and Roussillon. It was in these regions that the Greeks and the Romans first transmitted to France that wondrous heritage of wine which later winegrowers were able to exploit so well.

Thus the river Rhône has given the vineyards, along the almost 500 miles of land traversed, a thousand-year-old birthright to bring man pleasure. True, the winegrowers of Languedoc, Provence, Savoy and Valais must battle with various problems in order to succeed: the sun, so necessary to breathe life into the wine, is not always kindly; the vine-plants do not feed everywhere on the same soils; the geography of the area often brings a disordered layout to the winegrower's plans for planting. But the river itself has managed to smooth out many of these diversities of cultivation. Man, guided quite naturally by that flowing water, has been able to bring Mediterranean wine into the heart of Europe. Then, by dint of constant and profitable exchanges with his neighbours, he has striven to increase and improve his wines. The great fraternity of a common language, from Sierre to Marseilles, has joined that other fraternity of the wine to create an authentic Rhône mentality, as sung by Frédéric Mistral and Charles Ferdinand Ramuz.

The general description *"vins du Rhône"* unites under one term the wines of the Rhône Basin: those of the Valais, the Swiss shores of Lake Leman and Savoy, the wines of Côtes du Rhône from Lyons to the Camargue, and also the wines from neighbouring regions. These are on the one hand the French Jura area whose vineyards join the Rhône plain through the gap at Bresse, and on the other hand the regions of Languedoc-Roussillon and Provence, which join the main axis of the river at Avignon.

THE SWISS WINES OF THE RHÔNE VALLEY

French-speaking Switzerland stands out as having the largest production of wine of all Swiss viticultural regions. The vineyards are for the most part planted on the slopes along the Rhône, in the level area of the river plain and on the more or less steep slopes alongside Lake Leman. There is an important production of white wines, while that of red wine, about 25 per cent of its total, is constantly increasing. Geographically, politically, and qualitatively too, three characteristic regions are prominent along the Swiss run of the Rhône: the cantons of Geneva, Valais and Vaud.

The method of cultivation used is generally the low cultivation *en gobelet*, as practised in the Canton of Vaud. A few timid attempts have been made to introduce the semi-high and high methods of cultivation, usually on flat or almost-flat land. But the desire always to bring out the natural richness of the wines generally keeps the winegrowers faithful to techniques, well-tried and cheap, which they have used over the years, both for working the land and for thinning and preparing the vines. This latter is very delicate work, carried out during the month of June, and consists of tying the vine-shoots and stems to the vine-props. In former times, this work was done by the girls of the Aosta Valley (in Italy), Savoy (in France) and Valais (in Switzerland), who used to come into the Canton of Vaud for the occasion, but this custom is dying out now. Dressed in their beautiful local costumes, the girls left their neighbouring regions and, for ten or twelve days, worked the vines *en tâche*, that is, by small plots of just over an acre each.

Cultivating *en gobelet* allows the grapes, growing closer to the ground, to benefit from a more complete maturing and an optimal enrichment in natural sugar. Plants trained in this way have a single vertical trunk terminating in several arms following the shape of a goblet. The advantages of such a method are its simplicity and that no vine support is needed.

Canton of Valais

The traveller descending the Rhône valley sees the first vines appear soon after Brig, alongside the river and up in the lateral valleys. The land in Valais used for vine cultivation has usually a poor soil which has been improved over the centuries only by tremendous effort. Patient maintenance work is needed to maintain the little terrace walls which alone hold back the soil clinging to the mountainside. In this valley bordered by mountain peaks with eternal snow, the sun brings its warmth and blessing with great generosity.

The people of Valais are a sturdy race, proud of many traditions, who have known how to get the best results from the almost Mediterranean climate of the Rhône valley. The vine is queen in a canton where excellent fruit orchards produce apricots, asparagus and strawberries. It must have existed there since earliest times, but the vines which were cultivated in those far-off days have been almost completely abandoned in favour of varieties perfectly suited to the valley's soil and climate. The extent of the vineyard in Valais, which is still expanding, is about 10,000 acres, of which about 8,500 are on slopes and hillsides. To reap the full benefit of the sun the vines are mostly planted on the right bank of the river; and the vinegrowers cover the soil, or mix gravel or crushed shale into it, to catch and hold the warmth still more. The vinegrower of this land has an endless patience: he has gone close to the great mountain glaciers to seek the water source for the essential irrigation of his plants, and has led the precious liquid down to the vineyards by artificial canals or *bisses* along the mountainside, distributing it by trickling or sprinkling.

This is a deeply religious land, but one that is very realistic too. A famous vinegrower, now dead, liked to tell the following tale: "Back in the days when the Bishop of Sion, today the cantonal capital, was both spiritual and temporal prince of the Valais, an angel of the Lord appeared to him in his prayers and spoke as follows: 'The Lord has been touched by the great troubles of the people of Valais, whose vines dry up in the sun, while the people of Bern [the neighbouring canton, separated from Valais by a chain of mountains] receive a plentiful rain to produce beautiful green and lush grazings. Therefore my Master, in order to distribute better his blessings, will cause it to rain on Valais as on other parts of Helvetia. Its people will be able to abandon their costly and dangerous *bisses* and instead of killing themselves in this work of leading the water to the vines and watering, they will be able to relax and have a good time.' The bishop, deeply moved, thanked the angel profusely but asked leave for eight days before giving his assent to this generous celestial proposition, in order to be able to submit it to his dear brethren. Eight days later the angel, punctual at the rendezvous, received the following answer: 'My brethren thank the Lord for all his blessings, but as far as the matter of watering is concerned, they would prefer to look after it themselves, for they know better than anyone else what needs doing.' Since that time the sun shines for everyone, with special care for this rather privileged canton."

The steeply terraced vineyards of the Valais.

High above Lake Leman, the famous Riex-Epesses vineyards chequer the slopes of the lake. This general view shows the vineyards following the indentations of the lake. In the centre background, the Rhône enters the lake near Villeneuve.

Between Lausanne and Geneva lie the vineyards of La Côte. Benefitting from the sun and the microclimate of the Lake Leman, La Côte is the most important viticultural region of the Canton of Vaud.

The wines which are harvested in Valais and which have gained it fame carry the name of FENDANT for the white wines produced from *Chasselas* (*Fendant Roux* and *Fendant Vert*), and that of DÔLE for the reds. The latter is a harmonious mixture of wines derived from the *Pinot Noir*, which originates from Burgundy, and the *Gamay*, a typical Beaujolais vine-stock. Each year, some 7,700,000 gallons of FENDANT, DÔLE and other wines from special stock are harvested, to bring to sagacious drinkers fresh strength, a delight to the palate, warmth of heart and a flowering of the spirit.

The white wines of the Valais are very numerous and very different from each other, depending on the stock which produced them. But the best-known and most widely sold is certainly FENDANT; harvested for probably about a century, it comes from vine-stocks which originated in the neighbouring canton of Vaud, where they were already well acclimatized. It is an admirable wine which pleases at all hours by its balance, its restrained strength and even, in hot years, by its hidden violence; it is a dry wine without any residual sugar in suspension. It is chosen as the friend and companion of those evenings for eating the *raclette*, a well-known cheese dish typical of Valais.

It is JOHANNISBERG which occupies the second place of importance among the white wines. Produced from *Sylvaner* or *Plant du Rhin*, whose grape-bunches are recognizable by their small size and closely-packed clusters, this wine is warmer than FENDANT. It is selected with special care, is remarkable for its strength, but nevertheless combines a great distinctiveness with an exquisite and attractive charm. This wine makes a good companion to the locally grown asparagus.

The art of guiding the wine, of leading it to its perfect flowering, is very well-known here, and the concern and respect for the profession of oenologist have brought a wide fame to the wines of Valais. As with FENDANT, one must drink JOHANNISBERG while it is still young; it is not a wine that should be allowed to age too much.

Beside these two well-known wines, one must mention a few other specialities whose quantities are, however, very small, at the most not more than 5 per cent of the entire harvest of Valais.

PINOT GRIS or MALVOISIE (Malmsey) is a heady and strong wine which, in good years, does not manage to change all the natural sugar it contains into alcohol. It is especially a dessert wine, mellow and flavoursome, with its bright colour shining brilliantly in the glass like molten gold. MALVOISIE therefore charms the drinker as much by its beauty as by its taste and its bouquet, bringing a note of agreeable bliss to the conclusion of a meal that was perhaps full of extravagances, pomp and pageantry.

ERMITAGE is a firm, powerful and strongly-alcoholic wine, capable of being kept for a long time and with a bouquet which sings all the beauties of Valais.

Then there are PETITE ARVINE, AMIGNE and HUMAGNE, typical local wines which have not emigrated elsewhere. ARVINE is a virile and lively wine which sometimes has some bite; it resists the ravages of time thanks to its natural liveliness. AMIGNE (*vinum amoenum*) is a more delicate, more pleasant wine with a light bouquet; it holds its own at the beginning of a meal as well as at the end. HUMAGNE (*vinum humanum*), which is gradually disappearing, could be said to resemble certain old winegrowers of Valais: it not only has their brusqueness and sharpness, but also shares their frankness and nobility.

Some other wines also deserve mention, notably MUSCAT. Very little is harvested but it is vinified as a dry wine and then fermented to have more savour and bouquet: it is a wine which, if drunk while still young, flatters the most exacting noses and taste-buds by its aroma. Finally, one can mention two local specialities which are not commercialized and which one must be lucky enough to drink on the spot in order to appreciate fully their true qualities: PAYEN, made from a very old vine-stock, *Sauvagnin*, and VIN DU GLACIER, also from an old plant, *Rèze*. All these wines are specialities of Valais which are much discussed but which it is unfortunately very difficult to encounter, owing to their extreme rarity.

Among the red wines, DÔLE deserves a special mention: it is a wine which has body and mellowness yet which is nevertheless not heavy nor tiring. A delightful blending of *Pinot Noir* and *Gamay*, DÔLE can only carry this name if it contains a minimum amount of natural sugar, which is very closely checked and if the entire crop has been supervised by the Cantonal laboratory. If the alcohol content is not high enough, the wine will be named GORON: lighter and very pleasant, this never leaves the Valais.

Canton of Vaud

As far as Saint-Maurice, the Rhône valley is relatively narrow, but then it widens suddenly to form the vast Lake Leman, along all of which stretches the Canton of Vaud. To simplify, one may say there are three different viticultural regions in this canton; Chablais, Lavaux and La Côte.

In a general way, Vaud produces chiefly white wines, marketed under the name DORIN, although a production of red wines under the name SALVAGNIN has been increasing over the past ten years. This canton produces about 6,600,000 gallons each year, harvested from 8,000 acres of vines. All wines bearing the name

DORIN come from the *Chasselas* (*Fendant Roux* and *Fendant Vert*), a vine that has kept its name when commercialized.

DORIN, CHABLAIS, YVORNE and AIGLE have, in particular, built up a big reputation: these dry wines, true-bred, warm and of a great finesse—a major quality in wine—are much sought after. Among them, one must single out for special notice OVAILLES D'YVORNE, one of the best sites in the canton.

In the Lavaux region, the Dézaley wines are excellent; coming from vineyards hanging on steep slopes, these wines—aristocratic, rich, full—are dry with all the delicacy and exquisite bitterness needed to assure them a long life, and the slight hint of a flinty taste is a characteristic flavour. These are once more wines from the *Chasselas* grape, which because of its large yield and sturdiness and the earthy taste of the wine is still preferred by the conservative Swiss vinegrowers to the more noble vines that the vineyard would seem to favour. The Dézaley is a big terraced southern slope with glacial moraine overlying the original mollasse. It lies between Vevey and Lausanne and obtains its excellent microclimate mainly because of its proximity to Lake Leman. This vineyard was created around 1100, together with the other famous vineyards mentioned above, thanks to the untiring efforts of Cistercian monks. After the desecularization of the clergy it fell under Bern sovereignty and today belongs to the Wine Estates of the City of Lausanne.

In the canton of Vaud, wines are presented with the name of their commune of origin, so that one has for the region of Lavaux such famous labels as EPESSES, RIVAZ, SAINT-SAPHORIN (usually abbreviated to SAINT-SAPH), among others. The white wines of Vaud are, as a general rule, less tender than those of Valais, but also less lively than the wines of Geneva. These shades of meaning were much clearer in olden times, and winegrowers of Vaud, great ones for picturesque speech, liked to say that the wines of Geneva were *raides et pointus* ("stiff and pointed") like the North Wall of the Eiger, only to hear the Genevese Calvinists reply that the Vaud wines were as flat as the pages of the psalm-book! But progress in oenology has erased all these faults, so that today these wines are delicate, fruity, fresh and pleasant, as much at home during a meal as on any other occasion.

The slopes of La Côte, the most important viticultural region of the Canton of Vaud, are gentler, and if the wines harvested there are also less full-bodied and warm, they are nevertheless also appreciated for their remarkably fresh bouquet.

Large co-operative cellars and big firms have made the wines of this region well known, with such names as the famous VINZEL, MONT, FÉCHY, LUINS, TARTEGNIN and MORGES. There are, in addition, numerous châteaux along La Côte, rich in history and hiding in their cellars the inviting and exhilarating wines from the vineyards which surround them.

The red wines of Vaud carry the name SALVAGNIN (from the name of this old vine-stock); but only reds from noble stock (*Pinot* and *Gamay*) may in fact carry it, for this name is only given after a severe quality test. Elegant, balanced, velvety, flattering, well-bred, these slightly dark-coloured wines are warm enough and rich enough in alcohol to accompany spiced and seasoned foods. The ceaseless search for fresh markets leads some proprietors to offer their wines by separating the vine-stock used; the *Pinot Noir* can then do full justice to all its real magnificence and, as Latin-speaking winegrowers might be tempted to say, *in Pinot veritas*.

Red wines which do not have the SALVAGNIN name are sold under various trade names. In very great demand, these wines are served cool like Beaujolais wines and should also be drunk while young, unlike the PINOT which reveals itself, after a few years of ageing, as a wine of high class.

Special vine-stocks are much less cultivated in the Canton of Vaud than in Valais or Geneva; one does, however, find generous JOHANNISBERGS, sweet white PINOT-CHARDONNAYS, and RIESLING-SYLVANERS with a strongly muscat bouquet. But on the whole, these wines are rare as much by their high quality as by their small quantity, although they may well carry to a seventh heaven those who partake of them.

Canton of Geneva

Leaving the Canton of Vaud, the traveller arrives in Geneva, the site not only of a great international city with many attractions but also of a rich and flourishing vineyard of about 2,500 acres. One-fifth of this area is planted to red stock, and *Gamay*, which comes especially from Beaujolais, is the most-used vine-stock; *Pinot Noir*, however, of Burgundian origin, is carving for itself an increasing large share of the canton's wine production. The white wines come from different vine-stocks of which the most important, *Chasselas*, covers an area of 1,235 acres. About 740 acres produce wines which are original and full of personality; they come from special, well-acclimatized vine-stocks: *Riesling-Sylvaner*, *Sylvaner* and *Aligoté*. Some other plants, such as *Pinot Gris*, *Chardonnay* or *Pinot Blanc*, in particular, produce exquisite and well-bred wines in, alas, only small quantities. About 500 acres are planted to red vine-stock, producing, in a year and for an average total of 2,640,000 gallons, as much red wine as white.

On the banks of Lake Leman, above the village of Saint-Saphorin, the terraced vines of Lavaux turn towards the south-west to benefit from a triple share of the sun's warmth: that of the heavenly body itself, that received from the lake by reflection and, in the cool of the day, that returned to the soil from the little walls of sun-baked stones. In this vineyard, the most widely grown vine-stock is the *Chasselas*.

The winegrowers of Geneva are proud to be the descendants and the worthy successors of very long lines of antecedents. These vineyards, in fact, date back to the time of the Roman conquest, and several emperors have left their mark in various decrees. Domitian, trying to prevent the expansion of the vine, ordered the uprooting of half of those not belonging to Romans; Probus, on the other hand, favoured its cultivation and kept his soldiers busy in their spare time spreading the noble plant to numerous regions.

The vineyard of Geneva had a very chequered history over the centuries and the vinegrowers needed a firmly rooted faith to persevere in their work. Having survived the pillaging, pilfering and general murdering characteristic of, in particular, the sixteenth and seventeenth centuries, they saw towards the end of the nineteenth century two new pests emerge, as elsewhere in Europe: phylloxera and mildew. Powerless to fight against these two calamities, they suffered the disappearance of half their vineyards; but the

vineyards were re-planted and now extend in gentle folds between the Jura mountains and the Salève ridge.

The wines produced from *Chasselas* and called Perlan have gained for themselves an enviable place over the past few years: generally light, they are usually sold *sur lie*, that is, they have not been decanted. They have kept their natural carbonic acid gas, have a delicate perfume and rejoice the eye of the connoisseur as they sparkle gently in the glass. It has been said they are much like the Genevese: not very biting at one's first meeting, they turn out to be the most joyous and friendly of companions. These wines can be drunk still milky, before they have finished fermenting, although it is preferable to allow them to reach full maturity. However, they are not rich enough in alcohol to gain much by being kept for several years.

The success of the wines produced from special vine-stocks must be mentioned here. Talented winegrowers in this region offer, for example, Riesling-Sylvaner with a slightly musky perfume; dry and

95

strong, this is much drunk as an aperitif. SYLVANER or JOHANNISBERG take the richness of the vine from which they come and deserve encouragement from the drinker; thanks to the little-known *Muscat* plant, and also to *Aligoté* and *Chardonnay*, which are very high-class stocks, excellent and harmonious wines can be offered to the consumer.

The greater part of the wines of Geneva are very well produced, with modern methods and the large cellars grouped together under a single trade name. A few well-equipped individual proprietors produce, on their own, wines which are becoming better known.

A final mention must be made of the red Geneva wines GAMAY and PINOT NOIR: the former are produced in some quantity and are supple and friendly wines, not heavy, and excellent in company; the PINOT is a richer wine which has already brought joy to a few connoisseurs in good years.

The Bacchic Brotherhoods

Everywhere, be it in Geneva, Valais or Vaud, one sees the marvels and the gifts that wine brings in its train. One must admire not only the wine itself, but also the manner in which the ideas of the land are enriched, the customs strengthened and even the thoughts and way of life of Rhône-side dwellers heightened—wherever wine is present.

Recently, between the years 1950 and 1960, several brotherhoods of wine were formed in these three Swiss cantons, with the sole aim of making the varieties of wealth offered by the Rhône vineyards better known and more appreciated. The Académie du Cep in Geneva, the Channe in Valais and the Confrérie du Guillon in Vaud all organize great gastronomic dinners, usually in the château de Dardagny in Geneva, the château de Chillon (immortalized by the poet Byron) in Vaud, or a number of other famous places in Valais. The dishes and the wines are presented, served and commented upon with love, humour and competence. These well-dressed occasions see the friends of wine come running from just about everywhere, to meet *ce fils sacré du soleil* ("this sacred son of the sun") as Baudelaire put it, in order to prove that this drink mentioned in the Bible is admirably adept at forging faithful friendships, opening hearts, broadening the spirit and giving the final proof that wine throughout the world is the ambassador of civilization.

THE WINES OF SAVOY

Two writers of ancient Rome, Pliny the Younger and Columella, made famous the wines of Allobroge, the Savoy of today. The prince of Roman gourmets, Lucullus, had Savoy wines served at his table and the vinegrowers of Savoy are proud of the title of seniority that history has conferred on them.

With the exception of the local table wines drunk in the region, the wines of Savoy make up that honourable company called *vins délimités de qualité supérieure*, or more simply "V.D.O.S.". There is no outstanding vintage wine; there are simply good, honest wines which are, none the less, well known outside their place of birth.

The vineyard of Savoy can be divided into three zones:

1. To the north, the southern shores of Lake Leman, from Evian to Annemasse; the right bank of the river Arve from Annemasse to Bonneville, and the area along the Swiss frontier to Saint-Julien-en-Genevois. These make up a relatively homogeneous zone which is chiefly planted, as across the border in Switzerland, with *Chasselas*. The winegrowers produce fresh, light white wines, such as MARIN, RIPAILLE and MARIGNAN. First place, however, must go to COTEAUX-DE-CRÉPY and PETIT CRÉPY, both of them clear, semi-sparkling wines with a delicate perfume of almond, reputed also to be the most diuretic wines in France.

2. In the centre, the region of the Lake of Bourget, Seyssel and the left bank of the Rhône gives a very characteristic wine called Savoy ROUSSETTE, the principal vintages of which are FRANGY, MARESTEL, MONTHOUX and SEYSSEL. These wines have a good bouquet; fruity and full-bodied, they are the product of *Altesse*, a vine brought back, it is said, by the Count of Mareste from a crusade. Seyssel also produces a pleasant sparkling wine.

3. To the south, the vineyard encompasses the region of Chambéry, the right bank of the river Isère from Saint-Pierre-d'Albigny to Sainte-Marie-d'Alloix, and the Arc valley up to Saint-Michel.

Apart from the local wines, a few white wines have emerged from anonymity; these are the wines of Monterminod, Apremont, Abymes, Chignin, Cruet, Montmélian and Saint-Jean-de-la-Porte. To these white wines one can add a few reds and rosés, light, easy to drink and which, it is said, do not upset the drinker's temper.

The total production of the wines of Savoy is about 4,400,000 gallons.

THE WINES OF THE FRENCH JURA

The Roman naturalist Pliny, who also served in the armies of Germania, recalled "this grape needing no special preparations which produces the pitch-flavoured wine recently bringing pleasure to Sequani the area of the river Seine". If one is to believe this statement, the vine was established on the western edge of the Jura mountains right at the beginning of our historic age. There it prospered and the resulting VIN D'ARBOIS gained wide renown.

In the year 1885 occurred the first attack of phylloxera, which within the next ten years was to destroy the entire vineyard. The pre-phylloxera vines were cultivated with the aid of props and with no particular order or symmetry. The new vines were planted in lines and trained on to wire supports, a method allowing the use of a plough to work the land wherever it does not slope too much and an arrangement which also enables the grapes to soak up the maximum warmth of the sun. The first harvests of the twentieth century bear witness to the rebirth of this vineyard.

Today, the vineyard of the Jura, well situated and with a cold, humid climate in winter, extends from Salins in the north to Saint-Amour in the south, a stretch of some 50 miles in length by 8 miles at its widest part. It is planted to *Ploussard* or *Poulsard*, *Trousseau* and *Gros Noirin* for the red wines, and to *Naturé* or *Savagnin*, *Chardonnay* or *Pinot Blanc* for the white wines. Apart from the local table wines, the Jura produces three well-known wines:

The CÔTES-DU-JURA are full-bodied, heady red wines, earthy rosés, and dry whites which, although lively and fruity, are sometimes found to be a little acid when young.

The VINS D'ARBOIS are finer and more generous than the above-mentioned ones; the reds and rosés come from the *Ploussard* and, to a lesser degree, from the *Trousseau* and *Pinot Noir*. It is interesting to recall, in passing, that it was in Arbois, where he was born and where he owned a vineyard, that the illustrious Louis Pasteur worked on his study of fermentation.

The CHÂTEAU-CHALON is the wine *par excellence* of the Jura vineyards. This amber-coloured wine—hence its name *vin jaune*—is unusual in its production and handling. In the spring of the second year, after a normal vinification, it is transferred to a cask already impregnated with *vin jaune*. There it is left to age, without being touched in any way—not even the skin on its surface is disturbed—and it is bottled only after six years. This *vin jaune* is a truly original wine and one of the best white wines in France. Some of it is also produced under the name CÔTES-DU-JURA or ARBOIS, but it is the CHÂTEAU-CHALON which is the undisputed leader. It is the only white wine which must not be served chilled but slightly *chambré*, nearly at room temperature, in its specially shaped bottle called a *clavelin*.

The Jura vinegrowers also produce, apart from a sparkling wine processed by the *méthode champenoise* around Arbois, the so-called *vin de paille*, or straw wine. It is a wine of the winter frosts, made from grapes harvested at the end of the autumn which have been stored carefully on trays of straw until February; the grapes are then pressed, and the wine is kept in little oaken barrels. The *vin de paille* is a beautiful burned-topaz colour, a dessert wine with an unctuous bouquet.

Among the unusual Jura wines, one should not forget MACVIN, an aperitif produced by cooking the must from white grapes, infusing spices and, after filtering, adding *eau-de-vie de marc* (white brandy)

The annual production of the wines of the French Jura is now only about 660,000 gallons, not one-tenth of what it was before the advent of phylloxera.

THE WINES OF THE CÔTES DU RHÔNE

An infinite variety of locations and an infinite variety of wines—such are the characteristic features of the Côtes du Rhône region, stretching 125 miles along the majestic river, from Vienne-la-Romaine to Avignon, city of the Popes. In a few short hours by train or car, one passes from a northern world to a southern world, from forests of chestnuts to forests of olive trees. The wines produced in the various parts of the Rhône valley are different for reasons of variations of climate, of soil and also of vine-stocks.

The Côtes du Rhône region can be divided into two parts, separated by non-viticultural areas: the northern part from Vienne to Valence, and the southern part from Bourg-Saint-Andéol (just opposite Pierrelatte) as far as Avignon.

The cultivation of the vine has developed particularly in the vineyards of the CÔTES-DU-RHÔNE *appellation d'origine contrôlée*, but perhaps principally in the vineyards producing the basic type of wine. Thus, between 1956 and 1967, the area planted to vine increased from 31,085 acres to 60,330 acres, and wine production (including vintage wines) from 8,030,000 gallons to more than 22,000,000 gallons today (1967: 19,800,000 gallons of basic CÔTES-DU-RHÔNE, 4,400,000 gallons of vintage wines). As for the marketing side of wine production, the domestic demand has followed the increase in production, while exports have leaped ahead, from 1,386,000 in 1960 to about 3,216,400 gallons in 1967.

The basic regional name of the wine, which includes all types, is CÔTES-DU-RHÔNE. Within this vineyard, however, there are the following *appellations d'origine contrôlée* established by special decree of the French authorities: CHÂTEAUNEUF-DU-PAPE, CÔTE-RÔTIE, CONDRIEU, CORNAS, HERMITAGE, SAINT-PÉRAY, TAVEL, CHÂTEAU-GRILLET, CROZES-HERMITAGE, LIRAC and SAINT-JOSEPH.

CÔTE-RÔTIE: The vineyard of CÔTE-RÔTIE lies 22 miles south of Lyons and almost opposite Vienne, on precipitous slopes where the soil must be held in place by small walls. Two vine-stocks, *Viognier* and *Syrah*, produce a wine with a great fragrance and a delicate perfume which recalls violets and raspberries.

This red wine, harvested at Ampuis, develops its qualities to the full after ageing in casks for three or four years; it can be kept in the bottle for more than 20 years. The average production is 26,400 gallons.

CONDRIEU: This white wine comes solely from the white vine *Viognier* and must have an alcohol content of at least 11°. Its area of production includes the three communes of Condrieu (Rhône), Vérin and Saint-Michel (Loire). This gives an average production of about 4,400 gallons from the 17 acres of vineyards that the fifteen or so producers cultivate. Cultivation is carried out solely on small, stone-walled terraces, a type of exploitation of the land that is extremely difficult because it is impossible to employ mechanical aid. This difficulty accounts for the fact that these vineyards are being gradually abandoned.

The fermentation of Condrieu wines is allowed to proceed more or less slowly according to the prevailing temperature; it continues up to the end of the year when the rigorous winter stops the process. Fermentation re-starts in the spring and continues until some time in summer, if dry wines are being produced. To obtain the sweet wines, which contain 15-30 grammes of sugar per litre and represent 80 per cent of the total production here, fermentation is stopped by successive racking, combined with blending.

This wine is not drunk when it is old, because although it stands up to ageing very well, it loses that special fruitiness which has made its name. Bottling is therefore carried out, depending on the type of wine, during the first or the second year.

CHÂTEAU-GRILLET: This vintage wine is not cultivated very extensively and is confined to a few plots of land in the communes of Verin and Saint-Michel-sous-Condrieu (Loire).

The granite hillsides of Château-Grillet, facing south and dominating the Rhône, have a climate which is dry and hot during the summer and mild during the autumn, allowing the vine *Viognier* to attain over-maturity. The character of this tiny vineyard lies in its topography: the whole is made up of small, stepped terraces planted to not more than two rows of plants, and sometimes to only a few individual plants.

Harvested in late October, the must from these white grapes is put in casks and allowed to ferment very slowly over several months. It is racked a number of times to ensure a perfect clarification, and forms a very particular bouquet of violets. After two years of constant care, it is bottled, and it can then be kept for many years. Dry and fairly heady, it has some resemblance to Rhine wine, although it has more body and gives off a better developed perfume.

CROZES-HERMITAGE: This wine is produced in the communes of Serves, Erome, Gervans, Larnage, Crozes-Hermitage, Tain-l'Hermitage, Mercurol, Chanos-Curson, Beaumont-Montreux, La Roche-de-Glun and Pont-de-l'Isère.

The red wines are produced solely from the *Syrah* grape; the whites from the *Roussanne* and *Marsanne* varieties. However, the addition of *Marsanne* and *Roussanne* white grapes within the limits of 15 per cent is authorized for the production of red wine.

The hilly nature of the terrain makes cultivation here an extremely arduous affair. On the stepped-up terraces, all work must be done by hand, and fertilizers as well as the entire harvest can be carried only on the backs of men. The average production from 865 acres is 312,000 gallons.

These red wines are lighter and more purplish than the HERMITAGE wines which follow in these pages, and they retain a tang of the soil, although they are less mellow or fine.

The white wines are very slightly coloured and sometimes lack a certain flavour and strength; they are, however, fine and light, with a perfume of hazelnut.

L'HERMITAGE: The hillside of l'Hermitage, which produces the wine of that name, lies in the northern part of the Côtes du Rhône region, in the department of Dauphiné. It commands the little town of Tain-l'Hermitage, in the department of Drôme, situated beside the Rhône on Route Nationale No. 7 between Vienne and Valence.

The earliest vineyards here date back to the tenth century, but legend has it that Henri Gaspart de Sterimberg, a knight returning from the Crusades under Louis VIII and weary of wars, sought from Queen Blanche de Castille a corner of land to which he could retire. This would explain the origin of the name "Hermitage". HERMITAGE obtained its titles to nobility as a wine under Henry IV and Louis XIII and especially under Louis XIV. Up to the time of the phylloxera disaster at the end of the last century, this was universally considered to be one of the foremost wines of France, being the favourite vintage wine of the Czar's court in Russia. It was also much esteemed in nineteenth-century England.

The HERMITAGE vineyard is blessed with a quite exceptional geographical position: it faces south-west at an altitude of 894 feet above sea-level, only 6 ¼ miles from the 45° parallel of latitude.

The red wine is produced entirely from the vine *Syrah*, while the white wine comes from *Marsanne* with the addition of a small quantity of *Roussanne*. The 400 acres under cultivation are spread among 70 small viticultural properties. The wines of Hermitage are no longer the wines of the Lyons region, following on from those of Burgundy, nor are they wines of Provence yet; they are strictly Rhône wines.

SAINT-JOSEPH: The name of Saint-Joseph is a relatively recent one, since it was authorized by a decree dated June 15th, 1956. It had had, nonetheless, its "letters patent of nobility" for many years: according to Elie Brault in the book *Anne and her time*, Louis XII would allow on his table only the wines from his property at Beaune, his land at Tournon or his vineyards at Chenoves.

Six communes in the department of Ardèche are entitled to produce this wine, with the exception of lands which are unsuitable on account of their soil or their position are: Glunn, Mauves, Tournon, Saint-Jean-de-Muzols, Lemps and Vion.

For the red wines the *Syrah* grape is used while the *Marsanne* and *Roussanne* produce the whites.

The vine is cultivated on the steep slopes overlooking the right bank of the Rhône. Most of the work is done by hand, and the vintage is carried in on the grape-pickers' backs. The maximum yield permitted is 350 gallons per acre. The mean annual production is 33,000 gallons from 200 acres.

The SAINT-JOSEPH reds are fine wines with a perfumed bouquet although they are, perhaps, rather less full-bodied than the HERMITAGE wines. They have a fine ruby colour and are agreeable to drink after a few years in the bottle. The whites are fruity, supple and mellow; they should be drunk young while they retain their full perfume.

CORNAS. Every day throughout the centuries, as the rising sun sheds its rays on the Rhône valley, the first communes to benefit from them have been Châteaubourg and Cornas, situated as they are with their backs to the Cévennes. The commune of Cornas has a Provençal type of climate, as witness the olive, fig and almond trees which flourish in many a garden there. This privileged situation has encouraged the cultivation of the vine for more than a thousand years. A document of the time of Charles V reveals that the Great Companies halted at Cornas for far longer than was scheduled in their marching programme since they could not resist the good wine in the inns of this tiny piece of countryside.

The A.O.C. CORNAS covers the area around the village and the granite slopes; the alluvial soils in the Rhône valley are excluded. The vineyard has an area of only 300 acres.

The grapes grown in the vineyard are the *Syrahs*. Since they are not very productive, long shoots are permitted and this means that the shoots must be fastened to the props before the spring. All the work of cultivation on the terraces must be done by hand and the harvest seldom exceeds 44,000 gallons.

The best wine comes from the grapes ripened on the slope. It is richer and fuller bodied, fruitier and heavier with a characteristic taste of the soil due to its richness in tannin. In its first year, CORNAS may be a little sour and astringent; it reaches its peak of quality after three winters in the wood and two years in the bottle.

SAINT-PÉRAY. At the foot of Mount Crussol and in the latitude of Valence, we find the village of Saint-Péray. It would seem that the department of Ardèche has always been a favourite winegrowing country and, with CORNAS and SAINT-JOSEPH, SAINT-PÉRAY forms the trinity of fine Vivarais wines.

The vineyard, which is one of the oldest in the northern Côtes du Rhône area, is quite limited in area: 193 acres with 90 owners. The soil is tilled by hand because of the narrowness of the space between the rows of vines. In the parcels where the slope is less steep it is sometimes possible to use horse-ploughs or hand-ploughs.

The only white grapes permitted are the *Roussette* (or *Roussanne*) and the *Marsanne*. The *Roussette* is a fine grape variety and produces a high-class wine with a strong perfume, but since it is not very productive and is sensitive to disease, it is gradually being abandoned. Because of the soil type lighter wines are produced than on the other side of the Rhône.

Until the beginning of the nineteenth century, the Saint-Péray wines were served *nature*, i.e. as still wines. Attempts by local wine-merchants in 1828 to convert them into sparkling wines produced excellent results, and since then Saint-Péray has been available in that form also. Classical white-wine vinification is used. After pressing and drawing off, the must is fermented in 50-gallon hogsheads called *pièces*. The fermentation must be completed before winter. The dry white wines are usually bottled after two or three years.

The wines produced are marketed, therefore, either as still wines, as dry SAINT-PÉRAY, or as sparkling wines. It is the latter form—SAINT-PÉRAY MOUSSEUX —which is now the better known.

CHÂTEAUNEUF-DU-PAPE. This is the "Pontiff" of the Côtes du Rhône wines. In addition to possessing all the warmth of the Provençal sun, this wine is perfumed by the full aroma of that region's sparse soil. Between Orange and Avignon, dominating one of the widest and most breath-taking landscapes of Provence, an abrupt hill bears a picturesque village crowned by an imposing medieval ruin. The place was formerly selected by the popes as their summer residence. Climbing up the sides of the hill, the impressive vineyard of Châteauneuf-du-Pape reveals that the local winegrowers have lost nothing of the traditional renown attached to this soil. The wine produced is still in every way worthy of the pontifical table. The territory entitled to the A.O.C., i.e. the commune of Châteauneuf-du-Pape and parts of the communes of Orange, Courthezon, Beddarides and Sorgues, has been strictly limited since 1923. Incidentally, the national regulations on A.O.C.s, promulgated in December 1936, were inspired by what had been achieved at Châteauneuf-du-Pape.

The methods of cultivation, vinification and conservation have been fixed both by law and by the strong force of local tradition.

CHÂTEAUNEUF-DU-PAPE comes from thirteen grapes, seven of which, *Grenache, Clairette, Mourvèdre, Picpoul, Terret, Syrah* and *Cinsault*, are regarded as principal grapes, while the other six, *Counoise, Muscadin, Vaccarèse, Picardan, Roussanne* and *Bourboulenc*, are regarded as ancillary. Each of these grapes contributes its own special note to the wine produced: the *Grenache* and the *Cinsault* give it warmth, sweetness and mellowness; the *Mourvèdre*, the *Syrah*, the *Muscadin* and the *Vaccarèse* contribute colour, solidity and staying-power; the *Counoise* and the *Picpoul* supply wininess, taste, freshness and a special bouquet, while the *Clairette, Bourboulenc, Roussanne* and *Picardan* give it elegance, fire and brilliance.

The wines of Châteauneuf-du-Pape are always highly coloured and very warm. They have a powerful bouquet reminiscent of oriental spices. They are very varied in type: the pebbly soils give a great deal of strength while the sandy and sandy-clayey soils produce a wine of great finesse and elegance.

The vineyard covers over 6,000 acres which produce 176,000 gallons (15,400 gallons only of white wine). It has virtually doubled in the last twenty years.

Side by side with the great vineyards we have just mentioned, there is a host of small villages whose names strike no particular chord but which are excellent producers of wine with the A.O.C. CÔTES-DU-RHÔNE. This wine comes from no less than 138 communes with an average annual production of 13,200,000 gallons. Some of the areas involved are entitled to a stricter commune regulation, the place-name being granted to their wine after compulsory tasting. Cases in point are Cairanne, Gigondas, Vacqueyras etc.

Although the *Grenache* and the *Carigan* form the framework of the CÔTES-DU-RHÔNE wines, any or all of the following grape varieties can be used to distinguish one wine from another: *Clairette, Syrah, Mourvèdre, Terret Noir, Counoise, Picpoule, Muscardin, Bourboulenc, Ugni Blanc, Roussanne, Marsanne* and *Viognier*. It should be added that there are also variations due to the soil, the exposure, and individual cultivation which give each growth its originality. Everything is carefully regulated: the grape variety, the soil, the pruning of the plant, the degree of alcohol and the yield.

CAIRANNE. This is one of the oldest of winegrowing terrains. Almost all the Clairanne vineyard, which covers 3,000 acres, consists of slopes and terraces facing due south.

VACQUEYRAS and GIGONDAS. The main GIGONDAS grape is the *Grenache* while VACQUEYRAS is still largely based on the *Carignan*, which is gradually being replaced by the *Cinsault* and the *Syrah*. The red wines of the A.O.C. are of great quality and approach those of CHÂTEAUNEUF-DU-PAPE.

LIRAC. The LIRAC wines, whether red, rosé or even white, have each their own special type.

The principal grape, the *Grenache*, must make up at least 40 per cent of the planting for Lirac reds and rosés, the other 60 per cent consisting of *Cinsault* and *Mourvèdre*. Secondary grapes such as *Syrah* and *Picpoul* are permitted. In the case of the whites, 30 per cent of the planting must be the *Clairette* grape.

All these old local grapes, distributed throughout each vineyard in judiciously determined proportions and mixed together in the same vat at the harvest, produce these charming Lirac wines with such a pronounced bouquet and particular perfume.

TAVEL. A little village 8 miles from Avignon, Tavel, harvests from a particularly arid soil about 462,000 gallons on the average of a light red wine obtained from such old grape varieties as: *Clairette, Cinsault, Grenache* etc. This wine was very much appreciated by the Popes of Avignon, and by Philippe le Bel who claimed that "the only good wine is that from Tavel". It has an incomparable bouquet and, although strongly alcoholic, is light to the taste. Tavel can be taken as an aperitif or with red meat; it develops its full savour when it is put as an accompaniment to a young partridge or when served with a thrush with juniper berries.

RASTEAU. In this case, a single grape, the *Grenache*, has given birth to an excellent natural sweet wine. The must is vinified according to the classical method of obtaining naturally sweet wines. During fermentation, a certain amount of alcohol is added and this prevents the sugar from being completely transformed into alcohol. The wine thus retains a certain amount of sugar, which is the reason for its sweetness, while at the same time developing a high alcohol content.

BEAUMES-DE-VENISE. This is a natural sweet wine produced from various white *Muscats* with a special taste which are among the finest of their type. These wines are aged in casks or demijohns; when exposed to the sunlight, they develop a beautiful golden colour.

THE WINES OF THE CÔTES DE PROVENCE

The wines of the Côtes de Provence are of very ancient origin; under the name of "Provence wines", they were already known to the Romans. According to a statement by Justinian, it was the Gauls who cultivated the first vines brought from Italy and the near East by the Phocaeans, and they were already honoured during the reign of Caesar, who speaks of them in his Commentaries. The fame of the Provence wines continued through the Middle Ages and into the Renaissance; the Cartulary of Lérins mentions them and lords and abbots began to fix the rules for their production and marketing through such decrees as the Act of King Charles II in 1292, and the authorization by Queen Mary in 1391, both sovereigns of Provence.

In the seventeenth and eighteenth centuries, they were in high repute at the Court of the Sun King, where Madame de Sévigné became their best ambassadress. From this period dates the foundation by Louis de Vauvray, Naval Intendant at Toulon, of one of the first baccanalian orders, that of the "Knights of Medusa". In the nineteenth century and at the beginning of the twentieth, the *appellation contrôlée* and even the fame of the Côtes de Provence wines were in decline; under various names, some of these wines were used for blending and others for making vermouth. Only a few owners, proud of their growths and strong in the markets they had conquered, kept aloft the flag of this A.O.C.: under the auspices of the Syndical Association of the Winegrowing Landowners of the Var, established in 1931, they were to form the basis for the resurrection of the CÔTES-DE-PROVENCE.

The area of production is the result of a delimitation based on the geological, hydrological and climatic study of the land by a commission nominated by ministerial decree and composed of representatives of the National Institute of Place-Name Descriptions of Origin *(appellation d'origine)*, the General Inspectorate of the Ministry of Agriculture and the Science Faculties of the Universities of Marseilles and Montpellier. The area of production is limited to the following zones: the coastal zone of Provence from La Ciotat to Saint-Raphael; the Permian depression which stretches from Sanary through Toulon to Carnoules and Leluc; the triassic plateau of Lorgues-Carces; the terraces of the valley of the Var and the area described by geologists as the Eubeau Basin in the Alpes-Maritimes. A card index has been established for each producing commune and an individual card index per producer. They are all minutely followed.

The delimitation of the area of production, the fixing of a minimum production per acre and the determination of the grapes did not, in the eyes of the producers, constitute a sufficiently strict selection and they consequently imposed upon themselves the obligation to submit their produce, which already met the standards laid down, to an organoleptic analysis followed by examination by a tasting commission to decide if the wine were worthy of the *appellation contrôlée* CÔTES-DE-PROVENCE. In 1953 the wines were granted a statue allowing those of a sufficiently high standard to be sold as CÔTES DE PROVENCE V.D.Q.S. *(Vins Délimités de Qualité Supérieure)*, which is a secondary quality guarantee, and some wines are permitted to be sold as Classified Growths.

GRAPES. The varieties making up the CÔTES-DE-PROVENCE are fairly numerous. Some of them, however, play only a secondary part and occupy a limited area; everywhere the same basic grape varieties are cultivated.

Among the red grapes, the *Carignan* clearly heads the field, occupying as it does 25 per cent or more of the area of the vineyard. Late in budding, of average productivity but sensitive to oïdium, it gives full-bodied alcoholic wines which are sometimes rather sour in their youth. This bitterness rapidly disappears with age. A certain proportion of this grape is required.

The *Cinsault*, like the *Grenache* elsewhere, contributes suppleness, mellowness and bouquet. The same is true of the *Tibouren*, which is cultivated in a substantial area of the Maures mountains.

The *Mourvèdre*, an élite grape, formerly held a much more important place than at present; the irregularity

101

of its production has caused it to lose ground. However, under the impulse of a few progressive winegrowers, it is once again gaining a certain favour and is now definitely extending its sway. If it is included in suitable proportions, it should ensure that the wines age well and should distinctly improve their quality.

Among the white grapes, the *Ugni* and the *Clairette*, together with the *Rolle* in the Alpes-Maritimes, have an almost complete monopoly. To these principal grapes, however, are sometimes added some other high-quality varieties including the *Syrah*, the *Cabernet*, the *Barbaroux*, the *Picpoul*, the *Roussanne* and the *Pecoultouar*.

It is by a judicious association of grapes, each contributing its particular characteristics, that the CÔTES-DE-PROVENCE acquire their balance and their special quality. There is a growing trend toward increasing the proportion of high-quality grapes, and rapid progress is being made. We should mention that the law imposes a minimum alcohol content of 11º for the red and rosé wines and of 11.5º for the white wines.

VINIFICATION. On their arrival in the cellars, whether private or co-operative, the vintages are carefully selected so that only grapes entitled to the A.O.C. will be introduced into the vats. Since the use of the mustimeter and the refractometer have become generalized, the winegrowers wait until the grapes have reached complete maturity so as to have the maximum number of degrees.

Fermentation usually takes place in concrete vats; some owners of classed growths, however, vinify in wooden vats. On the other hand, wood is always used when storing the wine for any length of time; this is obligatory for producers who sell in the bottle. A frequent practice is to remove the stalks. Vatting is generally quite short: 4 to 5 days for red wines but somewhat longer for the white wines, which ferment for about a fortnight; and only 24 hours for the rosé wines which are the natural result of the first 100 per cent pressing of rosé grapes. The white wine is usually obtained by the so-called "bleeding" method. It consists in leaving open the drainage tap of the vat which contains the trodden vintage and withdrawing a certain proportion of the must.

The environmental conditions and the grapes cultivated make it possible to obtain, by rational vinification and careful storage, wines of the very first quality.

CLASSED GROWTHS. The Commission on Boundaries noted that, among the mass of producers, there were some who were organized to vinify in the best conditions and to store part of their harvest every year which was later sold, after ageing, in bottles. The Commission therefore adopted the idea of Classed Growths for any estate which had formerly practised ageing. It con-

sidered whether the fame of the wines from such-and-such a holding was justified on the basis of the environmental conditions, the grapes used, the cultivation methods, the vinification and growing processes used and the quality of the wines obtained. Moreover, it demanded a minimum ageing of 15 months for the red wines and 8 months for the rosé and white wines. Of more than 60 vineyards visited, the Commission decided that only 30 merited selection as CÔTES-DE-PROVENCE Classed Growths.

The fact that Provençal wines adapt easily to almost any dish might have accounted for the expansion of the A.O.C. to the detriment of certain wines.

The rosé, the great speciality of the CÔTES-DE-PROVENCE, is fruity and full-flavoured and has an irridescent robe. A choice companion to all dishes, it adds a note of high-quality, which is much appreciated by the epicures, to the festive board.

The white wine is generally dry, sometimes sparkling, but always full of the savour of the Provençal hills and proves a most happy foil to the fish and shellfish of the Mediterranean coast. The dace of the gulf of Saint-Tropez, the crayfish of the Corsican creeks, the red mullet from the rocky depths of the Var coast as well as the Mediterranean shell-fish take on their full gustatory value when set off by the bouquet of a bottle of CÔTES-DE-PROVENCE.

The red wine, which is very full-flavoured, is at its best when accompanying pâtés, pasties, game and roasts. It is the perfect foil to venison and brings out still further the delicate aroma of woodcock flamed in old armagnac.

As in the case of a number of other wines, a special shape of bottle has been created for CÔTES-DE-PROVENCE. It is derived from the original form of the Provençal bottle.

Wine Confraternity

Faithful to their tradition, the winegrowers of the Côtes-de-Provence, like those of many other wine-producing regions, have created a wine society or, more exactly, have revived a very ancient confraternity, founded in 1690, the Confraternity of the Knights of Medusa, from the name of one of the classical gorgons. Its first Grand Master was M. Dantan, its chief founder being the Naval Intendant at Toulon, M. Louis Girardin de Vauvray, who was named a benefactor member of the Order in 1697.

The rituals of the Order unfold in the sumptuous setting of the Château de Sainte-Roseline, at Arcs-de-Provence, in its cloisters and in its park, and they are presided over by Baron de Rasque de Laval and his Grand Council.

THE WINES OF LANGUEDOC AND ROUSSILLON

In Languedoc-Roussillon we find a very large wine-growing area which flourishes under extremely favourable natural conditions. The cultivation of the wine is at present the dominant activity of the region. In certain districts it is combined with other activities such as market gardening and fruit-growing on the Garde bank of the Rhône, cattle-raising in the region of Garrigues and the lower Montagne Noire, industry in the coalfields of Alès and near the urban centres of Montpelliers, Nîmes and Béziers and fishing along the coast, but it remains the sole activity for most of the communes in spite of the changeover which has begun.

Although 85 per cent of the wines are ordinary wines for current consumption, produced from the best grapes and vinified under first-class conditions, it should not be forgotten that 12 per cent are wines of simple *appellation d'origine* while 3 per cent are wines of *appellation contrôlée*. Over the last five years, wines for current consumption coming from vineyards free of hybrids and obtained from recommended grapes, which have satisfied a series of analyses and been passed by a tasting commission, can use the title of "selected wines" and be sold as such without blending.

These selected wines are beginning to take their places besides the growths of good repute such as SAINT-CHINIAN, COTEAUX-DU-LANGUEDOC, CABRIÈRES, FAUGÈRES, MEJANELLE, MONT-PEYROUX, PICPOUL DE PINET, PIC SAINT-LOUP, SAINT-CHRISTOL, SAINT-DREZERY, SAINT-GEORGES D'ORQUES, SAINT-SATURNIN and VESARGUES, all delimited wines of superior quality (V.D.Q.S.) produced in the department of Hérault. It should not be forgotten that the Hérault plain also produces some very aromatic muscat wines such as FRONTIGNAN, MUSCAT DE LUNEL, MIREVAL and CLAIRETTE DU LANGUEDOC.

In the department of the Gard, as well as the CÔTES-DU-RHÔNE wines with an *appellation d'origine contrôlée* —particularly the ROSÉ DE CHUSCLAN, TAVEL and LIRAC—the V.D.Q.S. COSTIÈRES-DU-GARD, with a production of 6,600,000 gallons from 15,000 acres, are agreeably fruity and palate-pleasing wines.

The second largest French department in terms of wines produced, with an average production of 154,000,000 gallons, the Aude produces about 48,400,000 gallons of guaranteed place-name description wines, including 20,900,000 gallons of CORBIÈRES and 8,800,000 gallons of MINERVOIS, as well as 1,540,000 to 1,760,000 gallons of A.O.C. wines, including 990,000 gallons of natural sweet wines. It should be added that, in the case of wines for ordinary consumption, there is a growing tendency to improve the grapes used (*Grenache* and *Cinsault*). Vinification is also being very appreciably improved. The 141 co-operative cellars in the department vinify between 55 per cent and 56 per cent of the wine production. The winegrowers to an increasing degree are producing wines which are drinkable "as they stand".

In the range of quality wines there are, in addition to CORBIÈRES and MINERVOIS, the names of FITOU, CLAPE, QUATOURZE, BLANQUETTE DE LIMOUX (374,000 gallons) and the natural sweet wines, with a comparable production, which have ensured the wine-growing reputation of the department.

Coming solely from the delimited Limousin slopes in the Upper Valley of the Aude, the BLANQUETTE DE LIMOUX is a sparkling white wine, prepared according to a very ancient method with Mauzac and *Clairette* grapes. For many centuries, BLANQUETTE DE LIMOUX has been favoured for its sparkle, elegance and fruitiness. It should be mentioned that the wine was granted an *appellation contrôlée* in 1938.

The Corbières vineyard, most of which is located in the department of the Aude, covers 74,130 acres. The vine is cultivated there according to careful and time-honoured local methods, with a respect for tradition calculated to maintain the specific characteristics of the wines. Judicious regulations have gone far to establish a balance between the necessary progress in technology and the improvement of the quality of the wines. These wines should have a minimum alcohol content of 11° and similar regulations are found in all French areas producing wines entitled to an *appellation d'origine* (delimitations of the parcels of land, grapes, degree, yield and viticultural practises). The annual production exceeds 22 million gallons.

The CORBIÈRES are, for the most part, red wines with a few rosé wines. White CORBIÈRES are much rarer.

The reds are substantial, complete wines whose quality improves with age. After a year, they lose a great deal of colour; after the second winter, their quality begins to blossom and they can be bottled. This produces a wine whose bouquet harmonizes well with pork, fowl, roasts, game and cheese.

The rosé wines are distinguished by their fruitiness, their elegance and their nervousness. They form a perfect accompaniment to fish and shell-fish; generally speaking, they have the advantage of being drinkable with all dishes.

As for the natural sweet wines of Roussillon and the Midi, the origin of the titles of nobility of which they are so proud is very ancient. The vineyards from which these wines come are to be found on steep terraces, on sunny slopes that overhang the sea as at Banyuls, or clinging to the last buttresses of the Pyrenees.

It is in the Pyrénées-Orientales, for the most part, that the BANYULS, MAURY, RIVESALTES, CÔTES-D'AGLY and CÔTES-DE-HAUT-ROUSSILLON wines are harvested. The southern winegrowing part of the Corbières of Aude, adjacent to Roussillon, also produces some of them but in much smaller quantities.

At Banyuls, the *Grenache Noir* predominates. It is cultivated under the direct influence of the winds from the sea, on the abrupt flanks of the last foothills of the Albères, in the small amount of arable land left by the slow crumbling of a bedrock of primary schists which has a rust-like colour and the appearance of old timber.

In the Fenouillèdes, near Maury, the *Grenache Noir* prevails once again in conjunction with an exceptional soil. The vineyard clings to rounded hillocks of dark flakey marls. Boxed in between two high white cliffs of hard limestone, the vineyard in its arid corridor profits by a particularly favourable concentration and a great intensity of sunshine. The first preoccupation of the purchaser and consumer should be carefully to verify the origin of the bottles he is buying. If it comes from Banyuls or Maury it will be a dark red or brick-coloured wine. Ageing brings reflections of purple and gold; when very old, the BANYULS and the MAURY often acquire the special taste described as *rancio* which is much appreciated by Catalan epicures. The experienced taster will recognize the special bouquet of the *Grenache Noir* in the BANYULS and the MAURY and will appreciate all the warmth and charm of these wines which are vinified by the maceration process. During fermentation, the must remains in more or less prolonged contact with the pulp and skin; macerated in this way, it acquires the most subtle of its qualities.

In the Côtes-d'Agly, as well as a large number of plantations of *Grenache Noir*, we find the *Grenache Gris* and the *Grenache Blanc* mixed together and supplemented by the *Maccabéo*. These grapes are planted mostly on secondary soils, but also on prime holdings constituted by the breaking up of primary ferruginous schists and black schists, the latter of which are appropriately called "grape schists"—schists which were once used to improve the soil of the vineyards.

At Rivesaltes, besides parcels of land completely planted to *Muscat*, the *Grenache Blanc* and the *Malvoisie* give wines of great elegance; most of the wine is established on terraces of ancient, very pebbly, alluvium between Salses, Rivesaltes and the "Crest" of Pia.

In the Côtes-de-Haut-Roussillon, the Aspres region, the *Grenaches* still have priority but they are giving way more and more to *Muscat* and *Maccabéo*, which contribute their very special bouquet. The ranks of the vines are planted on white gravelly or pebbly alluvial hills, red in colour, which were deposited at the tertiary period and then furrowed by erosion. This area is also very arid, hence its name Aspres.

White wines with a golden tint are also produced at Rivesaltes, the Côtes-d'Agly and the Côtes-de-Haut-Roussillon; in ageing, they often take on a beautiful burnt "topaz" tint. Once vinification is complete, these wines should have a minimum total potential alcohol content of 21.5º and titrate at least 15º.

The consumer should take care to cool his bottles to between 5º and 10º C; these are the ideal temperatures for consuming the natural wines. It should not be forgotten that the *Muscats* are always very sweet and should be ranked with the sweetest of natural sweet wines but that, under the other descriptions, several more or less sweet types can be found. Natural sweet wines based on *Malvoisie* and, particularly, on *Grenache* will, when aged in certain ways, acquire the much sought-after *Rancio* taste.

In their country of origin, the wines of Perpignan are regarded as the essential concomitant to various regional gastronomic manifestations. They prepare or conclude the *cargolades* at which the whole menu (snails, sausages, cutlets etc.) is grilled in the embers of a vine-shoot fire; they are used to accompany fruit dishes as well as Catalan pastries such as *bougnettes*, *rousquilles* and aniseed cakes.

The Catalan, settling himself firmly, drinks his wine through open lips from the *porrón*, a glass carafe with a finely drawn out conical spout which is held up at arm's length: a very fine jet of golden amber describes a harmonious and scintillating curve. In this skilful way of drinking *à la régalade*, the wine splashes out over the tongue, the palate and the taste buds. These natural sweet wines can be served as aperitifs. In this case, however, the drier types such as BANYULS and MAURY should be sought out. The wines of Perpignan are also particularly suitable as dessert wines or *digestifs*. Whether white, brick-coloured or of the muscat type, they should all be served very cold but not iced.

SWISS WINES OF THE RHÔNE VALLEY

CANTON OF VALAIS

WHITE WINES

Types of wine	*Appellation of the growth and commercial appellation*
Fendant	Fendant, Les Riverettes, Grand-Schiner Le Père du Valais, Brûlefer, Combe d'Enfer, Trémazières, Sur Plan d'Uvrier, Rives du Bisse, Réserve de Tous-Vents, Vieux Sion, La Guérite, Les Murettes, Etournailles, Vieux Sierre, Clos de Balavaud, Rocailles, Solignon, Montibeux, Grand Baillif, Pierrafeu, Vin des Chanoines, Etoile de Sierre, Ste-Anne, Réserve du Procureur, Fendant du Ravin.
Johannisberg	Johannisberg, Burgrave, Le Grand-Schiner Prince de l'Eglise, Johannisberg de Chamoson, Ravanay, Rives du Bisse, Brûlefer, Novembre, Salgesch, Mont d'Or, St-Théodule, Rhonegold, Grand Bouquet, Johannisberg Balavaud, Johannestrunk, Vin des Chevaliers.
Malvoisie	Malvoisie, Marjolaine, Combe d'Enfer, Malvoisie mi-flétrie, Rives du Bisse, Côte Dorée, Vieux Sierre, Rawyre, Vieux Plants, Brindamour, Malvoisie de la Fiancée, Malvoisie Pinot gris.
Amigne	Belle Valaisanne, Rives du Bisse, Raisin d'Or.
Arvine	Belle Provinciale, Petite Arvine de Chamoson.
Ermitage	Ermitage, Rives du Bisse, Hermitage, Ermitage « Cuvée réservée », Vieux Plants, Ermitage Vétroz, Les Chapelles.
Humagne	Humagne Vétroz.
Païen	Vin du Glacier.
Rèze	Vin du Glacier.
Riesling	Riesling, Goût du Conseil « Mont d'Or », Colline des Planzettes Sierre.

RED WINES

Dôle	Le Grand-Schiner Chapeau Rouge, Clos du Château, Combe d'Enfer, Dôle de Chamoson, Dôle-Pinot noir sur Plan d'Uvrier, Dôle von Salgesch (La Chapelle), Dôle Ravanay, Rives du Bisse, Hurlevent, Les Mazots, Dôle du Mont, Dôle de Salquenen, Vieux Sierre, Soleil de Sierre, Sang de l'Enfer, Clos de Balavaud, Dôle de Balavaud, Girandole, Crêta Plan, Chanteauvieux, Gloire du Rhône, Dôle-Pinot noir, Vieux Villa, Vieux Salquenen, Romane.
Merlot	Colline des Planzettes Sierre.
Pinot noir	Pinot noir de Chamoson, Le Sarrazin, Le Grand Schiner Saint Empire, Pinot noir du Valais, Rives du Bisse, Uvrier, Vendémiaire, Rhoneblut, Römerblut, Oeil-de-Perdrix, Millésime, Beau Velours, Colline des Planzettes Sierre, La Tornale, Ste-Anne, Vieux Cellier, Le Préféré, Chapelle de Salquenen, Johannestrunk, Pinot noir de Salquenen, Vin des Chevaliers, Crête de l'Enfer.
Rosé	Oeil-de-Perdrix, Rosé d'Eros.

CANTON OF VAUD

WHITE WINES • Dorin (Chasselas)

Appellation of communes	*Appellation of the growth and commercial appellation*
CHABLAIS	
Bex	Chêne.
Ollon	Côtes de Verschiez.
Aigle	Clos de Beauregard, Clos du Paradis, Clos de la Vineuvaz, Les Forteresses, Clos du Cloître, Crosex-Grillé, Aigle Royal, Hospices Cantonaux, Domaine de la Commune, Les Cigales, Merveilles des Roches, Les Murailles, Réserve du Vidôme.
Yvorne	Château Maison blanche, Vieux Collège, Clos de la George, Clos des Rennauds, Clos du Rocher, L'Ovaille, Le Chant des Resses, Les Fornets, Les Portes Rouges, Le Petit Vignoble, Plan d'Essert, Près Roc, Domaine de la Commune.
Villeneuve	Sur la Tour, Clos du Châtelard, De nos Domaines, Caves des Hospices cantonaux, Les Terrasses, Vin de l'Empereur.
Villeneuve (pinot gris)	Ovaille, Jeu du Roy.
LAVAUX	
Montreux	Rossillion, Château de Châtelard, Côtes de Pallens, Coteaux du Haut-Léman.
La Tour-de-Peilz	Clos des Mousquetaires.
Vevey	Caves de l'Hôpital.
Corsier	Cure d'Attalens.
Corseaux	Clos Châtonneyre, Clos sur la Chapelle.
Chardonne	Clos des Berneyses, Château de Chardonne, Cave des Allours, le Chantey, Le Fin de la Pierraz, Burignon, Clos de la Chenalettaz, Petite Combe.
Saint-Saphorin – Rivaz	Faverges, Les Rueyres, Blassinges, Charmus de la Cure, Château de Glérolles, Larchevesque, Les Fosses, Planète, Roches Brûlées, La Riondaz, Roche Ronde, Roc Noir, Pierre Noire, Grand Vigne, Domaine d'Ogoz, Le Grillon, Clos des Plantaz.

Appellation of communes	Appellation of the growth and commercial appellation
Dézaley	Chemin de Fer, L'Evêque, L'Arbalète, Chapotannaz, Clos des Abbayes, Dézaley de la Ville, Embleyres, Clos des Moines, Clos de l'Ermite, Clos du Philosophe, Château Marsens, Sous-Marsens, De la Tour, La Borne, La Gueniettaz, Mousquetaires, Renard, Pertuizet, Sur les Abbayes, La Médinette.
Epesses	Boux d'Epesses, Braise d'Enfer, Calamin, Chanteperdrix, Coup de l'Etrier, Crêt-dessous, Crêt-brûlé, La République, Terre à Boire.
Cully	Les Blonnaises, Chenaux, St-Amour, La Perle.
Riex	Maison Blanche.
Villette-Grandvaux	Bouton-d'Or, Belletaz, Bien-Venu, Clos des Echelettes, Clos des Roches, Daley Villette, Treize Vents, Domaine du Daley, En Genévaz, Côtes de Courseboux, Clos de la Cour.
Lutry	Bolliattaz, Grandchamp, Montagny, Clos de Chamaley, Joli Cœur, Ma Réserve, Boutefeu, Clos des Cloîtres, Châtelard, Clos des Brûlées, Bertholod.

LA CÔTE

Morges	Bravade, Clos des Abbesses, Marcelin, Domaine de la Commune.
Nyon	Château de Crans, Château de Duillier, Banderolle.
Aubonne	Curzille.
Allaman	Clos du Château, Ville de Lausanne.
Féchy	Clos des Bayels, Clos du Martheray, Vieux Coteaux, Mon Pichet, Joli Site.
Bougy	Domaine de Riencourt, Cave de Fischer, Château de Bursinel.
Gilly	Château de Vincy, Coteau de Gilly.
Perroy	Malessert, Clos de la Dame, Clos de la Donery, Abbaye de Mont Ville de Lausanne, Cave du Prieuré, Clos de l'Augmendaz.
Mont	Autecour, Haute-Cour, Crochet, Montbenay, Clos des Truits, Château de Mont, La Viborne, Chatagnéréaz, Mont-Crochet, Les Pierrailles, La Montoise, Beau-Soleil, Domaine de la Bigaire, Famolens, Beauregard.
Tartegnin	Clos du Rousillon, Clos des Panissières.
Vinzel	Domaine de la Bâtie, Château de Vinzel, Clos du Château de Bursins.
Luins	Château de Luins, La Capite, Domaine de Sarraux-dessous, Sarraux.

RED WINES

CHABLAIS	Salvagnin Eminence, Salvagnin Mille pierres, Clos de l'Abbaye, Clos du Châtelard, Clos de la George, Côtes de Verschiez, Bex, Pinot noir Monseigneur, Pinot noir le Notable.
LAVAUX	Salvagnin des Caves de l'Hôpital, Salvagnin de l'Hôpital des Bourgeois de Fribourg, Salvagnin Cep d'Or, Salvagnin Chevron rouge, Salvagnin Coteaux du Haut-Léman, Salvagnin Forban, Salvagnin Grain rouge, Pinot noir Coin des Serpents, Pinot noir Cuvée du Docteur, Pinot noir Grand-Croix, Pinot noir Sept Murs, Pinot-Gamay Montorgueil, Pinot-Gamay Roche rouge, Pinot-Gamay Saint-Saphorin printanier, Pinot-Gamay sous l'Auvent, Pinot-Gamay Burignon, Dôle d'Epesses.
LA CÔTE	Salvagnin Commune de Morges, Salvagnin Château de Saint-Saphorin, Salvagnin Domaine de Valmont, Salvagnin du Baril, Salvagnin Chapeau rouge, Salvagnin Croix du Val, Salvagnin Licorne, Salvagnin Piganot, Clos des Abbesses Clos du Paradis, Pinot noir Clos du Satyre, Pinot noir Grand Brocard.

ROSÉ WINES

Gamay	Bellarosa, Busard, La Caille, Perle Rose, Roussard, St-Martin, Vieux Murs.
Pinot	Oeil-de-Perdrix, Oeil-de-Perdrix - Clos du Terraillex, Oeil-de-Perdrix - Chantemerle.

CANTON OF GENEVA

WHITE WINES

Types of wine	Appellation of the growth and commercial appellation
Chasselas	Les Contamines, Chasselas Genève, Clos des Curiades, Clos de la Donzelle, Perle du Mandement, Coteau de Lully, Bouquet Royal.
Riesling-Sylvaner	Riesling-Sylvaner Satigny, Les Argoulets.
Aligoté	Lully, Clos des Curiades.
Pinot blanc	Les Curiades.

RED WINES

Gamay	Gamay de Gondebaud, Les Clefs d'Or, Gamay-Lully, Domaine des 3 Etoiles.
Gamay rosé	Rose Reine.
Gamay Pinot	Gamay Pinot, Pinogamay.
Pinot noir	Clos des Curiades, Le Damoiseau, Pinot noir Lully.

FRENCH WINES OF THE RHÔNE VALLEY

WINES OF SAVOY

Generic appellation	*Appellation of the growth or of the commune*
Vins de Savoie	Marin, Ripaille, Marignan, Coteaux de Crépy, Petit Crépy, Monterminod, Apremont, Abymes, Chignin, Cruet Montmelian, Saint-Jean-de-la-Porte
Roussette de Savoie . .	Frangy, Marestel, Monthoux, Seyssel.

WINES OF THE JURA

Generic appellation	
	Côtes-du-Jura, Château-Chalon, L'Etoile, Arbois.

CÔTES DU RHÔNE

WHITE WINES

Generic appellation	*Appellation of the growth or of the commune*
Saint-Péray	Amour de Dieu, Arboisset, Château de Beauregard, Bellevue, La Beylesse, Biguet, Biousse, Blaches, Bouzigues, Le Bret, Buissonnet, La Cacharde, Cerisier, La Chaume, Le Chêne, Combette, Coste Claude, La Côte, Coteau-Caillard, Coudiol, La Crozette, Déseret, Fauterie, Fourniers, La Gamone, Le Géant, Grand-Champ, Hongrie, Issartel, Jirane, Lubac, Maison Blanche, Malgazon, Marcale, Mois de Mai, Moulin-à-vent, Pateaud, Perrier, Pinchenas, La Plantier, Prieuré, Putier, Aux Putiers, Rochette, Ruines de Crussol, Sainte Fleurie, Les Sapettes, Soulignasses, Thioulet, Tourtousse, La Venance, Vergomars.
Château-Grillet	
Condrieu	Chéri, La Garenne, Vernon, Boucher, Château-Grillet, Laboye, Le Colombier.

ROSÉ WINES

Tavel	Aqueria, Blaise d'arbres, Bouvettes, Cabanette, Campey, Carcenies, Comeyre, Cravailleu et Alexandre, La Genestière et Fourcadure, Manissy, Montezardes et Trinquevedel, Olivet, Les Patus, Plaine de Vallongue, Plans et Palus, Les Prés, Roc Crispin et Malaven, Romagnac, Tavelet et les Oliviers, Vau et Clos, Vaucroze, Vaucroze et Vacquières, La Vaussière, La Vaute, Vestides, Le Village.
Côte-du-Rhône Chusclans	

WHITE WINES AND RED WINES

Châteauneuf-du-Pape . .	L'Arnesque, Barbe d'Asne, Bas-Serres, Beau Renard, La Bigote, Les Blaquières, Bois de Boursan, Bois de la Vieille, Bois Senescau, Les Bosquets, Le Boucou, Les Bourguignons, Les Brusquières, Cabrières, Cansaud, Castelas, La Cerise, Charbonnières, Chemin de Sorgues, Le Clos, Colombis, Combes d'Arnavel, Combes Masques, Coste-Froide, Coteau de l'Ange, Les Coulets, La Crau, La Croze, Devès d'Estouard, Les Esqueiron, Farguerol, La Font du Loup, La Fortisse, Four à Chaux, Les Galimardes, La Gardine, Grand chemin de Sorgues, Grand Devès, Grand Pierre, Les Grands Galiguières, Grandes Serres, La Grenade, Jaquinotte, Le Lac, Le Limas, Les Marines, Les Mascarrons, Mont de Viès, Montolivet, Mont Pertuis, Mont Redon, Moulin à Vent, La Nerthe, Le Parc, Les Parrans, Pelous, Petite Bastide, Petites Serres, Pied-de-Baud, Pied-Redon, Les Pielons, Pierre-à-Feu, Pignan, Les Plagnes, Les Pradels, Relagnes, Les Revès, La Roquette, Roumiguières, Saint-Joseph, Les Serres, Terres-Blanches, Les Tresquous, Vaudieu, Cabane Saint-Jean, Cansaud, La Chartreuse, Chemin de Châteauneuf, Les Combes, Le Coulaire, Coteau de Saint-Jean, La Crau, Croix de Bois, Duvet, Les Escondures, La Font de Michelle, La Font du Loup, Les Garrigues, Le Grand Plantier, Marron, Patouillet, La Petite Crau, Pied-Redon, Piegeoulet, Ras-Cassa, Reveirores, Sauvines, Terre-Ferme. La Barnuine, Barratin, Les Bédines, Chapouin, Coucoulet, La Crau, Le Cristia, Font du Loup, La Gardiole, Le Grès, Guigasse, La Jamasse, Le Mourre de Gaud, Le Mourre de Vidal, Le Mourre des Perdrix, Palinteau, Pignan, Le Pointu, Le Rayas, Saint-Georges, Saintes-Vierges, Les Saumades, Valori, La Bertaude, Boidauphin, Boilauzon, Cabrières, Maucoil, Palestor, Chafeune, Franquizons, Le Grand Collet, La Lionne.
Crozes-Hermitage	Bourret, Les Habrards, Martinet, Les Mejeans.
Hermitage or Ermitage . .	Beaumes, Les Bessards, La Croix, La Croix de Jamot, Les Diognères, Les Diognères et Torras, Les Greffieux, Les Gros des Vignes, L'Hermite, L'Homme, Maison Blanche, Le Méal, Les Murets, Péléat, La Pierrelle, Les Rocoules, Les Signaux, Varogne.
Lirac	
Saint-Joseph	
Côtes-du-Rhône	Rochegude, Saint-Maurice-sur-Eygues, Vinsobles, Cairanne, Gigondas, Rasteau, Roaix, Séguret, Vacqueras, Valréas, Visan, Laudun.

RED WINES

Côte Rôtie . . . . Les Arches, Basseron, La Blanchonne, Les Bonnevières, La Brocarde, Le Car, Chambre-tout, La Chatillonne, Les Chavaroches, La Chevalière, Chez Gaboulet, Chez Gueraud, Les Clos et Claperonne, Le Cognet, Le Combard, Combe de Calon, Corps des Loups, La Côte Baudnin, Le Crêt, Fontgent, Lefouvier, La Frizonne, Les Gagères, La Garde, Les Germines, La Giroflarie, Grande Plantée et la Garelle, Les Grandes Places, Le Grand Taillé, Grosse Roche et la Balayat, La Guillambaule, Janville, Les Journaries, Lancement, La Landonne, Les Lézardes, Le Mollar, Montmain, Montuclas, Le Moulin, Les Moutonnes, Nève, Le Pavillon Rouge, La Pommière, Les Prunelles, Les Rochains, Rosier, Les Sévenières, Thramon de Gron, Les Triottes, Le Truchet, La Turque, La Viallière, La Viria.

Cornas

PROVENCE AND THE SOUTH-EASTERN REGION

Generic appellation or appellation of communes Bandol, Bellet, Clairette de Die, Palette, Coteaux d'Aix-en-Provence, Coteaux des Baux, Côtes du Lubéron, Coteaux de Pierrevert, Côtes-de-Provence, Coteaux du Tricastin, Côtes de Ventoux, Haut-Comtat, Châtillon-en-Diois.

LANGUEDOC AND ROUSSILLON

Generic appellation, appellation of the growth or of the commune Corbières, Minervois, Costières du Gard, Coteaux du Languedoc, Coteaux de la Méjanelle, Saint-Saturnin, Montpeyroux, Coteaux de Saint-Christol, Quatourze, La Clape, Saint-Drézéry, Saint-Chinian, Faugères, Cabrières, Coteaux de Verargues, Pic Saint-Loup, Saint-Georges-d'Orques, Picpoul de Pinet, Fitou, Roussillon dels Aspres, Corbières du Roussillon, Corbières Supérieures du Roussillon.

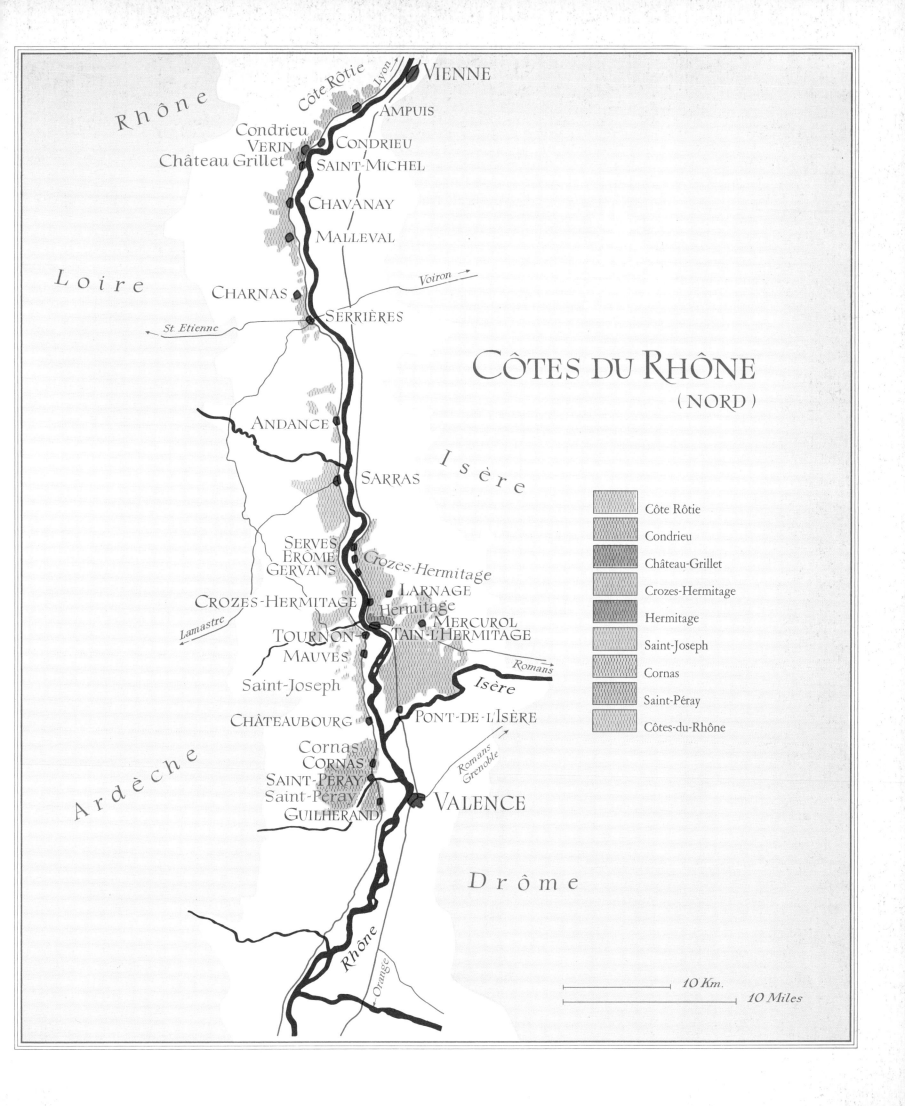

CÔTES DU RHÔNE
(NORD)

Rhône

VIENNE

Côte-Rôtie

Lyon

AMPUIS

Condrieu
VERIN
Château Grillet

CONDRIEU
SAINT-MICHEL

CHAVANAY

MALLEVAL

Loire

Voiron

CHARNAS

St Etienne

SERRIÈRES

Isère

ANDANCE

SARRAS

SERVES
ERÔME
GERVANS

Crozes-Hermitage

LARNAGE

CROZES-HERMITAGE

Hermitage

MERCUROL
TAIN-L'HERMITAGE

Lamastre

TOURNON-
MAUVES

Romans

Saint-Joseph

Isère

CHÂTEAUBOURG

PONT-DE-L'ISÈRE

Ardèche

Cornas
CORNAS

Romans
Grenoble

SAINT-PÉRAY
Saint-Péray
GUILHERAND

VALENCE

Drôme

Rhône

Orange

	Côte Rôtie
	Condrieu
	Château-Grillet
	Crozes-Hermitage
	Hermitage
	Saint-Joseph
	Cornas
	Saint-Péray
	Côtes-du-Rhône

10 Km.

10 Miles

RHÔNE SUISSE · SAVOIE

GRIGNAN

Nyons

VALRÉAS

Nyons

Rhône

Valence

Ardèche

BOLLÈNE

SUZE-LA-ROUSSE

SAINTE-CÉCILE-LES-VIGNES

VAISON-LA-ROMAINE

PONT-SAINT-ESPRIT

CAIRANNE

RASTEAU

V a u c l u s e

BAGNOLS-SUR-CÈZE

Aygues

ORANGE

GIGONDAS

VACQUEYRAS

BEAUMES-DE-VENISE

Ouvèze

Carpentras

Châteauneuf-du-Pape

ROQUEMAURE

CHÂTEAUNEUF-DU-PAPE

LIRAC

Lirac

G a r d

Tavel

TAVEL

CÔTES DU RHÔNE

(SUD)

Uzès
Nîmes
Toulouse

AVIGNON

Gard

Rhône

Durance

Tarascon

Marseille

Cavaillon

Châteauneuf-du-Pape

Tavel

Lirac

Côtes-du-Rhône

10 Km.

10 Miles

THE WINES OF THE LOIRE

ALEXANDER FRESNEAU

Long before the invasion of the Gauls the vine existed on the banks of the Loire. The Romans invaded this region 22 years after Christ, and probably found it growing wild. Its first cultivation, according to a popular legend, began in A.D. 380 when St. Martin and his disciples planted vines in the Abbaye de Marmoutier near Tours, which was founded at that time. These events are recounted by the historian Gregory, Bishop of Tours from 573 to 595, in his *Ecclesiastical History of France*, and by Fredegarius in his chronicles of the year 757. The vine flourished and spread rapidly; but in the thirteenth century it was restricted to the hillsides where it produced wines of a superior quality.

The first viticultural region along the Loire is the Massif Central, which contains the vineyards of Auvergne, Saint-Pourçain-sur-Sioule and Chateaumeillant. A little farther on the river crosses the chalky and flinty hills between Pouilly-sur-Loire, Sancerre and Menetou-Salon. Then come the two vineyards of Quincy and Reuilly, situated one near the other with identical soil, then the Val de Loire which one may consider as being on the very edge of the Loiret. This department also harbours the Giennois and Orléanais vineyards which have lost much of their importance in the last fifty years.

It is at Blois, the gateway to the Touraine, that the chalky soil has its beginning. It then stretches for miles and miles, following the course of the Loire and fertilizing the vineyards of Monts-Près-Chambord, Vendômois, Coteaux du Loir, Jasnières, Touraine, Vouvray, Montlouis, Bourgueil, Chinon and Saumurois, as far as the Angevine schists which introduce the Armorican Massif. The Angevine vineyard is the most important, and is responsible for nearly all the wines produced in this region. Aubance and Lyons bring one to the maritime zone of the Loire, and leaving Anjou behind one comes next to the MUSCADET vineyard in Basse-Bretagne. Special mention should be made of the Ancenis vineyard and the *Gros Plant* so sought after by tourists. From Orléanais to the ocean, the Val de Loire presents a soft and gentle spectacle to the traveller, with its sumptuous châteaux and variety of viticultural treasures. Other landscapes may offer fairer sights, but there is none more harmonious nor more compelling than these banks of the Loire.

In order to obtain choice wine, winegrowers have constantly taken pains to improve their vine-plants either through selection, by developing new varieties, or by importing well known grapes from distant parts.

It is possible that the vine-stocks developed by the monks in Touraine and elsewhere are derived from a particular type of vine which produced black grapes found growing wild in the forests. It is perhaps to this same wild lambrusca that the sixteenth-century poet Ronsard refers in his ode to Aubepin. This red vine was called *Pineau d'Aunis*, Aunis being a small village in Saumur. It deserves our gratitude, for it is thought that on some unknown date it produced, after selection, the white variety, *Chenin Blanc*, or *Pineau de la Loire*, a wonderful plant found in Touraine and Anjou. It is impossible to know exactly when this vine-plant was given the name *Chenin*, but it was already known as such in the early sixteenth century.

The *Sauvignon*, a noble plant found in Pouilly-sur-Loire, Sancerre, Quincy and Reugny is, however, of unknown origin. There is no document to show whether it is a plant indigenous to the region or whether it was imported.

On several occasions, numerous vines taken from foreign or other French viticultural regions were planted in these parts. It is not known exactly how or when the *Muscadet* grape came to the region of Nantes, but it would seem to date from the seventeenth century. When the frozen vines were replanted following the terrible winter of 1709, the *Muscadet* grape was introduced on a wide scale into the region. It would appear to have been brought from Burgundy, where it was known as *Melon*.

The *Gros Plant*, cultivated in the Atlantic Loire, originally came from Charentes through an exchange with Poitou, an intermediary province. Its wine was at first distilled, but today it produces a highly sought-after dry wine. It is of the same grade as the Muscadet.

The *Cabernet Franc*, which is cultivated in Touraine and in the regions of Bourgueil and Chinon as well as in Anjou, has a much disputed origin. According to some, it came from Rhuis, in Bretagne. According to others, and this seems more logical, the Bordelais grape was brought to the Loire valley either by Abbot Breton,

an administrator of Richelieu, when he inherited the property of the Abbey of Saint-Nicolas-de-Bourgueil; or even before, if we believe Rabelais when he speaks of "the good Breton wine, which does not grow in Bretagne but in this worthy land of Verron".

The *Côt* grape is cultivated in various places, but it certainly originated in Bordelais. The *Groslot de Cinq-Mars* or *Grolleau* was obtained around 1810 through the selection process in the region of Chinon.

Other grapes, such as the *Pinot Noir*, *Pinot Beurot*, and *Meunier* are thought to have come from Burgundy.

It is difficult to give any precise figures as to the number of fine quality vineyards in the *appellation contrôlée* category along the Loire. The *Chenin Blanc* or *Pineau de la Loire* covers about 37,000 acres, the *Muscadet* 21,000, the Sauvignon grape—which is constantly expanding—5,000, and the *Cabernet* 10,000. Other red grapes, apart from the *Cabernet*, probably cover a total area somewhat larger than that of the *Chenin Blanc* (*Groslot, Côt, Gamay, Pinot Noir, Pinot Meunier, Pineau d'Aunis*). White grapes other than the *Muscadet*, the *Sauvignon* and the *Chenin* cover around 5,000 acres of ground.

The vine region which produces the *appellation contrôlée* wines of the Loire Valley is about 74,000 acres in area. However the actual surface under cultivation is in fact bigger as part of the harvest is reserved for making table wines.

POUILLY-SUR-LOIRE - SANCERRE - QUINCY
REUILLY - MENETOU-SALON

The staple grape of these vineyards is the *Sauvignon*, blended at times with another variety.

POUILLY-SUR-LOIRE. Under this classification come all the wines produced in the communes of Pouilly-sur-Loire, Saint-Andelain, Tracy-sur-Loire, Saint-Laurent, Saint-Martin-sur-Nohain, Garchy and Mesvres-sur-Loire.

Depending on what grape variety they are made from, the wines of Pouilly-sur-Loire are known under one or the other of the following two categories: POUILLY FUMÉ (which should not be confused with another white wine, the POUILLY FUISSÉ produced in Burgundy) or BLANC FUMÉ DE POUILLY for those wines made from the *Sauvignon* grape alone; POUILLY-SUR-LOIRE in the case of wines derived from the *Chasselas* grape, whether blended with the *Sauvignon* grape or not. Only the communes of Pouilly-sur-Loire, Saint-Audelain and Tracy are true viticultural regions, although the actual area under cultivation is notably smaller. At present it includes about a thousand acres.

The commune of Saint-Audelain, larger than Pouilly-sur-Loire, has the most important vineyards, more so than those of Pouilly and Tracy. Other communes have a smaller area under cultivation. Since only about a thousand acres are capable of being harvested, it follows that each holding is quite small; there is one of more than 32 acres, but a dozen are on the order of 7 ½ acres each. The average production figure for POUILLY FUMÉ is about 46,200 gallons; for POUILLY-SUR-LOIRE about 154,000 gallons. POUILLY FUMÉ has a distinct and even sometimes pronounced bouquet; it is musky and smoky at the same time, a long-lived wine which ages well. The POUILLY-SUR-LOIRE, on the other hand, is considered to be best when drunk within the year.

SANCERRE. Thirteen communes come under this heading: Sancerre, Saint-Satur, Bué, Suvry-en-Vaux, Menetou, Ratel, Ménétréol Thauvenay, Vinon, Verdigny, Cresancy and some isolated parcels of land at Bannay and Veaugues.

Spread across some fifteen viticultural departments, from the Massif Central to the Atlantic Ocean, the famous vineyards of the Loire are ranged in tiers on the slopes which dominate the "royal river" and its tributaries. The wines of this charming valley are mainly produced in four major regions: the Centre (around Nevers, Giens, Bourges and Orleans), in Touraine, in Anjou-Saumur and in the region of Nantes.

The area under cultivation is some 1,500 acres, of which 1,300 acres grow the *Sauvignon* grape and the rest the *Pinot Noir*. Production has developed in the last ten years. During this time, the average yield was 143,000 gallons while present production, which is still increasing, gives an average yield of more than 330,000 gallons annually.

As in Pouilly-sur-Loire, the soil in which the vine grows is a calcerous-clay deposit, or sometimes mass formations of calcium formed on the slopes in the same geological era. The plains that dominate these slopes are clay-like and unsuitable for winegrowing. Each type of soil produces wine of a different character. The blended vines are sometimes of a higher quality than that of the components. SANCERRE is somewhat more mellow than the POUILLY FUMÉ and generally matures sooner than the latter.

These are pleasant, very fruity wines, though they cannot be compared to Burgundies made from the *Pinot Noir* grape. The red and rosé varieties have only recently qualified for the *appellation contrôlée*.

QUINCY. This vineyard is situated about 12 miles to the west of Bourges, along the right bank of the Cher. It is a small vineyard, of about 600 acres, which will probably develop in the next few years. It comprises the communes of Quincy and Brinay. The average wine-harvest is about 110,000 gallons, worked by 250 growers. The average grower cultivates about 2 acres and there are about twenty properties of 5 to 8 acres each and one of about 25 acres. QUINCY, which is nearly always dry, gets its fine quality from the grand soil which serves as its cradle and which makes it an excellent companion to oysters.

REUILLY. This name is given to the wine of four communes, two in the Indre, Reugny and Diou regions, and two in the Cher, Chery and Lazenay. Their vineyards are situated along the banks of the Arnon, 6 miles to the west of Quincy.

The area planted with the *Sauvignon* grape is definitely getting smaller. At present it is about 62 acres, almost entirely in Reuilly and Diou. Production is very much lower here: about 1,300 to 1,800 gallons yield a dry and semi-dry wine for local consumption.

MENETOU-SALON. Some 16 miles to the west of Vierzon is Menetou-Salon which has given its name to the youngest of the *appellation d'origine* wines of the Loire, created by decree in 1959. It is cultivated on a very small scale as its vineyard covers only 1,500 acres. It grows two grapes, the *Sauvignon* which produces a wine similar to that of Sancerre, though not nearly as well-balanced or as fine in flavour; and the *Pinot Noir* from Burgundy whose red and rosé wines have a most agreeable taste. The total production of this category varies yearly from 132,000 to 220,000 gallons.

115

TOURAINE

Touraine, so peaceful and welcoming, has been planted to vines since the fourteenth century, and the fame of its wines has grown with the years. Rabelais and Ronsard sang their praises, Alfred de Vigny and Balzac knew how to appreciate them and the beauties of their birthplace, and Alexander Dumas had the King's Musketeers drink them. Here, then, are the wines of which Jules Romain said "they are the very essence of French wit".

Their production is more varied than abundant. The white wines, whether dry, semi-dry or dessert wines, are fresh with full bouquets; the best of them are to be found in the lovely village of Vouvray. The delicate red wines of Bourgueil, Saint-Nicolas and Chinon are followed by a cheerful group of gay companions: red wines and rosés from the Côtes du Cher, white wines made from the *Pineau* or *Sauvignon* grape, which one must taste when visiting the châteaux.

A classic definition of Touraine describes this province as "a rough tweed trimmed with gold". The plains covered with forests, sandy moors and ploughed fields give the land an impression of sadness. There are the forests of Montrichard, Amboise, Chinon, Champeigne between Cher and the Indre, the Richelais and the Gâtine. But cutting across these unproductive regions are smiling valleys whose rich culture, sumptuous castles, white villas, and harmonious landscapes present such an enticing picture as to make a man believe that this is the very place where it would be wonderful to live.

The climate of Touraine is neither unbearably hot in summer nor excessively cold in winter, as the sea breeze modifies the differences in temperature.

Along the border, where the plains meet the valleys, on chalky slopes or terraced embankments pebbled by the Loire and the Vienne—this is where the Touraine winegrowers planted the present vineyards some fifteen centuries ago. The soil which nourishes the vine is often supported by yellow chalk or "Touraine tufa", in which the magnificent Vouvray caves have been carved. This immense blanket of chalk is covered with granitic sand sometimes mixed with silex clay which occurs when the chalk decalcifies.

The soil at the bottom of the slopes contains flinty sand, clay and chalk; it is the *aubuis* so perfectly suited to the *Pineau de la Loire*. It produces the finest and by far the most full-bodied wines.

On both banks of the Loire and the Vienne, in the Bourgueil and Chinon regions, the gravelly beds, brushed by the waters and mixed with sand clay, offer a soft and fertile soil for the *Cabernet Franc* grape.

The region of the white wines made from the *Pineau* grape extends from Tours to Blois, where the vines are cultivated on chalky slopes covered with the mixture locally known as *aubuis*. The vineyard of Vouvray is situated at the head of this region, near Tours.

In Loir-et-Cher, the Mesland region, with identical soil, offers excellent rosés and red wines produced from the *Gamay* grape, side by side with the clear fruity wines made from the *Pineau* grape. Farther south, along the chalky banks of the Cher and the Oisly plain where the ground is composed of sand over clay, red wines grow in the company of fine white wines made from the *Pineau* and *Sauvignon* grapes. In Touraine, the vine spreads over some 15,000 acres, producing wines of the *appellation contrôlée* category in the amount of 4,400,000 gallons per annum.

THE GREAT WHITE WINES. In Touraine as in Anjou, these are derived almost entirely from a single grape, the *Pineau de la Loire*. It alone is responsible for the reputation of the great wine of Touraine. The *Menu Pineau*, also called *Arbois*, gives more delicate wines and has decreased in quantity in Vouvray and Montlouis, but it still flourishes in Loir-et-Cher, the Contres plain, and Pontlevoy, as well as along the banks of the Cher. The *Sauvignon* grape in these regions has, in the past ten years, become more and more popular. Today it covers around 750 acres.

There are differences in pruning methods for the *Pineau de la Loire* and the *Sauvignon* which have important implications for their wines.

When pruning the *Pineau de la Loire*, it is desirable to cut well back into the stalk so as to produce wines with rich bouquets. However, this is not always possible, for this single most important operation in vine culture must take into account the strength on the vine-shoot, its stock and the nature of soil in which it is planted. The *Sauvignon*, on the other hand, need not be cut back too far, but should be dressed long, in the *Guyot double* manner with two long spurs and from six to eight buds.

The *Pineau de la Loire* grape is always cultivated close to the ground, at a density of about 2,240 plants per acre. *Sauvignon* vines, being taller (4 feet as against 3) are planted less densely, only 1,800 plants per acre. Attempts to raise the height of cultivation of the vine have proved inconclusive and unsatisfactory. The vine does not mature so well and has a stronger acid content; the wine is less robust and full-bodied.

The *Sauvignon* grape is picked before it reaches full maturity, usually towards the end of September. The *Pineau de la Loire*, however, is harvested according to

The Loire, that flows through the heartland of France, is naturally the link between many and various wine centres. Mentioned by Rabelais, the growths have a long history. Right, the fresh-picked grapes are poured into the press in a cellar hewn out of the rock.

Above: Typical of the Loire region is this two-wheeled cart, used to bring in the newly-picked grapes.

Right: A meeting of the *Confrérie des "Sagavins d'Anjou"*. At one time the Anjou region concentrated on the production of sparkling wine, but the demand has fallen off recently.

117

A ruined windmill stands guard over the widely-spaced rows of
vines in Anjou. The wine harvest is here again, and whole
families spend their days in the vineyards until the crop is picked.

the destination of its grape. If the wine-harvest is to be made into sparkling wines, the grapes must be picked before they are completely ripe, when their acid content is from seven to eight grams. If the proprietor wishes to produce a natural wine he must wait until the grape has become fully mature and then select his grapes. This can only be done in very good years. But these wines have a particularly fine bouquet, they are very sweet and at the same time fresh, delicate, robust, and of an exceptionally high quality.

GREAT RED WINES. The best of these, from Bourgueil and Chinon, are made from a grape cultivated in Gironde, especially in the Saint-Emilion region: the *Cabernet Franc* which must be pruned so as to leave a long stalk and a branch bearing seven to eight buds. The grower grafts a piece of bark containing sap on to the vine stalk so that the stem can grow. This stock is common but not extensive. It is considered exceptional to produce more than 400 gallons from an acre. The soil has a great influence on the wine. It might be difficult for the uninformed to distinguish a BOURGUEIL from a CHINON, but connoisseurs can easily tell the difference between a wine which has been planted in gravelly soil and one from a tufa soil.

The wines from grapes grown in gravelly soil are fine wines with good bouquets. They acquire their full qualities reasonably quickly, while the grapes planted in tufa are harder, do not bear fruit until a year later, and conserve admirably.

The wine of Bourgueil charms with its bouquet, its raspberry flavour and its invigorating freshness. It is a fruity, delicate wine, pleasant when young, but at its best after three or four years in a bottle. Some wines which are hard in the first years lighten with age.

CHINON differs from BOURGUEIL in its bouquet —which invokes violets—and its mellow warmth. It is particularly good when drunk young, full of a delicious sweetness. Demand for these wines seems to be growing. For some ten years the vineyards seem to have been developing, especially in the communes of Cravant and Chinon.

It should be mentioned, moreover, that these wines are made from stalked grapes. The stalks are removed as the clusters are picked from the vines by a special machine (known locally as a *rapoire* or *égrenoir*). It consists of a rotating funnel-shaped barrel with a wicker or wooden frame and a screen. The grater or stalker stirs the harvest with a long wooden paddle to separate the grapes from the stalks. Grapes are mechanically stalked by only one co-operative and six wineries, which represents less than 30 per cent.

Most wineries ferment wine in wooden vats with loose lids. Big wineries, however, ferment their wine in cement vats.

Contrary to the practice of many viticultural regions, the period of fermentation here is long, from 18 to 20 days. For example, in the wooden vats where the storage temperature is more than 17º-18º, the secondary fermentation takes place on the twelfth to thirteenth day, and thus the wine can be marketed quickly without any risk to the buyer afterwards. The alcohol content must not be below 9.5º for the wine to be entitled to the *appellation contrôlée* CHINON.

OTHER WINES OF THE TOURAINE. Aside from VOUVRAY, MONTLOUIS, BOURGUEIL and CHINON, Touraine has some other very charming wines which often equal these famous growths, but they are rarely to be found outside the region. Among these are:

AZAY-LE-RIDEAU. This region is better known for its castle than its wines. The communes around the area—especially Saché, where Balzac wrote *Le Lys dans la Vallée*—have always enjoyed a reputation for dry and semi-dry white wines, which are fruity and fresh and of which they produce 22,000 to 26,500 gallons. Unfortunately, since the Second World War, production of these wines has decreased, as the producers have replaced a considerable number of vines with apple orchards. They are also trying to orient their production towards sweet wines.

AMBOISE. The canton of Amboise, situated at the eastern tip of the department of Indre-et-Loire, is as famous for its castle as Azay-le-Rideau; however, it also produces fine quality wines which keep well. This is not surprising as both banks of the Loire form an extension of the vineyards of Vouvray and Montlouis. As always in Touraine, the wines are cultivated in a subsoil of calcareous tufa. This region also produces pleasant red and rosé wines made from the *Côt* grape, sometimes from the Beaujolais *Gamay* and less often from the *Cabernet* variety.

MESLAND. The Mesland region in Loir-et-Cher continues the Touraine vineyard along the right bank of the Loire, with Monteaux, Onzain and Chouzy-sur-Cisse. It produces from 330,000 to 440,000 gallons which is almost half the wine produced under the *appellation* TOURAINE in Loir-et-Cher.

All these wines are very agreeable when young, but the rosés made from the *Gamay* grape are the most successful, which perhaps accounts for the fact that more of them are produced. They get their fruitiness, lightness and fine texture from the granite sands which cover the chalky subsoil of Touraine.

JASNIÈRES and COTEAUX DU LOIR. At the far end of the three provinces, Touraine, Maine and Anjou, some 25 miles to the north, the valley of the river Loir offers the same favourable conditions for the vine as can be found in Touraine. The position of this little river, the nature of the soil, as well as the climate, are all the same here as above and below Tours. This region is at the northern tip of the viticultural zone and only in those years when the sun has been particularly generous does the *Pineau de la Loire* produce white wines of quality, and the *Pineau d'Aunis* become sufficiently ripe to give good red wines. This vineyard used to be far more important than it is today, but the wines have retained their reputation. Ronsard sang the praises of the wines of the Loir, and in *Pantagruel* Rabelais informs us joyfully that the little town of La Chartre was full of wine merchants and had at least twenty-seven inn-keepers.

SAUMUR AND ANJOU

The Saumur region used to be known as "Haut-Anjou". The Saumur wines at that time were the most prominent of this region. At the end of the eighteenth century, as Dr Maisonneuve tells us in his study of Anjou wines, a large quantity of white wine from Saumur were exported, the red wines being reserved for local consumption.

In those days, the winegrowers neglected natural wines somewhat in favour of sparkling wines, which were highly sought after. There, as in Vouvray, several wine-merchants or companies would produce some 7 million bottles of sparkling wine, 20 per cent of which were for export. In the last twenty years, however, this trade has undergone a slump, and today's figure is barely 3 ½ million bottles.

The sparkling wines made in Saumur have an advantage over those of Vouvray. The latter can only be produced from a single grape, the *Pineau de la Loire*, or *Chenin Blanc*. In Saumur, however, the regulations allow for a certain percentage of white wines made from red grapes to be added—up to as much as 60 per cent. This, as well as refining the froth, adds to the quality of the *cuvée* and reduces the somewhat objectionable tang of the soil. The *Cabernet* and the *Groslot* are the grapes which are used for this purpose. The former is of a higher quality and is sought after for the large vats.

The sparkling wines made in Saumur have distinguished qualities—fine, with agreeable bouquets, and a distinct, even personal character—which they owe to a privileged climate and soil as well as to selected grapes.

Apart from the sparkling wines, there are also some slightly effervescent white and rosé wines which are constantly growing in quantity and importance. The amount produced for commercial purposes has increased within the last fifteen years, and now equals that of sparkling wines. The bottling is similar to that of "still" wines; the cork is held by a thin wire fastener, as there is very little pressure.

ROSÉS OF CABERNET. The Saumur region produces rosé only from the *Cabernet* grape, while elsewhere in Anjou rosés are also made from *Groslot*. The *Cabernet Franc* and *Cabernet Sauvignon* grape varieties cover more than 6,000 acres which in turn produce an average of more than 2,200,000 gallons of wine per year.

The SAUMUR rosé made from the *Cabernet* grape is of a very light colour, as it is usually made from a white vinification, that is to say from grape pressings which have not been crushed, but allowed to ferment from their own weight. Their very pale colour means that they can be added without any difficulty to sparkling white wines.

Some rosé wines which have been slightly crushed have a stronger colour and a richer bouquet.

The other centres of production for rosé wines made from the *Cabernet* grape are the regions of Layon and Brissac in Aubance. In these regions the grapes are crushed and allowed to soak for a few hours. The cells of the broken skin of the grapes mix with the fermenting must, a more or less important part of coloration. The skins are broken and added for colour at the same time as the grapes are pressed. This process is carried out rapidly in order to achieve the finest quality wine. The pressure should not be too great in order to avoid breaking the stalks, which would make the wine astringent.

Wines which have fermented in a vat where the skins of the *Cabernet* grape were added are light pink; those which are pressed and go through a rapid vinification have a characteristic slightly yellow colour. If they have a strawberry hue, this means that a richly coloured juice was added afterwards.

These wines should only contain small quantities of anhydrous sulphur, to avoid discoloration. They should not have more than 11º to 12º in order to remain fruity and fresh. A drop of sweetening does them no harm and helps to cover slight faults. These wines are best when young, otherwise they lose some of their fruitiness and life.

ROSÉS OF GROSLOT. Before the war, these were almost the only wines cultivated in the area. They are fresh, light, and should be drunk within the year.

If there is only a little wine made from the *Groslot* grape, say about 350 to 450 gallons to an acre, then the wine is very pleasant with an alcohol content from about 9º to 10.5º or exceptionally 11º. The *Groslot* likes gravelly soils as well as clay or calcareous sands, and produces a special seed. The rosé it makes is much better dry; when sweet the wines tend to be heavy. To produce a very fruity, well-balanced, full-bodied rosé, one should add a small amount of *Gamay*, *Cabernet*, or *Pineau d'Aunis*.

ANJOU. The wines of Anjou have been praised by the poets of the Pléiade and enjoy a reputation which dates back to the sixth century when Apollinius praised the town of Angers as having been blessed by Bacchus. In the thirteenth century these wines gained great fame during the reign of the Plantagenets, who imported them to England. Still later, the Dutch and Belgians were good customers for more than two centuries. Boats laden with wine would travel up the Loire to depots at Chalonnes, Rochefort, and Ponts-de-Cé. The wine was brought to the river either by water (Layon, Thouet) or by land. In *Eugénie Grandet*, Balzac recounts an incident where "Père" Grandet tries to sell his wine-stock.

Boats no longer go up the Loire, but wine has found a new means of transport and has conquered new markets—a tribute to its quality and to the efforts made by winegrowers and wine-merchants. There is an infinite variety of Anjou wines. There are white wines made from the *Chenin* and *Pineau* grapes, reds and rosés from the *Cabernet* grape and rosés from the *Groslot* grape variety. There are also dry wines, semi-dry, sweet and dessert wines, still wines, slightly sparkling and sparkling wines, light or robust wines, which have been harvested in several stages by picking grapes which have attained the *pourriture noble* or "noble rot" category.

The Anjou wines are harvested throughout most of the south-east area of Maine-et-Loire, along the slopes which border the Loire below Angers, as well as from the land of the seventeen communes of Deux-Sèvres, from the area surrounding Bouillé-Loretz, and from eight communes along the Vienne River to the south of Saumur.

The largest wineproducing cantons are Thouarcé and Rochefort-sur-Loire where the vine covers 20 per cent of the area. Then come the viticultural regions that lie to the south of Saumur: Montreuil, Bellay, Doué-la-Fontaine, where the land under cultivation is 14 per cent.

The charm of Anjou lies in its climate—the deep blue sky, softened by a slight haze from the sea, the gentle winters, the early spring. Anjou is not a natural geographical region, but the focal point of several provinces which have widely diverging characteristics: the Vendean and Armorican mountain massifs, the mountain passes of Poitou and Touraine. Owing to this lack of homogeneity in its geographical make-up,

Anjou offers a varied soil which reflects almost every geological era: schists, sandstone, primitive calcareous rock, sands, clay, diorite-sand and especially calcareous tufa, chalky sands and a flinty, gravelly soil. To the west of Saumur, in the valley of Layon, the slopes are rich in calcareous sands which nourish a fertile vineyard which produces rosé and white wines. About 40,000 acres are covered in fine quality grapes. The white wines are produced from a single grape, the *Chenin Blanc*, which is planted over about 22,000 acres. A recent law has permitted, in certain circumstances, a small quantity of *Sauvignon* or *Chardonnay* grapes to be added. The best red grape is, as in Touraine, the *Cabernet Franc*. For about twelve years now, however, it has been either replaced to a certain extent by the *Cabernet Sauvignon* grape, which in the selection procedure produces a higher quality of wine, or else the two varieties are mixed. These two grapes are the ones most frequently used to produce red and rosé wines of superior quality. They cover more than 7,500 acres. The other grape varieties are used to produce rosés only. The *Groslot* grape, much cultivated during the reconstruction period, has now been replaced by the *Cabernet Sauvignon*, the *Gamay* and the *Pineau d'Aunis*. The red grapes, which ripen before the *Pineau*, are harvested earlier, usually from September 20th on. To make a rosé wine, the grapes are pressed immediately, without being crushed, in order to obtain a must with a very light colour. The must always ferments without any stalks. The grapes which go to make red Champignys are only pressed when all the stalks have been removed. Fermentation in open vats with unhinged lids or in cement vats lasts from eight to ten days. The wine is then preserved for a year in a large wooden barrel. For some years now, quite a significant amount of red wine has been produced by means of carbonis fermentation, a method yielding light, fruity wines which are most certainly considered to be at their best when young, rather than when aged. The *Pineau de la Loire* and *Chenin* grapes are picked first towards the beginning of October, but only in small quantities, for the grapes are still fresh and ripe. Later, when the *pourriture noble* (noble rot) sets in, they are picked again in larger and larger quantities. Often the harvest continues into the middle of November.

Fermentation takes place in wooden barrels, each of which contains 50 gallons. The temperature of the wine-cellars is from 10º to 35º, which enables these wines, through a slow fermentation, to attain the bouquet and finesse which is characteristic of them. Often the producer is obliged to heat the underground cellars during the first cold spells in order to bring them up to a temperature of 16º to 18º. In Anjou, as in all the other regions of the Loire, the wine benefits from being bottled in the early spring after having been racked, clarified and sometimes even filtered several times. When the wine is bottled later in the year, from May to September, the character of the wine changes, and the freshness and lightness which give it its essential quality are diminished.

Sulphur dioxide is indispensable. It acts both physiologically, since it stops fermentation, and chemically in that its anti-oxygen properties prevent premature ageing, the unwanted sweetness and colouring of maderization, and the spread of oxidasic casse. The anhydride is then eliminated by oxidation which leaves the wine clear and pure but retaining all its freshness and bouquet.

The average harvest of fine quality wines from the Anjou and Saumur regions is some 12,100,000 gallons.

Within Anjou there are two regional *appellations*: Anjou and Saumur. The Saumur region is in fact considered a part of Anjou, according to provisions of legislation passed by the Angers tribunal, and following decrees controlling both *appellations*: a wine made in Saumur may be sold as an Anjou, but not vice versa. The sub-regional *appellations are*: Coteaux du Layon, Coteaux de la Loire, Coteaux d'Aubance, Coteaux du Loir. The *appellations* of individual communes or vineyards are: Bonnezeaux and Quarts de Chaume, along the slopes of Layon; Savennières, along the Loire, as well as the Culée de Senant and Roche aux Moines varieties.

THE MUSCADET REGION

To leave Anjou at Ingrandes is to leave behind all the grape varieties discussed so far and to discover two new ones. Since 1955 a new trend has manifested itself in the Ancenis area: planting and propagating a *Gamay* grape for the production of red and rosé wines. In Basse-Bretagne, the area under vine cultivation at the time of the Romans was for a long time of small importance. In fact only the grounds belonging to the Abbey and its fortified enclosures were reserved for the vine.

When did the *Muscadet* grape first make its appearance in the Loire-Atlantique? Certain documents in Nantes disclose that in 1639, on numerous small farms, the red grapes were pulled out to be replaced by a good grape-stock from Burgundy. The terrible winter of 1709, however, almost entirely wiped out the vineyards. It was necessary therefore to replant completely, which required great effort. Leases provided that the replanting be in *Muscadet de Bourgogne* grapes. Thus it was in the year 1735 that the *Muscadet* grape of today was first known.

At the end of the last century, the *Muscadet* grape occupied approximately a third of the land reserved for the vine, the rest being taken up mainly by the *Gros Plant* grape, a variety of the *Folle Blanche* stock, a staple grape of the Cognac region.

When the vineyards were replanted again after the phylloxera epidemic, the *Gros Plant* lost out to the *Muscadet* grape.

The entire vineyard area here is situated on crystalline schists, on layers of gravelly soil, and on rare calcareous islets which in no way alter the lay of the land. The vine is planted on the gravelly slopes facing the south-west. The vineyards are concentrated in the regions to the south of the Loire, Sèvres and Maine. This region produces three-quarters of the Muscadet stock. It is also cultivated to the north of the Loire, mainly in the area between Nantes and Ancenis and around Grand-Lieu Lake.

The *Muscadet* grape ripens early. It is picked very early in the season, towards the beginning of September. Usually, already towards the 15th of this month, the harvesters are in full swing. The flat countryside offers no natural underground cellars; winecellars in this region consist of small buildings with tile roofs.

The wine is fermented in casks or tuns which hold a maximum of six litres (over 10 ½ pints). The process of fermentation is slow, in order that it may acquire a fine bouquet and fruity texture. The wine must be bottled in haste, in fact only a few months after the grapes have been picked. When bottled in its lees, with a small amount of carbonic gas, it retains a finesse and charm which make it very agreeable and much sought after as a companion to sea-food.

Muscadet generally has a slight acid content, is of a pale yellow colour and light character. It is very difficult to define its bouquet and flavour. The niceties are infinite, and vary considerably from commune to commune and even vineyard to vineyard.

It is possible, however, to distinguish other characteristics peculiar to each type of Muscadet. The wine comes from the hillsides along the Loire is particularly full-bodied, often with a higher acidity; this is not a fault since a lack of acidity would make this wine spiritless and sharp in character.

The area covered by the *Muscadet* grape is nearly 25,000 acres, producing an average of about 6,600,000 gallons per annum.

WINES OF THE LOIRE

CENTRAL REGION

	Name of the wine	*Principal growths*		
White wines	Pouilly Fumé	Château du Nozet	La Loge aux Moines	Côteau des Girarmes
		Coteaux des Loges		
	Pouilly-sur-Loire	Les Berthiers	Le Bouchot-du-Haut	Le Grand Bouchot
		Bois-Fleury	Les Cassiers	Le Grand Puizac
		Boisgibaud	Château du Nozet	Mezières
		Bouchot	Les Chétives-Maisons	Le Petit Soumard
		Le Bouchot-du-Bas	Les Girarmes	
	Ménetou-Salon			
	Quincy	Bourg	Les Chavoches	Les Gravoches
		Les Brosses	Cornançay	Rimonet
		Bruniers `	Le Grand Chaumoux	Villalin
White, red and rosé				
wines	Sancerre	Amigny	La Côte	La Perrière
		Coteau de Bannon	La Côte-de-Verdigny	Les Plantes
		Beauregard	Les Côtelins	La Porte du Clos
		Les Belletins	Les Coudebraults	La Poussie
		Chambraste	Les Crilles	Reigny
		Champtin	Clos de l'Epée	Les Rochons
		Les Chassaignes	Fricambault	Saint-Martin
		Château de Sancerre	La Grande Côte	Les Terranges
		Chavignol	Les Groux	Château de Thauvenay
		Chemarin	Lare	Le Thou
		Chêne Marchand	Les Montachins	Côte de la Vallée
		Les Chevillots	Les Monts-Damnés	Les Vicairies
		Les Coinches	La Moussière	Les Vignes-Chatton
		La Comtesse	Le Paradis	Les Vignes de Ménetou
	Reuilly	Beaumont	Les Couagnons	Les Marnais
		Les Beauregards	Le Figuier	Clos des Messieurs
		Les Bossières	Les Lignys	Les Varennes
		Chatillons		

TOURS REGION

	Name of the wine	*Commune*	*Principal growths*	
White wines	Touraine — Azay-le-Rideau	Azay-le-Rideau		
	Montlouis	Montlouis	Clos de la Barre	Clos Renard
			Clos de la Frelonnerie	Les Sicots
			La Milletière	
		Lussault	Cray	Pintray
		Saint-Martin-le-Beau . . .	Château du Boulay	Clos de Mosny
			Cange	
	Jasnières (in the Sarthe, a	Jasnières	L'Aillerie	Les Hussières
	fairly rare wine)		Les Beduaux	Les Jasnières
			La Bonatière	Les Longues Vignes
			Les Côtières	Les Mollières
			Les Fleuries	La Mule
			Les Gargouilles	Le Paradis
			La Gidonnière	Saint-Jacques
			Les Haurières	Sous-le-Bois
			Les Héridaines	Les Verboisières

VOUVRAY

	Commune	Principal growths		
White wines	Vouvray	Les Argouges	La Fontainerie	La Muscadelle
		Domaine de l'Auberidière	Les Fouinières	Clos Naudin
		Clos des Barguins	La Gaillardière	Clos de Nouis
		Clos de la Barre	Clos de Gaimont	Perrets de Minuze
		Clos Baudoin	Château Gaudrelle	Clos du Petit-Mont
		Clos Bel-Air	Clos des Girardières	Le Portail
		Clos des Bidaudières	Grand Echeneau	La Renardière
		Clos du Bois-Rideau	Clos des Gues d'Amant	Clos des Roches
		Les Bois Turmeaux	Le Haut-Lieu	Clos Saint-Come
		Clos Le Bouchet	Coteau J.-Jouffroy	Clos Saint-Mathurin
		Clos du Bourg	Clos des Lions	Sauzelles
		Clos de la Brianderie	La Loge	Clos Toulifaut
		Coteaux des Brosses	Clos la Lucassière	Vallée Coquette
		Les Brosses	Clos de Marigny	Clos de Val-Roche
		Les Brûlées	Monaco	Clos Vaufuget
		Coteau Chatrie	Château Montcontour	Clos les Verneries
		Clos Dubois	Clos le Mont	Clos le Vigneau
		L'Epinay		
	Chançay	Clos des Augustins	Croix-de-Vaux	La Pirée
		Clos Baguelin	Clos de la Forêt	Château Valmer
		Coteau de Chançay	Grand Bathes	Clos de Vau
		Clos de Charmigny	Château Gaillard	Coteau de Vaux
		La Croix-de-Bois	Petites Bastes	Veaux
	Noizay	Clos d'Anzou	Le Grand Coteau	La Roche-de-Cestres
		Les Barres	La Grotte	Clos de la Rochère
		Coteau de Beaumont	Les Hauts-Bois	Coteau de la Rochère
		Clos de Beauregard	Clos Hure	Roquefort
		Clos du Bois d'Ouche	Clos Marteau	La Tremblaie
		Bois Guyon	Molaville	Clos de Venise
		Clos de la Bretonnière	Château d'Ouche	Coteau de Venise
		Goguenne	Clos de la Roche	
	Rochecorbon	Clos de l'Alleau	Clos de la Bourdonnerie	Clos de l'Olivier
		Château les Armuseries	Les Chapelles	Clos des Pentes
		Château des Basses-Rivières	Clos de la Chasse-Royale	Clos de Sens
			Clos Château-Chevrier	Clos de la Taisserie
		Clos des Batonnières	Château de la Lanterne	Le Clos Vaufoinard
		Bois-Soleil	Château de Montgouverne	
	Sainte-Radegonde	Clos de l'Archerie	Clos Mon-Baril	Clos Saint-Georges
		Clos de la Hallotière	Clos de Rougemont	
	Vernou-sur-Brenne. . . .	Les Batailleries	Hardilliers	Perrets-de-Fou-Joint
		Bel-Air	Haut-Cousse	Les Pichaudières
		La Carte	L'Hermineau	Poupine
		Le Cassereau	La Joubardière	Clos de Pouvray
		Clos de Chaillemont	Clos des Longs-Reages	Clos Roc-Etoile
		Clos Chauvin	Clos des Madères	Rue Baffert
		Chopet	Clos Mauguin	Clos des Surins
		Le Clos	Clos de la Meslerie	Tabourneau
		La Coudraie	Mialet	Terne
		Les Deronières	Les Morandières	Clos Thenot
		Château de l'Etoile	Le Mortier	Clos des Thierrières
		Le Feau	La Neurie	Tortemains
		La Folie	Noyer-de-Cens	Vau-Louis
		La Follière	Pain-Perdu	Vaux-Barres
		Clos de Fougerai	Pâtureaux	Vignes-Morier
		Clos Franc	Peu-de-Cartes	Clos de Vilmier

CHINON

Name of the wine		Commune	Principal growths	
White, red and rosé wines	Chinon	Chinon	Les Aubuis	Repos de Saint-Martin
			Les Bruneau	La Rochelle
			Les Closeaux	Rochette
			Montrobert	Saint-Jean
			Clos du Parc	Saint-Louand
			Clos du Pin	La Vauzelle
		Avoine	Les Lignes	
		Beaumont-en-Veron . . .	Château de Dauzay	Les Peuilles
			Les Gresilles	Les Picasses
			Clos du Langon	Les Pineaux
			Le Martinet	Roche-Honneur
		Cravant-les-Coteaux . . .	Les Battereaux	Clos de la Haie-Martel
			Bel-Air	Les Quatre-Ferrures
			Les Coutures	La Semellerie
			La Gresille	Coteaux de Sonnay
		Rouzilles	Pelivet	
		Huismes	Bauregard	Clos Marie
			La Colline	Le Pin
		La Roche-Clermault . . .	Les Aiguillons	Les Rosettes
			Les Bessardières	Sassay
		Ligré	Clos de Galonnes	Clos du Saut-du-Loup
			La Noblaie	Saute-aux-Loups
			Le Paradis	Le Vau-Breton
		Panzoult	La Galippe	Clos Queron
			La Haie-Martel	Ronce
		Rivière	La Croix-Marie	Les Harrassons
			Les Croulards	Clos Saint-Hilaire
Red and rosé wines . .	Bourgueil	Bourgueil	Chevrette	Clos de l'Oie-qui-casse
			Les Galuches	Les Pins-Les Sablons
			Clos des Geslets	La Salpetrerie
		Benais	Beauvais	Petit-Mont
			La Chanteleuserie	Les Raguenières
		Chouzé-sur-Loire	Les Goutierreries	Les Grandes Ouches
		Ingrandes-de-Touraine . .	Clos de Blottières	La Gallotière
			Cru des Brunetières	Minière-Château
		Restigné	Les Evois	Château Louys
			Fougerolles	La Philebernière
			Domaine de la Gaucherie	Clos de la Platerie
			Les Grands-Champs	Les Rosaies
			Les Hauts-Champs	Clos du Vendôme
		Saint-Nicolas-de-Bourgueil	Beaupuy	La Jarnoterie
			La Contrie	La Martellière
			Clos de l'Epaisse	Port-Guyet
			Les Fondis	Clos de la Torrillère
			Forcine	Clos du Vigneau
			La Gardière	La Villatte

SAUMUR REGION

Name of the wine		Commune	Principal growths	
White wines	Coteaux de Saumur	Montsoreau	Clos des Rotissants	Clos des Pères
		Bizay	Clos des Treilles	
		Brézé	Les Clos du Château de Brézé	Château La Ripaille
				Clos des Carmes
		Parnay	Clos des Murs	Clos des Saints-Pères
		Saint-Cyr	Butte de Saumoussay	
		Turquant	Château Gaillard	
		Dampierre	Clos des Morains	
		Souzay	Champ Chardon	Clos de la Bienboire
		Saumur	Château de la Fuye	

	Name of the wine	Commune		Principal growths	
Red wines	Cabernet de Saumur	Souzay		Champigny-le-Sec	
		Saumur		Souzay	Varrains
				Parnay	Allonnes
				Saumoussay	Brain-sur-Allones
Rosé wine	Cabernet de Saumur				

ANGERS REGION

White wines

Name of the wine	Commune				
Coteaux de la Loire	Savennières	Principal growths	La Coulée de Serrant	La Roche-aux-Moines	
			Château d'Epire	Clos du Papillon	
	La Possonnière, La Pommeraye, Ingrandes, Montjean, Bouchemaine, Saint-Barthélemy, Andard, Brain-sur-l'Authion.				
Coteaux du Loir	Huillé	Principal growths	Clos des Tertres	Clos du Pineau	
			Clos Pilate	Clos la Patrie	
	Lézigné, Durtal, Baugeois.				
Coteaux du Layon	Rochefort-sur-Loire	Principal growths	Quart de Chaume	Les Guimonières	
			Clos de Sainte-Catherine		
	Beaulieu-sur-Layon	Principal growths	Château du Breuil	Les Mullonnières	
	Saint-Aubin-de-Luigné	Principal growths	La Roulerie	Plaisance	
			Château La Fresnaye		
	Rablay	Principal growths	L'Argonette	La Touche	
			Le Clos de la Roche	Les Sablonnettes	
			Les Gonnordes	Les Celliers	
	Faye-sur-Layon	Principal growths	Château de Chanze	La Saillanderie	
			Château de Mongeneau	La Pierre-Gauderie	
			La Madeleine	Les Jouets	
			Les Noëls	Le Miroir	
	Thouarcé	Principal growth	Bonnezeaux		
Other vine-growing communes .	Saint-Lambert-du-Lattay, Le Champ, Chaudefonds, Martigné-Briand, Chavagnes, Brigné, Concourson.				
Coteaux de l'Aubance	Murs-Erigné, Vauchrétien, Sainte-Melaine-sur Aubance, Quincé, Brissac, Juigné-sur-Loire, Saint-Saturnin-sur-Loire, Saint-Jean-des-Mauvrets.				

Rosé wines

Rosé d'Anjou	Dampierre, Varrains	
Cabernet d'Anjou	Chacé, Bagneux, Martigné-Briand, Tigné, Le Thoureil, Vauchrétien, Murs, Notre-Dame-d'Alençon, Brissac.	

NANTES REGION

White wines	Name of the wine	Principal growths	
	Muscadet de Sèvre-et-Maine	Vallet	La Chapelle-Heulin
		Mouzillon	La Regrippière
		Le Pallet	Saint-Fiacre-sur-Maine
	Muscadet des Coteaux de la Loire	Saint-Herblon	Liré
		Ancenis	Drain
		Saint-Géréon	

VINS DE LA LOIRE
ANJOU ET SAUMUR

Laval
Oudon
Mayenne
Loir
Sarthe
Rennes
Le Mans
Sarthe

BAUGÉ

Maine
et
Loire

ANGERS

Loire - Atlantique

Coteaux de la Loire

SAVENNIÈRES
Coteaux de l'Aubance
ROCHEFORT S/R LOIRE
BRISSAC

Nantes
Loire

ST. AUBIN- DE-LUIGNE
Quarts de Chaume
CHAUME
BEAULIEU
ST LAMBERT-DU-LATTAY
FAYE
RABLAY
BONNEZEAUX
THOUARCÉ
Coteaux du Layon

Anjou

Authion
Loire
Aubance

Indre-et-Loire

SAUMUR

CHAMPIGNY
Coteaux de Saumur
Tours
Vienne

Vendée

DOUÉ-LA-FONTAINE

Saumur

Layon
Thouet
Dive
MONTREUIL-BELLAY

CHOLET

Poitiers

Les Sables d'Olonne

THOUARS

	Coteaux de la Loire
	Coteaux de l'Aubance
	Coteaux du Layon
	Anjou
	Coteaux de Saumur
	Saumur

-------- limite de département
-------- department border

20 Km.

20 Miles

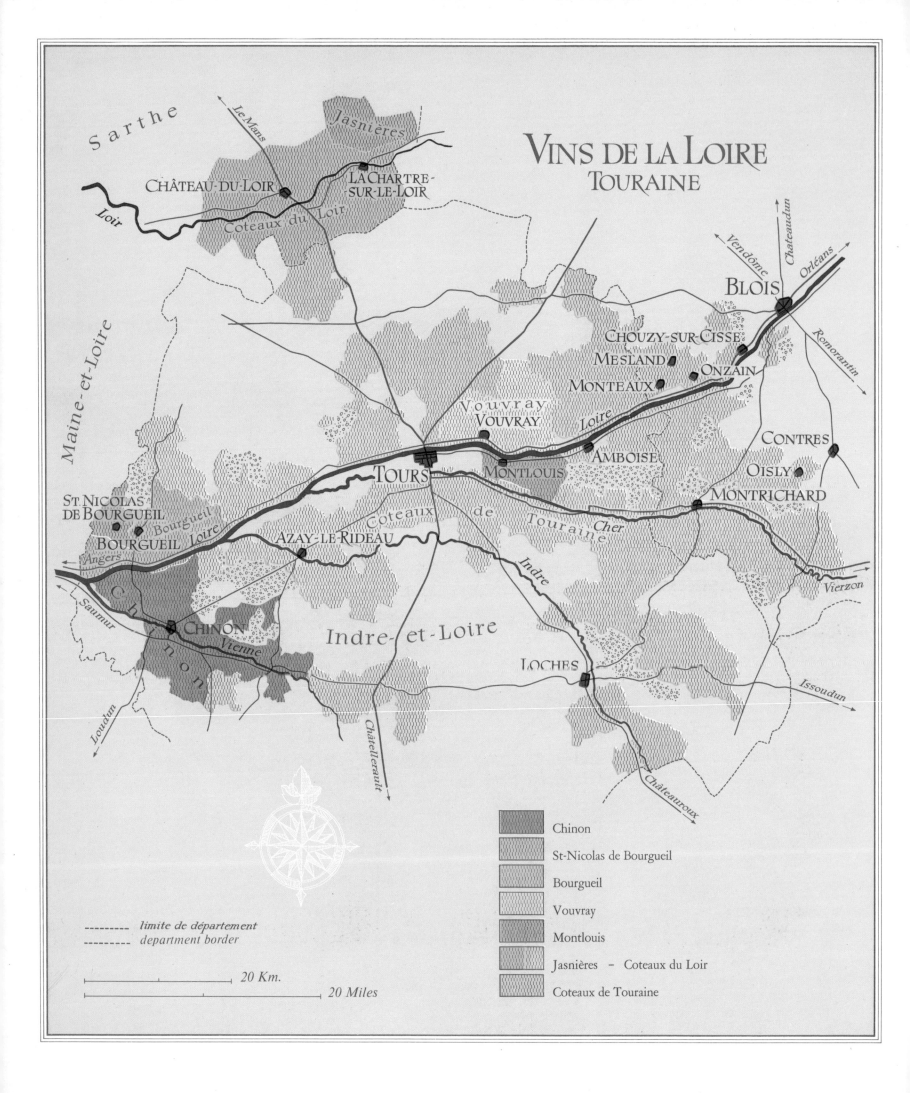

VINS DE LA LOIRE
TOURAINE

Sarthe

Jasnières

Le Mans

CHÂTEAU-DU-LOIR   LA CHARTRE-
                   SUR-LE-LOIR

Loir

Coteaux du Loir

BLOIS

Vendôme

Châteaudun

Orléans

CHOUZY-SUR-CISSE

Maine-et-Loire

MESLAND
MONTEAUX   ONZAIN

Romorantin

Vouvray
VOUVRAY

Loire

CONTRES

AMBOISE

OISLY

Montlouis

TOURS

ST. NICOLAS
DE BOURGUEIL

MONTRICHARD

Coteaux   de   Touraine

Cher

Bourgueil
Loire

BOURGUEIL

AZAY-LE-RIDEAU

Angers

Indre

Vierzon

Saumur

Chinon

Indre-et-Loire

CHINON

LOCHES

Issoudun

Vienne

Loudun

Châtellerault

Châteauroux

limite de département
department border

20 Km.

20 Miles

Chinon

St-Nicolas de Bourgueil

Bourgueil

Vouvray

Montlouis

Jasnières – Coteaux du Loir

Coteaux de Touraine

THE WINES
OF BORDEAUX

GASTON MARCHOU

Between the first and third centuries of the Christian era, the Bordeaux countryside witnessed the triumph of the medium-sized estate. The large Gallic domain, hitherto indivisible under the authority of the chieftain of the clan, began to break up. In most cases, the chief was anxious to obtain the title of "Roman citizen", which obviously implied an obligation to accept the conqueror's legal system. Since Roman Law did not recognize the right of inalienability, land was bought, sold and sub-divided. It became a matter for speculation, a means of self-enrichment and a way of paying debts. It could be bequeathed by will.

Agrarian reform, though almost imperceptible, was rendered inevitable by the interaction of customs and vested interests. When great landowners reappeared, even before the break-up of the Empire, the large domain was not re-established. Wealth no longer meant the ownership of a single immense territory but of a number of adjoining estates, each having its own economy. In some cases, in fact, there were no means of communication between such land-holdings.

The cultivation of the vine and the preparation of wine were much better suited to this sub-division than to the vast expanses of territory under a single head. Where necessary, in fact, it encouraged the process.

In A.D. 92, Domitian inaugurated a policy which was to continue until the present day, despite successive repulses and the harmful consequences it was to produce. This emperor, who has been harshly judged by history for other reasons, tried to remedy the shortage of wheat by prohibiting the planting of new vines on Italian soil and ordering that half those that existed in the western provinces should be uprooted. Montesquieu, it is true, gives another reason for Domitian's decision: "This weak and timid prince," he said, "caused the vines in the two Gauls to be grubbed up lest the wine should attract the barbarians." Possibly the author of the *Spirit of the Laws* was loath to leave a Roman emperor, even a mediocre one, in the company of the mid-eighteenth-century economists who advocated pulling up vines. Nevertheless, he was wrong to state as a fact that the Gallic vineyards even partly disappeared under Domitian. The governor of the province was obliged to grant official privileges and exemptions. Incidentally, the winegrowers of Bordeaux often dispensed with them both. They simply bribed the officials responsible for applying the edict.

Even in Rome itself, the winegrowing interests of Bordeaux were defended with typically Gascon asperity and irony. By means of clandestinely distributed pamphlets, the vine, condemned to death by Domitian but still very much alive, addressed the Emperor: "Eat me down to the roots," it said, "I shall still bear enough grapes for great libations to be poured on the day that Caesar is slain!"

Domitian was assassinated four years later. One cannot attack the vineyards of Bordeaux with impunity. The great French administrator Tourny was also to discover the fact. Although he sacrificed his fortune for the city and lavished his affection on it, he was disgraced because he forgot that the fame of its wine was more important than his own.

129

If the vine, which climbs in serried ranks up the slopes of the right bank of the Médoc, drives back the forest from the left bank and rushes through the sands of the delta to the ocean, has succeeded in defending itself against arbitrary central power, this is most clearly explained by the medium- and small-holding system. It would have been much easier for the officials to ensure that the vines were uprooted in the domains covering the area of a canton or several communes, it would have been far more serious for anyone to disobey the Emperor and the landowners would have been more vulnerable.

At the time of Domitian, the vineyards were grouped around the city; but Burdigala, as it was than known, was built on a very simple plan and was still rustic. The proprietor lived on his land, in his Gallo-Roman villa. He preferred the scent of new-mown hay and the strong perfume of his wine-cellar to the frenzied habit of writing verse which he was to contract at the time of Ausonius, when he was completely latinized. This final latinization of Aquitaine, incidentally, in the twilight of the Empire, coincided with a decline of Latin influence in the East.

While awaiting his conversion to poetry, the master of the villa trembled for his flowering vine if the nights of May were clear. In his short hood and gaiters, he would rise early in the morning to go and see it. He would take the fragile corollas delicately between index finger and middle finger and regard them with a paternal eye. He would meet his workmen, unless he was up before them. He would talk to them, ask the advice of the most experienced, look up at the sky, observe the colour of the river, sometimes shining like a silver lake, sometimes restless and yellow if heavy rain was approaching from the uplands. From his garden-neat vineyard, laid out in tasteful and human geometrical patterns, he had banished the fruit trees which were grown elsewhere. He personified the ageless proverb that Olivier de Serres was to borrow from the land of the Gironde:

The shadow of a good master
Makes the vine grow much faster

However, this good master was not only a wine-grower whose ear was the first to hear the cuckoo heralding the certain arrival of fine summer days. Since the villa had to provide for all its own needs, he was also an artisan or even an engineer. He brought to life the lost dream of self-sufficiency which is still evoked in Olivier de Serres' *Theatre of Agriculture and Field Management*. Every villa possessed a forge, a carpentry shop and a pottery kiln. It manufactured earthenware pottery, tools and instruments. The owner supervised everything, like a paterfamilias who,

living close to the land, was well aware of the limits of productive efforts and the precariousness of their results.

He stamped an impression on the soil of the Gironde which successive invasions were unable to efface. It is to the credit of the first Gallo-Roman landowner, to his peasant mentality, and the care he bestowed on his vine which he cherished like a queen, that the region, when the Gallic system of serfdom was renounced, refrained from introducing the despicable Roman custom of slave labour.

The seeds of what the all-embracing goodness of a Younger Pliny had attempted in Italy and what Christianity was to achieve in due course, were already present in the Bordeaux vineyards by the middle of the third century A.D. The Gironde landowner of the fifth century was thus appreciably better off than the debt-ridden Italian farmer of whom Columella tells us. He was a man who lived well from his free labour and harvested the fruits of the earth, at least partly to his own advantage. The famous wine which was drunk from silver cups in the palaces was also drunk by him from his rustic earthenware goblet. He caught the echo of the praises lavished on the "liquor of the Gods" like a father hearing a tribute to his infant prodigy.

The wine of Bordeaux was to become the sole pre-occupation of a whole population. Thanks to it, the social classes, so well-marked elsewhere, were inter-mingled in a common faith. Beyond the narrow compartmentation of feudalism, it opened up new horizons so attractive that archbishop and cobbler, noble and burgher were assembled together in a kind of superior guild. In the centuries to come, a singular wine-born aristocracy was to arise, in the eyes of which all other products of human activity, including politics and war, would be negligible or secondary.

In the first half of the eighth century, Bordeaux found itself briefly under Arab domination, the only régime which could definitely endanger the vine, since the Moors were conquerors who did not drink it. When deliverance came with Charles Martel, the city still had to face twenty years of war during which the dukes of Aquitaine defended their inheritance against the successors of Clovis. Finally, the Bordeaux country became a march of the Carolingian empire. A noble procession now passes by, a glittering interlude in the mediocrity of those remote ages. Charlemagne comes first, mounted upon his battle charger, holding his sword "Joyeuse" with its ruby-encrusted hilt, with which he will touch the sarcophagus of St. Seurin. Four pages on horseback hold a canopy above his head. Next come his three sons, then the bishops, the dukes, the Twelve Peers, the counts and the knights. The Emperor is interested in the winegrower's way of life; he visits the wineries. He forbids the custom of

Situated in the Haut-Médoc, on the left bank of the Gironde, the commune of Margaux owes its world-wide renown to Château Margaux, one of the great lords of the Bordeaux wine-country. In the middle of the eighteenth century, Monsieur de Fumel, the military Governor of Bordeaux, planted it with fine, carefully selected vines which quickly made the estate's name. It is shown here on a contemporary plan.

carrying Bordeaux wine in leather bottles and prescribes the use of hooped casks. He discusses vintages with the merchants and orders good years to be aged in jars.

The eternal wine of Bordeaux is a continuous creation; not only as regards winegrowing and viticultural techniques, in which scientific innovations must constantly be controlled by references to tradition, but also at the prestige level, where promotion efforts are ineffective unless constantly renewed. Hence, in the Middle Ages, after the marriage of the beautiful Eleanor of Aquitaine to Henry Plantagenet of England, the *Jurade* or City Council of Bordeaux based the whole of its foreign policy on the need to keep and develop the English market, the sole outlet for claret. After the reunion of Guienne with France, Bordeaux wine could no longer depend exclusively upon exports. Continental consumers had to be found. From the sixteenth century onwards, the city fathers carried out a systematic campaign to find them.

In 1555, the Mayor of Bordeaux visited the French Court, taking with him twenty *tonneaux* (four hogsheads) of wine for presentation to noblemen who were favourably disposed to the city and its trade. A year later, twenty *tonneaux* of Graves were sent to the Cardinal of Lorraine and to Marshal Saint-André for the same reason. In 1559, the Duke of Alba, while passing through Bordeaux, was visited by the *Jurats* or aldermen who offered him a present of wine. In 1596,

a Bordeaux *Jurat* named Pierre de Brach, on a mission to Paris, was instructed to distribute several *tonneaux* of wine to the best effect. He recounts the difficulty he had in bringing the wine into the capital: "An hundred times I wished the wine back on its vine, for truly I believe it less troublesome to bring a king into Paris than a little wine. There are fifty formalities, routines and prescripts." On June 3rd, 1681, the Muscovite Ambassador arrived in Bordeaux and, having greeted him, the *Jurats* presented him with several dozen bottles of fine wine and some brandy. It is noteworthy that bottled Bordeaux thus made its official appearance at the end of the seventeenth century, even if bottling was not yet the standard commercial practice. It was not until the following century that the establishment of the first industrial glass-works gave birth to the Bordeaux fine-wine business which was to produce the first classification by parishes and then by châteaux or estates.

In 1728, twelve years before Tourny was appointed intendant of Bordeaux, the Duke of Antin was able to write to Robert de Cotte: "The Bordelais prefer to sell their wine rather than to put up fine buildings." The fine buildings were not, in fact, to be put up (as later events were to prove) until the area became closely dependent on the central power. The Bordeaux wine trade, on the other hand, was still to remain for a long time yet the privilege of the people of Bordeaux.

The "Great Privilege" or "Wine Privilege" remained in force until the Revolution, when it was abolished as an unjust feudal institution. In fact, the privilege was perfectly justified. Quite apart from the guarantees it gave of quality production, the beneficiaries were responsible for maintaining the city and its ramparts. This very complex legal monument was the *Jurade's* masterpiece. Its purpose was to restrict access to the port of Bordeaux to wines produced in the seneschalcy.

In addition, everything connected with wine—brokerage, retail sale in the Bordeaux taverns and pot-houses, the shape and capacity of the *barrique* (a barrel containing about 50 U.K. gallons, the standard model for which was installed in the City Hall in 1597), everything was regulated and the regulations were scrupulously observed. Every *barrique* had to carry, at both ends, the growth mark, burnt in with a hot iron. This mark was removed once the *barrique* was empty, unless it was returned to the vineyard of origin. Its owner had to obtain a certificate ("stamp") from the local mayor or parish priest that the cask had been duly returned. The text of the "stamp" stipulated that "it is enjoined upon all merchants' masters of the wine-stores to erase immediately, under penalty of a fine of three thousand livres [about £600 or $1,440] and corporal punishment, the marks on *barriques* which have been broached in their stores whether for consumption, ullaging, fine bottling or cutting down."

This affair of the "stamp" brought the constant conflict between traders and producers to a height of tension. It aroused so many protests among the traders of Chartrons, the trading quarter of Bordeaux, that the regulation was annulled. It should be realized, incidentally, that the chief result of the "stamp" system, as elaborated by the *Jurats*, was not only to prevent the dilution of the wine but also to turn the merchants into habitual lawbreakers, since all normal work in a winestore became impossible. The sovereign power of the *Jurade*, no longer able to assert itself in grand designs, was degenerating into officiousness.

The quarter of a century between the treaty of 1763, which ended the Seven Years War, and 1789 was, roughly speaking, the period of the "Trade with the Isles". Never had the flame of enterprise burned more brightly in the "Port of the Moon". With a rapidity comparable to the lightning development of the towns of the American West in the nineteenth century, Bordeaux carried out the programme outlined by Tourny. The society which was to die under the knife for the crime of "merchandizing" was certainly the gayest and most artistic that the City of Montaigne had ever known. It had subtlety, poetry and a very lively taste for nature, though without the dialectic bent so dear to Rousseau. Each year when autumn

came the whole of that fashionable society, counsellors of the *Parlement* at its head, left the "Follies" of the suburbs embalmed in the fragrance of the wine-vat; Pomona's sleep began, and the port of Bordeaux awoke. The crescent-shaped roadstead was immense. It stretched from the old Salinières quarter to the more modern quarter of Chartrons, making a semi-circle in front of the classical perspective of the house-fronts.

Breaking the medieval records of which Froissart had spoken, the port was filled with as many as 300 ships, not counting brigs and brigantines. The vessels flew the flags of England, Holland, the Hanseatic towns, Denmark, the Baltic countries, Spain and the distant American republic. At that time, Bordeaux was the greatest distribution centre for colonial goods in all Europe and monopolized a quarter of France's foreign trade.

In fact, if the time of the "Trade with the Isles" is reduced to the period during which it was brilliant and stable, it will be realized that it lasted no longer than fifteen years! Fifteen years during which the *barriques* from those parishes of Médoc and Graves whose growths had, for the first time, been arranged in a hierarchy in 1755, were lined up and modestly concealed behind piles of exotic wealth.

The Jacobin incursion plunged Bordeaux into the same stupor as the arrival of the Barbarians had done. For that happy-go-lucky city, the Napoleonic wars were a long and sombre tunnel. When peace was restored, the port for a long time remained deserted and the "Trade with the Isles" became a shadowy memory. Happily, however, during those fifteen years the wine of Bordeaux had become a "European creation", as Gabriel Delaunay well put it. English, Germans, Dutch, Belgians and Scandinavians could no longer do without it. It was their fidelity to this unique product that saved Bordeaux. Stripping off the white gloves they had worn to handle samples of indigo, the people of Bordeaux had no recourse but to return to their vines and their winestores, and this they did. Since then, whatever the economic climate, however enticing the promise of an industrial future might be, the Bordeaux winegrowers have known where they are going. They will never again depart from their vine-bordered road.

I remember, during the war, a honey-sweet morning draped in a luminous, velvety mist. It was at a spot in that immense Central European plain where the very shape of a vine-stock is unknown. That morning, for the first time in months, I felt my distant birth-place refilling my void. Like many another, I knew that extraordinary, almost painful moment when the wearisome dizziness of captivity suddenly becomes fixed in a blinding revelation. By undreamt-of approaches, our lost France reclaimed her anonymous flock and gave each of us back his provincial identity. With the help of a sign, expressly given to us, marvellous images of the past rose up under our closed eyelids with a force, a truth, a wealth of detail which the seeing eyes can never achieve.

It needed that dawn in the early Silesian autumn, the melancholy of a desolate grassland on which innumerable rain-puddles reflected clouds driven by the West wind, the misty prospect of the huts and strange quality of the sounds in the atmosphere, to give me back the soft and magnificent "grape-gathering weather" in the middle of Elsterhorst Camp.

This well-known phenomenon of exile turned me into one of those naïve travellers of ancient times who would suddenly discover an unknown city from the brow of a hill. But my discovery was a symbolic one.

It gave me a destiny. I realized that the glory of Bordeaux both siezes upon the senses and obtrudes upon the intellect, for even before encountering the miraculous life of Joan of Arc, translating Voltaire or sending its women to Paris for their frocks, a civilized nation makes the acquaintance of Bordeaux wine.

On the other hand, there is a vine epic in the Bordeaux country. Through wine, the vine presides over the social, moral and political activities of every day; it regulates life, of which it is the essential framework. A child born on the banks of the Garonne cannot conceive of a countryside without vineyards.

Throughout the centuries, the vine has been the friend of man in every country where the grape ripens. But once and once alone, in the history of mankind, it hat been a whole people's reason for living; and that was in Bordeaux.

THE REGIONS OF BORDEAUX

If you look at a map of France, your eye will be caught by the blue indentation of the Gironde estuary. It is a vast gateway to the ocean, the longest and widest along the whole coastline. From Ambès Bill, where the Garonne and the Dordogne meet, to the sea is a distance of some 60 miles and, at that point, the river is 2 miles wide. Downstream, the two banks are more than 6 miles apart. This expanse of water is subject to tidal action. When the ocean rises, its irresistible mass pours into the estuary, hurling back the current. This is the phenomenon known as the "bore" which is more or less violent according to season. The tidal wave moves with the speed of a galloping horse, raising in front of it a wall of seething, yellowish water. The bore does not slacken off before reaching Bordeaux and the violent agitation is still visible well above the city.

In the age of wooden ships, the mouth of the Gironde, although it had not yet achieved its present configuration, was an excellent route for penetrating into the continent. No other European river could carry ships so far inland. If, however, the reader follows the course of the Garonne in an atlas, he will realize that the river is not only the "maryne-lyke waie to the see of Biscaye and the noble and puyssante citie of Bourdeaulx" as the old portulan maps put it. Crossing the Limogne, you reach the Naurouze plateau which connects the basin of the Garonne to that of the Aude. This is the easiest and most agreeable route between the Mediterranean and the Atlantic. Long before the conquest, the Romans of Narbonne used to send their merchants down the Garonne, whence they took ship for the British Isles and the ports of the north.

Although the right bank of the estuary, which is bordered by a succession of cliffs, has been unchanged for thousands of years, this is not true of the left bank. Even as late as the historical period, this was a confused jumble of dunes and marshes through which the waters of the river made their way, depositing silt. Not more than six or seven centuries ago, the river embraced part of the long riparian plain now called the Médoc before losing itself in the Atlantic. The island thus formed was, at high tide, crossed by other arms of the river which, although a true estuary to the east, opened out into a delta in the west.

The department of the Gironde, the limits of which more or less coincide with the frontiers of the ancient Guienne, is the largest in France and covers more than 2 ½ million acres. It can be divided into two distinct regions. The first, covering about 1,500,000 acres, is bordered by the ocean on the one side and, on the other, by the left banks of the Gironde, the Garonne, the Ciron and the Barthus. It is a well-wooded countryside which belongs to the great Landes forest. Near the river, however, an outcrop of quaternary gravels forms a ridge on which are found the most famous vineyards in the world. The second region consists of a succession of hills and plateaus on the right banks of the Gironde and the Garonne. Their soil varies considerably. Starting from the south, we come to the Réolais, consisting of more or less argillaceous sandstones, the Entre-Deux-Mers and, on the right bank of the Dordogne, the very characteristic sub-regions of the Fronsadais and the Saint-Emilionnais where the gravel becomes more and more clayey and gives birth to several Great Growths. The Blayais-Bourgeais region, which is opposite the Médoc, across the Gironde, borders the right bank of the estuary, like a predominantly limestone wall.

Even nowadays, despite the vine which reigns on both banks, despite the links forged between all the inhabitants of the Bordeaux country over two millenia, the great river still separates two different worlds. To the west, the impenetrable curtain of coniferous forest shuts off the horizon behind the vineyards. To the east, there rise up hills so steep that the whiteness of limestone outcrops can be seen on their flanks.

The mild winters of the Gironde are due to the Gulf Stream. The temperate summers with their golden light, which will be entrapped in the liquid prison of the grape, are saved from excessive heat by a protective bank of clouds. The wine of Bordeaux is as much the offspring of a climate as of a soil.

THE "APPELLATIONS CONTRÔLÉES"

What is meant by the three words: "Wine of Bordeaux"? Speaking at Nogent-sur-Marne one day, the late-lamented Jean Valmy-Baysse replied to that question with as much elegance as simplicity: "the wine of Bordeaux, gentlemen, is France personified!"

To the foreign consumer, the trademark "Bordeaux" does, in fact, mean the rarest and most sought-after of products, regular consumption of which is a sign of good taste and distinction.

Bordeaux wine is, as someone once put it, "something quite other than merchandise". It is a product which, according to Aristotle's definition, may be classified among the great universals. If, however, the universal makes the unity of the species, the particular makes its number. The legal descriptions of origin Bordeaux and Bordeaux Supérieur belong to the number.

Here we shall have to indulge in a little more history. These "descriptions of origin" are so loaded with references, they express the idea of collective heritage and ownership so well that, not so long ago, their delimitation gave rise to a hot dispute which was finally settled only by a decree published in the *Official Gazette* of February 19th, 1911.

Before they came to their decision, the legislators were bombarded with more or less justified claims that the description Bordeaux should be extended to wines which were sometimes far removed from the city of that name.

The archivist Brutails helped them to decide on the limits by bringing his historical knowledge to bear and making a clear distinction between the wines of the seneschalcy and those of the Uplands (Haut-Pays) in accordance with traditions dating from the Middle Ages.

In that distant era, the only wines entitled to the description Bordeaux were those harvested in the immediate vicinity of the city by winegrowers who were freemen of the city and dwelt *intra muros*. To guard the privilege King John had stated on April 15th, 1214: "We desire that all the wines of our citizens of Bordeaux, which come from the vines of their city, should travel freely on the river." In other words, all other wines were subject to a blockade and were discriminated against fiscally.

Like waves spreading out from a stone splashing in water, the description—or, more exactly, the privilege—was then extended to the 350 parishes of the seneschalcy of Guienne. Such was the legal position of the vineyards in 1789. It was not too critical.

The new administrative division of France into departments, on the threshold of the nineteenth century, once again extended the area of the description Bordeaux. Instead of the 350 parishes of the seneschalcy, it covered almost all the 554 communes of the Gironde. It was only a strike by the Council General that prevented the description being also extended to 63 communes of the Dordogne and Lot-et-Garonne.

After the decree of 1911, the winegrowers of the Lot-et-Garonne tried to call their wines "wines of the Bordeaux Uplands". This attempt was rejected by the courts since the description *Haut-Pays bordelais* was not a traditional one. Quite the contrary, in fact, since the term "Haut-Pays" was used to identify wines other than those known by the trademark Bordeaux. So much so, indeed, that cutting the city wines with wines from the Haut-Pays had always been prohibited, as is evidenced by numerous fiats of the Bordeaux *parlement* down the centuries. The Act of 1911 was thus perfectly straightforward. Its purpose was to fit the place-of-origin concept into the framework of modern law and to protect the description Bordeaux from the concept of "provenance" with all the possibilities of generalized fraud it entailed.

At this stage of regulation, however, the name "Bordeaux" covered all the growths of the Bordeaux region without distinction, including the Great Growths which had been the beneficiaries of the 1855 classification and which had made use of all their prestige to obtain the decree.

In early 1919, the problem of descriptions of origin came up again with a new urgency owing to the Peace

The Aquitaine basin is one of the principal winegrowing regions in France. The vine is mainly cultivated in the departmnt of the Gironde which groups, around the proud name of Bordeaux, a great number of famous designations such as Médoc, Graves, Sauternes, Barsac and St.-Emilion. Other vineyards are to be found around Bergerac and Monbazillac, in the middle reaches of the Dordogne; around Gaillac in the Albigeois and, finally, in the former province of Béarn, to the south of the Adour and the Gave de Pau.

Conference being held at Versailles. If respect for descriptions of origin was to be imposed upon Germany, internal regulations had to be set up. The Descriptions of Origin Act was promulgated on May 6th, 1919. From then on, legislation proliferated. The most decisive laws were the Capus Act of 1927 and the Decree-Act of 1935. The fact was that the winegrowers were unable to accept geographical origin as the sole criterion entitling to a "description". The 1919 Act was supplemented therefore by others which took account of new factors such as soil, vine species, degree of alcohol and yield per acre. Thus were born the *appellations d'origine contrôlée* (A.O.C.), the guaranteed descriptions of origin.

In the case of the Bordeaux region, the result of these provisions was a sort of hierarchy. It may, perhaps, have been a mistake to put the most limited description at the top and gradually descend to more and more general descriptions with an increasingly large production. Thus, in order of descent, a Pauillac growth was entitled to the descriptions PAUILLAC, MÉDOC and BORDEAUX.

To put it another way, a Pauillac wine which was considered to be unworthy of its name of origin and which lacked the characteristics required of a good Médoc could always be marketed as a BORDEAUX. This use of the description BORDEAUX as a catch-all was to produce great confusion in view of the world-wide renown of the greatest fine-wine producing region in France. However famous some celebrated châteaux or a few restricted descriptions might be, the foreign wine-lover had great difficulty in understanding that the word BORDEAUX standing alone indicated the more modest products of the Bordeaux region. The most recent example of this regrettable confusion was given by the world press when commenting on a speech made by the then French Minister of Agriculture, Mr. Edgard Pisani, during a visit to Bordeaux. He said: "I have been and still am struck by the fact that the 'Bordeaux' flag is fast reaching the stage when it waves over the most mediocre goods and that so much disorder has been created in this winegrowing area that the first care of every winegrower is to put on a château label instead of the Bordeaux one."

Being badly informed about the A.O.C. legislation, all that some journalists gleaned from his statement was the inference that Bordeaux wine was mediocre in general. Nonetheless the Minister's criticism was perfectly justified and the reluctance of some Girondin producers to use the name BORDEAUX was quite understandable. It does not mean, however, that they were entirely in the right. Although the descriptions BORDEAUX and BORDEAUX SUPÉRIEUR were used to denote the more mediocre products, the great mass of BORDEAUX wines in terms of the Capus Act were of excellent quality and widely used to improve growths better placed economically.

It was necessary to escape from that blind alley and take up the challenge to logic. The question was who would take the first step on the way back to a sound tradition. One solution would have been for the Great Growths to meet their historic responsibilities and once more inscribe the name of Bordeaux on the pediment of their fame. In that way, they would have taken up anew their centuries-old mission and, like true nobles, would have returned to the head of their troops and imposed discipline amongst them. The hesitation to sign such a blank cheque, however, was quite understandable. The other solution, more in keeping with the style of our era, was for those involved to take the revaluation of the description BORDEAUX into their own hands and that, in fact, was what they did.

Thanks to Mr. Pierre Perromat, President of the National Institute of Descriptions of Origin but who never abandoned the presidency of the BORDEAUX and BORDEAUX SUPÉRIEUR wine syndicate, these wines have, since 1967, enjoyed full descriptions of origin. They are subject to tasting and analytical tests like most of the other Gironde descriptions and have recovered their independence. There is no longer a catch-all description. Henceforth, the only refuge for disinherited Bordeaux descriptions is the category: "wines for everyday consumption".

The description BORDEAUX CLAIRET, which derives from the description BORDEAUX, has been highly fashionable in recent years. It is a rosé wine from any red grape already covered by the regional description and is obtained by "bleeding" the vat before the must has taken on its full colour. BORDEAUX CLAIRET has nothing in common with the old claret, which was a briefly fermented red wine. It is none the less a charming, fruity wine, both delicate and cheerful.

THE WINES OF THE LEFT BANK
OF THE GIRONDE AND THE GARONNE

MÉDOC

In 1855, a patriot of the Médoc, Mr. Saint-Amant, could write: "The Médoc appears rich and sumptuous: yet it both is and it isn't. A great year lavishes abundance there, but such a year arrives but once every three or four years. In other years, it is difficult to meet expenses, which are much greater on the large domains where people talk unceasingly of restricting their size without ever taking any measure to that end. The owner of a great growth of Médoc should not sink all his fortune in it, but half at most, in order to support the costs and be able to await the favourable moment to sell his wines. The revenue from the vines is precarious and unequal. Such a domain should be held as a subsidiary and its owner should glory in it."

A century ago, the great Bordeaux wines had reached their zenith. What would Mr. Saint-Amant write now about the wonderful vocation of an area which is noble among the noblest?

It will be realized that the period in which Mr. Saint-Amant was defining the viticulture of Médoc was also that of the celebrated "classification". The idea of the "parish" (which dated from 1755) gave place to that of the "château", the "manor-house", thereby marking a dual evolution in the vineyard: a technical evolution as the practice of château bottling developed and an economic evolution whereby the exploitation of the Médoc was improved by an injection of business capital. In 1855, Médoc viticulture was beginning to reveal a veritable humanism. A great Médoc winegrower proved it not so long ago by showing us his "book of reason". It was the treasured wealth of a long experience of husbandry. In it we find, indeed, traces of events which shook the world throughout the century: wars, revolutions and massacres; but what our venerable friend noted down was, perhaps, more important. It was the creation of that masterpiece, an eminent bottle of wine. Nothing but short remarks, dates and figures, but these notes have a Homeric quality, the flavour of an epic constantly rolled up and unrolled to the rhythm of the seasons and the rhythm of work. The patriarch had recorded, for future generations, the softness of a morning, the freshness of an evening, the time taken by a wagon to come from the vine to the wine-store, the song of the first cuckoo or the flight of the symbolic blackbirds which formed part of the folklore of the domain.

In Médoc, viticulture is first and foremost an act of faith. If the earth were to explode tomorrow, the justification of our existence would be that we are able to present to our Creator this book of reason in which a wise man questioned the whole of nature to discover the right moment for "pouring", bottling or ploughing.

To the extent that Médoc is unquestionably a work of art, its production, like that of the other great wines of Bordeaux, involves an irreducible minimum of traditional husbandry. This does not mean that, as Paul Valéry put it, the Médoc winegrower "backs into the future". He is by no means filled with nostalgia for the past. He refuses to subject the traditional vineyard to an experimental aspect of technology, but no one is more delighted when technology performs some function which is of service to the vineyard. If, for example, our planners clear away the spider's web of electricity and telephone wires from the Médoc skies, we shall see this "husbandman" immediately adopt the aircraft or the helicopter to spread insecticides or fungicides. If the agricultural machinery industry manages to supply him with a reasonable engine for his ploughing, he will abandon animal traction which, in some places, is still indispensable.

Over a distance of fifty miles in the direction of the river, with a depth inland of six to ten miles, the vineyards of Médoc produce wines which, though different, are all remarkable, even in years which are poor in alcohol content. There are no finer, more thoroughbred, more intellectualized wines. This nobility proceeds from their bouquet and aroma which are unique among the great French wines.

The truth is that a Médoc can hold its peak of perfection for a very long time. When President Albert Lebrun came to Pauillac to open the first of the famous festivals to longevity, it was not only the centenarian winegrowers who were fêted. An 1834 growth was tasted and that, too, was in excellent health.

The northern part of the Médoc Peninsula constitutes the generic place-name description MÉDOC.

This region stretches from Saint-Seurin-de-Cadourne to the Pointe de Grave and skirts the Gironde estuary over a distance of twelve miles, its width being from four to five miles.

At the very edge of the river, vineyards cover a strip of gravelly land, cut by shallow valleys, which is from one to two miles wide. It is this tongue of land which produces the best wines. On the other soils (clayey limestones), the wines produced are more commonplace but are held worthy of the name "Great Ordinary".

In the 1855 classification, Médoc was not allotted any classed or "Superior Bourgeois" growths but only "Bourgeois" growths. There were quite a number of these, however, and they often fetched prices well above their position in the Médoc hierarchy. Eleven communes possessed such "Bourgeois" growths: Saint-Germain-d'Esteuil, Ordonac-et-Potensac, Saint-Yzans, Couquèques, Blaignan, Saint-Christoly-de-Médoc, Bégadan, Lesparre, Valeyrac, Civrac and Prignac.

To the south of this region, towards Bordeaux, is the area which has earned the place-name description of origin HAUT-MÉDOC. It covers a number of sub-descriptions which are well-known throughout the world and are among the brightest jewels in the Bordeaux crown, MARGAUX glowing in their midst like a royal ruby. Since the dawn of time, several neighbouring parishes have shared in its ancient renown but nowadays four communes, in addition to that of Margaux, are entitled to the description, namely Cantenac, Soussans, Arsac and Labarde. CHÂTEAU MARGAUX, whose nobility is equalled only by the historic memories attached to the domain and the magnificent mansion of the same name, is a *Premier Cru Classé*, or "First Growth". The description MARGAUX as a whole connotes a great, sometimes very great, fine, full-bodied and elegant wine with a world-wide reputation.

Moulis is situated in the centre of the Haut-Médoc. At the end of the Hundred Years War, this little area was still more sylvan than viticultural and Pey Berland, the future Archbishop of Bordeaux, used to graze his father's flocks there. Moulis, however, with its good-quality gravel soils, clearly had a winegrowing vocation. Moulis growths are mentioned in the list drawn up by the Intendancy of Guienne in 1767 but, according to the 1855 classification, it contained only "Superior Bourgeois" growths.

The wines of MOULIS, which are very much appreciated in Germany, Belgium and the Netherlands, have the rare advantage that they will keep in perfect safety. In addition to the delicacy, bouquet and elegance of the great Médocs, they have also a balanced constitution which guarantees them a happy old age.

The Listrac vineyards occupy one of the highest hill-tops in the Haut-Médoc. The growths of this place-name description are reminiscent of the MOULIS in their body and vinosity. For centuries, this parish has also produced white wines, which strongly resemble the best white GRAVES. The 1855 classification gave no classed growths to Listrac but it had several "Superior Bourgeois" growths.

"Passers-by, you are now entering the ancient and celebrated vineyard of Saint-Julien, bow low. . . ." Such is the proud inscription at the boundary of Saint-Julien-Beychevelle. It is now applied to an excellent vineyard, one of the richest dependencies of the Haut-Médoc. It refers, however, to the sailors' custom of striking their sails in salute when passing the Château de Beychevelle, residence of the Duke of Epernon, Grand Admiral of France. SAINT-JULIEN can be distinguished from the other famous wines of the Haut-Médoc by its beautiful purple colour, its great elegance and its mellowness. More full-bodied than MARGAUX, less hearty than PAUILLAC; it can also be recognized by a very personal bouquet that develops quickly.

Encouraged by its winegrowing mayor, Saint-Julien is steadily increasing its fame. There is so much competition among the producers in this commune that several "Superior Bourgeois" or "Bourgeois" growths, which were formerly almost unknown, have become as much valued as a "classified growth".

Situated about thirty miles from Bordeaux, Pauillac is the most important of the winegrowing communes of the Médoc. It has a House of Wine and is the headquarters of the *Commanderie du Bontemps-Médoc*. This fraternity uses the town as a starting point for all its ceremonies, the most important of which, the Flower Festival, is the occasion for a gathering of lovers of Bordeaux wine from all over the world. The place-name description PAUILLAC also applies to the wines harvested in certain of the lands of Saint-Sauveur, Saint-Estèphe and Cissac. The Lesparre Decree, one of the most detailed instruments of viticultural jurisprudence, lists the vineyards, plot by plot, in which PAUILLAC is grown. In some cases, even the rows of vine-stocks are measured and numbered. This description, the most representative of the Gironde winegrowing region, is the only one which possesses two first growths, three seconds, one fourth, eleven fifths and a whole train of "Superior Bourgeois" and "Bourgeois" growths, the nobility and brilliant qualities of which are often very close to the Great Growths.

PAUILLAC wines, whether they have a great coat of arms or a simple shield, are the most masterful of the wines of the Médoc. The great years give them characteristics which can be rather surprising if they are drunk before the ageing process which develops their incomparable charms. Nevertheless a PAUILLAC, even when it is too young and astringent, charms the experienced palate. This wine is always promising and has never lied.

The place-name description SAINT-ESTÈPHE is reserved solely for growths from the commune of that name, one of the largest in the Médoc. The SAINT-ESTÈPHE wines have an individual bouquet, and are delicate, mellow and distinguished. The soil, which is gravelly over an iron-pan subsoil, produces five classified growths, two of them being seconds; numerous "Bourgeois" growths, and a whole series of "artisan" and "peasant" growths. This rather byzantine hierarchy is very often pushed aside, however, by the great reputation for quality of all the SAINT-ESTÈPHE wines.

The time has now come to speak of the famous "classification". To what extent did the grandeur and luxury of the Châteaux of Médoc affect the judgement passed on their growths? It would be difficult to say. It is certain, however, that the first Bordeaux labels using a château name were always adorned with the picture of a genuine château. It must also be admitted that great mansions are to be found throughout the Médoc area. For the most part, they reflect the taste of the early nineteenth century when they were built. They are reminiscent of the neo-Gothic style popularized by Sir Walter Scott in 1812, when he built his Abbotsford manor on the south bank of the Tweed.

The main factors taken into account in establishing a hierarchy of quality were, it is true, the taste of the wine, the price it fetched, the more or less cared-for appearance of the vineyard, technical details of wine-making equipment and a few historical references. Nevertheless, since the initiative for classification came from a Chartrons firm of wine merchants, then at the zenith of its power, which either owned or was closely connected with the largest domains in the Médoc, we may well think that the 1855 classification reflected a vague notion of "caste" (at least to the extent that subjectivity inevitably played its part).

Hence, the châteaux of the Médoc have, from the very beginning, been a commercial factor as well as an architectural one. They formed the backbone of the classification system and spread the fame of Bordeaux wine far and wide. Consequently, a château label was desired for every growth of any quality in the Bordeaux area, even if the winegrower lived in the simplest of dwellings. The multiplicity of châteaux in the Gironde is by no means a product of Gascon ostentation, of a rather childish arrogance; it is the result of hard economic facts. It became necessary, therefore, to regulate the legal use of the word château. The Decree of September 30th, 1949 fixed the following conditions for its use:

1. The wine must be entitled to a place-name description of origin.

2. The wine must come from an agricultural holding, designated by the word château or by an equivalent word, which must genuinely exist as an agricultural holding and be already precisely designated by these words and expressions.

3. The name of the château or its equivalent must be restricted to the produce of the agricultural holding designated by the proposed words.

Legal usage, by its interpretation of the word château, had already prepared the way for the evolution implicit in the Decree. A ruling by the Bordeaux Civil Court, dated May 8th, 1939, had declared that the word château denoted a given agricultural or viticultural holding.

It should not be hastily concluded, however, that the majority of the châteaux in the Bordeaux region are of recent construction or that they exist only in the official register of wine growths. The ancient seneschalcy of Guienne, with its fascinating history and wealth of legend, is a veritable goldmine for the archaeologist and the art-lover. Noble mansions abound, often surrounded by famous vineyards.

Thus we find in the Médoc, for example, the Château d'Angludet which, although rebuilt in the eighteenth century, was the lair of a notorious robber baron during the Hundred Years War. The Château d'Issan at Margaux also dates from the Anglo-Gascon alliance. With its nine pavilions and pyramid-topped towers, it has a fairy-tale appearance. The present buildings have succeeded two or three earlier structures at one time inhabited by famous French families.

Ornamented by its Grecian façade, Château Margaux is rather more than the most famous "label" in the world. It once belonged to King Edward III of England. In the twelfth century, it was known by the name of La Mothe. At that time it was, of course, a fortified castle. It was successively the property of the d'Albret, de Montferrand and de Durfort families. Towards the middle of the eighteenth century, its then owner, Monsieur de Fumel, assisted the Marquis de Lafayette to embark for America, despite the opposition of the Court. The present owner of Château Margaux is Mr. Pierre Ginestet, Grand Chancellor of the Bordeaux Wine Academy.

A little to the north, at Pauillac, Château Mouton-Rothschild has known four generations of the Barons de Rothschild since 1853. In the more remote past, the great winegrowers of Mouton were the Seigneur de Pons (1350), the Duke of Gloucester (1430), Jean Dunois, Gaston de Foix, the Dukes of Joyeuse and the Dukes of Epernon. Baron Philippe de Rothschild, the present proprietor, has established a superb wine museum adjacent to the wine-sheds of the Château. The objects on display are rich beyond compare but give not the slightest impression of ostentation. They include a Mycenean goblet of the thirteenth century B.C., masterpieces of the German goldsmith's art and paintings by Picasso, Giacometti and Juan Gris.

GRAVES

Since time immemorial, the lands of Graves have surrounded Bordeaux, except on the east where the ancient city is bounded by the river. Since the vineyards of Bordeaux are primarily a creation of the city, Graves has always been their focal point. It was not the vineyard which gave birth to the town but the citizens of Bordeaux who, having planted the civilizing grape, lavished the most constant and attentive care upon it and honoured it as a divinity. In the Middle Ages, the grape was still being harvested *intra muros*, in the very centre of Bordeaux. The Gascon terriers (land-holding registers) have revealed the existence of a vineyard entirely within the town, the harvest from which was sufficient to stock the cellars of the *Jurats* and the chapters. By the end of September, baskets were being filled with grapes in the Rue de Saint-Genès, near St. Nicholas' Church, at the Croix-Blanche, at Terre-Nègre, in the Place Dauphine, at the Palais-Gallien and the Rue des Capérans, charming spots which the ravages of urbanization have not spared. Nowadays, the vineyard of Graves begins at the Jalle de Blanquefort, the southern boundary of the Médoc. To the south, it extends as far as Langon, having left the river at Virelade to encircle the Cérons and Sauternes-Barsac areas as, to the north, it once encircled the former Burdigala. Its total length is 38 miles and its average width does not exceed six miles.

It was for the wine of Graves (and not for the others which were then too far from Bordeaux) that the collegiate government of the city proclaimed the edicts forming the basis of the most extraordinary legal monument of all time: the famous *Privilège des Vins*, as evidenced by the highly secret records of the deliberations of the *Jurade*, otherwise called the *Livre des Bouillons* from the copper bosses—*boullons*—which protected its cover.

Halfway through the Middle Ages, with the same eagerness to regulate everything, the *Jurade* of Bordeaux set up the official corps of Taverners. Although this seemed, at first sight, an attempt to introduce a police force into the wineshops and keep them orderly, the main objective of the *Jurats*, in this case, was to control frauds within the municipal jurisdiction. For example, to help sales of nondescript wines, it had been customary to cry "a very drinkable wine of Graves". This commercial misrepresentation now became impossible, and much too dangerous for an official clothed in all the majesty of the municipality.

Moreover, all the control measures applied at both the production and distribution stages and which had such a favourable effect on the reputation of Bordeaux wines, originated from the desire felt by the wine-growing burghers to protect their urban growths, i.e. the place-name description GRAVES. That is why the Bordeaux archives for the sixteenth, seventeenth and eighteenth centuries reveal the names and activities of the inspectors of urban vineyards, an office that was already of very ancient foundation.

Today, in our mind's eye, we can see these velvet-clad burghers jogging on horseback across the vineyards. The warm, juicy bunches are presented to them on white cloths and we see them, having brushed away a greedy wasp with a gloved and beringed hand, tasting a grape thoughtfully and then, raising their heads, gazing wisely and reflectively at the vine.

In permanent session throughout the harvest time, the *Jurade* would listen to the reports of its itinerant experts and, after debate, would fix the day on which the grape pickers, the *laborador de vinhas* could begin picking with the best chance of obtaining a wine of quality. The great bell of the City Hall would then "ring in the wine-harvest".

The period when there was no Bordeaux wine other than Graves was, *par excellence*, the time of CLARET. The English gave the name to the produce of a region much smaller than the Bordeaux region of today but the antiquity of which, as compared with the Bordeaux winegrowing area as a whole, is unquestionable.

Much closer to us, in the middle of the eighteenth century, any red Bordeaux exported to Germany became, for the importing wine merchant, Pontac wine, the name of the then owner of Château Haut-Brion, the uncrowned king of Graves. The future member of the "big four" served as an insignia for the whole vineyard, a century before the 1855 classification.

During the whole nineteenth century the place-name description GRAVES was predominantly "red". Nowadays, in the second half of the twentieth century, the grape distribution has virtually returned to what it was in its hey-day, namely, the era when the harvests of La Brède and Martillac were gathered by Charles Secondat de Montesquieu. This new balance between whites and reds is, perhaps, mainly due to the fact that the city of Bordeaux for the last two hundred years has been extending its limits, intensifying building operations and swallowing up communes which were formerly famous for their production of red wine: Caudéran, Talence, Mérignac etc. Moreover, ten miles to the south of Bordeaux, in centres such as Léognan which had been entirely devoted to red grapes before the phylloxera crisis, whole estates have been replanted with white grapes. At present, the figures for the production of GRAVES are 880,000 gallons of white wine and 330,000 gallons of red.

However that may be, the white GRAVES have often reflected great glory on the place-name and have been deservedly fashionable, as has once again been the case during the last twenty years. But this fashion has never been the result of a snobbish insistance that white GRAVES should be this or that, that it must be dry or semi-dry. It is what it has to be, whatever a few professional food-pundits may say. The white GRAVES harvested in the north of the region are naturally dry with a charming touch of acidity. At Martillac, La Brède, Saint-Morillon, Saint-Sèlve, Saint-Médard and Cadaujac, they are still dry but already softened by the suave bouquet characteristic of the soil of Léognan. Speaking of these thoroughbred wines, Rabelais described them as "gay and fluttering". At Portets, Arbanats, Landiras and Budos, they became more unctuous, trickling down the inside of the glass. The brokers distinguish these wines by saying they are fat. Lastly, the nearer we come to Langon, the more the wines are reminiscent of CÉRONS mellowness. In the Graves country, therefore, some less dry wines are found alongside the more numerous dry wines, all of them being admirable because they are quite natural.

Leaving aside all personal preference, however legitimate it might be, the soul of Bordeaux is undoubtedly to be found in a glass of red GRAVES.

As often happens in the case of the eldest of a large family, GRAVES bears the most striking resemblance to its father. MÉDOC, with its subtle and complex bouquet, or SAINT-EMILION, with its reckless gallantry, need envy their elder brother in nothing except the dominating fragrance which follows a red GRAVES everywhere like an invisible escutcheon. It is the perfume which has been transmitted from stock to stock and from vat to vat for over 2,000 years. One has to experience this privilege of the red GRAVES in order to become convinced.

That is what I must have perceived at a very early age when my grandfather first gave me a small piece of goatsmilk cheese (to clean my palate) and after it a finger of HAUT-BRION 1888. In that already remote period, the growth was not called a red GRAVES, as it is today, but a GRAVES DE BORDEAUX. The memory of that initiation and of that inward resplendence has, once and for all, enabled me to identify a Bordeaux wine, whether noble or artisan, red or white, from the left bank or the right bank of the Garonne.

Of course, one has to be up-to-date. It must be realized that there has been, not a development of taste—taste has not developed since the Parthenon—but a certain depravation of taste. Some will claim that henceforth the general public will be looking for supple, round red wines; in other words, wines stripped of their authentic character. With respect to some products without breeding or which have been badly vinified, the general public may be perfectly right. It may well be that agreeable mediocrity is preferable to decayed and aggressive nobility. This is a valid point of view but for anyone who tasted his first GRAVES three or four years after his last feeding bottle, the criterion could never be that of the wine-canning industry.

A good GRAVES remains "as eternity itself has shaped it". It is food for the body and the soul. It has a luminous robe the colour of those rustic window-panes through which our childhood reveries recreated a summer twilight in the midst of winter. It is as elegant as the solution to a Euclidian theorem. Above all, since it is from Graves, it has that bracing and discreet bitterness that makes it kin to all the savours of the Bordeaux soil.

Direct in its taste, frank in its attack, though full of mysteries and chaste aromas, GRAVES rises from the depths of memory like a promise of happiness and peace, so needful in this anguish-stricken world.

THE CÉRONS REGION

Situated 22 miles to the south-east of Bordeaux, on the left bank of the Garonne, the Cérons region is made up of three communes: Cérons, Illats and Podensac. The boundaries of this place-name description are slightly fictional. There are dry CÉRONS wines which possess the characteristics of the finest GRAVES, the only distinction being a particularly fruity aroma, while other CÉRONS are closely related to SAUTERNES-BARSAC. The sweet CÉRONS are, however, lighter than the growths obtained in the soil of Barsac.

The soil of Cérons, silicious gravel over clayey limestone, is virtually the same as in Sauternes. To obtain sweet CÉRONS, picking is carried out (as in Sauternes) by successive stages and the must, which is comparatively less rich, nevertheless produces wines with a strength of 12° to 15° of alcohol and, in addition, 1° to 3° of *liqueur*. The CÉRONS type is distinguished by its nervousness, elegance and extremely fine bouquet. All these qualities, combined with the ambiguous position of the Cérons region, have caused its produces to be described as a link between the best dry white wines and the most famous of the great sweet wines.

In Cérons more than elsewhere, we thus encounter those imponderables which make white Bordeaux so variable. The place-name description produces annually between 330,000 and 396,000 gallons.

The essential originality of the winemaking process in the Sauternes area consists, first of all, in the method of harvesting.

Normal ripening is insufficient. The winegrower has to wait for the grape to become "overripe" and develop a rot which is so special, so peculiar to the microclimate that it is described as "noble". It is caused by a characteristic mycoderm, which flourishes only in certain winegrowing regions and which is called *botrytis cinerea*, a minute fungus which, in great years, produces the famous "roast" that can be recognized in old bottles.

It is not always easy to turn the *botrytis* to best account. Its effect on a given bunch of grapes is not uniform. Hence the need to harvest by picking individual grapes. If it rains, picking has to be suspended until the grapes dry out. The result is that the harvest has to be staggered over a period of up to two months, and quantity is sacrificed to quality, yields being less than 170 gallons per acre.

Thanks to this process, which is quite unique in viticultural technology (it amounts to a veritable concentration of the vintage on the vine), the musts have a sugar content of between 15º and 20º or even more on leaving the press. In 1929, 25º were found while, in 1959, some musts were recorded which attained 30º.

In an average year, the ideal is to obtain a balance after fermentation between the alcohol content (14º) and the unconverted sugar content (4º of *liqueur*). In a very great vintage year, the divergence can be considerable. The care lavished on the wine-store is mainly aimed at activating alcoholic fermentation. As will be realized, the glory of SAUTERNES-BARSAC is an expensive one. There can never be any question, in this soil, of sacrificing the supreme, the "extravagant" quality to considerations of cost.

The wine of Sauternes-Barsac is still and will always remain one of the few things in this world whose inimitable nobility brushes aside the notion of "productivity", as conceived of by economists dealing in large quantities of ordinary consumer goods rather than rare products.

The Sauternais can best be compared, therefore, to a dream country ruled over by a wizard, the wizard being the most famous wine on earth, the wine of kings and the king of wines. The region must be entered deliberately, but once we are there, time seems to lose its meaning and the ordinary world, humming with cares and duties, drifts far away from our eyes and from our memories. All the enchantments of this magic land weave round us a fairy net which holds us willing prisoners in a life of rarest pleasure.

I can remember a fine afternoon in June. The park of the Château of Suduiraut appeared, under a thrilling sky, to be rising out of the vaporous haze which bathes Fragonard's *Fête de Saint-Cloud* or Jean-Baptiste Pater's *Garden Party*, or was it the slight mist of the *Embarkation for Cythera*? Maurice Chevalier was singing, clutching a jeroboam of CHÂTEAU D'YQUEM to his breast, proving that there are mysterious affinities between the most varied forms of art. The only condition to be fulfilled is that, however appearances may change, artistic creation must remain faithful to the classic standards of quality. What music, painting and song offer us in their highest forms is also to be found in the subtle bouquet of a SAUTERNES-BARSAC. That is why you should make the circuit of the Sauternes country (which is well signposted for the visitor) at a slow speed with the engine barely ticking over, just as you move slowly and appreciatively past the masterpieces in the Uffizi Gallery.

There are some discoveries that are worthless unless you make them for yourself. In the Palazzo Vecchio in Florence, for example, I came across the most intelligent of guides. He watches visitors coming, going, dreaming, strolling and sometimes retracing their steps (which is so important). Then, smiling, he intervenes, simply because someone has overlooked something he loves. I should like to imitate him and not drag the reader by main force to the entrance of a vineyard if he is attracted by the slate-crowned roof of a tower. Let it suffice that, en route, you do not neglect a growth which, once known, will have a permanent place in your heart and in your memory. Whether you approach the Sauternais circuit from the beginning or from the end, you will find only one road marked "No Entry": the road to mediocrity. It is a magic carpet straight out of a fairy-tale and, if the turnings appear frequent, it could be that your head might be turning round a little.

THE WINES BETWEEN
THE GARONNE AND THE DORDOGNE

PREMIÈRES CÔTES DE BORDEAUX

When the contemporaries of Ausonius visited him, they did so languorously stretched out in boats furnished with carpets and cushions, under canopies of laurel branches and with pennants streaming. This patrician luxury which was shared by winegrowers and poets, men of the world and philosophers in an intimate society marks the zenith of the region now called the Premières Côtes de Bordeaux. This place-name description covers thirty-four communes along the right bank of the Garonne, between Bassens and Saint-Macaire. It is essentially an area of abrupt slopes which dominate the river for 38 miles. The plateaux of Entre-Deux-Mers (Between the Two Seas) forms its hinterland as far as the left bank of the Dordogne.

Despite its exceptional length and the size of its production (3,300,000 gallons), the Premières Côtes region produces growths which head the list at international exhibitions. Although the northern part of the region is almost exclusively devoted to red wines, the southern part, beyond Gambes, covers what are usually called the great white wines of the right bank.

The red Premières Côtes de Bordeaux were undoubtedly among the first Bordeaux wines regularly exported. Pey Berland, the last Gascon Archbishop of Bordeaux, possessed an important red vineyard in the Parish of Bouillac. Under the archiepiscopal privileges, therefore, it was a Premières Côtes de Bordeaux growth which the English, on their arrival with the "wine fleet", would purchase as a first priority.

When young, these wines are robust, fruity, rich in tannin and very tonic. With age, they acquire considerable delicacy and the bouquet characteristic of the Bordeaux soil. As for the white, semi-dry or sweet Premières Côtes de Bordeaux, they sometimes reach such a degree of delicacy and elegance that their nobility requires some specific place-name descriptions in the form of enclaves: such is the case with Cadillac and Gabarnac.

LOUPIAC AND SAINTE-CROIX-DU-MONT

Loupiac and Sainte-Croix-du-Mont are also enclaves in the Premières Côtes de Bordeaux but have no legal connection with the latter place-name description.

Both Loupiac and Sainte-Croix-du-Mont belong to the kingdom of the *Semillon, Sauvignon* and *Muscadelle* grapes. Apart from this triumvirate, no other grape is permitted to enter into the composition of these illustrious sweet growths. On the abrupt and sunny slopes, the bunches of grapes are not picked until they have reached a subtle degree of over-ripeness. And yet, what delicacy, what tang of the soil is to be found in a Loupiac or a Sainte-Croix!

What gaiety is to be found in one or another of these bottles! Without wearing the sumptuous garb of a Sauternes, they too evoke the bronze satin in which Watteau dresses the beauties in his enchanted parks.

The sweet warmth of these wines, their bouquet, their topaz robe go beyond the vocabulary of the gourmet; it would need the music of a Verlaine poem to give an adequate impression of so much grace.

The boundary of the place-name description Loupiac is a little to the south of Cadillac, whose best growths are in no way inferior to those of the two gems of the Premières Côtes de Bordeaux.

HAUT-BENAUGE

The place-name description Haut-Benauge is restricted to white wines produced by the communes of Arbis, Cantois, Escoussans, Ladaux, Soulignac, Saint-Pierre-de-Bat and Targon. This region, although much smaller than the former county of Benauge, has nevertheless retained as its centre the enormous and majestic castle built by the redoubtable Lords of Benauge on the hill of Arbis. In former times, the county was called "Black Benauge" and was darkened by the oak forests from which was obtained the timber for the manufacture of the *barriques*. But the winegrowers cleared the land and, ever since, the serried ranks of vine-stocks have occupied the flanks of the valleys. Black Benauge is one of the world's most beautiful viticultural areas. It produces a white, semi-dry wine which has harvested awards and medals.

CÔTES DE BORDEAUX-SAINT-MACAIRE

The place-name description Côtes de Bordeaux-Saint-Macaire extends the Premières Côtes de Bordeaux towards the south. It covers the communes of Saint-Macaire, Pian, Saint-Pierre-d'Aurillac, Saint-Martin-de-Sescas, Caudrot, Saint-André-du-Bois, Saint-Martial, Saint-Laurent-du-Bois, Saint-Laurent-du-Plan and Sainte-Foy-la-Longue. Few white wines are so adaptable as Côtes de Bordeaux-Saint-Macaire. Robust and fine, they form an agreeable accompaniment to sea-food as well as to desserts and even certain roasts.

GRAVES DE VAYRES

In the vicinity of Libourne, on the ancient road which once linked Burdigala to Lutetia, the communes of Vayres and Arveyres, on the left bank of the Dordogne, constitute the winegrowing territory entitled to the place-name description Graves de Vayres. This designates a colourful and subtle red wine, of great delicacy, reminiscent of the second growth of Pomerol and endowed with the precious commercial quality of being drinkable at an early age. The white wines from the same soil can be distinguished from the excellent products of Entre-Deux-Mers by their mellowness and their very typical aroma.

ENTRE-DEUX-MERS

Entre-Deux-Mers is a name which really appeals to the imagination. It evokes all kinds of ideas of distant voyages and unknown lands. People who are unfamiliar with the place-names of these great winegrowing regions are generally disappointed to learn that "Between the Two Seas" refers to the territory between the right bank of the Garonne and the left bank of the Dordogne. The place-name description does not, of course, include those which have just been defined but it nevertheless extends over the largest and most productive part of the Bordeaux vineyard, and in fact, covers one-fifth of the area of the department. The spontaneous luxuriance of the vegetation in Entre-Deux-Mers and the survival of large tracts of oak, hornbeam and elm are relics of the ancient forest cleared by the Romans to plant the civilizing vine. After the Barbarian invasions, immense tracts of these woodlands reappeared and, this time, it was the monks who launched a new attack on the hardy forest mass. The Abbey of Saint-Girard, at La Sauve, was founded in 1090. For centuries, this community shared, with the monks of Sainte-Croix, at Bordeaux, the privilege of supervising the winegrowing destiny of Entre-Deux-Mers. In 1547, a wine of the region was selling for 20 to 25 crowns the *tonneau* as against only 18 to 22 crowns for a Libournais-Fronsadais product. The place-name description of origin Entre-Deux-Mers, which has been defined since 1924, became a guaranteed description by the decree of July 31th, 1937. According to this legal instrument, the place-name description can only be applied to white wines made exclusively from the noble grapes: *Sauvignon, Semillon, Muscadelle,* and *Merlot,* harvested within the area delimited. Red wines of the same origin must carry the place-name descriptions Bordeaux or Bordeaux Supérieur.

In the last few years, spurred on by the youthful officers of its viticultural syndicate, Entre-Deux-Mers has regained its ancient fame. This was achieved through a policy strongly emphasizing quality which is intended to give this dry white wine back its natural characteristics. Fifteen years ago, the persons responsible for the place-name description decided to increase the proportion of *Sauvignon* in the vineyards. As this trend has continued ever since whenever new vines were being planted, Entre-Deux-Mers has once again become a very fruity and recognizable wine, both fresh and nervous, which meets the requirements of the consumer of today. It should not be forgotten, however, that Entre-Deux-Mers is a Bordeaux wine. In other words, it is an hygienic wine, a healthy wine, just like the red wines of similar origin. In addition to the incomparable satisfaction to the taste buds, it possesses other important qualities which should be mentioned: its richness in vitamin P and its high bactericidal power which is completely independent of its alcoholic content. Invigorating, tonic and diuretic, it is just the wine for people who have difficulty in taking other white wines. It is an unfailing destroyer of the pathogens which are found in raw vegetables and well-informed doctors do not hesitate to attribute to it therapeutic virtues also. All this has been known empirically for a very long time, but serious studies carried out by learned professors and their pupils in the laboratories and universities on Entre-Deux-Mers have made it possible to formulate the benificent action of this growth in scientific terms.

After many years of endeavour, Baron Philippe de Rothschild at last achieved the reclassification of Mouton Rothschild from Second Growth to First. This was achieved in 1973, and crowns a lifetime's work in improving and cultivating the wine. In the background to this harvesting scene can be seen Château Mouton, which contains the famous wine museum.

The canton of Sainte-Foy-la-Grande comprises only fifteen communes, but the controlled place-name description SAINTE-FOY-BORDEAUX has nineteen. They have been detached from the north-eastern part of the vast Entre-Deux-Mers region to delimit a sweet or semi-dry white wine, the dominant characteristics of which are suppleness and elegance. Coming from the Périgord confines of the Bordeaux country, this white wine is, if dry, a perfect foil for the oysters, shellfish and delicious shad caught in the Dordogne.

THE WINES OF THE RIGHT
BANK OF THE DORDOGNE AND THE GIRONDE

SAINT-EMILION

On the right bank of the Dordogne, Saint-Emilion and its vineyards are high places where the wind of the spirit blows free. The whole of France and a good part of the civilized world can testify to that.

The "great" little city—with apologies for the paradox—has known a cosmopolitan animation every year since very ancient times. In fact, Camille Jullian, in his history of the Gauls, states that Saint-Emilion was one of the ritual stages on the journey to Compostella. A pious and motley crowd always filled the monolithic church. An extraordinary vitality and spirituality overflowed from those narrow streets and corbelled houses, and faith in a world in which men were brothers was proclaimed from all the towers in joyous peals of bells and in solemn fanfares of trumpets.

At Saint-Emilion, the tumultuous heartbeat of French history can be felt. Here and there, as you walk about the town, you suddenly encounter an astonishingly fresh vision of the past, whether it be the Tour du Roi or the Grotte des Girondins. But in this acropolis where all the friends of wine come to worship together in the high traditions of the past, there are other voices than those of stones, vigorous human voices raised in eloquent testimony of the centuries which have passed.

Today as yesterday, the vine and wine are the reason for living, the cause of happiness and, sometimes, suffering for the viticultural peoples of the eight communes which make up the place-name description: Saint-Emilion, Saint-Laurent-des-Combes, Saint-Hippolyte, Saint-Christophe-des-Bardes, Saint-Etienne-de-Lisse, Saint-Sulpice-des-Faleyrens, Saint-Pey-d'Armens and Vignonet. The area of the place-name description amounts to 11,250 acres.

In our days, the poets have glorified the powerful and noble wine of SAINT-EMILION, as did Henri d'Andeli in the eleventh century. In our days, we may compare SAINT-EMILION to the nectar of the gods, as Louis XIV did in 1650. It is not only the town of stone which is immutable. As well known in the past as the wines of Graves, the wines of Saint-Emilion continue their royal career without any artificial vinification. When the weight of years has broken down the other wines and has left in the bottles nothing but a tasteless and colourless water, then it is that SAINT-EMILION develops all its wealth and all its perfume. "The wine of Saint-Emilion," wrote Victor Rendu, "has body, a beautiful colour, an agreeable delicacy, generosity and a special bouquet which is found in particular in the best sections of this distinguished vineyard. Good Saint-Emilion wine should, after its early years, have a dark, brilliant and velvety colour and a touch of bitterness which flatters the palate. In addition, it must have body which does not prevent it from becoming very smooth at a later stage. It becomes very much finer after six months in bottle but does not reach its full perfection until it is from 6 to 10 years old."

The most prestigious domains of the place-name description have recently been granted a classification but are still subject to the rigorous quality control exercised by the illustrious *Jurade* and the Saint-Emilion Viticultural and Agricultural Syndicate, which is alone entitled to bestow upon the wine a "certificate of approval" for marketing.

In addition to the communes entitled to the simple place-name description, the following five others have obtained the right to add Saint-Emilion to their own names: SAINT-GEORGES-SAINT-EMILION, MONTAGNE-SAINT-EMILION, LUSSAC-SAINT-EMILION, PUISSEGUIN-SAINT-EMILION, PARSAC-SAINT-EMILION.

As for the special place-name description SABLES-SAINT-EMILION, this refers to a small part of the commune of Libourne, between Saint-Emilion and Pomerol, which produces excellent red wines which are subtle and fragrant and mature quite quickly.

POMEROL AND ITS REGION

The commune of Pomerol, which covers 1,550 acres, is a few miles to the north-east of Libourne. It is bordered by the vineyards of Saint-Emilion to the east and of Fronsac to the west.

As far back as history records, the existence of Pomerol is evidenced by memorials of every kind. This clayey-gravel plateau was crossed by a Roman road which the winegrower poet Ausonius had to take when travelling from the port of Condat, on the Dordogne, to his magnificent villa of Lucaniacus in the Saint-Emilion region.

In the Middle Ages, the Knights Hospitallers of St. John established their first commandery at Pomerol. From the twelfth century onwards, therefore, the famous borough was endowed with a fortified manor, a hospital and a Romanesque church which has now, unfortunately, disappeared.

With the Knights Hospitallers, as in the time of the Romans, the vine was in high honour in Pomerol. But the Hundred Years War which, of course, lasted three centuries, was not very kind to this ancient countryside. Time and time again, French and Anglo-Gascons turned the parish into a battlefield. Moreover, as long as Pomerol remained under the fleur-de-lis, its wine could not take the Bordeaux road, i.e. they could not be sold to its good and faithful English customers. However, after the decisive French victory at Castillon in 1453, which entailed the surrender of Guienne, the wines of Pomerol made rapid progress in gaining a reputation and soon became one of the most precious jewels in the Bordeaux crown.

For these are complete wines which gladden both the nose and the palate. These growths have a fine and generous vinosity which comes from grapes such as the *Bouchet* and the *Merlot*. While retaining the delicacy of the SAINT-EMILION wines, they also approach the wines of the Médoc. POMEROL wines go extremely well with red meat, game and cheese.

The guaranteed place-name description LALANDE DE POMEROL (about 1,250 acres), with its soil varying from siliceous clay to clayey gravel, produces fine red wines comparable with those of its famous neighbour. Next door, the commune of Néac, which corresponds exactly to the area of the place-name description, contains a 675-acre vineyard. The NÉACS are generally supple, velvety, full-bodied and have a strong bouquet. Although it is impossible to establish any absolute rule in this field, it is agreed that the First Growths of NÉAC are roughly comparable in quality with the second First Growths of POMEROL.

CÔTES DE FRONSAC

When crossing the Bordeaux country on his return from Spain, Charlemagne had fortifications built on the knoll of Fronsac which commands the Dordogne. This fortress became the bastion *par excellence* of the strategic region. The enormous castle still existed in the fifteenth century, but it could not survive three days of battering by the artillery of Jean Bureau, Master of Artillery of France under Charles VII. Even genius is powerless to control the future. If Fronsac with its knoll deserves to be called a high place, it is not because of its military history. Fronsac is glorious for its red wines. High-coloured, robust and plump, with age they gain an exquisite distinction. They have never betrayed the attention given them by the flower-bearded emperor and, in more modern times, by the Duke of Richelieu (1706-1788), who was as famous for his knowledge of wine as for his amorous successes. Richelieu, who also held the title of Duke of Fronsac, built on the knoll one of those charming "follies" that the eighteenth century sprinkled throughout the Bordeaux region. In that house, he gave fashionable parties. It was about the same time that Richelieu introduced the wine of Bordeaux to the Court of France.

On the legal plane, the description FRONSAC does not exist. The name forms part of two separate place-name descriptions: CÔTES DE CANON-FRONSAC, which includes the best slopes, particularly that of Canon; and CÔTES DE FRONSAC.

CÔTES DE CASTILLON

The Côtes de Castillon comprise the territory of Castillon-sur-Dordogne (recently rebaptized Castillon-la-Bataille) and of several neighbouring communes. This is not only an ancient winegrowing region but also an historic site. Castillon-sur-Dordogne became Castillon-la-Bataille in 1953 when the commune celebrated the fifth centenary of the last battle of the Hundred Years War. It was at Castillon that Talbot, the English general, fell and Albion's continental ambitions melted away in the smoke of Charles VII's mor-

CHÂTEAU CHEVAL BLANC

CHÂTEAU CHEVAL BLANC
1. 1a. Trade name "Château Cheval Blanc". This name is well-known to wine-lovers but the merchant-viniculturist gives further details on his label and indicates that the wine is a "first great growth". The vintage is also mentioned on the label. – 2. 2a. Place-name description of origin: Saint-Emilion, which is confirmed by the reference to "Saint-Emilion, first great growth". Nothing could be more explicit, therefore, than this label, and the knowledgable wine-lover will also be aware that the Cheval Blanc is one of the two "first great growths classed as (a)" in the area. – 3. Name of the merchant-viniculturist. – 4. The reference to bottling at the Château is compulsory for the great growths of Bordeaux; it is a guarantee of both quality and authenticity.

CHÂTEAU HAUT-MARBUZET
1. Trade name "Château Haut-Marbuzet". This growth did not appear in the list of growths classified in 1855 but was mentioned in the syndicate merit-list of March 3rd, 1966 with the annotation "exceptional great-bourgeois" (see page 158). – 2. Guaranteed descriptive name: Saint-Estèphe. The Saint-Estèphe area is in the Haut-Médoc near the border of the Bas-Médoc.

CHÂTEAU MOUTON-ROTHSCHILD
1. Trade name "Château Mouton-Rothschild". This label is laconic and, apart from its more elegant style, nothing distinguishes it from its next-door neighbour. As a great noble, Château Mouton-Rothschild does not mention its rank in the 1855 classification in which it was one of the eminent second growths (see page 158). – 2. Place-name description of origin: Pauillac. Some people will find it difficult to place Pauillac in the Haut-Médoc and to realize, at first glance, that Mouton-Rothschild is a Bordeaux wine. – 3. Name of the merchant-viniculturist. – 4. 4a. Careful details of the château bottling process are given, the bottle being numbered after the word "Ci". Confirmation of this operation is given in 4a.

CHÂTEAU RIEUSSEC

1. Trade name "Château Rieussec". We are immediately informed that it is a first great growth. – 2. 2a. Place-name description of origin: Sauternes. This is a great dessert wine. The year gives the knowledgeable wine-lover an indication of quality. The description of origin is in the prescribed form. – 3. Name of the merchant-viniculturist. – 4. Reference to bottling at the Château.

CHÂTEAU PÉTRUS

1. Trade name "Pétrus". The indication "great wine" is not very explicit. – 2. Place-name description of origin: Pomerol. – 2a. This area has no official classification like those of the Médocs and Saint-Emilions, but Pétrus is regarded as the best of the Pomérols. The description is repeated in the prescribed form. – 3. Reference to bottling at the Château. – 4. Name of the merchant-viniculturist.

CHÂTEAU LA MISSION HAUT BRION

1. Trade name Château la Mission Haut Brion. The reference to "classified great growth" make it immediately clear that this is a great wine; it should not, however, be confused with Château Haut Brion which is a "first classed great growth". – 2. Place-name description of origin: Graves. Since there are both red and white Graves, I should, perhaps, mention that Château la Mission Haut Brion is a red wine. – 3. Reference to bottling at the Château. – 4. Name of the merchant-viniculturist.

tars. A dreary plain? No, indeed! The symmetrical rows of the vines are interrupted by fields of clover, alfalfa and maize in which tractors and a last few patient oxen carry out their manoeuvres. In this fertile countryside, the ghosts of the past are imprisoned in a small circle traced out, from dawn to dusk, by the shadow of the cenotaph erected in memory of the illustrious defeated. Anyone, according to his sense of history, can put whatever he likes into an empty tomb. Filling one's glass is a much more serious procedure. Hence, no one should ever go to Castillon without taking the opportunity of tasting for himself the excellent wines which are entitled to carry this famous name. The red wines (80 per cent of the harvest) have a richly tinted robe, a generous fragrance and a full body which does not prevent them from acquiring great suppleness from at least the third racking onwards. In the spring following the vintage, they deserve a respectable place on the connoisseur's table. The white wines, which represent only a small part of the harvest, come from the north-west part of the area. Fine and delicate, they keep perfectly. (The recognition of CÔTES-DE-CASTILLON by I.N.A.O., the National Institute of Descriptions of Origin, is fairly recent.)

BOURGEAIS

The general appearance of the town of Bourg-sur-Gironde is that of a small fortified medieval city. It bears some resemblance to Saint-Emilion overhanging the valley of the Dordogne, but its origins may be even more ancient. Discoveries of the greatest interest dating from the palaeolithic and neolithic eras have been made in twenty-eight different spots at Bourg. Thousands of objects and tools have been found, tons of chipped flints and wall-carvings of great beauty. Many caves have yet to be explored. Such are the unquestionable proofs of the presence of prehistoric humanity in this large village.

It is clear that the first inhabitants of Bourg came from the Eyzies region through Rouffignac, the forest of La Double, the Entre-Deux-Mers and the Fronsac region. According to the theory dear to the heart of André Siegfried, they had quite naturally followed the "fall of the waters" and had halted in front of the immense estuary (which they took for the ocean itself), finally settling down to plant the vine on the slopes dominating its bank.

Some time ago, an English archaeological journal published an article on the villa of Ausonius at Bourg. It was situated on the outskirts of the town, towards the present Blaye-du-Bourg, on the slope facing the sea. Very comfortable and luxurious, like the other villas which the poet-consul possessed in Guienne, it was also the centre of an important vineyard. Ausonius himself speaks of it in clear and precise terms when singing the praises of the wine of Bourg. There seems good reason to believe that this vineyard had already been in existence for several centuries, since it takes much longer for a vine to produce a famous wine than for a poet to compose a poem!

From the Gallo-Roman epoch to the Middle Ages and the present day, the history of Bourg has been closely linked with that of Bordeaux. The two cities have the same love for the vine and for freedom.

Without a break since 1273, the winegrowers and burghers of Bourg have elected their mayor and corporation. The last *Jurats* (wearing a hood and a livery of red and white damask) were elected two years before the Revolution. This proud commune was never the vassal of any lord apart from the greatest lord of all, the King. When the king was English, Bourg took advantage of his remoteness to stretch its liberties and privileges as far as possible.

Thus the burghers of Bourg, unlike Archbishop Pey Berland, have felt the "wind of history" caress their walls and shiver among the vine shoots. They opposed no resistance to Charles VII. Basically animated by the same municipal passion as Bordeaux but more rural and less torn by Italian-style factions, Bourg was able to keep its unity and follow a single line of conduct while the metropolis of Aquitaine saw its cohesion break up under the pressure of events.

It is hardly possible to say whether the virtues and wisdom of the Bourg vintners were responsible for the fame of the wine of this region, or vice-versa. Anyway, the fact is that this fame, which goes back to the dawn of history, was confirmed once again at the end of the eighteenth century by the chronicler Abbé Baurein: "The wines of Bourg were so esteemed in the last century that private individuals with property in the Bourgeais and in the Médoc would only sell their Bourg wine on condition that the purchaser also agreed to take the Médoc." This evidence has been much contested in modern times but there are still proprietors with vineyards on both sides of the water.

The red wines of the Bourgeais are rich in vitamins, have a very agreeable bouquet and age excellently. As for the white wines, whether semi-dry or sweet, they are sturdy, nervous and full-bodied. It should be noted that some of the white wines do not have the right to carry the appellation BORDEAUX because of the types of grapes used to produce them.

A former staging point on the way to Compostella, the citadel of Blaye, built by Vauban in 1652 on the remains of a Roman *castrum*, is haunted by the ghost of Jauffré Rudel, the twelfth-century troubadour and poet of the Distant Love, and the more tragic shade of the Duchess of Berry, imprisoned in 1832 for attempting to organize an uprising against Louis Philippe.

The whole countryside is bathed in the poetry of the sea. It was selected as the locale for the film *Moderato Cantabile* with the 2 ½-mile wide estuary providing the backdrop. But the slopes overhanging the Gironde are covered with vines. "Opulent plains with gentle hillocks, sumptuous hills, abrupt spurs which defended Bordeaux against the Saracen and Norman invasions," so wrote E. Lacroix, "the lands of Blaye, coveted by the conquerors of the north and the south, still remain one of the finest flowers of the soil of France. Since the most ancient times, the vine, under a temperate sky, has occupied this privileged earth in which the limestones reluctantly surrender to the silicas and red clays which already announce the truffle-perfumed slopes of Périgord."

The wineproducing area of the place-name descriptions BLAYE and CÔTES-DE-BLAYE covers the cantons of Blaye, Saint-Savin and Saint-Ciers-sur-Gironde.

The simple description BLAYE deals expressly with both red and white wines. The first must come from the following grapes which, incidentally, are not all to be found elsewhere in the appellation BORDEAUX: *Cabernet*, *Béquignol* and *Verdot*. The use of any other grape cancels the right to the place-name description.

The white wines must be made from the following grapes: *Semillon, Sauvignon, Muscadelle, Merlot Blanc, Folle Blanche, Colombard, Pineau de la Loire* and *Frontignan*. The last four grapes are not encountered anywhere else in the place-name description BORDEAUX. In the place-name description CÔTES-DE-BLAYE, there is still some tolerance regarding grapes, at least as far as the red wines are concerned. In the case of the whites, only the classic trilogy of *Sauvignon, Semillon* and *Muscadelle* is permitted.

The reds are colourful, fruity and sweet, and gain by early bottling. The tannin and iron they contain recommend them as tonic wines. Of all the wines of the Gironde, they are perhaps the only ones whose savour recalls the good growths of Burgundy. The white wines are nervous and delicate. By one of nature's happy juxtapositions, they make an ideal accompaniment to the delicious oysters of Marennes whose beds are established on the near-by Seudre.

WINES OF THE NEIGHBOURING REGIONS

The basins of the Garonne, Dordogne and Adour are devoted to viticulture. We shall not go back to the problems which arose, at the beginning of the present century, with respect to these "marginal" vineyards when it was a question of marking out the boundaries of the production area of Bordeaux wine. In the long run, the autonomy granted to the "marginal" wines turned out to their advantage in that it made it possible for them to bring out their individuality.

Thus, the wine of Cahors, before being marketed in the "Port of the Moon" under the name of VIN DE HAUT-PAYS, had been sung by Horace and Virgil. Like the wines from the slopes of the Isle and the Lot and from around Bergerac, it is a powerful, highly-coloured red wine which, though rough in its youth, has a remarkable vinosity after a few years in the bottle. Its basic grape is the *Malbec* which gives it a very agreeable bouquet. The slopes of Marmandais, an area of mixed farming with an abundance of fertile orchards, also supply some agreeable red wines from near the great place-name descriptions of the Gironde. The CÔTES DE BUZET, also in Lot-et-Garonne, are

V.D.Q.S. red wines (delimited wines of superior quality) which are fruity and light, supple and round. The VILLAUDRIC are red wines harvested a few miles from Montauban which have the same qualities and also the advantage that they can be drunk young. On the Côte d'Argent and in the Basque country, the *gastronomade* (gourmet) takes pleasure in the growths of IROULEGUY, SAINT-ETIENNE-DE-BAIGORRY and ANHAUX. These are delicately fruity and act as an excellent foil to the local ham. The wines of Béarn are often vinified as rosé and are accommodating enough to go equally well with fish and with white meat. Astride two departments (Landes and Gers), the vineyard of Tursan was formerly quite famous and produces white and red wines as well as a few rosés with a very elegant bouquet. On the borders of Languedoc, Fronton also produces red, white and rosé wines, the principal outlet for which is Toulouse. Elegance and delicacy characterize the LAVILLEDIEU, red and white growths from Tarn-et-Garonne.

The wines of MONBAZILLAC can, in good years, compete with the best of the luscious white wines of

Bordeaux, although their aroma is rather less complex. In this soil, which has long been famous, the wine-growers must, as in Sauternes and Barsac, await the "noble rot" before harvesting. In the first two or three years after picking, the MONBAZILLAC wines are very attractive and run like liquid gold. It would be wrong, however, to yield to temptation. As they age, they acquire a deeper but no less luminous colour and, above all, develop their full character which then differs appreciably from that of a great luscious white wine of Bordeaux of similar age.

Without aspiring to the heights of the MONBAZILLAC, the dry, semi-dry or semi-sweet wines of BERGERAC have charm and a distinguished bouquet which, as André Lamondé wrote, make one celebrate the food-stuffs of that "land of Périgord paved with truffles and heavenly with *foie gras*". However, a type of BERGE-RAC of higher and more constant quality is to be found in the place-name descriptions CÔTES DE SAUSSIGNAC and CÔTES DE BERGERAC.

The Périgord poet Armand Got glorified MONTRAVEL in the following terms:

Montravel! Montravel!
Les sucs fruités, moelleux, d'un bouquet non pareil,
Les vins "de bonne foi" comme un "dict" de Montaigne,
Qui font "vivre à propos" et sont de bon conseil.

Montravel! Montravel!
Mellow, fruity juices of a fragrance clear and wise,
Doughty wines which savour of a saying of Montaigne,
Conducive to right living and magnanimous advice.

The simple place-name description MONTRAVEL is reserved for wines harvested in the plain. The place-name descriptions CÔTES DE MONTRAVEL and HAUT-MONTRAVEL cover less fertile soils and produce growths of a greater distinction. They are remarkably fruity and elegant. The best white wines of the Lot-et-Garonne are from the Côtes de Duras: less sweet than the MONTRAVEL wines, but fresh and delicate.

Decked in pale gold, ardent and heady, ROSETTE comes from the white grapes used in the Bordeaux country: *Semillon, Sauvignon* and *Muscadelle*.

The winegrowers of Gaillac were among those who, not so long ago, fought the most bitterly for inclusion in the place-name description BORDEAUX. Their wine is now managing very well on its own, thanks to the Confraternity of Bacchus to which part of their élite belongs. The sweet GAILLAC is a rough wine drunk very soon after the harvest. However, the guaran-teed place-name description of origin GAILLAC indicates a dry white wine without excess acidity which is light and very drinkable. GAILLAC PREMIÈRES CÔTES has a fine colour and a great frankness of taste which it keeps in its age and which it owes to its dominant grape, the *Mauzac*, which has the peculiarity of pro-

ducing a thick-skinned fruit which can ripen fully despite the rains of September. GAILLAC PERLÉ is a perfectly natural sparkling wine, no product other than the grape being used to obtain it. Without acidity or tartness, gushing with savoury cream, it is an exquisite "lady's wine", as the saying went half a century ago, in its lusciousness, delicacy and relatively low alcohol content. The red wines are unequal in quality but the best of them have body, a fine colour and travel well.

Surrounded by a large area which produces only white wines, Madiran has a shrine sheltering a small wooden Virgin of great antiquity named Our Lady of the Vines. The vines in question are red. The chief growths of this Bigorre soil are ANGUIS, LE PARSAN, LES TUILERIES, LES TURCOS and HECHACQ. They are made from the noble grapes: *Cabernet Sauvignon* and *Cabernet Franc* which are used in the best holdings of the Bordeaux country. These wines have an aroma which is reminiscent of that of the grape-flower, a spare, very fluid scent which is obviously due to the *Cabernet*. Unfortunately, more fertile grapes have been introduced into the vineyards on the pretext of productivity. In the context of the new outlets offered by the Common Market, it would no doubt be a wise policy to eliminate these intruders. Tonic and digestive, MADIRAN keeps for a very long time. However, a sediment forms which adheres to the side of the bottle and the wine must therefore be decanted.

Portet is the tiny capital of a winegrowing area which may, perhaps, be more ancient than that of Jurançon. It produces a white wine from a grape called *Pacherenc* with which the *Mansenc*, a Jurançon plant, is sometimes mixed. The harvest is late. Formerly, picking was still being carried out at Christmas. Nowadays, it is just about finished before the end of November. Hence the winegrowers of this countryside have been rather resistant to the benefits of modern oenology. The savours of their wine give themselves without evasion "like the virgins of Béarn" as Paul de Cassagnac, who admired this growth and its countryside, once wrote.

Caring little for fashion, PORTET is luscious, sweet or dry according to the caprices of nature. It maderizes readily but the winegrower is indifferent to this. He does not mind the maderized taste and he produces his wine for himself, not for the wine-merchant.

Some very interesting wines resembling the PORTET have been obtained at Lambeye, Montpezat and Crou-zeilles, which are communes of the Vic-Bilh.

Even if there is no historic proof that Henry IV had his lips moistened at birth with Jurançon wine, this legendary episode continues to shed an immortal glory on the slopes in front of which the town of Pau was built. What is more, the scene is part of the spiritual heritage of our civilization. Whether authentic or not, it generally annoys and irritates the enemies of wine in France. It it by no means necessary, however, to resort to this reference to prove the nobility of a growth harvested at the end of autumn in the communes of Jurançon, Gan, Laroin, Saint-Faust, Aubertin and Monein. It owes nothing to anyone. None of the grapes which compose it has been identified in any other viticultural region. Very sensitive to oïdium, the large and small *Mansencs*, the *Cruchen* and the *Courbu* produce tight bunches of juice-heavy grapes which are naturally reduced, dried and candied on the vine, producing a veritable concentration of the must before picking. The richness in sugar of this must is transformed into liquid without altering the delicacy of the bouquet which characterizes the finished product.

JURANÇON is in the first rank of the most famous sweet wines. It involves both the senses and the spirit and lends itself to that famous "after-taste" of which the great connoisseurs speak.

Around that great queen—a vintage bottle of Bordeaux we find a host of noble companions and maids of honour which, according to protocol, may be less beautiful but are sometimes so pretty that, in a sense, they become her equal. The wines of the south-west form the retinue without which there could, of course, be no sovereign.

THE LIFE OF THE WINE PEOPLE IN THE BORDEAUX COUNTRY

In the last fifteen years or so, something has changed in the hearts and spirits of the Bordeaux winegrowers. They have not lost sight of the fact that the area of production is of paramount importance as regards the quality of the growth, but they have remembered that the origin of a wine is not enough to make it good, any more than the highest birth and impeccable ancestry will make a gentleman if his education be defective.

The rebirth of the three great pilot-confraternities of the Bordelais (*Jurade de Saint-Emilion*, *Commanderie du Bon-Temps Médoc et des Graves* and *Connétablie du Guyenne*) is due to this new viticultural psychology, although, in some cases, it has been the cause of it. The confraternities, by bringing together the wine professionals on a more human and humanist level than could be achieved by the trades unions, by reviving ancient handicraft and corporative traditions and by excluding all demagogy and disputes from their meetings, have restored to a place of honour that comradely mentality which, in the past, was the glory of the guilds, even though the guilds were also syndicates which fought the authorities to retain their "privileges".

The modern Bordeaux confraternities have taken from these old associations only their noblest and most disinterested features and have left for the trades unions the technological and contentious aspects which all modern viticulture must entail, even if it has a thousand years of history behind it.

THE JURADE DE SAINT-EMILION

The development and prosperity of the Jurade de Saint-Emilion date from the twelfth century when Richard the Lionheart accorded it various privileges and freedoms. The most ancient document known concerning the town of Saint-Emilion is the Charter of Falaise, dated July 8th, 1199, in which on the death of his brother Richard, John Lackland confirmed the privileges granted by his predecessor. The great concessions made by the English kings were, of course, designed to create conditions under which the Bordeaux vintners could provide the best wine possible for the ever-thirsty English market.

This was the origin of the *Jurade*, composed, as the old writings put it, of "honest folk" elected by their fellow-citizens to administer with sovereign power the interests of the commune. As regards the cultivation of the vine and vinification, the *Jurats* displayed a tireless and scrupulous vigilance. They held the "vintner's mark" (a branding iron with the arms of the town), proclaimed the "ringing in" of the harvest, banned the sale of insufficiently "fine" wine and dealt rigorously with abuses and fraud.

From the tunning stage onwards, they watched over the quality of the growths, visited the wine-stores and cellars and checked the *barriques*. After which the "vintner" branded the casks of "good wine" with the coat of arms of the town. "Unworthy" wine was destroyed by fire. Lastly, the *Jurats* issued certificates without which it was forbidden to transport wine. These measures, which may appear excessively authoritarian, ensured the prosperity of the region through the resounding fame of SAINT-EMILION, which the English then called the king of wines.

The men of goodwill who, on September 13th, 1948, with due solemnity and authenticity reconstituted the *Jurade*, did not aspire to the political powers of their ancestors but limited themselves to the immense task of placing the wine of Saint-Emilion once again on the throne of its ancient splendours.

The *Connétablie de Guyenne*, here shown being solemnly received in the City Hall of Gouda in the Netherlands, in 1952 revived the title if not the administrative functions of an institution which in the Middle Ages had extensive influence in the Bordeaux country.

The first pressing operations often take place on the picking site. The baskets of the wine-pickers are emptied into the *baste*, a little tub of light wood containing about 5 ½ gallons. The grapes are rammed down in the rudimentary manner shown in the picture.

The most illustrious of the Bordeaux whites comes from the Château d'Yquem (above); among the reds, that of the Château Lafite-Rothschild (below) is one of the top prestige wines of the Médoc area.

THE COMMANDERIE
DU BON-TEMPS MÉDOC ET DES GRAVES

Likewise, in October 1951, the men of the Médoc desired one thing and one thing only: to establish an organization which, in modern society, could really serve the cause of their wine, irrespective of classification or privilege, great growths and modest artisan growths alike, with the sole proviso that they were the good Médoc wines on which the universal glory of Bordeaux was founded.

Thus, under the distant patronage of a winegrowing religious order formerly active in Médoc, this utterly unique society was formed. It comprises the winegrowers, whether owners of famous châteaux or simple "bourgeois" growers, the wine-brokers (the link between production and trade) and, lastly, the wine-merchants who for centuries have been exporting Médoc throughout the whole world.

The *Commanderie* has taken as its emblem the wooden bowl which was well-known to the image-carvers of the gothic churches. This *bontemps*, or *lou desquet* as it is called in the local dialect, is a tiny piece of winemaking equipment used for beating the whites of eggs which are then "whipped" in the *barrique* of new wine to clarify it. The commanders' hats are shaped like the *desquet* and are topped by a white cover reminiscent of the beaten egg-whites. It is also with *lou desquet* that, in the wine-stores of the Médoc, when summer has come again, the happy marriage between the new harvest and the wine ready for bottling is achieved.

For some years now, the Médoc *Commanderie* has had two offshoots in the white-wine country: the *Commanderie du Bontemps de Sauternes-Barsac* (dressed in golden velvets) and the *Commanderie du Bontemps de Sainte-Croix-du-Mont* (in light-yellow linen).

THE CONNÉTABLIE DE GUIENNE

The *Connétablie de Guienne*, much referred to throughout the Middle Ages in the Bordeaux country, was the link which bound to the great mother-city the small winegrowing daughter towns which are still dotted along the banks of the Garonne and the Gironde. The important administrative functions of the Constable, with his headquarters in the Palais de l'Ombrière, though carefully distinguished from the attributions vested in the *Jurats* of Bordeaux, were inspired by the same concern: to serve the viticultural interest of the seneschalcy by controlling the origin and the quality of the wines. Memory of those past ages aroused enthusiasm in the hearts of those who founded the contemporary *Connétablie*, in 1952. They were winegrowers from the Premières Côtes de Bordeaux, Entre-Deux-Mers, Benauge and part of Graves who were later joined by those of the Côtes de Bourg, Blaye and Saint-Macaire.

As the *Connétablie* marches by torchlight under the porticos of the quasi-royal Château of Cadillac-sur-Garonne, dressed in majestic black robes stamped with the golden cross, the moving rite of the enthronement unfolds in the barrel-vaulted crypt. While prominent personalities listen to the indictment which will open to them the gates of the Privy Council, the spectators feel themselves enveloped in ten centuries of history.

THE HOSPITALLERS OF POMEROL

It was at the beginning of the twelfth century that the powerful Hospitallers of St. John of Jerusalem chose Pomerol as the site for their first Commandery in Libournais. In the post-Roman era, it was they who, for nearly five centuries, cultivated the vine in that parish. From it they produced a wine regarded as a wonder for the comfort of pilgrims and the cure of the sick. In the spring of 1968, with the permission of the Sovereign Order of Malta, the winegrowers of Pomerol reconstituted the Commandery which joined the other confraternities in the Grand Council of Bordeaux.

GRAND COUNCIL OF BORDEAUX

The Grand Council of Bordeaux is not still another confraternity but a high assembly which, during the Middle Ages, presided over the destiny of the city and of the province. At times of crisis, all the corporate bodies of Bordeaux and Guienne met in the Great Council for joint deliberation as to the decisions which should be taken with respect, chiefly, to the production of and trade in wine. That is what still happens today. Although it is true that the city among the vines reigns over a great variety of soils, it has but one soul as it has but one history.

While respecting the personality of each of the viticultural regions of the Bordeaux country, the Grand Council is thus responsible for safeguarding and strengthening the idea of unity contained in the three words: wines of Bordeaux.

It has a dual significance. Within the limits of the Bordeaux country, it makes a reality of the necessary idea of association. Outside, particularly in new markets where the name of Bordeaux takes precedence over the numerous place-name descriptions of the Gironde, it makes it possible to fix the attention on a product whose great variety should not cause one to forget its unique provenance.

When all the confraternities are met together, the Grand Council holds chapters either at Bordeaux, in the House of Wine, headquarters of the Inter-Professional Wine Council of Bordeaux, or in great foreign cities during which, according to an ancient ritual, it awards to some rarely privileged persons the title of "Companion of Bordeaux".

THE BORDEAUX WINE ACADEMY

The Bordeaux Wine Academy, which is not a confraternity either, is entitled to a seat in the Grand Council. It is an academy in the full sense of the word. Around a few celebrated writers who are members of the French Academy, it groups in all 40 life members belonging to Letters, Science and the Arts, the owners of Great Growths, winegrower merchants etc. It sits either in the city of Bordeaux itself or in the great châteaux of the region.

The aims of the Academy are noble in their humanism. The company puts in the forefront of its work the defence and the glorification of Bordeaux wine by the exact observance of refined tasting usage and the study of viticultural and winegrowing dialectics. It publishes annually a code of vintages which is not a simple scale of values applied to Bordeaux growths but a mass of information concerning the development of a number of harvests since 1920.

WINES OF BORDEAUX
LEFT BANK OF THE GARONNE AND OF THE GIRONDE

SAUTERNES AND BARSAC REGIONS • WHITE WINES

CLASSIFICATION OF THE GREAT GROWTHS OF 1855

Superior first growth . . . Château d'Yquem . . . Sauternes

First growths

Château La Tour-Blanche . . .	Bommes	Château Rabaud-Sigalas	Bommes	Château Climens	Barsac
Château Lafaurie-Peyraguey . .	»	Château Rabaud-Promis	»	Château Guiraud	Sauternes
Clos Haut-Peyraguey	»	Château de Suduiraut	Preignac	Château Rieussec	Fargues
Château Rayne-Vigneau	»	Château Coutet	Barsac		

Second growths

Château de Myrat	Barsac	Château Filhot	Sauternes	Château Romer	Preignac
Château Doisy-Daene	»	Château Broustet	Barsac	Château Lamothe	Sauternes
Château Doisy-Védrines	»	Château Caillou	»	Château Nairac	Barsac
Château Doisy	»	Château Suau	»		
Château d'Arche	Sauternes	Château de Malle	Preignac		

OTHER GREAT GROWTHS OF SAUTERNES AND BARSAC

Château Raymond-Lafon . . .	Sauternes	Château du Mayne	Barsac	Château Montjoie	Barsac
Château Lafon	»	Château Camperos	»	Château Lapeloue	»
Château Lanère	»	Château Saint-Marc	»	Château Moura	»
Domaine du Coy	»	Château Gravas	»	Château des Rochers	Preignac
Château Comarque	»	Château Latrézotte	»	Château Bastor-Lamontagne . .	»
Château d'Arche-Vimeney . . .	»	Château Villefranche	»	Château d'Arche-Pugneau . . .	»
Château Haut-Bommes	Bommes	Clos des Princes	»	Château du Pick	»
Château Mauras	»	Clos du Roy	»	Domaine de Lamothe-Vigneau,	
Cru Bel-Air	»	Château Petit-Mayne	»	château des Remparts	»
Château Cameron	»	Château Brassens-Guiteronde . .	»	Domaine de la Forêt	»
Cru Bergeron	»	Château Fleury	»	Château Jonka	»
Château Le Hère	»	Château Simon	»	Château Saint-Amand	»
Château Lamourette	»	Château Jacques-le-Haut . . .	»	Château de Veyres	»
Domaine de Souba	»	Château Bouyot	»	Château d'Armajan-des-Ormes .	»
Château Cantegril	Barsac	Cru Hournalas	»	Château Guimbalet	»
Château Baulac	»	Château du Roc	»	Château Monteils	»
Château Piada	»	Château Grand-Mayne Guy-né-		Cru Peyraguey	»
Château Piot	»	Marc	»	Château Laribotte	»
Château Grillon	»	Château Simon Carrety	»	Château Fontebride	»
Château Mathalin	»	Château Menauta	»	Château du Mayne	»
Château Dudon	»	Château Coustet	»	Clos de l'Ecole	»
Château de Carles	»	Cru La Pinesse	»	Château Gilette	»
Château Guiteronde	»	Château Ducasse	»	Château Haut-Bergeron	»
Château La Clotte et Cazalis . .	»	Château Péchon	»	Château de Pleytegeat	»
Château Roumieu	»	Château Saint-Robert	»	Clos du Pape	Fargues
Château Massereau	»	Château Massereau-Lapachere .	»	Château de Fargues	»
Château Rolland	»	Château Mercier	»	Cru Fillau	»
Château Pernaud	»	Château La Bouade	»	Cru Mothes	»
Château Prost	»	Château Grand Carretey	»	Château Paillon-Claverie	»
Château Luziès	»	Château L'Haouilley	»	Château Portarrieu	»
Château Liot	»	Château Jany	»	Château de Touilla	»
Château Hallet	»	Château Menate	»		

CÉRONS REGION • WHITE WINES

Château de Cérons et de Calvi-mont	Cérons	Château Mayne-Binet	Cérons	Château Haut-Mayne	Cérons
Grand enclos du Château de Cérons	»	Cru Larrouquey	»	Clos Barail	»
Lalannette-Ferbos	»	Château Sylvain	»	Domaine des Moulins à Vent . .	»
		Château Lamouroux	»	Cru de Peyroutène	»

Domaine de Freyron	Cérons	Crus des Grands-Chênes	Cérons	Domaine de Castagnaou	Podensac
Château Beaulieu	»	Crus Ferbos-Lalanette	»	Château du Hau-Rat	Illats.
Château Grand Chemin	»	Cru des Moulins à Vent	»	Château Archambaud	»
Château Barthez	»	Clos des Moulins à Vent	»	Clos du Tauzin	»
Cru du Moulin-à-Vent	»	Domaine de Caillou	»	Château Cantau	»
Château des Bessanes	»	Château Méric	»	Château Beaulac	»
Cru Haut-Mayne	»	Cru du Moulin	»	Château Haut-La-Huntasse	»
Clos Bourgelat	»	Cru Haut-Belloc	»	Château Le Huzet	»
Château de l'Emigré	»	Cru Voltaire	»	Domaine de Calbet	»
Château Balestey	»	Clos Avocat	»	Château Thôme-Brousterot	»
Château du Seuil	»	Cru Larrouquey	»	Domaine de Prouzet	»
Cru de Du Peyrat	»	Cru Majans	»	Château Despeyrères	»
Clos de l'Avocat	»	Cru Cravaillas	»	Château Haut-Gravier	»
Château La Salette	»	Cru du Freyron	»	Domaine de Jaussan	»
Cru Dauphin	»	Cru Le Mayne	Podensac	Clos des Roches	»
Cru La Liste	»	Château d'Anice	»	Cru Navarot	»
Cru des Magens	»	Cru des Cabanes	»	Château Haut-Bourdat	»
Cru Menaut-Larrouquey	»	Château de Madère	»	Château Cazès	»
Cru Chacha	»	Cru Le Bourdieu	»	Clos du Bas Lançon	»
Cru de Pineau	»	Cru Boisson	»	Cru de Brazé	»
Clos Cantemerle	»	Cru Maucouade	»	Cru Haut-Boutoc	»
Cru Cleyrac	»	Cru du Brouillaou	»	Château Tinan	»
Château Lalanette	»	Cru Madérot	»	Cru de Lionne	»
Domaine du Salut, Château Huradin	»	A Mayne d'Imbert	»	Domaine de Gallier	»
		Domaine Le Cossu	»	Domaine de Menjon	»

GRAVES REGION • WHITE WINES AND RED WINES

CLASSIFIED GROWTHS • I.N.A.O. classification officially recognized by the decree of February 16, 1959

RED WINES

Château Haut-Brion	Pessac	Château de Fieuzal	Léognan	Château Malartic-Lagravière	Léognan
Château Bouscaut	Cadaujac	Château Haut-Bailly	»	Château Olivier	»
Château Carbonnieux	Léognan	Château La Mission-Haut-Brion	Talence	Château Pape-Clément	Pessac
Domaine de Chevalier	»	Château La Tour-Haut-Brion	»	Château Smith Haut-Lafitte	Martillac
		Château La-Tour-Martillac	Martillac		

WHITE WINES

Château Bouscaut	Cadaujac	Château Couhins	Villenave-	Château Laville Haut-Brion	Talence
Château Carbonnieux	Léognan		d'Ornon	Château Malartic-Lagravière	Léognan
Domaine de Chevalier	»	Château La-Tour-Martillac	Martillac	Château Olivier	»

The above classification is in alphabetical order, except for the Château Haut-Brion, classified in 1855

LIST OF THE PRINCIPAL GROWTHS

Château Haut-Brana	Pessac	Château Lespault	Martillac	Château des Fougères	La Brède
Château Haut-Carré	Talence	Château La Solitude	»	Château Guillaumot	»
Château Pique-Caillou	Mérignac	Château Lafargue	St-Médard-	Domaine de Lasalle	»
Château Chêne-Vert	»	Château Lamothe	Eyrans	Cru de Magneau	»
Château Baret	Villenave-	Château de La Prade	»	Cru de Méric	»
Château Cantebau-Couhins	d'Ornon	Château Lusseau	Aygue-	Clos du Pape	»
Château Pontac-Monplaisir		Château du Méjan	morte	Château Bel-Air	St-Morillon
Château Bardins	Cadaujac	Château Saint-Jérôme	»	Château Belon	»
Château Malleret	»	Château Boiresse	»	Domaine de Gravette	»
Château Lamothe-Bouscaut	»	Château de Beauchêne	Beautiran	Domaine du Jau	»
Château Poumey	Gradignan	Château Grand Bourdieu	»	Château Piron	»
Château de France	Léognan	Château de Tuquet	»	Château du Bonnat	St-Selve
Château Gazin	»	Château Ferrande	Castres	Domaine du Barque	»
Domaine de Grand-Maison	»	Château Foucla	»	Domaine de La Peyrère	»
Château La Louvière	»	Château Bas-Pommarède	»	Château Bernard-Raymond	Portets
Château Larrivet-Haut-Brion	»	Château Pommarède de Haut	»	Château Cabannieux	»
Château Le Pape	»	Château Lognac	»	Château Crabitey	»
Château Chaviran	Martillac	Domaine de Sansaric	»	Château de Doms	»
Château Ferran	»	Château de La Brède	La Brède	Château Jean-Gervais	»
Château Lagarde	»	Cru de Bichon	»	Château des Graves	»
Château Malleprat	»	Château La Blancherie	»	Château Les Gravières	»
Château Haut-Nouchet	»	Château de l'Espérance	»	Domaine de La Girafe	»
Château La Roche	»	Cru d'Eyquem	»	Château de Graveyrion	»

Château Lagueloup	Portets	Château de Virelade	Virelade	Domaine d'Ordonnat	Langon
Château Lhospital	»	Château de Gayon	»	Clos Léhoul	»
Château Madelis	»	Château des Tilleuls	»	Château Ludeman	»
Château Millet	»	Château d'Arricaud	Landiras	Château Péran	»
Château Le Mirail	»	Château Batsères	»	Domaine de Toumilot	»
Château Moulin	»	Château Pessille	»	Château Bellefontaine	St-Pierre-
Château Pessan	»	Cru de Baylen	Budos	Clos Cantalot	de-Mons
Château du Pingoy	»	Château de Budos	»	Clos Cazebonne	»
Château de Portets	»	Château des Charmettes	»	Château des Jaubertes	»
Château Rahoul	»	Cru de l'Hermitage	»	Clos La Magine	»
Château La Tour-Bicheau	»	Domaine de Courbon	Toulenne	Château Magence	»
Domaine de Videau	»	Château de la Gravère	»	Clos du Moulin-à-Vent	»
Château Vieille-France	»	Clos Louloumet	»	Château Peydebayle	»
Cru du Bérot	Arbanats	Château Respide	»	Château des Queyrats	»
Château Mamin	»	Château La Tourte	»	Château de Respide	»
Domaine des Places	»	Château Tustoc	»	Château Toumillon	»
Château Tourteau-Chollet	»	Château Chanteloiseau	Langon	Clos d'Uza	»
Domaine de Teychon	»	Domaine des Gluchets	»		

MÉDOC REGION • RED WINES

GREAT GROWTHS OF THE 1855 CLASSIFICATION

First growths

Château Lafite-Rothschild, Pauillac	Château Margaux, Margaux	Château Latour, Pauillac	Château Mouton-Rothschild, Pauillac

Second growths

Château Brane-Cantenac	Cantenac	Château Léoville-Lascases	St-Julien	Château Rausan-Ségla	Margaux
Château Cos-d'Estournel	St-Estèphe	Château Léoville-Poyféré	»	Château Rauzan-Gassies	»
Château Montrose	»	Château Léoville-Barton	»	Château Pichon-Longueville	Pauillac
Château Ducru-Beaucaillou	St-Julien	Château Durfort-Vivens	Margaux	Château Pichon-Longueville-La-	
Château Gruaud-Laroze-Sarget	»	Château Lascombes	»	lande	»

Third growths

Château Kirwan,	Cantenac	Château Palmer	Cantenac	Château La Lagune	Ludon
Château Calon-Ségur,	St-Estèphe	Château Desmirail	Margaux	Château Giscours	Labarde
Château Cantenac-Brown	Cantenac	Château Ferrière	»	Château Lagrange	St-Julien
Château Boyd-Cantenac	»	Château Malescot-Saint-Exupéry	»	Château Langoa	»
Château d'Issan	»	Château Marquis-d'Alesme-Becker	»		

Fourth growths

Château Beychevelle	St-Julien	Château Talbot	St-Julien	Château Prieuré-Lichine	Margaux
Château Branaire-Ducru	»	Château Duhart-Milon	Pauillac	Château Pouget	Cantenac
Château Saint-Pierre	»	Château La Tour-Carnet	St-Laurent	Château Marquis-de-Therme	Margaux
				Château Lafon-Rochet	St-Estèphe

Fifth growths

Château Pontet-Canet	Pauillac	Château Haut-Bages-Libéral	Pauillac	Château Pédesclaux	Pauillac
Château Batailley	»	Château Lynch-Bages	»	Château Clerc-Milon	»
Château Haut-Batailley	»	Château Lynch-Moussas	»	Château Belgrave	St-Laurent
Château Croizet-Bages	»	Château Dauzac	Labarde	Château Camensac	»
Château Grand-Puy-Ducasse	»	Château Mouton-Baron-Philippe	Arsac	Château Cantemerle	Macau
Château Grand-Puy-Lacoste	»	Château Le Tertre	Pauillac	Château Cos-Labory	St-Estèphe

EXCEPTIONAL GROWTHS

Château Angludet	Cantenac	Château Bel-Air, Marquis d'Aligre	Sousans	Château Moulin-Riche	St-Julien
Château La Couronne	Pauillac	Château Chasse-Spleen	Moulis	Château Ville-Georges	Avensan

LIST OF THE PRINCIPAL BOURGEOIS GROWTHS ACCORDING TO THE SYNDICAL PRIZE-LIST OF MARCH 3, 1966

EXCEPTIONAL GREAT BOURGEOIS GROWTHS

Château Agassac	Ludon	Château La Closerie	Moulis	Château Houissant	St-Estèphe
Château Andron-Blanquet	St-Estèphe	Château Citran	Avensan	Château Lanessan	Cussac
Château Beausite	»	Château Le Crock	St-Estèphe	Château de Marbuzet	St-Estèphe
Château Le Boscq	»	Château Dutruch-Gd-Poujeaux	Moulis	Château Meyney	»
Château Capbern	»	Château du Glana	St-Julien	Château Phélan-Ségur	»
Château Caronne-Ste-Gemme	St-Laurent	Château Haut-Marbuzet	St-Estèphe	Château Villegeorge	Avensan

GREAT BOURGEOIS GROWTHS

Château Belle-Rose	Pauillac	Château Hanteillan	Cissac	Château Paveil-de-Luze	Soussans
Château Bel-Orme	St-Seurin	Château Labégorce-Zédé	Margaux	Château Pibran	Pauillac
Château Bibian-Darriet	Listrac	Château Lafite-Canteloup	Ludon	Château Pomeys	Moulis
Château Le Bourdieu	Vertheuil	Château Lamarque	Lamarque	Château Potensac	Potensac
Château Le Breuil	Cissac	Château Laujac	Bégadan	Château du Raux	Cussac
Château La Cardonne	Blaignan	Château Lestage	Listrac	Château Rolland	Pauillac
Château Canteloup	St-Estèphe	Château Lestage-Darquier	Moulis	Château Saransot-Dupré	Listrac
Château du Castera	St-Germain	Château Liversan	St-Sauveur	Château Ségur	Parempuyre
Château Coufran	St-Seurin	Château Loudenne	St-Yzans		
Château Coutelin-Merville	St-Estèphe	Château Mac-Carthy	St-Estèphe	Château Sénéjac	Le Pian
Château Cissac	Cissac	Château Malleret	Le Pian	Châteaux Sociando-Mallet et Pontoise-Cabarrus	St-Seurin
Château Fonbadet	Pauillac	Château Morin	St-Estèphe		
Château Fonréaud	Listrac	Château Moulin à Vent	Moulis	Château du Taillan	Le Taillan
Château Fontesteau	St-Sauveur	Château Moulis	»	Château La Tour-de-By	Bégadan
Château Fourcas-Dupré	Listrac	Château Patache-d'Aux	Bégadan	Château Verdignan	St-Seurin
Château Grandis	St-Seurin				

BOURGEOIS GROWTHS

Château Bel-Air-Lagrave	Moulis	Château Haut-Padarnac	Pauillac	Château Romefort	Cussac
Château Bonneau	St-Seurin	Château Larrivaux	Cissac	Château Roquegrave	Valeyrac
Château Bellegrave	Listrac	Cru Lassalle	Potensac	Château La Rose-Anseillan	Pauillac
Château de Come	St-Estèphe	Château Mac-Carthy-Moula	St-Estèphe	Château Saint-Bonnet	St-Christoly
Château Chambert	»	Château Malescasse	Lamarque	Château Saint-Christoly	»
Château Donissan	Listrac	Château Maurac	St-Seurin	Château Tayac et Siamois	Soussans
Château Grand-Duroc-Milon	Pauillac	Château Monthil	Bégadan	Château Les Ormes-Sorbet	Couquèques
Château La Fleur-Saint-Bonnet	St-Christoly	Clos du Moulin	St-Christoly	Château La Tour-Blanche	St-Christoly
Château La Fleur-Milon	Pauillac	Château Moulin-Rouge	Cussac	Château La Tour-des-Termes	St-Estèphe
Château Fonpiqueyre	St-Sauveur	Château Pabeau	St-Seurin	Château La Tour-St-Bonnet	St-Christoly
Château Fort-de-Vauban	Cussac	Château Le Privera	St-Christoly	Château Victoria	Vertheuil
Château Gallais-Bellevue	Potensac	Château Labatisse	St-Sauveur	Château Vieux-Moulin	Cussac
Château Grand-Saint-Julien	St-Julien	Château Renouil-Franquet	Moulis		

SOME OTHER BOURGEOIS GROWTHS

Château Dillon	Blanquefort	Château Barreyre	Arcins	Château La Tour-Milon	Pauillac
Château Fongravey	»	Château Poujeaux	Moulis	Château La Tour-d'Anseillan	»
Château Grand-Clapeau	»	Château Duplessis Hauchecorne	»	Château La Garosse	St-Sauveur
Château de Parempuyre	Parem-	Château La Closerie Gd Poujeaux	»	Château Peyrabon	»
Cru Ségur-Fillon-isle-d'Arès	puyre	Château Robert-Franquet	»	Château La Tour du Mirail	Cissac
Château La Dame-Blanche	Le Taillan	Château Gressier-Grand-Poujeaux	»	Château La Tour Saint-Joseph	»
Domaine de Chalet-de-Germignan	»	Château Duplessis-Fabre	»	Château Le Roc	St-Estèphe
Château Ludon-Pomiès-Agassac	Ludon	Château Ruat-Petit-Poujeaux	»	Château Tronquoy-Lalande	»
Château La Providence	»	Château La Morère	»	Château Fonpetite	»
Château d'Arche	»	Château Médrac	»	Château de Pez	»
Château « Trois-Moulins »	Macau	Château du Testeron	»	Château La Haye	»
Château Maucamps	»	Château l'Érmitage	Listrac	Château Pomys	»
Château Fellonneau	»	Château Semeillan-Mazeau	»	Château Les Ormes de Pez	»
Château Larronde-Desormes	»	Château Semeillan Balleu-Faulat	»	Château Ladouys	»
Château Larrieu-Terrefort	»	Château Lafon	»	Château Saint-Roch	»
Château d'Arsac	Arsac	Château Fourcas-Hosten	»	Château Clauzet	»
Château Montbrison	»	Château Rose-Sainte-Croix	»	Château Grand-Village-Capbern	»
Le Moulin-Avensan	Avensan	Château Granins	»	Château Domeync	»
Château Rosemont	Labarde	Château La Bécade	»	Château Picard	»
Château Siran	»	Château du Cartillon	Lamarque	Château Mac-Carthy	»
Château Martinens	Cantenac	Château Cap-de-Haut	»	Château Laffitte-Carcasset	»
Château Montbrun	»	Château Moulin-Rose	»	Château Latour de Marbuzet	»
Château Rouge Port-Aubin	»	Château Lanessan	Cussac	Château Faget	»
Château Pontac-Lynch	»	Château Beaumont	»	Domaine de Pez	»
Château de Labegorce	Margaux	Château Lamothe-Bergeron	»	Château Reysson	Vertheuil
Château L'Abbé-Gorsse-de-Gorsse	»	Château Larose-Trintaudon	St-Laurent	Château La Gravière-Couerbe	»
Château La Gurgue	»	Château Larose-Perganson	»	Château Charmail	St-Seurin-
Domaine de Clairefont	»	Château Galan	»	Château du Haut-Carmail	Cadourne
Château La Tour-de-Mons	Soussans	Château Corconnac	»	Château Livran	St-Germ.-
Château La Bégorce	»	Château La Tour Marcillanet	»	Château Beaulieu	d'Esteuil
Château Haut-Breton	»	Château Gloria	St-Julien	Château Carcanieux-les-Graves	Queyrac
Château Marsac-Séguineau	»	Château Haut Bages Monpelou	Pauillac	Château La Croix-Landon	Begadan
Château de l'Aiguillette	»	Château Malécot	»	Château Bellegrave	»
Château La Tour-du-Roc	Arcins	Château Balogues	»	Château Bellerive	»
Château d'Arcins	»	Château Latour-L'Aspic	»	Château Les Lesques	Lesparre

REGION BETWEEN GARONNE AND DORDOGNE

CÔTES DE BORDEAUX SAINT-MACAIRE • WHITE WINES

Château Cordeliers	St-Macaire	Domaine de Flous	St-Pierre-d'Aurillac	Château Machorre	St-Martin-de-Sescas
Domaine de Belle-Croix	»				
Domaine des Charmettes	St-Martial	Château Perrayne	St-André-du-Bois	Château La Serre	Caudrot
Château Haut-Bardin	»			Domaine de Jacob	St-Laurent-du-Pian
Cru Terrefort	Le Pian	Château Malromé	»		
Château Fayard	»	Château d'Arche-Lassalle	»	Domaine de Beaulieu	Ste-Foy-la-Longue
Cru Rigal	»				

SAINTE-CROIX-DU-MONT • WHITE WINES

Château Loubens	Ste-Croix-du-Mont	Domaine de Morange	Ste-Croix-du-Mont	Château Terfort	Ste-Croix-du-Mont
Château de Tastes		Château La Gravière		Château Les Marcottes	
Château Bouchoc	»	Château Labory	»	Domaine de Roustit	»
Château Lafüe	»	Château Coullac	»	Cru des Arroucats	»
Château Laurette	»	Château Loustauvieil	»	Clos Belle-Vue	»
Château Bel-Air	»	Château Roustit	»	Château La Graville	»
Château de L'Escaley	»	Domaine du Tich	»	Cru de La Gravière du Tich	»
Château du Grand-Peyrot	»	Domaine des Sorbiers	»	Château Lapeyreyre	»
Château La Rame	»	Château Jean Lamat	»	Château Copis	»
Château La Mouleyre	»	Château du Pavillon	»	Château La Caussade	»
Château Médouc	»	Château Bertranon	»	Château du Verger	»
Château des Mailles	»	Clos de Verteuil	»		

LOUPIAC • WHITE WINES

Château de Ricaud	Loupiac	Château Lanusse-Couloumet	Loupiac	Château La Yotte	Loupiac
Château Mazarin	»	Château du Vieux-Moulin	»	Cru de Montallier-Lambrot	»
Château Dauphiné-Rondillon	»	Clos Champon-Ségur	»	Domaine du Chay	»
Château du Cros	»	Domaine de Turon-Lanere	»	Domaine de Barbe-Maurin	»
Château de Loupiac-Gaudiet	»	Château des Roches	»	Château Terrefort	»
Château Pontac	»	Domaine de Rouquette	»	Château Le Portail Rouge	»
Château Tarey	»	Château Le Tarey	»	Château de Martillac	»
Domaine de Malendure	»	Cru du Couloumet	»	Cru du Merle	»
Clos Jean	»	Domaine de Pasquet	»	Clos de Giron	»
Château de Rondillon	»	Château Pageot-Couloumet	»	Domaine de Miqueu-Bel-Air	»
Château La Nère	»	Château Peyruchet	»	Château Roustin	»
Domaine du Noble	»	Domaine de Roby	»	Domaine de Guinot	»
Cru de Couloumet-Les Boupeyres	»	Domaine du Rocher	»	Château de Beaupuy	»
				Château Margès-Dusseau	»

PREMIÈRES CÔTES DE BORDEAUX • WHITE WINES

Château Laurétan	Langoiran	Château Terrasson	Langoiran	Château de Plassans	Tabanac
Château Sauvage	»	Cru Baylibelle	»	Château Lucques Bessan	»
Château La Tour Maudan	»	Château Lagareyre	»	Château Lamothe	»
Château Pommarède	»	Domaine du Pin	»	Château Sentour	»
Château Biac	»	Château Barrère	»	Château Renon	»
Château Le Gardera	»	Domaine du Gourdin	»	Château La Providence	»
Château Tanesse	»	Domaine de Côte-Rôtie-Lamothe	»	Domaine d'Armaing	»
Château Faubernet	»	Château Dutoya	»	Château Laroche	Baurech
Château du Vallier	»	Château Chauvin	»	Domaine de Melin	»
Domaine de Bellevue	»	Domaine de Lagaloche	»	Château Puygueraud	»
Château Gourran	»	Château La Ronde	Le Tourne	Château de Lyde	»
Château Lapeyruche	»	Château Pic	»	Château Gaussens	»
Château Langoiran	»	Domaine de Moutons	»	Château Pressac	»
Château de l'Eglise	»	Château Le Mesnil	»	Château de Haux	Haux
Château La Ligassonne	»	Domaine de la Côte Rôtie	Tabanac	Château du Juge	»
Domaine Crassat-Gramman	»	Château Lagarosse	»	Château La Gorce	»

160

Château Peneau	Haux	Château Mony	Rions	Château Faugas	Gabarnac
Château Gréteau	»	Clos du Monastère du Broussey	»	Domaine de La Cure	»
Château Brigaille	»	Domaine de la Bastide	»	Cru du Bourdieu	Monprim-
Château Lamothe de Haux	»	Château des Remparts	»	Château Beau-Site Monprimblanc	blanc
Château du Grava	»	Château Peironnin	»	Domaine de Lagrange	»
Château de La Bézine	»	Clos de Ricouet	»	Clos La Burthe	»
Domaine de Bernadon	»	Domaine de Carsin	»	Domaine Lambert	»
Château du Courreau	»	Château La Roque	La Roque	Château de Teste	»
Château Jeanganne-Préfontaine	»	Château Peller	»	Cru de Vigneyre	»
Château Bellegarde	Paillet	Clos Dezarneauld	»	Domaine de la Frairie	»
Château Paillet	»	Château Haut-Laroque	»	Domaine de Poncet	Omet
Château l'Ermitage	»	Château Lassalle	»	Domaine des Biscarets	»
Château de Marsan	Estiac-sur-	Château Birot	Béguey	Domaine de Camelon	»
Au Moulin des Graves	Garonne	Domaine du Pin	»	Clos du Boudeur	»
Château du Peyrat	Capian	Château Peyrat	»	Domaine de La Bertrande	»
Château de Caillavet	»	Château Boisson	»	Château Mont-Célestin	Verdelais
Château Suau	»	Domaine de la Marquise	»	Château Pomirol le Pin	»
Château Barakan	»	Château de Garreau	Cadillac	Cru Cantegrit	»
Domaine de Sainte-Anne	»	Château du Juge	»	Domaine de Grava	»
Château de Grand-Mouëys	»	Château des Tourelles	»	Château Gravelines-Semens	»
Château Ramondon	»	Château Arnaud-Jouan	»	Domaine de Joffre	»
Domaine de Potiron	»	Château Fayau	»	Domaine de Lescure	»
Château de Grand-Branet	»	Château de Beaulieu	»	Cru du Haut-Roudey	»
Château Lezongard	Villenave-	Clos des Capucins	»	Cru de Nazareth	»
Château Fauchey	de-Rions	Château Lardiley	»	Domaine de Boustit	»
Domaine de Lamarque	Cardan	Château Côte-Belle	»	Château La Prioulette	St-Maixant
Château Janisson	»	Château Justa	»	Château du Point-de-Vue	»
Château Videau	»	Clos Saint-Cricq	»	Château Chante-l'Oiseau	»
Domaine de Bourgalade	»	Château de la Passonne	»	Château Malagar	»
Domaine de Lhoste	»	Château du Gard	»	Château Montonoir	»
Domaine de Mespley	»	Cru Peytoupin	»	Château Pique-Caillou	»
Château du Payre	»	Cru La Gravette	»	Château Lavison	»
Château Mageot	»	Domaine de Chasse-Pierre	»	Château Saint-Germain	St-Germain-
Château de l'Espinglet	Rions	Domaine de Saint-Cricq	»	Domaine de la Maroutine	de-Graves
Domaine du Broussey	»	Château du Pin	»	Château Génisson	»
Domaine de Hautes-Graves	»	Château Marcelin-Laffitte	Gabarnac	Clos de Millanges	»
Domaine de Cholet	»	Clos Pierre-Jean	»	Domaine de Goursin	»
Château Jourdan	»	Domaine du Moulin de Ballan	»	Château Saint-Germain	»
Domaine de Cardonne	»	Clos du Grand-Bonneau	»	Domaine du Fihl	Donzac
Château Caïla	»	Château Latour Feugas	»	Domaine du Haurin	»
				Domaine de Prentigarde	»

PREMIÈRES CÔTES DE BORDEAUX • RED WINES

Château Bassaler Castanède	Bassens	Château Léon	Carignan	Château La Rigaudière	Camblanes
Château Favols	Carbon-	(Domaine de Camelon)	»	Château de Courtade	»
	Blanc	Château Malherbes	Latresne	Château Damluc	»
Château La Croix	Lormont	Château Gassies	»	Domaine de Cluseau	»
Château de Cypressat	Cenon	Domaine de Pardaillan	»	Château Lestange	Quinsac
Château Costeriou	Bouliac	Domaine du Grand-Parc	»	Château Péconnet	»
Château Montjon-Le-Gravier	Ste-Eulalie	Château Pascot	»	Château de Pranzac	»
Château La Tour-Gueyraud	»	Château Rauzé-Sybil	Cénac	Domaine de Chastelet	»
Château de Chelivette	»	Château Haut-Brignon	»	Domaine de Castagnon	»
L'Abbaye de Bonlieu	»	Château Materre	»	Château Montaigne	»
Château Larose	»	Château Saint-Sève	»	Château Bel-Air	»
Château Malbec	»	Château La Mouline	»	Château Bellevue	»
Château d'Intrans	»	Château Duplessis	»	Château du Peyrat	Cambes
Château du Grand Jour	Yvrac	Château Rauzé	»	Château La Navarre	»
Château Bellevue	»	Domaine de Roquebrune	»	Château Maran	»
Domaine de Bouteilley	»	Château Latour	Camblanes	Château Puy-Bardens	»
Château Maillard	»	Château Bel-Air	»	Château Brémontier	»
Château Canteloup	»	Château Brethous	»	Château Lardit	»
Château Labatut	»	Château Courtade Dubuc	»	Château Roubric	»
Château Cayre	»	Château Lafitte	»	Château La Chabanne	»
Château Miraflorès	»	Château Lagarette	»	Clos de Gourgues	St-Caprais-
Château Tertre du Renard	»	Château Tapiau	»	Château Campet	de-
Château de Carignan	Carignan	Château du Tasta	»	Domaine de Luc	Bordeaux
Château Roqueys	»	Clos Haut-Forcade	»	Domaine des Conseillants	»

ENTRE-DEUX-MERS • WHITE WINES AND RED WINES

HAUT-BENAUGE

Château du Vert	Arbis	Domaine de Fongrane	Gornac	Domaine de la Grangeotte	Gornac
Domaine de Gouas	»	Château Cazeau	»	Château d'Ories	»
Clos de Terrefort	»	Château Martinon	»	Domaine de Pédebert	»
Château de Benauge	»	Château Pouly	»	Domaine de Troubat	»
Domaine de Meyssau	Cantois	Château d'Hauretz	»	Domaine de Peyrines	Mourens-
Domaine de Fermis	»	Domaine de la Gaborie	»	Domaine de Mondain	Monpezat
Domaine de Talusson	»	Domaine de Terrefort	»	Domaine du Ferron	Soulignac
Domaine de Pasquet	Escoussans	Domaine du Houre	»	Château de Toutigeac	Targon
Domaine de Nicot	»	Château La Mazerolle	»	Domaine de Brufanno	»

CANTONS OF BRANNE, OF PUJOLS, OF SAUVETERRE AND OF PELLEGRUE

Domaine de Fauchey	Branne	Domaine de Vignolles	St-Quentin-	Château de Pressac	Daignac
Château de Blagnac	Cabara	Clos Picard	le-Baron	Château Mauros	Guillac
Château du Grand Puch	St-Germain-Puch	Château de Bellefontaine	Baron	Château de Vidasse-Pessac	Pessac-s.-
Domaine Le Pin	St-Aubin-de-Blaignac	Château Raymond	»	Domaine Le Mayne	Dordogne
		Château Ramonet	»	Domaine de Glayse	»
Domaine de la Girolatte	Naujan-et-	Domaine du Grand-Canteloup	Nérigean	Domaine de la Rivière	Pujols
Château Beaufresque	Postiac	Château Martouret	»	Château de la Salle	Rauzan
Château de Naujan	»	Château de Montlau	Moulon	Château Villotte	»
Domaine de la Rouergue	»	Château Mouchac	Génissac	Château du Bedat	Blasimon
Château Bonnet	Grézillac	Château Rambaud	»	Château de Roques	Mauriac
Domaine de Cabirol	Camiac	Château du Burg	»	Château de Courteillac	Ruch
Domaine de Balestard	St-Quentin-le-Baron	Château Fantin	St-Jean-de-Blaignac	Château de Grand-Champs	St-Sulpice-de-Pomiers

CANTONS OF CARBON-BLANC AND OF CRÉON

Château du Burk	Ambès	Château La Mothe	Montussan	Clos de Dominge	Camarsac
Château Sainte-Barbe	»	Château La Tour	Sallebœuf	Château Seguin	Lignan
Château Parabelle	Ambarès	Château Grand-Monteil	»	Clos Saint-Jean	»
Château du Tillac	»	Château Pontac-Gasparini	»	Château de Tustal	Sadirac
Château Formont	»	Château de Lesparre	Beychac-	Domaine de Calamiac	»
Château du Gua	»	Château Quinsac	et-Cailleau	Château Guillaumet	»
Château du Peychaud	»	Domaine de La Grave	»	Château Lestage	»
Château Lagraula	St-Sulpice-	Château Senailhac	Tresses	Domaine de Landreau	»
Château Beauval	Cameyrac	Château Bel-Air	»	Château de Bergerie	St-Genès-
Château Quantin	»	Château Lestrilles	Artigues		de-
Château de Reignac	St-Loubès	Château Lafitte	»		Lombaud
Château Lescart	»	Château Landeron	Pompignac	Château Beauduc	Créon
Château Labatut	»	Château Rivasseau	»	Château Patrouilleau	La Sauve
Château Chelivette	»	Château des Arrouches	»	Domaine de Castebelle-	»
Château Les Dauphins	»	Château Beaulé	»	des-Praud	
Château La Tour-Puymirand	Montussan	Domaine des Carmes	»	Château Chateauneuf	»
Château Lavergne	»	Château de Camarsac	Camarsac	Château de Goélane	St-Léon
Château Fonchereau	»	Château Beauséjour	»	Château Le Cugat	»
				Château du Bedat	Blasimon

SAINTE-FOY-BORDEAUX REGION • RED WINES AND WHITE WINES

Château de Courauneau	Ligueux	Château de Langalerie	St-Quentin-	Château de La Tour Beaupoil	Pessac-sur
Château La Roche	Les Lèves	Domaine de Mayne	de-Caplong		Dordogne
Château des Vergnes	»				

GRAVES-DE-VAYRES • RED WINES

Château Bel-Air	Vayres	Château Bussac	Vayres

RIGHT BANK OF THE DORDOGNE AND OF THE GIRONDE

SAINT-ÉMILION REGION • RED WINES

GREAT GROWTHS OF THE 1955 CLASSIFICATION

First great classified growths (a)

Château Ausone . . . .   St-Emilion   Château Cheval-Blanc . . . . .   St-Emilion

First great classified growths (b)

Château Beauséjour	St-Emilion	Clos Fourtet	St-Emilion	Château Magdelaine	St-Emilion
Château Bel-Air	»	Château Figeac	»	Château Pavie	»
Château Canon	»	Château La Gaffelière	»	Château Trottevieille	»

Great classified growths

Château l'Angélus	St-Emilion	Château Le Grand-Corbin-		Château Le Couvent	St-Emilion
Château l'Arrosée	»	Pécresse	St-Emilion	Château Le Prieuré	
Château Balestard-la-Tonnelle .	»	Château Grand-Mayne	»	Saint-Emilion	»
Château Bellevue	»	Château Grand-Pontet	»	Château Mauvezin-La-	
Château Bergat	»	Château Les Grandes-Murailles .	»	Gommerie	»
Le Cadet Bon	»	Château Guadet-Saint-Julien . .	»	Château Moulin du Cadet . . .	»
Château Cadet-Piola	»	Château Jean-Faure	»	Château Pavie-Decesse	»
Château Canon-La-Gaffelière . .	»	Clos des Jacobins	»	Domaine Pavie-Macquin	»
Château Cap de Mourlin	»	Château La Carte	»	Pavillon Cadet	»
Château Chapelle-Madeleine . .	»	Château La Clotte	»	Château Petit-Faurie-de-Soutard	»
Château Chauvin	»	Château La Cluzière	»	Château Ripeau	»
Château Corbin	»	Château La Couspaude	»	Château Sansonnet	»
Château Corbin-Michotte . . .	»	Château La Dominique	»	Château Saint-Georges-	
Château Coutet	»	Clos La Madeleine	»	Côtes-Pavie	»
Château Croque-Michotte	»	Château Larcis-Ducasse	»	Clos Saint-Martin	»
Château Curé-Bon-la-Madelaine .	»	Château La Marzelle	»	Château Soutard	»
Château Fonplégade	«	Château Larmande	»	Château Tertre-Daugay	»
Château Fonroque	»	Château Laroze	»	Château Trimoulet	»
Château Franc-Mayne	»	Château La Serre	»	Château des Trois Moulins . . .	»
Château Grand-Barrail-		Château La Tour-du-Pin-Figeac	»	Château Troplong-Mondot . . .	»
Lamarzelle-Figeac	»	Château La Tour-Figeac	»	Château Villemaurine	»
Château Grand Corbin Despagne	»	Château Le Châtelet	»	Château Yvon-Figeac	»

Principal other growths

Château Badette	St-Emilion	Château Dassault	St-Emilion	Château Haut-Simard	St-Emilion
Clos Badon	»	Château Daugay	»	Domaine de Haut-Veyrac . . .	»
Domaine de Badon-Patarabet .	»	Domaine De Rey	»	Château Hermitage-Mazerat . .	»
Château Baleau	»	Château De Rol	»	Château Jacquemeau	»
Château Beau-Mazerat	»	Château Etoile-Pourret	»	Château du Jardin-Saint-Julien .	»
Château Belles-Plantes	»	Château Fongaban-Bellevue . .	»	Château du Jardin-Villemaurine.	»
Château Berliquet	»	Château Fonrazade	»	Château Jaugue-Blanc	»
Château Bézineau	»	Château Franc-Patarabet	»	Château Jean de Mayne	»
Château Bord-Ramonet	»	Château Franc-Pourret	»	Château Jean Voisin	»
Château Bragard	»	Clos du Grand-Châtelet	»	Clos Jean-Voisin	»
Château Cadet-Soutard	»	Domaine du Grand-Faurie . . .	»	Château La Clotte-Grande-Côte .	»
Château Cadet-Fonroque	»	Château Grand Mirande	»	Château La Croix-Chantecaille .	»
Château Cantenac	»	Château Guadet-Le-Franc-Grâce-		Château La Fleur-Mérissac . . .	»
Château Cardinal-Villemaurine .	»	Dieu	»	Château La Fleur-Pourret . . .	»
Château Cartau	»	Château Gueyrot	»	Château La Fleur-Vachon . . .	»
Château Cassevert	»	Château Haut-Berthonneau . . .	»	Domaine La Gaffelière	»
Château Cauzin	»	Château Haut-Cadet	»	Château La Gommerie	»
Château Champion	»	Château Haut-Fonrazade	»	Château La Grâce-Dieu	»
Domaine du Châtelet	»	Château Haut-Grâce-Dieu . . .	»	Château La Madeleine	»
Domaine de Chante-Grive-Badon	»	Château Haut-Grand-Faurie . .	»	Château Le Manoir	»
Château Châtelet-Moléonne . .	»	Château Haut-La Rose	»	Clos La Marzelle	»
Château Cheval-Noir	»	Château Haut-Mazerat	»	Château Laniotte	»
Château du Clocher	»	Domaine Haut-Patarabet . . .	»	Château Laplagnotte-Bellevue .	»
Château Cormey	»	Château Haut-Pontet	»	Château Laporte	»
Château Cormey Figeac	»	Château Haut-Pourret	»	Château La Rose	»
Couvent-des-Jacobins	»	Clos Haut-Pourret	»	Château La Rose Pourret . . .	»
Château Cravignac	»	Château Haut-Sarpe	»	Château La Rose-Rol	»
Château Croix-de-Chantecaille .	»	Château Haut-Segotte	»	Château La Tour-Fonrazade . .	»

163

Château La Tour-Pourret	St-Emilion	Château Vieux-Ceps	St-Emilion	Château Puy-Blanquet	St-Etienne
Château La Tour-Saint-Pierre	»	Château Villebout	»	Château du Rocher	de-Lisse
Château Magnan	»	Château Vieux-Grand-Faurie	»	Château du Vieux-Guinot	»
Château Magnan-La-Gaffelière	»	Château Vieux-Moulin-du-Cadet	»	Château Baladoz	St-Laurent-
Château Malineau	»	Château Vieux-Pourret	»	Clos La Barde	des-Combes
Château Martin	»	Domaine de Yon	»	Château de La Barde	»
Château Matras	»	Château Yon-Figeac	»	Château de Béard	»
Château Matras-Côte-Daugay	»	Château Barde-Haut	St-Christophe	Château Bellefont-Belcier	»
Château Mazerat	»	Château Les Basiliques	des-Bardes	Château Belle-Isle-Mondotte	»
Château des Menuts	»	Château Brun	»	Château La Bouygue	»
Clos des Menuts	»	Château du Cauze	»	Château Godeau	»
Côte Mignon-Lagaffelière	»	Château Coudert	»	Château Haute-Nauve	»
Château Montlabert	»	Château Fombrauge	St-Emilion	Château Pipeau	»
Château Moulin-Saint-Georges	»	Château Gaubert	»	Château du Sable	»
Château Petit-Figeac	»	Château Grangey	»	Château Villebout	»
Château Mouton-Blanc	»	Château Guillemot	»	Château Larcis-Ducasse	»
Château Clos de l'Oratoire	»	Château Haut-Sarpe	»	Château Capet	St-Hippo-
Château Le Palat	»	Château Lapelletrie	»	Château de Ferrand	lyte
Château Patris	»	Château Laroque	»	Château Capet-Guillier	»
Château Petit-Cormey	»	Château Larquet	»	Château Haut-Plantey	»
Château Petit-Faurie-Trocard	»	Château Marrin	»	Château Lassègue	»
Domaine Petit-Val	»	Château Panet	»	Château Maurens	»
Château Peyraud	»	Clos des Moines	»	Château Monlot-Capet	»
Château Peygenestou	»	Château Quentin	»	Château Pailhas	»
Clos Picon-Cravignac	»	Château Rol-de-Fombrauge	»	Château Pipeau-Ménichot	»
Château Pindefleurs	»	Château Saint-Christophe	»	Clos des Sarrazins	»
Château Pontet	»	Château Sarpe-Grand-Jacques	»	Château Gros	St-Pey-
Château Pontet-Clauzure	»	Clos de Sarpe	»	Château Fourney	d'Armens
Château Pontet-Fontlabert	»	Château Sarpe Pelletan	»	Château Jean-Blanc	»
Château Puygenestou	»	Château La-Tour-St-Christophe	»	Château La Chapelle-de-Lescours	»
Château Régent	»	Château Vieux-Sarpe	»	Cru Peyrouquet	»
Château Royland	»	Château Bel-Air-Ouy	St-Etienne	Château de Saint-Pey	»
Clos Saint-Emilion	»	Domaine du Calvaire	de-Lisse	Château Saint-Pierre	»
Château Saint-Julien	»	Château Canterane	»	Château Le Castelot	St-Sulpice-
Domaine de la Salle	»	Château Côte Bernateau	»	Château Grand-Pey-Lescours	de-Faleyrens
Château Simard	»	Château de Lisse	»	Château Lande de Gravet	»
Château Soutard-Cadet	»	Château La Fagnouse	»	Château de Lescours	»
Enclos de Soutard	»	Domaine de Haut-Bruly	»	Château Monbousquet	»
Château La Tour-Pourret	»	Château du Haut-Rocher	»	Château de Faleyrens	»
Château Trianon	»	Domaine de Haut-Veyrac	»	Château Saint-Martial	»
Cru Troquart	»	Château Jacques-Blanc	»	Château Trapeau	»
Château Truquet	»	Château Lamartre	»	Château Quercy	Vignonet
Château Vachon	»	Château Mangot	»	Château Peyroutas	»
Clos Valentin	»	Château Mont-Belair	»	Château Rouchonne-Vignonet	»
Château de la Vieille-Cloche	»	Château de Pressac	»		

SABLES-SAINT-ÉMILION • RED WINES

Château Martinet	Sables-	Château Garde-Rose	Sable-	Château Cruzeau	Sable-
Clos de la Bordette	St-Emilion	Château Doumayne	St-Emilion	Château Gueyrosse	St-Emilion
Château de la Capelle	»	Clos Froidefond	»	Château Quinault	»

MONTAGNE-SAINT-ÉMILION • RED WINES

Château Bayard	Montagne-	Château Haut-Plaisance	Montagne-	Château La Tour-Montagne	Montagne-
Château Beauséjour	St-Emilion	Château Jura-Plaisance	St-Emilion	Château La Tour-Paquillon	St-Emilion
Château Bellevue	»	Château La Bastienne	»	Château Maison-Blanche	»
Château Calon	»	Château La Bichaude	»	Château des Moines	»
Château Corbin	»	Château Lafleur	»	Château Montaiguillon	»
Château Coucy	»	Château La Papeterie	»	Château Mouchet-Montagne	»
Château de Fontmurée	»	Château La Picherie	»	Château Moulin-Blanc	»
Château Gay-Moulin	»	Château La Tête-du-Cerf	»	Clos des Moulins-de-Calon	»
Château Haut-Goujon	»	Château La Tour-Calon	»	Château Négrit	»
Château Les Hautes-Graves	»	Château La Tour-Corniaud	»	Château Paradis	»

Château Petit-Clos	Montagne-	Château Les Tuileries-de-Bayard	Montagne-	Domaine de Faizeau	Montagne-
Château Pierrot-Plaisance ...	St-Emilion	Château Vieille-Maison	St-Emilion	Domaine de Fontmurée	St-Emilion
Château Plaisance	»	Château Le Vieux-Logis	»	Domaine de Gillet	»
Château Rocher-Corbin	»	Vieux Château Goujon	»	Domaine de La Barde	»
Château Roudier	»	Domaine de Beaudron	»	Domaine de Labatut.	»
Château Saint-André-Corbin ..	»	Domaine de Cazelon	»	Domaine de La Clotte	»
Château Saint-Jacques-Calon ..	»	Domaine Croix-de-Mission ...	»	Domaine de La Vieille	»
Château des Tours.......	»				

SAINT-GEORGES SAINT-ÉMILION • RED WINES

Château Bellevue	St-Georges-	Château La Tour du Pas-Saint-	St-Georges-	Château Samion.	St-Georges-
Château Calon	de-Montagne	Georges	de-Montagne	Château Tourteau	de-Montagne
Château Bel-Air Haut-Mont-		Château Macquin	»	Château Troquard	»
guillon	»	Château Saint-André-Corbin ..	»	Château Vieux-Guillou......	»
Château du Châtelet	»	Château Saint-Georges	»	Domaine de Maisonneuve ...	»
Château Guillou	»	Château Saint-Georges Cap-d'Or.	»	Domaine de Grimon	»
Château Haut-Troquard	»	Château Saint-Louis	»		

LUSSAC SAINT-ÉMILION • RED WINES

Château Belair	Lussac	Domaine de Lagrange	Lussac	Château Petit-Refuge	Lussac
Château Bellevue	»	Château La Tour-de-Ségur ...	»	Château Poitou-Lussac	»
Clos Blanchon	»	Château Lion-Perruchon	»	Château Souchet-Piquat	»
Domaine du Courlat	»	Château de Lussac	»	Château Taveney	»
Château Croix-de-Blanchon ..	»	Château du Lyonnat	»	Château Terrien	»
Château Haut-Larose	»	Clos du Lyonnat	»	Château Tiffray-Guadey	»
Château Haut-Piquat	»	Domaine de Rambaud	»	Château La Tour-de-Grenet. ..	»
Château La Fleur-Perruchon ..	»	Château La Ferrière	»	Château Les Vieux-Chênes ...	»

PUISSEGUIN SAINT-ÉMILION • RED WINES

Château Beauséjour	Puisseguin	Château Guibot-la-Fourvieille .	Puisseguin	Château de Puisseguin	Puissseguin
Cru Belair	»	Château Haut-Bernon	»	Château du Roc de Boissac ...	»
Château Chêne-Vieux	»	Château La Clotte	»	Clos du Roy	»
Château Durand	»	Château des Laurets	»	Château Teyssier	»
Château Guibaud	»	Château du Mayne	»		

PARSAC SAINT-ÉMILION • RED WINES

Château Langlade........	Parsac	Château Malagin	Parsac	Château Piron	Parsac
Château Lestage	»	Château Musset........	»		

POMEROL • RED WINES

Château Beauchêne (former Clos		Clos du Clocher	Pomerol	Château Grandchamp	Pomerol
Mazeyres)	Pomerol	Château Conseillante.	»	Domaine des Grands-Champs ..	»
Château Beauregard......	»	Château La Croix-Saint-Georges.	»	Château Grate-Cap	»
Clos Beauregard........	»	Clos l'Eglise	»	Château Guillot........	»
Château Belle-Brise	»	Domaine de l'Eglise	»	Clos des Hautes Graves	»
Château Bourgneuf-Vayron ..	»	Clos l'Eglise-Clinet	»	Domaine de Haut-Pignon ...	»
Château Brun-Mazeyres	»	Château l'Enclos	»	Château Haut-Plateau	»
Château Le Caillou	»	Château L'Evangile	»	Domaine Haut-Pomerol	»
Château de Cantereau	»	Château Ferrand	»	Château Enclos Haut-Mazeyres .	»
Château Carillon	»	Château Feytit-Clinet	»	Château La Cabanne.	»
Château Certan-Demay	»	Château Gazin	»	Château La Croix	»
Château Certan-Marzelle	»	Château Gombaude-Guillot et		Château La Commanderie ...	»
Château du Chêne-Liège	»	Grandes Vignes Clinet réunis .	»	Château Lacroix-de-Gay	»
Château Clinet	»	Château Gouprie	»	Château Lafleur	»

La Fleur du Gazin	Pomerol	Clos Mazeyres	Pomerol	Château Saint-André	Pomerol
Château La Fleur-Petrus	»	Château Monbran	»	Château Saint-Pierre	»
Château La Ganne	»	Château Monregard La Croix	»	Château de Sales	»
Château Lagrange	»	Château Moulinet	»	Château Samson	»
Château La Grave-Trigant-de-Boisset	»	Château Mouton-Mazeyres	»	Château Sudrat-Boussaton	»
Château La Pointe	»	Château Nenin	»	Château du Tailhas	»
Château Latour à Pomerol et Grandes Vignes réunies	»	Cru de La Nouvelle-Eglise	»	Château Taillefer	»
Château La Violette	»	Château Petit-Bocage	»	Clos des Templiers	»
Château La-Vraye-Croix-de-Gay	»	Château Petit-Village	»	Clos Toulifaut	»
Château Le Gabachot	»	Château Petrus	»	Château Tristan	»
Château Le Gay	»	Château Plince	»	Château Trotanoy	»
Château Le Prieuré La Croix	»	Château La Providence	»	Château de Valois	»
Château Mazeyres	»	Clos René	»	Château Vieux-Certan	»
		Clos du Roi	»	Vieux Château Cloquet	»
		Château Rouget	»		

LALANDE-DE-POMEROL • RED WINES

Clos des Arnaud	Lalande-de-Pomerol	Clos l'Etoile	Lalande-de-Pomerol	Château de Musset	Lalande-de-Pomerol
Château de Bel-Air		Domaine de Grand-Moine		Château Perron	
Château Bourseau	»	Château Grand-Ormeau	»	Sabloire du Grand Moine	»
Petit Clos de Brouard	»	Château La Gravière	»	Château Sergant	»
Château de la Commanderie	»	Clos Haut Cavujon	»	Château Templiers	»
Château La Croix-Saint-Jean	»	Château Laborde	»	Château de Viaud	»
Château Les Cruzelles	»	Château des Moines	»	Domaine de Viaud	»
Clos de l'Eglise	»	Clos des Moines	»	Clos de la Vieille-Forge	»

NÉAC LALANDE-DE-POMEROL • RED WINES

Domaine du Bourg	Néac	Château Garraud	Néac	Domaine de Machefer	Néac
Château Canon Chaigneau	»	Château Gachet	»	Château Moulin-à-Vent	»
Clos du Castel	»	Domaine des Grands-Bois-Chagneau	»	Château Moulin-Blanc	»
Château Chaigneau-Guillon	»	Domaine du Grand-Ormeau	»	Château Moncets	»
Château Châtain	»	Château Haut-Ballet	»	Château Nicole	»
Clos du Châtain	»	Château Haut-Chaigneau	»	Domaine du Petit-Bois	»
Domaine du Châtain	»	Château Lacroix	»	Château Saint-André	»
Vieux Château Chevrol	»	Château La Croix-Saint-André	»	Château Siaurac	»
Château Les Chaumes	»	Château Lafaurie	»	Domaine de Surget	»
Château Chevrol-Bel-Air	»	Château Lafleur-Lambaret	»	Château de Teysson	»
Château Drouilleau-Belles-Graves	»	Château Lavinot-la-Chapelle	»	Château Tournefeuille	»
Château Fougeailles	»			Château Yveline	»

CANON FRONSAC • RED WINES

Château Vray-Canon-Boyer	St-Michel-de-Fronsac	Cru Gros-Bonnet	Fronsac	Château Capet-Bégaud	Fronsac
Château Canon		Château de Toumalin	»	Clos Lariveau	St-Michel-de-Fronsac
Château Vrai-Canon-Bodet-La Tour	»	Château Barrabaque	»	Château Pey-Labrit	
Château Vrai-Canon-Bouché	»	Domaine de Trepesson	St-Michel-de-Fronsac	Cru La Tour-Ballet	»
Château Canon-Lange	Fronsac	Domaine de Trepesson-Lafontine	de-Fronsac	Domaine de Roulet	Fronsac
Château Junayme	»	Château Bodet	Fronsac	Domaine de Bourdieu-Panet	»
Château Canon	»	Château Panet	»	Château Toumalin-Jonquet	»
Château Comte	»	Domaine du Haut-Caillou	»	Domaine de Margalis	»
Château Belloy	»	Château Gaby	»	Château Coustolle	»
Château Mazeris-Bellevue	St-Michel-de-Fronsac	Château Moulin-Pey-la-Brie	»	Château Pichelèvre	»
Château La Fleur-Canon		Cru Casi-Devant	St-Michel-de-Fronsac	Cru Combes-Canon	St-Michel-de-Fronsac
Château du Pavillon-Haut-Gros-Bonnet	Fronsac	Domaine du Haut-Mazeris		Clos Nardon	
Château Mazeris	St-Michel-de-Fronsac	Château Cassagne	»	Clos Toumalin	Fronsac
Château des Combes-Canon		Château La Marche-Canon	Fronsac	Clos Haut-Cailleau	»
Château Grand-Renouil	»	Château Vincent	»	Château Canon-Bourret	»
Château Maussé	»	Château Haut-Ballet	St-Michel-de-Fronsac	Château Canon de Brem	»
Château Lariveau	»	Crus Moulin-à-Vent		Château La Tour-Canon	»
Château La Chapelle-Lariveau	»	Château du Gazin	»	Château Lamarche-Candelayre	»
		Château Cassagne	»	Château Roulet	»
		Château Larchevesque	Fronsac		

CÔTES DE FRONSAC • RED WINES

Château des Trois-Croix	Fronsac	Château La Tour Beau-Site	Fronsac	Château de Carles	Saillans
Château Gagnard	»	Domaine de la Croix	»	Châteaux de Malgarni et Coutreau	»
Château de Pontus	»	Clos Bellevue	St-Michel-	Château Mayne-Viel	Galgon
Château La Dauphine	»	Château Queyreau-de-Haut	de-Fronsac	Cru Vincent	St-Aignan
Château La Valade	»	Château Tasta	St-Aignan	Château Vincent	»
Château La Fontaine	»	Château Tasta-Guillier	»	Domaine de Vincent	»
Château Arnauton	»	Château Jeandeman	»		

BOURGEAIS REGION • RED WINES AND WHITE WINES

Château du Bousquet	Bourg	Château de Blissa	Bayon	Château Mendoce	Villeneuve
Domaine du Boucaud	»	Clos Nodot	»	Château Peychaud	Teuillac
Château du Haut-Gravat	»	Château Rousset	Samonac	Château Cottière	»
Château Croûte-Charlus	»	Château Barrieux	»	Domaine de Rivereau	Pugnac
Château Croûte-Mallard	»	Château Macay	»	Domaine de Viaud	»
Château Mille-Secousses	»	Domaine de Bel-Air	»	Château Lamothe	Lansac
Château Lalibarde	»	Domaine de Bouche	»	Château de Taste	»
Château Rider	»	Château de Thau	Gauriac	Château La Barde	Tauriac
Château Cambes-Kermovan	»	Château du Domaine de Desca-		Domaine de Guerrit	»
Château de la Grave	»	zeaux	»	Château Nodoz	»
Château Rebeymond-Lalibarde	»	Château Poyanne	»	Château de Maco	»
Domaine de Paty	»	Domaine de Bujan	»	Château Grand-Jour	Prignac et
Château Rebeymont	»	Domaine de Peyror	»	Château Le Mugron	Gazelles
Château Belleroque	»	Clos du Piat	»	Château de Grissac	»
Domaine de Noriou-Lalibarde	»	Clos de Seillas	»	Domaine de Christoly	»
Château Gros-Moulin	»	Domaine de Bonne	»	Château Laureusanne	St-Seurin
Château Lagrange	»	Château La Grolet	St-Ciers-	Château Berthou	Comps
Domaine de Lalibarde	»	Château Rousselle	de-Canesse	Domaine des Augiers	»
Château Tayac	Bayon	Château Guiraud	»	Domaine de Fonbonne	Teuillac
Château Eyquem	»	Château La Tour-Seguy	»	Château des Richards	Mombrier
Château Falfas	»	Domaine de Grand-Chemin	»	Château Guienne	Lansac
Château de la Croix (Millorit)	»	Château de Barbe	Villeneuve		

BLAYAIS REGION • RED WINES AND WHITE WINES

Château Cazeaux	St-Paul	Château Breuil	St-Martin-	Château Meneau	Mazion
Château Lescadre	Cars	Château La Brousse	Caussade	Château La Cure	Cars
Château Crusquet	»	Château Petit-Trou	»	Château Les Alberts	Mazion
Château Barbet	»	Château La Garde	St-Seurin-	Château Le Virou	St-Girons
Château Bellevue	Plassac		Cursac	Château Chasselauds	Cartelègue
Château Les Chaumes	Fours	Château Clos d'Amières	Cartelègue	Château Le Coudeau	Cars
Domaine du Chai	»	Château Le Cone Moreau	Blaye	Château Dupeyrat	St-Paul
Château Pardaillan	Cars	Château Le Cone Sebilleau	»	Château Guillonnet	Anglade
Château Gontier	Blaye-Plassac	Château Berthenon	St-Paul	Château Gordat	Cars
Château Monconseil	Plassac	Château Perreyre	St-Martin	Château Haut-Cabat	»
Château Le Cone Taillasson	Blaye		Caussade	Château Lagrange Marquis de	
Château Gigault	Mazion	Château Pinet La Roquete	Berson	Luppe	Blaye
Château Le Menaudat	St-Androny	Château Lamothe	St-Paul	Château Puy Beney	Mazion
Château Les Petits-Arnauds	Cars	Château Ricadet	Cartelègue	Château La Garde Roland	St-Seurin-
Château Sociondo	»	Château Rebouquet	Berson		Cursac
Château Charron	St-Martin	Château La Girouette	Fours	Château La Hargue	Plassac
Château Saugeron	Blaye	Château Pinet	Berson	Château Gadeau	»
Château Les Moines	»	Château La Bertonnière	Cartelègue	Château Lafont	Cartelègue
Château Le Mayne Gozin	Plassac	Château Peybrune	Plassac	Château Pomard	St-Martin
Château Lassale	St-Genès	Château La Perotte	Eyrans	Château Boisset	Berson
Ancien Manoir de La Valette	Mazion	Château Le Mayne Boye	Cars	Château Cantemerle	St-Genès
Château Puy Beney Lafitte	»	Château La Cave	Blaye	Château Perrein	Mazion
Château Segonzac	St-Genès-	Château Chaillou	St-Paul	Château Mazerolles	Cars
	de-Blaye	Domaine de Graulet	Plassac	Château Les Bavolliers	St-Christ.-
Château La Cabane	St-Martin-	Château Les Ricards	Cars		de-Blaye
	Caussade	Château La Tour Gayet	St-Androny	Moulin de la Pitance	St-Girons
Château La Taure Sainte-Luce	Blaye	Château Mayence	Mazion		

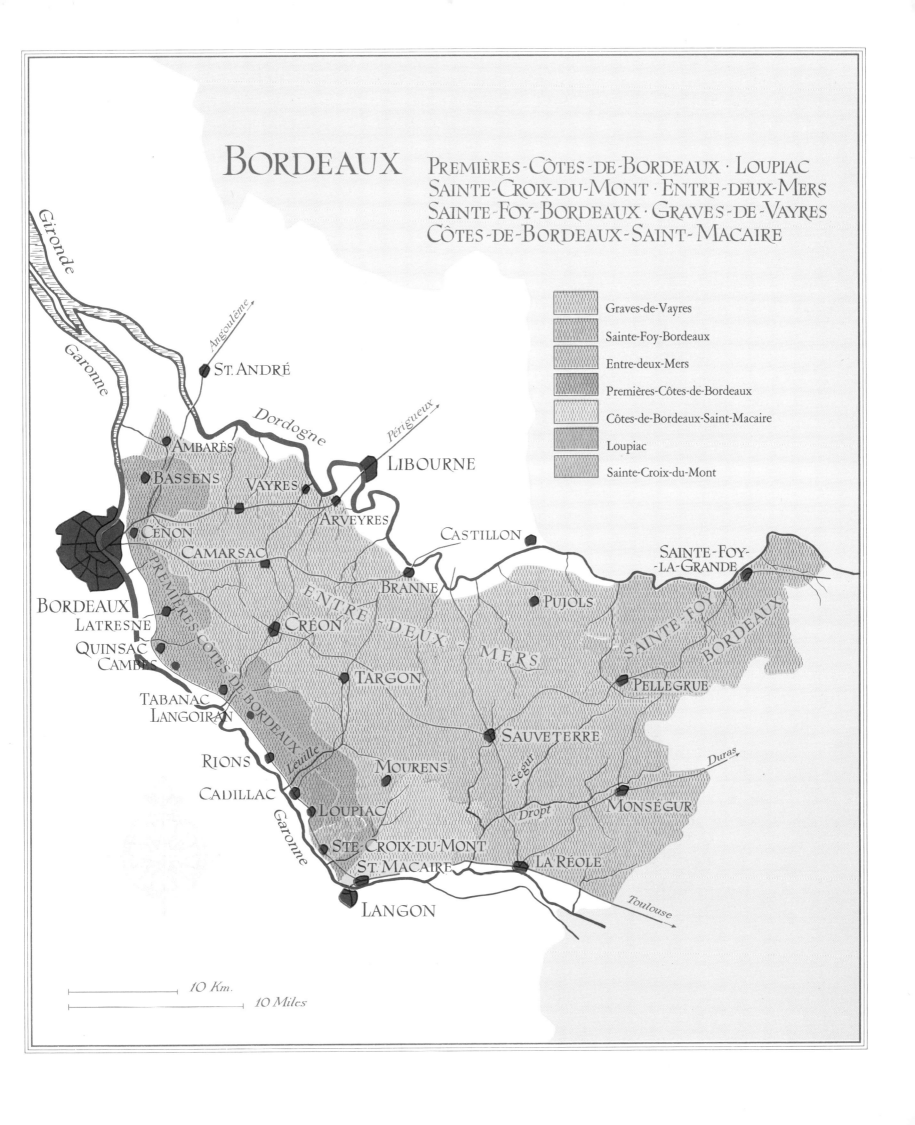

BORDEAUX

PREMIÈRES-CÔTES-DE-BORDEAUX · LOUPIAC
SAINTE-CROIX-DU-MONT · ENTRE-DEUX-MERS
SAINTE-FOY-BORDEAUX · GRAVES-DE-VAYRES
CÔTES-DE-BORDEAUX-SAINT-MACAIRE

Graves-de-Vayres
Sainte-Foy-Bordeaux
Entre-deux-Mers
Premières-Côtes-de-Bordeaux
Côtes-de-Bordeaux-Saint-Macaire
Loupiac
Sainte-Croix-du-Mont

Gironde

Garonne

Angoulême

ST. ANDRÉ

Dordogne

Périgueux

AMBARÈS

BASSENS

VAYRES

LIBOURNE

ARVEYRES

CÉNON

CAMARSAC

CASTILLON

SAINTE-FOY-
LA-GRANDE

BORDEAUX

BRANNE

PUJOLS

ENTRE-DEUX-MERS

SAINTE-FOY-BORDEAUX

LATRESNE

CRÉON

QUINSAC

CAMBES

PREMIÈRES-CÔTES-DE-BORDEAUX

TARGON

PELLEGRUE

TABANAC

LANGOIRAN

Leuille

SAUVETERRE

Ségur

Duras

RIONS

MOURENS

CADILLAC

LOUPIAC

Dropt

MONSÉGUR

Garonne

STE-CROIX-DU-MONT

ST. MACAIRE

LA RÉOLE

LANGON

Toulouse

10 Km.

10 Miles

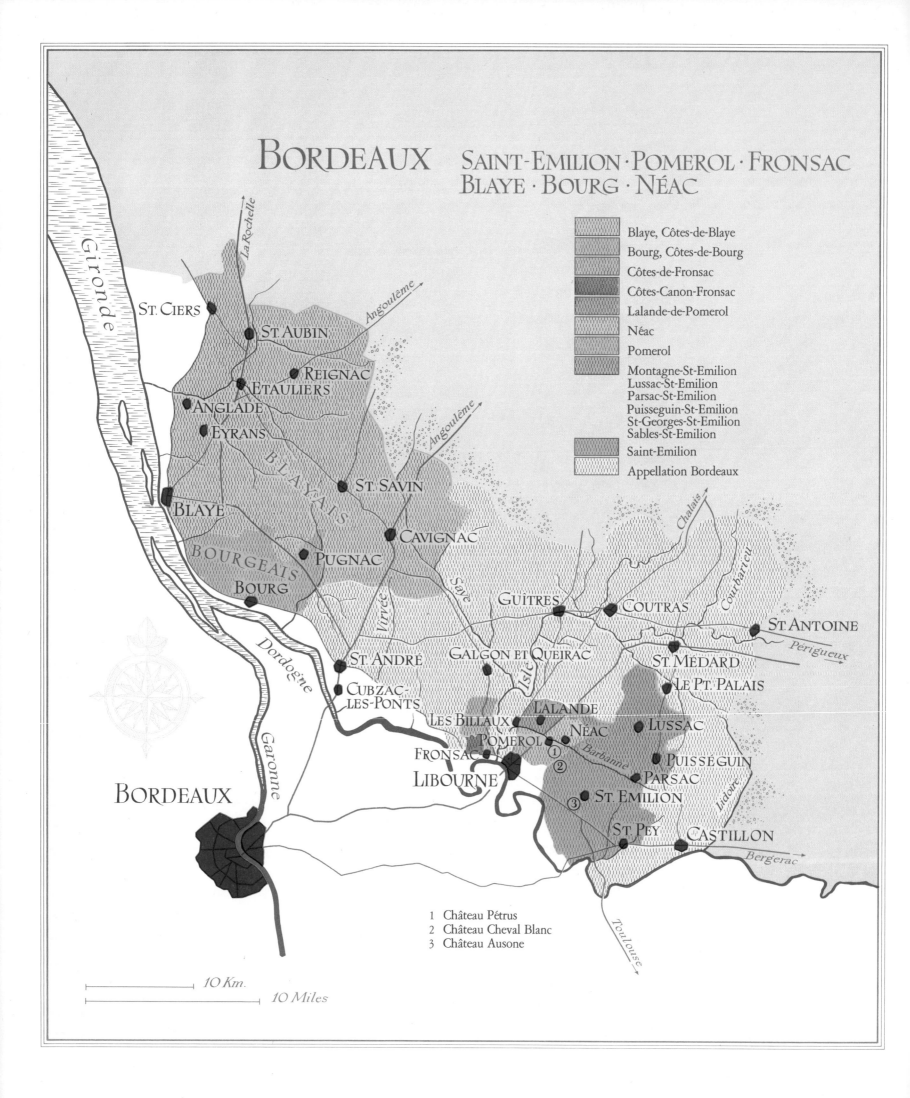

BORDEAUX

SAINT-EMILION · POMEROL · FRONSAC
BLAYE · BOURG · NÉAC

Blaye, Côtes-de-Blaye
Bourg, Côtes-de-Bourg
Côtes-de-Fronsac
Côtes-Canon-Fronsac
Lalande-de-Pomerol
Néac
Pomerol
Montagne-St-Emilion
Lussac-St-Emilion
Parsac-St-Emilion
Puisseguin-St-Emilion
St-Georges-St-Emilion
Sables-St-Emilion
Saint-Emilion
Appellation Bordeaux

GIRONDE

La Rochelle

Angoulême

ST. CIERS

ST. AUBIN

REIGNAC
ETAULIERS

ANGLADE

EYRANS

BLAYAIS

ST. SAVIN

BLAYE

CAVIGNAC

Chalais

BOURGEAIS

PUGNAC

Courbarieu

BOURG

GUÎTRES

COUTRAS

ST ANTOINE

Saye

Périgueux

Vivrée

ST. ANDRÉ

GALGON ET QUEIRAC

ST. MÉDARD

Isle

LE PT. PALAIS

Dordogne

CUBZAC-
LES-PONTS

LES BILLAUX

LALANDE

NÉAC

LUSSAC

POMEROL   ①

Barbanne

②

FRONSAC

PUISSEGUIN

LIBOURNE

PARSAC

③   ST. EMILION

Lidoire

BORDEAUX

Garonne

ST. PEY

CASTILLON

Bergerac

Toulouse

1 Château Pétrus
2 Château Cheval Blanc
3 Château Ausone

10 Km.

10 Miles

THE WINES OF SPAIN

ELADIO ASENSIO VILLA

Legend says the vine was first brought into Spain under some very ancient civilization. Indeed, in some parts of southern Spain it is even said that the Phoenicians came to Spain, in the course of their Mediterranean trading, to buy the wine grown there. Historically, however, it has been proved irrefutably that it was the Romans who introduced winegrowing into Spain under the Empire. Thereafter, it spread over the north-eastern provinces, the coast of the Spanish Levante (the east coast from Tarragona to Alicante) and to Andalusia, where it flourished exceedingly, especially under the Arab rulers. Later, the vine began to be cultivated in the temperate zones farther inland. Gradually the large number of varieties of vine which Spain produces today began to be planted in the valleys, on the slopes and on the foothills (up to 3,000 feet) and in the coastal area of the Spanish Levante. The geographical distribution of the vine in Spain is as varied as the character of the regions. Another factor is the widespread existence of small-holdings, since, originally at any rate, winegrowing was particularly suited to one-family farming. There are a number of other special features, notably the fact that winegrowing is carried on side-by-side with the cultivation of the olive, the other great Mediterranean crop, and in some cases vineyards and olive groves are inextricably mingled.

Wine was one of Spain's largest resources in the Middle Ages, as it was in other Mediterranean countries. The trade in Spanish wines really began to flourish in the tenth century, carried by sea and river to the north-ern European countries and to some areas in eastern Europe. This prosperity continued until the end of the eleventh century. In the twelfth century the economic, and one might even say cultural, renaissance of wine took place. Consumption increased in the wealthiest northern and central European countries as well as in the Mediterranean countries, where it was already the usual beverage and where the wines produced in Spain were well known.

Because of its geographical location, Spain was to some extent outside the main flow of European trade, and this placed it in a very special position. Under these conditions, wine could not be exported, and so it came to be consumed domestically. But once it was possible to establish normal trade from the ports of Barcelona and Valencia, Spain made a great effort to conquer the foreign markets and sell its most typical commodities, especially its wines, which already enjoyed a great reputation.

The Spanish wine trade, however, like the trade in other Spanish commodities, suffered greatly from the repercussions of economic crises in several European countries. This state of affairs was reflected in the measures taken by several of the Spanish kingdoms before the unification of Spain. This continued until 1868, the year in which the great French vineyards were invaded and ruined by the phylloxera, for this opened up new outlets for Spanish wines throughout the world. Spanish winemaking techniques also profited, for a great many French growers settled in the best Spanish winegrowing districts after their own vineyards had been destroyed and introduced their skills and practices. But, as always happens when success comes too suddenly, disorganization prevailed in the Spanish markets abroad and Spain neglected to consolidate the markets it had gained as a result of the disappearance of French wines. Winegrowing in Spain, too, underwent a severe crisis when the phylloxera crossed the Pyrenees and made its appearance there in turn, wiping out numerous vineyards and leading to very serious economic and social consequences which left deep traces on the history of the vine in Spain and indeed on Spanish agriculture in general.

Over the past forty years Spanish wine production has been very unequal in quantity. It has been influenced not only by climate but also by unfavourable natural phenomena occurring in other countries. It may, however, look forward to a more promising future, since the public authorities are taking a greater interest in it and the trade itself is eager for more effective organization. According to the official statistics of the Ministry of Agriculture for 1965, the total area planted to vines was 4,273,000 acres, of which 485,960 were also planted to mixed crops; but since the vine in fact covers 75 per cent of the area of mixed cultivation, it can be said that the actual area of the Spanish vineyards is about 4,151,300 acres. It is estimated that about 3,953,600 acres are planted to wine grapes and the rest to table grapes and raisins. In area, therefore, the Spanish vineyards are the largest in the world, more extensive even than the French and Italian.

The importance of wine and grape production to Spanish agriculture and the economy of Spain is due to the fact that the area planted to vine accounts for 3.73 per cent of the total cultivated area, and especially to the fact that the area planted to the wine grape accounts for 3.62 per cent of it. A comparison of the winegrowing area with that under other crops shows that it is exceeded only by grain and olives.

Average production in 1963-1966 was 63,230,000,000 gallons. This is a significant figure which may be taken as representing the potential of Spanish grape production. The 1964 harvest can be considered a record; it was due to a combination of favourable climatic conditions in that year.

As we have seen, the Spanish vineyards are distributed all over the Peninsula, since its climatic conditions are everywhere favourable to the vine, which requires above all long periods of unbroken sunshine. The roots remain in the ground for fifty years, sometimes longer, and this is a factor contributing to keeping the population on the land.

A glance at the map of the agricultural regions in Spain shows that every province, including the Balearic and Canary islands, has its winegrowing districts. As to area, La Mancha and the region of Utiel and Requeña (province of Valencia) take first place, followed by Catalonia and the area between Alicante and Jumilla (province of Murcia), where over 30 per cent of the land is planted to vine. Classifying groups of provinces by the area of vineyards, the order is:

Group I (over 250,000 acres per province): Ciudad Real, Toledo, Valencia and Albacete; the four provinces total 1,542,000 acres, or over one-third of the total area planted to vine in Spain.

Group II (from 123,550 to 247,100 acres): Saragossa, Tarragona, Cuenca, Badajoz, Alicante, Barcelona and Murcia; these seven provinces have 1,290,000 acres of vineyards.

Group III (61,775 to 123,550 acres): Zamora, León, Malaga, Navarre, Madrid, Logroño and Valladolid; the vineyards in these seven provinces cover 551,033 acres.

Group IV (24,710 to 61,775 acres): Cadiz and Cordoba, two provinces with wines of a high quality.

Group V (12,355 to 24,710 acres): Pontevedra, Gerona, Granada, Segovia, Seville, Almeria, Álava, Lugo and Guadalajara. The vineyards in these nine provinces cover 67,000 hectares. Winegrowing is less important here, but the province of Álava should be mentioned for its wines of exceptionally good quality and the provinces of Gerona and Pontevedra, which produce very acceptable wines.

Lastly, in Group VI (under 13,000 acres) are the provinces in which winegrowing is only of secondary importance: Balearic Islands, Santa Cruz de Tenerife, Jaen, Soria, Las Palmas, Corunna, Oviedo, Santander, Vizcaya and Guipuzcoa.

To sum up, the area of the winegrowing districts varies between a maximum of 646,000 acres in the province of Ciudad Real and a minimum of 64 acres in Guipuzcoa. Average yields and number of plants per acres vary a great deal from region to region in accordance with the climate, the grape varieties and the categories of the wines.

The total area of grape growing in irrigated regions is only 96,430 acres, 66,250 of which only are planted to wine grapes. Planting is forbidden by law nowadays on land that is not irrigated. The vineyards that existed on this land at the time when they became restricted areas are liable to a graduated tax.

Wines are classified according to their colour (red, white, other). Production (official figures for 1965) is: red wines 40.5 per cent, white wines 41 per cent, other 18.5 per cent. In the "other" class are musts, fortified wines, rosé wines, vermouths and aperitifs blended

Enjoying as it does a splendid climate, the Spanish winegrowing region is one of the largest in the world and few provinces do not produce wines of their own. The principal wine regions include the Rioja, Navarre, the province of Saragossa, the east coast from Barcelona to Alicante, La Mancha and the southern provinces with Malaga and Jerez de la Frontera, and the Canary and Balearic Islands.

with quinquina. White wines predominate in New Castile, Andalusia and Catalonia, red wines elsewhere. Comparing the regions by vineyards which bottle in their own cellars, we find that in the north-west (Galicia and Asturias) there is a definite breakdown into very small properties so far as winegrowing is concerned. Western and eastern Andalusia, the Spanish Levante and New Castile have a more rational and consequently more profitable structure. In general, the co-operative movement is continuously expanding, speedily rationalizing the sectors in which reforms are most urgently needed. It promotes the concentration of cellar-bottling, which is essential from the economic point of view, and likewise an improved quality, for the small growers do not possess the skills and technical equipment necessary to guarantee at least a minimum

of quality, classification and presentation. Vinification is carried out practically in the vineyard itself, as the grape does not travel well to the vat, even in co-operatives. As a rule, the larger co-operatives are no more than some six miles away from the vineyards. The wines may be classified as, first, the ordinary *(corrientes)* for immediate national consumption, and, second, the better wines for maturing.

The wines, of course, differ from each other owing to the differences inherent in the climate, nature of the soil, exposure, variety of grape and method of vinification, so that the wines from different regions have from the outset very marked characteristics of their own. Different methods of vinification within the regions produce further variations, as can be seen from the many different types of sherry.

THE WINES OF THE RIOJA

The winegrowing region of the Rioja covers the region of that name comprising the provinces of Logroño and Álava and some communes in Navarre. It is the region of quality wines; they are some of the most sought-after of the wines of guaranteed origin, the Spanish equivalent of the French *appellation d'origine contrôlée*. It stretches from around Haro to Alfaro in the valley of the Ebro and beyond its banks. It may be divided into three main districts: the Lower Rioja between the Yregua and the right bank of the Ebro; the Upper Rioja, a more humid area, the centre being Haro and taking in the north-western part of the province of Logroño on both sides of the Ebro; and the Rioja Alavesa, formed by the valleys of several tributaries of the Ebro, the Oja, Tirón, Najerilla, Leza and Cidacos; it is a transitional land in which the natural characteristics of the Basque provinces, Castile and Navarre all blend.

In most of the districts in the Rioja winegrowing is extremely important. The area planted to vine in the provinces of Logroño, Álava and Navarre is 203,000 acres, 188,300 solely to vines and the rest mixed cultivation.

The region produces a very wide range of wines, all of them differing in strength, taste and bouquet. This is due to the large number of grape varieties and the proportions in which they are used, which differ from district to district. All of them, however, obviously belong to the same family because of the characteristics they have in common.

In the Upper Rioja the red varieties are the *Tempranillo*, *Mazuela*, *Graciano* and *Garnacha* and the white the *Viura* and *Malvasia*. The red wines, mostly

from the *Tempranillo*, are very well-balanced, robust, well built, with a good acidity and a prominent bouquet, well suited for maturing. They run from 10.5° to 12° in strength, according to their origin. The white wines are rather lower in alcohol content; they are dry and have a fair bouquet.

The Lower Rioja is the largest district, stretching from the town of Logroño to Alfaro. The *Garnacha* predominates, and so most of the wines are red. They are very full-bodied with an extremely high alcohol content, ranging from 14° to 16°; they are thick, hardly acid at all and rather sweet. Co-operatives are very common in this region.

The Rioja Alavesa, a long narrow strip north of the Ebro, is protected by the Cantabrian Mountains and, owing to its exposure, gets more sun than the Upper Rioja. The wines are typically very well-balanced, very full-bodied, very heavy and excellent for maturing. Their taste and bouquet have a character all their own, and their average strength may be as high as 14°.

Ageing of the wines is considered of great importance in the Rioja: they must be matured within a carefully delimited zone for a period of at least two years, one year of this in oak casks.

RIOJA is aged in fairly small oak Bordeaux casks (225 litres—about 50 gallons) in underground cellars called *calados*. The must and grapes are carefully selected, since not all the wines are suitable for ageing. With some varieties of grape the colour is not stable enough and the wines therefore do not keep. The *Tempranillo* variety ages best.

The first stage (maturing in Bordeaux casks) should last from two to five years, according to the character of the wine and the type of wine desired. The necessary racking is done during this period and slow oxidation occurs in the cellar, which is kept at a constant and cool temperature. This stabilizes the wine.

The second stage consists in reduction. The wine is bottled and kept for a period that depends on the results of the first stage. This is the stage in ageing during which the aroma begins to develop. The red wines acquire a ruby tint and are quite clear, with an intense and characteristic bouquet.

The Rioja wines most widely sold are usually first-year wines that are shipped by the growers or co-operatives themselves. The wines called *corrientes*, or ordinary light carafe wines, are wines which have been stabilized and bottled during their first year.

Stabilized wines bottled and kept for two years are commonly known as harvest wines or second-year wines, and are white, red or rosé. Wines of a light-red colour (darker than rosés, but lighter than reds) are called Rioja Claretes. These are the wines that generally reach the foreign market and are served in the better Spanish restaurants.

Lastly, wines aged in oak casks before bottling are designated as third, fourth, etc. year wines, or *viejas reservas* (old reserve). They include reds, claretes, dry whites, sweet whites and rosés. Unfortunately some of these lose much of their charm from being over-aged.

Switzerland imports a great deal of Rioja, some 1,430,000 gallons. The U.S. market is promising and the Cuban market is fairly promising but irregular.

THE WINES OF NAVARRE

In the province of Navarre, adjacent to the Rioja, the valley of the Ebro broadens and the river receives as tributaries the Ega, Arga and Aragón. Navarre stretches along the foothills south of the Pyrenees and the region is one of fertile valleys and slopes with a very good exposure, moderately sunny and sheltered from the prevailing winds, two ideal conditions for winegrowing. The wine district comprises roughly the southern half of the province, hence the name guaranteeing the origin. The principal grape variety is the *Garnacha*; the *Tempranillo* is also used, but to a lesser degree, like the *Viura* and the *Malvasia*. The *Moscatel* is used for making dessert wines.

Climatic conditions, which are quite different in northern and southern Navarre, obviously influence the characteristics of the vineyards and consequently the wines. In the north, where the rainfall ranges from 30 to 40 inches, the wines are not as high in alcohol content as in the Ribera district, where the rainfall is 20 inches at most. Both districts produce very tolerable wines, allowing for their special characteristics.

The wines produced on 8,055 acres of vineyards within the province of Navarre and in the communes adjacent to the province of Logroño are entitled to carry the Rioja label.

The winegrowing area producing Navarra wines may be divided into three quite different regions: the Lower Ribera, made up of the area near the Ebro in the south of the province, which produces very strong red wines, sometimes as high as 18°, and very good fortified wines; the district of Valdizarbe, where the wines are not so strong (from 11° to 15°) and more acid than the Ribera wines; and the district of Montaña, whose wines do not sell as well as those from the other two districts. Some of the better Navarre wines are the light wines of Estella, on the banks of the Ega, the reds and claretes of Peralta, Salces and Artajona in the valley of the Arga, the reds of Olite and Tafalla on the banks of the Cidacos and the reds and claretes of Murchante, Cintruénigo and Cascante on the banks of the Ebro. Most of the wines are sold for local consumption, although a proportion is exported each year.

THE WINES OF CARIÑENA

The board of directors in charge of awarding guarantees of origin has recently awarded the label to Cariñena, defining its production area as a fairly small one in the province of Saragossa south of the former capital of Aragon. It is made up of the communes of Aguaron, Alfamén, Almonacid de la Sierra, Alpartir, Cariñena, Cosuenda, Encinacorba, Tosos, Langares, Paniza and Villanueva de Huerva. In this area, whose name

covers the reputedly best regional vineyards, various types of wine are made, very typical of those harvested all over the province of Saragossa.

The traditional grape varieties are the *Cariñena*, *Black Garnacha* and *White Garnacha*, which produce very full-bodied, heavily coloured wines with a high degree of dry extract. The first variety produces wines of a strength ranging from 14° to 17°, seldom less than

13º and sometimes rising to as much as 18º. This is the same as the maximum strength obtained experimentally in the laboratory. The dry extract ranges from 20º to 32º according to the type of wine. The wine is fermented in underground wells and in spite of the advent of co-operatives with their modern techniques some treading still goes on. There are red table wines, dry table *claretes* and various kinds of sweet and fortified dessert wines.

The communes of Alfamén, Alpartir, Almonacid de la Sierra and the lower part of the commune of Sariñena produce wines for blending. The communes of Langares, Cosuenda, Aguaron, Tosos and Villanueva de Huerva produce *corrientes*. The higher parts of these communes and of the communes of Encinacorba and Paniza make wines which, aged by well-tested techniques, display the characteristics of fine table wines: they are very well-balanced, they have an agreeable and delicate flavour and their alcohol content does not run much above 14º.

The whole region produces the classic Aragon *claretes*, which are somewhat like the light-coloured red wines from some other regions. Brilliant in colour, these are highly appreciated table wines; they have a high alcohol content similar to that of the usual red wine. Both the red wines and the *claretes* are very suitable for blending, the reds especially, because of their deeper colour.

THE WINES OF THE EAST COAST

TARRAGONA. The region which produces Tarragona wines, comprising part of the province of that name, is made up of a large number of communes. The most characteristic varieties of grape are the *Cariñena*, *Garnacha* and *Picapoll* for the reds, and the *Macabeo*, *Malvasia*, *Moscatel*, *White Picapoll* and *Pansa* for the whites. Mixed cultivation is sometimes practised.

The TARRAGONA CAMPO wines should be distinguished from the TARRAGONA CLASICO. They are red and white sweet dessert wines, from 2.5º to 7º Beaumé, with an alcohol content ranging from 14º to 23º. The very typical Tarragona vinification process is rapid oxidation of the must at very high temperatures. The cellars are not underground, but very well-aired and subject to abrupt changes in temperature. The wine is stored in glass containers. With the current trend towards dry wines and spirits the sweet TARRAGONA CAMPOS are not as widely seen as they used to be.

PRIORATO. The name of this region derives from the priory of a fifteenth-century Carthusian monastery, the ruins of which are still to be seen. These wines are produced in an enclave within the region covered by the TARRAGONA guaranteed origin label. The region is made up of several communes and the towns of Reus, Valls and La Secuita where the maturing is done. The permitted grapes are the *Cariñena*, the *Garnachas*, the *Macabeo* and the *Pedro Ximénez*.

The Priorato wines make excellent table wines and are good for blending. They have a high alcohol content, from 14º to 18º, while the fortified and aged dessert wines may run as high as 22º.

PANADÉS. The district which produces the Panadés wines, which are good table wines, mostly white—is made up of parts of the provinces of Barcelona and Tarragona. The wines enjoy the guarantee of origin and are derived from the *Macabeo, Xerel-lo, Parellada, Sumoll, Merseguera, Moscatel, Garnacha* and *Malvasia* grape varieties for the whites; the main varieties for the reds are the *Black Sumoll, Cariñena, Morastrell, Black Garnacha* and *Tempranillo*. The first-year wines have a low dry extract, a moderate alcoholic content (10º to 12º in general), but a high acidity, so that they are very suitable for making sparkling wines.

These cellar-bred wines are matured with the greatest biochemical care. The first-year wine is bottled with the yeast and the racking liquor to produce the second fermentation characteristic of wines made by the Champagne method. The bottles are laid flat in underground cellars to enable the added sugar to ferment and produce the carbonic acid gas characteristic of wines of this type, which escapes when the bottle is uncorked. The maturing of the sparkling wine really begins after the second fermentation. The quality of the sparkling Panadés wines has been constantly improved. More and more different varieties of this wine are being produced and the market is continuously expanding.

ALELLA (370 acres). This small district, with two quite different slopes, the larger with a southern exposure towards the sea, the other facing north, is part of the province of Barcelona. It produces delicate table wines, very pale whites, light reds and rosés. The drier wines run to between 11º and 13º. The grape varieties used are the *Pansa, Garnacha, Picapoll, Macabeo* and *Malvasia* for the whites and the *Black Garnacha, Tempranillo* and *Sumoll* for the reds.

MALVASIA DE SITGES. This wine comes from a very small district planted solely to the *Malvasia* grape. Sweet, very agreeable to the taste, old gold in colour, it is greatly appreciated as a dessert wine but it has a very small yield.

CONCA DEL BARBARÁ. The winegrowing district of this name is situated in the south of the province of Tarragona below the Priorato; there are some very good table wines similar to those coming from Alella and Panadés. Together with two other East Coast regions, Barcelona and Malvasia de Sitges, Conca del Barbará comes under the official place-name control (denominacion de origen) regulations, a programme for which was established some years ago.

ALICANTE. The Alicante winegrowing district may be divided into two parts. The first, running west from Alicante itself, produces wines for blending and some table wines; the second, in the north-east of the province where the soil varies considerably and the main variety of grape is the *Moscatel*, supplies mostly fortified wines. The deeply coloured red wines, which are used for blending, have an alcohol content between 14º and 18º and their dry extract titrates between 25º and 35º Beaumé. The alcohol content of the *clarete* and red table wines does not exceed 14º, while that of the fortified wines varies between 14º and 17º, with a Beaumé measurement ranging from 7º to 10º.

VALENCIA, UTIEL-REQUENA and CHESTE. These three wines of guaranteed origin are regulated by the Board and are divided into three sections corresponding to the three growing districts.

The Utiel-Requena district is in the west of the province of Valencia. The Cheste district is an enclave in the centre, and the Valencia district proper covers the remainder of the province.

The Utiel-Requena district is the highest-lying and most rugged, and so the reds, *claretes* and rosés have a lower alcohol content (10º to 13º). They are very suitable for ageing owing to their high fixed acidity. Grapes used are the *Bobal*, *Garnacha* and *Crujidera*.

The Cheste wines are made from a wide range of varieties, the *Pedro Ximénez*, *Planta Fina*, *Moscatel*, *Merseguera*, *Macabeo* and *Planta Nova*. All of them are white wines running between 11º and 15º. The wines in the third district, Valencia, are very varied. The grape varieties are the same as for the Cheste wines, with, in addition, the *Malvasia* for the whites and the *Garnacha Tintorera* and *Monastrell* for the reds. This district produces red table wines, fortified and dessert wines and sweet wines named after the grape from which they are derived: *Malvasia*, *Pedro Ximénez* or *Moscatel*. The alcohol content of the dessert wines can be as high as 23º.

THE WINES OF THE CENTRE AND THE SOUTH-EAST

The districts that produce the wines of the central and south-eastern part of Spain are part of the provinces of Ciudad Real (the MANZANARES and VALDEPEÑAS) and Toledo (the NOBLEJAS), which, with the provinces of Cuenca and Albacete, make up La Mancha. Vines take up the greater part of the arable land in this region. The province of Ciudad Real comes first with 645,000 acres, or 23.6 per cent of the cultivated area; then Toledo with 332,450 acres, or 12.8 per cent, followed by Albacete with 247,100 acres (12.9 per cent) and Cuenca with 221,033 acres (12 per cent). The vineyards of these four provinces account for about 35 per cent of the total Spanish winegrowing area. The figures show the vast importance of grape and winegrowing in this part of Castile. Here, as in the Catalan and Andalusian regions, whites predominate, though the few red wines produced are very good.

La Mancha is a broad plain between 1,500 and 2,400 feet above sea-level. The climate is dry and semi-arid, which accounts for the comparatively low yields of the vines. Indeed, La Mancha is a name that has derived from the Moorish word *marzo*, meaning "dry land". The wines from all the communes in La Mancha have certain characteristics in common, due both to identical climatic conditions and to the fact that the processes of vinification used are fairly similar.

Most of the grape varieties are white, like the wines themselves; the *Airen* is by far the most common, the *Pardillo*, *Verdencho*, *Albillo* and *Macabeo* less widely grown. The most characteristic red varieties are the *Cencibel*, with some *Garnacha*. The varieties with the largest yields are the *Airen* among the whites and the *Cencibel* among the reds. In the province of Ciudad Real the average yield is about 6 hundredweight per acre, slightly higher in Cuenca. La Mancha is the main region producing *corrientes*, dry wines with an alcohol content of 11.5º to 13º, with a moderate degree of fixed acidity. They are used all over Spain as table wines and aperitifs, especially in the capital, Madrid. Most of the La Mancha wines are vinified in *tinajas*, the large vats of baked clay typical of the region. Although more modern vats are to a certain extent taking over from the *tinajas*, the old-fashioned clay pots are still widely used and are generally preferred by the vintners. Each vessel is made by hand and may hold as much as 2,500 gallons of wine.

The most characteristic of the La Mancha wines is the VALDEPEÑAS from the *Cencibel* grape. It is ruby-

177

coloured with fine shadings and up to 14° alcohol content. The wines called ALOQUE, from the same district, are pleasant-tasting *claretes* which are almost rosés. The generic guaranteed origin label MANCHA covers growths from a wide area made up of a large number of communes, the principal being Alcazar de San Juan, Campo de Criptana, San Martin de Valdiglesias, Socuellamos, Ciudad Real, Manzanares, Méntrida, Tarancón, Ocaña, Noblejas, El Bonillo and Villarobledo. To be entitled to the label the wines must be at least two years old and have been matured for at least one year in oak casks. The wines of Manchuela and Almansa, which also are entitled to a guaranteed origin label, deserve a mention here.

By far the majority of the commonest regional white wines are derived from the *Airen* grape. Their alcohol content is 12° to 14°. They are golden, clear, but not very brilliant, and their fixed sulphuric acidity is low (2.40°). They are usually drunk in their first year. The wines made from the *Pardillo* grape at Tarancón and the red wines of Belmonte, the *claretes* of Noblejas and the wines from Yepes, Ocaña and Esquivias are well liked in some parts of the country, especially in the province of Cuenca, and have a strong local following. Excellent local wines are produced in this central region, in the provinces of Toledo and Madrid. Very deep-coloured wines with a high alcohol content and a high dry extract are produced in the districts of Méntrida (province of Toledo) and Navalcarnero (province of Madrid) and in the communes of Arganda and Colmenar. The Méntrida wines are entitled to the guaranteed origin label.

The grape varieties are the Madrid *Red Garnacha* and some *Cencibel* for the reds, and the *Jaen, Torrentes* and *Pardillo* for the whites. The red wines of Arganda, Colmenar and San Martin de Valdeiglesias run to 15° and are slightly astringent, low in acid and usually with a good taste. Some dessert wines are made, notably the MOSCATEL.

The very reputable wines from the province of Avila, north-west of the province of Madrid, may also be included in this region. The *Garnacha* and *Tempranillo* grapes are most used for the reds and mainly the *Jaen, Malvar, Torrentes* and *Verdejo* for the whites. The village of Cebreros produces the best known of the Avila wines, red wines without much colour, almost *claretes* in fact, and white wines with a good taste but little body. Quite agreeable dessert wines are made from the reds. The white table wines are golden in colour, light and generally dry.

THE WINES OF JUMILLA (MURCIA)

The province of Murcia is not part of Andalusia, even though it is in southern, or rather south-eastern, Spain. It produces wines which are highly spoken of, mostly from the *Monastrell* grape, with some from the *Garnacha*. They are entitled to the JUMILLA label. The JUMILLA-MONASTRELL wines range from 14.5° to 18° alcohol content, and this strength is wholly natural, since no alcohol is added during fermentation. There are some other types of wine also entitled to the label, running between 12.8° and 15°, made from grape varieties of which the *Monastrell* accounts for at least 50 per cent. This, of course, tends to promote the growing of this variety, for, even though its yield is small, its quality is excellent. The Board is therefore quite right in keeping the wine under control. The reds and *claretes* from this district are greatly liked in Spain and abroad. They have a high dry extract and their deep, rich red colour reflects the amount of tannin in them. They age very well, though they are very often drunk young as *corrientes*.

THE WINES OF SOUTHERN SPAIN

In the Montilla-Moriles district the first-year wines are rather insipid but are very suitable for maturing, which gives them a remarkable aroma and other fine qualities. They are produced all over the province of Cordoba from the vineyards on the limestone of the Sierra of Montilla and Moriles Altos. Their guaranteed origin labels are MONTILLA ALBERO and MORILES ALBERO. They are matured in a district made up of Montilla, Los Moriles, Aguilar de la Frontera, Lucena, Cabra and Doña Mencia, Puente-Genil and Cordoba.

By far the largest proportion of the wines of the Montilla and Moriles district are made from *Pedro Ximénez* grape; the *Lanren, Baladi, Baladi-Verdejo* and *Moscatel* are also cultivated but in far smaller amounts. The continental climate, the soil and the slopes are very well suited to these varieties. The traditional types of these wines, all of them white, are known as *fino, fino viejo* (or *amontillado*), *oloroso* and

This painting by Velasquez (1595-1660) is entitled the Triumph of Bacchus. A good jug of wine has made these wretched Castilian peasants forget their worst misfortunes and at the culminating point of their joyful drunkenness they render solemn homage to Bacchus and to wine.

oloroso viejo. The first-named has an alcohol content of 16º to 16.5º, the *fino viejo* 17º to 17.5º, the *oloroso* 18º to 19º and the *oloroso viejo* 19º to 21º. Although these wines are blended to match the standard sherry grades no alcohol at all is added, whereas in the sherry vinification process grape alcohol is used to stabilize and fortify the wine. The wines are pale greenish-gold in colour, limpid and transparent, with a very prominent bouquet and a special taste which marks them out from the sherries (q.v.) of the same name. Light and dry, they have a delicate bitter-almond flavour.

MALAGA. Wine has been grown in this district from remote ages. The winegrowing district of 89,000 acres of vineyards covers the whole province, with a definite predominance of the *Moscatel* and the *Pedro Ximénez.* The *Moscatel* makes raisins, the *Pedro Ximénez* produces sweet and semi-sweet wines, old gold in colour, with an alcohol content of 14º to 23º. This type is known as the LACHRYMA CHRISTI. With their low acidity, Malaga wines are famous throughout the world for their incomparable bouquet and taste.

HUELVA. This province is in western Andalusia and its winegrowing district was once known as the Condado de Niebla (County of Fog). The main winegrowing districts are Niebla, Bollullos del Condado, Paterna, Almonte, Bonares and Moguer. The main varieties are the *Palomino, Garrido Fino, Mantuo de Sanlucar* and *Listan.* The wines are golden and very fragrant, and they are sweeter in the Moguer district than elsewhere. The wines are something like those of Jerez owing to the similarity of climate, soil and grape, but do not in general have such a delicate flavour.

179

OTHER WINE DISTRICTS

RIBEIRO. There are three separate winegrowing districts in the Galician province of Orense. The largest is Ribeiro in the western part of the province, west of the town of Orense. The *Treixadura* is most used for the white wines, and to a lesser extent the *Albariño*; the *Garnacha, Caiño* and *Brancellao* for the reds. The alcohol content of the white wines run to 10º to 11º, the reds to 10º to 12º. These sharp, clean, light wines with their slight sparkle are appreciated locally. The red wines are deeply coloured and acid.

VALDEORRAS. The second district is Valdeorras, a region of gently sloping hills where the vine is always planted above 2,500 feet and trellised against cryptogamic diseases. White wines are made from the *White Godello* and the red wines from the *Garnacha, Alicante* and *Mencia*.

MONTERREY. In the third district, the valley of Monterrey, the vines are grown on gentle slopes, not above 2,500 feet. The rainfall is nearly 40 inches and the vine is usually trellised. The grape varieties are the same as in the other districts. The red wines are rather more full-bodied than elsewhere in the province.

ESTREMADURA. In the provinces of Badajoz and Caceres, which make up Estremadura, *corrientes* are produced among which that from Almendralejo is notable. In the Barros district the vineyards cover 20 per cent of the cultivated area. The wines are drunk locally or taken elsewhere to mature. Most of the whites come from the *Unite Jaen*, but the *Airen* is also grown. The *Garnacha* and the *Morisca* are used for the reds. The *Pedro Ximénez, Palomino* and *Macabeo* are grown as table grapes.

The white wines of Almendralejo are light, sweet and golden, not very acid and run to 13º. Those of Villanueva de la Serena are rather more straw-coloured

and also rather stronger, about 15º, and are often drunk as aperitifs. The red wines of Guarena are pleasantly fresh and almost purple in colour. Stronger red wines are made in the Salvatierra de los Barros district, and rosés in Fregenal. In the province of Caceres the *Jaen, Cayetana* and *Airen* are used for the whites, and the *Garnacha* and *Negra de Almendralejo* for the reds. Both the reds and whites are of very unequal quality. The best are the whites from Cañamero, the *claretes* from Montehermoso and the reds from Montanchez.

RUEDA and TORO. The Castilian province of Valladolid and the provinces of León and Zamora produce a great deal of *corrientes* and a few wines with some character. In the province of Valladolid the best wines come from Rueda, La Nava, Peñafiel, Cigales and La Seca, in León from La Bañeza and in Zamora from Toro. The *White Verdejo* and the *Red Garnacha* are the main varieties in the Rueda district. The climate is dry, the mean rainfall 16 inches. The alcohol content of the Rueda wines is 13º, sometimes higher; they are straw-coloured and are drunk locally. The white wines of La Seca and Nava del Rey are well spoken of. The *clarete* of Cigales and the wines from Mucientes and Fuensaldaña, which enjoy a deserved reputation, are not quite so strong. Very full-bodied, thick, purple red wines are produced around Peñafiel. Besides these *corrientes* there are some special wines which, when matured and bottled, are much sought after in the domestic market. Light, sharp, slightly acid, pleasant-tasting wines are made from the *Red Mencia* and *Prieto Picudo* grapes in the province of León. Lastly, in the north of the province of Zamora, the district known as Tierra del Vino (Wineland) produces the Toro wines, *corrientes* of good quality which, however, unfortunately do not age.

THE WINES OF JEREZ

The town of Jerez de la Frontera (province of Cadiz), situated in the centre of the district which has given its name to sherry, was founded by the Phoenicians. The name Xera, "a town situated close to the Pillars of Hercules", is found in documents dating from the fourth century B.C. Martial (A.D. 40-104) mentions the wines of Ceret in some of his epigrams. When the Moors occupied Andalusia, they called the town Sherisch, from which comes the English "sherry", the name by which the Jerez wines are generally known. In 1894 the phylloxera destroyed almost all the vine-

yards, but there were luckily enough vine stocks left to re-establish vineyards with qualities similar to the pre-phylloxera ones.

The wine known as JEREZ or SHERRY, the label of origin being legally protected, is made exclusively from grapes gathered within a restricted area in the north-west of the province of Cadiz comprising the communes of Jerez de la Frontera, Puerto de Santa Maria, Sanlucar de Barrameda, Chiclana, Puerto Real, Chipiona, Rota and Trebujena. The outstanding vineyards are those on the calciferous soils of the communes of Jerez de la Frontera, Puerto de Santa Maria and Sanlucar de Barrameda. These communes, together with the neighbouring communes of Rota and Chipiona, make up the district of Upper Jerez.

GRAPE VARIETIES. The two varieties best suited to sherry-making are the *Palomino* and the *Pedro Ximénez*. The two sub-varieties of the *Palomino*, the *Palomino Fino* and the *Jerez*, are white, and account for more than 70 per cent of the vineyards in the district. The *Palomino* is particularly well suited to the local soil and climate, and its shoots take very well on the stock of the *Berlianderi*, the best American vine for calciferous soil. The *Pedro Ximénez* supplies first-rate 13º to 14º musts, and with enough exposure to sun the grapes can produce wines with an alcohol content running as high as 30º to 32º. When semi-fermented, these musts produce the PEDRO XIMÉNEZ, a natural sweet wine with very special organoleptic characteristics.

The cultivation of the vineyards in all its details is far too vast and specialized a subject to go into here, but it may be noted that throughout the district the vines are treated with as much loving care as a great and stately garden.

HARVESTING and PRESSING. The vintage usually starts in the first two weeks of September, but the date, of course, varies with the weather. The grapes are never gathered until they are fully ripe, for it is only then that they produce the maximum quantity of juice and, as their sugar content is at its height, they give the alcoholic strength desired. The ideal time to begin the vintage is shown by the changes in the grapes' colour from green to a dark tobacco brown and in the stalks, which become woody.

The grapes are picked in stages, since only the fully-ripened bunches are gathered. They are then placed in baskets which hold about 25 pounds each and are transported to the *almijar* with which all large vineyards are equipped.

The *almijar* is a very clean platform of beaten earth on which the bunches of grapes are spread in the sun on woven esparto mats and left for varying periods according to the type of wine to be made. The grape throws off any remaining humidity. At night the grapes are covered with mats to protect them from the dew. This age-old practice causes certain changes in the grape and must which affect the character of the wine. In the first place, the evaporation of the humidity reduces the weight; this brings about a concentration of the juice and consequently gives the must a higher sugar content, an increased total acidity and an increase in the alkaline content of the cinders. It is interesting that despite the increase in overall acidity, part of the malic acid disappears, so that its concentration is halted or even reduced. This should be borne in mind, for this acid affects the wine's aroma and flavour. The grapes are then taken from the *almijar* to the presses. The must is expressed by various methods ranging from the classic grape-treading by men in spiked leather boots to mechanical presses. In every case the juice which exudes naturally from the press before pressure is applied is kept separate from the juice extracted from the mush after pressing. In other words the first juice is expressed by light pressure on the grapes (the weight of the man who treads them, for instance). The presses may either be screw-presses, the oldest and best-known type, or modern variable-pressure machines. The juice from the mush alone will make lower-quality wines, which are generally used for distilling.

Besides exposing the picked grapes to the sun, another very typical process it used from time immemorial in the Jerez de la Frontera district. This is "plastering", which is the addition of gypsum or calcium sulphate to the musts to induce the necessary degree of acidity. There is a great deal of controversy about this method with regard to the way calcium sulphate acts on the musts. They become brighter, fining is speeded up, the colour brightens too, large deposits are formed and the alcohol content rises because of the completer fermentation. The amount of gypsum that is used in this method is about 26 ounces to 32 ounces in an 110-gallon cask. Plastering, however, is subject to strict regulation, since the limits are fixed by law in a number of countries, including Spain itself. But broader limits are tolerated for sherry and other fortified wines. The wine-making equipment and containers are normally sterilized with sulphuric acid (sulphur anhydride or sulphur dioxide) or with potassium bisulphite or liquefied pure SO_2. The purpose of this sterilization is to prevent infection by microbic flora which may damage the musts or wines. Though this method is lethal to micro-organisms if enough sulphur is used, it does not damage the yeasts most suited to vinification.

VINIFICATION AND MATURING. If a wine is to be entitled to bear the label SHERRY with its guarantee of origin, it must undergo a process of maturing and ageing in wood within a district defined by regulation, that is to say, in cellars situated within the communes of Jerez, Puerto de Santa Maria and Sanlucar de Barrameda. It may not be matured in any of the other communes. The maximum permitted production is 700 gallons per acre in the Upper Jerez district and 900 gallons elsewhere. The purpose, of course, is to protect the wine's quality.

Maturing sherry is a delicate affair, for it has to be geared to the musts each year, since owing to the factors set out earlier in this section each vintage produces different musts. The Jerez cellarers are past masters in the art of maturing their wines and are able to co-ordinate the various factors which continually affect it at this stage of its vinification so as to obtain sherries of such uniform and constant quality that they live up to their brand name.

The must obtained by one of the processes described above is drawn off straight into casks holding 30 *arrobas*—about 110 gallons—which are immediately taken to the cellar.

A few hours after treading and pressing, the first fermentation, called "lively fermentation", begins. It is therefore essential to transport the casks as quickly as possible to the cellars (which are usually close to the towns) since too high a temperature may damage the normal proliferation of the yeasts which are to convert the glucose into alcohol. Disease germs may also develop at this stage, reducing the sugar content which, in turn, would reduce the alcohol content and could even produce acetic acid.

The cellars in the Jerez de la Frontera district are not constructed underground, as in the other winegrowing districts. They are long buildings made up of several cellars some twenty feet high, separated by long galleries. The casks are stacked lengthwise one above the other, in several rows, usually three, on either side of the cellars, leaving access corridors down the middle of each cellar. To get as much fresh air as possible and, above all, ensure a stable temperature, the cellars are built some miles from built-up areas, with thick walls and in an open space facing south-west or south, where they catch the sea-breeze. Since a great deal of oxygen is needed in maturing sherry, the cellars have small windows some way up the walls and they are always left open in order to set up a constant draught. The floor of the cellar is of beaten earth and is frequently watered to keep the air fresh and the temperature even. It is covered with small oak squares at places where the casks are rolled or any work is to be done.

Since the climate in this region is temperate in September, there is no need to fear any sudden rise in temperature during the fermentation, which might have a harmful effect on the wine, in particular a reduction in the alcohol content. This danger is further mitigated by the fact that the casks hold so little. Nevertheless, a constant strict watch is kept to prevent any accidents. When the lively fermentation is completed, the cellarer inspects the wine-musts (the local name for musts less than a year old) to see whether they have kept dry; if so, the fermentation is completed. He then waits until January, February, or March at the latest, to start the racking in order to separate the wine-musts from the deposits or lees formed at the bottom of the cask. During the racking he engages in

one of the most delicate of the operations which are to determine the future wine: an initial classification of the contents of each cask by its special characteristics, such as delicacy of flavour, aroma and colour. A mark is then placed on the bottom of each cask: one or more *palmas* (stylized palms) if the wine is likely to be fit for *finos*; one or more *rayas* (stripes) if it is fuller-bodied; one or more stripes barred diagonally, whence the name *palo cortado* (cut stick) when it is sweeter and sharper, though still fairly full-bodied. After the classification has been made, the next stage, in March, is fortification, consisting in adding a certain amount of alcohol. The casks are then transferred to the ageing cellar where the real sherry process takes place. This process gives the wine the strength it lacks and raises the alcohol content to 15.5°, or slightly more for the wines of the *rayas* and *olorosos* type.

One of the most interesting things in the making of sherry is the action of certain micro-organisms which live in the wine and feed on its components. They cause chemical reactions which liberate aldehydes and free acids; these determine the aroma and taste peculiar to sherry. They are known as *flor*, or flower. The flor is composed of yeasts which form a very thin film on the top of the wine at the beginning of the second stage in their development, and this film gradually thickens if the temperature and humidity are right. While the flor is forming, the casks are examined frequently to watch the characteristics—consistency, colour and so on—and at the same time to see whether the wine is still in the same class as it was—*palmas*, *rayas* or *palo cortado*—or if its classification has changed. The flor does not act continuously in the maturing of sherry, but only when the temperature and humidity are favourable, i.e. first about April and then in August or September. During these two periods white spots appear on the surface of the wine and spread till they form irregular patches resembling small flowers—hence the name. The patches gradually expand until they form a species of thin white coating which finally attains the thickness and consistency of cream. The chemical and biological transformations of these yeasts which live and grow on the wine combine to make up one of the major characteristics of maturing sherry.

With the type of wine called *finos* (pale dry) of the *amontillados*, the formation and development of the flor is allowed to proceed during the first years of ageing until the wine is bottled. With the *olorosos* (sweet, dark), *paloscortados* (midway between the *finos* and the *amontillados*) and in the final stage of the *amontillados* the development is muted by the addition of a little wine alcohol, which raises their alcoholic content slightly. This and fortifying are the only things added in the course of maturing the wine.

Ageing by the *solera* system works differently. Its purpose is to keep indefinitely a specified type of wine which will always have exactly the same characteristics no matter when it is drunk. Losses either by racking and filtering or from natural causes are made up by adding younger wines. In this method of ageing a number of casks are used, all of them containing wines which may be old or young, but are invariably of the same type and in the same classification while maturing.

In the cellars of Jerez the casks are ranged above each other in three or four rows. The lowest are the casks called *sole*, the row nearest the ground—hence the term *solera*. To avoid confusion, it should be explained that this term is also applied to very old and noble dark wines, since all the dark sherries, whether *finos* (fine), *palidos* (pale) or *añejos* (aged), come from the *sole* casks. Above the row of *sole* casks are ranged two or three rows of casks known as *criaderas* (breeders).

The wines to be marketed are drawn from the *sole* row; they are the oldest. Great care is taken not to draw off more than half the contents of each cask. The *solera* casks are filled up with slightly younger wine from the *criaderas* row. The *criaderas* in turn, are filled up with younger wine from the third row. The number of *criaderas* varies with the types of wine; there are usually more for the *finos* than for the *olorosos* and *amontillados*. In blending care is taken to add a smaller amount of young wine than the amount of old wine left in the cask, so that the older wine may act on the younger, imparting to it its better qualities. The cellarers are very skilled in making these careful blends and in adapting each type of new wine to the wine of previous years and the result is that the oldest casks remain always the same in quality.

The maturing of MANZANILLA must be described separately, as it has features of its own. The general process is similar to that we have just described, but in the Sanlucar de Barrameda district the harvest is brought in fairly early, about the first week in September. Exposure to the sun, which raises the alcohol content of the wine-must to 12°-13°, does not take place, nor are the musts for making MANZANILLA given the *añada* treatment for more than twelve months. The *solera* and *criadera* casks must never be full; a void corresponding to at least 22 gallons is essential. There should be ten or twelve casks in the *sole* row. Too much wine should not be drawn off in the racking, but it should be racked frequently; four or five cellar jugs (capacity about 20 pints) should be drawn off monthly or even every five days. The alcohol content should not exceed 15.5° while the dry MANZANILLA are maturing. If it does, it has to be lowered with young wine; but if it falls below 14.8°, it must be raised by adding wine with a higher alcohol content or an admixture of sherry or alcohol known as *miteado* or *combinado*. The dry MANZANILLAS become MANZANILLAS *pasadas* if the process is prolonged, the alcohol content gradually increasing to 17° or 20°. Owing to this high alcohol content, the flor dies, but the wine already has all the qualities to which it owes its great reputation.

When the wines from the *soleras* are drawn, they are clarified to stabilize them and to keep them perfectly clear and bright. This is done with beaten egg-whites, five to twenty per 500-litre (about 110 gallons) cask.

The regulations for the SHERRY guarantee require four groups of cellars: vinification cellars, production cellars, maturing and storage cellars, and maturing and shipping cellars. This last group is sub-divided into cellars for shipping to Spain and shipping abroad.

The regulations also prescribe that no cellar to which they apply may sell or export more than 40 per cent at the most of its reserves in hand at the beginning of each crop year. No wine may use the guaranteed origin label unless it is at least three years old. A Board exists to see that the regulations are observed.

Export sales of sherry to the United Kingdom in barrel are by far the largest, with some 6,600,000 gallons, increasing fairly regularly each year (by an average of 374,000 gallons). Annual shipments to Denmark and Sweden are also increasing; they are 550,000 and 330,000 gallons respectively. Sherry exports to the United States have doubled since 1961.

The following general characteristics of sherry should be particularly born in mind:

1.   There is no such thing as a vintage sherry, that is a sherry produced from the wine harvested in one particular year. The year of bottling is sometimes seen marked on the cork, but since this does not indicate a "vintage" it is of no special interest.

2.   An eighty-year-old sherry does not mean a wine that is eighty years old, but a sherry from a cask first filled eighty years ago. It is possible that traces of the original wine are still present in the sherry but the usual interpretation is that the particular blend has been maintained unchanged for eighty years.

3.   The longevity of sherries in the bottle is very hard to determine and depends on the quality. A good quality sherry from a well-reputed house can be kept in the bottle for many years. Since this wine is fortified it travels much better than fine wines and the consumer can buy it when he needs it.

4.   The sherry bouquet is produced by the oxidizing effect of certain varieties of yeast that form a film on top of the wine which "blossoms" into flors twice a year. This flor is carefully watched by the cellar masters and the casks are only part-filled to give the air access to it.

MANZANILLA

1. Name of wine; Manzanilla. Manzanilla is a very pale, dry light sherry with a special bouquet and an alcohol content between 15.5° and 17°. – **2.** Reminder: Manzanilla comes from the restricted region of Jerez. – **3.** Origin. – **4.** Grower and shipper's name.

MANZANILLA
SHERRY

"Para conservar el conocimiento,
vete al vino con tiento;
pero, si el vino es de Jerez,
perderás el tiento alguna vez".

Produced and Bottled by
WILLIAMS & HUMBERT
JEREZ and LONDON
PRODUCE OF SPAIN
Registered Trade Mark

RGTO. EMB. No. 206   PRINTED IN SPAIN

DON ZOILO
(lower left)

1. Trade name "Don Zoilo". – **2.** "Very Old Dry Sherry" describes the wine; it has no vintage year, so the shipper has to produce a sherry that will be precisely the same year after year. Actually, the real name is Don Zoilo Dry. – **3.** Origin. – **4.** Grower and shipper's name. The wine's quality is bound up with the shipper's reputation.

PEDRO DOMECQ

1. Trade name "Primero". – **2.** Type of sherry: amontillado. The wine has a more pronounced bouquet and taste than Manzanilla and is older. "Medium Dry Nutty" are details of the wine. This is the most typical sherry; alcohol content ranging from 16° to 18°, old amontillados from 22° to 24°. – **3.** Origin. – **4.** Grower and shipper's name.

DON ZOILO

VERY OLD
DRY
SHERRY
PRODUCE OF SPAIN

ZOILO RUIZ-MATEOS, S.A.
JEREZ

LIT HURTADO JEREZ

Pedro Domecq
ESTABLISHED 1730

MACHARNUDO CASTLE PROPERTY OF THE FIRM

Primero
AMONTILLADO SHERRY
MEDIUM DRY NUTTY

PRODUCED AND SHIPPED BY PEDRO DOMECQ
JEREZ DE LA FRONTERA, SPAIN

IMPORTADO DE JEREZ ESPAÑA

"BROWN BANG" SHERRY
(GOLDEN OLOROSO)

SANDEMAN BROS. & CO.
JEREZ DE LA FRONTERA SPAIN

(REGISTERED TRADE MARK)

SANDEMAN

ESTABLISHED IN THE YEAR 1790

SOLDADO
SELECTED OLD BROWN
SHERRY

PRODUCE OF SPAIN

BODEGAS DE SAN PATRICIO
ESTABLISHED 1780

JEREZ DE LA FRONTERA (SPAIN)

GARVEY

SOLDADO
1. Trade name "Soldado". – 2. "Old Brown" sherry is sometimes called "Raya"; it is dark brown and sweeter than oloroso, stronger, 18° to 20°, but with less bouquet. – 3. Origin. – 4. The shipper mentions the "bodega" where the sherry was matured. – 4. Grower and shipper's name.

BROWN BANG SHERRY
1. Trade name "Brown Bang Sherry". – 2. Oloroso has more body and bouquet than amontillado; this wine is golden; some olorosos may be slightly lighter in colour (tawny). – 3. Origin. – 4. Grower and shipper's name. – 5. This shows that this wine was served to King George VI.

DIAMOND JUBILEE
1. Trade name "Diamond Jubilee". – 2. This sherry of the "cream" type is sweet, with a very strong flavour and great vigour. – 3. General origin. – 4. Grower and shipper's name. This name should not be confused with the name of the sherry; this is not quite clear from the label.

TYPES OF SHERRY

FINOS. Drier, less full-bodied and not so strong as the *olorosos*. There are two types.

— the *finos* proper, straw-coloured, pale, with a sharp and delicate aroma, which may be compared to that of almonds; they are light, dry and not very acid; the alcohol content is between 15.5º and 17º.

— the *amontillados*, amber-coloured, very dry, with less bite, soft and full in flavour, nutty; alcohol content 16º to 18º.

OLOROSOS. Darker, heavier and stronger than the *finos*. There are several types:

— the *rayas* are lower-class *olorosos*, old gold in colour, fuller-bodied and less delicate in aroma. They sometimes taste somewhat sugary, possibly because fermentation was not completed; strength 18º and over.

— the *olorosos* proper, dry, dark golden, with great aroma, though less bite than the *finos*. Their delicate taste may be compared to that of the walnut. They are called *amorosos* when they are sugary and rather fuller-flavoured. The alcohol content is the same as the above.

— the *paloscortados*, midway between the *amontillados* and *olorosos* proper; they may be called the higher-class *oloroso* type. They have the aroma of *amontillados* and the flavour of *olorosos*; colour and alcohol content similar to the latter.

— the "creams", rather sweet, with the body of *olorosos*. A judicious blend of dry *olorosos* with some PEDRO XIMÉNEZ. The blends are matured in *soleras* before they are sold.

DULCES. These are deep-coloured sweet wines from various grape varieties:

— PEDRO XIMÉNEZ is a natural sweet wine, its sweetness due to the exposure to the sun of *Pedro Ximénez* grapes after they are picked in order to obtain a must at nearly 30º Beaumé which is subjected to partial fermentation. In some cases, the grapes intended for this type of wine are exposed for as long as twenty days, so that complete fermentation is not possible. The wine is dark, with an alcohol content between 10º and 15º.

— MOSCATEL, a natural sweet wine from grapes of this variety, between 10º and 20º Beaumé.

MANZANILLA. A dry wine produced in the Sanlucar de Barrameda district. It comes under the Sherry Regulation Board, but has a different label from SHERRY. The two types of MANZANILLA come from the same district and the same variety of grape. The difference begins at the maturing stage. MANZANILLAS must by law be matured in cellars at Sanlucar de Barrameda. MANZANILLA is a delicate, light, very pale and very aromatic, dry and only slightly acid wine with a slightly bitter taste and an alcohol content between 15.5º and 17º. There are two types: MANZANILLA FINA is smooth and slightly bitter and does not age; MANZANILLA PASADA acquires a special taste by ageing and has a more prominent aroma, somewhat like that of the *olorosos*, but the taste is dry and has the characteristics of MANZANILLA FINA.

The sherries that are produced in California or in the South African Republic are wines produced in the same way as those of the Jerez region. But the differences in soil and climate give wines of the sherry type, wines that are analogous but not identical to the original sherries. To taste and compare for oneself is the only means by which one can form a judgement on this subject. The same comparison can be made between the true Champagne vinified in France and the innumerable sparkling wines that sometimes carry the name of Champagne.

Sherry is believed to have been introduced into what is now the United States of America by the Spanish explorer Álvaro Núñez who discovered Florida in 1528 and who came from a long line of vintners and cellar owners in Jerez. Something is even known of the price of sherry in Spain during those epic days of discovery since there is an account of a certain gentleman paying sixteen golden pesos (8 ½ dollars, 70 shillings) for a *botija* or jar of wine.

In conclusion let us move forward a few years to Shakespeare's time and repeat what he had to say in Henry IV Part 2 about the "sherris" drunk in England in the sixteenth and seventeenth centuries: "A good sherries-sack hath a twofold operation in it. It ascends me into the brain; dries me there all the foolish and dull and crudy vapours which environ it; makes it apprehensive, quick, forgetive, full of nimble, fiery and delectable shapes; which delivered o'er to the voice,—the tongue,—which is the birth, becomes excellent wit. The second property of your excellent sherries is,—the warming of the blood; which, before cold and settled, left the liver white and pale, which is the badge of pusillanimity and cowardice; but the sherries warms it and makes it course from the inwards to the parts extreme; it illumineth the face; which, as a beacon, gives warning to all the rest of this little kingdom, man, to arm: and then the vital commoners and inland petty spirits muster me all to their captain, the heart, who great and puffed up with this retinue, doth any deed of courage; and this valour comes of sherries...."

(Act IV, Scene III)

WINES OF SPAIN

NORTH-WESTERN SPAIN

RIBEIRO

Dry white wines . . . . . .   Pazo   Albariño

NORTHERN SPAIN

RIOJA

Dry red wines . . . .   Banda Azul   Castillo Ygay   Royal   Viña Tondonia
                                    Banda Roja   Imperial   Viña Monty   Viña Vial
                                    Bordon   Marques Riscal   Viña Pomal   Viña Zaco
                                    Castillo de las Arenas Reserva Yago   Viña Real

Dry white wines . . . . . .   Castillo Ygay Reserva Marques Riscal   Rinsol   Viña Sole
                                    Corona   Monopole   Viña Paceta   Viña Tondonia
                                    Etiqueta Blanca

Medium-sweet white wines . .   Diamante   Monte-Haro   Viña Zaconia

Dry rosé wines . . . .   Brillante   Castillo de las Arenas

RIOJA ALTA

Red wines . . . .   El Siglo   Monte Real   Viña Ardanza   Viña del Perdon
                                    Glorioso reserva   Viña Albina Vieja reserva Viña Ercoyen

White wines . . . .   Canchales   Metropol

Rosé wines . . . .   Viña Ercoyen

NAVARRE

Red wine . . . .   Castillo de Tiebas

CARIÑENA

Dry red wine . . . .   Cariñena

EASTERN SPAIN

ALELLA

Dry red wine . . . .   Marfil

Sweet red wine . . . .   Lacre Violeta

Dry white wines . . . . . .   Lacre Gualda   Marfil   Super Marfil reserva

Red wines . . . .   Oro Viejo   Zumilla

Dry rosé wine . . . .   Marfil

PRIORATO

Dry red wines . . . . . .   Falset Garnacha Priorato High Priorato   Priorato Reserva especial

Sweet red wines . . . . . .   Priorato extra Rancio Solera 1918   Vicosa Generoso Priorato

PANADÉS

Sweet white wines	Malvasia	Moscatel
Red wine	Sumoll	

TARRAGONA

Dry red wines	Spanish Red Wine 1955	Viña Vinlo
Red wines	Aureo	Tarragona-Tawny
Dry white wines	Dry Grand Solera	

JUMILLA

Dry red wine	Solera
White wine	Oro Viejo Solera 1902

CENTRAL SPAIN

NOBLEJAS

Red wine	Noblejas	
White wine	Ocaña	Yepes

VALDEPEÑAS

Red wines	Cencibel (Tinto fino)	Garnacha	Tinto Basto
Dry white wines	Airen (Lairén)	Cirial	Pardillo

SOUTHERN SPAIN

MORILES-MONTILLA

Dry wines	*Amontillado*	Alvear Montilla	
	Amontillado pasado . .	Flor de Montilla	
	Fino	Moriles extra san Joaquin	Los Palcos
	Moriles	Seneca	Tercia
	Oloroso	Oloroso Alvear	
	Oloroso viejo	Diogenes	
	Blanco seco	Solera 1906	

MALAGA

Sweet wines	*Moscatel*	Moscatel Delicioso
	Moscatel dorado	Cariño
	Extra viejo	Pedro Ximenez FP
	Lágrima selecte	Los Frailes
	Dulce	Lacrimae Christi
	Dulce añejo	Malaga
Medium-sweet wine	*Vieja solera*	Pajarete 1908

188

Manzanillas	Aris	Eva	La Piconera	Pochola
	Atalaya	Fina	Macarena	Rayito
	Bertola	Garbosa	Mari-Paz	Rechi
	Bone Dry	Gloria	Merito	Regina
	Caricia	Greta	Montana	Sirena
	Carmelita	Hilda	Olorosa Angelita	Solear
	Carmen	La Ballena	Osborne	Torre Breva
	Carola	La Capitana	Papirusa	Varela
	Clasica	La Especial	Pemartin	Villamarta
	Cochero	La Goya	Petenera	Viva la Pepa
	Deliciosa	La Jaca Andaluza	Piedra	Wisdom & Warter
	Duff Gordon	La Lidia		
Finos	Agustinito	Deportivo	Jardin	Pedro Dry
	Alvaro	Don Algar	La Ina	Pemartin
	Apitiv	Don Zoïlo « Dry »	La Condesa	Pinta
	Banquete	Ducal	La Panesa	Preferido
	Barbadillo	Eco	Loredo	Quinta
	Benito	El Catador	Los Compadres	Quisquilla
	Bergantin	Faena	Mantecoso	Redoble
	Betis	Fajardo	Marinero	Rivero
	Bombita	Feria Sherry	Marismeño	Sancho
	Camborio	Finito	Matador Pale Dry	San Patricio
	Campero	Fino F.M.	Menesteo	Tio Mateo
	Canto	Flamenco	Merito	Tio Pepe
	Casanovas	Gaditano	Micalet	Tres Palmas
	Clarita	Hernan Cortés	Olivar	Varela
	Chiquilla	Hidalgo	Palma	Victoria
	Coronel	Inocente	Pando	Viña del Carmen
	Cuesta Alta	Jarana	Pavon	Viña del Cuco
Amontillados	Abolengo	Dry Pale	John Peter	Principe
	Algar	El Botanico	King Alfonso	Rosa
	Amontillado 50	El Cid	La Capilla	Salinera
	Amontillado S.S.S.	El Duque	La Uvita	Salvador
	Anticuario	El Gallo	Lord Sherry	Sancho
	Ataulfo	El Navio	Luque	Santa Cruz
	Barbadillo	El Tresillo	Martial	Siglo de Oro
	Baroness Cocktail	Escogido	Matador	Solito
	Benito	Escuadrilla	Merito	Tio Diego
	Botaina	Fairyland	Millonario	Tio Guillermo
	Buleria	Finest	Miranda	Tito Jaime
	Carta Blanca	Fino Ideal	Nila	Tocayo
	Carta Real	Fino Zuleta	N.P.U.	Tulita
	Casanovas	Florido	Old Dry Classic	Ultra
	Chambergo	Guadalupe	Oñana	Varela
	Club	Guapito	Pemartin	Viejo M.M.M.
	Coquinero	Guerrero	Pizarro	Viña AB
	Del Abuelo	Imperial	Predilecto	Viño del Virrey
	Diestro	Jauna	Primero	Vintners Choice
	Dry Don			
Olorosos	Alfonso	Cacique	Don Quijote	España
	Almirante	Capitan	Don Zoïlo « Medium »	Fandango
	Autumn Leaves	Cartujo	Doña Juana	Favorito
	A Winter's Tale	Casanovas	Double Century	Fenecio
	Bailen	Chambelan	Dry Sack	Galarza
	Barbadillo	Diestro	D.S.	Gran Señor
	B.C. 200	Dique	Duque	Harmony
	Black Tom	Don Gonzalo	El Cesar	La Espuela
	Blazquez	Don Nuño	El Patio	La Infanta

La Merced	Molino	Regio	Solera P.J.
La Novia	Montado	Rio Viejo	Solera Tizon
La Raza	Navigator	Royal Double	Solera Victoria Regina
Long Life	Nina	Sancho	Tercios
Los Flamencos	Nº 10 R.F.	Solariego 1807	Torrecera
Martial Golden	Nº 28	Solera E	Trafalgar Solera 1805
Mayoral	Nutty Solera	Solera Florido	Valdespino
Medium Golden	Ochavico	Solera Granada	Varela
Mercedes	Orrantia	Solera 1842	Viña Isabel
Merito	Pemartin	Solera 1865	Wisdom's Choice
1874	Real	Solera Misa V.O.B.S.	Zuleta

Palos cortados . . . .

Deportivo	Don José	Ojo de Gallo	Superior
Diestro	Eva	Romate	Tres Cortados

Pedro Ximenez . . . .

Bobadilla	El Abuelo	Niños	Solera 1847 (Brown)
Cardenal Cisneros	Gonzalez	Osborne	Solera Superior
Carla	La Goleta	Pemartin	Superior
Cartago (Brown)	Legionario	Procer	Superior
Cob-Nut (Brown)	Martial (Brown)	Reliquia	Valderrama
Consejero	Matador (Brown)	Romate	Venerable
Diestro	M.G.L.	Royal (Brown)	Vintners (Brown)
Diestro (Brown)	1827	Soldado (Brown)	Wisdom
Ducha	1870		

Moscatel . . . .

Ambrosia	Evora	Padre Lerchundi	San Pedro
Atlantida	Fruta	Payaso	Tambora
Baron	Gran Fruta	Pico Plata	Toneles
Duquesa	Laura	Polca	Triunfo
Evangelio	1870	Promesa	Vitoria

Creams . . . .

Abraham	Dalgar	Harmony	Real Tesoro
Armada	Descarado	Infanta	Reverencia
Benito	Diamond Jubilee	Laurel	Romate
Bertola Cream	Diestro	Luque	Royal
Blazquez	Don Zoïlo « Cream »	Matador Cream	Sancho
Carlton House	El Monasterio	Meloso	San Rafael
Carmela	El Tutor	Merito	Sherry Joselito
Casanovas	Eva	Nectar	The Dome
Celebration	Felicita	Orleans 1886	To-Night
Coronation	Flor de Jerez	Osborne	Varela
Cream 201	Gentileza	Palomino	Vintners
Cream Sherry	Grape Cream	Pemartin	Wisdom's Cream
Cristina			

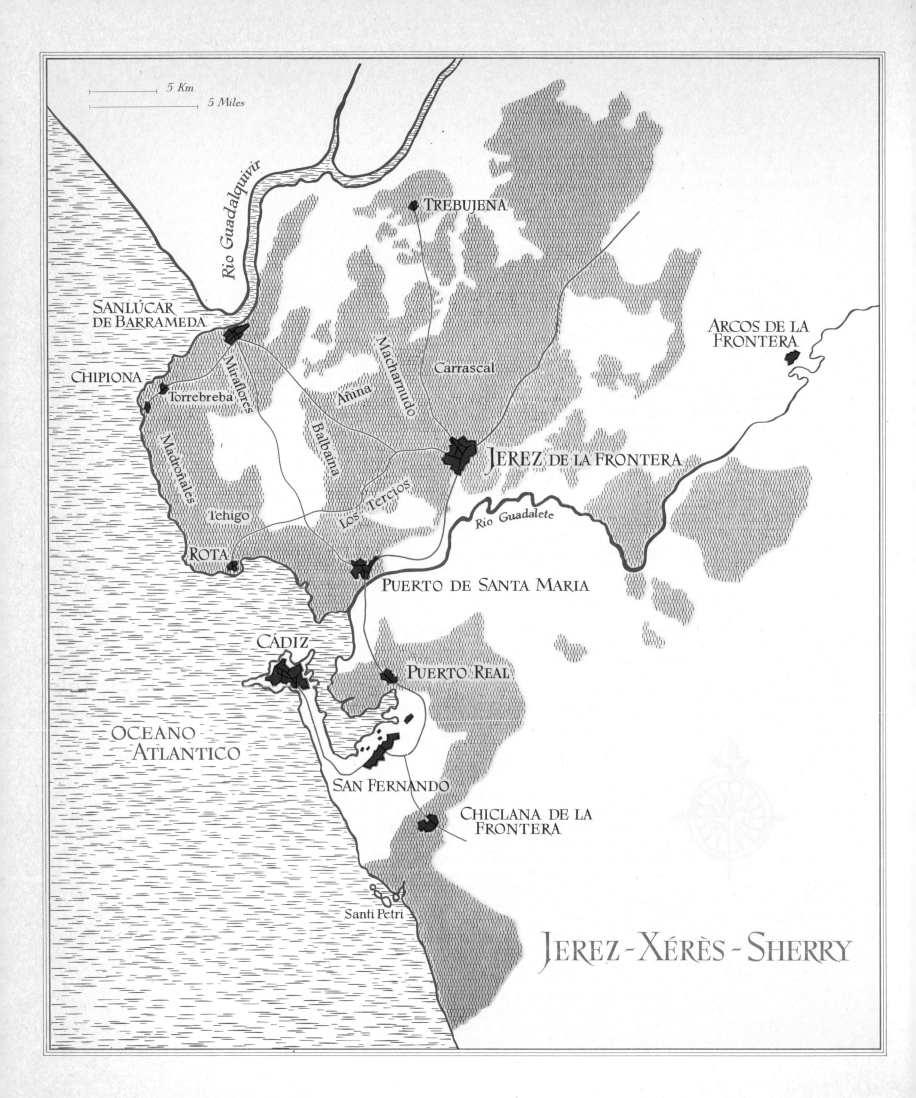

5 Km.

5 Miles

Río Guadalquivir

TREBUJENA

SANLÚCAR
DE BARRAMEDA

ARCOS DE LA
FRONTERA

CHIPIONA

Miraflores

Carrascal

Torrebreba

Añina

Machamudo

JEREZ DE LA FRONTERA

Madronales

Balbaina

Tehigo

Los Tercios

Río Guadalete

ROTA

PUERTO DE SANTA MARIA

CÁDIZ

PUERTO REAL

OCEANO
ATLANTICO

SAN FERNANDO

CHICLANA DE LA
FRONTERA

Santi Petri

JEREZ - XÉRÈS - SHERRY

THE WINES
OF PORTUGAL

SUZANNE CHANTAL DOS SANTOS

Although in world ranking Portugal stands in only sixth position for the total quantity of wine produced annually—behind Italy, France, Spain, the U.S.S.R. and Argentina—she is in fact the world's number one producer when one relates the density of production to the total area of land (metropolitan and insular) under cultivation. The Portuguese is a great drinker of wine, with an average annual consumption of 25 gallons per head. Despite this, he remains a sober citizen, for he has always known how to drink his wine; also, although flavoursome, it has a low alcohol content and it is as rare to see any drunkenness in the countryside as it is in the towns.

Portugal is a country conditioned by the extreme changeableness of its sky and by the great geological variety of its soils. This diversity is reflected in the some 330,000,000 gallons of wine that she drinks or exports each year. The country is very much under the influence of the great ocean winds, which favour a climate not unduly dry, except in the plains south of the river Tagus where, in any case, wheat is grown and not vines. Blessed with sunshine, the climate favours viticulture quite outstandingly. One can find traces of the vine in the very earliest history of the land: for example, on the sarcophagus of Reguengos, dating from two thousand years ago, can be seen the detailed figures of men treading the grape. Much has been said and written on the subject of who first introduced the vine-plant into Portugal, one argument being that it came from Gaul with the Romans, another that it was brought by the Greeks and Phoenicians who, from earliest times, had navigated along the shores of Portugal and had eventually established trading here.

This Lusitania of Roman times was famous for its oil and its wines, since its olive-groves and vineyards made excellent neighbours. So much so that Rome became alarmed at the popularity of the wines, which were competing seriously with those of Italy. The Emperor Domitian decreed severe laws forbidding the cultivation of the vine in the provinces under Roman occupation, often even going as far as having it uprooted and replaced by cereal crops. The vine nevertheless survived this treatment, while both the Barbarians, who drank beer, and the Moors, who tolerantly would allow local customs to be continued in the territories they dominated, left it to prosper and develop. At the time of modern Portugal's birth, in the twelfth century, when young Afonso Henriques was recruiting troops for the Crusades to the Holy Land—as well as to chase the occupying Arab armies out of his future kingdom—we find one of these knight-errants making a prophetic statement: Arnulfo, an Englishman, in a letter which has come down to us, praised highly the merits of the wine from Douro. It was a precursor of what was to be seen, centuries later, as a root of one of the oldest alliances in the world, that of the Portuguese, who make the wine, and the English, who like to drink it. When Afonso Henriques captured Lisbon in 1147, vine-plants were found under the defensive walls of the future capital. As the young kingdom became more populated, the monks planted vineyards in the vast domains which were entrusted to them; and this not merely to obtain their altar wine. The wonderful illustrations of the Apocalypse by Lorvao show the wine harvest and the grape-presses. The Burgundian dynasty, also, was so conscious of the richness that viticulture represented for this country which it dominated for more than two centuries that a decree by Sancho I, at the beginning of the thirteenth century, prescribed that "whomsoever shall destroy with premeditation a vine-plant shall be brought in judgement as it were for the death of a man".

One of the earliest and the most successful commercial exchanges between Portugal and the northern countries of Europe (England, Germany and The Netherlands) was with wine, which was shipped from Viana do Castelo. The cultivation of the vine, in which the Portuguese excel both by nature and by taste, then took on a new importance. The vineyards spread to the banks of the rivers and into the harshest regions: the sea-shore sands of Colares as well as the rocky ravines of Douro. But of course the day came when wine was over-produced at the expense of its quality, and viticulture, far from nourishing people in Portugal, almost condemned them to die of hunger. Strict measures had again to be taken, as in the days of Rome: wine production was limited, and thousands of inferior-quality vine-stocks were uprooted, to be replaced by more useful crops. In fact, all through its history, the Portuguese vineyard has known a series of crises and successes, and one of the constant factors of its evolution has been the anxiety of the authorities to safeguard the quality of the wine used for export. Divergent claims have been made as to whether this policy has been to the detriment or to the benefit of the wines or vineyards considered of secondary importance, since in this sector conditions of production are up to the local growers and there is no outside control.

World events have also had a marked influence on Portuguese viticulture. The sixteenth century seemed almost to be dedicated to the desertion and neglect of the vineyards, as all the fever and ambition of the Portuguese adventurers and explorers was diverted overseas to the newly-discovered foreign lands. Within a very few years, the vines were taken over by heaths and waste-lands. After the wars with Louis XIV of France, England prohibited the importation of the wines of Aquitania and signed, in 1703, the Treaty of Methuen with Portugal which guaranteed a vital exchange—that of a monopoly in Portuguese wines for one in English wools. The wine trade picked up again: from 632 casks (of about 120 gallons each) exported in 1687, it rose spectacularly to 17,000 casks in 1757. England drank mostly the wines from Douro, and a large number of English wine merchants moved to the Continent and established themselves at Porto, where they could buy the standing harvests and closely supervise the shipment of the casks. From the very special conditions of this collaboration was to be born the most famous of Portuguese wines: port.

Although the nineteenth century saw improvements in cultivation and in the processes of vinification, successive disasters descended on the unfortunate Portuguese vineyards. In 1832, during the fratricidal warring between the rival kings Pedro and Miguel, Pedro landed in Porto and drew the chaos and horrors of battle into that region. Crops were neglected or pillaged, the winemaking plant in Porto set afire and the wine stocks destroyed.

In 1846, an insidious illness appeared: oïdium. It was necessary to clean out the vineyards, replacing most of the plants with new stock. Then twenty years later came another catastrophe, which was at first attributed to abnormally hot and dry summers and cold and humid winters. Vinegrowers wore themselves out in ineffectual and unorganized battle until it was discovered that this was an epidemic caused by an insect then unknown in Europe: phylloxera. Many growers gave up, discouraged by the terrifying devastation it had wrought. But others persevered, imported American plants to restock and by dint of years of courage, patience and hard work gradually rebuilt the kingdom's vineyards.

Today, vineyards account for more than 10 per cent of the total agricultural area under cultivation (excepting forestry regions) in Portugal; and the vine, which by its very nature is already diversified, has become even more so under the local methods of cultivation and vinification. But this suits the Portuguese agricultural system, parcelled out as it is into small-holdings, dependant on the family unit, where everyone likes to grow the wheat, rye or maize for his bread, the olives for his oil and the grapes for his wine. This means that many winegrowers drink their own wine—which does not therefore appear in any official production statistics—and have an annual production which is too small to be marketable. Under present conditions, the majority of winegrowers belong to co-operatives, working under the direction and supervision, and also with the assistance, of special organizations.

The great majority of the Portuguese vineyards lie to the north of Lisbon. The most important are those of the Upper Douro region, home of the celebrated port wine. Those of the Minho region produce the *vinhos verdes* ("green wines"); then come the vineyards of Dão, Colares and Bucelas. South of the capital, only the vineyards in the region of Setúbal are of any size.

COCKBURN'S

REGISTERED TRADE MARK

PORT

"Vintage Character"

ESTABLISHED 1815

SHIPPED BY

COCKBURN SMITHES & CO LTD
OPORTO

PRODUCE OF PORTUGAL

QUINTA DO NOVAL

1963

VINTAGE PORT

This wine has been produced on the **150**th anniversary of the Shipper ANTÓNIO JOSÉ DA SILVA
VINHOS, S. A. R. L.
VILA NOVA DE GAIA – PORTUGAL
and bottled in 1965, **250** years after the first known records of the Quinta do Noval - 1715

PORT: VINTAGE CHARACTER

1. Name of the wine: "Port". This generic term seems to suffice. – 2. The mention "Port" is here amplified by the expression "Vintage Character". This means that although not vintage nor free from any blending, this port wine has been treated in the manner of a vintage port, i.e. bottled after a few years in the wood and sold while still fairly young. One can therefore expect a good red semi-sweet port. – 3. Name of origin. There is no exact or obligatory formula. – 4. Name of the merchant. The connoisseur will give his preference to a particular firm, or to a particular port from a particular firm and another port from another firm. In this realm, there is nothing to beat experience.

VINTAGE PORT

1. Type of port: "Vintage Port". This is a good red port, from the best growth of a good year. Free of any blending additive, it has been bottled after 2-3 years in the wood. Caution! It is probably necessary to decant it. – 2. Date of vintage. This mention is obligatory for every true vintage port. – 3. This mention indicates the vineyard of origin. – 4. Name of the merchant-producer. – 5. This port was bottled in 1965.

ROYAL OPORTO WINE C°.

FOUNDED BY ROYAL CHARTER IN 1756

WHITE PORT

EXTRA

(DRY)

PRODUCT OF THE ALTO DOURO

REAL
COMPANHIA VELHA

COMPANHIA GERAL DA AGRICULTURA DAS VINHAS DO ALTO DOURO

V. N. DE GAIA – PORTUGAL

O VINHO DO PORTO É UM VINHO NATURAL, SUJEITO A CRIAR DEPÓSITO COM A IDADE RECOMENDA-SE QUE SEJA SERVIDO COM O CUIDADO INDISPENSÁVEL PARA NÃO TURVAR.

WHITE PORT

1. Name of the wine: "White Port". Here again, this mention seems sufficient, particularly as it will be appraised in relation to the name of the merchant. – 2. The mention "extra dry" draws attention to the fact that this white port is very dry; it is in fact an aperitif wine. – 3. Another version of the name of origin. – 4. Name of the merchant. The Real Companhia Velha was, from 1756 onwards, behind the origin of the regulations for port wine.

2

1

3
2a

4

SIBIO

1. Trade name: "Sibio". – 2. 2a. This name is amplified: dôce = sweet; tinto = deep red; tipo vintage = vintage type (in other words, not aged in the wood). This is therefore a young port, deep-red coloured, with violet reflections. – 3. Name of origin. – 4. Name of the merchant.

PARTNERS' PORT

1. Trade name: "Partners' Port". – 2. In the mention "Finest rich ruby", the word ruby holds the attention and indicates not only its colour but also its age of the wine. "Ruby" also indicates that this port has a beautiful red colour, with reflections as in a precious stone, and an age of 10-15 years. – 3. Name of origin. – 4. Name of the merchant. The connoisseur will appraise the label as a whole when judging the quality of a port, since the name of the merchant cannot be dissociated from the trade name.

EL-REI D. JOSÉ

1. Trade name: "El-Rei D. José". – 2. "Alourado" gives the colour (tawny in English). This type of port will be 15-20 years old. Meio dôce = semi-sweet, this is therefore a dessert wine. – 3. Name of origin. – 4. Name of the merchant.

1

2

4/3

4

4

4

1

2/3

THE GREAT WINEGROWING REGIONS OF PORTUGAL

Certain regions have types of wines with such clear-cut characteristics that their zone of cultivation has been legally, and severely, delimited; by the same token, this has given them the right to an *appellation contrôlée*. This is the case with eight of the fourteen great wineproducing regions of Portugal: Bucelas, Carcavelos, Colares, Dão, Douro, Entre-Douro-e-Minho, Madeira and Setúbal.

WINES OF DÃO: Dão is a green and fertile region, both thickly wooded and intensely cultivated, which rises in tiers from the foothills of the two mountainous "spines" of Portugal: the Serra d'Estrela and the Caramulo. The farmer of these parts is stubborn, vigorous, resistant; his wine tends to resemble him, being strong and full-bodied. It ages well, possesses a good and velvety aroma and a deep colour that seems to come from the rolling landscapes with their low-toned tints, pines, purple heather and rocky outcrops.

This wine, long cultivated as a family affair and pressed in the open-air, is rightly considered to be Portugal's best table wine. Several varieties exist, as a result of the great diversity of soils (where sometimes shale is mixed with granite) and of the vineyards' varying exposures to the sun. One can find the vine-plant at an altitude of more than 1,600 feet on the heights of Tarouca and Castro Daire, or tumbling along the banks of the Mondego (SANTA COMBA, TABOA, MORTAGUA) and on to the plain (MANGUALDE, VISEU). All these wines are therefore quite distinct, although at the same time related through a common stock: *Tourigo*, a vine which provides a high sugar content and a slightly astringent taste. By mixing red grapes and white grapes, a naturally oily, sweet wine is obtained. The red wines, although having a low alcohol content, are full-bodied, with beautiful deep-ruby reflections, while the whites are light, fresh, clear and very perfumed. In 1966, the area of the vineyard was 46,386 acres, producing 19,712,000 gallons.

WINES OF COLARES: It is really astonishing to see, between Cintra and the coast, within almost a stone's throw of Lisbon, the vine being cultivated along the sea-shore and on sandy lands now left high-and-dry by a retreating sea, particularly in the silted-up estuary of the old river Galamares. Yet the vineyards of Colares are among the very oldest in Portugal. Stretching to the south of Cabo da Roca, the westernmost point of the European continent, through the regions of Turcifal and Fontanelas and right on to Azenhas do Mar, they have the noteworthy distinction of having survived the terrible phylloxera epidemic, simply because this insect was not able to live in the sand.

The cultivation of these vineyards is extremely difficult and sometimes even dangerous, for the first step entails digging trenches five to ten yards deep in light, running soil in order to get down to the more solid clay layers where the vine-plants can take root. Each plant spreads its roots sideways along the trenches, which are gradually filled in as new shoots appear. The vinegrower carefully layers his stock, enabling each layered shoot, once covered over, to become the basis of still more new shoots. But the extraordinary intricacy of the procedure in encouraging these last shoots means that, in reality, they are still part of the original vine-plant. Sometimes whole rows of vine-plants are thus made up of one solitary vine-plant at the bottom of the original trench, while up above ground, sheltered by heather or leafy screens and cut back very hard to stand up against the strong Atlantic winds, the vines twist and stretch on their way like strange muscular serpents.

With the arrival of summer, the bunches of grapes must be propped up so that they are not dried by the burning sand. The harvest is brief but picturesque and even in these times it is often carried on the backs of donkeys. In present days, too, a local *adega* weighs the grapes on the spot, and they are treated at once. Periods of rest in the cask before and after the press enriches the must in tannin and colouring matter. COLARES wine must be kept in the cask for two years, and attains its best form from the age of five years onwards. The site of the vineyard, the influence of the sea fogs and winds and of course more particularly the *Ramisco* (vine-plant of the sands) all give COLARES a special flavour, full-bodied yet velvety. Even the red wine is extremely light because of its low alcohol content, while the white is highly perfumed. The production of this unusual wine is very small: only 88,000 gallons for a vineyard of 620 acres which, alas, is getting ever smaller as amenities for tourists gradually invade the Lisbon Peninsula.

WINES OF CARCAVELOS: The Carcavelos region is composed of alluvial deposits on the banks of the Tagus estuary, a soil much less dry and sandy than that of the Colares and producing a wine which is quite different.

The vine *Galego Dourado* gives a quick-fermenting must of a clear colour; the wineproducer adds a completely fermented wine called *abafado* which lends a certain velvety texture to this liqueur, dry rather than sweet, with a rather surprising almond flavour and an alcohol content of at least 19º to 10º. Much appreciated in the seventeenth and eighteenth centuries, CARCAVELOS has now become a rare wine (an area of

77 acres produce no more than 5,500 gallons) which is bought up almost entirely by Great Britain and the Scandinavian countries.

WINES OF SETÚBAL: Scarcely 25 miles from the capital but on the southern bank of the Tagus lies the region of Setúbal, with its pines and rice-fields.

A centuries-old reputation enhances MOSCATEL DE SETÚBAL: this was the wine—along with GARNACHE and MALVASIA, both wines from plants of those same names—that was so lauded among the *vins étranges* appreciated in the Paris of the fifteenth century. Rabelais mentions it when describing the *Temple de la Dive Bouteille*, Louis XIV insisted on having it in his cellars at Versailles and Voltaire had it brought to his property at Ferney.

The stalks of the grapes are left in the must, which gives the MOSCATEL its lively perfume, its strong colour and its characteristic taste. The wine is never drunk until it is at least five or six years old, and there are some MOSCATEL, called "museum wines", which are very old indeed and quite unexcelled: the 1920 vintage is perhaps the best of these. This MOSCATEL DE SETÚBAL, particularly appreciated in Canada, has been called by experts "the quintessence of liqueur wines"; it is sweet, light, fruity yet less musk-scented than FRONTIGNAN and lively enough to be excellent when drunk as an aperitif provided it is iced. It goes very well with second courses and desserts or, better still, with cheese, especially Azeitao ewe's cheese with its original flavour and taste of aromatic herbs.

The Estremadura Transtagana (south of the Tagus) produces other good wines: for example, the region of Palmela has light-red clarets and red table wines, notably PIRIQUITA, which is silky, supple yet robust. And Azeitao is the home of FAISCA, a very pleasant rosé which is extremely popular abroad: its delightful colour and thirst-quenching freshness (for it must, of course, be drunk iced) attract the drinker without startling him. Under the trade-name LANCERS, it is one of the best-selling wines in the United States.

WINES OF BUCELAS: The wines of the region of Bucelas, which are produced from the *Arinto* vine of the Tagus estuary, are dry and somewhat acid wines the colour of yellow straw. Much appreciated by Wellington's officers and men during his Peninsula War against Napoleon, they afterwards found a great success in England. Charles Dickens mentions them as among his favourite wines, along with SAUTERNES and sherry, and Lord Byron praises their qualities, to which George III of England adds that of having cured him of a troublesome kidney disease.

VINHOS VERDES: While such wines as DAO, COLARES, BUCELAS, CARCAVELOS and even MOSCATEL have their imitators in other countries, the noted VINHOS VERDES ("green wines") are 100 per cent Portuguese all along the line. Their unusual name does not come from their colour (they are in fact red or white) but from the amount of ripening, for these wines are produced from plants in northern Portugal which are pruned espalier fashion and whose grapes never reach maturity.

These VINHOS VERDES, lively, slightly acid and always extremely young, have a very long history behind them and seem to have been known to Strabon.

Minho, home of VINHOS VERDES, is at the same time Portugal's most densely-populated province and that with perhaps the most difficult land, for its granite-like soil is unforgiving and unrelenting. Centuries-old parcelling of the land has resulted in an infinite number of tiny properties each hardly able to support a family—this is the region of traditional emigration to seek new hope, even though the vineyards hold man close through the unceasing cares which they demand and the joys and benefits they return. Human wisdom over the years has dictated that these vineyards must not be given a soil so dearly needed to feed so many mouths, and by law the vine may be cultivated only on waste ground, along the edges of fields or by paths and roads. So the farmer of Minho plants his vines in espaliers, as high hedges or even, very frequently, on living supports such as chestnuts, sycamores, poplars, cherry-trees or alders. The vine-plant is tied to the tree by fine willow stalks and the vine-shoots are allowed to hang down. These "grape-bearing trees" which delighted Jean Giraudoux, these "hanging vines", these paths of trellis give the landscape a gentle shade and cut up the country roads with a lace-like pattern of chiaroscuro. Their tart grapes come from very old selected vine-stocks: *Vinhão*, *Borracal* and *Espadeira* for the black grapes and *Azal* or *Dourado* for the white grapes.

The vines of the Minho basin remain undisturbed for long years and the plants become almost arborescent. The roots descend deep into a soil dug and fertilized with green heather and animal manure, while above ground, the knotted and muscled stem and the long supple vine-shoots often reach a height of 15 feet. The humidity of this region encourages plant sickness, which means an unrelenting struggle with long sprays, using special products against the mildew and phylloxera. Harvested in September and racked at the end of the year six weeks after they have been bottled, these VINHOS VERDES are already a sparkling wine— and there is one of their characteristics, even one of their charms. The white wines are thirst-quenching, light and harmless, admirably suited to picnics and summer lunches, with an alcohol content of only 6° to 9°. The red VINHOS VERDES are also of low alcohol content, but these full-bodied wines are of a dark purple colour, with a crimson foam which stains the glass.

The VINHOS VERDES have been long appreciated for their refreshing taste of fruit and their lively youthfulness, but for many years they were drunk only locally, for it was said they travelled badly. Rich in lactic acid and malic acid, they were volatile and lacked body. More recently, it has been possible to stabilize them and they are now exported to Belgium, Africa and Great Britain, not to mention even to France where an equivalent wine does not exist. The price of modern progress has to be paid, however, and today bottles of uniform contents have replaced the attractive little stoneware jugs, the shape and size of which were seldom quite uniform.

There are 90,000 producers of VINHOS VERDES; of these, only 33,000 produce more than 11,000 gallons each a year, while 54,000 of them produce only about 200 gallons! The success of these wines has seen exports rise to 1,320,000 gallons out of a total production of 66,000,000 gallons, the balance being drunk in the country and making up 33 per cent of the home consumption of Portuguese wine.

OTHER WINEPRODUCING REGIONS: Several other regions of Portugal are of quite some interest to viticulture, particularly eight of them which are expected to become delimited zones, with the production of their wines strictly controlled. These are the wines of Pinhel, light and pleasant clarets; the wines of Lafoes, non-sparkling but otherwise similar to the VINHOS VERDES and grown on trellises (these *verdascos* are usually red wines and total about 1,540,000 gallons a year); the wines of Bairrada, semi-sparkling whites or reds which come not far from Dão with its ANADIA wines; the wines of Buçaco, rich and strong yet smooth; wines from the region of Sangalhos with reds which come close to the best of those from Dão, and whites which rival those of Anadia; the wines of Alcobaça, where Cistercian monks in the twelfth century cleared the barren lands to plant the vineyards; the wines of Ribatejo, where the plants stand high to escape the periodical floodings of the Tagus, with notably ALMEIRIM, CARTAXO and several ordinary wines, including the full-flavoured "ordinary" red wine, of a low alcohol content but keeping its quality well, which flows freely during the *festas bravas* that accompany the bullfights and the popular feasting on roast kid; finally, the wines of Torres Vedras, full-bodied tannin-rich ordinary red wines used for blending and also simple wines for café-restaurants and family tables; over towards Obidos, the GAEIRAS and especially the white type is very worthy.

It is noticeable that, with the exception of MOSCATEL DE SETÚBAL, all these good quality wines are grown north of the Tagus, although the southern provinces do have some of their own. In Alentejo, for example, the names of such places as Cuba, Vidigueira, and so on, would seem to indicate that the vine was once cultivated there, but the region, which is thinly populated, was devoted to other crops—cereals, cork oak and olives, all better adapted to large seasonal monocultures. A few vineyards of Alentejo which escaped the oïdium infection were able to produce, around the end of the nineteenth century, some strong and aromatic wines which were practically unknown outside the region, although one should mention the wine of Borba.

The province of Algarve, in the extreme south, long had the unfair reputation of producing the country's most mediocre wine. It was unfair because here too the vine had to give way to other crops such as almonds, figs and locust-beans, although the local population is considerable and well used to the multiple tasks of small cropping and make good winegrowers. The grapes grown are excellent: the black grapes from *Pauferros* produce a wine with a very good bouquet and the white grapes from *Tamarez* produce a very sweet wine, of which Lagõa is the main producer. The Portuguese government is encouraging viticulture in the province of Algarve and various schemes are in progress for reviving once-popular wines.

Fuzeta and Moncarapacho produce a Malaga-type dessert wine while AFONSO III, a liqueur wine, is a good aperitif with the warmth of sherry.

In the far north of the country, Chaves offers a wine with many connoisseurs called "wine of the dead" because it is sometimes buried to hasten its ageing.

Finally, Portugal produces some natural sparkling wines, notably at Lamego, with also some much appreciated rosés such as the already-mentioned FAISCA. MATEUS ROSÉ is also exported in the whole world—Europe, the United States, Canada, Australia, Hong Kong—and demand for the wine is so high (13 million bottles in 1967) that it absorbs the entire harvest, from its home province of Trás-os-Montes to around Anadia.

This abundance (304,681,828 gallons in 1966), this diversity, this often exceptional quality, this long and solid reputation mean that wine is a major trump-card for Portugal in the international market-place. Many of these wines are, however, enjoyed locally, perhaps particularly by the French, whose country sets restrictive measures with very limited quotas to protect the French national wine trade against imports of all wines, except those which have no equivalent in France, such as port, Madeira, VINHOS VERDES and some rosés. Portuguese wines exported in the bottle (only 7 per cent of the total, however, because of transport costs) carry a seal of guarantee, but the remainder of the production is exported in casks. In 1967, the total of wine exports exceeded 7,920,000 gallons, or a value of 1,350 million escudos.

PORT WINES

This famous wine owes to Porto only its name, for the vineyards which produce it are stepped along the ravine sides of the Upper Douro valley, and it is the town of Vila Nova de Gaia (across from Porto itself) where the wine is treated and aged, over many years, in the shade and silence of the great winemaking plants.

But it is from Porto, since time immemorial, and from Porto alone that this famous wine has been shipped to the four corners of the world, and it is the name Porto that one reads today, as one did a hundred years ago, on the casks rolled so gaily along the riverside quays. Some relate the tale that the name *rio douro* means "river of gold" and that this heavy and slow-running water does indeed run over nuggets of gold. The truth, however, is elsewhere and quite different, and one can perhaps remember Jean de La Fontaine: the treasure of the Douro, he maintained, must be wrenched from it with grit, with hard sweat, with faith and with love. For this most generous of wines is born of the most ungenerous and avaricious of lands, and throughout its long life it remains at the mercy of a thousand different perils: drought, wind, frost, fog, storms and all the illnesses of the vine. Just one week, if conditions go wrong at the moment the grape is ripe, is sufficient to ruin a whole harvest.

The port must is also a fragile substance, which must be observed and handled with loving and knowing care if one is to extract the very best qualities from it. It is sensitive to heat, to air currents, to odours, to any delay in pressing the grapes or in fermentation. It passes long years maturing in large casks where it sheds its skin and absorbs enrichment at the same time, yet this very sojourn reduces also its vitality, for the rate of evaporation can reach as much as 4 per cent a year. Port wine demands a great deal of vigilance and care and costs its producer much. In Douro, from the vinegrower to the consumer, the whole world lives a veritable cult of the wine.

Many people claim that the plants which produce port wine came originally from Burgundy. However that may be, it is known that, at the end of the eleventh century, Henry, grandson of Robert I, Duke of Burgundy, had won fame at the side of El Cid in the fighting against the infidels. As a reward, he was given the lands of Douro and Minho and he later married a natural daughter of Alfonso VI, King of Leon and of Castille, receiving also the title of Count of Portugal. As Henry then settled down in his property and seems to have had few other worries than to make the most of his land, it is quite probable that he cultivated the vine and preferred the vine-stock of his home. In any case, it was to be many years before the vineyards of Douro became famous, for in reality their history begins only with the eighteenth century.

The wines at this time were very full-bodied, heavy and loaded with tannin; furthermore, in an effort to heighten their colour, elderberries were added, while various methods of stabilization were attempted so that the wine might survive the voyage to the English shores. It can be admitted outright: the wines were abominable and the English would certainly have preferred the wines of Bordeaux had not their endless quarrels with the French led to a complete ban on the import of the wines of Aquitania. Yet the English soldiers and sailors remembered very well having drunk some very satisfactory local wines in the harbour bars and other places during their campaigns.

The demand for the wines, as a result of the Treaty of Methuen in 1703, encouraged farmers without any experience to try cultivating vine-plants, and the prospect of easy gains had already incited the wine-growers to cut corners on wine production. One must bear in mind, too, that at this time wines were everywhere drunk very young and the secret of ageing the great vintage wines had been lost over the years in the same way as the use of impervious jars. The wine quickly went bad in the barrels and survived no better in the skin containers.

Since they were in any case obliged to drink this unpleasant wine, bought, understandably, at the nearest point to their land, in northern Portugal, the English decided to go and see on the spot how it was made. Merchants established themselves at Porto, although at first they opened only transport offices, later risking their capital by buying the standing harvest. In this way, they discovered the Douro and became winegrowers: they had the necessary capital and made the law of the vineyards, and they could also choose the best musts. But overproduction very rapidly brought the prices down and the valley lived wretchedly.

The REAL COMPANHIA: Bartholomeu Pancorvo, a man richer in ideas than in gold, was the first to understand the vital need to take the whole production of wine in hand in Douro, in order to keep a check on quality and prices. The English, however, caused his plan to fail and the poor man did not survive his ruin. But the idea was now in the air and a monk, Brother Mansilha, in high favour at Court, developed a scheme to win the game. He had the backings of the great Duke of Pombal. He instigated the founding of the *Real Companhia dos Vinhos do Alto Douro* (Royal Company of the Wines of Upper Douro) in 1756 and took up both the monopoly of trade with England and Brazil and the production of wine-based spirits.

Brother Mansilha began by countering the manoeuvres of the English, who were baulked in their attempted take-over of the vineyard. But, as is often the case, he was opposed even more violently by the very people he hoped to help, for in 1759, three years after the foundation of the Royal Company and at the time of the great popular drinking feasts and carnivals, the price of wine had gone up a few pence in the bars. There was a riot in Porto and the mob, feeding on its own fury, pillaged the premises of the Royal Company and burned all the books. The repression was brutal—people were jailed, hanged, quartered—but order was finally restored.

One of the first jobs for the Royal Company, henceforth sovereign in the field, was to mark out the best region for producing a high quality wine. The exceptional qualities of the wine meant that, with appropriate treatment and ageing, it could become not merely a table wine but a vintage wine. Many mediocre vine-plants were sacrificed and on the confined space remaining, experiments were patiently carried out with more and more rigid methods of vinification.

At the same time, success was achieved in developing mass production of glass vessels in which the wine could rest sheltered from the air. Inaugurated in Portugal, this procedure was to permit the whole world to find again the powerful yet delicate flavour of the ancient wines, while the Upper Douro was to discover the secret of its incomparable port. This wine very rapidly met an immense popularity in England for, warm, comforting, tonic, it brought into the humid mists of the long English winters the living light and the warmth of a beautiful fire in the hearth. Even today port is more popular in colder countries than in its native Portugal, where a lighter wine is preferred,

Porto benefited from the wealth of the vineyards. Always hardworking, thrifty and valiant, the old town had never been very smart. But the gold from port wine now gave her palaces and churches in which one might see, as in San Francisco, vine-shoots and grape-clusters stretching right on to the altars. Roads and bridges were built for transporting the wine, and soon, too, appeared more winemaking plants, official and private offices, and spacious and beautiful houses. English merchants established themselves in a road which was named Street of the English, and built, at great expense, a *factorerie* where they could discuss their business. The Portuguese, for their part, had become aware of their national heritage: proprietors of lands set their estates (called *quintas*) in order and established firms to produce and sell their own wines.

Thus two groups, with the same aims, associated yet at the same time competitors, and living even in the heart of a relatively small town two absolutely separate existences, were working side by side—in the vineyards of Douro, in the winemaking plants of Vila Nova de Gaia and in the offices in Porto.

From this comes something of the special physiognomy of Porto. It is certain that its pearly skies, its frequent mists, its freshly cool climate were already making it a "northern capital". And one can understand that the English felt at home, for the natives of Porto were, by nature, hard-working, provident, enemies of waste and false manifestations, to which qualities this contact with the English added efficiency and exactness, as well as a taste for elegant and family comfort. In Porto, behind the austere granite of the house façades, one finds beautiful mahogany, fine carpets, precious silverware, added to the dignity of old port decanted in crystal flasks.

THE VINEYARDS OF DOURO

Any good vine-plant, once acclimatized to Douro, would give port wine, but a vine-plant of Douro transplanted elsewhere would cease to produce port wine. This strange alchemy which, it is believed, presides over the making of this wine is the work of Nature, which has brought together on the banks of the Upper Douro and its tributaries (Corgo, Torto, Tua) conditions which are special, exceptional, mysterious and delicate. Here the vinegrower comes to grips with lava terrains, rugged and rocky. He plants his vine on a chaotic accumulation of eroded, crumbled and broken-up land, the work of the torrents and rivers, for it is true that for a long time there have grown on these ungrateful slopes only scrub brush and the aromatic grasses that the mountain goats feed on.

Down in the deep river gorges, the winter air currents are icy and fog collects like thick cottonwool. When summer comes, the storms build up and their effects are felt from valley to valley, until, finally, the sun begins to heat the stone. The valleys become ovens of 40° C. and even 50°, enveloping without a breath of air the whole "land of wine", the region so minutely and strictly laid out in vineyards whose product can be turned into *approveitado* (approved) port wine. The part of the Douro production not used for port will give table wines or wine alcohol.

In 1966, the total production of these vineyards, an area of nearly 60,000 acres, was 33,000,000 gallons, of which only 6,930,000 gallons were *approveitado*.

This goes to show that apart from the position of the lands, their soil composition and their exposure to the sun, one must also count the local conditions, meteo-

This view of the site of Cachao de San Salvador da Pesqueira, near Beira, shows us the landscape of the Upper Douro valley as it was about the middle of the eighteenth century. This is the period that saw, under the impulse of the institute of the *Real Companhia dos Vinhos do Alto Douro*, the restoration of the vineyards and the birth of port wine, a wine which was to extend its reputation across the entire world.

rological or otherwise, which increase or reduce the quality of the must each year. And even before the harvest, it was necessary to create the vineyard—with the hand of man and on the back of man. The hard, laminated, slated rock had to be broken up with the hand-pick, crumbled and laid out in terraces, open to the maximum amount of sun and rain. These terraces held by small stone walls, climb the steepest slopes, with the lowest plants at water-level: it is said that the best grapes are picked where they have ripened "listening to the creaking of the river boats' heavy rudders". The plants do not grow above an altitude of 1,000 feet; any higher and ripening cannot take place satisfactorily.

The terraces give the landscape a strange and imposing aspect. As far as the eye can see, the hillsides are striped and patterned as if with giant fingerprints, and everywhere one looks, the plants line up rank on rank, held by vine-props and wires. The shoots hang fairly close to the ground, benefiting from all the emanations of the soil, but care has been taken also to see that the grape-bunches are neither soiled nor damaged by contact with the ground. To conserve the

rains of winter and keep a reserve of freshness during the heat of summer, a large ditch is dug and filled with rough stones at the foot of each plant, whose roots go six feet under ground. No secondary crops; the entire vitality of this soil is dedicated to the vine. The leguminous plants between the vine-plants are mulched in as additional fertilizer. The whole winter is spent clearing, cleaning and tidying the vineyard. Working under enormous capes of maize straw for protection against the frequent rain between October and March, the vintners repair the little walls, disinfect and consolidate the vine-props, layer, graft and prune the vine, until along the lines not a dead leaf nor a stone is to be seen. The vine-shoots turn green, the grape-bunches begin to lengthen. It is the perilous time when a morning frost can turn it red and kill it. Throughout the workers must fight parasites, be prepared for storms, watch the sky; and then comes the summer, with its terrible dryness and burning winds. The harvest, in September, is at once a task, a ritual, a feast. It is a final effort, crowning a whole year of hard labour and bringing its reward or, sometimes, withholding it.

THE HARVEST AND THE PRESSING

The ideal moment of ripening of the grapes has to be seized on, a moment that varies for each *quinta* and even for each slope of the hillside. Then the women, with their scissors and baskets, crouch beside the vine-plants, cut the grape-bunches and check each to make sure that not a single spoiled or unripe bunch goes to the press. Under the slight shade of the leaves, the workers suffocate in the heat mirrored by the stones, too hot to rest a hand on them. The baskets are emptied into hods at the end of each row, collected by groups of *barracheiros*, the stalwarts who can carry a load of 165 pounds of grapes well balanced on the nape of the neck with a leather strap and steadied with a steel hook. They walk in a long single file, with a heavy step, in time to the rhythm of the stick of the leader, who guides them down the stone steps and steep paths of the vineyards. The presses are set up as low down the hills as possible, yet high enough to escape the danger of the sudden and violent floods of the often torrential rivers.

In the vastness of the landscape, men trudge onwards like ants, glistening with sweat. The sticky juice glues to their skin the jute sacking with which they protect their backs. These *barracheiros* are irreplaceable, because no other method of transporting the grapes has been found which can be used in these steep vineyards.

At the presses, everything has been made ready. Over the past months, new barrels have been carved and the old ones cleaned. For centuries, the grape was pressed with the feet, because this was believed to be the only way of extracting all the goodness from the pulp and skin of the grape without crushing the grape-pips. Tiring work, in the vats filled with wet and slippery grapes, which had to be pressed till they were crushed and split open and were transformed into a gluey porridge-like mass. The pressers had to bring air down into the mass too, by constantly lifting their knees high, in order to break up the crust that the waste products formed on the surface of the liquid. A team of six men would take twenty hours to extract some 200 gallons of must. But a joyous exaltation seemed to lie over this work, reminiscent of a birth: the pressers, already a little dizzy with the vapours rising from the vat, were encouraged with songs and music, and the womenfolk danced all night long around the stone vats by the light of lanterns. Today, this pressing with the feet has become difficult because of lack of seasonal labour, and is being replaced more and more by a mechanical process, called the Ducellier process, which gives, after a mechanical stoning, excellent results: a system of valves, set in action by the fermentation, simultaneously stirs and aerates the must.

Another critical moment comes with the decision of how much wine alcohol should be added to the must in order to stop the transformation of sugar into the alcohol which results from fermentation. The quantity depends itself on the richness of the must: too much rain, before or during the harvest, swells the grapes but may reduce their sugar content by several degrees, while drought and dry periods give a rich but rarer grape. In Douro, nothing ever seems to be given in quite the right quantities. The measured addition of wine alcohol will therefore give a wine which is more or less dry or sweet.

Suitably "dosed" in this way and allowed to settle, the must is left in the freshness of the cellars of the *quinta*, until in the springtime it is transported to the winemaking plants of the estuary. For many years a curious type of boat was used for this, with a flat bottom and a high poop on which an experienced helmsman ruled. The Douro is treacherous, even impetuous here, seamed with hidden reefs or shoals, and the old-fashioned *barcos rabelos* have given way little by little, first to trains and then to heavy road transport. The valley's charm is the loser, for nothing was more picturesque than this sight of the sailing boats or the *rabelos*, sometimes towed by oxen, sometimes beating against the wind.

TYPES OF PORT

Until its arrival at Vila Nova da Gaia, the wine is still young and a little rash, but it will now undergo a long retirement, during which it will learn the best of wisdom. Depending on the characteristics which they show right at the start of their life, that is to say when they leave the presses, the new wines will belong to one or other of the two great port "families": that of the "blends", which are the more numerous, or that of the highly prized "vintages".

The blends, which cover the majority of the port wines, are as their names indicate, blends aged in the wood. Once the must has settled, after two years in the cask, it is again weighed, tasted and appraised. Other types of must are then sought which can be added, bringing with them characteristics of their own which will underline or complement those of the original must. Some of the blending musts may bring strength, others colour, others again bouquet. Any port worthy of the name is made up of at least sixteen varieties of vine-stock. Like a florist making up a display, or a painter mixing the colours on his palette, or a perfumer dosing out the essences, the port experts compose, mix and dose the different port wines.

They work surrounded by retorts, test-tubes, bottle-racks, note-books, in veritable laboratories that the

All along the Douro, thanks to centuries of work by the vinegrowers, the vines climb across the steep hillsides and give the landscape the aspect of some enormous staircase fashioned by giants. Even today, springtime still sees the wine moved by boat along the river. The old-fashioned *barcos rabelos* transport the barrels of must to the famous winemaking plants at Vila Nova da Gaia, opposite Porto.

Above: A view of the terraces that produce Port, laboriously hacked out of the stony ground by hand in the valley of the Douro, Portugal. Left: Labourers plant and tend the vines with loving care, planting each in a sort of basin surrounded by big stones to conserve the water. Below: In the Douro valley, where extremes of heat and cold are known, the vintners wear capes of maize straw in bad weather.

winemaking firms have fitted out. To inspiration must be linked experience. For it is not purely a question of inventing a new port, but of establishing a successful formula which can be followed and above all maintained, in order that a trade product can be confidently and successfully marketed.

Listed, their composition carefully analysed, the blends are then put into enormous wooden casks, in order to prevent both their oxydation and too rapid an evaporation. The wines remain there under constant supervision. They are measured, sounded, tasted, and the attentive ear of the master winemaker watches out for and notices the noises, deep or light, which come from the immense *cuvée*. This latter remains alive and moving for, as it takes on greater age, the wine is enlivened and enriched with the careful addition of young and strong musts. No port wine may be drunk before it has aged five to six years in the wood. It reaches its fullness after about thirty years, but one can drink ports of sixty years and more which have remained absolutely marvellous. It is impossible and in fact a vain effort to try to date the different blends; one can merely say that they are *cuvées spéciales*.

For reasons of convenience and economy, the blends are usually exported in barrels and bottled by the importers. The importers of a few large brands, to ensure the unbroken quality of their chosen *cuvée*, insist on bottling in the winemaking plants before the wines are sold, and in this case, the bottle is sealed by the Port Wine Institute. This institute works with two other bodies, the Port Wine Shippers Guild and Douro House, to control and regulate the cultivation, vinification and exporting of port.

Contrary to the blends, the port vintages always have a birth certificate. It is always a *very* good year. When a harvest has been outstandingly good in quality, a vintage year is decided. The must, which is usually treated and kept in the wood for two years, is put straight into bottles without any blending, and the bottle, hermetically sealed, is put in the winemaking plant. There, the wine ages, in austere and silent solitude, for ten, twenty, thirty years or even more. It skins and enriches itself by natural means. It is a *millésimé* port. The vintage ports are more appreciated in England, or at any rate were so in earlier days: the old connoisseurs of Thackeray and Dickens' times valued them more than any other. But the vintage ports, one can well imagine, are fragile: they demand a lot of care in the conservation, transport and even in the drinking. Furthermore, even if their fine uprightness is admirable, they do not have the clever complexity that enchants the connoisseurs of the blended ports. Great vintage years are very rare; one can mention the years 1890, 1900 (still to be found on the market), 1908, 1927, 1931, 1945 and 1947. According to the vine-plant used in their production, vintage ports are more or less light or dark, and with age, darken or lighten, although most vintage ports gradually become "tawny", that is to say, the colour of light mahogany.

In addition to this fundamental difference between blends and vintages, port is divided into extra-dry, dry (usually white port), semi-dry and sweet (red). Ageing, by decanting the colouring matter, touches all with gold, and the shades of colour spread out from light topaz to bronze. The official colours are: deep red, red, ruby (these are the "fulls"), light gold, onion peel (the "tawnies"), pale white, pale straw and golden.

The "fulls" are fairly young port wines, rich, full-bodied, ruby-coloured or deep garnet. The "tawnies" are old wines which have taken on the colour of amber or wild honey. A good port can be recognized first by its aroma, and secondly because it "weeps", that is to say it lets slide down the sides of the glass a long, slow unctuous tear.

PORT IN THE WORLD

England, for some time, has been no longer the world's major importer of port: between 1900 and 1919, the British drank each year 13,200,000 gallons but in 1939 they bought only 6,380,000 gallons.

Up to the war of 1914-1918, port, with Madeira, was intimately linked with the daily life of the upper-class English. It was the sole wine judged worthy of using for the Sovereign's Toast, at the end of a meal. Chosen with the greatest care—and tastes in port could be discussed all night—a bottle was served to the gentlemen, while the ladies "withdrew", going to the drawing-room (or withdrawing-room) for infusions of herbs or tea and light conversation. The men emptied the bottle between them while chatting. Each gentleman's club knew exactly the preferences of its eminent members and kept in reserve a suitable supply of their port and cigars. The great families had their cellars, where reserves were built up, either as a financial investment or for sentimental reasons. A similar custom, still preserved in Douro, established for each child born into a family a stock of bottles which was increased from year to year. The lucky child who came into the world the year of a vintage port could be assured of an outstanding wine with which to celebrate its coming-of-age or its wedding.

But while England began reducing its consumption of port, others, France among them, began to discover it. Or rather, re-discover it, for this wine had been much appreciated long ago, especially after the Napoleonic invasions at the beginning of the nineteenth century. The archives of the region of Douro hold the requisition orders signed by the general occupying Porto, be he the English ally or the French enemy. It is amusing to note that some of these carry the same date: for example, March 29th, 1809 was the day that Wellington, landing unexpectedly, interrupted the lunch of Marshal Soult.

Despite its relatively limited area, the Douro vineyard presents a rich variety of vine-stocks. One remembers, too, that the blends, spread out over ten years or more, obey subtle and supple rules. This is why port wines are so varied and why they suit all tastes and all climates.

HOW AND WHEN TO DRINK PORT

One must first know just what one expects of port. If it is a question of serving a refreshing aperitif which at the same time sets an "ambiance", one should choose a dry white port, and serve it chilled, either by chilling the glasses with an ice-cube or by putting the glasses themselves in a chilling recipient. This is the way the French usually drink port wine. For an afternoon refreshment, a five-to-seven reception or the end of a meal, a "tawny" or a "full" is preferable. A semi-dry or a sweet port makes a delightful accompaniment to dessert pastries and to certain fruits, but not citrus varieties.

One should not, moreover, neglect to serve port with the cheese. It is no doubt to enhance the taste of the port that the English brought into fashion savouries or hot dishes, usually with cheese and spiced and offered right at the end of the meal, when the bottles or decanters are going round. It is also the English who put port into their famous Stilton cheese, cutting into the centre and filling the hole with good port as cutting proceeds, which allows the wine to permeate the creamy mass. All the cheeses in the world—Danish, Dutch or Swiss cheese, Portuguese, Spanish or Italian cheese, and of course the inexhaustible plateau of French cheese—have a common denominator: they enhance the port which, in its turn, exalts the cheese.

In Douro and in Portugal in general, port is drunk according to a certain ritual. It must never, even in a public establishment, be served open; the law requires that the bottle be presented. In private homes, the wine is not brought in its bottle; it is considered more elegant, and shows a better knowledge of port itself, to transfer it a few hours beforehand into a decanter, where it may rest and take the air. A vintage port is never uncorked, for in the ten or twenty years of its life, the best of corks would have spoiled and mildewed and thus, inevitably, cork dust would fall in the wine. Real connoisseurs therefore, to open a bottle of a really great port, use a pair of special pliers heated red-hot in a fire, with which they decapitate the bottle.

Although such refinements have largely fallen into disuse, both port wine and the mistress of house who intends to offer it have everything to gain in observing the niceties. There is a wide choice of decanters, some old, engraved, cut, filled gold, others modern, heavy, belted with leather. They usually carry a metal medallion round the neck marked with the word "Port" in more or less fancy letters. The glass, on the other hand, should be very simple, in fine crystal, with a foot, and all in one piece in the shape of a tulip or a balloon. One can thus better appraise the colour of the wine, and the bouquet is more concentrated. Connoisseurs say port should be "chewed" before it is swallowed, after having lengthily held the glass (except in the case of the fresh white ports) in the hollow of the hand. Thus port gratifies all the senses.

These days one can forget the old rule that port is always served in a clockwise direction; but remember that connoisseurs never re-cork a bottle: once opened, it is drunk. If, however, one should wish to keep an opened bottle and not be able to finish it in the following days, it should be decanted into a smaller flask where it will be free from air.

Port for anniversaries and tête-à-tête meals; as a pick-me-up for grandfather or the overworked student; port to warm the hunter after the stalk or the traveller after the long trip; prelude and conclusion of a large banquet; port in a reducing diet; port drunk with friends informally at a bar or at an important ceremony in an official reception—in brief, port, the truly grand seigneur, is everywhere at home.

On the official level, port is also the Portuguese wine which is most carefully watched over by the authorities. Several official organizations watch to ensure that it is cultivated, vinified and marketed according to very strict rules. The Casa do Douro supports, advises and sometimes finances the vinegrowers; the Gremio dos Exportadores, at Porto, organizes and co-ordinates the trade in wine; and the Instituto do Vinho do Porto heads all these other activities, checking and controlling all the wines which will be put on the market and which may not be sold in Portugal without a guarantee seal. This small seal, marked "I.V.P.", seen on a bottle is a sign which does not mislead. Many wines are exported in casks, with a certificate of origin. Some frauds can be carried out when the wine is bottled, but fortunately many countries, including France, have enough respect for great wines, of whatever origin, to punish fraud energetically and effectively. It is therefore possible anywhere to drink a port wine which is just as good as in the cellars of Gaia, where Portugal likes to greet visitors and let them taste these jewel-shaded wines.

THE WINES OF MADEIRA

The equerries of Henry the Navigator landed in Madeira in 1419 after years of searching for the Fortunate Isles. Stranded after a terrible storm on an almost barren island which out of gratitude they had baptized Porto Santo, the voyagers had for months seen a misty silhouette appearing and disappearing on the horizon, a real "enchanted" island. They landed there at last, disembarking in a rocky creek occupied by sea animals and which they describe in their portulan as *Camara de Lobos*. All around were dense forests, made up of trees whose odour was so strong that men became dizzy when cutting them down. They called the island Madeira, which means wood in Portuguese.

As a result of the travellers' reports men were sent to colonize the islands and they planted both European-style and tropical crops. In this way, Madeira grew and side by side flourished cane sugar and grape-vines.

Right from the start, the Madeira wine proved to be excellent. Ca da Mosto, the celebrated Venitian navigator, in 1455 praised the wine drunk in these new isles. The whole of Europe became enthused. The Duke of Clarence, locked up in the Tower of London, chose to drown himself in a barrel of Malmsey wine to escape the vengeance of his brother. Falstaff, as Shakespeare claimed, sold his soul one Friday for a glass of good Madeira and a cold leg of chicken. François I insisted on always having some in his castles in Touraine. Portugal granted special privileges to the English merchants established at Funchal, where trade was brisk, and the wines of the island, which were traded against wheat and dairy produce of Ireland, wood and rice from America, and fish from Newfoundland, provisioned the long-haul sailing ships.

William Bolton, the British Consul at Funchal, a shipowner and banker, played an important role in the development of the Madeira vineyard, and in 1699, complained that the supply could not meet the demand, particularly from the American colonists. The future George IV, the first gentleman of Europe, lent them his prestige in England: nothing else was drunk at Carlton House and 22,000 pipes (a pipe was large-size cask) of wines were exported to Great Britain in 1813. But there was another side to the coin.

In 1852, a terrible disease attacked the island's vineyards: oïdium. Whole plants were decimated. Twenty years later, phylloxera struck. The plants would have been abandoned had it not been for the stubborn work of enlightened winegrowers, who managed to save a part of the vineyard and rebuilt some stocks. Thanks to their patience and devotion, Madeira wine little by little took its place in trade

again. Today its role in the country's economy is important: Portugal in 1966 exported 1,017,786 gallons of Madeira out of a total production of 2,200,000 gallons.

THE VINES OF MADEIRA

The island of Madeira is very small—only 30 miles long by 16 miles wide—and one-third of it is hardly suitable for cultivation. It is an old volcano, jutting up out of the ocean, defending itself with high cliffs and caves as deep as 2,400 feet. As in Douro, arable land must be created out of nothing, patiently, tenaciously, by breaking up the lava with the pick. The farmer of Madeira cultivates the smallest patch of ground that can be reached, even if it hangs out into space. The vine is his little luxury, his joy and his pride, so that one sees it growing on trellises along the edges of paths and covering the tiled roofs shadowing the little courtyards where the women sit and embroider. Those grapes are for the family table. But the great wines of Madeira come from the land with the best exposure, in the south-west. The plots are so narrow that the regions are called *estreitos* (straitened). Among the most famous are Campanario, Ponta do Pargo and Madalena.

In order to make use of this area so meagrely awarded, the winegrowers *roll* the vines in numerous tight coils, held up by wires, and strip off the leaves from the vine-shoots so that the grape-bunches may drink in the sun all day long. The sun gilds them, ripens them, gives them their sugar: the grapes must be picked when very ripe, but not one shrunken or spoiled grape must reach the press.

THE HARVEST AND THE TYPES OF WINE

The harvest is a festival. For the same reasons as in Douro, everything must be carried on the backs of men, even the must, which is brought to the winemaking plants in goatskins or in small 80-100 pint barrels.

This must is kept in a barrel open to the sun; there, it gradually reduces and caramelizes (the method particularly used for sweet wines). Nowadays, a system of hot-baths heats the must to 50°. The fermented must gives the *vinho claro* which is then left to rest in order to obtain the *vinho trasfugado*.

As with the wine of Porto, Madeira includes two family types: the vintage wine, which is must from an outstanding harvest, aged in closed bottles and with nothing added; and the Madeira *solera* (from the Portuguese for sun), which is a wine aged always in the

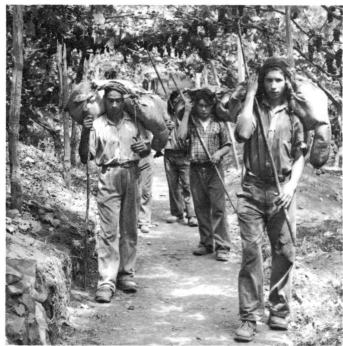

Harvest time on the isle of Madeira. The vinegrower works standing, picking at his own height the bunches of grapes swollen with sugar. These are collected in baskets and sorted on the spot, before being carried down to the presses. As in the Douro region, the must is transported by *borracheiros*, carrying goatskins with capacities of about eleven gallons.

same barrel. But in the latter, the inevitable evaporation is compensated for each year by filling the barrel to the brim with wine of the same type but one year younger. The date of a vintage *solera* is therefore that of the original must. There still exist on the island a few flasks of a venerable wine called MADÈRE DE NAPOLÉON, produced in 1792. The British Consul at Funchal offered some to Napoleon in 1815 on his way to St. Helena. The exiled emperor was ill and did not touch any of the precious barrels, which were returned after his death to the Consul; the latter sold the Madeira to Charles Blandy, who had it bottled in 1840. One can still sample some of this old Madeira today, although this is indeed an exceptional case. Normally, one is advised to choose from Madeiras of between twenty and thirty years old.

In contrast to port, which demands peace and quiet in its life, Madeira seems all the better for long voyages. This was established in the seventeenth century, on sampling MALVASIAS which had been shipped to America: the rocking of the ships and the heat of the tropics seemed to be so advantageous to the ageing of Madeira that the custom developed of "sending it out on a voyage": so much so that a shipment of wine which had made the round trip to India was very much sought after by connoisseurs. A cargo of MALVASIA was a great prize for pirates and certain shipments are known to have changed the colours under which they were sailing three of four times during the course of a voyage.

The English, during the eighteenth and nineteenth centuries, were great connoisseurs of Madeira. Ladies used it to perfume their handkerchieves and officers on campaigns demanded fifteen bottles a month. The truth is that, in addition to the pleasures it brings, Madeira has great tonic qualities; from 1785 on, it was much recommended for sick or over-worked people and was nicknamed the "milk of the old".

Madeira is also a marvellous wine for cooking, and sets off admirably such dishes as consommés, filet of beef, game, liver and lights, dishes in aspic, punches; and of course it is the essential ingredient of the well-known garnish, Madeira sauce. For cooking, one should use young Madeiras, above all never confusing those used in the kitchen and those drunk in the drawing-room.

A happy and very fashionable innovation consists of giving a reception where only two types of Madeira are served: one very dry, the other sweet and velvety. The first accompanies canapés and salted biscuits, the second, sweets.

There are four great Madeiras, of which the first is MALVASIA or MALMSEY obtained from pressing the ripest of the grapes. This was the very first to be cultivated on the island and was produced from vine-plants which came from Candia. Cultivated in the hottest part of the isle, its grapes are long, conical and very golden. The juice from these grapes is full of the sun's warmth; it is velvety and takes on the appearance of liquid gold, with a smoothness of honey.

MALVASIA has long been the great favourite among the wines of Madeira, for it expresses all the sensual, intoxicating and slightly mysterious charm of this island of perfumes. It is especially suitable as a dessert wine and is drunk at room temperature. On the other hand, SERCIAL, which is produced from vine-plants originating in the Rhine valley, is dry, amber and strong. It evokes quite another aspect of the island: the abysses, the peaks which pierce the clouds, the wild and grandiose landscapes. The best SERCIAL wines come from the vineyard where the soil is the most barren, not far from the abyss above which perches the *Curral das Freiras*, a convent built to escape the pillaging of barbarians. SERCIAL should never be drunk until it has at least eight to ten years of age, and should be served chilled as an aperitif.

VERDELHO, a semi-dry, and BOAL, a semi-sweet, are stronger wines than MALVASIA but do not have its mellowness; on the other hand, if they lack the haughty austerity of SERCIAL, they are more pleasant, more complete and more suitable for every occasion.

Madeira must be served with the same care as port, decanted into a flask before being drunk from fine and transparent glasses.

Finally, one must say a word about the wine of Porto Santo, the neighbouring island of Madeira, and especially the wine of Pico, in the Azores, which also had its moment of glory in the eighteenth and nineteenth centuries at the Russian Court. The vineyards —destroyed by an epidemic and only now just beginning to re-establish themselves—grow on soil which is as black as charcoal. The region is called the Land of Mystery, at the foot of a volcano which is the highest peak in Portugal. Walls of pumice-stone protect the plants, which grow, stunted and clinging to the very stone, never more than a few together. The wine of Pico is dry, lively, a little rough: it could be described as a sort of wild sherry.

In the very strange church of Jesus, at Setúbal, a panel of *azulejos* (Moorish tiles) represents the Tree of Jesse: the tree is a vine-plant which sprouts from the abdomen of the patriarch and then, spreading out, represents the Son of God. Nothing could better express the vital and sacred character of this most noble crop which, in Portugal, reunites the two most precious things: bread and wine. The vine nourishes man, and brings him joy, strength and hope.

WINES OF PORTUGAL

DRY WHITE WINES

Bucelas	Dão U. C. B.	Vinho Verde Casal Garcia	Vinho Verde Quinta da Aveleda
Bucelas Velho	Douro Favaios	Vinho Verde Casal de Pejeiros	Vinho Verde Quinta do Tamariz
Dão Cabido	Vinho Verde Agulha	Vinho Verde Casal da Seara	Vinho Verde Reserva da Aveleda
Dão Caves Império	Vinho Verde Alvarinho-Cepa Velha	Vinho Verde Casalinho	Vinho Verde Valverde
Dão Grão Vasco	Vinho Verde Amarante	Vinho Verde Casal Miranda	Vinho Verde Verdeal
Dão Monástico	Vinho Verde Aveleda — 1 R	Vinho Verde Deu-la-Deu	Vinho Verde Lafões
Dão Real Vinícola	Vinho Verde Casa do Landeiro	Vinho Verde Lagosta	Vinho Verde Sico

SWEET WHITE WINES

Arealva	Casalinho	Emir	Monte Serves
Borlido	Corveta	Grandjó	Murtelas

ROSÉ WINES

Aliança	Faísca	Mateus	Spiral
Dom Silvano	Isabel	Grandélite	Barros

RED WINES

Aliança	Dão Monástico	Messias	Vinho Verde C. Mendes
Arealva	Dão Real Vinícola	Palmela-Clarete	Vinho Verde Casal Garcia
Carvalho, Ribeiro & Ferreira	Dão Sóvida	Periquita	Vinho Verde Folgazão
Colares M. J. C.	Dão U. C. B.	Quinta do Seminário	Vinho Verde Moura Basto
Colares V. S.	Dão Vale da Fonte	Reserva Sogrape	Vinho Verde Quinta do Tamariz
Dão Cabido	Evel	Romeira	Vinho Verde Verdeal
Dão Caves Aliança	J. M. da Fonseca	Serradayres	Vinho Verde Lafões
Dão Caves Império	Lagoa	Solar	Vinho Verde São Gonçalo
Dão Grão Vasco	Lagos	Vinho Verde Casal da Seara	Vinho Verde Valverde

VARIOUS GENEROSOS WINES

Carcavelos-Quinta do Barão	Estremadura Silveira	Moscatel de Setúbal - Setúbal	Moscatel de Setúbal - Setúbal Roxo
Carcavelos-Quinta da Bela Vista	Estremadura Lezirão	superior	Palmela superior

NATURAL SPARKLING WINES

Assis Brasil	Grande Natal	Neto Costa	Raposeira
Danúbio	Monte Crasto	Principe Real	Companhia Velha

MADEIRA

| Sercial | Verdelho | Boal | Malmsey (Malvoisic) | Rainwater | Solera |

PORT WINES

VERY DRY WHITE WINES (BRANCOS)

Casino Dry White	D. Fernando Extra Dry White	Porto Aperitivo	Port Dry White Estoril
Dow's Dry White Aperitif Port	Prince Henry	Porto Fino	Carito
Dry Tang	Cocktail Port	Golden Crown White Extra Dry	Dry Tua
Branco Extra Seco	Revisec Extra Seco	Extra Dry White	Souza Port Dry White
Chip Dry			

DRY WHITE WINES (BRANCOS)

Very Dry, Old	Superior Alto Douro Dry White	Dry Port	Special White Dry
Very Dry White Port	Port	Aperitive	Porto Dry White Estoril
Rainha Santa Dry White	Porto Imperial Dry White	Dry White Port	Dalva's Dry White Port
Top Dry	Argonauta Dry White	Dry Old Port	Dryor
Secco Branco	Dry Finish White Port	Clipper	Porto Triunfal (White Dry Port)
Brig's Port White Dry			

DRY RUBY WINES (ALOIRADOS-CLAROS) DRY TAWNY WINE (ALOIRADO) MEDIUM-DRY WHITE WINE (BRANCO)

D. Velhissimo	Gotas de Ouro (seco)	Velho Seco	Special Pale Dry

MEDIUM-DRY TAWNY WINES (ALOIRADOS)

Directors Reserve	Dow's Boardroom Port	Choco	Commendador	Victória	Dalva's Port

SWEET LIGHT TAWNY WINES (ALOIRADOS-CLAROS)

Fine Royal Choice	Warre's Nimrod Port	Quinta do Bom Retiro	Fine Port	Duque de Bragança

SWEET TAWNY WINES (ALOIRADOS)

Douro Velho	Imperial	Superb Old	Porto Clube
Royal Diamond	Quinta do Junco	Shippers	Very Superior Old Port
Senex	Royal Port No. 3	Old Lodge	Royal Delicate
Medieval Port	Cintra Grand Corona	Lança 2 Coroas	Porto Antonat Tawny
Top Honours	Vintners Choice	Revinor	Porto Nogueira Genuíno
Particular	Emperor	Imperial Tawny Doce	Ultra Tawny
Noval 20 Anos	Boa Vista	Tawny Superior	Porto Cruz
Directorial	His Eminence's Choice	Very Old Superior	Atlantic
Special Reserve	Rodo	Royal Port No. 1	Vasconcellos
54 Port	Acordo Finest Old Tawny Port		

SWEET WHITE WINE   VERY SWEET TAWNY WINES (ALOIRADOS)   WHITE LAGRIMA (BRANCO)

Lacrima Christi	Porto V V	Royal Esmeralda	Lacrima Christi

SWEET RUBY WINES (TINTOS-ALOIRADOS)

Quinta das Quartas	Marquês de Pombal	Crasto V. O. R.	Century Port Abelha

SWEET RED WINES (TINTOS)

Rainha Santa 840	Imperial Crown

DOURO

Mirandela

Bragança

MURÇA

ALIJÓ

Chaves

VILA REAL

PENAGUIÃO

MESÃO FRIO

← *Porto*

Rio Douro

LAMEGO

← *Aveiro*

ARMAMAR

Moimenta

TABUAÇO

Moimenta

S. JOÃO DA PESQUEIRA

Penedono

QUINTAS

1	Quinta do Roco	26	Sernadelo Baranda	53	Quinta do Portelo	
1A	» Pedregal	27	» Val do Locaio	54	» Frades	
2	Sernadelo	28	» Mourão	55	» S. Joaninho	
2A	» Telhada	29	» Varaes	56	» Ferrader	
3	» Pitarrela	30	» Abraham	57	» Carvalhosa	
4	» Loureiro	31	» Couto	58	» Val Moreira	
5	» Osorio	32	» Val dos Sapos	59	» Val Mór	
6	» Lagares	33	Quinta do Terrão	60	» Antonio de Melo	
7	» Travassos	34	» Marrocos	61	» Costa	
8	» Bairro	35	» Sta Barbara	62	» Caleiro	
9	» Partelo	36	» Covaes	63	» Pasteleira ou Sobreira	
10	» Gervide	37	» Garcia	64	» Bom Dia	
11	» S. Gonçalo	38	» Torre	65	» Crasto	
12	» Boavista	39	» Bouca	66	» Lagoa Alta	
13	» Gonte	40	» Matta	67	» Borges	
14	» Forrester	41	» Val de Lagea	68	» Napoles	
15	» Val de Fogo	42	» S. Joaninho	69	» Tedo	
16	» Loureiro	43	» Deveza	70	» Alegria	
17	» Mourisca	44	» Fonte do Peso	71	» Lobata	
18	» Garcia	45	» Val Bom	72	» Figueiredo	
19	» Romarigo	46	» Canal	73	» Pessanha	
20	» Retorta	47	» Zambujal	74	» Trancada	
21	» Firveda	48	» Enxudreiro	75	» Serra	
22	» Vacaria	49	» Cabanas	76	» Jocozelo	
23	» Valado	50	» Bagauste	77	» de la Rosa	
24	» Carneiro	51	» Foz de mil lobos	78	» Cachuxa	
25	» Pacheca	52	» Barrilar	79	» Nova	

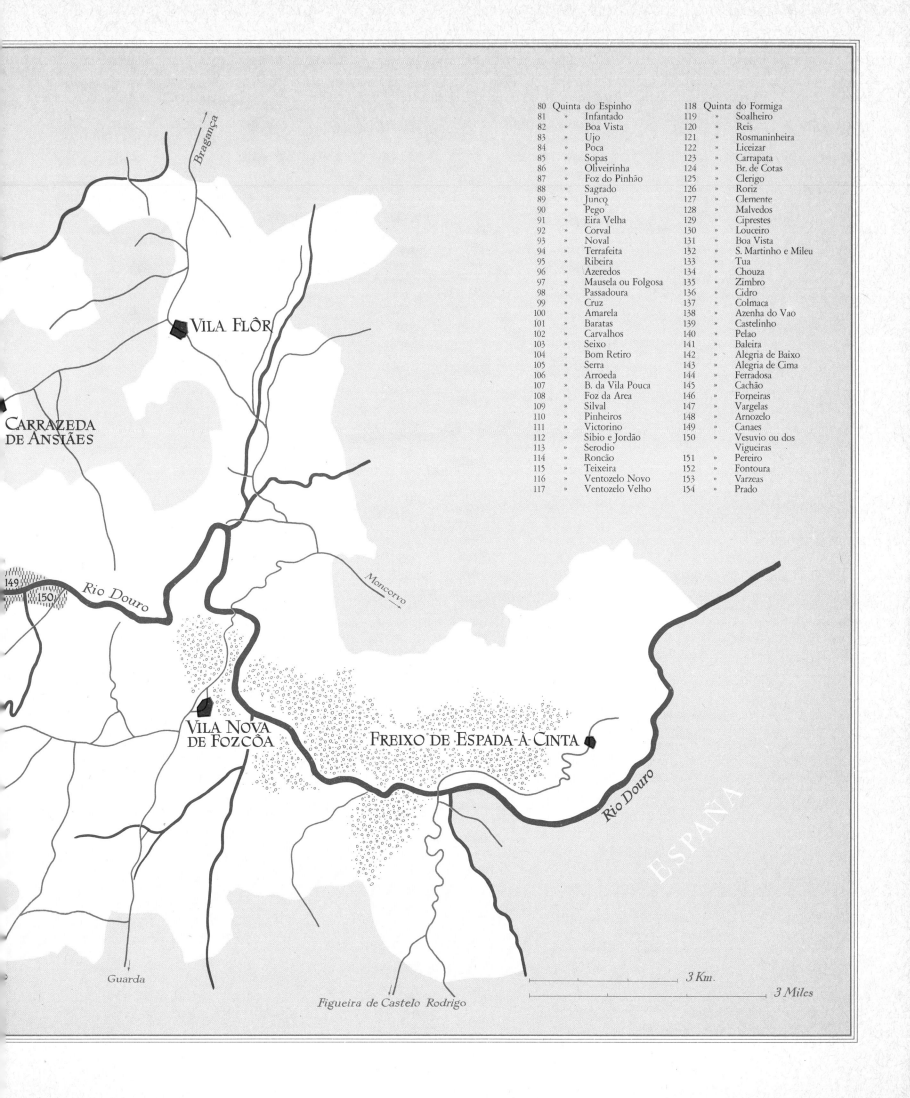

80	Quinta	do Espinho	118	Quinta	do Formiga
81	»	Infantado	119	»	Soalheiro
82	»	Boa Vista	120	»	Reis
83	»	Ujo	121	»	Rosmaninheira
84	»	Poca	122	»	Liceizar
85	»	Sopas	123	»	Carrapata
86	»	Oliveirinha	124	»	Br. de Cotas
87	»	Foz do Pinhão	125	»	Clerigo
88	»	Sagrado	126	»	Roriz
89	»	Junco	127	»	Clemente
90	»	Pego	128	»	Malvedos
91	»	Eira Velha	129	»	Ciprestes
92	»	Corval	130	»	Louceiro
93	»	Noval	131	»	Boa Vista
94	»	Terrafeita	132	»	S. Martinho e Mileu
95	»	Ribeira	133	»	Tua
96	»	Azeredos	134	»	Chouza
97	»	Mausela ou Folgosa	135	»	Zimbro
98	»	Passadoura	136	»	Cidro
99	»	Cruz	137	»	Colmaca
100	»	Amarela	138	»	Azenha do Vao
101	»	Baratas	139	»	Castelinho
102	»	Carvalhos	140	»	Pelao
103	»	Seixo	141	»	Baleira
104	»	Bom Retiro	142	»	Alegria de Baixo
105	»	Serra	143	»	Alegria de Cima
106	»	Arroeda	144	»	Ferradosa
107	»	B. da Vila Pouca	145	»	Cachão
108	»	Foz da Area	146	»	Forneiras
109	»	Silval	147	»	Vargelas
110	»	Pinheiros	148	»	Arnozelo
111	»	Victorino	149	»	Canaes
112	»	Sibio e Jordão	150	»	Vesuvio ou dos Vigueiras
113	»	Serodio			
114	»	Roncão	151	»	Pereiro
115	»	Teixeira	152	»	Fontoura
116	»	Ventozelo Novo	153	»	Varzeas
117	»	Ventozelo Velho	154	»	Prado

Bragança

VILA FLÔR

CARRAZEDA DE ANSIÃES

149

150

Rio Douro

Moncorvo

VILA NOVA DE FOZCÔA

FREIXO DE ESPADA-À-CINTA

Rio Douro

ESPAÑA

Guarda

Figueira de Castelo Rodrigo

3 Km.

3 Miles

THE WINES OF ITALY

GIOVANNI DALMASSO

Tracing the origins of winegrowing and winemaking is not an easy undertaking. History from its very beginning often accumulates legends, myths and traditions; reality is distorted by poetry, folklore or fantasy. In Italy this is particularly true. There the cultivation of the vine goes back to very ancient times. Man apparently discovered in the Neolithic age the quasi-magic properties of the fermented grape, which conferred on the moderate drinker the "wise forgetfulness of life" of which Dante speaks. The vine in those times grew freely in its wild state in the forests, winding itself around the trees and climbing to a considerable height. Man learned to cultivate it and produce the still-mysterious process of alcoholic fermentation.

One point remained in dispute for a long time: should our vine, commonly called the European vine (the plant *vitis vinifera*) be considered as a native plant or was it on the other hand imported into Italy on the tide of the great human migrations from Asia Minor or North Africa? Doubtless both theories have a basis in fact. The crossing of the different vine-plants gave birth to the innumerable varieties of vines which led Virgil to exclaim in his *Georgics*: *Quem scire velit, Libyci velit aequoris idem* ("He who would know [the infinite variety of vines] would just as well [count] the grains of sand in the Lybian desert").

Certainly even in Homeric times Sicily was producing abundant quantities of wine. One episode in the *Odyssey* seems to point to this: when, near Etna, the Cyclops Polyphemus, whom Ulysses had blinded, falls stupefied by drink into a deep sleep. The Etruscans,

who had settled in Italy perhaps about 1000 B.C., must certainly have contributed to disseminating the vine. They came from the East, where agriculture had already reached a certain stage of evolution, which no doubt included vinegrowing and winemaking. But when the Etruscans landed on the Tyrrhenian sea coast they probably found old and sturdy vines already growing there, since Pliny had asserted that a statue in Populonia was carved from a single vine plant.

There is no doubt that in the time of Pliny the Elder, Italy already led the world in the quantity and excellence of her wines, outstripping even Greece, whose pupil she had been in winegrowing. In his *Naturalis Historia* Pliny speaks of 195 kinds of wine, of which over half were produced in Italy. What were some of the wines of ancient Italy? The MAMERTINO around Messina, the TAUROMENITANUM from the region of Taormina, the POTULAMUM, the SIRACUSANUM, the wines of Agrigente and Selinonte and the BIBLINO in the region of Syracuse. In Calabria the most appreciated were the BRUTIUM and, moving northwards to Lucania, the wines of Consentia, Tempio, Rhegium and Buxentium. Apulia also produced well-reputed wines, notably those of Tarente, Babia, Brindisi, Canosa and Aulon. However the region which in the times of the Empire produced the wines praised most highly by the Latin poets was the area dominated by Naples, Campania, which could boast its FALERNO, its CECUBO, its CALENO, its FORMIANO and the wines of Vesuvius.

Latium supplied numerous wines to the capital of the ancient world, but none was of outstanding quality.

The same could be said, moving north, of the wines of Umbria, the Marches and even Tuscany, which today is such an important wineproducing area. It is not until one comes to the Upper Adriatic, around the Gulf of Trieste, that one finds one of the most famous wines of Antiquity: the PUCINUM, produced near the mouth of the Timaro, not far from Aquileia.

The north of Italy produced another great wine, the RETICO, which Virgil himself claimed was rivalled only by the FALERNO. It is nevertheless difficult to know for certain whether it resembled the excellent wines of today from the region of Verona, or those of the Valtelino or even the Trentino.

The fame of Italian wines has in no way diminished over the centuries. Italy today has the world's second largest winegrowing area and is the biggest producer of wine and of dessert grapes. Her average annual production over the last decade (1958-1967) was 1,408,000,000 gallons. In 1967 it even reached 1,650,000,000 gallons. Apulia headed the list of regional harvests in 1967 and has done so for several years; this province alone produces more than 264,000,000 gallons of wine. In second place comes Veneto, with some 220,000,000 gallons: third, Sicily, 198,000,000; fourth Emilia-Romagna (187,000,000) and fifth Piedmont (154,000,000); sixth comes Latium (110,000,000); seventh Tuscany (88,000,000); eighth Campania (72,600,000); ninth Lombardy (66,000,000) and tenth the Marches (59,400,000), followed by the Abruzzi, the Trentino-Upper Adige, Sardinia and Calabria. One of the essential characteristics of Italian winegrowing is its repartition in two forms: monoculture and mixed culture. Italy is the only country in the world where the cultivation of vines alongside other plants, either climbing or herbaceous, is still very widespread. In 1967, for 3,075,000 acres of vineyards under monoculture there were 5,137,500 acres under mixed culture.

As for the distribution of vineyards according to altitude, the Virgilian precept *Bacchus amat colles* ("Bacchus loves the hills") is still true today in Italian agricultural economy and continues to give a very typical appearance to the countryside of peninsular Italy. In many regions, for example the Monferrato and the Langhe of Piedmont, or the region of Pavia in Lombardy, the hills which stretch as far as the eye can see are often entirely covered by a mantle of vineyards which seem almost to have been etched there by a calligrapher of olden days.

In many places the way of life and social standards have changed, accompanied inevitably by a progressive reduction in the rural population, which is increasingly attracted by the salary of the urban worker. The labour shortage has brought about a marked change in Italian winegrowing. Mechanization has been introduced almost everywhere. Machines have been tried out for the wine harvests, but sometimes the whole appearance of vineyards on the plains had to be changed. This is why vines "married" to trees (elms, maples, poplars) are gradually giving way to close-set, regular rows of plants which make possible much more rational methods of cultivation.

NORTHERN ITALY

Northern Italy, which in all produces around 660,000,000 gallons of wine (almost half the national production) has a great variety of reds, whites and rosés. They are mainly ordinary, fine or superior wines, but they also include special wines such as sparkling wines and aromatized or *passiti* wines.

It would take too long to list them all; better to limit oneself to a few notes on the best ones, on a geographical basis, taking the winegrowing regions in order from west to east.

PIEDMONT. Although, as mentioned earlier, other regions of Italy are bigger producers of wine, there is probably not one which surpasses Piedmont in the variety of quality wines yielded by the vineyards which cover its hillsides as far as the eye can see.

In general red table wines predominate, classed according to quality as ordinary (for everyday consumption), fine and superior. But there is no lack of whites—dry table wines or luxury wines, sparkling, aromatized or not, and there are even some dessert wines.

Beginning with the red wines and passing over the ordinary wines, which are often produced by mixing various grapes, the *uvaggi*, we find that one of them outclasses all the others: it is referred to as "the king of Italian wines" and "the wine of kings": BAROLO. It wins such praise both because of its intrinsic quality and because in the nineteenth century it was the favourite of the monarchs of the House of Savoy, who even envisaged growing it on their estates. Its production zone (quite a small area) is found in the Langhe district, a region of hills around Alba (the ancient Albe la Langhe, rival of Rome) and which includes, besides Barolo, a dozen other districts. The grape that produces this superb wine is the NEBBIOLO, a vine which was already under cultivation about A.D. 1300, not only in this region but in other areas of Piedmont and

Suisse

Trentino

Alto Adige

Trento

Österreich

Friuli

Piave

Veneto

Trieste

Lombardia

Aosta

Milano

Venezia

Piemonte

Adige

Torino

Po

Liguria

Po

Emilia

Bologna

Genova

Firenze

Marche

Ancona

Arno

Mare Ligure

Toscana

Mare Adriatico

Umbria

Tevere

Abruzzo

Molise

ROMA

Lazio

Mare Tirreno

Campania

Puglia

Napoli

Basilicata

Tirso

Sardegna

Calabria

CAGLIARI

Mare Ionio

PALERMO

Reggio

Sicilia

Mare Mediterraneo

In Italy, where vines are cultivated in all twenty administrative regions, the system of naming wines varies from one region to another and even from one district to another. Sometimes the name of the wine is derived from that of the vine, such as the Barbera and the Dolcetto, or the district where it is produced, as with Marsala. Other names, such as Sangue de Giuda or Lacryma Christi, evoke the legendary past.

under other names, as in Lombardy and Valtelino. This aristocratic plant requires a carefully chosen climate and soil. It is not a prolific plant, yet it is capable of producing wines of a very high quality. BAROLO is an excellent *da arrosto* wine, in other words a wine to drink with roasted or grilled meats. It is a superior quality red with a strong alcohol content (13°-14°), a lot of body, a harmonious flavour and a rich and fine bouquet. When young it has a sharp taste, due to its acid and tannin content; it requires a long ageing process. Today its authenticity is guaranteed by the regulation on production that forms part of the Presidential Decree of May 6th, 1966. This law stipulates that the name BAROLO may be given to wine produced in the above-mentioned region only if it has been kept at least three years in oak casks; this gives it a beautiful orange-red colour. Its delicate bouquet has overtones of violets, mixed with a slight odour of tar; it has a somewhat dry flavour, which is always rather austere yet at the same time harmonious and velvety. All this makes for a wine particularly well-suited to red meats, such as game, roasts and braised beef (sometimes accompanied by truffles). It is served at a temperature of 20° C. and should be opened an hour beforehand, to allow a slight oxydation.

A wine which has a great deal in common with BAROLO is the BARBARESCO, which also comes from the *Nebbiolo* vine. It derives its name from the district where it is produced, land clinging to the steep slope of a hill on the right bank of the Tanaro, not far from Alba and overlooked by a Roman tower. It also must be aged in oak but matures more quickly than BAROLO.

In Piedmont the *Nebbiolo*, also called *Spana*, yields other good quality *da arrosto* wines, produced in even smaller quantities than the two named above. They are GATTINARA, LESSONA, MOTTALCIATA, GHEMME, SIZZANO, FARA and BOCA, found in the provinces of Vercelli and Novarro, at the foot of the Biella Alps. All these wines have a sharp taste when young and take a long time to mature. With time, however, they take on an admirably harmonious flavour.

On the rocky slopes of the hills which lie on the borders of the province of Turin and the Aosta Valley it is once more the *Nebbiolo*—which changes its name yet again, to become this time the *Picotener*—which produces another much sought after *da arrosto* wine: the CAREMA. Slightly lighter in colour, it is, once suitably aged, an outstandingly fine wine.

Another Piedmontese wine, produced on a much wider scale, is the BARBERA, which takes its name from the vine. The size of the area producing it and the quantities in which it is produced make it the most representative of Piedmont's wines. At an estimate, half the wine production in Piedmont is made up of BARBERA. It originates in the Astigiano, but is also found in a large part of the province of Alessandria and in the provinces of Cuneo and Turin. Genuine BARBERA D'ASTI, if correctly matured (not less than three to four years), is looked on as an excellent quality wine which with time acquires a harmonious flavour.

Many of the characteristics of BARBERA may also be attributed to another wine, the FREISA, which also takes its name from its vine. It is produced in large quantities and comes, in part, from the same wine-producing area. It is grown in the Astigiano and on the hills which reach from Asti almost to the outskirts of Turin. The centre of this area is Chieri. Two quite distinct types of FREISA are made: one is dry, the other a more popular speciality. If sufficiently matured the former improves greatly (for a shorter time, however, than the BARBERA). It develops a delicate violet flavour and loses much of the acid taste of its youth.

A third red table wine, produced in large quantities in another part of Piedmont, is the DOLCETTO. It takes its name from a vine bearing a very sweet grape which matures very rapidly. The wine, however, is a dry one. It has developed all its qualities by the first or at the latest the second year. It has body and a moderate amount of acidity. It has an agreeable, well-rounded aroma, slightly but pleasantly bitter. A slightly sparkling variety, best appreciated outside meal-times, is also produced. The DOLCETTO vineyards go as far as the Langhe region, which is made up of a series of hills. These divide in two, part of them lying between Alba and Mondori in the province of Cuneo, the other centred on Acqui in the province of Alessandria. Since the *Dolcetto* matures so quickly, it is also grown above 1,800 feet.

Another wine that improves with age is the GRIGNOLINO, produced in a very small area lying for the most part in the province of Asti, but also to a lesser extent in the province of Alessandria (near Casalemonferrato). Many consider it to be the best of Piedmont's table wines because of its fresh, delicate and harmonious flavour, its fragrant aroma, its fine, light ruby colour and its moderate alcohol content (11°-12°).

As has already been pointed out, there are, in comparison to the red wines, very few white wines. The best-known and most prevalent of these is the CORTESE, produced almost entirely in the province of Alessandria. It is a very pleasant wine, with a reasonable alcohol content (10°-11°), a fine straw-yellow colour and a flavour which is dry, light, fresh and delicately perfumed and goes very well with fish.

Another fine white wine comes from the Canavese region in the province of Turin, principally from Caluso, the centre of the area. The vine used for this wine is the *Erbaluce*, hence the name ERBALUCE DI CALUSO.

The same vine also yields small quantities of a famous dessert wine, the CALUSO PASSITO, obtained after a lengthy fermentation of the grapes.

But Piedmont is also proud, and rightly so, of its "special" wines, of which the best examples are the MOSCATO D'ASTI and the ASTI SPUMANTE. The grape from which they are made is the *Yellow Muscat* also called *Muscat di Canelli* after a small town in the centre of the production area and the industrial zone. Here are produced the famous sparkling wines that have won such favour on the national and international markets. These wines are subjected to a complex and detailed treatment, now perfected, and acquire a distinctive personality much prized by the general public.

Among the other special wines of Piedmont is the BRACHETTO, grown on a small strip of land between Asti and Acqui. It is a wine with a delicious aroma recalling both the *Muscat* and roses; it is one of the rare good-quality sparkling red wines. Finally, a red MALVASIA SPUMANTE, produced in the province of Asti, has quite recently come to the fore.

LOMBARDY. Lombardy is certainly not one of the main wineproducing regions of Italy, but it can lay claim to several quality wines. The vineyards are divided into three distinct areas: the Oltrepò of Pavia, the Valteline and the western shores of Lake Garda.

The first of these would seem to be the prolongation of the hills of Piedmont, or more precisely of the hills of Monferrato. It lies in the province of Pavia and appears to be an endless series of hills, covered with magnificent vineyards producing excellent red and white wines. Of the red wines, the majority are produced from the Piedmontese *Barbera* and local vines: *Ovattina* (also called *Bonarda*), *Uva Rara* or "rare grape", and *Ughetta*. Their names are well known to connoisseurs today: BUTTAFUOCO ("fire-propagator") BARBACARLO ("Charles' beard") SANGUE DI GIUDA ("blood of Judas") CLASTIDIO, FRECCIAROSSA, MONTE-NAPOLEONE. Brilliant ruby red in colour, with a good bouquet and a dry flavour, they are on the whole mellow, well-constituted table wines which if matured correctly ripen into good *da arrosto* wines appreciated in particular by the Milanese. Their alcohol content reaches 11º-13º and their rather pronounced acidity is yet not excessive. Besides these dry wines, there are other agreeable wines, such as the CANNETO DOLCE, the BONARDA AMABILE, the NEBBIOLO DI RETORBIDO, held in great esteem for drinking between meals.

In the white wines of the Oltrepó of Pavia, the most outstanding come from the *Riesling* vine (mainly Italian, to a lesser extent Rhenish) the *Pinots* or the *Cortese*, such as the FRECCIAROSSA, the white CLASTIDIO or the white CANNETO. All are good dry white wines with a delicate bouquet.

Another major winegrowing area of Lombardy producing excellent quality wines is the Valtelino, in the province of Sondrio. The quality of its wines has been acknowledged for centuries, though it is open to doubt whether the famous RETICO of the Rhaetian vines which was such a favourite of the Emperor Augustus is in fact the ancestor of today's Valtelino wines.

The work of the vinegrowers of the valley of the Adda, in the province of Sondrio, who crawl on to narrow vertiginous terraces to tend their vines, deserves to be admired. From these exposed sites they obtain first quality *da arrosto* wines. These are *Nebbiolo* vines, which we have mentioned before, but here they change their name to *Chiavennasca*. They produce lively, rich, smooth and harmoniously flavoured wines, deep and intense in colour, dry, with a subtle bouquet and rather full-bodied. They are identified by the names of the districts where they are grown. The best-known are the SASSELLA, GRUMELLO, INFERNO, FRACIA, VALGELLA, and VILLA. These are wines which are particularly sought-after by the Swiss, many of whom are moreover proprietors of vineyards in Valtelino, which is a sort of natural prolongation of their own lands.

One particular type of Valtelino wine whose prestige has revived recent years is the SFURZAT. It is a wine which responds to a long maturing process, when it changes into a real dessert wine (with an alcohol content of 15º-16º). It tastes rather sweet at first, then takes on a smooth, well-rounded, rich flavour and turns almost orange in colour.

The third well-known winegrowing area in Lombardy is the western bank of Lake Garda, in the province of Brescia. It has been famous for many years for its excellent red and rosé fine table wines. The most popular, in Lombardy principally but also abroad, are those from the Valtenesi. A sixteenth-century sage, A. Bacci, declared that the wines of Saló on Lake Garda were sold as far away as Germany; he mentioned the SCHIAVA and GROPELLO. Confining ourselves to the present day, we find a predominance of red and rosé wines. These are made principally from the *Gropello* and *Merzemino* vines. The red wine is ruby coloured, with an aroma which develops progressively and a slightly bitter but harmonious and velvety flavour. The rosé is cherry-coloured and both its bouquet and its flavour are sweeter.

Another wine which comes from this same province of Brescia, near the southern slopes of Lake Garda, is the LUGANA, a dry, high quality white wine. It is produced in limited quantities on the clay lands of the plain from the *Lugana*, a particular type of *Trebbiano*. It has an almost green straw colour, a delicate bouquet, a fresh and harmonious flavour and goes extremely well with fish. The same region also produces the

PUSTERLA, a fine wine which is found as red, white and rosé. It comes from quite a small vineyard which lies to the north of the castle of Brescia.

LIGURIA. Although winegrowing plays only a small role in the economy of this region, Ligurian wines nevertheless have a very good reputation. Among the most important is the VERMENTINO, a good quality dry white wine found on the western Riviera between Genoa and Ventimiglia. It has a fine dark straw-yellow colour, a pleasant bouquet and a moderate alcohol content. Close to the same area, the red vine *Rossese* yields the DOLCEACQUA, a particularly well-known wine, which improves with age. Garnet-red in colour, it is particularly pleasant, very slightly alcoholic and with a delicate bouquet.

Along the Eastern Riviera the most famous wines are those of the CINQUETERRE ("Five Lands") which take their name from a picturesque part of the province of Spezia. Winegrowing here is quite an extraordinary process, carried out according to tradition on the dizzy slopes which rise above the sea. The vines cling to the rock-face, producing, very sparingly, small clusters of white grapes of the *Rosco*, *Albarolo* and *Vermentino* varieties. These vines ripen perfectly, giving a must with a very high sugar content which is turned into dry wine, or after a brief fermentation period, into dessert wines which go by the curious local name of SCIACCHETRA.

THREE VENETIAS. This large area of northern Italy today competes with Apulia for first place as the biggest producer of wine. It can also pride itself on possessing an extremely large number of quality wines of all categories. Moving still from west to east in this rapid survey one arrives, after Lombardy, in the neighbouring province of Verona. Here one must first of all go up the River Adige as far as Tridentine Venetia in the provinces of Trentino and Bolzano.

In the province of Trentino are found both white and red table wines qualifying for the "fine" or "superior quality" label. One of the most characteristic fine wines is the TEROLDEGO. It comes from a vineyard lying at the junction of the Noce and the Adige rivers called the "Campo rotaliano" which is almost entirely covered with the famous "Trentino trellises". This wine, produced from the *Teroldego* vine, is quite different from the other Trentino wines. It has a bright ruby colour, with a strong bouquet, which, as the wine ages, takes on a hint of raspberries and violets. The MARZEMINO is a noticeably different wine, light ruby in colour, with a delicate aroma which asserts itself very gradually; it is subtly full-bodied with a refined flavour.

Besides these two local wines the Trentino also produces from imported vines wines such as the CABERNET, the MERLOT and the PINOT NOIR. All are

wines which after a short ageing period can be reclassed as "superior quality" wines. First place among the whites must be given to the TRAMINER: it is a very fine wine which takes its name from a vine from the Tridentine district of Termeno. It has a delicate aroma and a dry and velvety taste. Another superior quality white wine with a great deal of distinction is made from a species of *Riesling* which grows in Trentino, the *Riesling Italico*. Finally, the *Pinot Blanc* gives excellent semi-sparkling and sparkling wines.

The province of Bolzano (Upper Adige) produces a wide variety of quality wines, especially superior quality red table wines. Of these the most outstanding is the SANTA MADDELENA, obtained from the *Schiave*. This vine is cultivated on the abrupt and picturesque slopes that tower above the town of Bolzano and behind which rises the magnificent silhouette of the Dolomites. CALDARO, produced in great quantity, originates in the terraced vineyards bordering the Lago Caldaro, part of which moreover belongs to the province of Trentino. It is a wine with a very slight alcohol content and an extremely agreeable taste: at once dry and mellow, it gives off a light aroma of almonds. Finally there is the LAGREIN rosé wine, coming from the grape of the same name, which is a delicately perfumed wine with a dry, fresh and harmonious flavour.

Among the most reputed of the whites are the TERLANO, a dry, light, greenish-yellow wine, and those mentioned already, such as the TRAMINER, the PINOT —especially the BORGOGNA (WEISSBURGUNDER) and the PINOT GRIS (RULÄNDER)—the RIESLING RENANO and the SYLVANER VERDE, which is a speciality of the Bressanone vineyard. All these local wines benefit from extremely painstaking production and cultivation techniques which give each a distinct personality.

Turning back down the Adige river one arrives in Veneto proper, or "Euganea" Venetia, a vast and varied region with many vineyards, producing charming wines of all categories including excellent fine or superior quality reds and whites.

The BARDOLINO, VALPOLICELLA and VALPANTENA red wines come from the most famous vineyards. They are produced from a mixture of various native vines, especially the *Molinara* (or *Rosara*) the *Corvina Veronese* and the *Negrera* with *Rondinella* and *Rossignola*. All these wines are ready for consumption after only a few months of fermentation, but improve greatly if aged for two to three years. They then acquire characteristics which raise them into the category of superior quality wines. Generally, however, they are less robust and less austere, as well as lighter in colour, than the Piedmontese wines.

A very well-known quality white wine from Verona is the SOAVE, the product of a small vineyard on the

The Oltrepò of Pavia is an extension of the Piedmont hills, and produces excellent red and white wines from vineyards that climb the hills and descend the slopes.

The grapes are being povred into this traditional cart, usually
hauled by two white oxen, in this scene at Asti, home of the
famous spaskling Asti spumante.

frontier of the province of Vicenza. It is made from two vines, the *Garganega* and the *Trebbiano*. Straw-yellow, with a dry harmonious flavour and a delicate bouquet, it is a light-bodied wine with a low alcohol content. Nor should one overlook the RECIOTO, a famous, special, almost liqueur-like red wine, whose production is an ancient tradition in the province of Verona—some even seek to trace it back to Theodoric the Great, King of the Ostrogoths (A.D. 454-526). It comes from the same vines as the VALPOLICELLA and undergoes a long period of fermentation.

A wine similar to the SOAVE, the GARGANEGA DI GAMBELLARE, is produced in the province of Vicenza in an area bordering on the preceding one. Other excellent white wines, such as the PINOT (white or *gris*) or the VESPAIOLA are found in the same region. Just recently the production of fine red table wines has been developed, especially in the region of Breganza. These are obtained from imported vines such as the *Merlot*, *Cabernet* and *Pinot Noir*, and from the *Tokay*.

We now come to the province of Padua. Ten years ago it could boast of only a small number of fine and superior quality table wines, produced on an unusual hill formation of volcanic origin, the Colli Euganei, which rise from the immense plain characteristic of most of the province. These wines have a very ancient reputation, which today has been reinforced by the introduction, side by side with the old local vines (*Gargenaga, Pinella Serpina*), of foreign vines such as the *Pinot Blanc*, the *Sauvignon* and the *Riesling*. Formerly vines such as the *Pattaresco* and the *Corbinella* and another variety, the unassuming *Friularo*, used for producing red blending wines, flourished in this region. Today cultivation is concentrated on quality vines such as the *Cabernet Franc* and the *Merlot* which can yield good and even excellent red wines.

The province of Venice, which is the natural continuation of Padua, is a plain where, thanks to the introduction of rigorously selected foreign vines, good red wines are produced from the *Cabernet* and *Merlot* and reasonably fine white wines from the *Riesling Italico* or the *Sauvignon*.

It is worth pausing a moment in the province of Treviso: this is one of the most varied and pleasant of the Venetias. Its claim to fame lies in having founded, in 1877, Italy's first school specializing in winegrowing and oenology, the School of Conegliano, which has made a considerable contribution to the development of these subjects. It was next to this school that in 1923 an experimental laboratory opened that has made a decisive contribution to vinegrowing and the wine industry in the Venetias.

The province of Treviso has acquired a solid reputation for the white wines grown on its hills and the few red wines produced in the plain. Among the white wines, those produced on the hills of Conegliano and others from the hills of Valdobbiadene are deservedly famous: the former are golden-yellow in colour and come mostly from the *Prosecco*; the latter, paler in colour, come from the *Verdiso*. The best of them are used to make excellent sparkling wines.

Besides white wines this region also produces good fine red table wines, especially from the *Merlot*, to a lesser degree from the *Cabernet Franc* and a very old local plant, the *Marzemino*. Formerly the RABOSO DI PIAVE, an extremely acid and deeply coloured wine, was also much-prized, especially as a wine to mix with others. It has been largely replaced by the RABOSO VERONESE, which is in itself an honest table wine.

Now for the easternmost region of northern Italy, where the Friuli and the Julian Venetia meet. The people of Friuli have always been extremely proud of their wines, even if in the past they were not always of very good quality. Among the traditional wines made from local plants should be mentioned the REFOSCHI among the reds, and the VERDUZZO among the whites. Of the latter the one most worthy of mention is the TOCAI FRIOLANO, made from a plant which has been grown widely for a long time in part of the plain (towards Portogruaro) where it yields an exquisite wine, harmonious in flavour, fresh and extremely pleasant. It should be stressed that this wine has no connection with the famous Hungarian TOKAY, which is produced from quite different vines. Nevertheless the vintners of Friuli still produce (as did the great lords of the past) a liqueur-like wine, resembling the TOKAY ASZU, which takes its name from the vine, the *Piccolit*, so called because its grape seeds, due to a malformation, are very small in size. The fruit is left to decay before being pressed, in order to give a wine with a high alcohol content, but which is also deliciously sweet and perfumed and of a golden-yellow colour.

Towards the east we come to the province of Gorizia, which suffered severely during the last war. Today its winegrowing is limited to the Collio Goriziano, a small hilly area bordering the Friuli. Its vineyards produce, albeit in limited quantities, a variety of white and red wines of undeniable quality. Among the whites: the RIESLING ITALICO, the TOCAI, the PINOT BLANC, the PINOT GRIS, the SAUVIGNON, the TRAMINER, the MALVASIA (a non-aromatic Malmsey, probably coming from Istria); and among the reds the MERLOT, the CABERNET FRANC, the PINOT NOIR. A white wine which is no longer very common but was formerly well-known is the RIBOLLA GIALLO (from the name of the vine); a red wine, the old TERRANO, produced in limited quantities on the Karst de Gorizia from red *Refoso*, should also be mentioned here.

EMILIA ROMAGNA. As far as production is concerned, Emilia Romagna is one of the most important wine-growing regions of Italy. Here the vines stretch across a plain whose climate is eminently suitable to their growth. The red wines grown here belong to the LAMBRUSCHI family and are widely appreciated. All these wines have some characteristics in common: a very bright colour, a very pronounced bouquet and flavour, a typical acid taste, often tempered by a slight sweetness and, finally, an abundant but shortlived froth. They all fit perfectly with Emilian cooking, which is highly flavoured and rather greasy, based as it is largely on pork. The LAMBRUSCHI come from different varieties of the *Lambrusca* vine grown on the Emilian plain in the province of Parma above all, but also in Reggio Emilia, Modena and Bologna. They are not all of the same quality. The best wine is certainly the SORBARA, named for the district of Modena where it predominates. While possessing the same characteristics as the others, it is a finer, more graceful and undoubtedly superior wine. It turns sparkling if produced carefully by the appropriate technique. However, a fault in the flowers of the sapling considerably reduces its productivity and restricts its cultivation.

Other good LAMBRUSCHI are the SALAMINO (or LAMBRUSCO DI SANTA CROCE) and the GRASPAROSSA (or LAMBRUSCO DI CASTELVETRO). Finally the LAMBRUSCO MAESTRI and the LAMBRUSCO DI MONTERICCO should also be mentioned.

Besides the LAMBRUSCHI, Emilia produces several red wines for everyday consumption and for blending purposes. Only the part of the province of Plaisance bordering on Lombardy and Piedmont produces fine table wines. One of these is the GUATTURNIO of the Colli Piacentini, produced from the Piedmontese *Barbera* and *Croatina* vines grown in the foothills of the Apennines. Among the white table wines are those derived from the *Otrugo, Trebbiano, Romagnolo, Sauvignon, Pinot*, and some special aromatic wines obtained from the *Malvasia di Candia* and the *Yellow Muscat*.

If we go from Modena to Bologna and from there to the provinces of Forli and Ravenna (and so enter Romagna), we find, beside the extensive cultivation of the vine on the plain, winegrowing in the hills. Among the vines of the plain a white vine predominates, the *Trebbiano Romagnolo* which gives everyday wines. Of the hillside vines, another white grape vine, the *Albana*, grown most of all between Imola and Cesena, has given a top quality wine for centuries. The most famous is the BERTINORO, an excellent dry white wine, golden yellow, with a delicate, fruity flavour, which can take on the agreeable personality of a dessert wine.

CENTRAL ITALY

The six regions of Central Italy (Tuscany, the Marches, Umbria, Latium, Abruzzi and Molise) produce in all only 242,000,000 gallons of wine (about one sixth of the country's total production). Two of these regions have a very old reputation as winegrowers.

TUSCANY. Of Tuscany, one could say the same as of Piedmont: although it is not one of the biggest wineproducers in the country (it maintains an average of 88,000,000 gallons), the proportion of fine wines and superior table wines certainly exceeds that of other regions of Italy. About 80 per cent of these wines are reds. The most important and the best known internationally—it is often taken as a synonym for "Italian wine"—is CHIANTI. Its name comes from a small area in the centre of Tuscany, between the provinces of Sienna and Florence. The name CHIANTI appears in very reliable documents as early as 1260, but old texts refer most frequently to a CHIANTI of 1378, when the "CHIANTI League" was instituted (by an official Act of the Republic of Florence). It comprised the present districts of Gaide, Radda and Castellina. The production zone has, however, slowly been extended with the passage of time to include the districts of Poggibonsi, San Sasiano, Val di Pesa, Castelnuevo Berardenga and other Tuscan vineyards more or less bordering on it, all of which have produced for a long time a wine which has the same biochemical qualities as the original CHIANTI. As the demand for this wine keeps on growing both in Italy and abroad and it becomes increasingly difficult to refuse the right to the name CHIANTI to wines grown in these neighbouring vineyards, the problem has been discussed on many occasions and was even taken up by Parliament. The result was a ministerial decree in 1932, followed by a decree of the President of the Republic in 1967 which brought the controversy to an end. The latter decree stipulated that the name CHIANTI belonged to all the wines produced in a clearly defined area. This area was subdivided into six strictly defined sub-areas which use in addition to the name CHIANTI CLASSICO for the whole area, the names MONTALBANO, RUFINO, COLLI FIORENTINI, COLLI SENESI, COLLI ARETINI and COLLINE PISANE.

The predominant vines remain the traditional ones. The regulation on the production of CHIANTI lays down that the basic vines must be: 50-80 per cent *Sangiovese*,

10-30 per cent *Canaiolo Nero* and 10-30 per cent *Malvasia del Chianti*. Among the complementary vines are the *Colorino*, the *Mammolo* and the *Bonamico*.

There is one traditional and characteristic practice in the winemaking process of CHIANTI, called the *governo* ("government"). It consists of adding to the new wine during the month of November a small quantity (5 to 10 per cent) of must made from grapes which have been specially conserved on trellises or hung up on hooks. If the cellar is kept at the right temperature this grape ferments and if the casks are hermetically sealed, the carbon dioxide dissolves in the wine, giving it a characteristic tang and adding a surprising but agreeable taste to the young Chianti. Tuscans say it "kisses and bites". CHIANTI can be drunk in its first year, at the latest in late spring. But the best is aged in casks for two or three years. After at least two years it can be labelled CHIANTI VECCHIO, and after three years of ageing it earns the right to the description *réserve*.

The characteristics of CHIANTI are: a very bright ruby-red colour which tends to garnet as it ages; a strong bouquet when young but which turns with time to an aroma of violets or iris; a dry flavour, slightly impregnated with tannin, which becomes delicate, mild and velvety with age. The alcohol content of CHIANTI must be at least 11.5°; that of the wine entitled to the label CHIANTI CLASSICO 12°.

Most Chianti is sold commercially in *fiaschi* with a straw covering. These *fiaschi* formerly contained around two litres. Then one-litre half-fiaschi were introduced, followed by half-litre bottles and finally quarter-litre ones. The oldest CHIANTIS, the "reserves" of very famous houses (such as Ricasoli, Antinori, Frescobaldior, the more modern ones of Rufino and Melini) are always put in dark glass bottles.

CHIANTI is not, however, the only highly-prized wine of Tuscany. To mention only those superior red table wines most closely resembling CHIANTI, there is first and foremost the BRUNELLO DI MONTALCINO from the gentle countryside of the same name near Sienna. It too is produced from the *Sangiovese*; its alcohol content is between 12.5° and 13°. It has more body than CHIANTI and needs maturing for at least three years before becoming smooth and perfectly harmonious and acquiring its delicious aroma of violets. It is unfortunate that this wine cannot be produced in larger quantities.

Next comes the NOBILE DI MONTEPULCIANO (which also takes its name from a small area in the province of Sienna). It is a wine with a rather dark, almost garnet colour and a very slightly bitter taste. It too requires ageing for at least two years. It was an extremely popular wine in the seventeenth century.

Some other famous red wines should also be mentioned which often bear the names of families of the Tuscan nobility; the BRIOLI of Ricasoli, the ANTINORI, the POMINO, the NIPPOZANO of Frescobaldi, the ARTIMINO and the CARMIGNANO. Nor should one forget the MONTECARLO, a light red wine produced on the hillsides of the province of Lucques, which was already well-known in the thirteenth century.

Although produced in much smaller quantities than the red wines, some of the whites deserve mention; above all the VERNACCIA DI S. GIMIGNANO. It is an excellent dry white wine which comes from a small area of the same name in the province of Sienna and from a vine which also has the same name. It should be pointed out here that the VERNACCIA of Tuscany bears no relation to the more famous VERNACCIA of Sardinia and Oristano. This is a wine whose praises were sung by poets and minstrels as long ago as the fourteenth century. It is never more than 12° and has a very slight acidity.

CHIANTI also takes the form of good dry white wines (in small quantities) which are often rather loosely termed CHIANTI BIANCO. One of the best is the ARBIA BIANCO of Ricasoli. But dry white wines are produced in greater quantities in the province of Arezzo: for instance those called the BIANCHI VERGINI ("virgin whites"), which are only slightly alcoholized, but have a very strong acid content. There is also a MONTECARLO BIANCO which was highly prized by the Medici when they were masters of Florence.

Even better known are the white wines of the Isle of Elba. Associated with the memory of Napoleon's exile, this iron-bearing island in the Tyrrhenian Sea, the largest of the Tuscan archipeligo, produces several quality wines in the vineyards which cling in dizzy flights of terraces to its mountainsides. The vines grown there are the *Biancone di Portoferraio* and the *Procanico*, a sub-species of the *Trebbiano Toscano*. Suitably treated, they yield wines which are highly esteemed as an accompaniment to fresh seafood or the island's delicious crayfish.

Besides the ELBA BIANCO a red wine is also produced from a base of *Sangiovese*, mixed with a little *Canaiolo* and the white grapes spoken of earlier. These are wines with a very slight alcohol content and which have relatively little acidity.

The Isle of Elba also produces some good special wines: chief of these is the ALEATICO DI PORTOFERRAIO. Ruby-red, with a bouquet and flavour which become more pronounced with the passage of time, it brings to mind the sweet, velvety, highly-alcoholized *Muscat*. There is in fact a MOSCATO DELL'ELBA, golden-yellow, sweet and wonderfully aromatic, made from the semi-dried grapes of the *Moscato* plant.

The amount of Tuscan wine for sale has grown progressively smaller over the last 50 years, partly because of the ravages of phylloxera, but also because of serious economic difficulties, arising chiefly from high production costs. However, for the last ten years production has again been on the increase, due to the slow but fundamental transformation of the traditional mixed culture into monoculture. Thanks also to the effect of a new law protecting the nomenclature of the better-known wines, production should soon reach its original level, with the added benefit of a guarantee to the consumer that the wines bearing such impressive labels are authentic.

THE MARCHES. In this province, on the Adriatic side of Tuscany, mixed culture still outweighs the specialized methods, but as the old plantations of climbing vines disappear they are replaced by short vine-stocks.

On the whole the proportion of white wines produced in the Marches is higher than in other regions of Italy. At an estimate, about 50 per cent of its production is taken up by red wines, 47 per cent by whites and the rest by rosés. Without a doubt, the best and the most characteristic wines are to be found among the whites. First comes the VERDICCHIO DEI CASTELLI DI JESI, produced in the province of Ancona. The hills it grows on and the vine it comes from bear the same name. It is one of Italy's most pleasant dry whites.

Another very similar wine is the VERDICCHIO DI MATELICA. The same grapes are used as for the first VERDICCHIO, but they are generally mixed with a small proportion of *Trebbiano Toscano* and *Malvasia Toscana*. It, too, is a straw-yellow, dry-tasting wine, but with a slightly bitter after-taste. Its alcohol content is usually around 12º, which is quite high for a dry white wine.

Another good wine from the Marches is the BIANCHELLO DEL METAURO, produced in the undulating countryside of the province of Pesaro from a mixture of white grapes in which the *Bianchello* (or *Biancame*) predominates. Usually it is a wine for everyday consumption; it can rise to heights if it comes from the best vines and undergoes very careful vinification.

In general the reds of the Marches are looked on as good ordinary wines, but some are of a quality which enables them to challenge the most famous Tuscan wines. The best-known is the Rosso CONERO, named after the mountain which rises above the town of Ancona and the corresponding area along the Adriatic coast. The basic vine used is the *Montepulciano*, which should not be confused with the Tuscan vine mentioned in connection with the NOBILE. The area where it is produced comprises various districts lying between Ancona and Osimo-Castelfiardo to the south and Falconara to the north. It is a pleasant, fine dry wine, with a brilliant ruby colour, a pleasing bouquet and a delicate flavour. It has a moderate alcohol content (in general 11.5º) and a reasonable acidity level.

The province of Ascoli Piceno produces another red wine known as the PICENO which is made from a mixture of grapes in which the *Sangiovese* and the *Montepulciano* predominate. It closely resembles the preceding wine but has in addition just a slight suspicion of bitterness.

Although it is impossible to list all the wines of the Marches, many of which are produced in very small quantities from imported vines such as the *Barbera*, the *Merlot*, the *Cabernet Franc*, the *Carignan* or the *Pinot Noir*, one special wine cannot be omitted: the VERNACCIA DI SERRAPETRONA, from the province of Macerata, a sweetish sparkling red which is made from slightly fermented grapes.

UMBRIA. Wine production in Umbria exceeds 17,600 gallons only in the very best years. And, what is extremely rare in Italy, it produces more white wine than red (respectively 60 and 40 per cent). Generally its wines are of an ordinary quality. Of course, some quite fine products can be found among the old-established firms or from the most advantageously sited vineyards: for instance the FONTESEGALE, the MONTECASTELLI and the AMELLA in the upper valley of the Tiber; the wines from the hills of Perugia; or the white GRECO DI TODI and the SACRANTINO DI MONTEFALCO, a sort of fermented red wine, very sweet and strongly alcoholized. But these are without any claims to a premier quality rating.

There is, however, one wine which on its own earns a well-deserved reputation for the wine production of Umbria: the ORVIETO, one of the most famous of Italian white wines. It is made from grapes grown in the tiny vineyard of the district of Orvieto, where the soil is mainly tuff mixed with volcanic materials. The main plant is the *Procanico* (which is simply the *Trebbiano Toscano* combined with other vines such as the *Grechetto* and the *Verdello*). Two types of wine are produced from this ORVIETO; one, a dry wine, is the best known today; the other, a pleasant wine which can be drunk at any time of the day, with a very distinguished golden colour, was very popular in days gone by. In the sixteenth century it was the favourite of Pope Paul III Farnese, who was a great lover of good wine. To prepare this type of wine it was customary in those days, much more than today, to put the must of very ripe grapes (sometimes they were even allowed to start rotting) to ferment in small vats inside deep, cool caves which had been hollowed out of the tuff. This encouraged the development of the very finest bouquet and flavours.

Italy, where artists find inspiration in the limpid light, where historians and archaeologists explore ancient ruins and sweethearts admire each other to the sound of love songs and mandolins. But Italy would not of course be Italy without the abundantly flowing wine, uniting young and old, men and women, as in this romantic painting of an Italian wine shop by Pietro Lucatelli (1634-1710).

But apart from the vineyards of Orvieto, it must infortunately be concluded that winegrowing in Umbria will remain as it is, due to the rather unfavourable ecopedological conditions in the region.

LATIUM. The fame of the wines of Latium goes back in time to the heydays of the Roman Empire. At that period Latium extended into the present-day Campania and the wines most highly praised by the Latin poets came in fact from this region.

Latium is today looked on as one of the most important winegrowing regions of Italy. Its annual production averages around 88,000,000 gallons (but in 1967 it was more than 110,000,000). A particularly outstanding feature is the marked predominance of white wines over the reds: in the provinces of Rieti, Frosinone and Latina, some 65 per cent of the wines are white; in Rome and Viterbo white wines make up 90 per cent

of the total! And a large number of these are good enough to be classed as quality wines; today most of them qualify for an *appellation d'origine*.

The most famous wines of Latium are those known by the generic name of DEI CASTELLI ("castles"). All are wines produced in the unusual region of volcanic hills to the south of Rome (more precisely the Colli Albani) which are practically covered with flourishing vineyards growing almost nothing but white grapes. They are chiefly: the *Malvasia di Candia*, the *Malvasia del Lazio*, the *Trebbiano Giallo* (or *Greco*) and, to a lesser extent, the *Trebbiano Toscano*, the *Bellone* and the *Bonvino*. The vines are all short bushes and the vineyards often stretch beyond the horizon. Although the appellation DEI CASTELLI is a generic one applying to an area of about 50 square miles, there are particular appellations according to the districts of production.

229

Among the best known and appreciated wines of the region is the FRASCATI—produced mostly in the district of the same name, but also throughout its designated region. In most cases it is made from the grapes of the *Malvasia del Lazio*, the *Greco* (or *Trebbiano Giallo*), the *Trebbiano Toscano* and also from a little of the *Bellone* and the *Bonvino*. It has always been quite an agreeable wine and when it is sweet it is called *cannellino*. In olden times it was dark yellow in colour because the musts were left to ferment at length on the grape marc and the grapes were picked when they were over-ripe and already starting to decay. They were then called *uve infavate*. Today however, thanks to more rational techniques, wines are produced with a straw-yellow, slightly golden colour and a very low tannin content. Their bouquet and flavour may be less pronounced but they have gained in subtlety.

Two other Roman CASTELLI which have recently won legal recognition of their *appellation d'origine* are the MARINO and the COLLI ALBANI. Their name is now officially acknowledged by the National Committee for the Protection of "Appellations d'Origine". The MARINO is made from a mixture of grapes of *Malvasia di Candia*, of *Malvasia del Lazio*, of green and yellow *Trebbiano Toscano* and of *Bonvino* in an area close to the Lake of Albano and Castelgandolfo. Straw yellow in colour, it is a rich, sweet wine with a delicate bouquet and a pleasant dry flavour. The COLLI ALBANI wine comes from much the same plants, grown in a region close by the preceding one. It resembles the MARINO very closely and their chemical composition is practically the same. Both are agreeable fine table wines which are much appreciated not only by local consumers but also by the numerous visitors to Rome.

The Latium also produces a whole category of quite different wines, several of which can claim an impressive and long-established reputation. One of them most frequently mentioned, because of its strange name, is the EST! EST!! EST!!! of Montefiascone. It is a dry white wine which, though it lacks any bouquet, has a pleasant taste and a fine gold colour. It has a moderate alcohol content (11º) and acidity level. The grapes which between them produce this wine are the *Procanico* (or the *Trebbiano Toscano*), the *Malvasia di Candia* and the *Rosetto (Trebbiano Giallo)*.

The most widely produced of Latium's red wines is the CESANESE, which comes from a vine of the same name. The most popular is the wine of Affile, a small area some 50 miles from Rome. This dark-red wine comes in two varieties, dry and sweet; it has a full-bodied flavour and characteristic agreeable bouquet. Equally popular is the red wine CESANESE DEL PIGLIO, which is grown not only in the district of the same name but also in neighbouring districts to the south-

east of Rome. Ruby-red, with a very strong bouquet, it is full of flavour and body. It is both dry and smooth to the taste, well alcoholized (11º to 12.5º) but with a moderate acid content. Sometimes it is left to age, to produce an even better quality wine.

A naturally sweet wine is the beautiful garnet-coloured ALEATICO of Gradoli (province of Viterbo) which comes from a vine of the same name. To keep it sweet, the must undergoes various filtrations which prevent it fermenting. When it is ready for sale it has an alcohol content of 10º and 9 per cent of sugar. Another, sweeter variety is more alcoholic. In flavour the ALEATICO is reminiscent of *Muscat*.

Among the outstanding wines of Latium of relatively recent date (in contrast to so many others whose history goes back to pre-Christian times), the wines of Aprilia ought to be mentioned. This name was given to one of the settlements which followed the draining of the Pontine Marshes a few years before the Second World War. It was a bold venture: flourishing towns and villages, gentle countryside, orchards and vineyards sprang up where once had been only evil-smelling marshland. The wines of Aprilia, to speak of just these wines, come from an area south of the Roman CASTELLI some seven miles from the Tyrrhenian Sea coastline (close to Anzio and Netturo). The soil there is volcanic in origin, part sand, part clay and part what is clearly volcanic matter. Several *appellation contrôlée* wines come from there: TREBBIANO DI APRILIA, SANGIOVESE DI APRILIA and MERLOT DI APRILIA. All are fine table wines which stand up very well to comparison with wines of much older ancestry.

The TREBBIANO DI APRILIA comes from the *Trebbiano Giallo* or *Trebbiano Toscano* vines. It is straw-yellow, with a very definite bouquet and a delicate, dry and agreeable flavour. It is a pleasant wine, which like the other wines of Latium, is suitable for all kinds of meals. The SANGIOVESE DI APRILIA, made from the *Sangiovese* vine (the same basic vine as for CHIANTI) is a rosé wine with an orange tinge; it has a personable aroma and a dry, well-balanced flavour.

The MERLOT DI APRILIA (from the *Merlot* vine) has met with a great deal of success in Venezia. A garnet-red wine with a very pronounced aroma, it is dry and full-bodied, though not excessively so.

Another designated area producing good red and white wines known by the appellation CORI, after the wineproducing centre of the region, is to be found on the hills of Aprilia. The vines here grow in volcanic soil and enjoy a mild climate, thanks to the Lepini hills which shelter them from the cold winds, a combination of natural circumstances particularly conducive to the production of quality wines. The CORI BIANCO is made from the grapes of the *Malvasia di Candia, Bel-*

lone, *Trebbiano Toscano,* and the *Trebbiano Giallo;* the Cori Rossi from the *Montepulciano,* the *Sangiovese* and other local vines. Neither of these table wines is lacking in quality; the white may be dry or sweet, with an alcohol content of around 11º. The red is always dry, but smooth, fresh and with a moderate degree of alcohol.

After the draining of the marshes a model wine-growing centre was established, the Maccarese estate, which produces highly-reputed red and white wines sold under the name of Castel San Giorgio, as well as other, more ordinary wines.

Abruzzi and Molise. This is a predominantly mountainous region containing the highest peaks of the Appennines (Gran Sasso and Maiella); at the other extreme it is practically at the level of the Adriatic Sea. In between stretches a succession of hills, a constantly changing countryside of picturesque villages each with their architectural peculiarities and folklore.

The first point to note about winegrowing and production in this region is that here, contrary to the regions north of the Abruzzi (the Marches), specialized culture far outstrips mixed culture. In addition, more than half of the grapes produced are grown as a fruit crop and not for wine. The average wine production of the past few years was around 50,600,000 gallons, of which some 30 per cent was white wine, 40 per cent

red wine and 30 per cent rosé wine, among which are some classified as "fine" wines. One of the most typical is the Cerasuolo d'Abruzzo, so-called because of its cherry-red colour. It is produced mainly in the provinces of L'Aquila, Chieti and Pescara. Its colour comes from a technical peculiarity of the winemaking process; the must (of black grapes) is fermented away from the grape marcs. It is made almost entirely from the *Montepulciano d'Abruzzo* vine, which is the most widespread in the region. It is essentially dry, but it is often smooth, agreeable and quite strongly alcoholized. It should not be confused with another wine which is produced in larger quantities and takes its name from the same vine: the Montepulciano d'Abruzzo. In contrast to the Cerasuolo, its must is fermented on the marc, giving a full-bodied ruby-coloured wine, with a good bouquet. Dry or slightly mellow, with a good alcohol content (12º-13º), it is capable of turning into a notable *da arrosto* wine after a short period of ageing.

The most typical white wine is the Trebbiano d'Abruzzo from the *Trebbiano* vine, produced mostly at Francavilla, Ortona, Città Sant'Angelo and Montesilvano. It is usually quite a dark straw-yellow colour, with a pleasant bouquet, a dry flavour and around 11º to 12º of alcohol. Another good white wine is the Peligno, from Pratola Peligna, a village of L'Aquila.

SOUTHERN ITALY

Oenologically speaking, southern and insular Italy have many similarities. According to the most recent official statistics (those of 1967), out of a total area of 2,840,000 acres of vineyards under monoculture, 1,635,000 were in southern or insular Italy. It should be added that most of the lands under viticulture in these vast regions have a very clear "winegrowing vocation" and could hardly be used for any other crop.

Apulia. Even disregarding the particularly good wine harvest of 1967 (278,630,000 gallons), wine production exceeded 220,000,000 gallons in four of the seven past years. The five provinces which make up the region of Apulia—Foggia, Bari, Brindisi, Tarento and Lecce—all produce wine; the most important are Bari and Lecce. Whites, reds and rosés are all represented. Superior red table wines have been produced for a long time in some of the centres of the province of Foggia, for example at Cerignola, where the Santo Stefano is produced from a mixture of local vines —*Troia, Montepulciano* and *Lascirma*—or such other varieties as *Alicante* and *Barbera.* The red Castel del Monte, produced in the area of the Murgi hills

from the *Bombino Nero, Troia* and *Montepulciano* grapes, has an alcohol content of 12º to 13º. If aged a little it turns into an excellent table wine.

Today, the production of quality wines is spreading to a remarkable extent in Apulia, partly because of the introduction of better vine plants and partly due to a change from the traditional methods of pruning the vines (a system of low, heavily pruned bushes recalling the "goblet" shape of the South of France) into the cultivation of taller, more productive plants. These have been introduced wherever the depth, fertility and moisture, either natural or irrigation-produced, of the soil have made it possible. Much better grape harvests are obtained by these methods, and because of their very low sugar content, the grapes can be used to make table wines of every-day quality.

The rosé wines of Apulia have increased in number, especially since the last war. A rosé type of the Castel del Monte mentioned earlier is made, with an unusual bouquet and a dry but delicate and velvety taste. Another agreeable rosé wine is produced in the area of the Castellana hills, in the province of Bari, while still others, such as the GIGLIANO rosé, produced at Copertino from the *Malvasia Nera* and the *Negro di Amaro* vines, come from Cerignolo and the Salentino.

Of the white wines, the SANSEVERO, from the province of Foggia, deserves to be mentioned; it comes from the district of the same name and others close by. Made from the *Bombino Bianco* and the *Trebbiano Toscano* in almost equal quantities, it is a straw-yellow colour, with a pleasant bouquet and a fresh, dry, harmonious flavour. It has been granted an *appellation d'origine contrôlée*. There is also a red and a rosé SANSEVERO. The LOCOROTONDO and the MARTINAFRANCA are made from a mixture of two plants, the *Verdeca* and the *Bianco d'Alessano*.

An important centre for the production of white wines is Ostuni-Cisternino-Ceglie, bordering on the district of Martina. It provides a good white wine which goes by the name of OSTUNI and is made from a combination of the *Verdeca* and *Bianco d'Alessano* vines.

The hilly region of Conversano in the province of Bari produces another white wine from a mixture of *Verdeca*, *Malvasia* and *Bianco d'Alessano*: it too is a dry, well-balanced wine.

Finally Apulia itself produces a number of special wines, mainly sweet wines, but also some aromatic varieties. Among these latter is the MOSCATI DI TRANI, made from the *Muscat Blanc*, the same vine which produces the famous ASTI SPUMANTE and the COLLI EUGANEI, as well as the *Muscats* of the Isle of Elba, of Syracuse in Sicily and Tempio in Sardinia.

The Trani wine is a true sweet wine, golden-yellow, with a delicious aroma. Prepared from slightly rotten grapes, it not infrequently has an alcohol content as high as 17°. A very similar wine is the MOSCATO DI SALENTO, which is also called SALENTO BIANCO LIQUO-ROSO. The ALEATICO DI PUGLIA is made from the

In olden days, vines in Italy frequently grew up trees. This made for wine harvests as picturesque as this one painted by Philip Hackert at the end of the eighteenth century in the countryside around lovely Sorrento.

same vine which produces the ALEATICO of the Isle of Elba. It is produced in small quantities in the provinces of Bari, Brindisi, Lecce and Tarento and bears a slight resemblance to *Muscat* with its warm, slightly sweet flavour. It may have as much as 15º to 17º alcohol and generally it is left to age for two or three years.

CAMPANIA. The vineyards of this very rugged and picturesque region are shrinking noticeably, particularly in the provinces of Naples and Salerno. The most northerly part of the region, bordering on Latium in the province of Caserta, produces a wine which was famous in olden times: the FALERNO, described as fiery by Horace, fuming by Tibullus and immortal by Martial. The vine which produces this illustrious wine is the *Aglianico*, also called *Ellanico*. Today's FALERNO is a heavy, dull-red, full-bodied wine with a rather bitter taste due to its high tannin content (which comes from the prolonged fermentation of the must with the skins). A warming wine because of its high alcohol content (from 13º to 16º) it is slightly acidified and often retains a certain amount of non-decomposed sugar, which introduces a sweet note into the bitterness. This wine should undergo quite a long ageing process to bring out all its qualities and it deserves to be produced in a more rational manner..

Equally famous is the LACHRYMA CHRISTI, which originates on the slopes of Mount Vesuvius. This is the legendary symbol of the tears which Our Lord is supposed to have shed on Capri, land of sin, after Lucifer, banished by God, stole the island from Paradise and let it fall in the Gulf of Naples. It is a fine dry white wine notable for its golden-yellow colour, its subtle, perfumed bouquet, its velvety flavour and its moderate alcohol content. It is made from the *Falanghina*, *Greco di Torre* and *Fiano* vines. There is also a red LACHRYMA CHRISTI, but it is quite an ordinary wine.

Moving down to the peninsula of Sorrento, we come to a very well-known red wine, the GRAGNANO, produced in a hilly region near Castellamare di Stabia. It is made from the *Aglianico*, *D'Olivella* and *Piè di Palumbo* vines. It is an excellent table wine, full-bodied and rather tart, a quality which increases its appeal for Neapolitan consumers. Among the other wines of Sorrento, the RAVELLO deserves a brief mention. There exists a white type, a rosé type and a red which is obtained by mixing the grapes of the *Bianca di Sorrento*, the *Pinot Blanc* and the *Pinot Noir*. All these wines are around 12º.

One should not leave the Gulf of Naples without mentioning the principal wines of its islands. The white CAPRI wine was long sought after as one of the best dry Italian wines. The main vines used to produce it are the *Greco* and the *Fiano*. Present-day production of this wine is on a considerably smaller scale. On the next island a white ISCHIA is made from a mixture of *Forastera* (predominantly), *Biancolella* and *San Leonardo*. It has a straw-yellow or slightly golden colour, an agreeably delicate bouquet and a dry, harmonious flavour. Red ISCHIA is made from *Guarnaccia*, *Piedirosso* and a little *Barbera*.

Among the wines of the province of Salerno are the wine of Corbera and those of Monte Julio and of Cilento, which if suitably aged may well turn into superior quality red table wines. They are exported in large quantities for blending with South American wines.

The province of Avellino (or Irpinia) is almost entirely covered by hills and mountains, which form three distinct winegrowing areas: the del Sabato valley, the region of Taurasino and the Colle del Partenio. The most important and the most popular of the red wines is the TAURASI, produced in the district of the same name and in the districts adjacent to it. It is without a doubt one of the best superior Italian table wines. It is made from the *Aglianico*, which is one of the most widely grown vines both in Campania and the adjoining Basilicato, mixed with 20 per cent of other vines *(Piedirosso, Montonico, Barbera)*. Among the white wines the GRECO DI TUFO (or GRECO DEL VESUVIO) should be mentioned; it is also to be found in the Benevento and the province of Naples. The vine of the same name is centuries old; it is even thought to be the *Aminea Gemella* of Columella. The FIANO is a similar white wine made from a vine which the Latin people called *Vitis Apiana* because it was such a favourite with the bees.

The neighbouring province of Benevento produces quality white and red wines, particularly in the areas of Solopaca, in the Telesina valley and towards the borders of Campania and Molise. The white wines are made from a mixture of *Greco Bianco*, *Trebbiano* and *Malvasia Bianca*; they are light golden-yellow in colour, with a very pleasant bouquet and a dry, velvety and harmonious flavour. The red wines come from a mixture of *Olivella*, *Montepulciano*, *Sangiovese*, *Aglianico* and *Mangiaguerra*. They are bright red, with a strong bouquet and pleasing, harmonious flavour.

Another wine of Campania which deserves mention is the ASPRINIO DELL'AVERSANO, made from a vine which grows up the very tall poplars of the plain. It has a very light alcohol content (7º to 8º) but is on the other hand quite acid. To protect it from the summer heat it is stored in deep caves and served very cold.

BASILICATO. This region lies between Apulia to the east and Campania to the west. It is mainly mountainous woodland and only a limited area can be used for winegrowing. Most of the wine production of the region is carried out in the district of Vulture, an old volcanic mountain chain in the north of the region.

Here vines grow at heights of as much as 2,400 feet above sea level. The districts of Barile, Rionero, Rapolla, Melfi, Maschito, Venoso and others, all land of volcanic origin, are covered with vineyards yielding quality wines. The most outstanding of these is the AGLIANICO DEL VULTURE, one of the best fine red wines of southern Italy. When young it is a splendid ruby-red which turns to garnet with age. It is a generous wine with a very pronounced acidity. Suitable ageing for three to four years develops its bouquet and lends it a sweeter taste.

CALABRIA. This region is almost entirely surrounded by the sea and is an essentially mountainous, wooded land. Vines grow in a very scattered fashion in only a small part of the region. Calabria's wines were famous even in antiquity and the wines of Sybaris, the BALBINO and the AMINEI, were equally well known.

One of the wines which has remained famous for its excellent quality throughout the centuries is the CIRO, produced in the province of Catanzaro. It is made from the black grapes of the *Gaglioppo* and a small proportion of *Greco Bianco* and *Greco Nero*. The POLLINO and the SAVUTO DI ROGLIANO, which come from much the same vines, have similar qualities to the CIRO. But in the past Calabria also produced good sweet wines, now limited to the Muscat of Cosenza and Salento and the Malvasia of Brindisi. Steps should be taken to prevent their disappearance.

SICILY

In the days of Pliny, Sicily could pride itself on possessing several of the most highly prized wines of Roman Italy. Among these were the MAMERTINO which was so popular with the court of Caesar, the TAUROMENITANUM, the POTULASUM and the BIBLINUM. Today Sicily ranks third among the wineproducing regions of Italy. Its expansion has been considerably fostered by aid from the Regional Institute of Vines and Wine, set up in Palermo in 1950.

Because of its southerly latitude and the fact that it is an island, Sicily generally has a hotter climate than any other region of Italy. Vines are not only grown all along its splendid beaches with their rich crops of citrus fruits, but are also cultivated inland to quite an altitude, as, for instance, on the slopes of Mount Etna. Every province of the island can boast the production of quality wines. From the province of Messina comes a wine with a particularly well-established reputation: the FARO, made from the *Nerello Cappuccio, Mascalese, Nocera, Nerello d'Avala*, etc. It is a generous, harmonious, ruby-red wine. After ageing, it takes on all the qualities of an excellent *da arrosto*. The MAMERTINO, which has such a distinguished name, is produced on the heights above Messina from white grapes, especially the *Cataratto*, mixed with *Inzolia, Grillo* and other vines. It is in fact more of a dessert wine than a table wine, and is produced in very small quantities.

The wineproducing area of the province of Catania is made up of a strip of land running around the cone of Mount Etna from the north to the south and the east. It includes all or a part of the districts of Paternó, Nicolosi, Viagrande, Zafferana, Milo and Linguaglossa. The vines from which its wines are made are principally: the *Carricante* and the *Cataratto Bianco* for white wines; the *Nerello Mascalese* and the *Nerello Mantellato* for the reds and the rosés. White ETNA is dry and straw-yellow in colour. After a brief ageing period it matures into a *da arrosta* wine.

The province of Syracuse offers a wide variety of wines, either for direct consumption, or, more often, for blending with other wines. The best blending wines come from Pachino in the far south of the island. They are strong, richly coloured, full-bodied wines which never have less than a 15º of alcohol content. This province also produces some very reputable, fine and superior-quality wines such as the white or red ELORO. The white is made from *Cataratto, Inzolia, Grillo* and *Albanello*; the red comes from the *Calabrese*.

The adjoining province of Ragusa produces another excellent wine, which goes by the name of FRAPPATO DI VITTORIA, made from the *Frappato* and *Calabrese* vines; and a special wine called the CERASUOLO DI VITTORIA because of its cherry colour. It is strongly alcoholic (15º to 16º) and is frequently exported to other parts of the country as a blending wine.

In western Sicily the white CORVO, a wine served with entrées, is made from 40 per cent of *Cataratto* and the remainder from *Inzolia*; the red is made from *Perricone* and *Catanese*. Well matured, CORVO becomes a wonderful *da arrosto* wine. Western Sicily is, however, primarily the land of MARSALA. For close on two centuries it has been by far the best known and most prized of Sicilian wines. Its origins go back to 1773, when an Englishman, John Woodhouse, who exported the produce of western Sicily to England, discovered the quality of the wines of the Marsala vineyards, cultivated in those days by somewhat primitive methods. He developed the production of these wines and was responsible for their rise in popularity. MARSALA is made from the *Grillo* and *Cataratto* vines and, to a lesser extent from the *Inzolia* and *Catanese*: all bear grapes with a high sugar content and little acidity. The vineyards of Marsala, which jut out into the provinces of Palermo and Agrigente but lie otherwise almost entirely in the province of Trapano, enjoy a hot climate. MARSALA is made by adding cooked concentrated must to fermented must. The different types of MARSALA, varying in sweetness and alcohol content are the result of variations in the proportions of this mixture. The alcohol content ranges from 17º to 20º and the sugar content from 5 to 10 per cent. One of the most highly rated MARSALAS is the SUPERIOR OLD MARSALA (S.O.M.) with 18º of alcohol. A prerequisite for obtaining the best quality MARSALA is to let it mature in wooden casks. A remarkable thing is that this process takes place in large buildings, even on the ground floor, where the wine is subject to sudden changes in temperature.

Among the many "special" wines of Sicily is the MOSCATO DI SIRACUSA, made from the white *Muscat*, the *Inzolia*, the *Cataratto* and the *Albanello*, whose grapes are gathered only when they begin to show the first signs of decay. It is a true sweet wine, dry, delicious, full-bodied, with an alcohol content of about 14º to 17º. Other liqueur-like Muscats are produced in western Sicily, especially in the province of Palermo. One of the best is the LOZUCCO, originally named after a vast property belonging to the House of Orleans, but which today is almost non-existent. On the other hand large quantities of an aromatic Muscat are still produced on the picturesque island of Pantelleria. The vines which grow on its mountainous and volcanic terrain yield some excellent wines. The most important variety is the *Zibbibo* whose fruit is left to rot for the purpose of making either raisins or wine.

Another outstanding liqueur-like wine is the MALVASIA DI LIPARI. It is produced in the archipelago of the same name on the small islands of Salina and Stromboli. The grapes are left to decay for a week, in order to make a very alcoholic wine (from 15º to 16º).

SARDINIA

Sardinian oenology was always particularly noted for its special wines, but several table wines in the ordinary, fine and superior classes have also long claimed attention. Among the superior wines should first be mentioned a white from the province of Cagliari with the historic name of NURAGUS. The *Nuragus* vine from which it is made is in fact reputed to be the oldest of all vines, going back to prehistoric times. It produces an excellent fine table wine, with a light bouquet and a dry, fresh, subtle taste. The VERMENTINO, from the province of Sassari, is another fine dry white wine, with an amber-like colour, a delicate bouquet and a very slightly bitter taste. There are some quite respectable, if slightly sweet, red wines made in the Ogliastra from the *Cannonau* vine. Among the superior quality wines, pride of place should go to the VERNACCIA DI ORISTANO, "the most Sardinian of Sardinian wines", whose austere taste is well-suited to the fierce temperament of the island's inhabitants. It is a dry, strongly alcoholic wine. The vine it comes from is grown in the deep cool soils of the Tirso Valley, the only place where it gives really good wine. Light amber-yellow in colour, with a powerful and distinctive bouquet, its mellow flavour has just a hint of bitterness. Its alcohol content varies between 15.5º and 17º. Lengthy ageing in oak casks enables its much-prized qualities to develop to the full. Among the special white wines should be mentioned the famous Sardinian MALVASIA, with its golden hue and bouquet reminiscent of almond flowers. Another sweet white wine is the typically Sardinian NASCO from the province of Cagliari, which is undoubtedly one of the most delicious of Italian sweet wines. Lastly there is the MOSCATO DEL CAMPIDANO of Cagliari. In contrast to the *Muscats* of northern Italy, it is produced by a special technique: once the must has reached a 10º to 12º alcohol content fermentation is stopped by the addition of very pure ethyl alcohol. This method gives a delicious wine of 15º to 16º.

Among Sardinia's range of special red wines is the famous OLIENA which Gabriele D'Annunzio hailed as the "Nepenthe of Oliena". It is a strongly alcoholic wine (from 15º to 17º) but not at all sweet; it has a strong bouquet and a mellow, slightly bitter taste. As it ages it turns somewhat orange in colour. The *Cannonau*, which is the main vine used in the production of OLIENA, also supplies another special red wine, the CAMPIDANO DI CAGLIARI. Ruby-red when young, it takes on an orange hue with age, and at the same time acquires a pleasant bouquet and a smooth, generous flavour. It is held to be one of the most tonic of dessert wines. Two other sweet wines should also be mentioned: the MONICA and the GIRO, both probably of Spanish origin. Some, in fact, compare the Sardinian sweet wines to the same type of wines produced in Spain, in particular to MALAGA and MADEIRA wines.

WINES OF ITALY

PIEDMONT

Dry red wines	Barolo	Boca	Barbera d'Alba
	Nebbiolo d'Alba	Barbaresco	Barbera del Monferrato
	Carema	Ghemme	Dolcetto delle Langhe e d'Ovada
	Gattinara	Sizzano	Freisa di Chieri e d'Asti
	Lessona	Barbera d'Asti	Grignolino d'Asti
Medium-sweet red wines	Brachetto d'Acqui	Barbera d'Asti	Freisa di Chieri
	Malvasia di Casorso	Barbera d'Alba	Freisa d'Asti
	Nebbiolo Piemontese	Barbera del Monferrato	Grignolino d'Asti
Dry white wines	Cortese di Gavi	Erbaluce di Caluso	
Sweet white wines . . .	Moscato d'Asti	Asti spumante	Caluso Passito

LOMBARDY

Dry red wines	Barbacarlo dell'Oltrepo pavese	Grumello	Riviera del Garda
	Buttafuoco dell'Oltrepo pavese	Inferno	Franciacorta
	Sangue di Giuda Oltrepo pavese	Sassella	Botticino
	Freccia Rossa di Casteggio	Valgella	Cellatica
Medium-sweet red wines .	Barbacarlo dell'Oltrepo pavese	Canneto	Clastidium
	Sangue di Giuda dell'Oltrepo pavese	Bonardo amabile	Nebbiolo di Retorbido
Dry white wines	Riesling dell'Oltrepo pavese	Frecciarossa di Casteggio	Tocai di San Martino della Battaglia
	Cortese dell'Oltrepo pavese	Lugana	Pusterla
Medium-dry white wine .	Clastidium di Casteggio		
Sweet white wines . . .	Spumante di S. Maria della Versa	Moscato di Casteggio	
Dry rosé wines	Chiaretto del Garda	Pusterla	

LIGURIA

Dry red wine	Rossese di Dolceacqua		
Dry white wines	Vermentino	Polcevera	Cinqueterre
	Coronata		
Sweet white wine	Cinqueterre passito (Sciacchetrà)		

TRENTINO-ALTO ADIGE

Dry red wines	Lago di Caldaro (or Caldaro)	Marzemino	Cabernet
	Santa Maddalena	Lagrein	Merlot
	Terodelgo	Termeno	Pinot
Dry white wines	Pinot	Riesling renano	Sylvaner verde
	Ruländer	Traminer	Terlano
Sweet white wines . . .	Moscato trentino	Moscato atesino	
Rosé wines	Lagarino rosato (Lagrein)	Mazermino d'Isera	

VENETIA

Dry red wines	Bardolino	Valpolicella	Merlot delle Venezie
	Valpantena	Cabernet delle Venezie	Rosso dei Colli veronesi
Sweet red wines	Recioto della Valpolicella	Recioto Veronese	
Dry white wines	Soave	Bianco dei Colli Berici	Valdobbiadene
	Bianco di Breganze	Bianco dei Colli Euganei	Verduzzo
	Bianco di Gambellara	Prosecco di Conegliano	Pinot
Medium-dry white wines	Bianco dei Colli Berici	Colli Trevigiani	

FRIULI AND JULIAN VENETIA

Dry red wines	Rossi dei Colli Friulani	Cabernet friulano	Merlot friulano
	Rossi del Collio Goriziano	Tocai friulano	Refoschi
Dry white wines	Bianchi dei Colli Friulani	Bianchi del Collio Goriziano	Tocai Friulano

EMILIA AND ROMAGNA

Dry red wines	Lambrusco di Sorbara	Lambrusco grasparossa di Castelvetro	Sangiovese di Romagna
	Lambrusco Salamino di S. Croce	Guatturnio dei Colli Piacentini	Grasparossa
Dry white wines	Albana di Romagna	Trebbiano di Romagna	Bertinoro
Sweet white wine	Albana di Romagna		

TUSCANY

Dry red wines	Chianti	Chianti Rufino	Nipozzano
	Chianti classico	Chianti Colline Pisane	Artimino
	Chianti Colli Aretini	Brunello di Montalcino	Carmignano
	Chianti Colli Fiorentini	Vino nobile di Montepulciano	Monte-Carlo
	Chianti Colli Senesi	Antinori	Rosso delle Colline Lucchesi
	Chianti Montalbano	Brolio	Elba
Sweet red wine	Aleatico di Porto-Ferraio		
Dry white wines	Vernaccia di San Gimignano	Arbia	Bianco dell'Elba
	Bianchi vergini dell'Aretino	Moscadello di Montalcina	Monte-Carlo
Sweet white wines . . .	Moscato dell'Elba	Vino Santo toscano	

THE MARCHES

Dry red wines	Rosso Conero	Rosso Piceno	
Sweet red wine	Vernaccia di Serrapetrona		
Dry white wines	Verdicchio dei Castelli di Jesi	Verdicchio di Matelica	Bianchello del Metauro

UMBRIA

Red wines	Torgiano	Sacrantino de Montefalco	
Dry white wines	Orvieto	Torgiano	Greco di Todi
Sweet white wine	Orvieto		

LAZIO

Dry red wines	Ceasanese	Sangiovese di Aprilia	Merlot di Aprilia
	Ceasanese del Piglio	Falerno	Castel San Giorgio
Medium-dry red wine . .	Ceasanese del Piglio		
Sweet red wine	Aleatico viterbese		
Dry white wines	Est ! Est !! Est !!!	Frascati	Cori
	Colli Lanuvini	Marino	Trebbiano di Aprilia
	Colli Albani	Velletri	Falerno
	Colonna	Montecompatri	
Medium-dry white wines	Est ! Est !! Est !!!	Colonna	Malvasia di Grotta-ferrata (or Grotta-ferrata)
	Colli Albani	Frascati	
	Colli Lanuvini	Marino	Cori
Sweet white wines . . .	Moscato di Terracina	Colonna	Frascati

ABRUZZI

Dry red wines	Cerasuolo di Abruzzo	Montepulciano di Abruzzo
Medium-sweet white wine	Cerasuolo di Abruzzo	
Medium-dry white wines .	Trebbiano di Abruzzo	Peligno

CAMPANIA

Dry red wines	Aglianico Lacrima Christi del Vesuvio Falerno	Taurasi Vesuvio	Ischia Ravello
Medium-sweet red wines	Conca	Gragnano	Solopaca
Dry white wines	Capri Ischia Greco di Tufo	Lacrima Christi del Vesuvio Ravello Falerno	Furor divina Costiera Asprinio Bianco d'Avellino
Medium-dry white wines .	Solopaca	Greco di Tufo	
Dry rosé wine	Ravello		
Medium-dry rosé wine .	Solopaca		

APULIA

Dry red wines	Castel del Monte Santo Stefano di Cerignola	Primitivo di Gioia e Manduria	Barletta
Medium sweet red wine .	Castel Acquaro		
Sweet red wine	Aleatico di Puglia	Moscato del Salento (or Salento)	Zagarese
Dry white wines	Sansevero	Martinafranca Locorotondo Ostuni	Torre Giulia
Sweet white wines . . .	Moscato di Salento (or Salento liquoroso)		Moscato di Trani
Dry rosé wines	Castel del Monte	Gigliano	

BASILICATA

Dry red wine	Aglianico del Vulture	
Dry white wine	Provitaro	
Sweet white wines . . .	Malvasia del Vulture	Moscato del Vulture
Medium-dry rosé wine .	Malvasia di Lucania	

CALABRIA

Dry red wines	Cirò di Calabria Savuto di Rogliano	Pollino	Lacrima di Castrovillari
Dry white wines	Provitaro	Balbino	
Sweet white wines . . .	Greco di Gerace	Moscato di Cosenza	Malvasia di Cosenza
Rosé wine	Pellaro		

SICILY

Dry red wines	Faro Etna	Eloro Corvo di Casteldaccia	Frappato di Vittoria Cerasuolo di Vittoria
Dry white wines	Corvo di Casteldaccia Etna	Eloro Lo Zucco	Bianco di Alcamo
Medium-dry white wines .	Mamertino	Marsala vergine	
Sweet white wines . . .	Malvasia di Lipari Mamertino Marsala	Moscato Lo Zucco Moscato di Siracusa Moscato di Noto	Moscato Passito di Pantelleria Cerasuolo di Vittoria
Dry rosé wines	Eloro	Etna rosato	

SARDINIA

Dry red wines	Oliena	Cannonau del Campidano	Campidano di Cagliari
Sweet red wines	Cirò di Sardegna	Monica di Sardegna	
Dry white wines	Nuragus Vernaccia di Oristano	Vermentino di Gallura Vernaccia di Sardegna	Malvasia di Bosa
Sweet white wines . . .	Nasco	Moscato del Campidano	Moscato di Tempio

238

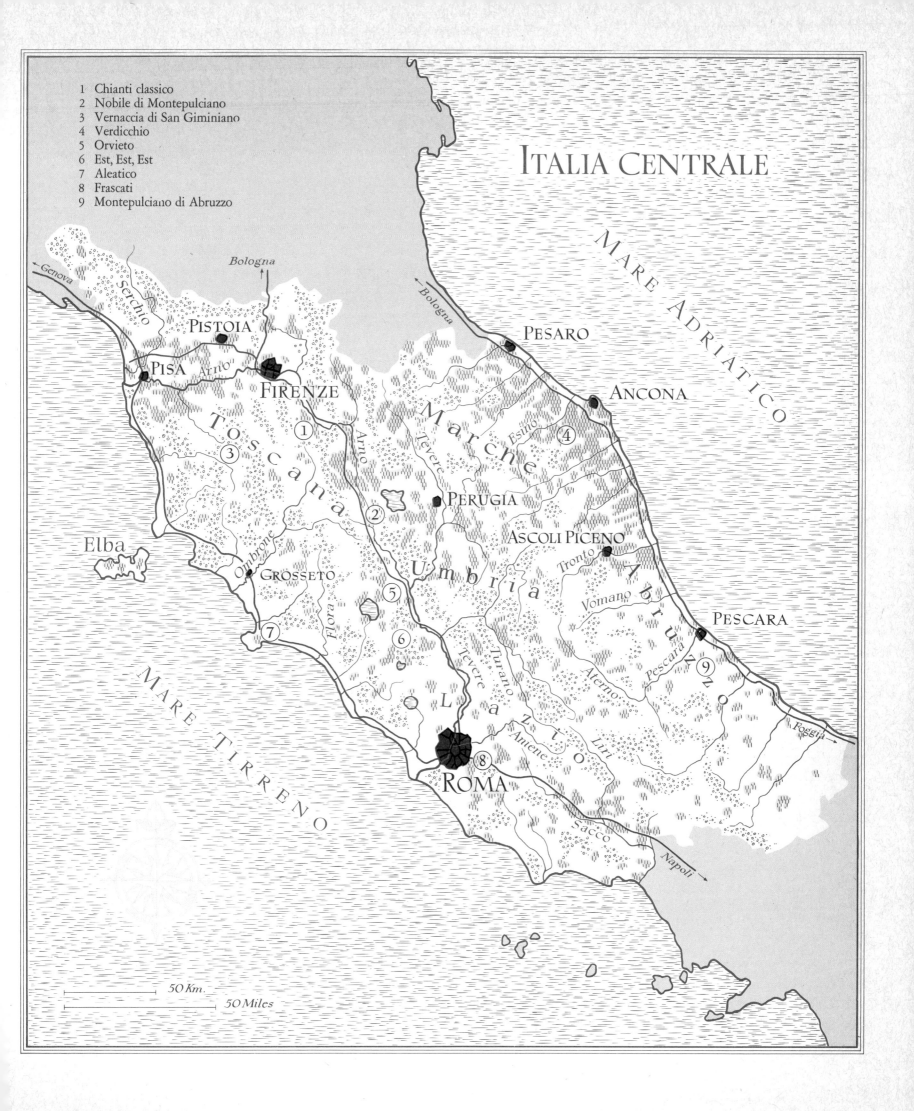

ITALIA CENTRALE

1 Chianti classico
2 Nobile di Montepulciano
3 Vernaccia di San Giminiano
4 Verdicchio
5 Orvieto
6 Est, Est, Est
7 Aleatico
8 Frascati
9 Montepulciano di Abruzzo

MARE ADRIATICO

Genova
Serchio
Bologna
Bologna

PISTOIA
PISA
Arno
FIRENZE

Toscana

①
③
②

Elba

Ombrone

GROSSETO

⑤

Flora

⑦

MARE TIRRENO

⑥

Tevere

PESARO

ANCONA

Marche

④
Esino

PERUGIA

Umbria

ASCOLI PICENO
Tronto

Vomano

Tevere

Turano

Aterno

Pescara

Abruzzo

PESCARA

⑨

Liri

Poggia

Aniene

Lazio

⑧
ROMA

Sacco

Napoli

50 Km.

50 Miles

ITALIA SETTENTRIONALE

1 Freisa
2 Nebbiolo
3 Barbaresco
4 Barolo
5 Barbera d'Asti
6 Grignolino
7 Dolcetto d'Ovada
8 Cortese
9 Lagrein
10 Merlot
11 Soave
12 Valpolicella
13 Bardolino
14 Lambrusco
15 Sangiovese
16 Oltrepò

SUISSE

FRANCE

Ticino

Simplon

Grand Saint-Bernard

Lago Maggiore

Lago di Como

Valt

Valle d'Aosta

AOSTA

Sesia

VARESE

COMO

BERGAMO

NOVARA

MILANO

VERCELLI

Po

Ticino

Adda

Po

① TORINO

⑤

⑯

Piemonte

Po

⑥

⑧

② ③

⑦

④

Liguria

50 Km.

50 Miles

Nice

GENOVA

LA SPEZIA

GOLFO DI GENOVA

MARE LIGURE

MARE ADRIATICO

50 Km.
50 Miles

1 Falerno
2 Lacryma Christi
3 Malvasia
4 Etna
5 Corvo
6 Alcamo
7 Pachino
8 Faro
9 Marsala

← Roma

Pescara
Candelaro
Celone

FOGGIA

Volturno

Ⓐ①

C
a
m
p
a
n
i
a

NAPOLI ②
SALERNO
Sele
Calore

Ofanto

P
u
g
l
i
a

BARI
MATERA
Bradano
Basento

Platano

Basilicata

Agri
Sinni

BRINDISI

TARANTO ③
LECCE

GOLFO DI TARANTO

Crati
Trionto

C
a
l
a
b
r
i
a

Savuto

MARE TIRRENO

MARE IONIO

Sardegna inset:

Mannu
SASSARI
Tirso

S
a
r
d
e
g
n
a

NUORO

50 Km.

Mannu
Flumendosa
Cixerri
CAGLIARI

PALERMO
MESSINA ⑧
REGGIO CALABRIA

TRAPANI
⑥
⑤
⑨

S i c i l i a

Simeto

④

ENNA

CALTANISSETTA

Platani

CATANIA

Salso

AGRIGENTO

Acate

SIRACUSA

⑦

MARE MEDITERRANEO

ITALIA MERIDIONALE E INSULARE

THE WINES
OF THE RHINE

JOSEPH JOBÉ, JOSEPH DREYER and HELMUT ARNTZ

Had not the Rhine river carried its civilizing influences northward, the vine would have remained confined to the basin of the Rhône. As early as the fourth century B.C. Greek adventurers pushed their way up the Rhône to the Swiss plateau and very probably made contact with the Celts along the Jura as far as Basel long before the Romans arrived. They probably introduced vines which they had acclimatized in Gaul. The process was completed by the gradual Romanization and, later, the Christianization of Central Europe. Once the vine had crossed the barrier of the Alps, it became established in the east wherever the altitude permitted, and permanent vineyards grew up round the veterans' colonies and the earliest monastic establishments on the Rhine until at last a new chain of vineyards stretched from Chur to Bonn.

The source of the Rhine, or at least of the larger of its two branches known as the Upper Rhine, is not very far from the source of the Rhône. The stream issuing from Lake Tuma is only a few miles from the Furka glacier; but the two rivers flow in different directions, turning, as it were, their backs on each other. The Rhine, starting higher up, goes farther and is slower to decide on its final course. The vine in the Grisons grows lower down than the vine in the Valais—not above 1,800 feet—where the Rhine first definitely flows northwards. It favours the red grape, which, indeed, is the predominating variety all along the Upper Rhine. The landscape, with the Alps in the background, often verges on the sublime. The language along the river moves on from Romanche to the various

dialects of eastern Switzerland, while the impetuous stream is tamed by man and becomes international. The right bank borders the Austrian Vorarlberg and the tiny Principality of Liechtenstein, where the vine is scanty, but where the inhabitants, looking to Switzerland, have always felt that the Rhine brings them closer to the Swiss rather than separating them.

Now the river comes to Lake Constance, where, like the Rhône in Lake Leman, its waters slow down and disappear in the broad expanse. To the north, the first German vineyards shimmer on the foothills of the Black Forest. Opposite, the red grapes of the Rheintal in St. Gallen and the Untersee in Thurgau counterbalance the whites of Baden. The town of St. Gallen, a far-famed bulwark of medieval culture, is not far away—one more link in the chain of episcopal and university towns of the Middle Rhine, like Constance, Basel, Freiburg-in-Breisgau and Strasbourg.

Flowing through Lake Constance the river makes a deep bend, turning sharply east and west; and it maintains this course as far as Basel. Over a hundred yards wide here, it flows past the vineyards of the Klettgau in the Canton of Schaffhausen and narrows somewhat in the loom of the Swabian Jura just before it makes an impressive leap of over sixty feet that sends it hurtling through the Cantons of Zurich and Aargau. There, as it flows past the vineyards of Baden to the north, its tributary, the Aare, which links it to most of the Swiss lakes, flows in from the left. The vineyards of Zurich, the Bernese Jura, Fribourg and Neuchâtel are thus connected up with the Rhine.

Indeed, the connection has always been very close, as is shown by the alliance concluded in the sixteenth century between the people of Strasbourg and the people of Zurich. The good burghers of Zurich, to show how speedily they could come to Strasbourg's, aid, rowed down the Limmat, the Aare and the Rhine and reached the city in less than eighteen hours, "before a dish of millet had time to cool". Neuchâtel, it should be noted, was subject to French influence; here the *Riesling*, the traditional variety of the Rhine, yields to a stock brought in from the west, the *Chasselas*.

The Rhine achieves its maturity at Basel. Meeting the buttress of the Jura's eastern end, it turns definitely north along the passage formed by the parallel ranges of the Black Forest and the Vosges. It is still seven hundred and fifty feet above sea-level and it takes it some five hundred miles to descend to the sea. The wine road, continuous on the right bank, does not start again to the west until Mulhouse, where the famous Alsatian winegrowing region begins. The vineyards on the French bank, carefully terraced on the last outcroppings of the Vosges, exposed to the rising sun and with an extremely favourable climate, are parcelled out in very small lots. Their wines have been distributed for ages throughout Europe by the Rhine itself and, in medieval times, many a boat carried the precious SYLVANERS and RIESLINGS to the courts of Swabia, Bavaria, Sweden and England.

To the east the vineyards of Baden and Württemberg are separated by the Black Forest, joined nowadays in a single *Land* of the Federal Republic of Germany. The wines of the Neckar were as celebrated in feudal Europe as those of the Main, the Moselle and the Aare.

Although the vineyards are so densely concentrated, this has in no way detracted from the personality of each region. The Rhine wines are derived from a very few varieties of grape and would seem to be closely akin, but each vineyard has a pronounced character of its own and its neighbour has no wish to imitate it. The Palatinate, to which the river now brings us, is simply a natural extension of Alsace, and yet the soil has changed. Our hearts were won by the GEWURZTRAMINER, but now we are enchanted by the celebrated growths of Forst and Deidesheim. It is hard to choose between them, for it is very true that "the sky, the climate and the land are all in every glass" of these delightful wines.

The landscape gradually changes from Karlsruhe to Mainz, becoming less abrupt; the rapids gradually disappear, as do the alluvial deposits between its many branches, and the river spreads in a broad stream over a deep and stable bed, with firm banks: it becomes navigable. The towns, which hitherto seemed to shun the banks, are now situated closer to the river, like Worms, whose lofty Romanesque cathedral surveys the ripening Palatinate wines to the south and the wines of Rheinhesse to the north.

From Mainz the vineyards follow the winding route of the Main, threading eastward through Franconia to successfully invade Bavarian territory, despite its apparent total occupation by the hop. At Bingen, on the other bank, at the very moment when the Rhine at last emerges from the vast curve it had described downstream from Worms, the Nahe takes over the vine and carries it up into Rheinhesse.

Now we come to the heart of the romantic Germany, the fantastic stage-setting of marauding Burgraves and elves, massacres and sorceries, Fürstenberg, Gutenfels, the Pfalz, that lowering pile jutting out of the waters, the Cat and the Mouse, still defying each other, and Rheinfels—ruined towers, jagged keeps, massive and disturbing shades, and among them on either bank the vineyards of the Lower Rhineland, a miracle of life amidst all this ancient death.

At Koblenz, at the junction with the Moselle, and not far from the junction with the Lahn, the wine road becomes a three-pronged fork, the middle prong going as far as Bonn. Thereafter, reaching the northern limit of the area dictated by nature, the vine becomes scarce. Rotterdam and the sea are too far away for wine to reach them except by import. But, if only along one half of its course, the story of the vines of the Rhine gives us a convincing example of what a natural means of communication can bestow upon man by way of increasing his pleasure and his profit. Despite many bloody episodes, the Rhine has been more than a left and a right bank; there has been an upstream and a downstream as well, a flowing route which, as the centuries passed, spread the art of printing, the humanism of Erasmus, the fantasies of Romanticism and, more recently, the European spirit. More celebrated here than anywhere, the vine has, through undisclosed channels, contributed to an awareness of the Rhine's high mission.

"Wines of the Rhine" covers the wines of the Upper Rhine (the wine-growing cantons of German Switzerland), the wines from the shores of the Lake of Neuchâtel, those of Alsace, and the German wines of Baden, Württemberg, the Palatinate, Rheinhesse, the valley of the Nahe, Franconia, the Rheingau, the valleys of the Moselle, Saar and Ruwer, and of the Ahr and the Middle Rhine (or Mittelrhein).

THE WINES OF THE UPPER RHINE

The wine districts of eastern and northern Switzerland are all part of the Rhine basin. It seems to suit them less well than the Valais and the shores of Lake Leman, though the winegrowing tradition is quite as ancient. The growers formerly produced mainly white wines, but the reds predominate nowadays, except in the vineyards of the Lakes of Biel and Neuchâtel.

In this part of Switzerland the vine seems more threatened than in the Rhine Valley, for various reasons, including the constant growth of industrialization and urbanization and competition from foreign wines. Some vineyards are now mere fossils, such as those of Basel-City, Lucerne, Solothurn and Schwyz, none of which exceeds 20 acres.

Of the old white varieties, the *Elbling* has practically disappeared and the *Raüschling* and *Completer* are merely curiosities; they have been replaced by the *Riesling-Sylvaner*, which is as preponderant in these areas as the *Chasselas* in western Switzerland. The *Riesling-Sylvaner* was produced in 1882 from a cross between the *Riesling*, a late-ripening grape with a high acid content, and the green *Sylvaner* (or *Johannisberg*), also a late ripener. In Germany this variety has kept the name of its inventor, *Müller-Thurgau*. After several years of experiment and improvement, he produced a new variety, stable, prolific, rather low in acid and not exacting about soils. It is the variety best suited to the local climatic and soil conditions. The *Riesling-Sylvaner* gives a wine with a fine bouquet, light-bodied and fresh, with a slight muscat flavour.

The commonest red variety is the *Pinot Noir*, called here the *Blauburgunder*, or *Blue Burgundy*. It was introduced into the Grisons between 1630 and 1635 by the Duc de Rohan who was in command of French troops at Maienfeld. The variety became common in other regions later, especially in regions with a good exposure and a deep, rich, loose soil. The *Pinot Noir* wines produced in the Grisons are, together with the wines of Neuchâtel, the best in Switzerland, but do not give the highest yields.

CANTON OF THE GRISONS. Travelling down the Upper Rhine, we come to vineyards downstream from Chur, those of Costamser, Trimmis and Zizers. Here the *Pinot Noir* produces a light red wine and the *Riesling-Sylvaner* a white with a strong bouquet.

After the junction with the River Landquart, the Lower Rhine Valley seems more suited to the vine, and the vineyards of the Grisons Seigneury—the Bündner Herrschaft—spread over the communes of Malans, Jenins, Maienfeld and Fläsch. By far the commonest variety (99 per cent) is the *Pinot Noir*, which was introduced during the Thirty Years War. This region of the Grisons, less frequented by tourists than the Engadine, enjoys a very pleasant climate, especially in September and October; fog is virtually unknown and though the *fœhn*, the warm south wind, is unpleasant to man, it is beneficial to the grape, which thus ripens in conditions more favourable than those in many other parts of German Switzerland.

Most of the vineyards are owned by smallholders who trellis the vine and devote to its care about 400 to 600 hours per acre per year. Though this vine has never been afflicted with the phylloxera, it is being gradually replaced with resistant stocks. A variety of unknown origin, the *Completer*, is still to be found in the commune of Malans; it produces a white wine which is a local speciality. The best Grisons growths are the reds, which are fragrant and well-balanced. They are drunk young and preferably on the spot. The yield is very variable, but averages 132,000 gallons.

CANTON OF ST. GALLEN. Further down the Rhine we enter the Canton of St. Gallen. The area under wine cultivation may be divided into three regions:

1. The southern region, with the vineyards lying between the districts of Bad Ragaz, Sargans and Lake Walen. The wines are mainly red, and the best-known growths include the SCHLOSS WERDENBERG and the PORTASER from Pfäfers.

2. The northern region comprises the vineyards situated between Hub and the entry of the Rhine into Lake Constance. As in the northern part of the Grisons, the valley of the Rhine is suitable here for vinegrowing, but the area under cultivation has shrunk by three-quarters since the end of the last century. The best red wines bear the names of BALGACHER, SONNENBURGER, REBSTEINER, MARBACHER, PFAUENHALDE, ROSENBERG, EICHHOLZ, MONSTEINER, BERNERKER and BUCHENBERG, the latter known as "the pearl of the Rheintal". The FORSTWEIN from Altstätten fetches remarkable prices. All these wines are from the *Pinot Noir* grape, locally known as *Blauburgunder*. The two winegrowing communes of the Canton of Appenzell, Wolfhalden and Lutzenberg, may be added to this region; they produce, half and half, red and white wines for local consumption.

3. The small vineyards in the north-west of the Canton, Bronschhofen and Wil, where the WILBERG is highly appreciated. Growers in this region make a wine from red grapes after removing the stalks, known as BEERLIWEIN; it is full-bodied and fragrant and has a heavy bouquet.

CANTON OF THURGAU. The vineyards of Thurgau lie between the lower arm of Lake Constance, the Rhine and the Thur. Most of them (80 per cent) produce a red wine from the *Pinot Noir*, the remainder being a white from the *Riesling-Sylvaner*.

The ARENENBERG DOMANE is worth bearing in mind and tasting locally. Further south, the vineyards of Stettfurt produce the famous SONNENBERG, a growth of admirable consistency.

Almost all the wines in this region are drunk locally. The tourist will certainly drink them with the local dishes—*féra*, a fish from Lake Constance, with a white wine from the Untersee; and slices of liver pâté, Thurgau style, with a red from Warth.

CANTON OF SCHAFFHAUSEN. In the Schaffhausen region, the vine crosses the Rhine to the right bank. The foothills at the end of the Jura form a protecting screen. The *Pinot Noir* is grown on the heavier soils, the *Riesling-Sylvaner* on the chalk regions.

In 1900, the area grown to vine was 2,710 acres; it has stabilized in recent years at between 890 and 940 acres.

Some 90 per cent of the area produces red wines from the *Pinot Noir*. The whites come from the *Riesling-Sylvaner* and are distinguished by a very strong bouquet. Some other varieties (*Pinot Gris* and *Elbling*) are rarely to be found. Hallau is the largest winegrowing commune, and its most notable wine is the HALLAUER "IM HINTERE WAATELBUCK", a red of first-rate quality. Passing through Schaffhausen, where the traveller will visit the Zu Allerheiligen Museum or the Falls of the Rhine, according to his taste, he will be able to sample a full-bodied red, the MUNOT, which takes its name from the squat keep which dominates the town and the Rhine valley.

CANTON OF ZURICH. Further south again, in the Canton of Zurich, residential and industrial areas have gradually encroached upon the winegrowing area, which has shrunk from some 12,400 acres at the beginning of the century to 740 today. The climate is less suited to the vine in this region than on the banks of the Rhine, particularly because of the spring frosts. The vine clings, however, to the most sheltered and sunniest slopes. This winegrowing area may be divided into three regions:

1. In the north: the Zurich vineyards—the district is called the *Weinland*, or wine country—follow on from those in Thurgau and, like them, produces red wines from the *Pinot Noir* and whites from the *Riesling-Sylvaner* and the *Raüschling*, full-bodied wines which are suitable for laying down.

2. Farther to the west, the Zurich Unterland is still part of the Jura and produces a great variety of wines,

mostly reds from the *Pinot Noir* and whites from the *Riesling-Sylvaner*. These are local wines for local consumption.

3. In the south: the shores of the Lake of Zurich and the banks of the Limmat, downstream from Zurich, produce wines which are well reputed. Stäffa, the largest winegrowing commune in the canton, is proud of its STERNENHALDE and its LATTENBERG; Herliberg produces a CLEVNER SCHIPFGUT, well-reputed among local connoisseurs. Other wines are APPENHALDE, CHORHERRENHALDE, ÄBLETEN and TURMGUT. Weiningen, on the slopes of the Limmat, is the second largest winegrowing commune in the canton.

The people of Zurich have many local dishes and it is not hard to find a range of wines worthy to go with them. However, these pleasures of the table are confined to those who can take advantage of an undisturbed sojourn in the canton, since none of the wines grown under what are called "regional agreements" may be exported.

CANTON OF AARGAU. The course of the Limmat takes us quite naturally into the Canton of Aargau. Here the vine spreads along the slopes of the Aare and its tributaries, the Limmat and the Reuss, on the sheltered slopes of the Jura and the north-eastern shore of Lake Hallwil. The area covers no more than 740 acres. The *Riesling-Sylvaner* (27 per cent) and the *Pinot Noir* (55 per cent) are the two main varieties. The wines are light and fragrant, with a low alcohol content. The white wines, such as the SCHINZNACHER RÜHBERG, have a bouquet that is highly appreciated; the reds, especially the NETTELER, GOLDWAND and BRESTENBERGER, are excellent table wines.

The vineyards in the Canton of Lucerne, an extension of the Aargau vineyards southwards, are certainly more of a curiosity than anything else, since they cover only 4 acres (171 ares).

CANTON OF BASEL. From the border of the Canton of Schaffhausen to Basel there are no vineyards along the Rhine. The twin cantons of Basel-City and Basel-Country each possess some vineyards. That of Basel-City—there is only one—is on the other side of the Rhine at Riehen, is called *Im Schlipf* and is only about 2 ½ acres in area. Basel-Country is rather better off (about 125 acres), particularly on the end slopes of the Jura and along the Birs. Very little but white wines are produced, from the *Chasselas* and the *Riesling-Sylvaner*, and they are curiosities more for the local fancier than the passing tourist.

CANTON OF SOLOTHURN. Going up the Aare from Basel we cross the Canton of Solothurn, which produces local wines with an alcoholic content varying from 9º to 11º. The white wines are from the *Chasselas*, locally known as the *Gutedel*, and the reds from the *Burgunder*. The winegrowing area in Solothurn has been greatly reduced in less than a century and today covers only about ten acres.

CANTON OF BERN. We now come to the Lake of Biel, the north shores of which, backed by the Jura, form a winegrowing district from Vingelz-Biel to La Neuveville, extending westwards into the Canton of Neuchâtel. It is planted almost entirely with *Pinot Noir* and *Chasselas*, the latter greatly predominating. These wines are light, fragrant and sharp, and are best drunk young. The best-known are the TWANNER and the SCHAFISER. A long way upstream, at the very threshold of the Alps, there lie the vineyards of Spiez and Oberhofen, which produce white wines from the *Riesling-Sylvaner* and reds from the *Pinot Noir*.

THE WINES OF NEUCHÂTEL

Although they are part of the Rhine basin, the vineyards along the shores of the Lake of Neuchâtel are in French Switzerland, a Latin country. That is perhaps why a local poet has asserted that "The land of Neuchâtel is not yet of the South, but is by no means any longer of the North."

In this region, transitional both geographically and historically, the vine seems to have been known even before the coming of the Romans. Winegrowing in this district has been established with certainty by a document dating from A.D. 998; Rodolphe, Lord of Neuchâtel, donated a vineyard at Bevaix to the Abbey of the Benedictines at Cluny. Today, the winegrowing region of the Lake of Neuchâtel extends along the lower foothills of the Jura from the Lake of Biel to the banks of the Orbe; the western part, in fact, lies within the Canton of Vaud. This region takes the form of a long ribbon some 30 miles in length by less than a mile in breadth. Along the lake it is about 1,300 feet above sea-level; the highest vineyards are at 1,800 feet, but most lie between 1,300 and 1,600 feet. These benefit from the lake's heat and stabilizing influence; at Neuchâtel itself the mean winter temperature is 1 to 1.5 degrees higher than at Fribourg or Bern. In summer the vine receives light and heat reflected from the lake, but it is subject to spring frosts despite the range of the Jura which protects it from the cold north winds. The area under vine cultivation is at present 1,560 acres in the Canton of Neuchâtel and 500 acres in the Canton of Vaud.

The markets for Neuchâtel wine trade have varied greatly. At times the trade was mainly with Bern, at others with Solothurn when that city received the foreign ambassadors accredited to the Federal Diet. There is a story that the boatmen carrying barrels of Neuchâtel to Solothurn sometimes succumbed to the temptation to sample the goods, replenishing the casks with the same volume of water.

The wines of Neuchâtel are well known today far beyond the frontiers of Switzerland. They are now sold under the generic name of NEUCHÂTEL, since the quality of the vineyards is remarkably homogeneous. Some growers and estate-bottlers add a place or growth name. The knowledgeable wine-lover may well choose a NEUCHÂTEL-SAINT-BLAISE or a NEUCHÂTEL-CORTAILLOD, denoting communes, or a NEUCHÂTEL-CHÂTEAU D'AUVERNIER or NEUCHÂTEL-HÔPITAL DE POURTALÈS, denoting a growth. Bottlers and shippers undertake to sell only Neuchâtel wines. There is an official inspection for quality and production. For over twenty-five years the State of Neuchâtel has exercised a control over the alcohol content at harvest time, and this induces growers to defer the picking and pay special attention to quality. The inspectors are paid by the State, must hold themselves available to the bottler and inspect every *gerle* (about 22 gallons) as it reaches the vat.

The Neuchâtel red wines are some of the best in Switzerland. They are splendidly rich in colour and have a strong bouquet, they are fragrant and fairly sharp and develop a delicate and well-bred aroma. One of the best is that of Cortaillod. All are derived from the *Pinot Noir*. The ŒIL DE PERDRIX (partridge eye) also comes from the *Pinot Noir*, but is slightly fermented in the vat; it is a light wine of an intriguing shade and one which is drunk young.

All the white wines (about three times as many as the reds) come from the *Chasselas*. Bottled while they are still on the lees, they retain enough carbonic acid gas to make them slightly sparkling. Locally they are said "to make the star"—i.e. they show the sparkle. They are light and fresh, with a very delicate floweriness. Some may find they have a flinty taste. Besides the wines from the *Chasselas* it is possible to find—but in limited quantities only—whites from the green *Sylvaner*, delicate and well-balanced, from the *Riesling-Sylvaner*, with a strong muscat flavour; from the grey *Pinot*, flowery, supple and bland; and from the white *Pinot*, very delicate indeed. Throughout the region the *Chasselas* whites go extremely well with the fish which are characteristic of the Lake of Neuchâtel, notably those called *palée* and *bondelle*. The reds from

This print of the Romantic period shows the Neuchâtel winegrowing district seen from the south-west near Colombier, looking towards Auvernier and Neuchâtel. The vineyards stretch in a ribbon some 30 miles in length and an average of less than one mile wide. The lake mitigates the harsh climate and the range of the Jura protects the vineyards from the north winds; but frost can do a great deal of damage.

the *Pinot Noir* go very well with red meat or game. Total production year in and year out stands at between 1,320,000 and 1,540,000 gallons.

The westernmost part of the region, which is in the Canton of Vaud, is also planted to *Chasselas* and *Pinot Noir*, as well as some special local varieties. Some growers make the wine "Neuchâtel style", i.e. on the lees, and produce wines comparable to the true Neuchâtel. Others vinify "Vaudois style", by racking, and produce a more supple wine, which, however, in the opinion of some people, loses something of its original quality. Most of these wines are sold under the name BONVILLARS. Both the reds and the whites are typical local wines *(vin du pays).*

Whereas the Vaudois wines of La Côte, Lavaux and the Chablais (see chapter on wines of the Rhône) usually have an alcohol content of 10.5º to 13º, these run from 9.5º to 11º, occasionally to 12º. They are wines which sparkle gaily, but are not treacherous; and they are believed to encourage liveliness and wit in those who drink of them.

In the Rhine basin, too, we should mention the winegrowing district on the southern slopes of Mont-Vully, between the Lake of Neuchâtel and the Lake of Morat. The white *Chasselas* wines are light, acid and fresh; the few red wines from the *Pinot Noir* or the *Gamay* have a fine colour and a distinctly agreeable bouquet. These, too, are local wines.

249

THE WINES OF ALSACE

Alsace lies in a rift-valley running north and south, originating in an ancient massif the remains of which form the Vosges on the west and the Black Forest on the east. Shut in by the Jura on the south and the hills of Lower Alsace on the north, it forms a "punch-bowl" with a continental climate, cold in winter and hot in summer, with its maximum rainfall in July and August and its minimum in winter.

The Alsatian winegrowing district covers the foot-hills of the Vosges from Thann in the south to Marlen-heim in the north. Here, between the Belfort Gap and the Col de Saverne are the only breaches in the mountain wall through which air flows in from the west, to disturb the thermal and climatic balance of the part of Alsace centring on Colmar. This area is practically on the 48th parallel, the same latitude as Orleans. The prevailing winds are south in winter and north in summer. On an average computed over fifty years there are about sixty days of frost annually at Colmar; they occur even at the beginning of May, on the three days known as the *saints de glace* ("the ice saints"). Serious damage is, however, comparatively rare and remains localized. The reason is that the vineyards are situated at a height between about 550 and 1,200 feet, above the fogs that form in the flatlands, and the exposure to the sun and the geological conditions for heat storage are far more favourable than they are in the flatlands. The mean annual temperature at Colmar is 10.8º C.; on the slopes it is several tenths of a degree higher. Since the Vosges themselves catch most of the rain, the rainfall in the foothills is slight, from 20 to 28 inches annually.

The climatic conditions of the Alsatian winegrowing district are therefore extremely favourable. The annual cycle usually follows the same rhythm: budding in mid-April, flowering in mid-June, ripening in mid-August and harvest about October 10th; this gives the grapes about 115 days to develop, spread over a spring which is usually fine, a hot and thundery summer and a sunny autumn. The Alsatian vineyards also benefit from exceptional geological conditions. The foothills of the Vosges are the outcrop of the rift-valley and have a very complex geological structure; triassic, liassic and tertiary jurassic rock lie side-by-side and are blended with modern alluvial deposits, partly covered by older gravelly layers, with scree talus of glacial origin or surface deposits of loess from the flatlands. These climatic and geological conditions are the key to the special characteristics of the wines of Alsace, as compared with other wines, and the key to the principles of Alsatian winegrowing.

CHARACTERISTICS OF THE WINES OF ALSACE

Wine is, of course, produced by the fermentation of the juice of grapes; and grape juice possesses in a latent state all the qualities which the wine may later aspire to. A wine can never be improved; all that can be done is to preserve the qualities it already possesses. The heat stored up during the process of ripening comes out in the sugar concentration and determines the subsequent strength of the wine; the soil forms its body, and the variations in temperature caused by the inflow of continental or oceanic cold air modulate its fragrance. Therefore, as we move from a warm to a cooler region, the sugar content lessens and the strength diminishes; conversely, the acidity increases and reaches the maximum permissible limit near the northerly limit of winegrowing, while the fruity aromas thin out and are finally lost in an acid tartness. This may be demonstrated by following the white wines from south to north and examining the relationship between their two antagonistic components, acidity and sugar. A white wine from the south naturally has an excess of natural sweetness and an inconsistent acidity (Bordeaux wines, MONBAZILLAC, etc.). North of a certain latitude all the sugar can be fermented; this produces a dry wine. If the acidity is comparatively low, the wine takes on fragrance by developing the body (Burgundies, MACON in particular); as it increases, the aromas of the fruit become more prominent and more delicate and the wines become fruity (Alsatian and Austrian wines). Again, if there is a great deal of natural acidity in the grape juice, vinification becomes difficult, for simultaneously to lessen the concentration of acidity and to accentuate the compensating sweetness requires great technical skill and knowledge of vinification.

In Alsace vinification is simple: it is designed purely to keep the wine in its natural state. The alcohol content is usually between 11º and 14º, and in good years many growths retain a few grammes of residual sugar per litre. The tartaric acid content of the matured wines ranges from 5 to 7 grammes per litre. The prerequisites for producing a well-balanced wine are therefore excellent. But to preserve the original and special character of an Alsatian wine it is essential to preserve the taste of the fruit, that is its fruitiness and its youth. Hence oxidation must be prevented at all costs, since that would mean vinifying in the Burgundy manner, and this would completely change the wine's type. This technical detail of winemaking is a very delicate matter and requires constant vigilance, which accounts for the fact that the winegrowers of

Alsace refuse to deliver in cask and bottle their own wines in their own cellars as early as the month of May.

To sum up, the wines of Alsace have three basic characteristics: freshness, fruitiness and youth, owing to the triple balance between body, acidity and the taste of the fruit. They therefore give an impression of freshness, delicacy and "race", varying with the variety of the grape and the relation between the three components. People accustomed to the creamy quality called *moelleux* are somewhat startled by their first taste of an Alsatian wine, since the threefold balance typical of it is almost unique among the French wines and even among the German; but they speedily acquire a taste for these attractive and well-bred wines which conceal a relatively luxuriant substance behind a cool approach; they are always natural, frank and genuine.

THE PRINCIPLES OF ALSATIAN WINEGROWING

Alsatian winegrowing is governed by climatic and geological imperatives and by tradition.

Except for a few climatically similar districts in Central Europe, there is no winegrowing district where the vine grows as densely as in Alsace. Mounted on stakes, the vines usually grow to about 7 feet 8 inches (2.4 metres) and consequently bear a high yield. The district, therefore, is naturally propitious to quantity production, and efforts have always been made to push it in that direction, whereas the Alsatian grower in his wisdom, taking advantage of the extreme geological variety of the soil, has devoted all his attention to finding the variety of grape that will enable him to combine satisfaction of the market demand with the essential maintenance of the quality of his wines.

It has been stated in various works on the subject that the Alsatian winegrowing region has been considerably reduced in area. In actual fact it has remained practically the same for centuries, but it must be understood that "the winegrowing district of Alsace" means the traditional winegrowing region on the foothills of the Vosges, about 30,000 acres under production and 5,000 to 7,500 acres fallow or being readied, in accordance with the normal growing cycle. Since 1961 the whole of this region has been officially recognized as a winegrowing district entitled to the so-called *appellation d'origine contrôlée* (A.O.C.). It produces some 15,400,000 gallons annually, 99 per cent of it white wine. This delimitation is the outcome of constant efforts over many years to recover the stability and quality control which was formerly customary in the towns and villages in the district, which did their utmost to reduce or even eliminate winegrowing on the flatlands and to prevent the planting of coarse varieties with excessively large yields.

A ministerial decree with force of law issued in 1945 defined the varieties permitted. There are now considerably fewer, only those which furnish the most dependable quality having been retained. A distinction is drawn between the noble varieties—*Riesling, Muscat, Gewürztraminer,* the *Pinots* (white, grey, or Alsatian *Tokay,* and red) and *Sylvaner*—and the ordinary varieties, the *Chasselas, Knipperlé* and *Goldriesling.* All the others listed in the older classifications have disappeared.

These varieties are of very ancient stock; most of them, mentioned from the sixteenth century onward, have been selected by centuries-old tradition and long deliberation. Each requires the appropriate soil, the limestone supplying lightness and elegance and the clay body and solidity. Whereas the *Sylvaner* is fairly indifferent to the type of soil, the *Pinots* prefer chalk and the *Muscat* and the *Gewürztraminer* soil rich in clay; the *Riesling,* on the other hand, does best on primary formations. Given the extreme variety of the soils, each commune is able—some, of course, more successfully than others—to grow most of the varieties.

THE WINES OF ALSACE

The ZWICKER is a light and pleasant wine with no great pretentions, generally served as a carafe wine. It comes from several varieties of grape, usually the *Chasselas,* and legally must be from a noble variety.

The SYLVANER is fruitier and sharper, with an apparent sparkle, and is very pleasing to drink. It is of good quality at Barr; very full-bodied in the Haut-Rhin; and really appetizing at Westhalten.

The PINOT BLANC is a very well-balanced wine which could be described as discreet and distinguished. It is currently very popular.

The ALSATIAN TOKAY, from the grey *Pinot,* is a wine of rare elegance with a regal build; it is the richest of the Alsatian growths and has a most attractive velvety flavour. It is called Tokay because of the tradition embodied in an ancient legend that General Lazare de Schwendi, warring against the Turks in Hungary around 1560, brought back some roots which he cultivated in his conservatory at Kientzheim. This wine is still grown around Kientzheim in the central district of the Haut-Rhin area, between Eguisheim and Bergheim, where the best-known Alsatian vineyards are situated.

The ALSATIAN MUSCAT is the wine with the strongest but also the freshest bouquet in the whole range of Alsatian wines. Its fruitiness is very characteristic; it faithfully reproduces the savour of the fresh grape.

The GEWÜRZTRAMINER, which is known outside Alsace sometimes simply as "Gewürz" and sometimes as "Traminer", is the great Alsatian speciality. This wine is clothed in velvet, it is perfumed, it is brilliant and it seduces the ladies, for it is potent and enchanting.

The RIESLING is an elegant and distinguished wine, with a great deal of discretion. Delicate and fragrant, it has a fine and subtle bouquet. Many Alsatians call the RIESLING the emperor of Alsatian wines. The RIESLINGS of Turckheim and Bergheim in the Haut-Rhin and Dambach in the Bas-Rhin are highly spoken of. These wines age extraordinarily well.

FROM PRESS TO TABLE

Until a few years ago the whole grape harvest was pressed by the grower and the wine was sold by the barrel in the grower's own cellar after tasting, comparing and discussing the price with the shipper, innkeeper or private buyer through a local expert broker. Since 1945 the Alsatian wine district has undergone a great, though necessary, change; but a change that is rather to be regretted nevertheless. Formerly all the growers used to keep their own wines in their own cellars and people visited them there, tasted, laughed, spent whole nights among the vats, sang, emptied glasses and ate bacon or smoked ham with the wine.

This atmosphere is now to be found only at the cellars of a few large growers. The handlers, who bring in their own grapes, vinify their wines and sell them direct to the consumer. Many of the growers' cellars are empty and the magnificent oak barrels ring hollow; the grapes are sold to the trade or taken to the co-operative, which does the winemaking and marketing. Some of the poetry is lost, but quality is gained.

Growers, co-operatives and handlers very seldom sell their wines by the barrel, but in bottles known as Alsace *flûtes*, holding 72 centilitres (about 24 fluid ounces) for quality wines or a litre for carafe wines. The ordinary wines are bottled in March and the better wines in May or June. All these bottles bear a label which must state *Appellation Alsace Contrôlée*, usually with the addition of the name of the grape variety and the shipper. Sometimes such qualifications as *grande réserve*, *grand vin* or *vin fin* are added; these are conventional terms for wines which must by law be over 11° in strength. The consumer thus receives wines which are absolutely reliable.

All that the buyer has to do, therefore, is to lay the bottles down in a cool and slightly damp cellar kept in the dark at a temperature of about 12° C. If this is done, a quality wine will keep from five to ten years depending on whether it is a full-bodied wine, that is to say, of a sunny vintage year, or a lighter wine of a year in which there was not much sun. The Confrérie Saint-Etienne, the main selling and connoisseur organ-ization, even has bottles of the 1834 and 1865 vintages, over a century old but still in perfect condition; actually, 1834 was a fairly difficult year but 1865 was the great year of the century.

Alsace wine is drunk cool, but not iced, at a temperature of about 12° C. If the chill is taken off slightly, it develops its bouquet deliciously, but keeps its youthful flavour. It may, of course, be drunk by itself as a thirst-quencher; the CHASSELAS, ZWICKER and SYLVANER are wines of which one can never grow tired. Even better, for sipping, are the PINOT BLANC or the EDELZWICKER, while on great occasions one of the Big Four, RIESLING, MUSCAT, TOKAY or GEWÜRZ-TRAMINER, with a slight preference for a fine MUSCAT.

The Alsatians always take some rather out-of-the-way snack with their wine, such as walnuts and wholemeal bread with a new wine, or unsweetened tarts with cheese puff paste or almonds or olives, before they sit down to a board amply stocked, but not as groaning as it was in the old days. Alsace, despite its many misfortunes, has always been a wealthy region and for centuries the granary and cellar of a large part of Europe. It had everything—fish, fowl, meat of all kinds, game, frogs, snails, white bread, cheese, and, above all, splendid wines which were exported in all directions from as early as the seventh century to stock the tables of prince and wealthy merchant.

Alsace has the reputation of always keeping a decent balance from every point of view, and all excess at table is frowned upon. Libations are copious, true, but never to excess; the Alsatian knows by nature how to drink decently, and he never fails to stop before laughter degenerates into imbecility. At table the wines are married to the dishes in accordance with simple rules conforming to the methodical Alsatian nature. An ordinary carafe wine is adequate with a good choucroute, a baeckaeffa or cold meats for a modest meal. Or, if something rather better is wanted, a PINOT BLANC or a modest RIESLING. For a more elaborate meal, with cheese and dessert, a bottle of TRAMINER is opened towards the end of the meal. The number of glasses beside each place increases for a banquet, for each dish calls for its own wine. Thus, a RIESLING is proper—or, going down the scale, a PINOT or a SYLVANER—with dishes which are not highly seasoned, such as asparagus, shell-fish, trout *au bleu* or white meat. The GEWÜRZTRAMINER is essential with a lobster *à l'américaine* or a well-ripened, strong munster or roquefort cheese, for it marries with them inimitably. For rich food, such as Strasbourg foie gras, the TRAMINER, and especially the TOKAY, is essential for the marriage. For the main dish the choice is wide open, though a really good vintage TOKAY is not to be sneezed at on occasion.

Alsatian women are excellent cooks, but a bottle of wine beside the pot is needed, for plenty of wine used in cooking a country dish makes it far more digestible.

The Alsatian philosophy of the table is that you must never eat purely for eating's sake nor drink simply to drink; but you should eat to drink better and drink to eat better. And the Alsatians take great care to stick to this maxim.

The Alsatian vineyards are among the oldest in France; they appeared soon after those around Narbonne. They experienced great prosperity from the seventh century onward, growing with that of Strasbourg, long the largest river port on the Rhine and the most famed wine market in central Europe; and this lasted until the Thirty Years War, which brought endless disturbances in its train. The winegrowing district was rich, but not opulent; it was and still is bourgeois; there are no châteaux, only cities and affluent market towns with a rigid sense of duty.

The Alsatian winegrower is a bourgeois; he is his own master; serfdom and share-cropping have never existed. He buys his land, never rents it; he makes his wine and he ensures that it is good enough for himself and his friends. This accounts for his character, and, too, the degree to which in Alsace, a wealthy and generous land, everything is imbued with balance.

THE WINES OF GERMANY

Germany, together with Canada and the U.S.S.R., is the most northerly winegrowing country in the world. Comparatively weak sunlight lasting over a long period creates the ideal conditions for white wines with a low alcohol content, an acid freshness and a bouquet not blurred by a high sugar content.

Winegrowing reached the Celtic area on the left bank of the Rhine before the Roman era, and excavations in the valleys of the Moselle, the Ahr and the Middle Rhine have demonstrated conclusively that the Romans cultivated the vine on the left bank. On the right bank in Roman times there was some trade in wine, and it has been proved that in the Frankish period (about A.D. 800) winegrowing was carried on everywhere where the vine still grows, while during the warm period of the Middle Ages it extended in a most remarkable way throughout the territory of the Germanic Holy Roman Empire. In the twelfth century the vine was grown in East and West Prussia and in Mecklenburg, and even in parts of Schleswig-Holstein and in Denmark.

A regression began in the sixteenth century and has not yet been halted. The deterioration of the climate after 1550 was only one factor. Imports of better quality at moderate prices by the League of Hanseatic towns and the dissolution by the Reformation of the monasteries which had hitherto been the main centres of winegrowing were disastrous to North Germany. In other regions, such as Württemberg, winegrowing never recovered from the Thirty Years War.

In addition, consumers' tastes changed. Wine had conquered regions whose climate was generally unfavourable to the slow ripening of grapes. It would hardly be true to say that the Germans of the Middle Ages preferred bitter drinks as well as having a documented predilection for bitter foods. The wine often produced nothing but alcohol; it was sweetened with honey, spiced and very often heated and drunk as a sort of hot punch. Until the end of the sixteenth century the consumption of wine must have been ten times higher than it is now. Bavaria, nowadays considered to be wholly devoted to beer, grew wine in the fifteenth to seventeenth centuries even in the Upper Bavarian regions.

But around 1500 the art of winning alcohol by distilling other fruits became widespread in Germany, and beer, which was dearer than wine till about 1550, became much cheaper. All these reasons, not to speak of the huge burden of customs duties and excise, account for the fact that the winegrowing area today is considerably less than half what it was around 1550.

In recent years the yield of must has been some 132,000,000 gallons. The greater proportion of this, 90,200,000 gallons, is supplied by three adjacent regions: the Palatinate, Rheinhesse and the valleys of the Moselle, Saar and Ruwer. Comparatively insignificant districts such as the Ahr (74,000 acres) and the Middle Rhine, including Siebenbergen (173,000 acres), remind us that the vine was once grown much farther to the north until the competition from wines imported from southern Europe, through Hamburg especially, became so fierce that German wine production fell off steeply, a decline hastened by the devastations of the last of the great religious wars. Present-day consumption amounts to an average of 28 pints per capita; 36.4 per cent of it is met out of imports.

GRAPE VARIETIES. Some of the whites—*Riesling, Sylvaner, Traminer, Ruländer*—do not give of their best except in good years and in very sunny exposures. This is notably the case with *Riesling*. Others, however, like the *Müller-Thurgau*, ripen more quickly and produce an agreeable wine even if there is not much sun.

The soil also makes a great deal of difference; indeed, it and the variety together determine the wine's character. This particular feature distinguishes Germany sharply from the other winegrowing countries. It is due to the low alcohol and sugar content; since neither of these two components are present in large quantities to affect the wine's smell and taste, the delicate qualities derived from the rocks in the sub-soil which do affect nose and palate come into their own.

Germany leaves the pre-eminence in the red varieties to her neighbour to the west. But the *Spätburgunder*, the German version of the Burgundian *Pinot Noir* grape, grown on red sandstone and schist, gives a ruby wine of a firm ripeness, outstanding in quality, deep burgundy in shade, with a character that yields nothing to wines from other countries. This is true, too, of the garnet-coloured *Frühburgunder*; the wine is first-rate, full-bodied, sometimes velvety; the *Portugieser* produces a paler wine, which has little bouquet and is lighter; it is sensitive to frost and early-ripening, and it is drunk young. In good years it is warm and velvety and its colour becomes dark red.

The better German wines have a character all their own—fruity acidity, balanced, flowery bouquet, a low alcohol content and lightness—and are thus a type of wine for which there is an evergrowing demand.

BADEN

The winegrowing region of the Upper Rhine, incorporated by referendum since 1952 in the *Land* of Baden-Württemberg, is divided up into six completely different winegrowing districts. In the south-west, on the shores of Lake Constance—at Meersburg to be exact—there is the SEEWEIN. This sharp and full-bodied wine from the *Ruländer*, *Traminer* and *Burgunder* varieties grown on moraines suffers from the altitude, and this is only partly counterbalanced by the southern climate and the broad stretch of water. Here, as elsewhere in Baden, is the famous WEISS-HERBST, derived from a *Burgunder* vinified as a white wine. It is full-bodied with a fine bouquet.

On the deep clayey soils, partly covered with loess, of the Margraviate, between Basel and Freiburg-in-Breisgau, the *Gutedel*, or *Chasselas*, imported from Geneva in 1780, produces a soft, perfumed wine of low acidity. Between Freiburg and Baden-Baden three regions share the warmth of the upper valley of the Rhine and the protection of the range of the Black Forest against the east winds: Breisgau, the vineyards of the Kaiserstuhl and Ortenau. On the Kaiserstuhl the vine grows on volcanic tuff, in Breisgau on loess, in Ortenau on granite, near Freiburg and in the valley of the Glotter on gneiss.

A wide range of grape varieties are grown on this variety of soils, no one of them predominating. The 20,600 acres of the winegrowing area in Baden are planted 23.4 per cent to *Müller-Thurgau* and 21 per cent to *Blue Spätburgunder*; *Gutedel (Chasselas)* 16.2 per cent, *Ruländer* (grey *Pinot*) 13.5 per cent, *Sylvaner* 8 per cent and *Riesling* 6.8 per cent. But 11 per cent is still left for the *Traminer*, *Portugieser*, old varieties such as the *Elbling* and *Raüschling*, and new selections such as the *Freisamer*. The must harvest amounts to an average of 154,000,000 gallons a year.

At Neuweier and in neighbouring areas the MAUER-WEIN is bottled in flagons, or *Bocksbeutel*, as in Franconia; elsewhere in long bottles, as in the Moselle. One sixth of the 400,000 farms cultivate the vine as well as other crops. Baden is a *Land* of wine co-operatives; there are about 110 of them and they account for two-thirds of the production. They are managed by an organization called the Central Federation of Wine-Growers' Co-operatives.

Among the Breisgau wines the GLOTTERTÄLER is famed and, indeed, rather feared for its effects.

The best wines come from the Kaiserstuhl, which dominates the plain of the Rhine. The principal places are Achkarren (SCHLOSSBERG), Ihringen (WINKLER BERG, FOHRENBERG, ABTSWEINGARTEN), Bickensohl (STEINFELSEN, EICHBERG, HOCHSTATT), Oberrottweil (HENKENBERG, KIRCHBERG, EICHBERG), Bischoffingen (STEINBRUCK, ROSENKRANZ) and the State domains of Blankenhornsberg. The vine grows everywhere on the eroded basaltic tuff of the old volcano, producing wines of a *Sylvaner* type, full and ripe, the *Riesling*, acid and elegant, the *Spätburgunder*, outstanding, and the *Ruländer*, ardent and impetuous with a soft and exquisite fruity flavour.

In the Ortenau, where the *Riesling* is called *Klingelberger* after the castle around which it was first planted in 1776, there are also some wines of quality at Durbach, Ortenberg, Neuweier and Oberkirch, for instance; the best red wines of the Ortenau are derived from the *Blauer Spätburgunder*. The MAUERBERG at Neuweier and the SONNENBERG, the KLOSTERBERG and the NÄGELSFÖRST at Varnhalt are wines of repute. This district also produces perfumed TRAMINERS reminiscent of the Alsatian wine.

In the Bühlertal red wines predominate, such as WALDULM, KAPPELRODECK, BÜHLERTAL and AFFEN-

TALER, the label of the latter being decorated with a monkey, although the name really comes from the Latin greeting *Ave*.

Northern Baden up to Heidelberg once had extensive vineyards, but in many places they have been reduced to insignificance by industrialization. But on the slopes of the Kraichgau and the Odenwald, BERGSTRASSENWEINE (wines of the mountain road) are still produced, as well as table wines from north of Heidelberg. Lastly, at the north-eastern end, the Taubergrund produces a wine which is almost contiguous at Wertheim-am-Main with the Franconian wines, which it closely resembles.

The Badeners' "wine road" is considerably longer than the Palatines', for Baden extends for 125 miles. A Baden label guarantees the quality of the wine.

WÜRTTEMBERG

The vineyards are terraced in the valleys of the Neckar and its tributaries, the Jagst, Kocher, Rems, Enz, Murr, Bottwar and Zaber. The soil is partly triassic and partly conchiferous limestone. The triassic soils are heavy and chalky, especially where they are broken down by deposits of marl. The conchiferous lime is lighter and warmer.

Until the Thirty Years War the Swabian wine district covered a million acres. Today it has only 15,750 acres producing 10,120,000 gallons of wine. The main variety is the *Trolinger* (28.4 per cent), which is found only in Württemberg and produces a brick-red, full-bodied wine; 24.8 per cent is planted to *Riesling* and 13.1 per cent to *Sylvaner*. The remainder is divided between the *Portugieser* (10.6 per cent), the *Müller-Thurgau* (6.3 per cent), the dark red *Limberger* (6 per cent), the *Samtrot* and the *Schwarzer Urban*.

Near Reutlingen the vineyards climb to over 1,700 feet. The cultivation is a typical co-operative enterprise. In 1920 the co-operatives took over a district which had gone completely out of cultivation for many years and have brought it to a level which can bear comparison with other districts. The Württemberg wines are hard to find on the market; apparently, the growers drink their wine themselves, usually very young, in the first two years.

One of the Württemberg specialities is the SCHILLERWEIN, something like the French rosé. It is made either by blending red and white grapes in the press or by leaving the skins of red grapes in the must for a short time (which is how the WEISSHERBST is produced in Baden). Another Württemberg speciality is a young wine which has not completed the fermentation process; it is called SUSER and is a very good and easy wine to drink. The communes of Cannstatt, Untertürckheim and Feuerbach produce excellent growths.

Stuttgart, the capital of Baden-Württemberg, is not only a large centre of the wine trade but still has an 2,000-acre vineyard. A French saying of about 1630 claimed that "if the grape of Stuttgart were not picked, the city would drown in wine".

The *Sylvaner* grape produces fresh green wines in the upper valley of the Neckar. There are fragrant, full-bodied Rieslings in the valley of the Rems as well as luscious Sylvaners. The Rems valley produces the famous STETTENER BROTWASSER. The valleys of the Murr and the Bottwar shelter Steinheim, Kirchheim, Murr, Kleinbottwar, Grossbottwar, Lombach and Marbach, the home of the poet Schiller, whose family is said to have given its name to the SCHILLERWEIN.

There is another place with the name of Stetten in the red wine district of Heuchelberg and, farther on, Schwaigen. In the valley of the lower Neckar there is Lauffen, where the vine grows on conchiferous lime, as at Heilbronn and Flein. It is on this soil too that the *Riesling* and *Sylvaner* of Taubergrund ripen. Maulbronn and Gundelsheim, as well as Schnait in the valley of the Rems, produce wines which are well spoken of.

THE PALATINATE

The Palatinate in the *Land* Rhein-Pfalz has 45,000 acres of vineyards and produces 37,400,000 gallons of must on an average; it is the largest wine-growing region in Germany. The *Sylvaner* is the principal variety of vine-plant grown in this district, with 39.6 per cent of the total area, followed by the *Müller-Thurgau* with 20.4 per cent, the red *Portugieser* with 17.7 per cent and the *Riesling* with 13.6 per cent. As early as the period of the Holy Roman Empire the Palatinate was known as "the wine-cellar of the Empire". This region is particularly favoured by nature; it gets an average of 1,875 hours of sunshine and the winter lasts less than three months. The vineyards are mostly on the flatlands and are easy to farm mechanically; only in a few places are they situated as high as 900 feet. The Haardt mountain range, which is an extension of the Vosges, protects the Palatinate plain from the bitter north winds and from the rain and snow from the west. Indeed, so sheltered is the district and so mild the climate that even figs and lemons, apricots and peaches can flourish there. The vine stretches in a ribbon 50 miles long by some two to four miles wide from the Alsatian border northwards to the edge of the Rheinhesse along the *Weinstrasse* (wine road) from the Wine Gate at Schweigern to Grünstadt.

The region is rich in archaeological finds which prove that the Romans cultivated the vine here on a large scale. Many of these finds are to be seen in the Wine Museum at Speyer, the largest in Germany. The importance of this winegrowing district at the time of the Frankish kingdoms was due to the fact that by the Treaty of Verdun in A.D. 834 which parcelled out the empire of Charlemagne, the region of Speyer, Worms and the Nahe was given to Germania because of its wealth of wine *(propter vini copiam)*.

The Palatinate comprises three winegrowing regions: the Oberhaardt, the Mittelhaardt and the Unterhaardt. The Oberhaardt, or Upper Haardt, is covered with fertile loess on which the *Sylvaner* produces a fresh and generous table wine for ordinary consumption *(Konsumwein)* in more than 50 communes between the Alsatian border and Neustadt. The *Traminer*, with its noble and discreet bouquet, also prospers. Hambach, Maikammer and Edenknoben are noted for their high yields. The best growths are to be found between Gleisweiler and Hasbach; Edenknoben and Diedesfeld are the best-known communes, producing sound and characteristic wines.

Farther north, the transition to the Mittelhaardt, or Central Haardt, is virtually imperceptible; the best-known communes are Deidesheim, Ruppertsberg, Forst and Wachenstein. The district extends to Dachenheim and Weisenheim-am-Berg. The soils are lighter on the whole, compounded of sand and warm gravel; the rainfall is slight. The Forst and Deidesheim vineyards are improved with powdered basalt, which makes them even warmer.

On the escarpments of the Haardt range there are triassic, red sandstone and schist outcrops, besides granite, gneiss and schist, and chalky and clayey alluvial deposits at the foot of the range. The *Riesling* is not much grown, but produces a vigorous and fruity wine here, with the very prominent tang of the local soil called *Schmeck*; but the *Sylvaner* is also represented by soft and rather sweet wines of a high quality—as, indeed, are the *Gewürztraminers*, which produce wines that are both fiery and round.

The Mittelhaardt produces the heaviest must in Germany. In 1959, a hot year, the must of the Haardt wines sometimes titrated at over 300° Ochsle. In the large vineyards which produce these selected and dried-out grapes they remain on the stem until as late as mid-November even in average years.

The nearly 3,500 different types of wine are being systematically reduced. Besides the great internationally famous estates (such as Bassemann-Jordan, von Buhl and Bürklin-Wolf) there are co-operatives which own huge vineyards. A large percentage of vinegrowers vintage their wines at these co-operatives, of which there are usually two in each village, divided as they are by their religious or by their political leanings.

A list of the most famous names in the Central Haardt would certainly include the following growths (classified by commune): at Forst DOPP, GRAINHÜBEL, HOCHENMORGEN, KIESELBERG, LEINHÖHLE, MÄUSHÖHLE, MÜHLE, MÜHLE UND GEHEU and RENNPFAD; at Ruppertsberg HOFSTUCK, HOHEBURG and NUSSBIEN; at Wachenheim BÖHLIG, GOLDBÄCHEL, LUGINSLAND and RECHBÄCHEL; and at Bad Dürkheim HOCHMESS, MICHELSBERG and SPIELBERG.

Second only to these great wines there comes a group which includes some other first-rate wines. For example: at Forst KRANICH, LANGENBÖHL, MUSENHANG, PECHSTEIN, WALSHÖHLE and SCHNEPPENPFLUG; at Deidesheim BILDSTÖCKL, HAHNENBÖHL, HERRGOTTSACKER, HOFSTÜCK, LANGENBÖHL and LANGENMORGEN; at Königsbach IDIG, ROLANDSBERG and BENDER; at Wachenheim DREISPITZ, FUCHSMANTEL, GERÜMPEL and SCHENKENBÖHL; at Bad Durkheim FROHNHOF, HOCHBENN, KLOSTERBERG and NONNENGARTEN.

There are also wines of quality at Gimmeldingen (MEERSPINNE and SCHILD), Kallstadt (NILL and SAUMAGEN), Ungstein (HERRENBERG, HÖNIGSÄCKEL and SPIELBERG) and at Freinsheim, Herxheim-am-Berg and Mussbach.

The Unterhaardt, or Lower Haardt, which stretches as far as Rheinhesse and the Nahe, supplies *Konsumwein* and table wines, the ZELLER SCHWARZER HERRGOTT being the best of them. The Unterhaardt accounts for about 13 per cent of the Palatinate production, the Mittelhaardt for about 35 per cent and the Oberhaardt for 52 per cent. A poet has said of Palatinate wine that in combining maturity with gentleness it is the maternal female among wines, and another has described it thus: "The wine of the Palatinate has the advantage over its two brothers (the Rheingau and the Rheinhesse) of having its own very special temperament, which ranges from the gracious levity of adolescence to the impetuous passion of the grown man, from blooming, perfumed and frivolous youth to noble, polite and dignified maturity."

256

The Rheingau, where some of the best-known vineyards of Germany line the right bank of the Rhine, which here flows east and west, giving the vines a southern, sunny aspect.

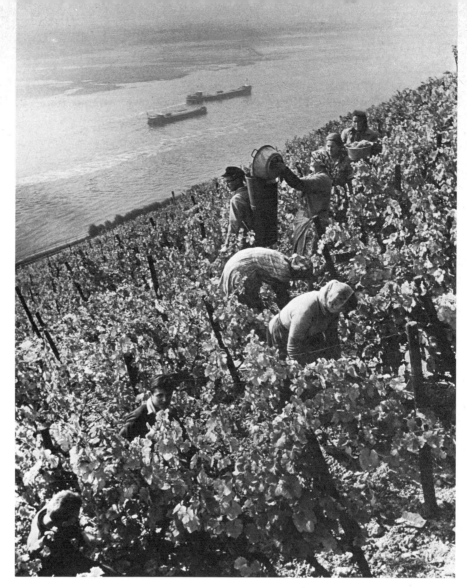

The Kaiserstuhl, the remains of an old volcano, dominates the Rhine plain and produces some of the best wine of Baden from its tufa soil.

RHEINHESSE

From the name one would suppose that Rheinhesse was the old *Land* lying between the Imperial Cathedral Cities of Worms and Mainz, but that disappeared from the political map in 1945. Rheinhesse is now a region of the Rheinpfalz, a *Land* of the Federal Republic, with Mainz as its capital. In the south the Palatinate vineyards near Worms merge into the Rheinhesse. In the north and east the border follows the bend of the Rhine from Bingen to Worms, and in the west it extends up the valley of the Nahe. Legend is fond of associating the cultivation of the vine in the Rheinhesse with Charlemagne, but, as in other regions, there is evidence that it existed there as early as A.D. 753.

The Rheinhesse is the second-largest winegrowing district in Germany. Extending over 176 communes, 40,500 acres are planted to vines, 8.5 per cent to red varieties (almost all *Portugieser*). The *Sylvaner* predominates among the whites (with 47 per cent), followed by the *Müller-Thurgau* (33.2 per cent) and the *Riesling* (6.2 per cent). The harvest of must amounts to one quarter of the entire German yield.

The *Sylvaner* grows best on heavy soils, producing a sweet wine with a rich bouquet. This valley country has chalky and marly soils as well as clayey soils which, though none too good in wet years since the water does not drain off easily, are very favourable to the grape in hot summers. Loess and friable sandstone are also common, particularly between Worms, Osthofen and Oppenheim. On the mountain slopes in the south-eastern part of the region the vineyards are set on porphyritic quartz with a high potassium content. On the other hand, around Nachenheim and Nierstein there are surface outcrops of red sandstone and sandy clay of the Permian period. Near Bingen the vineyards are set on quartz shales, the soil best suited to the *Riesling*, and produce a light, luscious wine with a natural sweatness smacking of the grape.

The Rheinhesse wine best known abroad is not a growth. Large vineyards cultivated by monks stretch round the church of Our Lady of Worms. "Monk" is *minch* in the local dialect and becomes *milch*, and this is the origin of the name Liebfrauenmilch, which has been adopted for all the sweet wines of the Rheinhesse that have the fine qualities of Rhine wine. Even the neighbouring wines of the Palatinate claim the right to sell under the LIEBFRAUENMILCH label.

The quality wines in the strict sense come from the district along the Rhine. The hinterland to Alzey and the valley of the Nahe supplies *Konsumwein*. Mainz and Worms are the capitals of the German wine trade. The vineyards are mostly owned by small-holders, medium-sized holdings and co-operatives, but, for all that, Bingen, Nierstein and Oppenheim have estates which enjoy a world-wide reputation.

Oppenheim, with its chalk and marl, produces *Auslese* (wines from carefully selected bunches of grapes) and *Beerenauslese* (selected berries, i.e. wines made from overripe grapes that have acquired the noble rot—the *Edelfaüle*—picked immediately after the harvest and pressed separately). These wines can attain great age. The Oppenheim wines are heavy and ripe, particularly such great growths as KREUZ and KRÖTENBRUNNEN, together with the world-renowned REISEKAHR.

On the red sandstone spur which crops out at Nierstein white wines are produced which are indubitably among the best-known in the world; they have a fruity bouquet and great elegance. Thirty years ago an attempt was made to reduce the vast number of names which had led to a great deal of confusion, especially abroad. A single name was selected for each growth to include all the others, but this necessary reform is still only a project. The names of the wines with a world-wide reputation are AUFLANGEN, REHBACH, BRUDERSBERG, ÖLBERG, GLÖCK, PETTENTAL and FLÄSCHENHALL. Just behind them come HEILIGENBAUM, ORBEL, FUCHSLOCH, KRANSBERG, FLOSS, HIPPING, KEHR and SANKT KILIANSBERG.

But Rheinhesse is, of course, more than the OPPENHEIM, NIERSTEIN and LIEBFRAUENMILCH names combined, although the ROTTENBERG from Nackenheim and the STEIG from Dalsheim are perhaps the only other "internationally reputed growths" besides those already listed. Above Bingen the Rochusberg—with the SCHLOSSBERG, SCHWÄTZERCHEN and ROCHUSBERG—and the Scharlachberg produce very high quality wines; and the following are also certainly worth mentioning: HOCH SANKT ALBAN, WESTRUM and SILBERBERG from Bodenheim; ENGELSBERG and FENCHELBERG from Nackenheim; and STEIG and RODENSTEIN from Dalsheim.

We come at length to Ingelheim, where the blue *Burgunder* produces the famous reds of SONNENBERG, PARES and GRAVER STEIN.

Shortly after 1800 the Romantic poet Ludwig Tieck described the Rheinhesse wines in the following terms: "These excellent spritely waves which range from the light LAUBENHEIM to the strong NIERSTEINER in whetting your whistle flatter the palate, purifying, refreshing and toning up the senses. To what should they be compared but to the tranquil steadiness of good writers, to generosity and fullness devoid of chimeras and gothick allegory?"

THE VALLEY OF THE NAHE

The winegrowing valley of the Nahe stretches from Bingerbrück at the junction of the Nahe and the Rhine to Martinstein, with the lateral valleys of Guldenbach, Trollbach, Grafenbach, Alsenz and Glan. An area of 7,500 acres is planted to the vine, almost entirely of white varieties. The *Sylvaner* predominates with 40 per cent; the rest is half-and-half *Riesling* and *Müller-Thurgau*. The annual yield is some 5,280,000 gallons. Politically, the Nahe region was part of Rhenish Prussia until 1940; it is now a region of the Rheinpfalz.

The soil in the upper Nahe valley, terraced between the Hunsrück and the Soonwald, is Devonian, whereas the deeper and narrow valleys are mostly schist. The wines are fresh and metallic, something like those of the Saar. This is the country of Monzingen, whose wines were lauded by Goethe, and the Ebernburg, "the asylum of justice", where Franz von Sickingen gave refuge to the exiles of the Reformation.

The soil of the Middle Nahe is clayey and sandy, composed of calcareous sand and porphyry. Where the valley widens along the prehistoric Rhenish sea the vine springs up on clay, marl and loess. The variety of soils is reflected in the great variety of the wines, unexampled in such a small area.

The KUPFERGRUBE of Schlossböckelheim, the KAUTZENBERG, BRUCKES, KRONENBERG, KRÖTENPFUHL and NARRENKAPPE of Bad Kreuznach, the ROTENFELS of Münster-am-Stein and the HERMANNSBERG, HERMANNSHÖHLE, ROSSEL and ROSENBERG of Niederhausen are internationally renowned. The other growths from Schlossböckelheim, Waldböckelheim, Kreuznach, Münster-am-Stein, Niederhausen and Norheim are well spoken of, and the Alsenz and Glan valleys produce equally good wines, especially those from Altenbamberg, Ebenburg and Dielkirchen.

The State lands around Schlossböckelheim and Niederhausen originated on land cleared of forest. The area was later extended by taking over abandoned farms and by buying up vineyards near Altenbamberg which had long lain fallow after the ravages of the phylloxera. The nobel wines come from the State domain of Niederhausen, between Schlossböckelheim and Bad Kreuznach, and the volcanic soils near Münster-am-Stein. They are fruity and luscious, at times oncoming and vigorous, at times gently mature, with a special and attractive character all their own.

For centuries the pun was repeated (in German) that the *Weine bei der Nahe* (wines beside the Nahe) were *beinahe Weine* (almost wines). In 1816 only 2,500 acres were planted to the vine. The area has multiplied three fold in 80 years when many other winegrowing districts were diminishing.

FRANCONIA

At the beginning of the nineteenth century there were still some 27,000 acres planted to vines in Franconia in the Free State of Bavaria; today, there are only 5,700 acres, with an average annual yield of 2,640,000 gallons of must.

The Franconian vineyards stretch from Hanau in the west to Bamberg in the east, and in the north from a line running from Bad Kissingen to Hammelburg to near Ansbach in the south. The climate is oceanic west of the Spessart range and continental east of it. Geologically, Franconia is Triassic marl from Zeil-am-Obermain to the Aichgrund, conchiferous lime from Schweinfurth to Ochsenfurth and variegated sandstone on the western slopes of the Spessart. The pebbly soils are in many places covered with loess and sand. The yield per acre is only 350 to 1,100 gallons, but this means that the wine has all the more body and bouquet. The bouquet and not the alcohol content has given it the reputation of a heady wine. The *Sylvaner* predominates, with 55.2 per cent.

The *Müller-Thurgau* accounts for 31.7 per cent and the *Riesling* is inconsiderable, with only 4 per cent, though it should be said that the *Riesling* is the variety that produces the best growths from Würtzburg, the capital, namely the sweet and round LEISTE and the STEIN, sharp and perfumed, the wine which has lent its name to the typical wine of Franconia, the STEINWEIN. The wines from Eschendorf, Randersacker and Iphofen are equally good. Eschendorf produces the best, LUMP, KIRCHBERG, EULENGRUBE and HENGSTBERG; the vines grow on chalk-and-clay strata here, with loam and silt. Randersacker has the PFÜLBEN, a wine with a world-wide reputation, and the HOHBURG, SPIELBERG and TEUFELSKELLER; Iphofen produces the JULIUS-ECHTERBERG and KRONSBERG KALB UND KAMMER. But Hörstein and Frickenhausen also produce wines of the best quality, as does Klingenberg, where the *Burgunder* grows on variegated sandstone.

Besides such celebrated vineyards as the Juliusspital and Bürgerspital there are several co-operatives. The

KREUZNACHER HINKELSTEIN

This straightforward label gives the following details: 1. Name of region: valley of the Nahe. – 2. Name of growth and vintage. – 3. Grape variety: Ruhländer, the German name for the grey Pinot. – 4. Auslese means that the grapes were specially selected at harvesting. – 5. Grower's name.

RAUENTHALER GEHRN

This is a rather more elaborate label. – 1. Wine from the Rheingau. – 2. Name and vintage of wine. – 3. Grape variety: Riesling. – 4. Spätlese: late-gathered, therefore a fairly sweet wine. – 5. Grower's name. – 6. Naturrein – i.e. natural wine with no sugar added. – 7. Cabinet: special reserve. – 8. Estate-bottled.

IHRINGER WINKLERBERG

The Baden vineyards lie in German territory opposite Alsace. This is a wine of the Oberrhein-Baden region, situated along the Rhine north of Basel. – 1a. The Kaiserstuhl vineyards lie on the slopes of the volcanic mountain of that name in Breisgau. – 2. Growth: Winklerberg from the village of Ihringen. – 3. Grape variety and vinification: Pinot Noir pressed to produce a rosé. – 4. Auslese: specially selected grapes. – 5. Grower's name. – 6. Estate-bottled.

IPHÖFER KAMMER

The Franconian wines are put up in broad-beamed flagons called "Bocksbeutel", hence the unusual shape of the label. 1. Region: Franconia. – 2. Growth: Kammer from the village of Iphofen, and vintage. – 3. Grape variety: Sylvaner; special reserve; no sugar added. – 4. Estate-bottled and grower's name.

WEINSBERGER SCHEMELSBERG

This label denotes a type of red wine very popular in Germany. –
1. Wine from Württemberg. – 2. Growth: Schemelsberg from the village of Weinsberg, and vintage. – 3. Grape variety: Spätburgunder. – 4. Grower's name.

FORSTER JESUITENGARTEN

The Palatinate wines have a great reputation and this is a very celebrated label. – 1. Name of region: Rheinpfalz, or Palatinate. – 2. Growth: Jesuitengarten from the village of Forst, and vintage. – 3. Grape variety: Riesling; Trockenbeerenauslese – selected grapes gathered when overripe and dried out, therefore a sweet wine. – 4. Grower's name. – 4a. The grower is sole proprietor of this growth. – 5. Estate-bottled.

WEHLENER SONNENUHR

Moselle is so well known for its Riesling grapes that the grape variety is not mentioned on this label. – 1. Region: Mosel-Saar-Ruwer. – 2. Growth: Sonnenuhr from the village of Wehlen, and vintage. – 3. Eiswein Auslese means a wine made from grapes caught by an early frost, carefully gathered and immediately pressed. This is therefore, an "ice wine", rare and with a very special bouquet. – 4. Grower's name. – 5. Estate-bottled. – 6. The grower is a member of growers associations to promote the sale of wines of high quality.

Arranged like a sort of giant stairway for heroes from the Niebelungen saga, this vineyard surrounds Schloss Ehrenfels, which dominates the gorge of the Rhine at Bingen opposite the Mouse Tower. Here is one of the most celebrated growths of the district, the "Rüdesheimer Schlossberg".

largest State domain in Germany is in Franconia, covering about 400 acres. The Carolingians bestowed large donations of vineyards upon the monasteries scattered throughout the region. After the separation of Church and State, all the Church property reverted to the Free State of Bavaria. The properties include some of the most famous Franconia wines, especially the STEIN at Würzburg, the SCHALKSBERG and the LEISTE on the other bank of the Main and, farther upstream, the RANDERSACKER, and downstream the THÜNGERSHEIM. The Bavarian Wine Institute, of which the former Royal Bavarian Cellars at Würzburg and the State Wine Institute at Veitshochheim are branches, has a great reputation for experimental cultivation. With few exceptions, the wines of Franconia are put up in the special flagon called *Bocksbeutel*.

The wine of Franconia smacks of the soil that produces it. It can be full-bodied and down to earth, but it may also be well-bred and fresh. In any particular year, its quality greatly depends on the weather. This wine has all the variations of cold steel, from the supple Damascene blade to the Turkish scimitar.

THE RHEINGAU

The 7,584 acres of the Rheingau vineyards are divided up among no more than twenty communes and stretch for some 30 miles along the right bank of the Rhine between Wiesbaden and the valley of the Wisper near Lorch (Hochheim-am-Main also belongs to the Rheingau). The region was part of Rhenish Prussia until 1946, after which it was included in the *Land* of Hessen, the capital being Wiesbaden, itself a winegrowing commune of the Rheingau. The Rhine, which elsewhere flows north and south, here flows east and west. The vineyards in the "elbow of the Rhine" enjoy a full southern exposure, so that they have a truly southern winegrowing climate, especially as the Taunus range of hills protects the Rheingau from the cold north winds and the river bends enough to cut off most of the wind from the east or the west.

An inland geological sea and its deposits which were covered with a layer of clayey loess in the Diluvian epoch gradually built up the Upper Rheingau in terraces from Hochheim to Rüdesheim. The southern slopes, which rise to 600 feet, draw additional warmth from the sun's reflection from the Rhine, which is some 800 yards wide in this part. The warm summers and the humidity from evaporation make up for the frequently inadequate warmth of the soil.

Upstream from Rüdesheim the river flows between high cliffs and its bed is 600 feet deep. The shores are no longer gentle slopes, as in the Upper Rheingau, but sheer drops, terraced with innumerable low walls climbing from the river to the top of the cliffs some 900 feet above. The Rhine flows through Assmannshausen, which produces from the *Spätburgunder* a red wine with a strong flavour of almonds. But white varieties are grown in the rest of the Rheingau.

In area the Rheingau is only the seventh-largest German winegrowing district, but in quality its wines rank with the best in the world. The Hochheim wines have such a reputation in Britain that all Rhine wines are called hock there. The saying "a good hock keeps the doctor away" was probably coined at the time Queen Victoria visited Germany, but the wines from the Rheingau had been celebrated since the sixteenth and seventeenth centuries, owing particularly to the highly skilled viniculture practised at the Abbeys of Johannisberg and Eberbach. It was here that the first *Spätlese* wines were made, from overripe grapes picked after the ordinary harvest, and especially the *Trockenbeerenauslese*, wines made from overripe grapes which have acquired the "noble rot" and have been left to dry on the vine, somewhat like corinth currants. Ten women have to work for two whole weeks to gather enough grapes to make 20 bottles of these wines. It is no accident that such wines are found only here, for the autumn mist that rises from the Rhine, known as the *Traubendrücker*, or grape-presser, causes the grapes to become overripe and to acquire the noble rot *(Edelfäule)* and, if the weather is suitable, the grapes may be picked as late as the second fortnight in November. One of the regional specialities is the EISWEIN ("ice wine") which comes from sudden frosts; the frozen water remains in the press and the vat collects only an extract of the ethers of sugared oils and perfume.

All the best growths are produced by the *Riesling*, which accounts for 77 per cent of the area planted to vines; the remainder is partly *Müller-Thurgau* (17.9 per cent) and partly *Sylvaner* (7.6 per cent). The average yield is about 4,620,000 gallons. The vineyards, because of the inheritance laws, are mostly smallholdings. The large properties, however, are also very productive. There are hardly any co-operatives.

The wines from the *Riesling* combine an elegant fruitiness and sweetness with acidity in a noble harmony which the connoisseur calls *finesse*, meaning something like "supreme delicacy". The bouquet is flowery and elegant. Though made from overripe grapes, the wines of the Rheingau are light, considerably lighter, for instance, than the fine wines of Baden or the Palatinate. This is due in great part to the soils. On the terraces above the Rhine the vine grows on sericite and clayey shale and often, too, on quartz. The eroded rocks have broken down into clayey and loamy soil and the alluvial loess has a high lime content.

It is hard to choose among so many very great wines. Of those with a world-wide reputation Hochheim would undoubtedly be represented primarily by the DOMDECHANEY, KIRCHENSTÜCK, RAUCHLOC and STEIN. Eltville produces the KALBSPFLICHT, KRUMBCHEN, MONCHHANACH, SONNENBERG, TAUBENBERG and the ELSFELD, Elsfeld being the former name of the place at the time when the Archbishops of Mainz resided there. The wines from Eltville, like those from the large vineyards owned by the Graf von Eltz and the Barons Langwerth von Simmern, are of great character.

Erbach too has wines with a world-wide reputation, such as the famous MARKOBRUNN from a vineyard bordering Erbach and Hattenheim, and the BRÜHL, HOHENRAIN, RHEINHELL and SIEGELSBERG; Hattenheim can boast of the ENGELMANNSBERG, HASSEL, MANNBERG, NUSSBRUNNEN and WISSELBRUNN; Östrich the DOOSBERG, EISERWEG, KELLERBERG and LENCHEN. The EDELMANN and OBERBERG are the two main growths from Mittelheim. All these are wines of the *Riesling* type, full-bodied and with a magnificent bouquet.

Immediately thereafter comes Winkel; Goethe esteemed its noble wines, such as the DACHSBERG, HASENSPRUNG, JESUITENGARTEN and OBERBERG. In the commune of Winkel, too, there is Schloss Vollrads, which has been in the possession of the Greiffenklaus family since the fourteenth century, and nearby is Schloss Johannisberg, presented by the Emperor of Austria to Prince von Metternich in 1816. Some connoisseurs consider the SCHLOSS JOHANNISBERGER the king of German wines, but the HOLLE, MITTELHOLLE, KLAUS and KLAUSER BERG are equally magnificent.

Geisenheim produces the ROTHENBERG, DECKER, HOHER DECKER, KOSACKENBERG, LICKERSTEIN and MÄUERCHEN; and the next town, Rüdesheim, boasts internationally reputed wines: the RÜDESHEIMER BERG, BRONNEN, BURGWEG, DICKERSTEIN, HAUPTMANN, HELLPFAD, LAY, MÜHLSTEIN, PAARES, ROSENECK, ROTTLAND, STUMPFENORT and ZOLLHAUS and the BISCHOFSBERG and SCHLOSSBERG growths. The Rüdesheim wines are reputed to be particularly full-bodied.

Assmannshausen is known for its red wines from the *Spätburgunder* grape, the main growths being the HÖLLENBERG and HINTERKIRCH. Some connoisseurs consider that the red wines of Assmannshausen are the best in Germany. The most important vineyard in the region, the ancient Höllenberg, was already under cultivation at the beginning of the twelfth century. Rauenthal produces the BAIKEN, GEHRN, HERBWEG, ROTHENBERG, WÜLFEN and WIESHELL. These upland wines have a remarkable body and bouquet, and some people say they are for gentlemen only, but their velvety suppleness and delicate perfume recommend them to the ladies too.

Of the wines of Kiedrich we may mention the GRÄFENBERG, WASSEROS, SANDGRUBE and TURMBERG. A few miles farther on grows the STEINBERG, the vineyard, like the Abbey of Eberbach, being State property. The name alone has such a reputation that the grower adds only the description of the method used—*Kabinett* (or "special reserve"), *Spätlese* (late picking), *Auslese* (specially selected berries, or grapes), *Beerenauslese* (specially selected berries, or grapes) or *Trockenbeerenauslese* (selected overripe grapes left on the vine till dried in order to achieve the maximum sugar content possible). There only remains Hallgarten,

with its DEUTELSBERG, HENDELBERG, JUNGFER and SCHÖNHELL; its clayey marl produces wines highly esteemed for their great elegance and full-bodied character. The vineyards here rise to 900 feet.

The State domains in the Rheingau date back to 1866, when the Duke of Nassau had to cede his possessions to the King of Prussia. The Steinberg, the largest single vineyard, is 125 acres in extent. The domain also includes vineyards at Rüdesheim, Hattenheim, Rauenthal, Kiedrich and Hochheim, as well as the Assmannshausen vineyards, which produce mainly red wines. The State owns in all over 350 acres, almost all the whites coming from the *Riesling* grape.

The Institute for Tree, Wine and Horticultural Research, founded at Geisenheim in 1872, is in the forefront of wine research in Germany, while the former Cistercian Abbey at Eberbach is a kind of pilgrims' shrine for wine-lovers.

An English poet who compared the German wines to people called the Rheingau wine "a noblewoman". It should be respected accordingly.

MOSELLE - SAAR - RUWER

The three valleys of the Moselle and two of its tributaries, the Saar and the Ruwer, extend for some 190 miles. The winegrowing district of the Moselle stretches from Perl to Koblenz for 125 miles. From the ancient and fairy-tale-like village of Serrig to the junction with the Moselle near Konz the Saar district spreads for some 30 miles, and Waldrach-Sommerau is some 75 miles from the junction of the Moselle with the Ruwer. There are also some good vineyards along such tributaries of the Moselle as the Dhron and the Lieser. Most of the district is in the Rheinpfalz, and only a very small part of it, with 125 acres of vineyards, encroaches upon the Saar.

The three valleys form a unit, though their wines have characteristics all their own. All of them share the typical *Riesling* bouquet and have a fine and fruity acidity. The Saar wines are sparkling and well-bred; the Ruwer wines are noted for their so-called smoky taste and elegant acidity. The Moselles are usually fuller-bodied. The district is divided into the Upper, Middle and Lower Moselle. The vineyards are protected by the cliffs of the Hunsrück and the Eifel. They follow the windings of the river, which wanders so much that, especially in the Middle Moselle, the loops seem to cross their own course and the river triples its length. Hence the exposure keeps changing, so that many sunny slopes facing east and south give way without transition to shady woods and pastures. The canalization of the Moselle has proved advanta-

geous because of the intenser reflection of the sun due to the uniform raising of the water level.

Unlike the vineyards in the Palatinate and the Neckar valley, the vineyards here are situated on the slopes. They are so steep in the Lower Moselle that all farming has to be done by hand. As at Bremm, the growers have to carry back in hods the earth washed down by the rains. Here the vineyards can no longer compete within the Common Market with vineyards that can be worked by machine.

The banks of the Moselle between the Lorraine border and the junction with the Saar are made of white chalk; thence to the junction with the Ruwer they are the red sandstone of the Trier basin. Only thereafter begin the blueish banks of shale.

Winegrowing in the valley of the Moselle is the oldest in Germany. It may well have been introduced into the Trier region, then Celtic, by Greek colonists from Massilia (Marseilles) before the Roman conquest of Gaul.

The old grape variety *Elbling*, which was the only one grown along the Moselle before the Thirty Years War, now covers only 11 per cent of the 25,000 acres of vineyards, which produce only whites. The *Riesling* is ahead with 79 per cent; the remainder is *Müller-Thurgau*. The average yield is 19,800,000 gallons.

The Upper Moselle, stretching from the Luxembourg border to the junction with the Saar near Trier, produces lesser table wines, which are also used for the manufacture of sparkling wines. The Lower Moselle between Boulay and the junction with the Rhine produces ordinary *Konsumwein*, but in places some very decent table wines, at Bremm, Ediger, Beilstein, Valwig, Pommern and Winningen. Sometimes they have some of the characteristics of Rhine wines. The growers gather them with some difficulty from the parcels terraced steeply above each other.

The Middle Moselle is one great vineyard from the old Imperial Roman City of Trier to Alf and Bullay. The most famous villages are Trittenheim with its ALTÄRCHEN, APOTHEKE and LAURENTIUSBERG; then Neumagen (ROSENGÄRTCHEN, ENGELGRUBE and LAUDAMUSBERG), Dhron (HOFBERG, ROTERD and SÄNGEREI) and Piesport (GOLDTRÖPFCHEN, GÜNTERSLAY and FALKENBERG). Piesport is world-famous for the unequalled *finesse* of the perfume of its wines. After Wintrich, with the Ohligsberg and Geierslay, we very soon come to Brauneberg, which until only fifty years ago was still called Dusemont (from the Latin *in dulce monte*—"on the sweet hill"), a very appropriate name for it, for all the Great Growths, such as the FALKENBERG, HASENLAUFER and JUFFER, have a southern

exposure and produce a very delicate bouquet. The following villages produce wines with a world-wide reputation: Lieser (NIEDERBERG), Bernkastel, Kues, Wehlen, Graach, Zeltingen, Erden, Ürzig and Traben-Trabach. The BERNKASTLER DOKTOR, also sold under the name of DOKTOR UND GRABEN, and facing it, at Bernkastel-Kues the JOHANNISBRÜNCHEN, KARDINALSBERG and PAULINUSHOFBERG open the way to the culminating point of the Moselle vineyards, Ürzig. The famous wines of Wehlen are the LAY, NONNENBERG and SONNENUHR; at Graach the ABTSBERG, DOMPROBST and HIMMELREICH; at Zeltingen the HIMMELREICH and SONNENUHR again and the SCHLOSSBERG; at Erden the BUSSLAY, HERRENBERG, PHÄLAT and TREPPCHEN; at Ürzig the WÜRTZGARTEN; and at Traben the GAISPFAD, GEIERSLAY, KRÄUTERHAUS and WÜRTZGARTEN.

The Saar produces wine on its lower stream after emerging from the industrial region. It then becomes a narrow picturesque valley in which the vine roots bristle from the steep and rocky slopes. The vineyards begin near Staadt, and there are decent wines at Serrig, Saarburg and Irsch (HUBERTUSBERG), and especially

The painter Janscha produced this watercolour in 1789; it shows the village of Oestrich beside the Rhine and, on the far right, Schloss Johannisberg. The Emperor Francis II of Austria presented this property to Prince von Metternich in 1816 in gratitude for his restoration of Austrian power in Europe. Today, Schloss Johannisberg produces the greatest and the most famous wines of the Rheingau district.

The commune of Zeltingen, in the central part of the valley of the Moselle, contains three of the greatest growths in this district: Zeltinger Rotlay, Zeltinger Himmelreich and Zeltinger Schlossberg. These vineyards, with a fine sunny exposure and a very considerable yield, were a source of contention between the Archbishops of Trier and Cologne for centuries; neither would yield these fine wines to the other.

good ones at Ayl (KUPP), Ockfen (BOCKSTEIN, GEISBERG and HERRENBERG), Wavern (HERRENBERG) and Wiltingen (SCHARZHOFBERG, BRAUNE KUPP and DOHR). Wiltingen is the largest viticultural commune in the Saar valley. Its most famous vineyard, the Scharzhofberg, was not planted until 1750.

Some of the best wines from Oberemmel are the AGRITIUSBERG, SCHARZBERG and HÜTTE. The ALTENBERG, SONNENBERG and HÖRECKER are the best from Kretnach; Filzen produces a HERRENBERG; and, lastly, the FALKENSTEIN, from Konz, like the SCHARTZHOFBERGER from Wiltingen, needs no commune name.

The Ruwer produces great wines at Waldrach (HAHNENBERG, HUBERTUSBERG, JESUITENGARTEN, JUNGFERNBERG and KRONE), at Kasel (NIES'GEN, KERNAGEL and KÄULCHEN) and from the two large vineyards at Grünhaus (MAXIMIN GRÜNHÄUSER) and Karthaüserhof, which belonged to the Carthusian Order from the fourteenth century on (EITELSBACHER KARTHÄUSER HOFBERG). There is also the vineyard at Avelsbach (ALTENBERG, HERRENBERG and HAMMERSTEIN). All over the Moselle, Saar and Ruwer districts one is struck by the abundance of ecclesiastical names. The Bishop of Trier and the monasteries, which have done so much for the cultivation of the vine since the establishment of Christianity in these parts, still own the best vineyards, such as the Bernkastel Hospital, founded at Küs by Cardinal Nicolas de Cusa.

The State domain in the Moselle was founded at the beginning of this century. It did not acquire existing

266

vineyards, but planted new ones, originally as a social measure. As the tanners' bark from the oak forests had been replaced by chemicals in the tanneries, the plantations of oak on the slopes of the Saar and the Ruwer ceased to be profitable. But good quality wines could prosper here, and so 198 acres were planted at Ockfen in 1896 and more later at Avelsbach and Servig.

Moselle wines cleanse the palate and stimulate the appetite. They go best with fish, hors-d'œuvres and salads. Lively, a soft green in colour, they are of invigorating freshness. When young, Moselle contains a little carbonic acid gas and pricks the tongue; it is slightly sparkling. It is drunk young, for its freshness and character are liable to go off with age. Moselle needs sun; it does not attain its natural sweetness in years when there is not much sun and has to be improved artificially. "Nowhere else," Baudelaire said, "is so much hard work, so much sweat and so much ardent sun needed to bring the grapes to life and to imbue the wine with soul."

THE VALLEY OF THE AHR

The Ahr virtually follows the northern border of the Rheinpfalz. Winegrowing is restricted to a strip some 15 miles long in the lower valley, where the vine is set on shale. It grows on rocky terraces, very narrow in places, where a thin layer of earth often holds only a few roots. With its 16 winegrowing communes and 1,312 acres, producing 660,000 gallons of wine at most, at the most northerly limit of winegrowing in the world, the Ahr wine district is romantic. Moreover, it is the largest red wine district in Germany, though the 31.1 per cent of *Portugieser* and 23.2 per cent of *Spätburgunder* are supplemented by 43 per cent of white grapes, 23 per cent *Riesling* and 16 per cent *Müller-Thurgau*. It is to be hoped the region will remain faithful to the *Spätburgunder*, which derives a warmth and special fineness from the sun-drenched schist. Especially round the State domain, the former monastry of Marienthal, noble, velvety and soft red wines are produced in good years. The winegrowing district begins at Altenahr, where the Ahr finishes its romantic course between cliffs, continues via Rech, Mayschoss and Dernau to Ahrweiler, Marienthal and Walportzheim, and ends at Bad Neuenahr and Heimerzheim.

Co-operatives first arose in the Ahr district, which formerly experienced great difficulty in marketing its wines, and spread throughout Germany; the fact that holdings were only about an acre in extent made it necessary to regroup them if they were to survive.

THE MIDDLE RHINE

All the wines from north of a line running from Bingen to Lorchhausen—except the valleys of the Moselle and the Ahr—are designated as coming from the Mittelrhein, or Middle Rhine. The region is part of the Rheinpfalz, except the northern part, which encroaches upon Rhein-Westfalen. The winegrowing area, stretching for more than 75 miles and containing 104 communes, totals 2,412 acres. It has constantly diminished over the past few centuries; in 1883 it was still 7,907 acres. As late as 1828 there were 2,903 acres of vineyards in the district of Neuwied; there were no more than 534 in 1949. Red wine exists in any quantity only in the Siebenbergen district. The *Riesling* predominates in the Middle Rhine proper (87.7 per cent). The *Müller-Thurgau* accounts for as much as 34.6 per cent in the Siebenbergen, but elsewhere for only 6.2 per cent. The total yield is some 1,540,000 gallons.

This decline is not due only to a falling-off in quality. Industry has drained off labour from winegrowing, and on the flatlands other kinds of fruit are more profitable. The phylloxera, too, was a decisive factor in this reconversion. Faced with such economic risks, most of the Mittelrhein growers decided not to replant vines. On the left bank there are no vineyards north of Koblenz. The main winegrowing districts on the left bank lie south of Koblenz at Steeg, Bachrach, Oberwesel and Boppard, while Kaub and Braubach are on the right bank. On the right bank the vineyards stretch to Königswinter and Niederdollendorf via Leutesdorf, Hammerstein and Leubsdorf. Bachrach was a famous German wine centre until the eighteenth century, mainly because it was the place where the wines from the Palatinate and the Rheinhesse were transhipped because they could not pass the falls upstream from Bingen.

The rock was formed by the erosion of clayey shales, carboniferous sandstones and, in places, quartzite soils which generally warm up readily. The wines have great body and may be described as sturdy, but have a rather high acidity.

THE WINES OF THE RHINE

SWISS WINES OF THE UPPER RHINE

CANTON OF THE GRISONS

White wines . . . . . . Malanser Completer, Malanser Tokayer, Tokayer Eigenbau, Churer Tokayer aus dem Lochert

Red wines . . . . Malanser Blauburgunder, Malanser Blauburgunder Fuchsen, Malanser Blauburgunder Rüfiser, Churer Süssdruck Lürlibader, Churer Costamser Beerli, Süssdruck Duc de Rohan, Süssdruck Bündner Rheinwein, Malanser Rüfiwingert, Schloss Freudenberg, Maienfelder Blauburgunder Kuoni-Wii, Maienfelder Schloss Salenegg, Jeninser Chüechler Beerliwein, Malanser Beerli Weisstorkel

CANTON OF ST. GALLEN

White wines . . . . . . Tokayer Hoch Chapf Eichberg, Balgacher Riesling-Sylvaner

Red wines . . . . Altstätter Forst, Altstätter Rebhaldner Blauburgunder, Balgach Beerli Blauburgunder, Rebsteiner Süssdruck Blauburgunder, Hoch Chapf Eichberg, Bernecker Blauburgunder, Sarganser Langstrich Blauburgunder, Bernecker Rosenberger, Balgacher Buggler, Walenstadt Beerli Felixer am Ölberg, Melser Beerli Ritterweg, Portaser Blauburgunder, Baccastieler-Beerli Sevelen, Freudenberger Beerli

CANTON OF THURGAU

White wines . . . . . . Kalchrainer Tokayer, Arenenberg Domaine

Red wines . . . . Nussbaumer, Götighofer, Kalchrainer Blauburgunder, Hüttwiler Stadtschryber

CANTON OF SCHAFFHAUSEN

White wines . . . . . . Löhningen, Munötler Tokayer

Red wines . . . . Buchberger, Gächlinger, Osterfinger, Trasadinger, Steiner, Wilchinger Beerli, Hallauer Blauburgunder, Siblingen Eisenhalder, Osterfinger Blauburgunder, Osterfinger-Beerli Badreben, Hallauer Beerli Graf von Spiegelberg, Blauburgunder Beerli Munötler, Löhninger Clevner Beerli, Chäfer-Steiner Blaurock, Hallauer Süssdruck vom Schälleweg

CANTON OF ZURICH

White wines . . . . . . Riesling-Sylvaner Berg am Irchel, Riesling-Sylvaner Meilen, Meilener Räuschling, Riesling-Sylvaner Stäfner, Tokayer Weiningen, Riesling-Sylvaner Weinigen, Eglisauer Riesling-Sylvaner, Eglisauer Tokayer, Weininger Räuschling, Flurlinger Tokayer, Räuschling Kusnacht, Riesling-Sylvaner Sternenhalde

Red wines . . . . Blauburgunder Oberembach, Blauburgunder Schlosshof Berg am Irchel, Birmenstorfer Klevner, Eglisauer Blauburgunder, Stammheimer Blauburgunder, Eglisauer Stadtberger Beerli, Weiniger Klevner, Worrenberger Blauburgunder Rebhüsli, Blauburgunder Burg Schiterberger, Blauburgunder Schloss Goldenberg, Clävner Sternenhalde, Rudolfinger Beerli Blauburgunder, Stammheimer Beerli Blauburgunder, Clevner Sternhalden Stäfa

CANTON OF AARGAU

White wines . . . . . . Zeininger Riesling-Sylvaner, Bözer Riesling-Sylvaner, Tokayer Schlossberg Villingen, Mandacher Riesling-Sylvaner, Riesling-Sylvaner Würenlingen, Schinznacher Riesling-Sylvaner, Schinznacher Rütiberger

Red wines . . . . Birmenstorfer Klevner, Blauburgunder Klingnauer Kloster Sion, Blauburgunder Schlossberg Villigen, Brestenberger Klevner, Döttinger Clevner Auslese, Döttinger Süssdruck, Elfinger Blauburgunder Schlotterboden, Ennetbadener-Beerli, Goldwändler, Klevner Villiger Steinbrüchler Beerliwein, Rütiberger, Wettinger Herrenberg Blauburgunder, Wettinger Kläfner, Wettinger Scharten, Zeininger Clevner

CANTON OF LUCERNE

White wine . . . . . . Riesling-Sylvaner Schloss Heidegg

Red wine . . . . Schloss Heidegg Clevner

CANTON OF BASEL

White wine . . . . Arlesheimer Schlossberg Gutedel

Red wines . . . . Arlesheimer Blauburgunder, Benkener Blauburgunder, Liestaler Blauburgunder

WINES OF LAKES BIEL AND NEUCHÂTEL

CANTON OF BERN

White wines . . . . Ligerzer, Ligerzer Kirchwein, Schafiser, Schafiser Bois de Dieu, Schafiser Engel, Schafiser Stägli-Wy, Schafiser Schlössliwy, Twanner, Twanner Engelwein, Twanner Engelwein pinot gris, Twanner Kapfgut Clos des Merles, Twanner Kapfgut Sous la roche, Twanner Steinächt, Twanner Auslese Johanniter, Der edle Twanner Chroshalde, Twanner Closer, Tschugger, Erlach Chasselas Lamperten, Schlossberg Erlach Gutedel

Red wines . . . . La Neuveville Oeil-de-Perdrix, Twanner Blauburgunder, Schafiser Pinot noir, Tschugger Pinot noir, Schlossberger Erlach Blauburgunder

CANTON OF NEUCHÂTEL
Compulsory generic trade name : Neuchâtel

White wines . . . . Pinot gris, Cortaillod, Auvernier, Cressier, Domaine de Champréveyres, Champréveyres de la Ville, Château d'Auvernier, Domaine de Chambleau P.H. Burgat, Goutte d'or, Domaine du Mas des Chaux, Chasse-Peines, Cru des Gravanys, Hôpital Pourtalès, Cressier La Rochette, La Grillette, Clos des Sous-Monthaux, Francœur, Cru des Bourguillards, Cru des Chair d'Ane, Cru des Merloses

Red wines . . . . Pinot noir, la Béroche, Oeil de Perdrix, Cru d'Hauterive, Francarmin, Cru des Gravanys, Hôpital Pourtalès, Pinot noir Cru des Chanez, Cru de la Ville, La Grillette, Clos des Sous-Monthaux, Tour de Pierre

CANTON OF VAUD

Red wines . . . . Salvagnin Clos du Manoir, Salvagnin Grand Nef, Clos Chenevières, Domaine du Château de Valeyres, Pinot noir Clos du Terraillex, Pinot noir Vin des Croisés

WINES OF ALSACE

Zwicker, Edelzwicker, Sylvaner, Pinot blanc-clevner, Riesling, Muscat, Gewürztraminer, Tokay d'Alsace

WINES OF GERMANY
BADEN

Munzingen	Lindenberg, Berg, Kapellenberg, Steinern
Tiengen	Rebtal, Hauser
Oberrimsingen	
Niederrimsingen	Bürkele, Scheibenbuck, Attila Felsen, Sonnenberg
Opfingen	Vogler, Kessler, Biergarten
Merdingen	Bühl, Mättenziel, Abbeureben
Gottenheim	Kriegacker, Ober-Kirchtal, Hahlen, Unterrain, Oberrain, Besteurein
Wasenweiler	Berg, Kreuzhalde-Staig, Eichen, Bösselsberg-Wanne, Kinzgen-Lot, Grub-Höge, Mamberg, Görn, Flanzer, Schlichten
Breisach	Eckartsberg, Schlossberg, Augustinerberg, Münsterberg
Ihringen	Winklerberg, Fohrenberg, Abtsweingarten, Himmelburg, Vorderer Winklerberg
Blankenhornsberg	Blankenhornsberger
Achkarren	Schlossberg, Büchsenberg, Bömisberg, Traubengarten, Rittersprung, Steinfelsen
Bickensohl	Steinfelsen, Eichberg, Bitzenberg, Käferhalde, Erlenhalde, Roggenberg, Hochstadt
Oberrotweil	Eichberg, Henkenberg, Kirchberg, Käselberg, Steingrubenberg, Wittel, Badenberg, Blindstöckle
Bötzingen	Weingarten, Eckberg, Kirchberg, Ganghalde, Laiere
Eichstetten	Lerdenberg, Mühlenberg, Eichenlaub, Rutzenhalden, Silbern
Burkheim	Burgberg, Käsleberg, Feuerberg, Schlossgarten, Haselberg
Bischoffingen	Enselberg, Hüttenberg, Rosenkranz, Steinbuck
Jechtingen	Eichert, Hochberg
Sasbach	Limberg
Endingen	Herzen, Steingrube, Buchberg
Ortenberg	Schlossberg, Freudentaler Berg, Im Silberlöchle, Im Rot, Im Käfersberg, Im Sonnenschein, Messerschmitt, Trottberg, Im Köpfle, Himmelsleiter, Käfersberger, Gottesacker
Zell-Weierbach	Abtsberg, Bittigrain, Stein, Riesenberg, Schmiedenbrünnle, Kohlenberg, Steinberg
Durbach	Schlossberg, Plauelrain, Herrenberg, Steinberg, Schwarzloch, Annaberg, Staufenberg, Josephberg
Schloss Staufenberg . . .	Schlossberg, Klingelberg
Waldulm	Pfarrberg, Russhalde
Neuweier	Mauerberg, Altenberg

WÜRTTEMBERG
Region of Stuttgart and Essling

Esslingen	Neckarhalde, Schenkenberg, Burgberg
Esslingen-Mettingen . . .	Mettinger Schenkenberg, Mettinger Lerchenberg
Esslingen-Sulzgriess . . .	Sulzgriesser Rosenholz
Stuttgart-Obertürkheim .	Obertürkheimer Kirchberg, Obertürkheimer Ailenberg
Stuttgart-Rotenberg . . .	Rotenberger Schlossberg, Rotenberger Hinterer Berg
Stuttgart-Untertürkheim .	Untertürkheimer Blick, Untertürkiehmer Mönchsberg, Untertürkheimer Goldberg, Untertürkheimer Altenberg, Untertürkheimer Hetzen, Untertürkheimer Semlis, Untertürkheimer Diethof
Stuttgart-Uhlbach . . .	Uhlbacher Steingrube, Uhlbacher Haldenberg, Uhlbacher Götzenberg
Stuttgart-Rohracker . . .	Rohrackerer Edenberg
Stuttgart-Hedelfingen . .	Hedelfinger Linsenberg
Stuttgart-Bad Cannstatt .	Cannstatter Zuckerle, Cannstatter Steinhalde, Canstatter Wolfersberg, Cannstatter Berg
Stuttgart-Mühlhausen . .	Mühlhäuser Berg, Mühlhäuser Wolfersberg
Stuttgarter Stadtgebiet. .	Neue Weinsteige, Mönchshalde, Kriegsberg, Lenzhalde, Obere Weinsteige, Feuerbacher Lehmberg
(the town of Stuttgart)	

REMSTAL

Fellbach	Lämmler, Wetzstein, Berg, Vorderer Berg, Hinterer Berg
Schait	Sonnenberg, Sandmorgen, Halde, Altenberg
Stetten	Häder, Lindhälder, Pfaffenberg, Pulvermächer, Brotwasser
Beutelsbach	Burghalde, Kappelberg, Rossberg
Endersbach	Klinge, Wetzstein
Grossheppach	Wanne, Klingenberg, Altenberg
Kleinheppach	Greiner, Sonnenberg
Korb	Kopf, Sommerhalde, Wanne
Strümpfelbach	Sonnenbühl, Fronklinge
Hanweiler	Berg, Bubenhalde, Kelterweinberg
Grunbach	Halde, Berg, Klingle
Winnenden	Holzenberg, Stöckach

MIDDLE NECKAR

Besigheim	Wurmberg, Neckarhälde, Niedernberg, Enzhälde
Mundelsheim	Mühlbächer, Käsberg, Rozenberg, Himmelreich, Pfaffenklinge, Steig
Hessigheim	Felsengarten, Wurmberg, Katzenöhrle
Walheim	Schalkstein, Eichquell
Gemmrigheim	Niedernberg
Kircheim	Kapellenberg
Höpfigheim	Königsberg
Hofen	Berg
Erligheim	Kirschgarten, Lerchenberg
Asperg	Berg

LOWER NECKAR

Neckarwestheim	Schlossberg, Herrlesberg
Lauffen	Katzenbeisser, Krappenfelsen, Mauerseugen, Nonnenberg
Talheim	Haigern, Geigersberg, Schlossberg
Schozach	Blauer Berg, Roter Berg, Mühlberg
Klingenberg	Schlossberg
Heilbronn	Stiftsberg, Wartberg, Staufenberg, Stahlbühl, Hundsberg, Riedenberg
Flein	Altenberg, Eselsberg, Sonnenberg, Staufenberg, Kirchenweinberg, Grafenberg, Klosterberg
Neckarsulm	Scheuerberg, Haag, Hägelich
Erlenbach	Petersbühl, Schönbühl, Herzgrüble, Sommerberg, Kay
Gundelsheim	Himmelreich, Hoheneck, Wolkenstein

BOTTWARTAL

Grossbottwar	Harzberg, Wunnenstein, Schmiedberg, Köchersberg
Kleinbottwar	Götzenberg, Linsenberg, Brüssele
Oberstenfeld	Forstberg
Hof und Lembach	Lichtenberg
Winzerhausen	Wunnenstein
Unterheinriet	Sommerberg, Nährnberg
Beilstein	Wartberg, Vogelsang, Steinberg, Burgberg
Burg Wildeck	Burg Wildecker

WEINSBERG VALLEY AND ÖHRINGEN REGION

Weinsberg	Burgberg, Schemelsberg, Ranzenberg, Wildenberg, Glückenhälde
Ellhofen	Berg
Lehrsteinfeld	Rosengarten, Steinacker, Althälde
Grantschen	Wildenberg, Rosenberg, Altenberg
Willsbach	Dieblensberg, Beerlesberg, Zeilberg, Rosenberg
Wimmental	Freudenberg, Eselsberg
Sülzbach	Altenberg, Ranberg
Affaltrach	Salzberg, Dorfberg
Eschenau	Salzberg, Paradies
Hösslinsülz	Weinhalde
Hölzern	Berg, Weinsteige
Gellmersbach	Dezberg, Kirchberg
Weiler	Berg, Schlierbach
Eberstadt	Eberfürst, Nonnenberg
Eichelberg	Hundsberg
Löwenstein	Wohlfahrtsberg, Eulenberg, Lerchenbühl
Verrenberg	Goldberg
Heuholz-Harsberg	Dachsteiger, Spielbühl
Geddelsbach	Schneckenhof
Siebeneich	Himmelreich
Adolzfurt	Berghäusle
Michelbach	Rosenberg

ZABERGAU AND LEINTAL

Bönnigheim.	Steingrube, Kapellenberg, Pfaffenwerg, Kirchweg, Spiegel
Brackenheim	Mäusekammer, Zweifelberg, Burg
Haberschlacht	Dachsberg, Langhälde, Gaisengrund
Neipperg	Burgwengert, Schlossberg, Seeberg, Altenberg, Steingrube
Stockheim	Schöllkopf, Altenberg
Dürrenzimmern	Feuer, Mönchsberg, Kehle
Hausen	Vogelsang, Staig, Seeberg, Steinhalde
Grossgartach	Annung, Sonntagsberg, Ehrenberg, Grabensgrund
Schwaigern	Grafenberg, Sonntagsberg, Vogelsang, Ruthe, Breiten
Stetten a. H.	Sonnenberg, Vorderer Berg, Hinterer Berg
Nordheim	Sonntagsberg, Auerberg, Sommerberg, Gräfenberg
Kleingartach	Leinburg
Cleebronn	Michaelsberg, Ruith
Güglingen	Hummelsberg, Hegnach
Hohenhaslach	Kirchberg
Knittlingen	Reichshalde
Eilfingerberg	Eilfingerberg
Oberderdingen	Brehmich, Wilfenberg, Kupferhalde, Hagenrain
Steinbachhof	Steinbachhöfer
Ochsenbach	Rohrsteig
Sternenfels	Sandberg, Schiedberg
Rosswag	Halde
Mühlhausen.	Mönchsberg, S chlossweinberge, Felsen
Horrheim.	Rieser, Röckenberg
Maulbronn	Scheuelberg, Klosterberg

KOCHERTAL – JAGSTTAL – TAUBERTAL

Bad Ingelfingen	Schlossberg, Hoher Berg
Criesbach	Burgstall
Niedernhall	Burgstall, Heyerberg, Bromberg, Engweg
Forchtenberg	Haardt, Kocherberg
Weikersheim	Karlsberg, Schmecker
Markelsheim	Mönchsberg, Probstberg, Tauberberg
Laudenbach	Heimberg, Schafsteige

UPPER NECKAR

Neuffen	Schlosssteige
Linsenhofen	Sand
Beuren	Fels
Weilheim	Limburg
Metzingen	Berghalde, Florian

THE PALATINATE

Neustadt	Erkenbrecht, Grain, Vogelsang, Guckinsland, Mandelgarten, Ritterberg, Mandelgewann
Hardt	Bürgengarten, Kirchenstück, Herrenletten, Herrengarten, Herzog, Mandelring, Hofstück, Kalkgrube, Aspen, Knappengraben, Schlossberg
Mussbach.	Räppel, Eselshaut, Hundsrück, Hohlbaum, Katzenhauer, Glockenzehnt, Hundertmorgen, Knappengraben
Deidesheim	Leinhöhle, Grainhübel, Kalkofen, Kieselberg, Mäusehöhle, Hohenmorgen, Grain, Geheu, Kränzler, Vogelsang, Linsenbusch, Hofstück, Reiss, Paradiesgarten, Hahnenböhl, Rennpfad, Klostergarten, Langenböhl, Langenmorgen, Petershöhle, St. Michelsberg, Sonneneck, Herrgottsacker
Gimmeldingen	Schild, Kapelle, Meerspinne, Bienengarten, Hofstück, Kirchenstück
Königsbach	Idig, Mückenhaus, Ölberg, Jesuitengarten, Reiterpfad, Hitzpfad, Bender
Ruppertsberg	Hoheburg, Nussbien, Mandelgarten, Reiterpfad, Linsenbusch, Goldschmied, Hofstück, Geisböhl, Kreuz, Mandelacker
Forst	Kirchenstück, Jesuitengarten, Kranich, Ungeheuer, Freundstück, Pechstein, Ziegler, Langenmorgen, Mäuerchen, Linsenstück, Musenhang, Mariengarten, Schnepfenflug, Hellholz, Hahnenböhl, Elster, Altenburg, Fleckinger, Langenacker, Langenböhl
Wachenheim	Goldbächel, Rechbächel, Gerümpel, Luginsland, Böhlig, Königswingert, Mandelgarten, Oberstnest, Schenkelböhl, Fuchsmantel, Wolfsdarm
Gönnheim	Sonnenberg, Mandelgarten
Friedelsheim	Schlossgarten, Tiergarten, Neuberg
Bad Dürkheim	Michelsberg, Spielberg, Hoehbenn, Hochmess, Schenkelböhl, Fronhof, Proppelstein, Feuerberg, Fuchsmantel, Forst, Klosterberg
Ungstein	Herrenberg, Michelsberg, Spielberg, Weilberg, Kreuz, Kobnert, Nussriegel, Bettelhaus, Osterberg, Honigsäckel
Leistadt	Annaberg, Kalkofen, Spiessberg, Frohnberg, Kirchenstück, Herzfeld, Herrenmorgen
Kallstadt	Saumagen, Nill, Horn, Kobnert, Steinacker, Kreuz, Kirchenstück, Kreidkeller
Herxheim	Himmelreich, Steinberg, Felsenberg, Honigsack, Kirchenstück, Goldberg, Berg, Steinberg, Sommerseite
Freinsheim	Oschelkopf, Gross, Rosenbuhl, Hochgewann, Liebfrauenberg, Musikantenbuckel, Mandelgarten, Goldberg, Gottesacker, Hahnen
Weisenheim/Berg	Feinerde, Mandelgarten, Sonnenberg
Kircheim	Römerstrasse, Schwarzerde
Dirmstein	Hochgewann, Mandelpfad
Bockenheim	Burggarten, Dom, Sonnenberg
Zell	Schwarzer Herrgott
Bissersheim	Goldberg
Kieln-Karlbach	Hofstück, Herrenberg
Gross-Karlbach	Orlenberg
Sausenheim	Hochgewann, Klostergarten
Laumersheim	Kirchgarten
Grünstadt	Bergel
Kindenheim	Burgweg
Schweigen	Sonnenberg, Vogelsang
Bergzabern	Altenberg, Steinbühl
Billigheim	Pfaffenberg
Eschbach	Hasen, Schlossberg
Wollmesheim	Mütterle
Mörzheim	Schreckenberg
Ranschbach	Seligmacher
Birkweiler	Kastanienbusch, Herrenberg, Mandelberg
Siebeldingen	Starkenberg, Sonnenschein, Forst
Nussdorf	Kaiserberg
Burrweiler	Schäwer
Flemlingen	Zechpeter
Edesheim.	Forst
Edenkoben	Blücherschanze, Heiligkreuz
Rhodt	Rosengarten, Herrengarten
St. Martin	Schlossberg, Ritter v. Dalberg
Maikammer	Heiligenberg, Alsterweiler Kapellenberg
Diedesfeld	Brühl, Johanniskirchel
Duttweiler	Mandelberg
Hambach.	Schlossberg, Grain

RHEINHESSE

Worms	Katterloch, Stiftsgarten, Kirchenstück, Liebfrauenstift
Osthofen	Rosstal, Goldberg, Klosterberg, Hasenbiss, Wölm, Liebenberg
Westhofen	Kirchspiel, Gries, Roterde, Ring
Dalsheim	Steig, Rodenstein, Sauloch, Bürgel, Wingertsstätte
Oppenheim	Reisekahr, Kreuz, Krötenbrunnen, Kreuzkugel, Schützenhütte, Herrenberg, Zuckerberg, Goldberg, Daubhaus, Herrenweiher, Kehrweg, Kugel, Sacktärger, Schlossberg, Steig
Nierstein	Auflangen, Rehbach, Brudersberg, Ölberg, Glöck, Pettental, Fläschenhahl, Heiligenbaum, Orbel, Fuchsloch, Kranzberg, Floss, Hipping, Kehr, St. Kiliansberg, Rehbach, Schnappenberg, Streng, Gutes Domtal, Domtal, Paterberg, Findling, Schmitt, Spiegelberg, Flockenberg
Nackenheim	Rotenberg, Engelsberg, Fenchelberg, Kreuz, Fritzenhölle, Kapelle, Kirchberg, Spitzenberg
Mettenheim	Michelsberg, Schlossberg, Goldberg
Dienheim	Tafelstein, Hofstück, Goldberg, Gumben, Ebenbreit, Guldenmorgen
Bodenheim	Hoch, St. Alban, Westrum, Silberberg, Kahlenberg, Burgweg, Johannisberg, Heitersbrünnchen, Kapelle, Mönchpfad, Leidhecke, Neuberg, Leistenberg
Laubenheim	Damsberg, Neuberg, Hitz, Kalkofen, Klosterberg, Vogelsang
Gau-Bischofsheim	Herrenberg, Brühl, Pfaffenberg, Kellerberg, Kirscheck, Glockenberg, Gickelsberg, Kreuzwingert, Pfaffenweg
Ingelheim	Sonnenberg, Horn, Pares, Grauer Stein
Bingen	Schlossberg, Schwätzerchen, Scharlachberg, Rochusberg, Ohliger Berg, Auberg, Mainzerweg, Rosengarten
Alsheim	Frühmesse, Rheinblick, Fischerpfad
Guntersblum	Bornpfad, Himmeltal, Sonnenberg, Eiserne Hand, Wohnweg, Vögelsgärten, Steig, Hasenweg
Bechtheim	Hasensprung, Geyersberg, Pilgerpfad, Gotteshilfe
Pfaffenschwabenheim . .	Hölle
Alzey	Sibillenstein
Gau-Odernheim	Petersberg
Nieder-Saulheim. . . .	Goldberg, Probstei
Uffhofen	Laroche

NAHE

Bingerbrück	Schloss Leyer, Pittermännchen
Münster-Sarmsheim . . .	Kapellenberg, Langenberg, Daubenpflänzer, Pittersberg
Winzenheim	Rosenheck, Berg
Bretzenheim	Kreuzberg, Schützenhöll, Steinweg
Dorsheim	Burgberg
Windesheim	Fels
Bad Kreuznach	Brückes, Narrenkappe, Kauzenberg-Stübchen, Krötenpfuhl, St. Martin, Kahlenberg, Steinberg, Hinkelstein, Mönchberg, Osterhölle, Gutental, Mollenbrunnen, Forst, Monart, Rosengarten, Vogelsang, Kauzenberg, Belz
Ebernburg	Erzgrube, Schlossberg, Götzenfels, Feuerberg
Roxheim	Birkenberg, Mühlenberg, Höllenpfad, Hüttenberg, Neueberg, Wiesberg
Norheim	Dellchen, Kafels, Kirschheck, Hinterfels, Schmalberg
Altenbamberg-Alsenz . .	Kehrenberg, Rothenberg, Laurentiusberg, Treuenfels, Pfarrwingert, Bangert
Schlossböckelheim . . .	Königsfels, Kupfergrube, Felsenberg, Mühlberg, Königsberg, In den Felsen, Pühläcker, Heimberg
Niederhausen	Hermannshöhle, Felsensteyer, Mönchberg, Hermannsberg, Mfingstweide, Rosenheck, Rossel, Fels
Odernheim	Weinsack, Disibodenberg
Monzingen	Frühlingsplätzchen, Lay, Rosenbaum, Gabelstich, Kronenberg, Halenberg
Meddersheim	Altenberg
Waldböckelheim.	Mühlberg
Langenlonsheim	Löhr, Sonnenborn
Wallhausen	Pastorenberg, Johannesberg

FRANCONIA

Volkach	Ratsherr, Berg, Kirchberg
Obereisenheim	Höll
Escherndorf	Lump, Eulengrube, Fürstenberg, Hengstberg, Berg, Kirchberg
Nordheim	Vögelein, Kreuzberg
Sommerach	Katzenkopf, Engelsberg, Wilm
Dettelbach	Berg, Rondell
Abtswind (Steigerwald). .	Schild, Altenberg
Castell	Schlossberg, Hohnart, Bausch
Wiesenbronn	Wachhügel
Rödelsee	Küchenmeister, Schlossberg, Schwanleite, Hoheleite

Iphofen	Julius Echterberg, Kammer, Kronsberg, Kalb, Burgweg
Einersheim	Vogelsang
Hüttenheim	Tannenberg
Bullenheim	Paradies
Ippesheim	Herrschaftsberg
Kitzingen	Eselsberg, Buchbrenner Berg
Sulzfeld	Cyriakusberg, Altenberg, Maustal
Marktbreit	Sonnenberg
Frickenhausen	Kapellenberg, Babenberg, Fischer
Sommerhausen	Steinbach, Altenberg
Randersacker	Pfülben, Teufelskeller, Hohbug, Spielberg, Sonnenstuhl, Marsberg, Kapellenberg, Ewig Leben, Lämmerberg
Würzburg	Stein, Jesuitenstein, Harfe, Schalksberg, Felsenleiste, Innere Leiste, Leiste, Neuberg, Rossberg, Abtsleite, Schlossberg, Pfaffenberg, Guthentahl, Lindleinsberg
Veithöchsheim	Abtsberg, Neuberg, Fachtel, Wölflein
Thüngersheim	Scharlach, Ravensburg, Johannisberg
Stetten	Im Stein, Loch, Rosstal
Schloss Saaleck	Schloss Saalecker
Hammelburg	Liebental, Fürstenberg, Bach
Homburg	Kallmuth
Bürgstadt	Mainhölle, Martinskirch, Hohenlinde
Grossheubach	Bischofsberg, Engelsberg
Klingenberg	Schlossberg, Felsenrot
Erlenbach	Altenberg, Krähenschnabel
Hörstein	Reuschberg, Abtsberg, Schwalbenwinkel

RHEINGAU

Hochheim	Domdechaney, Kirchenstück, Stein, Rauchloch, Stiehlweg, Königin-Viktoria-Berg, Hölle, Neuberg, Sommerheil, Steinern Kreuz, Daubhaus
Wiesbaden-Schierstein . .	Dachsberg, Hölle, Homberg, Marschall, Schäferberg
Wiesbaden-Frauenstein . .	Mühlberg, Herrenberg, Sand
Niederwalluf	Walkenberg, Berg-Bildstock, Oberberg, Mittelberg, Unterberg, Steinritz, Rötherweg
Oberwalluf	Sonnenberg, Langenstück
Eltville	Sonnenberg, Taubenberg, Langenstück, Mönchhanach, Kalbspflicht, Klümbchen, Siebenmorgen
Rauenthal	Baiken, Gehrn, Wieshell, Rothenberg, Herberg, Langenstück, Pfaffenberg, Burggraben, Siebenmorgen, Steinmächer
Martinsthal	Steinberg, Langenberg, Pfaffenberg, Wildsau, Heiligenstock, Mauer, Kirchgarten, Rödchen
Kiedrich	Gräfenberg, Sandgrub, Wasserros, Heiligenstock, Klosterberg, Scharfenstein
Erbach	Marcobrunn, Siegelsberg, Honigberg, Michelmark, Pellet, Kahlig, Steinmorgen, Hohenrain
Hattenheim	Nussbrunnen, Wisselbrunn, Hassel, Mannberg, Steingberg, Hinterhaus, Pfaffenberg, Schützenhaus, Engelmannsberg, Heiligenberg, Klosterberg
Hallgarten	Jungfer, Schönhell, Kirschenacker, Deutelsberg, Sandgrub, Hendelberg, Rosengarten, Mehrhölzchen, Geiersberg, Würzgarten
Oestrich	Doosberg, Lenchen, Pfaffenpfad, Hitz, Deez, Hölle, Eiserberg, Klosterberg, Mühlberg, Räucherberg
Mittelheim	Edelmann, Honigberg, Sonnenberg, St. Nikolaus, Rheingarten
Winkel	Hasensprung, Bienenberg, Honigberg, Dachsberg, Guthenberg, Jesuitengarten, Steinchen, Hellersberg, Erntebringer
Johannisberg	Schloss Johannisberg, Kochsberg, Hölle, Steinstück, Hansenberg, Vogelsang, Schwarzenstein, Kerzenstück, Nonnenhöhle, Goldatzel, Erntebringer
Geisenheim	Rothenberg, Kläuserweg, Fuchsberg, Mäuerchen, Morchberg, Kosakenberg, Katzenloch, Lückerstein, Hinkelstein, Mönchpfad
Rüdesheim	Berg Bronnen, Berg Rottland, Zollhaus, Berg Schlossberg, Berg Burgweg, Berg Roseneck, Berg Ramstein, Bischofsberg, Drachenstein, Sonnenberg, Kirchenpfad, Backhaus, Klosterlay, Magdalenenkreuz, Dechaney, Klosterberg
Assmannshausen	Höllenberg, Frankenthal, Bohren, Steil, Hinterkirch, Kapellenberg, Assmannshäuser Berg, Silberberg
Aulhausen	Kaisersteinfels, Orleans, Frenz
Lorch/Rheingau	Bodenthal, Lehn, Pfaffenwies, Kapellenberg, Schlossberg, Krone, Niederflur
Lorchhausen	Seligmacher, Rosenberg, Schönberg, Galgenpfad, Kapellchen

MOSELLE

Winningen	Uhlen, Röttgen, Hamm, Rosenberg
Müden	Hohenlay, Rotenburg, Himmelsberg
Pommern	Rosenberg, Goldberg, Greisenmund, Kapellenberg
Cochem	Pinnerberg, Langenberg, Schloss, Schlossberg, Kreuzberg, Tummetchen
Valwig	Herrenberg, Schwarzenberg

274

Bruttig.	Kuckucksberg, Siebenköpfchen, Brandenberg, Johannisberg, Kreuz, Rathausberg
Senheim	Kirchrech, Wahrsager, Bienengarten, Lay, Rosenberg, Schwarzberg
Ediger	Feuerberg, Osterlämmchen, Pfaffenberg, Elzoberg, Hasensprung
Bremm.	Kalmont
Alf	Herrenberg, Astasberg, Frauenberg, Kapellenberg, Kronenberg
Bullay	Domherrenberg
Merl	Stefansberg, Königslay, Klosterberg, Fettgarten, Schafenstein, Münchslay, Adler
Zell	Burglay, Domherrenberg, Schwarze Katz, Nussberg, Petershorn, Heiligenhäuschen, Kapertchen
Reil	Vom heissen Stein, Falkly, Goldlay, Weingrube, Görlay, Mauseberg, Mulley-Hofsberg, Pfefferberg, Sorrent, Staaden
Enkirch	Steffensberg, Monteneubel, Herrenberg, Edelberg, Weinkammer, Hinterberg
Traben-Trarbach	Schlossberg, Würzgarten, Geisspfad, Kräuterhaus, Ungsberg, Königsberg, Burgberg, Halsberg, Hühnerberg, Backhaus, Bergpächter, Rickelsberg, Steinbacher
Kröv	Steffensberg, Herrenberg, Engelberg, Paradies, Petersberg, Letterlay, Halsbach, Heislay, Niederberg, Petersberg, Nacktarsch
Kinheim/Kindel	Rosenberg, Hubertusberg, Eulenlay, Hubertushofberg, Löwenberg, Petrusberg
Erden	Treppchen, Prälat, Busslay, Himmelreich, Herrenberg, Herzlay, Filisberg, Frankenlay, Hötlay, Kaufmannsberg, Rotkirch, Schönberg
Ürzig	Würzgarten, Urlay, Schwarzlay, Lay
Zeltingen	Sonnenuhr, Rotlay, Himmelreich, Schlossberg, Kirchenpfad, Bickert, Kirchlay, Stefanslay, Steinmauer, Schwarzlay, Welbersberg
Graach	Josephshöfer, Himmelreich, Domprobst, Abtsberg, Obstberg, Goldwingert, Bistum, Kirchlay, Lilienpfad, Petrus, Rosenberg, Stablay, Heiligenhaus, Hömberg, Münich, Münzlay, Tirlei
Wehlen	Sonnenuhr, Lay, Abtei, Münzlay, Nonnenberg, Klosterlay, Rosenberg, Wertspitz
Kesten	Paulinshofberger, Herrenberg, Niederberg
Bernkastel	Doktor, Doktor und Graben, Badstube, Olk, Kirchgraben, Graben, Schlossberg, Rosenhang, Königsstuhl, Lay, Bratenöfchen, Pfaffenberg, Pfalzgraben, Schwanen, Altenwald, Held, Eich, Lay, Johannisbrünnchen
Kues.	Kardinalsberg, Weissenstein, Herrenberg, Kalbrech, Lay, Rosenberg
Lieser	Niederberg, Schlossberg, Kirchberg, Paulsberg, Pfaffenberg, Rosenberg
Brauneberg	Juffer, Hasenläufer, Bürgerslay, Burgenberg, Falkenberg, Nonnenlay, Kammer, Mandelgraben, Lay, Obersberg, Sonnenuhr
Maring	Römerpfad, Brauneberg, Klosterberg, Schwarzlay, Rosenberg, Sonnenuhr
Mülheim	Sonnenlay, Mühlheimer, Johannisberg, Elisenberg, Bitsch, Kloster
Veldenz	Geisberg, Kirchberg, Bitsch, Elisenberg, Neuberg
Wintrich	Grosser Herrgott, Rosenberg, Olk, Sonnenseite, Simonsberg, Geierslay, Ohligsberg, Geyerskopf, Neuberg
Minheim	Grauberg, Rosenberg, Lay, Christenlay
Piesport	Goldtröpfchen, Hubertuslay, Güterslay, Grafenberg, Falkenberg, Taubengarten, Treppchen, Lay, Bildchen, Hohlweid Pichter, Michelsberg
Niederemmel	Lay, Taubengarten, Gunterslay
Dhron	Dhronhofberger, Roterd, Sängerei, Kandel, Pichter, Grosswingert, Hengelberg
Neumagen	Laudamusberg, Engelsgrube, Rosengärtchen, Sonnenuhr, Hengelberg, Layenberg, Pichter, Pfaffenberg, Thierlay, Kirchenstück, Lasenberg
Trittenheim.	Apotheke, Altärchen, Laurentiusberg, Clemensberg, Fahrsfels, Falkenberg, Laurentiusberg, Neuberg, Sonnenteil, Vogelsang, Weierbach, Olk
Leiwen	Klostergarten, Laurentiuslay
Klüsserath	Bruderschaft, Königsberg, St. Michael
Thörnich	Ritsch, Engass, Ley, Schiesslay
Detzem	Würzgarten, Klosterlay, Königsberg, Maximiner Klosterlay, Stolzenberg
Mehring	Zellerberg, Plattenberg, Goldkupp, Huxlay, Kuckuckslay
Schweich	Annaberg, Herrenberg, Marienpichter
Longuich	Herrenberg, Probstberg, Maximiner Herrenberg, Kirchberg
Eitelsbach	Karthäuser Hofberg
Trier	Römerberg, Rotenburg, Vogelsang, Deutschherrenköpfchen, Pichter, Augenscheiner, Geisberg, Johannisberg, Neuberg, Herrenberg, Klosterberg

THE SAAR

Konz-Karthaus	Zuckerberg, Jesusberg, Kelterberg, Falkensteiner
Obermenning	Zuckerberg
Filzen	Urbelt, Herrenberg, Neuberg, Pulchen, Vogelberg
Wawern	Herrenberg, Jesuitengarten, Ritterpfad, Goldberg
Kanzem	Berg, Altenberg, Hörecker, Sonnenberg, Unterberg, Kelterberg, Wolfsberg
Wiltingen	Braune Kupp, Scharzhofberger, Dom Scharzhofberger, Kupp, Gottesfuss, Braunfels, Scharzberg, Klosterberg, Johannislay, Rosenberg, Schlangengraben, Schlossberg, Dohr, Neuberg
Oberemmel	Hütte, Agritinsberg, Karlsberg, Altenberg, Eltzerberg, Junkersberg, Lauterberg, Raul, Rosenberg, Scharzberg, Scharzberger
Schoden	Herrenberg
Ayl	Kupp, Herrenberg, Neuberg, Euchariusberg, Junkerberg, Scheiderberg, Silberberg, Sommerberg
Ockfen	Bockstein, Herrenberg, Geisberg, Heppenstein, St. Irminer

Saarburg Beurig	Mühlenberg, Layenkaul, Rausch, Antoniusbrunnen, Klosterberg, Berggarten
Irsch.	Hubertusberg, Sinnenberg, Wolfsberg
Serrig	Vogelsang, Kupp, Würzberg, Saarstein, Trutzberg, Antoniusberg, Schloss Saarfelser, Hindenburglay, Wingertsheck, Würzburger Helenenberg, Würzburger Marienberg

RUWER

Mertesdorf	Maximin Grünhäuser Herrenberg, Maximin Grünhäuser Bruderberg, Mertesdorfer, Lorenzberg, Spielberg, Treppchen
Eitelsbach	Karthäuserhofberg, Sonnenberg, Grossenberg, Sang, Burgberg, Kronenberg, Marienberg, Rothenberg, Marienholz
Kasel	Kernagel, Pichter, Herrenberg, Hitzlay, Niesgen, Taubenberg, Hiesgen, Steininger, Kohlenberg, Katharinenberg, Käulgen, Lorenzberg, Paulinsberg
Waldrach.	Jesuitengarten, Krone, Ehrenberg, Kloserberg, Meisenberg, Schloss Marienlay
Pölich/Mosel	Held, Südlay

AHR

Altenahr	Eck, Zapfenberg, Übigberg
Rech.	Herrenberg, Schieferstein
Reimerzhoven.	Ravenley
Laach	Berg
Mayschoss	Mönchberg, Silberberg
Dernau.	Hardtberg, Goldkaul, Sondersberg, Burgberg
Ahrweiler.	Rosental, Daubhaus, Silberberg, Berg
Walporzheim	Domberg, Kräuterberg, Gärkammer, Himmelchen
Marienthal	Jesuitengarten, Klosterberg, Trotzenberg, Klostergarten, Klosterley
Bad Neuenahr	Schieferley, Sonnenberg
Heimersheim	Landskroner Berg
Bachem	Karlskopf, Sonnenberg

MIDDLE RHINE

ST. GOAR REGION

Alken	Bleidenberg, Lay, Kölscheberg, Burgberg, Hunnenstein, Sonnenring
Bacharach	Posten, Hahn, Wolfshöhle, Kloster Fürstental, Mühle, Dell, Schlossberg, Bill
Bad Salzig	Römerberg, Sazbornberg, Altlay
Boppard	Hamm, Ewig Bach, Gietel, Feuerlay, Wiesborn, Mandelstein, Kerler, Hetz, Ohlenberg
Breitscheid	Steeger Mühlberg, Breitscheid und Rechtel
Brodenbach.	Hunnenstein, Neuwingert, Burgberg, Geisseberg, Schlossberg
Burgen/Mosel	Bischofsteiner, Klopplay, Kuckucksberg
Damscheid	Goldemund, Geissberg, Schippen, Frankenhöll
Dellhofen	Hambach, Sayen
Hirzenach	Staat, Probsteiberg, Röttgen
Langscheid	Pützbach
Manubach	Retz, Mühle, Mönchwingert, St. Oswald, Grube, Langgarten
Niederburg	Knüppelberg, Kohlgrube, Büttenberg
Niederfell.	Rotmauer, Grub, Fächern, Kochlay, Goldlay, Münichsberg
Niederheimbach	Raifersley, Löwenhell, Soonecker Schlossberg, Fron-Weingarten
Niederspray	Bopparder Hamm, Niederspray
Oberdiebach	Fürstenberg, Mittelberg, Mühlberg, Bischofstube, Glasten, Kräuterberg
Oberfell	Ringmauer, Brauneberg, Kebelberg, Marienberg
Oberheimbach	In der Sonne, Brückenstück, Wahrheit, Anweg
Oberspray	Bopparder Hamm
Oberwesel	Rheinhell, Ölsberg, Bernhell, Hangestein, Engehell, Hardthell, Lauerbaum, Bernstein, Würgehöll
Perscheid	Mittelhöll, In und ober der Hartel, Niedersagen
St. Goar	Hasenflöz, Bank Riesling, Kuhstall
Steeg	St. Jost, Kripp, Flur, Bocksberg, Hambuch, Mühlberg
Trechtingshausen	Morgenbach, Kieslau, Bodental
Urbar	Beulsberg, Oelsberg
Weiler bei Bad Salzig . .	Mühlenberg, Ziehberg, Rheinberg
Werlau	Ameisenberg, Frohwingert, Hasenflöz

ST. GOARSHAUSEN REGION

Bornich	Rieslingberg, Rothenack, Vordere Reste, Hintere Reste
Braubach.	Mühlberg, Kapellenberg, Koppelstein, Walkenberg, Liebedell, Marmorberg, Jagenstiel, Stiel
Dürscheid	Rosengarten, Mühlenstein, Hochstadt, Kolben
Fachbach.	Sommerberg
Kamp-Bornhofen	Schlossberg, Bornhofertal, Hohenstock, Gies, Schädert
Kaub	Schlossberg, Blüchertaler, Silbernagel, Pfalzgrafenstein, Backofen, Sonnenberg
Kestert	Liebensteiner, Kirchköppel, Nadenkopf, Im Stenner
Nochern	Hohe Lay, Rabenack, Am Brünnchen, Im Kanzler, Fensel
Oberlahnstein	Koppelstein, Karstel, Helmestal
Ostersprai	Bopparder-Hamm
Patersberg	Herschelberg, Schützenhaus, Herzenhöll, Mittelpfad
St. Goarshausen	Hessern, Loreley-Edel, Hühnerberg, Heiderstein, Burg Katz
Wellmich	Auf Roth, Hietzert, Oberberg, Auf der Mauer, Ohlenberg

UNTERLAHN REGION

Nassau	Haniob, Plattenstück, Niederberg
Obernhof	Goetheberg, Schreiberlay
Weinähr	Giebelhölle, Ackerbergen, Bollwerk, Rother-Pfad

KOBLENZ REGION

Dieblich	Fahrberg, Heilgraben, Fächer
Güls	Pattig-Heyerberg, Bienengarten
Kobern	Uhlen, Pappenscheren, Weissenberg, Rossenberg
Koblenz-Stadt	Moselweisser-Hamm, Römerheg, Aveberg, Kreuzberg
Lay	Hamm, Ankelspfad, Kützenberg
Rhens	Obersberg, Sonnenlay, König Wenzel
Urbar	Besselicher Klostermauer, Besselicher lange Zeilen
Vallendar/Rhein	Rheinnieder
Winningen	Rosenberg, Weinhex, Kirchenberg, Sternberg, Brückstück, Röttgen, Hamm, Uhlen

NEUWIED REGION

Bad Hönningen	Schlossberg, Feigenberg, Burgberg, Elsberg
Dattenberg	Domtaler, Tempelberg, Gertrudenberg
Erpel	Hühner-Berg, Karrenweg, Strohberg, Müdersgass, Leitzberg, Schwalkaul
Hammerstein	Schlossberg, Vorderberg, Hölle, Leyfelsen
Leubsdorf	Stehleberg, Daufenberg, Oberau
Leutesdorf	Laurentiusberg, Rosenberg, Martinsley, Gartenley, Forstberg, Olterberg
Linz	Rheinheller, Kaiserberg
Rheinbrohl	Monte Jupp, Römerberg, Pflanzenberg, Rheinbrohler Ley
Unkel	Unkeler-Berg, Mannberg, Sonnenberg

SIEBENGEBIRGE

Oberdollendorf	Laurenziusberg, Sülzenberg, Rosenhügel, Grafenberg
Niederdollendorf	Kellerberg, Longenburgerberg, Heisterberg
Königswinter	Drachenley, Kuckstein
Rhöndorf	Domley, Ulananeck, Mönchenberg

WEINBERGE DES OBERRHEINS

Rhein

DEUTSCHLAND

FRANCE

BASEL

Basel

LIESTAL

Aarg.

AARAU

ERLINSBACH

Birs

Ergolz

OLTEN

Aare

Solothurn

SOLOTHURN

La Chaux-de-Fonds

BIENNE

Lac de Bienne

Bern

La Neuveville

Aare

Neuchâtel

NEUCHÂTEL

BOUDRY

Lac de Neuchâtel

Lac de Morat

BERN

MORAT

Aare

YVERDON

FRIBOURG

Fribourg

THUN

Vaud

Thuner See

Brienzer See

SCHAFFHAUSEN

STEIN AM RHEIN

Thurgau

Rhein

Bodensee

Thur

FRAUENFELD

SULGEN

ROMANSHORN

RUGG

BADEN

Glatt

WINTERTHUR

WIL

ST. GALLEN

Limmat

ALTSTÄTTEN

ZÜRICH

Töss

Appenzell

Reuss

Zürich

APPENZELL

Zürichsee

St. Gallen

ÖSTERREICH

ZUG

Zuger See

Walensee

WALENSTADT

LUZERN

GLARUS

See

SCHWYZ

SARGANS

Bündner Herrschaft

Vierwald

stätter See

ALTDORF

Graubünden

CHUR

Rhein

20 Km.

20 Miles

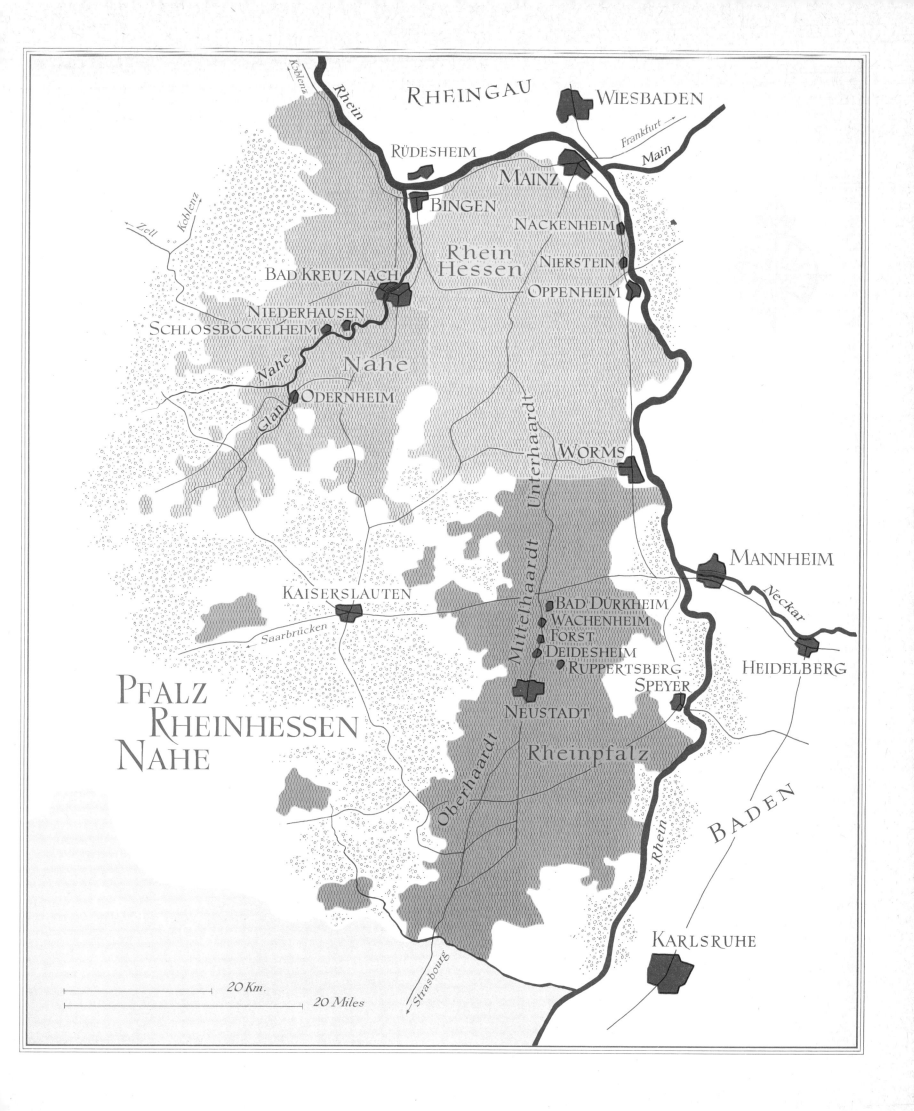

RHEINGAU

WIESBADEN

Koblenz

Rhein

RÜDESHEIM

Frankfurt

Main

MAINZ

BINGEN

Zell

Koblenz

NACKENHEIM

Rhein
Hessen

NIERSTEIN

BAD KREUZNACH

OPPENHEIM

NIEDERHAUSEN

SCHLOSSBÖCKELHEIM

Nahe

Nahe

ODERNHEIM

Glan

Unterhaardt

WORMS

MANNHEIM

Neckar

KAISERSLAUTEN

Mittelhaardt

Saarbrücken

BAD DÜRKHEIM

WACHENHEIM

FORST

DEIDESHEIM

RUPPERTSBERG

SPEYER

HEIDELBERG

PFALZ
RHEINHESSEN
NAHE

NEUSTADT

Rheinpfalz

Oberhaardt

Rhein

BADEN

20 Km.

20 Miles

Strasbourg

KARLSRUHE

LORCHHAUSEN

LORCH

PRESBERG

Wisperstrasse

R h e i n g a u g e b i r g e

STEPHANSHAUSEN

KLOSTER EBERBACH

HALLGARTEN

17   16

Rhein

26 AULHAUSEN

ASSMANNSHAUSEN

JOHANNISBERG

Schloss Vollrads

15   14

OESTRICH

EIBINGEN

19

Schloss Johannisberg

21

18

25   24

RÜDESHEIM

23   22

20

HATTENHEIM

MITTELHEIM

WINKEL

Nahe

GEISENHEIM

BINGEN

1   Hochheimer Kirchenstück
2   Hochheimer Domdechaney
3   Wallufer Walkenberg
4   Eltviller Sonnenberg
5   Rauenthaler Gehrn
6   Rauenthaler Baiken
7   Rauenthaler Wieshell
8   Eltviller Taubenberg
9   Erbacher Steinmorgen
10 Erbacher Hohenrain
11 Erbacher Marcobrunn
12 Hattenheimer Nussbrunnen
13 Hattenheimer Mannberg

5 Km.

5 Miles

BAD SCHWALBACH

BAD SCHLANGENBAD

W.-DOTZHEIM

RAUENTHAL

W.-FRAUENSTEIN

WIESBADEN

KIEDRICH

5

6

DIEDENBERGEN

7

MARTINSTHAL

NORDENSTADT

WALLAU

8

OBERWALLUF

W.-SCHIERSTEIN

W.-ERBENHEIM

9

10

4

3

WICKER

ERBACH ELTVILLE   NIEDERWALLUF

W.-BIEBRICH

HOCHHEIM

MZ-KASTEL

1

MAINZ

2

14 Hattenheimer Wisselbrunn
15 Hattenheimer Heiligenberg
16 Hattenheimer Steinberg
17 Hallgartener Jungfer
18 Winkeler Hasensprung
19 Schloss Johannisberg
20 Geisenheimer Kläuserweg
21 Geisenheimer Rothenberg
22 Rüdesheimer Bronnen
23 Rüdesheimer Zollhaus
24 Rüdesheimer Roseneck
25 Rüdesheimer Schlossberg
26 Assmannshäuser Höllenberg

MZ.-KOSTHEIM

Rhein

Main

RHEINGAU

20 Km.
20 Miles

1 Wehlen
2 Graach
3 Zeltingen
4 Ürzig
5 Kröv
6 Traben-Trarbach

Rhein
Bonn
NEUWIED
KOBLENZ
WINNINGEN
Lahn
Mosel
MÜDEN
SANKT GOARSHAUSEN
DAUN
COCHEM
BREMM
SANKT GOAR
Rhein
Mainz
WITTLICH
ZELL
Aachen
Köln
BITBURG
Kyll
4
5
3
2
1
6
BERNKASTEL-KUES
KLÜSSERATH
BRAUNEBERG
SCHWEICH
TRITTENHEIM
Sauer
Our
TRIER
KASEL
Ruwer
KANZEM
WILTINGEN
Namur
Alzette
SAARBURG
LUXEMBOURG
SERRIG
DEUTSCHLAND
Mosel
Metz
Nied
Saar
Saarbrücken
FRANCE

MOSEL · SAAR · RUWER

THE WINES
OF CENTRAL EUROPE,
THE BALKANS, THE USSR

JOSEPH JOBÉ and BORIS POGRMILOVIC

At the time of the Roman Empire, the vine was cultivated in Spain, Gaul and Helvetia as well as along the frontiers of the Empire, on the Rhine and on the Danube. In the Middle Ages, all the countries of central Europe produced some wine. However the climate and geological conditions as well as the economic and political fluctuations were less favourable to wine production in these countries than, for example, in France and Italy.

Today Czechoslovakia, of all the central European countries, is the one where the least wine is produced and drunk; just over a gallon per person per year. It is easy to understand this: the vineyards, situated at the farthest point north of the viticultural zone, are only cultivated on a marginal basis. However, at the beginning of the seventeenth century, before the Thirty Years War, even Bohemia, and in particular the area around Prague, was a country of vineyards and rich in wine. Before phylloxera attacked the stock, the Czech vineyards were as important as those of the present republic of Austria. It is true that the last few centuries have seen a slight change in climate which has adversely affected the vine, but there are other reasons for this regression. Czechoslovakia, Austria, Hungary and part of Yugoslavia all once belonged to a single large conglomeration of which Austria was the predominant element. Within this Empire, an increase or a reduction in the amount of land allotted to the cultivation of the vine depended not only on climatic conditions but also on historical events. Moreover, certain provinces, especially Hungary, suffered from the influence and invasion of the Moslem Turks, who were not wine drinkers. As wine was sometimes scarce in the most highly productive areas, a greater effort was required from the winegrowers in other regions of the Empire. At the end of First World War, each of the new states born of the fall of the Austro-Hungarian Empire had to view the future in a new light.

The Austrian vineyards, more ancient than the name of the country, have made very little progress. The vine here is cultivated on a very small scale and is confined to the eastern part of the country.

In Czechoslovakia, however, the vine covered 42,000 acres in 1917 and 25,000 acres in 1947; today it covers about 61,800 acres. The Hungarian vineyards have developed on quite a different scale. Here, apart from the years 1955 to 1958, production has always been maintained at around 495,000 acres. Hungarians drink from 5 ½ to 6 ½ gallons of wine per person per year, and export 20 per cent of their production.

The Greeks as much as the Romans were responsible for the introduction of the vine to Yugoslavia, where its development was further encouraged by the lords of the land and the monasteries. Under Turkish domination, the actual area under cultivation dwindled, but it did not disappear entirely. Since the beginning of this century, the area under vines has doubled. Consumption *per capita* is on a par with the neighbouring countries of Austria, Hungary and Bulgaria.

285

In Rumania and Bulgaria it would seem the vine was first introduced by the Greeks and later by the Romans. These two countries have better climatic conditions than Czechoslovakia, and in Rumania especially, the influence of the Black Sea does much to temper the excesses of the continental climate. In this country, the vine grows wherever the soil is favourable and the sun shines sufficiently. Despite a long period of submission to the Turkish Empire, the Rumanians continued to grow the vine though their overlords cared little for the fruits of their labour.

In 1913, Rumania had only 178,000 acres of soil under cultivation; today it has about 740,000. It produces more white wine than red, while in Bulgaria the opposite is the case. The increase of production continues under the incentive of the co-operatives and of the research institutes set up by the Government.

In Bulgaria, the soil planted to vines in 1913 was 131,000 acres; today it is about 445,000 acres and consumption has more than doubled in the last ten years. It is now 3 to 5 gallons per person per year.

A similar situation exists in southern Russia: in 1914 the vineyards were spread over 526 acres, while today they have developed to cover about 2 ½ million. It is true that the Russians are not great consumers of still wines; they prefer sparkling wines to the extent of about 200 bottles a year per thousand inhabitants.

Throughout the whole area, which stretches from Prague to the Black Sea and the Adriatic, there is only one wine as famous as the "great" wines: TOKAY.

AUSTRIA

Today Austria produces much less wine than it once did. The ebb and flow of history are responsible for this decrease. The Romans most probably introduced the vine to the banks of the Danube 2,000 years ago. After the invasion of the Barbarians who destroyed the Roman colonies, the vines were replanted under Emperor Otto I, from the year 955 onwards. Towards the end of the Middle Ages, the vine covered 200,000 acres in Lower Austria alone. When neighbouring Hungary was occupied by the Turks in 1526, the whole wine trade—and the competition in wines—between the two countries came to an end. As one result, for one and a half centuries the amount of land under cultivation in Austria increased greatly. The present area under cultivation is only a tenth of what it used to be at its zenith. Today, some 99,000 acres of vineyards produce 33,000,000 gallons of wine. As the country imports 11,000,000 gallons, it may be deduced that every Austrian drinks an average of 6 ½ gallons of wine a year, as against 15 gallons of beer. Austria exports 330,000 gallons of wine a year, nearly all in white wines.

In fact, most of the wine produced (85 per cent) is white wine made from various grape-stocks. The best known are the *Riesling*, the *Traminer*, the *Sylvaner*, as well as the *Grüner Veltliner*. Sometimes the *Sauvignon*, *Rotgipfler* and *Muskat-Ottonel* are also used.

Austrian wines have been much appreciated for many years. Nearly four centuries ago, in 1580, Johannes Rasch wrote an important work on viticulture in this country. At the end of the seventeenth century wines were already classified according to their quality, and the classification was ratified by the Imperial Court in 1673.

In 1780, the Empress Maria Theresa promulgated a law on wine which still affects the industry today. Certain provisions of this law stated that every vineyard had the right to sell the wine from its vines without paying taxes. When a wine-merchant had wine in his cellar, he would place a crown of leaves or straw above his cellar-door to indicate to the passer-by that he was welcome within. Here, he might rest himself and partake of some liquid refreshment. This was the origin of the famous *Heurigen*, where every year the Viennese and countless numbers of tourists go to enjoy a few moments of laughter and merry-making. Under the shady bowers, amidst a lovely countryside and preferably in good company, the lover of white wine can savour the best local products such as GRINZING, SIEBERING and NUSSDORF, as well as WIENER NUSSBERG, probably the best of all. Let us hasten to add that the vineyards around Vienna are neither the only ones, nor even the best in the country.

The winegrowing area of Burgenland includes the banks of Lake Neusiedel and, farther south, the area around the town of Eisenberg. Usually, local wines are drunk in such places as Oggau, Mörbisch, Rust, St. Margarethen, Eisenstadt, Mattesburg and Oberpullendorf. Some wines, naturally, are better than others: among the white wines these are the RUSTER GREINER, RUSTER SATZ, RUSTER TURNER, while among the red wines there are the RUSTER BAUMGARTEN, RUSTER G'MÄRK, RUSTER MITTELKRÄFTEN, and especially the RUST LIMBERGER, a *Pinot Noir*. Styria, in the Mur valley, near the lower part of Graz and Sulm, mainly produces white wines. The best-known vineyard is situated in the commune of Klöch, and some consider the KLÖCHER BERG one of the best *Traminers*

In this painting by Lucas van Valckenborgh (1530-1597) peasants gather apples, coopers prepare barrels, some winegrowers harvest the grapes while others trample the vintage. The mildness of these last fine days, the abundance of the earth's gifts and the promise of good wine has incited their masters to pass the day in the country: at midday they assemble to eat lunch to the strains of a violin.

in Europe. Other local wines highly-thought of by the Austrians are the HARTBERGER RING, the HARTBERGER LÖFFELBACH, the GRASSNITZBERG, the OTTENBERGER WITSCHEINBERG and the KOBELBERG.

In the Baden region to the south of Vienna—a region also called Südbahn—the best-known white wines are those of Gumpoldskirchen, in particular the GUMPOLDSKIRCHNER SPIEGEL, the GUMPOLDSKIRCHNER WIEGE and the GUMPOLDSKIRCHNER SONNBERG. Of the red wines, which are fewer, the VÖSLAUER ROTWEIN deserves particular mention.

The winegrowing areas, which produce local wines, white for the most part, are north of the Danube in the Weinviertel, which along the length and the western side runs from Vienna to Czechoslovakia, as well as along the banks of the Danube from Vienna to the confluence of the river Kamp, including Klosternberg, the Kamp valley and Langenlois.

However, it is especially the region of Krems and of Wachau above Krems that produce the best Austrian wines. In the past, these wines were not so well thought of because of their somewhat high acid content—in fact a well-known saying had it *sauer wie der Wachauer* ("as sour as Wachauer wine"). The winegrowers of Krems, a dynamic and pretty little town, were however able to produce Rieslings with a full-flavoured bouquet. The best of these may be compared to the Moselle Rieslings. To name but a few, the KREMSLER KÖGL, KREMSER KREMSLEITEN and KREMSER WACHTBERG may be recommended.

Farther up-stream is Dürnstein, a very picturesque place with the ruins of a feudal castle. It is well-known for its DÜRNSTEINER LIERENBERG, and for the DÜRNSTEINER HOLLERIN, which was served in 1955 at the time of the signing of the Austrian State Treaty which proclaimed Austria's independence. Yet farther up-stream, the Stein vineyards produce the STEINER GOLDBERG, made from the best *Müller-Thurgau* grape in Wachau. The Loiben wines are some of the best white wines to come from the banks of the Danube: wines such as the LOIBENER KAISERWEIN and the UNTERLOIBENER BRUGSTALL.

The traveller faced with a list of Austrian wines is often puzzled, as the names by which these wines are known are not always mentioned as fully or as systematically on the wine-list as is the practice elsewhere. For some wines only the place of origin is given—for example, WACHAUER 1959, a wine produced in Wachau in the year 1959. Others are known by the name of the grape used, without mentioning the place of origin, as in the case of VELTLINER 1959; this simply designates a wine produced from the *Grüner Veltliner* grape in the year 1959. Yet others mention the grape used preceded by the name of the commune; for example, the STEINER VELTLINER 1959, produced from the *Grüner Veltliner* grape in the commune of Stein in the year 1959. It should be noted, however, that the best wines, especially those we have referred to, mention the name of the commune or the village, followed by the name of the vineyard. For example: DÜRNSTEINER LIEBENBERG, designating a wine grown in the vineyard of Liebenberg in the commune of Dürnstein. A wine-lover who choses any of these wines will be sure to have chosen from among the best wines of Austria.

Austrian wines are little known abroad; for the most part they must be drunk in the country itself. The white wines are considered the best, but they should not be compared to the German wines made from the same stock. Those drunk in the "Heurigen" near Vienna have a low alcohol content; they are pale-coloured wines, sometimes of a milky white hue, fresh wines which are sometimes slightly effervescent.

HUNGARY

The most famous Hungarian wine is TOKAY. Associated with the names of emperors and kings, lords and poets, it has overshadowed all the other wines of the country. For Hungary is a country rich in vineyards and wines; it has 543,600 acres of vine and produces nearly 88,000,000 gallons of wine, which places it in about tenth position among the wineproducing countries of Europe.

The Romans introduced the vine to the Hungarian plains. Since those days, the vine there has undergone many vicissitudes. First cultivated by the Magyars, it was neglected when the Tartars laid the country waste in 1241. Later again, settlers from the west brought with them a new vine-plant, *Furmint*, from which TOKAY was produced. Afterwards, when for 173 years (from 1526 to 1699) the country was occupied by Moslem Turks, the vine was once again neglected. In the eighteenth century, however, the Hungarian wine-cellars were among the best-stocked in Europe, thanks to Count István Szecheny.

Today Hungarian production fluctuates around 88 million gallons of wine, a quarter of which, at the most, is for export. Hungary produces mainly white wines (60 per cent). It also produces rosés (25 per cent) and a little red wine (15 per cent). These wines are usually known by a compound name; the first indicates the place of origin, the second the grape. For example, BADACSONYI KEKNYELÜ means that the wine is made from the *Kéknyelü* ("blue stalk") grape, in the Badacsony region. The white wines of Sopron, Somló, Villány-Pécs, Gyöngyös-Visonta are ordinary wines mainly for local consumption.

Red wine can be found in Sopron, which is near the Austrian border, in particular in the district of Szek-szárd, to the south of Lake Balaton. Most of the reds come from an original Balkan grape, the *Kadarka*.

The western bank of Lake Balaton, on the slopes of Mount Badacsony, is particularly favourable to the cultivation of grapes such as *Kéknyelü*, *Furmint*, and *Szürkebarát (Pinot Gris)*. BADACSONY KEKNYELÜ is a dry white wine with a pleasant bouquet and an attractive colour bordering on green, while BADACSONY SZÜRKEBARAT is a semi-sweet white wine which, when mature, has a rich amber colour. Nevertheless, it does not have the distinction of the *Pinot Gris* wines in other parts of Europe. RIESLINGS are cheap white wines of Italian origin, very different from those produced in the Rhine districts.

The Mór region, farther to the north, is one of Hungary's oldest viticultural areas. The MÖRI EZERJO, which means "the one-thousandfold good Mor", is a dry wine with a very lovely light green colour and an agreeably sharp tang.

The DEBRÖI HÁRSLEVELÜ is another typical Hungarian white wine. The grape *Hárslevelü* ("lime-blossom") is cultivated in the mountainous region of the north; it produces a sweet wine which is highly thought of by the Hungarians.

The EGRI BIKAVER, or "Bull's Blood of Eger" is the only Hungarian red wine known abroad, no doubt because of its name. The Eger region is situated between Budapest and the Tokay region. The EGRI BIKAVER has a dark rich colour and a slightly bitter taste. It is made from a mixture of several vines: the *Kadarka*, *Médoc Noir* and *Bourguignon*. In Hungary it is much recommended during convalescence owing to its tonic properties. The EGRI LEANYKA is a white wine made from an indigenous grape, the *Leanyka*.

TOKAY is by all odds the best-known. The town which gave its name to the wines of this region is situated on the Bodrog, at the foot of the Hégalja, which dominates the Tisza plain. This is an area of orchards and vineyards where only 28 villages have the right to call the wine they produce TOKAY. (It should be stated quite clearly that the name TOKAY does not cover the whole range of wines produced in this region.) The excellence of this wine springs from a wonderful harmony that exists between the soil and the climate, the grape and the process of vinification. The soil consists of a layer of crumbled lava which covers alluvial mountain deposits on a bed of volcanic rocks. The climate is varied; the summers are very hot and very dry, the autumns long and sunny, but the winters are harsh. The altitude of the vineyard varies from 500 to 650 feet above sea-level. The grape which gives TOKAY its special character is the *Furmint*. Students of the vine are divided in their opinions as to its origin, but agree that in this country it has found the soil and the climate most suitable for it. It is believed that settlers coming from the west brought the *Furmint* to prominence. Its name is probably derived from the French *froment* (wheat) which has become *Furmint* in Magyar; no doubt it has to do with the colour of the grapes. To this grape, which is always the predominant one in TOKAY, are sometimes added small quantities of *Hárslevelü* and *Muscat Jaune*. The third factor responsible for its success is the process of vinification and the special cellars in which it is stored.

First, there is the TOKAY FURMINT, or FURMINT DE TOKAY, a wine made according to traditional methods, by pressing the juice of the *Furmint* grape-clusters without using the dry grapes. This is a full-flavoured, fruity wine. Often the year of manufacture is mentioned on the label.

The TOKAY SZAMARODNI or SZAMARODNI DE TOKAY is made from the fermentation of grapes which have not been specially selected but picked late and so have clusters which are dry or have reached a stage of *pourriture noble* (noble rot). Its alcohol content is higher than that of the TOKAJI FURMINT; it can be sweet, as it is in sunny years, but when dry makes an excellent aperitif. The label on the bottle will indicate the year and type of wine.

The TOKAJI ASZU or ASZU DE TOKAY is the most famous of all the TOKAYS and is usually the one referred to when speaking simply of TOKAY. It is said to owe its origin to a seventeenth-century local war, which caused a delay in the vine-harvest; the winegrowers thus rediscovered the advantages of a late wine-harvest which had already been known to their forefathers. Late in the season, sometimes even after the first snow has fallen, when the grapes are overripe and have reached a *pourriture noble,* the wine-harvesters pick them one by one. The grapes are then crushed and stirred together until they form a kind of crust. When this process has been completed, 2 to 6 basketfuls (puttonos) weighing 33 pounds each of the final mixture are added to every hogshead of 30 gallons of must or wine, whether it is young or old, which is produced in the same region.

The sugar and aroma from the pressing of dried grapes dissolves in the must or wine, which after a second slow fermentation produces the world-famous TOKAY ASZU. The number of basketfuls poured into each hogshead depends on several factors: on the one hand on the quality of the must or wine which is being used—this varies from year to year—on the other hand on the type of TOKAJI ASZU one wishes to produce. For this wine can be sweet or semi-sweet.

The TOKAJI ASZU maintains essentially the same degree of excellence from year to year largely owing to the art of the master winemakers. The TOKAJI FURMINT and the TOKAJI SZAMARODNI, however, vary from year to year depending on the quality of the wine-harvest. When buying TOKAJI ASZU, one should know that the label on the bottle always mentions how many basketfuls of concentrated grapes have been put into each hogshead. For example: "3 puttonos" means that the wine is sweet, yet not nearly as sweet as a wine with a label reading "6 puttonos". This is the maximum. Moreover, the TOKAJI ASZU bottle has a traditional shape; it is pot-bellied like a Burgundy bottle, with a well-defined neck longer than that of the claret bottle. The wine will keep for a long time, like a sherry or Madeira. It is a wine known the world over, made famous by Voltaire, Goethe and Burns, while Louis XIV is said to have called it "the wine of Kings and the King of wines".

The TOKAJI MASLAS is produced by fermenting must or wine on the lees of TOKAY, usually on the lees of the ASZU or the SZAMARODNI. In order to produce the desired results the must stands for several months in small barrels called *Gönci*.

The TOKAJI ESZENCIA, or ESSENCE OF TOKAY is made by fermenting a thick must made from overripe grapes or those which have reached a state of *pourriture noble*. It is a very sweet, liqueur-like dessert wine.

TOKAY is produced in several countries (Alsace, northern Italy and eastern Switzerland), but only those wines referred to here come from Hungary and are authentic TOKAYS. They are exported by the Hungarian Board of Foreign Trade (Monimpex). Rarely, one does find a very old bottle of TOKAY, a delight to the connoisseur or anyone nostalgic for the charm of the gay nights in Budapest at the time of the Austro-Hungarian monarchy or between the two wars.

CZECHOSLOVAKIA

Czechoslovakia, of all the countries which were part of the former Austro-Hungarian Empire, is certainly the one which produces the least wine. Its output is about 6,600,000 gallons a year, half as much as Alsace alone produces, and even if some years happen to be more abundant, such as 1964 when production reached 16,479,716 gallons, Czechoslovakia has nevertheless not recovered from the ravages of phylloxera.

Bohemia, in the Melnik region, Roudnice and Litomerice, to the north of Prague, produce an ordinary white wine called LUOMILLA, made from the *Sylvaner* and *Traminer* grapes. The red wines are made from *Bourguignon Bleu*, *Portugais* or *Saint-Laurent* grapes. Because of its geographical position Bohemia produces wines similar to those of certain German wine regions.

Morovia has little wine, and almost all of it comes from the region near the Austrian frontier: the Rhine Rieslings, the Italien Rieslings and the Veltline.

Of the three main regions in the country, Slovakia is the best developed from the point of view of viticulture and gives about three-quarters of the national yield. Near the Hungarian frontier, to the north of the Tokay region, the Mala Trna and Nove Mestro vineyards also produce so-called TOKAY. Elsewhere, in the Bratislava area, they make the usual wines: Veltliner, Riesling or Sylvaner.

Czechoslovakia has to import a certain amount of wine: in 1965 it imported 9,752,468 gallons, and 4,110,876 gallons in 1966. Wine here is by no means a national drink; the average Czech drinks only about ten pints of wine a year. As there are no great wines, the tourist must console himself with the local white wines. These are light, fruity, and of low alcohol content and may be enjoyed in charming surroundings. The Czech wines have much improved since the establishment of a control over their quality.

RUMANIA

The Rumanian winegrowers have for centuries managed to maintain a difficult balance between the soil, the climate and the art of cultivating the vine. Although the country geographically belongs in a temperate zone considered favourable for the vine, its climate is nevertheless extreme: very hot in the summer, very cold and windy in winter. Yet wine has been produced in this country since before the seventh century B.C. When the Greeks founded their Black Sea colonies they cultivated the vine here in order to produce wine which they then stored in huge pot-bellied amphoras and sent throughout the civilized world.

By the development of the nurseries and the application of modern scientific methods of viticulture and viniculture the area of Rumania's winegrowing districts has been greatly enlarged in the past few years. The present Rumanian vineyard covers more than 741,300 acres and produces more than 132,000,000 gallons of wine, most of it white wine.

The principal vineyards are the Cotnari and the Murfatlar, producing dessert wines; the Tirnave; the Dealul-Mare, the Focsain and the Banat, producing both red and white table wines. The best-known and the most renowned of the Rumanian white wines come from the Tirnave Mare and Tirnave Mica valleys, in the centre of the country. The TIRNAVE PEARL, a wine made from a mixture of several grapes which give it a very well-balanced bouquet, is well known outside Rumania.

Other white wines are made from a single vine-plant whose name they carry; for example, the FETEASCA DE TIRNAVE, RIESLING DE TIRNAVE, or RIESLING DE DEALUL-MARE, near Ploesti in Munténie.

The KADARKA is the most common red wine in the Balkans; the wine from Teremia, near the Yugoslav border, is often referred to; and there is also the SEGARCEA CABERNET, made from the *Cabernet* grape. It comes from the vineyards of the *Valea Calugaresca* (Valley of the Monks) which lies to the east of Ploesti. The SADOVA is a slightly sweet rosé from the Dragasani region, where the vine is often more than a century old. The white dessert wines from these parts are very highly thought of. In the north, the COTNARI wine is sweet and fruity. The MURFATLAR, from near the Black Sea, has a fine orange-blossom bouquet which is probably unique.

Rumanian wines are exported mainly to Germany, Austria and the Eastern European countries, although the Focsani Fructexport also sells a certain amount of wine to such countries as Switzerland, Belgium, Holland, Sweden, Denmark, France and Great Britain. Rumania has many indigenous stocks, but is making a real effort to improve the quality of its wines through a progressive elimination of hybrids and a selection of vine types. The new co-operatives have also done much to improve the standard in vine culture and turn the country's great wine potential to the best account.

BULGARIA

Before World War II, the vineyards of Bulgaria spread over an area of 331,200 acres; in 1968 they covered 494,200 acres. This increase is due on the one hand to a major change in the system of ownership, and on the other to a systematic reconstruction of the vineyards so that mechanization could be introduced on a large scale. The country today produces 66,000,000 gallons of wine per year; 52 per cent red wines, 48 per cent white wines. Although it is divided into viticultural regions, it would not be correct to attribute a particular wine to a given region. It might also be practical to mention only the better-known Bulgarian wines.

The *Dimiat* is the best-known grape. It grows near the Black Sea, in the Choumen regions and farther west in the province of Tarnovo. It produces a dry but fruity wine of a rich golden-green colour. Wines are named by their grape or by regional names, and sometimes by a combination of both. (WARNENSKI DIMIAT means a DIMIAT from Warna.) These wines recall the Rieslings, while the wines from the *Misket* grapes, in particular the MISKET KARLOVA or the MISKET DE KARLOVO, bring to mind the Sylvaner, as does the SONGURLARE MISKET which is produced on the coast. Other, more common white wines are the BALGARSKE SLANTSE or BULGARIAN SUN made from the *Furmint* grape; the DOUNAVSKA PERLA or PEARL OF THE DANUBE, and the SLANTCHEV BIRAG or SUNSHINE COAST, made from a Georgian grape, the *Rehaziteli*. The SLAVIANKA is a wine made from the *Muscat* grape; it is golden and full-flavoured, with the characteristic savour of the grape.

Although there are many more red wines, they are much less varied. Usually they are known by their grape. PAMID is purely for domestic consumption. GAMSA (the Bulgarian name for KADARKA) is an agreeable wine, with a pleasant bouquet, especially when young. Sometimes it is known by a local name such as KRAMOLINSKA, or wine from Kramoline.

MAVROUD, produced in the Assennovgrad region, has a rich dark red colour, and is somewhat acid, with an alcoholic content of 11 to 12 degrees. This wine is often used for blending with lighter red wines.

MELNIK is a wine from the north-west region. It is dark red, somewhat full-bodied, but of good quality. The *Melnik* grape variety has been cultivated in Bulgaria since ancient times and is probably a plant of French origin. The CABERNET is another Bulgarian wine made from the *Cabernet-Sauvignon* grape, which was introduced into the country.

YUGOSLAVIA

The history of Yugoslav vine culture and wines is similar to that of Italy, France and Spain. They all use the same vinification methods and even the same grapes: the *Burgundac* or *Pinot Noir*, the *Cabernet*, the *Merlot* and the *Riesling*. The Yugoslav climate and soil give a particular character to its wines. The vineyards cover 640,000 acres and produce, apart from table grapes, 110 to 132 million gallons of wine. The vine is cultivated throughout the country, from north to south in the following six regions: Slovenia, Istria, Crotia, Dalmatia, Serbia and Macedonia.

Slovenia has a flourishing vineyard situated in the Save and Drave valleys, including the districts of Ljutomer, Ormoz, Ptuj, Radgona and Maribor, as well as along the Adriatic to the Italian frontier. In this area, most of the white wines are made from the grapes of the *Traminer, Riesling Rhenan, Riesling Laski,* the *Sauvignon, Pinot Blanc* and *Sipon*, the local counterparts of the Hungarian *Furmint*. The Slovenia region produces 486,000 bottles of wine annually, about 9 per cent of the national output.

Istria is known for its red wines made from the grapes of the *Feran, Bogonja (Gamay), Merlot* and *Cabernet* varieties. Two white wines are also produced here, one made from the *Pinot* grapes, the other from the *Malvasia* or Malmsey grape. The Istrian growers employ the Italian methods of mixed cultivation, so that other plants can be seen growing side by side with the vines.

Croatia is one of the most important winegrowing regions in Bulgaria. The north produces white wines, light but somewhat acid, or wines with a rich bouquet and very high alcohol content. *Traminer, Riesling, Sauvignon* and *Semillon* grape varieties are greatly cultivated in this area. The coastal wines are red, similar to the full and heady wines from the Mediterranean. This area produces 5,038,000 gallons of wine, 35 per cent of the national yield.

The most famous grape-vine in Dalmatia is the *Plavac*, which produces a red wine of the same name. It is a full-bodied, ruby-red wine with a very special bouquet. Dalmatia also makes some semi-dry red wines known as DINGNAC and POSTUP. An unusual type of sweet wine called Prosek can be found in this area but it rarely appeals to the taste of foreigners.

The Serbian vineyard is the largest of all the Yugoslav vineyards and is responsible for half the wine produced in Yugoslavia. It makes mainly white wines and just a few red wines such as the Zupa. The area around the town of Smederevo grows a white wine called Smederevka, similar to Chablis from Burgundy. Other celebrated white wines are the Fruska Gora, the Vrsac and the Subotica. Elsewhere in Serbia, an indigenous grape, the *Prokupac*, is cultivated. It makes a very good table wine. Macedonia mainly produces ordinary red wines. Yugoslavia also exports wines from Herzegovina: the Zilavka, a dry white wine from Kosovo and Metohija. This is known in West Germany as Amselfelder Spätburgunder.

Since the end of World War II, the establishment of co-operative underground-cellars has done much to improve methods of vinification and wine-storage. Yugoslavian wine (8,800,000 to 11,000,000 gallons per year) is exported mainly to East Germany, Czechoslovakia, Poland and Italy.　B. Pogrimilovic

THE SOVIET UNION

Russia is the fifth largest wineproducing country in the world, after Italy, France, Spain and Argentina. Whether it be a good or a bad year, it produces 330 to 396 million gallons of wine. The viticultural zone forms a large semi-circle in the south of the country, stretching from the Rumanian frontier to the borders of Iran, India, Turkestan and Mongolia. However the most important ones are going from the west to the east: Moldavia, the Ukraine, the Crimea, the lower waters of the Don, the Krasnodar region, Russian Georgia and Usbekistan.

Vine culture in these region goes back for many years. Long before the emergence of man, the vine itself existed in a wild state in the land now occupied by the Soviet Union. Russian botanists have discovered on the shores of the Black Sea at least sixty varieties of wild vine, several of which were probably domesticated as far back as the stone age. Viniculture was developed in the bronze age in Georgia at least, where objects dating from this period and representing drinking scenes have been discovered. Much later Homer, Xenophon and Heroditus refer to it in their works.

Moldavia, which was formerly Bessarabia and was part of Rumania, produces mainly table wines. Pinot and Aligoté are among the white wines, Bordo is a red, no doubt made from the *Cabernet-Sauvignon* of the Bordeaux type. Some Moldavian wines may be found on the markets of Western Europe: the Negri de Purkar and the Cabernet, both reds, and the Fetysk, a white wine. Ukrainian white wines are made from the *Riesling* and *Aligoté* grapes, the red wines from the *Cabernet* grape variety.

The Crimea has a wide range of wines. Dry white wines are the Semillon Oreanda, the Riesling Massandra and the Aligoté Ay-Danil. Dry red wines are the Cabernet Livadia, the Saperavi Massandra, and the Bordo Ay-Danil. There is also a wide range of dessert wines: white, rosé or red. Among the white wines, the more celebrated are the Muscat Massandra and the Muscat Livadia, the rosé Muscat Alupka and, of the reds, the Muscat Kuchuk-Lambat. The Crimea also produces wines known as Port, Madeira and Tokay. Of course these wines are named by type, not by origin.

The subtropical climate of Georgia is ideal for cultivating the vine. It produces white wines such as Napureouli and Tsinandali, and red wines like the Mukuzani and Saperavi which are to be found on sale, for example, in Great Britain.

Armenia, where the vine is said to have originated, produces Tokay and dessert wines. Uzbekistan, on the border with Iran, has mainly dessert wines, red or white, and port-type wines.

Sparkling wines, whether red or white, such as the Tzymliansk and rosé, are produced today by the so-called *en continu* method from the vineyards of the Crimea, Krasnodar and the Kouban valley. The well-known "Donski" is a sparkling wine made along the banks of the Don. Sparkling wines made from the *Muscat* grape also deserve a mention.

It is strange but true that the U.S.S.R. produces six times more sweet and dessert wines than dry wines —this is partly because in Russia wine is consumed mainly on festive occasions rather than every day.

WINES OF CENTRAL EUROPE

AUSTRIA

WACHAU

White wines	Loibener Kaiserwein	Dürnsteiner Liebenberg	Weissenkirchner Achleiten	Undhof Wieden Spät- und
	Unterloibener Rotenberg	Kremser Pfaffenberg	Undhof Wieden-	Auslese Grüne Veltliner
	Unterloibener Burgstall	Steiner Pfaffenberg	Weissburgunder	Dürnsteiner Muskat-Ottonel
	Kremser Kögl	Steiner Schreck	Weisser Burgunder	Zöbinger Muskat-Ottonel
	Steiner Goldberg	Dürnsteiner Hollerin	Ruländer	Sonnenkönig
	Kremser Kremsleiten	Dürnsteiner Himmelsstiege	Neuburger	Heiligensteiner Sauvignon
	Kremser Wachtberg	Weissenkirchner Klaus		Undhof Goldberg

Red wines . . . . . Alter Knabe - Saint Laurent

VIENNA-SÜDBAHN

White wines . . .	Wiener Nussberg	Klosterneuburger	Kahlenberger Traminer	Kavalier-Zierfandler
	Gumpoldskirchner Spiegel	Rheinriesling	Sauvignon	Zierfandler Ried Kramer
	Gumpoldskirchner Sonnberg	Nussberger Schwarze Katz	Weisser Burgunder	Gumpoldskirchner
	Gumpoldskirchner	Original Gumpoldskirchner	Klostercabinet	Zierfandler
	Goldknöpfel	Rheinriesling	Franzhauser Kabinett-	Goldknöpferl-Rotgipfler
	Gumpoldskirchner Rasslerin	Neuburger	Neuburger	Rotgipfler Spät- und
	Gumpoldskirchner	Neuburger Spät-	Grüner Veltliner	Auslesen
	Grimmling	und Auslesen	Jungherrn Müller-Thurgau	Kreuzweingarten-Spätlese
	Gumpoldskirchner	Badener Lumpentürl-	Königswein Zierfandler	Zierfandler-Rotgipfler
	Stocknarrn	Neuburger	Zierfandler	Sonnberg
				Spätrot-Rotgipfler

Red wines	Blauburgunder	Saint Laurent		
	Soosser Blauer Burgunder	Soosser Blauer Portugieser	Saint-Laurent-Ausstich	Vöslauer Rotwein

BURGENLAND

White wines	Ruster Greiner	Ruster Ruländer	Original Golser	Ruster Ausbruch
	Ruster Satz	Original Joiser Ruländer	Welschriesling	Müller-Thurgau
	Ruster Turner	Ruster Muskateller	Weisser Storch Ruster	Beerenauslese
	Ruster Vogelsang	Muskat-Ottonel	Welschriesling	Oggauer Ambrosi
	Muskat-Traminer	Welschriesling-Spätlesen		

Red wines	Ruster Baumgarten	Rust Limberger	Oggauer Blaufränkisch	Schützenberger Rotkelch
	Ruster G'märk	Ruster Blaublurgunder	Blaufränkisch	Blaufränkisch Spätlesen
	Ruster Mittelkräften	Blauer Burgunder Spätlese	Pöttelsdorfer Bismarckwein	

STEIERMARK

White wines	Klöcher Berg	Köbelberg	Silberberg	Hochbrudersegg
	Hartberger Ring	Sulztal	Hochkittenberg	Muskat-Sylvaner
	Hartberger Löffelbach	Glanzer Berg	Morillon	Sausaler Welschriesling
	Grassnitzberg	Steinbach	Ruländer	Müller-Thurgau
	Ottenberger Witscheinberg	Schlossberg	Muskateller	

Red wine . . . . . Schilcher

CZECHOSLOVAKIA

Furmint   Harchlevelu   Lipouvina   Muskat de Lunel   Muskat Ztly

HUNGARY

White wines	Tokaji Szamorodni (dry)	Badacsonyi Kéknyelü	Balatonfüredi	Debröi Hárslevelü
	Tokaji Furmint	Badacsonyi Szürkebarát	Móri Ezerjó	Léanyka

Red wines	Egri Bikavér	Soproni Kékfrankos		

Dessert wines	Tokaji Aszu (3-5 puttonos)	Tokaji Szamorodni (sweet)		

WINES OF THE BALKANS

YUGOSLAVIA

White wines	Banatski rizling (Kreaca) — dry Belan — dry Graševina (Italian Riesling) — dry	Grk Malvazija — dry and sweet Maraština — dry and medium-dry Muskat Ottonel — medium-dry and sweet	Pošip — dry Rebula — dry Silvanac — dry and medium-dry Smederevka — dry	Traminac — dry and medium-dry Vugava Žilavka — dry
Rosé wines	Cviček — dry	Opol dalmatinski — dry	Ruzica — dry	
Red wines	Burgundac crni (pinot noir) — dry Dingač — medium-dry Frankovka — dry	Kavčina (Žametna črnica) — dry Kraski teran — dry Kratošija — dry	Muskat ruza (Moscate rosa) — medium-sweet and sweet Plavac — dry Postup — medium-dry	Prokupac — dry and medium-sweet Refošk — dry and medium-sweet Vranac — dry

BULGARIA

White wines	Pomoria Dimiat Preslav Dimiat Tchirpan Dimiat	Varna Dimiat Euxinograd Hemona	Songurlaré Misket Liaskovetz Riesling	Riesling of the Valley of Roses
Red wines	Chipka Novosseltzi Gamza Pavlikeni Gamza	Soukhindol Gamza Kalouger Kramolin	Loud Guidia Assénovgrad Mavroud Melnik	Pamid Pirgovo
Dessert wines	Bisser Hebros	Kadarka "Valley of Roses" Vratza Misket	Pomoria Slavianka	Tarnovo Varna

ROUMANIA

White wines	Dealul Mare Diosig Drăgâsani	Husi Murfatlar Muscel	Nicoresti Teremia-Tomnatic-Comlos Valea lui Mihai	Valea Târnavelor Cotnar
Red wines	Sarica-Niculitel	Cotnar		

WINES OF THE SOVIET UNION

White wines of the Crimea	Aligoté Ay-Danil Riesling Massandra	Riesling Alkadar	Semillon Oreanda
White wines of Krasnodar	Riesling Abraou	Riesling Anapa	
White wines of Georgia	Gurdjurni Manadis Mukuzani	Myshako Riesling Mzvane	Napurçouli Tsinandali
Red wines of Azerbaidjan	Chemakha	Kurdamir	Matrassa
Red wines of the Crimea	Bordo Ay-Danil	Cabernet Livadia	Saperavi Massandra
Red wines of Krasnodar	Cabernet Abraou		

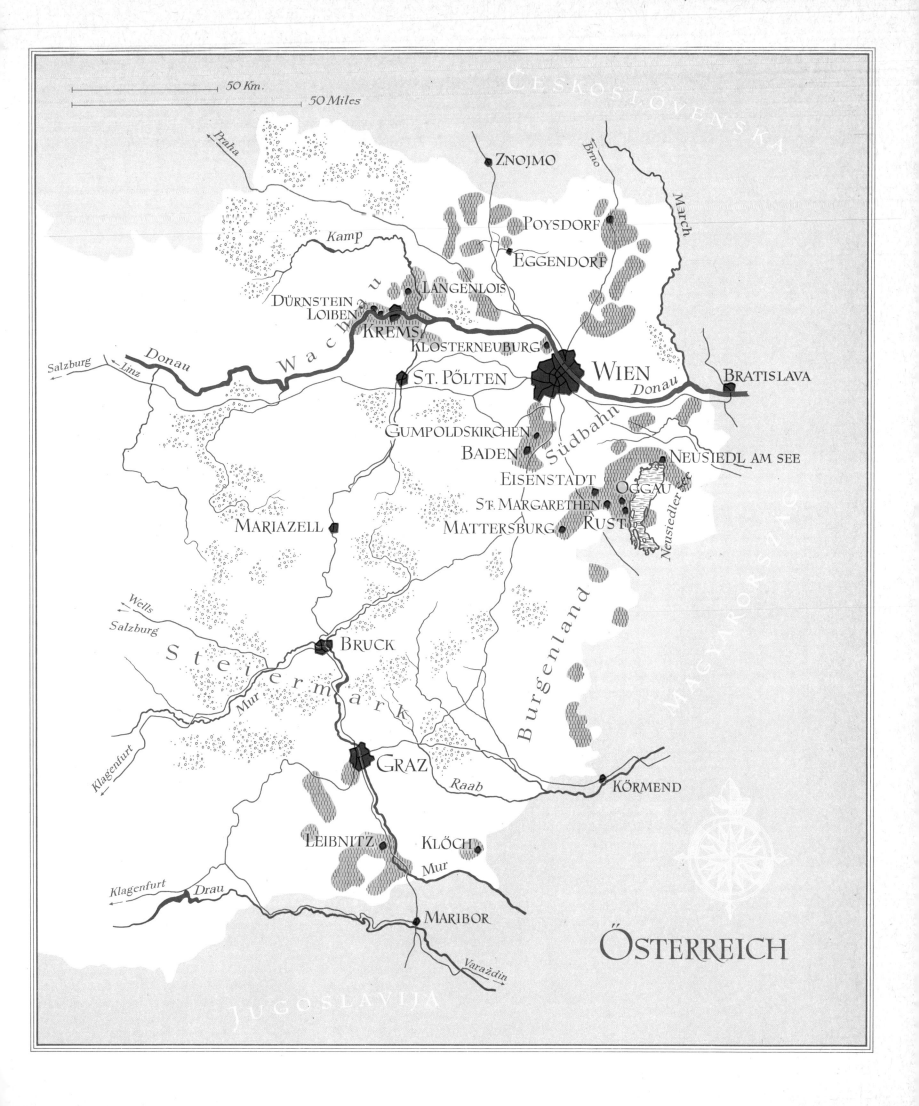

ČESKOSLOVENSKÁ

50 Km.
50 Miles

Praha

Brno

March

ZNOJMO

POYSDORF
EGGENDORF

Kamp

Wachau

LANGENLOIS

DÜRNSTEIN
LOIBEN

KREMS

KLOSTERNEUBURG

Salzburg Linz Donau

St. PÖLTEN

WIEN

Donau

BRATISLAVA

GUMPOLDSKIRCHEN

Südbahn

BADEN

NEUSIEDL AM SEE

EISENSTADT

OGGAU

St. MARGARETHEN

RUST

MARIAZELL

MATTERSBURG

Neusiedler See

Burgenland

MAGYARORSZÁG

Wells

Salzburg

Steiermark

BRUCK

Mur

Klagenfurt

Raab

KÖRMEND

GRAZ

LEIBNITZ

KLÖCH

Mur

Klagenfurt Drau

MARIBOR

ÖSTERREICH

Varaždin

JUGOSLAVIJA

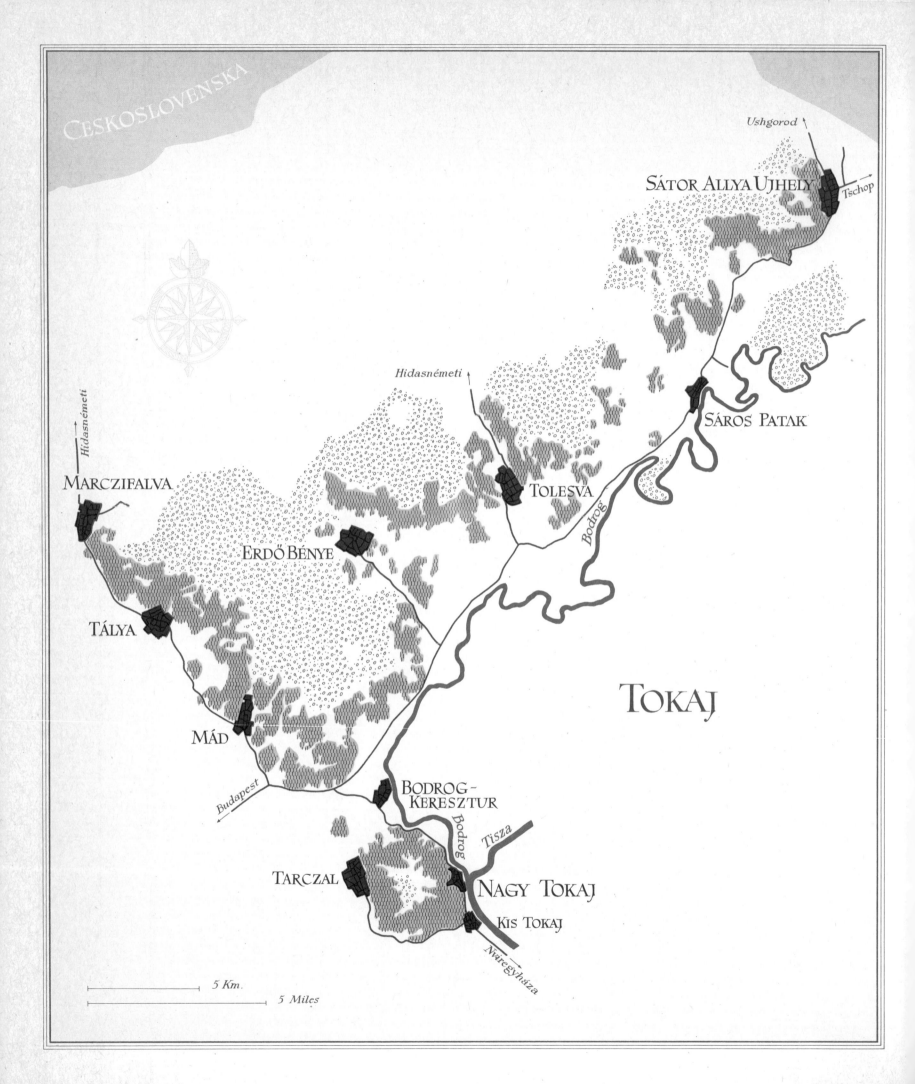

CESKOSLOVENSKA

Ushgorod

SÁTOR ALLYA UJHELY

Tschop

Hidasnémeti

SÁROS PATAK

Hidasnémeti

MARCZIFALVA

TOLESVA

Bodrog

ERDŐ BÉNYE

TÁLYA

TOKAJ

MÁD

Budapest

BODROG-
KERESZTUR

Bodrog

Tisza

TARCZAL

NAGY TOKAJ

KIS TOKAJ

Nviregyháza

5 Km.

5 Miles

THE WINES OF THE EASTERN MEDITERRANEAN

JOSEPH JOBÉ

All the countries of the Eastern Mediterranean basin have cultivated the vine since ancient times. The Egypt of the Pharaohs, the Promised Land of the Hebrews, the vast Persian Empire as well as the ancient Greek cities all produced wine. Under the benevolent eyes of the gods, the poets sang its praises, artisans and artists immortalized it on bas-reliefs and frescoes. The aged Homer celebrated "wine that gives us a manly heart"; Archilochus put the following truculent lines into the mouth of a galley-slave:

> One cannot mount guard
> While dying of thirst

The gentle Anachreon had a more melancholy turn of phrase:

> When I drink wine
> My pain is driven away
> And my dark thoughts
> Fly to the ocean winds

Like an echo come the words from the Book of Proverbs (xxxi, 6-7): "Give strong drink unto him that is ready to perish, and wine unto those that be of heavy hearts. Let him drink, and forget his poverty, and remember his misery no more."

When paganism gave way to Christianity the people of the Mediterranean basin continued to cultivate the vine and to produce wine right up to the Moslem era.

The later history of the vine in these regions may be explained in part by the ebb and flow of Christianity and Islam. Even today, Moslem influence is predominant in Egypt and Jordan; it is also felt in Moslem Turkey and, more surprisingly, in Christian Greece through the marketing of a considerable part of the vine-harvest, not as wine but as dried grapes or raisins (more than a hundred thousand tons are produced per year in each country).

After World War I, cultivation of the vine in this part of the world increased at a phenomenal rate. The surface under cultivation in Greece multiplied fifteen-fold and production of wine rose ten times. Cyprus, on the other hand, made somewhat slower progress. But in Turkey, between 1939 and 1966, the number of vineyards doubled and wine production rose by four times. The evolution of the vineyard in Israel shows remarkable variations: the area under cultivation rose from 30,000 acres in 1936 to 45,000 acres in 1946, only to decrease in 1948 to 13,500 acres, rising again between 1956 and 1966 to 25,000 acres. However, despite these fluctuations, the actual production of wine has been constantly on the increase. From 506,000 gallons in 1936 it rose to 8,095,120 gallons in 1966. This means that from approximately the same area of vines as were under cultivation in 1936, sixteen times as much wine was being produced 30 years later. Egypt and the Lebanon have also increased their viticultural areas and their production of wine, but to a lesser degree. At present Egypt produces about 990,000 gallons and the Lebanon 836,000 gallons of wine; these are negligible amounts in comparison with the large viticultural regions of France. The Greeks and the Cypriots are, needless to say, the heaviest wine-drinkers of all these peoples.

GREECE

In Greece, vineyards and wine are as old as the gods, the land and the poets. Dionysus cultivated the vine and Homer sang the praises of wine in the Iliad and the Odyssey. More important still, the Greeks transplanted the vine to their colonies. Thus it is that many famous vineyards like those of Sicily, Malaga, Jerez and the Rhône valley are of Greek origin.

The present viticultural area is 500,000 acres which produce 83,600,000 gallons of wine, 150,000 tons of dessert grapes and as many dried grapes. The Greek likes his wine, and drinks about 50 to 70 pints a year. The country exports nearly 11,000,000 gallons a year.

The Peloponnese is the most important viticultural region. Its wines are mentioned on most wine-lists in hotels. They are dry white wines, such as the DEMESTICHA, the SANTO HELENA, the ANTIKA or the SANTA

"Let us drink wine, the wine of noble Bacchus; when we drink it our troubles sleep." The words of the Greek lyricist Anachreon convey exactly the spirit of this scene decorating an antique vase.

LAOURA. The Peloponnese vineyard may be divided into three regions. The central part produces a well-balanced white wine, the MANTINEIA, around the ruins of the same name. The Patras region produces excellent dessert wines, such as the MAVRODAPHNE (red) or the MUSCAT DE PATRAS (white). In the third part, along the banks of the Gulf of Corinth and in particular at Nemea, a red full-bodied wine is made, the NEMEA or the HIGH NEMEA, depending on the altitude of the vineyard; these start at sea-level and reach up to about 2,500 feet in the interland.

On the mainland, Attica, already a land of wines and olives in ancient times, today produces a whole range of white wines made from the *Saviatiano* grape. The PALLINI is the best wine in these parts, though it is not the best-known. Attica is also famous for its RETSINA, which in the opinion of many is the best wine in the land. The tourist who likes to taste the local wines will find something to satisfy his curiosity almost everywhere. For the benefit of those who visit the beautiful ruins of the site dedicated to Apollo, there is the wine of Arakhova, a village near Delphi. Macedonia offers the best red wine, NAOUSSA, made from the *Popolka* grape which is also known as the *Noir de Naoussa*. Thessalia has two red wines, the RAPSANI and the AMBELAKIA; Epirus makes only one semi-sweet white wine, the ZITSA.

The soil and climate of the Greek islands are usually favourable to the vine, and nearly every island has its own vineyard. Crete, for example, has a very important growth. In the east, there are fortified red table wines, wines of substance though not much spirit, made from the *Leatiko* grape; farther west, the Heraklion region produces red wines made from the *Ketsifali* and *Mandilari* grape varieties; these are full-bodied, rich wines with a heavy bouquet. At the farthest point west, in the region of Canea, only the red grape *Romeikon* is cultivated. On the other hand, the little island of Santonni is very fertile thanks to its volcanic soil, and produces such dry white wines as the NYCHTERI or sweet white wines like the VINO SANTO. The island of Samos offers a whole range of white wines, dry wines, resinated wines and sweet dessert wines, known as MUSCAT DE SAMOS. The islands of Rhodes and Zakinthos also have dry white wines, while the island of Leucadia produces red wines.

Greece is, of course, also the country of the RETSINA, a wine which has a very special taste. It is a bitter taste, acquired by flavouring the wine with resin during the process of fermentation. The resin comes from a pine-tree—the *calitris quadrivalvis*—which grows in that region. As the Retsina takes on a bitter taste only after it has aged one year, those who are tasting it for the first time are advised to try a youthful Retsina, preferably from the Attica area; the resin flavour is not to the liking of all visitors.

Well-known and highly thought of are the dessert wines of Greece, starting perhaps with the Muscat de Samos already mentioned, and going on to the Mavrodaphni, a very sweet red wine, a type of Malaga. We might also mention that the *Malvasia*, or Malmsey grape, originated in Peloponnisos. Today, the grape can be found in many other countries, Italy, France, Spain and Madeira for instance, where it has adapted well to local conditions and gives excellent white wines.

Greece can legitimately be proud of its viticultural history—was not Homer, 2,800 years ago, already singing the praises of the wine of his country? "There is no moment more pleasurable than when the guests, sitting around a well-laden table, lend their ear to the voice of a singer, whilst the cup-bearer, having drawn wine from the amphoras, moves round the table to pour into each and every cup in turn."

CYPRUS

Thanks to its privileged geographical situation, Cyprus not only cultivated the vine at a very early date but participated throughout ancient times in the flourishing wine trade between Egypt, Greece and Rome. After the fall of the Roman Empire in the west in A.D. 476, there followed a long night of seven centuries for the vine.

The Crusaders and the Knights Templars were responsible for the revival of viniculture in Cyprus. But again, when the Turks arrived in 1571, the vine suffered another period of neglect although it did not disappear completely. It survived in the south-west part of the isle on the sunny slopes of Mounts Troghodhus and Makhera. From the grapes which grow in these parts, the Cypriot winegrowers make mainly ordinary table wines: red full-bodied wines, with a high tannin content, such as Afames and Othello. There are fewer white wines. The driest and the best are Aphrodite and Ansinoe. A rosé, Kokkinelli, is a

fresh, semi-sweet wine, although it is somewhat darker in colour than most rosés. The best Cypriot wine is a dessert wine called Commandaria. Named after the Knights Templars who guarded the Temple of Colossus, it is made from white or red grapes, specially dried in order to increase their sugar content. Usually the red grapes are used as they are more abundant. Only about twenty villages (Kalokhono, Zoopiyi, Yerass, Ayias and Mancas are the better known) are authorized to produce Commandaria, and experts can distinguish the qualities which each village gives to the Commandaria just as a connoisseur of Burgundy can tell from which particular vineyard along the Côte de Nuits or Beaune the Burgundy he is tasting has come.

Cyprus exports a good third of its wines, in particular red wines and Commandaria.

As a final point of interest, one should mention that it was vine-shoots from Cyprus that produced, in the fifteenth century, the first Madeira wine.

TURKEY

If one believes, as many do, that Anatolia is the mother-country of the European vine, then Turkey has indeed a long heritage of viticulture. For as long as there were non-Moslem peoples living within the Turkish frontiers in Europe, there were Turkish wines for sale on the domestic and foreign markets. At the beginning of the twentieth century, following a period of political unrest, wine production went into a steep decline, but the whole picture changed with the establishment in 1928 of a Monopolies Board. From its lowest ebb in 1928 of 590,000 gallons, production reached 9,556,000 gallons in 1966. However, only 2 to 3 per cent of the grapes grown are used to make wine. Turkey has white wines *(beyez)* and red wines

(kirmizi) which are found mainly in Thrace and along the shores of the Sea of Marmara, in Izmir (Smyrna) and in Anatolia. The best of the dry white wines usually come from the *Hasandede*, *Narince* and *Emir* grape varieties. The best red wines are made from the *Oküzgüzö-bogazkere*, *Papaskarasin* and *Kalecikkarasi* grape varieties; these wines have a very dark colour.

Well known on the international market is Buzbag, a wine from Anatolia made from the *Bogazkere* grape, and Trakya, a dry red or white wine from the European part of Turkey. Sweden imports Beyaz, a semi-dry white wine, which comes from Tekirdag in Thrace.

Other wines of quality are the red Adabag and Kalebag. The Turks like sweet wines and the term "sarap" on a label indicates a very sweet wine, too sweet for the Western palate. Among the best of the dessert wines can be named the TEKEL GAZIANTEP and the TEKEL KALEBAG ANKARA, which are both red wines, and a white wine the TEKEL MISBAG IZMIR. There are also some ordinary local wines: for example, in Istanbul there is the GÜZEL MARMARA, either a red or a white dry or semi-dry wine; Ankara has the GÜZELBAG, which is also either a red or dry or semi-dry white wine; Izmir produces the IZMIR, once again a red or dry white wine and from Central Anatolia comes both red and white ÇUBUK.

ISRAEL

The Bible attests that the people of Israel cultivated the vine. If ever a cluster of grapes was famous, it is surely the one brought back by the Hebrew scouts from Canaan. And if there ever was a famous drunkard, albeit an involuntary one, it is certainly Noah.

In the same way that Palestine has a turbulent history, so too was the history of its viticulture, for the vine was destroyed by some, replanted by others; reintroduced by the Crusaders, only to be finally abandoned for many centuries.

When the first Zionists started to filter into Palestine around 1882, they planted, on the advice of the Rothschilds, French vine-plants. With time, the surface under cultivation increased, and today it reaches about 25,000 acres. Vineyards which produce grapes for making wine are planted in different regions of the country stretching from the south to the north: in the Negev, along the coast-line and on the foothills of Judea, in the mountains around Jerusalem, in the Sharon valley, on the hills of Samaria as well as in Upper and Lower Galilee. The average rainfall varies from 8 inches a year in the Negev to 27 inches in the mountains of Upper Galilee.

The *Cargnan* (41 per cent) and the *Alicante Grenache* (32 per cent) are the most common grape varieties. The winegrowers and viticultural co-operatives produce every conceivable type of wine, even sparkling Champagne-like wine made by the *méthode champenoise*. To name a few: The AVDAT WHITE (dry) and the CARMEL HOCK (semi-dry) are white wines; the MIKWE ISRAIL (dry) and the ADOM ATIC (semi-dry) are red wines, and the BINAYMINA is a rosé. There are also some white dessert wines (MUSCATEL) or reds (INDEPENDENCE WINE). Annual production reaches a total of about 7,920,000 gallons of which about 330,000 are for export.

An Israeli drinks only seven to nine pints of wine a year but he eats 26 to 28 pounds of table grapes.

The viticultural area in the neighbouring countries of Syria, the Lebanon and Jordan is much larger than in Israel. But as these three countries are of the Moslem faith, the produce of their vineyards is marketed, locally or abroad, in the form of table grapes or dried grapes; very little is made into wine. Jordan produces from 22,000 to 330,000 gallons of wine; Syria about 550,000 gallons, and the Lebanon 836,000 gallons, while the State of Israel produces more than five times as much from an area which is ten times smaller than that of her three neighbours put together. There is also a small vineyard in Iran, in the Azerbaijan and Teheran regions. Kurdistan is noted for its wine which on pressing acquires the scent of violets. Even in the best years, however, this country does not produce more than 88,000 gallons of wine.

EGYPT

The paintings on the tombs of the Pharaohs bear witness to the antiquity of the vine in this country (see page 12). However, after the arrival of the Arabs on the scene, vine cultivation fell into a decline, and wines became either very rare or very bad. Towards the beginning of this century, however, the vines were replanted, and after thirty years of hard work, Egyptian wines have once again found their qualities of yesteryear. And even if Egypt does not figure in many books on viticulture and wine, nor is usually referred to in statistical data, the country of the Pharaohs nonetheless produces each year an average of about 990,000 gallons of wine, and excellent wine at that.

The Maryat region, west of the Nile delta, was already famous for its wine in ancient times: Cleopatra offered Caesar a wine from Mareotide when he came to pay her a visit. This region produces two white wines, the CLOS MARIOUT and the CRUS DES PTOLÉMÉES, as well as a red wine, the CLOS MATAMIR.

As Egypt is a Moslem country, its consumption of wine is very low and its imports are negligible. A third of its production is exported.

WINES OF GREECE

DRY WHITE WINES

Agrylos	Gerania	Lindos de Rhodes	Pallini	Verdes
Arcadia	King Minos	Mantineia	Samos	Votrys
Demesticha	Lefkas	Marco	Santa Helena	Ymettos
Peza				Santa Laoura

MEDIUM-SWEET WHITE WINES

Gerania	Pallini	Samos	Zitsa

SWEET WHITE WINES

Samos	Muscat Rion de Patras	Muscat de Limnos	Paros	Rhodes Kair (or Chevalier de Rhodes)
Muscat de Samos	Muscat Achaïa de Patras	Vino Santo de Santorin	Pilion	Ymettos
Muscat de Rhodes				

DRY RED WINES

Agrylos	Halkidiki	Demesticha	Lefkas	Nadussa
Archanès	Castel Danielis	Peza	Marco	Nemea

SWEET RED WINE

Mavrodaphni

SPARKLING WINE

Zitsa

WINES OF ISRAEL

DRY WHITE WINES

Askalon Blanc 1963	Avdat White	Binyamina Blanc	Ein Guedi White	Mikwe Israel Blanc

MEDIUM-DRY WHITE WINES

Carmel Hock	Doron	Ein Guedi	Hock d'Askalon	Hock Patron

DESSERT WINES

Ashdod	Golden Cream	Muscat Supérieur	Muscatel - 19°	Topaz Ein Guedi

ROSÉ WINES

Binyamina Rosé	Mikwe Israel	Pink (dry)	Rose of Carmel (medium-dry)	Vin Rosé d'Askalon

DRY RED WINES

Arad	Avdat Red	Ben-Ami 1965	Binyamina Red	Mikwe Israel

MEDIUM-DRY RED WINES

Adom Atic	Askalon Rouge 1965	Château Binyamina	Ein Guedi Red	Mont Rouge

DESSERT WINES

Château Richon Red	Hadar	Mikwe Israel-Dessert	Porath Atic	Poria
Ein Guedi Red Wine	Independence Wine			

WINES OF CYPRUS

DRY WHITE WINES	RED WINES	ROSÉ WINES	DESSERT WINES
Aphrodite	Cyprus	Othello	Commandaria
Arsinoe	Afames	Kokkineli	Muscat de Chypre

WINES OF EGYPT

RED WINES

Clos Mariout   Cru des Ptolémées

WHITE WINES

Clos Matamir

WINES OF TURKEY

DRY WHITE WINES

Barbaros	Doluca	Kulüp beyaz	Merih	Tekel ürgüp
Diren	Kalebag	Marmara Incisi	Quakaya yildizi	Trakya

MEDIUM-DRY WHITE WINES

Beyaz   Narbag

SWEET WHITE WINES

Tekez Misbag izmir   Adabag

RED WINES

Buzbag	Kalebag	Kulüp	Merih	Trakya	Yakut Damcasi

HELLAS

SHQIPERIA

JUGOSLAVIJA

BULGARIJA

TÜRKIYE

Skopje

Sofija

Plovdiv

Skopje

Makedonija

Nestos

Istanbul

ALEXANDROUPOLIS

THESSALONIKI

Thasos

KOZÁNI

Aliakmon

Thessalia

Olympos

Limnos

KÉRKYRA

LÁRISA

VÓLOS

Lesvos

Kérkyra
(Korfu)

Ípiros

LAMÍA

Evvoia

AIGAION PÉLAGOS

EGE DENIZI

Acheloos

Mórnos

Evvoia

Skyros

Chios

ARGOSTÓLION

Aitolia

PATRAI

Pineios

Peloponnesos

NEMEA

GAVRION

Andros

Samos

VATHY

Kephallinia

PYRGOS

ATHINAI

EVDILOS

MYTILINOI

Zákynthos

MANTINEIA

Tinos

TINOS

Ikaria

TRÍPOLIS

Kyklades

Kos

KALÁMAI

Evrotas

GYTHEION

MILOS

Kos

RODOS

IONION PÉLAGOS

Kýthira

KRITIKON PÉLAGOS

Rodos

OLYMPOS

Karpathos

PIGADIA

KOLYMPÁRI

IRÁKLION

Kriti

100 Km.

100 Miles

THE WINES OF AFRICA

DENIS BOUVIER and KENNETH MAXWELL

NORTH AFRICA

In the nature of its soil and its climate as much as the affinity of its distant past to Latin antiquity, North Africa resembles much more closely the European shores of the Western Mediterranean than the rest of the African continent. The Africans themselves, in fact, call it *djezira el Maghreb*, meaning "the Western Isle". The vine, like some messenger running ahead to announce the arrival of Mediterranean civilization, first saw life in the south, on the spurs of the mountains of Daïa, at the very doors of the Sahara. On this side, towards the north, begins the outer desert, which girdles the Mediterranean. From east to west, the vine runs along the coastal plains, up the hillsides and on the mountains, up to an altitude of about 3,600 feet, stretching from Kelibia in Tunisia as far as Bou Assida in Atlantic Morocco.

Here, as elsewhere, the vine has periodically appeared and disappeared throughout its history. There are many reasons for this, among them the continuous rivalries of nomadic and non-nomadic peoples, the conflicts between Christianity and Islam, and—nearer to our own times—the compelling demands of changing economics and politics.

No trace remains today to show whether the vine existed before the arrival of the Tyrians, who came to found Carthage. It is more than likely that they planted it themselves, in the valley of Medjerdah, before developing it further in their coastal colonies of

Northern Africa. But it was Rome who first undertook to colonize this province of Africa which she had taken over from Carthage. The legions sent by Caesar and later by Augustus put to good use their talents as builders, farmers and winegrowers. From Carthage, restored from its ashes, to Lixus, near today's Larache in Morocco, where legend has situated the Garden of the Hesperides, the very end of their world, Rome turned Mauritania into the cellar of its empire. The vine grew near the ports or, farther inland, on the slopes around Roman farms such as we see, for example, on the mosaics of Tabarka. This wine of Africa, so much appreciated in Rome, was equally appreciated in Byzantium, which gave a new impulse to the vine by converting the Berber tribes to Christianity and so spreading the influence of wine right into the mountainous regions of the Atlas.

This agricultural and vinicultural life, however, had soon to give way to a pastoral existence when the Moslem hordes from Arabia undertook, in the seventh century, to conquer North Africa and convert its people to Islam. The former Roman Empire fell then into total chaos. The winegrowing gave way before the increasing, often forced conversion to Islam of Christian or Israelite populations, and the vine was almost totally wiped out. It would be a mistake, nevertheless, to believe that as a result of the many fights inside the country and the invasions which followed each other, all contact ceased between the Maghreb and Christian Europe. There still existed in the Algeria of the tenth century nearly 40 cathedral cities, and there is every reason to think that cultivation including that of the vine was continued around them. In other regions more under Arab influence, as in Tunisia, Christian colonies began to spring up after the Eighth Crusade and, although they were very much spread out, wine trading could be established by Tunis between these colonies and Marseilles. In the *fondouk* of Tunis—the fondouk being the walled area reserved for Europeans outside a Moslem town—wine was sold both wholesale and retail, using hall-marked measures. In this way, the "presence" of wine was maintained, incredible as it may seem in a period when Christianity was finding itself in an almost continuous battle with Islam.

This presence was maintained until the arrival of the Turkish sultan's Janissaries who, in their turn, stained the history of the Maghreb with blood. Winegrowing died out rapidly, to revive only at the beginning of the eighteenth century. At this time, and notably in Tunisia during the Hussein Dynasty, a more settled way of life developed: the stone-built house reconquered the ground where previously nomads had pitched their tents. A few vineyards were recreated then, chiefly for consumption of the fruit: Tunisia possessed more than 5,000 acres of vines before the French began administrating the land.

The first colonists to follow the conquest into this land cared little about this local cultivation, although a few did take the risk of trying to produce wine in the African climate and with methods not yet adapted to local conditions. They soon ran into the problem of the musts, for in Mediterranean North Africa autumn is still a hot season. The temperature of the winemaking plants is still very high, fermentation takes place too rapidly, and the quality of the wine suffers. Several factors, however, contributed later to the development of this winegrowing, notably the arrival from 1871 on of settlers from Alsace and Lorraine, after the Franco-Prussian War. Others followed who had been defeated at home by the phylloxera epidemic of 1880. They came from all the vineyards of France, bringing with them a wide variety of vine-plants which they were able to exploit fully on this immense land, in a climate ideal for viticulture. To this could be added the opportunity of winning the French mainland market, where phylloxera had wiped out entire harvests. These winegrowers seized the chance of increasing the volume of production, both in Algeria and in Tunisia. But soon, the situation changed. In France, the vineyards were replanted with phylloxera-resistant American stock,

while North Africa saw the disease reach its own shores, although its spread was quickly stopped. France thus found herself, within a very few years, in possession of two important winegrowing regions, and it became essential to take steps to prevent a dangerous over-production. Vines producing only an ordinary wine were uprooted on a large scale. Fortunately, the Algerian wines—heavy, full-bodied, richly-coloured—harmoniously complemented the lighter and more acid wines of Languedoc-Roussillon of southern France. A permanent organization to export Algerian blending wines to France could thus be established. The North African vineyard was modernized and developed; the wines improved in quality, thanks also to planting new vines such as *Alicante-Bouschet, Cinsault, Carignan, Clairette* and *Grenache*. Better methods of vinification, more suited to the climate, were also introduced.

From 1919 to 1955, the North African vineyard progressed by leaps and bounds. Cultivation methods were rationalized and winegrowing became an industry, with increased mechanization, new transport and modern distribution methods. Even the actual vinification was now viewed as an industrial operation: the work, from the harvest to the bottling, was simplified to a maximum degree to make up for a lack of qualified labour. Some care was taken, too, to train the local inhabitants as vineyards workers by giving them agricultural instruction in specialized centres. While this effort was only limited in scope, a number of local winegrowers, in Oran especially, began to cultivate the vine for wineproduction, and began selling their produce, either direct to the market, or through the numerous agricultural co-operatives.

It is true that troubles due to over-production were never lacking and rivalry never disappeared in the various parts of the Mediterranean. But North Africa had acquired, with its vineyards, a new-found economic dimension of considerable importance.

Can one now look at the future of the North African vineyard more optimistically, after all the political upheavals which Morocco, Tunisia and Algeria have seen in turn? While that question perhaps cannot be answered yet, it would seem that wine production can be kept up provided two main conditions are borne in mind. The first is that the vines must not monopolize land in areas where the government would like to develop food production or industry. The second is that wine exports to foreign markets must be solidly covered by bilateral agreements with European countries and, more particularly, with France. This latter point clearly demonstrates how closely the North African viticultural industry is linked to and indeed controlled by economic and political contingencies.

TUNISIA

When one looks at a map of the Mediterranean around Tunisia, the little port of Kelibia appears like an island, surrounded by the sea on one side and by fields of olives and vines on the other. It is the first vineyard one meets in Tunisia when arriving from the east. Its wine grapes, *Muscat d'Alexandrie*, give a wine full of savour, as if impregnated with the perfumes of the Orient. But one must reach Carthage to be really in the heart of the great Tunisian vineyard. Here some Punic sculptor of long-ago has cut wine-grapes into the stonework of a monument to the goddess Tanit. In its modern form, this vineyard of 111,200 acres is the work of European colonists. To supplement the few local vines of table grapes spread along the coast, new vine-plants were introduced, such as *Grenache*, *Carignan*, *Alicante-Bouschet*, *Mourvèdre*, *Morastel*, *Vocéra*, *Pinot Noir* for red wines, and *Pedro-Ximenez*, *Sémillon*, *Sauvignon*, *Clairette de Provence*, *Beldi*, *Ugni*, *Merseguera*, *Muscat d'Alexandrie* and *Terracina* for whites.

The Tunisian vineyard, hit by phylloxera only in 1936, faced ten catastrophic years from 1943 to 1953. It managed to make a fresh start with regular expansion of production, despite the departure of many European winegrowers after Tunisia's Declaration of Independence in 1956. Today, 900 small concerns have regrouped themselves into well-equipped co-operatives; the cellars can hold more than ten million gallons of a wine which, thanks to the care given it by qualified workers, can be of a very good quality. But this already considerable stock of wine could be doubled, even tripled, for the French market, which is still the main customer. Home consumption of wine is dropping and new commercial outlets are urgently needed.

Going from west to east, the Tunisian vineyard is located in the regions of Bizerte, Mateur and Raf-Raf in the north; Tebourba, Massicault, Sedjourni and Carthage around Tunis; Khanguet, Grombalia, Bou Arkoub, Bir Drassen and Kelibia on Cape Bon. It thus forms a giant crescent around the Gulf of Tunis. Farther south, there are smaller vineyards, those of the Gulf of Hammamet and Zaghouan in the north, and Thibar at the foot of the Teboursouk mountains in the Caidate of the same name.

Tunisian law protects three types of wine. First of all, the VIN SUPÉRIEUR DE TUNISIE, a red, rosé or white wine with an alcohol content of 11° to 13°, depending on the region and the yield, and aged at least one year. Muscat is next, either with a simple *appellation d'origine* MUSCAT DE TUNISIE, or else with an *appellation d'origine contrôlée*, in which case it is sold under the name of the commune where it was produced, such as MUSCAT DE RADÈS or MUSCAT DE THIBAR. Finally, there are the vintage wines, with an *appellation d'origine contrôlée* but where the name of the vine does not appear, such as RADÈS and KELIBIA.

Most Tunisian wines are exported, but one can sample on the spot and with much pleasure a good SAINT-CYPRIEN or a THIBAR from the St. Joseph property.

ALGERIA

The colonization of Algeria was certainly responsible for the proper exploitation of its soil, the development of techniques for production, vinification and sale of their wines, all of which have placed Algeria among leading wineproducing countries.

Seven years after it gained its independence, the young state has kept alive its viticulture, despite the departure of its qualified European workers and the consequent disappearance of its non-Moslem domestic market. All honour to the nation. It is in any case absolutely essential for Algeria to maintain its viticulture: more than 50 per cent agricultural employment comes from the vineyards. The latter are in an even more important position when one realizes that not only do they produce the wine which provides, when sold, half of Algeria's total exports and cargoes for her merchant ships, the vineyards also supply the raw materials for a number of industries born of vinicultural side-products, such as the manufacture of alcohol, tartrates, oil, fertilizers and fodder. This trade requires costly and extensive equipment and installations, and the economic and social importance of the vini-viticultural production becomes even clearer. The government thus has not only the first preoccupation of making sure this colonial heritage produces profitably, but they must at the same time increase professional training and put a brake on the exodus from the countryside, which has been noticeable since 1962. A certain preference can understandably be seen, however, in favour of the conversion of the viticultural regions to cultivation of some product more independent of the French market, for the shipments of wine are at present only saleable in the former mother country, and the government must remember also that these sales are made thanks largely to commercial agreements which French vintners would be only too happy to see go.

The Algerian vineyard lies between La Calle in the east and Nemours (today called Ghazaouet) in the west, extending also from north to south, from the shores of the Mediterranean to the slopes of the Atlas upper plateau. Its total area is about 865,000 acres but its distribution has no uniformity, for Algeria is a very undulating land.

Apart from a few plants of local origin (*Hasseroum, Grilla, Farhana*), all the vine-plants grown in Algeria come from Europe, and have been grafted with American stocks to combat phylloxera. The red wines are usually wines for blending, full-bodied, with a high alcohol content and a good deal of tannin, although they can also be good vintage wines classified as of superior quality, or given a simple *appellation d'origine*. They come from vine-plants such as *Carignan, Cinsault, Alicante-Bouschet, Morastel, Mourvèdre, Gamay, Pinot Noir* and *Cabernet*. The white wines, which are usually of good quality, full-bodied, rather perfumed, and well alcoholized, come from plants such as *Clairette, Grenache, Ugni Blanc, Faramon, Macabéo* and *Merseguera*, although *Alicante* or *Cinsault* are also used. The climate, the nature of the soil, the exposure to the sun and type of vine-plant all have the usual influence on the wine produced, but here the altitude of the vineyards appears to play a particularly important role. The wines of the plain are usually light and do not keep well; the wines from the mountains are usually full-bodied, rich, heavy and thick, and the wines of the slopes, between the plains and the mountains, are of an intermediate type, fine, lively and with a delicate bouquet. Annual yield is about 198,000,000 gallons.

EASTERN ALGERIA

DEPARTMENT OF ANNABA (BÔNE). Coming in from Tunisia by the Medjerdah Valley, one meets the first mountain vineyards around Souk Ahras, at an altitude of about 2,100 feet. Their wine is supple but full-bodied, with a good colour. Continuing west from Souk Ahras on towards Medjez Sfa, one enters the Wadi Seybouse which leads, northwards, to the Bône plain and, westwards, to the region of Guelma. There are some very fine vineyards here, stretched along the flanks of the valley at an altitude varying between 300 and 900 feet, near Guelma, Heliopolis and Petit. They produce full-bodied but supple wines with a slightly earthy tang. Up towards Bône itself, vines are much rarer and one must edge over to Aïn Mokra, west of Seybouse Valley, to find them again, or else run eastwards along the valley to La Calle, where the wine is clean-tasting, light and with a good body.

DEPARTMENTS OF CONSTANTINE, BATNA AND SÉTIF. Returning from the Wadi Seybouse and following, beyond Guelma, the Wadi Bou Hamdane and the Wadi Zenati, the traveller passes the Kroub to reach Constantine in the north, and Lambèse and Batna in the south. The region just around Constantine produces excellent wines, those of Lambèse and Batna being rather more full-bodied and supple. Beyond Constantine and the Col des Oliviers, the region of Azzaba (Jemmapes) produces very honest table wines. But the palm of victory for the wines of the Constantine region must go, along with those of Souk Ahras, to the wines of BÉNI MELEK, with its vineyards laid out along the Eocene slopes of Skikda (Philippeville). The white wines of this part are much sought for their vigour and robustness. Still farther west of Constantine, one meets the vineyards of Petite-Kabylie and their light, lively and almost colourless wines, lacking somewhat in acidity and body; they are to be found around Djidjelli, Chefka, the foothills of Djebel Seddets and in the Wadi Djinedjerre. Finally, there are two vineyards encircling Petite-Kabylie: Sétif, in the south, at an altitude of 3,300 feet, and Akbou-El Maten-El Kseur in the Wadi Soummam which separates Petite-Kabylie from Grande-Kabylie in the west. The savour and bouquet of these wines is very fine.

CENTRAL ALGERIA

DEPARTMENTS OF ALGIERS AND TIZI OUZOU. The central region of Algeria has immense vineyards and is certainly the second most important of the country's viticultural areas. But here the estates formerly owned by Europeans have passed into the management of the Algerians themselves, and the inexperience of these new winegrowers, who took over from the colonists from one day to the next, shows in the many vines, notably in Mitidja, which were worn out before their time and are now abandoned. Viticulture nevertheless remains one of the primary agricultural activities here, in Mitidja and Sahel d'Alger, from Thénia to Ténès.

Following the Mediterranean shore, one finds east of the capital the vineyards of Thénia, Rouïba, Bou Bérah and Abbo, followed, south-east of Reghaïa, by those of St.-Pierre and Arbatache, then those of Souk el Haad, Chabet-et-Ameur, Isserville-les-Issers and Les Isserts in the Department of Tizi Ouzou. This region produces very well-balanced wines. Nearer Algiers stretch the vineyards of Aïn Taya, Dar el Baida (Maison-Blanche) and El Harrache (Maison Carrée). In the coastal region are the vinegrowing communes of Boufarik, Hadjout, Sidi Moussa, then Mouzaïa, Blida and El Affroun and, along the slopes, Bouzaréa, Montebello, Beni Mered, Guyotville, Cheragas, Zeralda, Douera, Mahelma,

Kolea, Bou Aroun, and so one. Their wines are cool and fruity, with an alcohol content of 10° to 12°.

DEPARTMENT OF EL ASNAM (ORLÉANSVILLE). The vineyards in this Department are in the north, in Sahel; Villebourg, Novi, Gouraya and Ténès; then in Dahra, west of Hadjout, Meurade and Bou Yersen. They produce "wines of the slopes" that are solid, lively and well-coloured. The best-known wines of this Department are, in fact, the Côtes du Zaccar, produced above Miliana and along towards Rouïan and Orléansville; they are fairly full-bodied wines, robust and lively and with an alcohol content of 11° to 13°. Many people do not hesitate to compare them with the French CÔTES DE RHÔNE wines.

DEPARTMENT OF MÉDÉA. There are vineyards at an altitude of 2,100 feet around the towns of Médéa, Damiette, Hassen ben Ali and Lodi, and farther east at an altitude of 1,800 feet, in the region of Sour el Gozlan, Bir Rabalou and Aïn Bessem. The reputation of the MÉDÉA and AIN BESSEM wines is already firmly established and they can be compared to those of Bouïra at the foot of Djurdjura in the Department of Tizi Ouzou. All are classified as of superior quality.

WESTERN ALGERIA

DEPARTMENT OF MOSTAGANEM. This region still has very many private estates which, up to the time of independence, made up part of the vast Department of Oran, producer of two-thirds of the country's total wine harvest and undoubtedly of the best wines in Algeria.

Going down the right bank of the Wadi Cheliff and leaving behind the vineyards of the Zaccar slopes, one finds not far from the mouth of the watercourse, on the slopes of Dahra, wines which are fine yet fruity and which keep well. South of the Wadi, vineyards of the plains on argillo-siliceous soil, around Mohammédia and Relizane, criss-cross those of the slopes near Mostaganem, Mesra, Rivoli, Mazagran, Aïn Tédelès and so on. Their wines have an alcohol content of only 10° to 12°, but they are honest and robust types, while those of Mostaganem have the right to the appellation V.D.Q.S.,

as do also those of Mascara, the large viticultural area south of the Beni Chougran mountains. The wines known under the appellation COTEAUX DE MASCARA have probably the finest reputation of any in Algeria. The wines called MASCARA, on the other hand, produced from vines at a lower altitude, are of a lesser quality.

DEPARTMENT OF ORAN. The vineyard of this Department is divided into four large regions. East of the provincial capital, in a magnificent plain reminiscent of the French landscapes of Languedoc, the vines stretch as far as the eye can see from Sidi Chami to Arzew, past Assi Bou Nif, Fleurus, Gdyel, Renan and Ste. Léonie. Farther south is the little vineyard area of St. Lucien, in the Wadi Tlélat. West of Oran, facing the sea on both sides of Sahel, are the vines of Aïn el Turk and Bou Sfer; then those of Misserghin and Brédéah, turned towards Sebkra d'Oran and the slopes of M'silah. These vines produce lively wines with a pronounced bouquet. South-west of Sahel d'Oran is the area producing the Aïn Témouchent and Aïn Kial wines, while those of Rio Salado and Hammam bou Hadjar come from the Metla plain, at an average altitude of 1,200 feet. Finally, the last viticultural region of this department is that of the Tessalah mountains, which produces excellent reds, whites and rosés deserving the classification of "superior quality". The main centres are Sidi bel Abbès, Sidi Daho, Sidi l'Hassen, Sidi Khaled, Lamtar and Wadi Imbert.

DEPARTMENTS OF TLEMCEN AND SAIDA. Adjoining the frontiers of Morocco, the Department of Tlemcen produces vintage wines of which the best is COTEAUX DE TLEMCEN. Outside of Tlemcen, there are vines in the communes of Bréa, Négrier, Mansourah, Aïn Fezza, Lamoricière and Wadi Chouly. There is a small vineyard at Marnia, north-west of the Tlemcen mountains and near the Moroccan frontier, which produces the same type of wine as the preceding areas.

This tour of the vineyards of Oran and Alger ends in the Department of Saïda, where, backed up against the Daïa mountains and facing the great Sahara, is the vineyard of Saïda, while at the westernmost point of Algeria is Aïn el Hadjar and its excellent wine.

MOROCCO

Tingitan Mauretania, the name given by the Romans to their colony in Morocco, has known the vine since earliest antiquity. Today, the most up-to-date vineyards rub shoulders with the traditional vine which produces grapes for the table. There are in all some 185,000 acres planted to the vine, of which four-fifths produce wine, to the extent of 55,000,000 gallons.

Most Moroccan wines are either reds or rosés, with only a small quantity of whites being produced. The red wines are generous, supple and rich, well-balanced but perhaps lacking a little in spirit, with an alcohol content of 12° to 14°. The rosés are clear, limpid and lively, with an agreeable fruitiness. The whites are distinguished as elegant, warm but a little heavy, with a good bouquet. At Boulaouane, El Jadida (south of Casablanca) and Demnate in the area of Marrakech, there is a production of "grey" wines, which are dry and fruity, and also of table wines made from the *Muscat d'Alexandrie*. The most commonly met vines are *Cinsault, Carignan, Grenache* and *Alicante-Bouschet* for the red wines, and *Pedro Ximenez, Plant X, Clairette* and *Grenache* for the white wines. The main viticultural areas are Oujda, Berkane, Anged El Aioum and Taourirt in the east; around Taza, Fez and Meknès (whose red wines, fairly light, are the best in Morocco) in the centre; and around Rabat and the Chaouïa Plain towards the west. Other vineyards are spread across southern Morocco between Safi and Mogador, and farther east along the Wadi Tensift up to Sidi Addi, and finally at Bou Assida, on the south-west slopes of the High Atlas, where the vineyards are rather few and far between.

SOUTH AFRICA

In the fertile soil of the Cape of Good Hope, the vine has found superb conditions for growth, and it has prospered there for more than three centuries. Today, the vineyards stretch across the hillsides and valleys of the hinterland, from the foot of the mountain which rises above Table Bay to the chain of purple peaks whose imposing stature confers on the Cape such magnificence and such beauty.

Against this backdrop of hills and mountains, the vineyards of the Cape survey one of the most enchanting panoramas in the world. The farms with their gabled-ends and their whitewashed façades are pure history, the history of the first colonists, and they reflect the perseverance and character of the people who conceived this famous Dutch-style Cape architecture.

Three years after the first Dutch settlement was established at the Cape of Good Hope, in February 1655, a packet of the Dutch East India Company sailed into Table Bay, carrying a few European vine-plants. Johan van Riebeeck, Governor of the Colony, had these plants set out in the gardens of the Company, at the foot of Table Mountain. Four years later, South Africa's viticulture was born when grapes from those vine-plants were pressed to make the first Cape wine. Some twenty years after that, Governor Simon van der Stel himself set out 100,000 roots of vine in a model-farm in Constantia Valley, thus encouraging the colonists to develop cultivation of the vine. And at the end of the seventeenth century, a large number of French Huguenot refugees poured into the Cape, bringing with them the experience and the secrets of winemaking. They settled in the valleys of Stellenbosch, Paarl, Drakenstein and Franschhoek, building up the viticulture there and greatly improving the quality of the region's wines. Some of these farms and workings carry their original French names to this day.

The harvests increased and wine could soon be exported to Batavia. For one must remember that the original reason for the Dutch settlement at the Cape was as a port of call where ships could take in fresh supplies on the voyage from the Netherlands to India. Nevertheless, as the Cape wine became known and appreciated in Europe, considerable quantities were shipped to Great Britain and the Continent of Europe.

Most of the South African wine was at that time being produced in the Constantia Valley by the Groot-Constantia farm, which was then the property of the Cloete family. The Muscat from Constantia was, in fact, described as "undeniably a dessert wine, strong but delicate, and having in its bouquet something singularly agreeable". In 1805, Great Britain, then fighting against Napoleon, occupied the Cape for the second time: her vessels came to take on supplies there, being no longer able to do so in France. The wine-growers were encouraged to produce vintage wines for export, and an official wine-taster was appointed to sample the export wines and ensure that they had the required quality and ageing. The British Government wished to stimulate the export of wines still more, and in 1813 introduced a preferential customs tariff for imported colonial wine. The result of this colonial preference was absolutely staggering. The production of wines of all kinds, both natural wines and sweet and liqueur wines, shot up. From 930,000 gallons in 1813, the South African wine production rocketted in 1824 to 2,442,000 gallons, of which nearly one-half (1,011,000 gallons) were exported. These preferential tariffs were, however, progressively cut back in later years, until they were finally abolished in 1861 by William Gladstone's government.

Phylloxera ravaged the vineyards of the Cape in 1885, leaving the winegrowers in a very poor situation. The disease was finally eliminated in the same way as in Europe, by grafts on American stock resistant to the parasite. But after this cure, the revitalized wines met a fresh problem in the first part of the twentieth century—over-production. Their yield was so generous that in 1916 winegrowers had to be content with

310

a one-penny profit per bottle of good quality wine. To cope with this overabundance and avoid a recurrence of the crisis, a co-operative organization was formed. The principal vinegrowers had already met several times in 1916 to discuss the advisability of setting up a central organization which would protect their interests. No one who saw this body founded realized that it would become an all-powerful apparatus of control, directing and ruling the activities of vinegrowers and wineproducers alike. A proposal for a central co-operative body was drawn up, and presented at a huge assembly at Paarl. The result was the foundation, in 1918, of the body known as the *Ko-operatieve Wijnbouwers van Zuid-Africa* (K.W.V.), or Wine-Growers Co-operative of South Africa. It was then and still is today mainly made up of Afrikanders, and had as its principal aim the conduct, control and regulation of the sale and disposal of its members' production; it also guaranteed or tried to guarantee that their profits would be consistent with their production. Today, nobody can produce wine without the authorization of the K.W.V., which decides the maximum annual production of each vineyard and the minimum prices of good wines and distillation wines, and also calculates the "surplus" factor or proportion of each wineproducer which then has to be delivered free of charge to the K.W.V. No producer may sign a sales contract with a merchant without the prior approval of the K.W.V., which receives the payments due, nor may a producer sell any part of their harvest to individuals without the express consent of this governing body.

WINEGROWING REGIONS

The South African vineyard is situated in the south-west part of Cape Province, and is divided into two distinct zones. The first part includes the areas around Stellenbosch, Paarl and Wellington, then the area from Malmesbury to Tulbagh, and finally the Cape Peninsula and the famous Constantia Valley. The climate there is temperate: mild in spring, hot and even very hot in summer, either mild or hot in autumn, cold and humid in winter. This comparatively small region —very small, in fact, when one compares it with the regions which produce the many types of European wine—can produce most of the well-known wines thanks to the wide variety of soil and land; most of the South African natural wines of everyday type are to be found there.

The other major wine-producing zone is at a higher altitude. Known as the Little Karoo, it extends from Ladysmith to Outshoorn, between the Drakenstein and the Swartberg, and includes Worcester, Robertson,

Bonnievale and Swellendam. The climate here is much more severe than in the coastal region—less rain and more heat, hence the need to irrigate the land—but there is a good production, largely in the domain of dessert wines, sherries or ports.

TYPES OF VINE-PLANT. A wide variety of grape grows in these two regions, with the vine-plants used for white wines *(Riesling, Stein, Blanc Français, Clairette Blanche)* doing well along the coast. The *Hermitage, Cabernet Sauvignon* and *Shiraz* give light red wines, while the *Pinot, Gamay, Cabernet, Hermitage, Shiraz* and *Pinotage* give full-bodied reds. As far as the wines themselves are concerned, the strongest are produced in the regions close to the coast (Constantia, Somerset-West and certain parts around Stellenbosch), with the better wines coming from Paarl, Stellenbosch and Tulbagh; the light red wines come from around Paarl and Durbanville. A vine called *Pinotage*, developed by one of K.W.V.'s research workers who crossed *Hermitage* with *Pinot*, is very well known in South Africa and is planted quite extensively. Its wine combines the best qualities of the two separate species: a full-bodied red of good quality, with a fruity and perfumed bouquet which somehow recalls the French Beaujolais. In the Little Karoo region, the *Blanc Français, Hermitage, Hanepoot, Muscat* and *Sultana* vines produce dessert wines.

THE CLIMATE. Although in the southern hemisphere, the whole calendar of vine growth is, naturally, entirely different from that of Europe, the influence of each season is nevertheless very similar. Spring, from September to November, is the busiest time of the year for the vinegrower. In summer, from December to February, the grape ripens; the harvest is carried out in the southern autumn, between March and May. The cold, humid winter is in the middle of the year.

The South African climate is almost over-generous; in fact, the sun presents some serious problems for the vinegrowers. While in Europe the harvest ripens in the cool of autumn after a relatively short summer, in South Africa it ripens during the heat of midsummer, which creates special problems in the fermentation and ageing. On the other hand, grapes that ripen under a strong sun always contain a high proportion of sugar, which does not always balance out the natural acidity. One can say, too, that the South African winegrower is much less bothered by the capricious moods of the weather than his European counterpart. In the Cape, *every* wine-year is a good year. There is, however, a constant search to profit from what little amount of freshness can be found or engineered during the ripening of the grape, for it facilitates the conservation of the bouquet and aroma in the wine, particularly in the white wines. An interesting difference of opinion is seen in this connection: some farmers use vine-props to lift the vine clear of the ground during the torrid midsummer period, while other farmers take quite the opposite viewpoint and leave the vine close to the ground, claiming that the vine leaves protect the grape from the sun's strength. A great deal of attention is paid to the orientation of the vineyards. It has been proved that the vines which are grown on the cooler southern slopes (remembering that this is the southern hemisphere) produce better white wines, while for good red wines the winegrowers prefer the sites facing north, that is, towards the prevailing sun.

GENERAL CHARACTERISTICS OF THE WINES

The products of the Cape vineyards can never be the same as the European wines of similar type, however much the South African growers may simulate European production methods by using modern refrigeration and modern control systems during the fermentation and ageing processes. And even were the vine and the soil identical to those in Europe, the sheer heat of the Cape climate raises the sugar content, reduces the acidity, and consequently gives an entirely different wine. In this respect, wine-lovers who attempted to find in the Cape wines the exact replicas of the European wines they know, would be depriving themselves of a rare chance for enjoyment: the Cape wines possess their own aroma and characteristics, despite their apparent resemblance to European wines.

The production of Cape vintage wines has been made possible by the introduction of temperature control in the cellars. By using great stainless-steel or steel containers, the winegrower can now control the speed of fermentation at a low temperature, and can thus re-create the fresh European climate which is needed if the wine is to retain its delicate perfume and its taste. This can be achieved in one of three ways. The required low temperature can be maintained by pumping cold water through pipes which pass through the must, or the must itself can be circulated through a refrigerating circuit, or the temperature of the air in the cellar itself can be lowered by air-conditioning.

The slightly-sweet wines so popular in South Africa are obtained by cutting short the fermentation, either by using a sulphureous gas, or else by compressing or chilling the must so that the wine, which already contains the authorized 2 per cent amount of sugar, keeps in addition a part of its natural sweetness. After ageing in cool cellars, the wine is clarified by being racked and filtered. In South Africa, white wines are bottled and drunk while they are still very young, sometimes after a mere six months and while they are still fresh, sparkling and deliciously fruity.

RIESLING is probably the best Cape white wine, followed closely by STEIN. The RIESLING wine tends to be the drier of the two; yet it is not, as the Cape climate might lead one to suppose, as dry as the German RIESLING. The STEIN wine is usually semi-sweet but it can be dry on occasion, in much the same way that the RIESLING can be semi-dry or semi-sweet. These wines, which have such an agreeable taste, fruitiness and aroma, tend, however, to be more full-bodied than the semi-sweet European wines. The wines made from *Clairette Blanche* vines are more delicate, and when drunk young, have an admirably mordant freshness and perfumed aroma.

The alcohol content of the Cape white wines, at 11° to 12° by volume, is slightly higher than the European white wines. These growers now also produce a SPÄTLESE, a white *mi-flétri*, which by virtue of letting the grapes dry longer before pressing them has a distinctly higher alcohol content. Good wines of a deep yellow colour, they are made from *Steen, Riesling*, or even *Hanepoot* vines.

As for the Cape red wines, they are usually aged for two or three years before being bottled, at which stage they are very drinkable, since most of them are dry and have a very pleasant perfume. To improve their quality still more, connoisseurs keep them yet another two or three years. There are, unfortunately, only a very few wineproducers who take the trouble to indicate the harvest-year on the bottle labels, and even then, these are wines from small winegrowers whose vines are renowned for their quality. A few experienced *restaurateurs* are careful to cellar the wine for two years or so, to avoid the possibility of any disagreeable surprises and to allow it to assert its best qualities.

It is the red wines of the Cape which come closest to European wines. The full-bodied reds, made from *Cabernet, Pinot Noir, Gamay* and *Hermitage* vines in the regions of Paarl, Stellenbosch and Durbanville, are of a Burgundy type, with all the qualities which that can imply. The light reds tend more towards the Bordeaux type and come from vines in Constantia Valley, around Stellenbosch and Somerset-West. The *Shiraz* vine does very well in the Cape climate, producing a red wine with a rich bouquet; blended with *Hermitage* or *Cabernet*, it gives a full-bodied wine of a certain distinction if it has been allowed to age. The red wine made from the crossed vine *Pinotage*, with its bright colour, its fruitiness and its pronounced bouquet, is one of the best full-bodied reds in the country.

The rosé wines, which are much lighter, are finding increasing approval, their freshness being particularly welcome in the South African heat. They have the colour of red wines but the main characteristics of whites; they tend to be astringent and to lack body.

APPELLATIONS. There are no provisions in South African law covering the use of the term *appellation d'origine contrôlée*. In point of fact, such a definition is not suitable for the wines of South Africa. Very many wines are described as "bottled" on such-and-such an estate, but most often they certainly do not come from vines harvested on one single estate; they may even come from a mixture of wines of quite different origins. One can also add that any mention on the label of the A.O.C. would probably not interest the South African consumer, who has more confidence in the guarantee of a standard quality offered in wine coming from the big estates. The name of the vine is sometimes given on the label, an advantage for the lover of good wine who is able to make his choice between wines from *Riesling* or *Cabernet* or *Pinotage*. As so many wines carry only the name of a winegrower, the only really reliable method of investigating their quality is by the tried and trusted one of tasting them. Some labels, however, carry the word "selected", which is usually an indication either that the grape was carefully selected before pressing, or the wine, while still young and before being treated and aged, was picked out as being of excellent quality. This solitary one-word mention is by no means negligible when it comes to judging the quality of the bottle's contents. The year of the wine-harvest is, as already pointed out, very rarely given: the South African consumer seldom pays any attention to it and the winegrowers claim that since the climatic conditions are always constant and perfect the quality of the wine is equally so !

On this ticklish point of appreciation of the quality of wines, one can mention that the foreign consumer might consider as too sweet or too heavy certain wines which are highly appreciated by the South Africans. Conversely, of course, the connoisseur of European wines might very well find happiness in a wine considered very "so-so" by the South African standards. More than 90 per cent of the wines which have some *appellation d'origine* are produced and sold by only four firms. These establishments, which are both wineproducers and merchants and are equipped with enormous cellars and the latest modern machinery, obtain their grapes either in their own vineyards or from neighbouring estates, and their wine either from their own production of from other wineproducers or co-operatives, in which case they buy young wine.

The Stellenbosch Farmer's Winery (S.F.W.), which also includes the Monis group, has the largest choice of wines. Those from Zonnebloem are its first line and are excellent white wines made from *Riesling*, with a dry and full-bodied CABERNET of delightful bouquet. There is also a semi-sweet, well-ripened ZONNEBLOEM *mi-flétri*.

Another branch of the S.F.W.'s activities concerns the so-called Lanzerac, whose origins date back to 1692. A magnificent and well-preserved Dutch-style farmhouse has been converted into a hotel which today has an international reputation. Here the wines of Lanzerac may be enjoyed, sold in bottles shaped like a dew-drop. They comprise two whites, a dry wine made from *Riesling* called RIESENSCHON and a semi-sweet made from *Stein* called GRÜNMÄDCHEN; while the red wines of Lanzerac are a full-bodied CABERNET and a good specimen of PINOTAGE, lighter than the Cabernet but still fairly full-bodied. There is also a light and semi-sweet rosé.

From the "Oude Libertas" cellars of the S.F.W., dating back to 1707, come very popular moderate-priced wines: GRATITUDE, a type of dry Chablis, and TASHEIMER GOLDTRÖPFCHEN, which is like a semi-sweet Rhine wine. Their CHÂTEAU LIBERTAS, carrying the name of these famous cellars, is a very well-known Burgundy-type wine.

The Stellenbosch Farmer's Winery also produces a whole series of ordinary wines which are very widely distributed. These include a Burgundy-type, TASSEN-BERG, and a semi-sweet wine called ZONNHEIMER which has a taste of *Hanepoot*. Probably the most popular of their wines is LIEBERSTEIN, a semi-sweet white wine which has been highly publicized.

The Nederburg property, which has recently linked up with the S.F.W., was the first concern in the Cape to experiment with German methods of vinification for fermentation and low-temperature ageing. Furthermore, this property will only plant and develop vines of pure stock. A very nice choice of white wines comes from their cellars. HOCHHEIMER, a Rhine riesling type, and MI-FLÉTRI, for those who prefer the rather sweeter *Spätlesen*, are both outstanding. SYLVANER-NEDERBURG is a pleasant and fairly dry white, but SELECTED RIESLING and RIESLING are the best-selling moderate-priced white wines. The CABERNET from this cellar is full-bodied with a nutty taste. One should note that the Nederburg winery does not produce any ordinary wines.

Gilbey-Santhagens, at Stellenbosch, offer wine drinkers several wines labelled TWEE JONGEZELLENS ("the two young bachelors")—for example, RIESLING "39", a dry Rhine-type wine with a very pleasant bouquet, and the semi-dry STEIN SUPERIOR. The cheapest wines in this series are the dry RIESLING, the semi-dry STEIN, the semi-sweet LIEBFRAUENMILCH, and a sweet rosé.

The Distillers Corporation of South Africa markets two medium quality wines which come from the Clos de la Résidence and which are much appreciated by those who seek inexpensive refreshment. THEUNIS-KRAAL, pleasantly dry and with a good taste, is a

Riesling, while Alto Rouge is a tasty dry wine made from *Cabernet*. Grünberger, a semi-dry stein-type wine contained in bottles of a special shape, Villa Bianca and Villa Rosa, both semi-dry, all come from these same cellars. The Corporation also offers ordinary wines from the well-known Witzenberg series.

The Castle Wine and Brandy Company of Capetown offers a range of white wines under the name Vlottenheim Estates of Vlottenberg. One finds a very pleasant semi-dry Sylvaner, a Schlossberg, a good quality dry Riesling Kabinett and a semi-sweet Honigberg. Apart from these wines, the best known is Rougemont, a very popular mellow Burgundy. For the rest, the firm's products are mostly very ordinary kinds of wines.

There are a certain number of private vineyards whose wines are worth searching for, although their combined production is very small compared with that of the big concerns. One can find these wines only in their home region, for their producers do not need to find other markets. Taking them in alphabetical order, the list begins with Alphen, the two-centuries old property in Constantia Valley. Alphen produces an Alphen Riesling Selected and two light Burgundies, as well as good sherries and good dessert wines. The Bellingham property (Groot-Drakenstein) is trying to match European A.O.C. wines with a balanced range of high quality products, and offers a remarkable Blanc Sec Premier Grand Cru, a semi-dry Johannisberg, a delicious Shiraz, a Stein and a rosé. The Delheim vineyard at Koelenhof produces a *mi-flétri* Spatzendreck for those who like a rather sweeter wine, and very worthy red wines which include a full-bodied Pinotage and a Burgundy-type wine, Cabernet-Sauvignon.

From Muratie, also at Koelenhof, come some very attractive red table wines: their Cabernet-Sauvignon is a light and perfumed Burgundy, the full-bodied Gamay Pinot-Noir has Burgundy-like qualities and their Bordeaux brings a light taste of *Hermitage*. The Schoongezicht property, near Stellenbosch, produces two wines much sought after by wine-lovers, particularly the Rustenberg, a dry and full-bodied wine made from *Cabernet* which has many of the characteristics of a Médoc and has crowned many a harvest with excellent success. The other is a Schoongezicht white wine full of taste and with a rich bouquet which takes it name from the property where it is harvested; *Clairette Blanche* grapes are also used for this wine. The Uitkyk vineyard, at Mulders in Vlei, produces two wines which should be better known: the first is a dry white wine sold under the name of Carlsheim, the other is Carlonet Cabernet, a full-bodied and very fresh red wine.

In sparkling wines, Grand Mousseux from the Stellenbosch Farmer's Winery, ranging from extra-dry to sweet, is by far the most popular. These wines have a very fruity taste and are just a little sweeter than European sparkling wines.

South Africa has without any doubt really excellent products in the field of *liquoreux* wines. The range of dessert wines is simply immense, and covers all types. As examples one might mention Mooiuitsig Wynkelders, from Bonnievale; Monis Marsala, an excellent product from the S.F.W., and the same firm's delicious Muscadine. Two firms offer from their cellars wines which, it seems, are identical to that famous eighteenth-century wine of Constantia: Constantiaberg from Bertrams of Constantia and the Schoongezicht Frontignac.

The range of ports to be found in the Cape is also very large. The *topazes ambrés* are the lightest, going from very light reds to deep reds; the rubies are of a richer colour and more full-bodied. The vintage ports, which are produced only in limited quantities, are a deep red and full-bodied, their mellowness coming from ten to fifteen years of ageing in the bottle.

The best South African ports are made in the coastal region around Paarl and Stellenbosch. Most of the vines come originally from the Portuguese district of Douro, where port wine itself originated. *Pontac*, *Mataro* and *Shiraz* vines are used in order to be able to blend better, and care is taken to age the port sufficiently, even though the length of time needed in the South African climate is shorter than in Europe.

South African sherries come from authentic *xérès flor* vines, and the South African sherry vineyards are in the same southern latitude as the Spanish sherry vineyards are in the northern hemisphere. Furthermore, the principally used vine is *Palomino*, the "foundation stone" of Spanish sherries. The vines giving light sherries grow at Paarl, Stellenbosch, Tulbagh and Goudini in the south-western part of the Cape, while the more full-bodied sherries come from Worcester, Robertson, Mongatu and Bonnievale. The K.W.V. organization is quite certainly the largest producer and exporter of Cape sherries; many millions of gallons of stock are in the process of ageing.

Although the very dry and pale sherry sought in Europe is unknown in South Africa, there are nevertheless other very excellent sherries. The driest sherries —although even these are much less dry than their Spanish cousins—are the *finos* and the *amontillados*, fairly pale in colour and of a delicate flavour. The *oloroso* are darker, much sweeter and more full-bodied. As for the sherries aged by the *solera* system, they have a much darker colour and a much sweeter taste than the European varieties.

WINES OF AFRICA

ALGERIA

Aïn Bessem-Bouira	Coteaux de Médéa	Côtes du Zaccar	Miliana
Aïn El Hadjar	Coteaux de M'Silah	Haut-Dahra	Monts du Tessalah
Coteaux de Mascara	Coteaux de Tlemcen	Mascara	Mostaganem-Dahra

TUNISIA

Cap Bon	Kélibia	Muscat de Thibar	Sidi-Tabet
Carthage	Muscat de Kélibia	Radès	Thibar
Coteaux de Khanguet	Muscat de Radès	Saint Cyprien	Tébourba

SOUTH AFRICA

SUPERIOR QUALITY WINES

Dry white wines	Bellingham Premier Grand Cru	Lanzerac Riesenschön	Nederburg Selected Riesling
	Carlsheim 8	Nederburg Riesling	Twee Jongegezellen Riesling « 39 »
Medium-dry white wines . . .	Bellingham Late Vintage	Nederburg Sylvaner	Twee Jongegezellen Stein Superior
	Bellingham Vintage Johannisberger	Twee Jongegezellen Stein	Vlottenheimer Sylvaner
Medium-sweet white wines . . .	Bellingham Selected Steinwein	Delheim Selected Stein Goldspatz	Nederburg Stein
	Blumberger Late Harvest	Kupferberger Auslese	Tulbagher
	Charantelle	Lanzerac Grünmädchen	Twee Jongegezellen Spätlese
	Delheim Late-Harvest	Nederburg Hochheimer	Vlottenheimer Schlossberg
	« Spatzendreck »	Nederburg Late Harvest	Zonnebloem Late Harvest
Dry red wines	Lanzerac Pinotage	Nederburg Selected Cabernet	Zonnebloem Cabernet
	Lanzerac Cabernet	Stellenrood	Alphen Special Old Vintage
Medium-dry red wines	Bellingham Shiraz	Carlonet Cabernet	
Dry rosé wines	Bellingham Rosé	Nederburg Rosé Sec	
Medium-dry rosé wine	Bellingham Almeida		
Medium-sweet rosé wines . . .	Lanzerac Rose	Nederburg Rose	

VERY GOOD QUALITY WINES

Dry white wines	Alphen Dry White	La Gratitude	Schoongezicht
	Alphen Selected Riesling	La Residence Theuniskraal	Stellenvale Selected Riesling
	Bellingham Riesling	J.C. le Roux Mont Pellier	Stellenvale Selected Stellenblanche
	Constantia Riesling	Molenburg Riesling	Theuniskraal
	Culemborg Selected Riesling	Muratie Riesling	Twee Jongegezellen Liebfraumilch
	Delheim Riesling	Muratie Stein	Twee Jongegezellen Riesling
	Delheim White-French	Paarl Valley Old Riesling	Vlottenheimer Riesling Kabinet
	De Rust Riesling	Prestige Selected Riesling	White Leipzig
	Huguenot Riesling	Prestige Selected Stellenblanche	Witzenberg
Medium-dry white wines . . .	Delheim Selected Riesling	Tafelheim	Vlottenheimer Selected Riesling
	De Rust Stein	Villa Bianca	Witzenberg Grand
	Grunberger Stein		

Medium-sweet white wines . . .	Amaliensteimer	Liebfrauborg	Stellenvale Estate Riesling
	Bruderberg Na Œs (late harvest)	Lombards Liebfraumilch	Tasheimer Goldtröpfchen
	Capinella	Molenberg Stein	Vlottenheimer Honigberg
	Constantia Valley Stein	Molenhof Stein	Volson
	Culemborg Selected Stein	Monis Steinheimer	Winterhock Stein
	Gezellen Liebfraumilch	Stellenvale Hochheimer	Witzenberg Spatlese
	Kloosterberg		

Slightly sparkling white wines .	Culemborg Perlé	La Provence	Nauheimer

Dry red wines	Bodenheim	Delheim Pinotage	Rustenburg
	Bruderberg Selected Cabernet	La Résidence Alto Rouge	St. Augustine
	Château Alphen	Muratie Claret	Valais Rouge
	Château Constantia	Muratie Pinot noir-Gamay	Vredenburg
	Château Le Roux	Nederburg Cabernet	Alphen Red
	Château Libertas	Province Red	Muratie Cabernet Sauvignon
	Château Monis	Rougemont	Vlakkenberg
	Delheim Cabernet-Sauvignon		

Medium-sweet red wines . . .	Back's Claret (light-bodied)	Stellenvale Cabernet (light-bodied)

Dry rosé wine	Valrosé

Medium-dry rosé wine	Villa Rose

Medium-sweet rosé wines . . .	Culemborg Rose	Rosala	Witzenberg Grand Rose
	La Provence	Twee Jongegezellen Rose	

DESSERT AND APERITIF WINES

Dessert wines	Amarella	Malvasia	Mooiuitsig White Muscadel
	Consanto	Miranda	Liqueur Wine
	Constantia Berg	Monis Barbola	Morilos Marsala
	Golden Bonwin	Monis Marsala	Muscadine
	Golden Mantilla	Monis Moscato	Ruby Bonwin
	Kloovendal	Mooiuitsig Red Muscadel Liqueur	Rynilla
	La Rhone	Wine	Stellenvale Marsala
	Malaga Red		

Port wines	Castelo Port	Government House Port	Mooiuitsig Fine Old Port
	Devonvale Port	Libertas	Muratie Port
	D.C. Vintage Port	Monis Cardinal Port	Santyis Old Ruby Vintage Port

Very dry sherries	Gonzales Byass Dry

D.G. Flor No. 1 sherries . . .	Harvey's Extra Dry	Old Master Amontillado	Libertas
	Karroo Sherry	Devonvale Solera Dry « Flor »	Monis Palido Sherry
	Mattersons Fine Dry	Harvey's Dry Sherry	Tayler's Pale Dry Sherry

Medium-dry sherries	Bertrams Biscuit Sherry	Monis Dry Cream Sherry	Tudor Medium Cream Sherry
	D.G. Flor No. 2	Tayler's Mmooth Medium Sherry	

Medium-sweet sherries	Bertrams Oloroso Sherry	Gonzales Byass Medium	Sedgwick's Medium Cream
	Devon Cream Sherry	Roodezand Sherry	Vlei Sherry

Sweet sherries	D.G. Olorose	Harvey's Full Cream Sherry	Tayler's Full Cream Sherry
	Gonzales Byass Sweet	Libertas	Tayler's Rich Brown Sherry

REPUBLIC OF
SOUTH AFRICA

Province of the Cape of Good Hope

50 Km.
50 Miles

PIKETBERG

Berg River

TULBAGH

CERES

MALMESBURY

MATROOSBERG

LADISMITH

CALITZDORP

WELLINGTON

WORCESTER

MONTAGU

OUDTSHOORN

PAARL

CAPE TOWN

STELLENBOSCH

BARRYDALE

SWELLENDAM

RIVERSDALE

CAMPS BAY

CONSTANTIA

STRAND

Riviersonderend

Breede River

Gouritz River

CALEDON

Cape of
Good Hope

BREDASDORP

ATLANTIC OCEAN

CAPE AGULHAS

INDIAN OCEAN

MAROC

OCÉAN ATLANTIQUE

DÉTROIT DE GIBRALTAR

TANGER

MER MÉDITERRANÉE

ALGÉRIE

BERKANE

RABAT

CASABLANCA

FEZ

OUJDA

MEKNÈS

O. Mellah

O. Moulouya

O. Oum er Rbia

MARRAKECH

SAHARA

AGADIR

BOU ASSIDA

Aaiun

200 Km.

200 Miles

MER MÉDITERRANÉE

Dahra

Haut Dahra

EL ASNAM

MOSTAGANEM

ARZEW

Mostaganem

Oued Cheliff

ORAN

Sebkra d'Oran

AÏN-TÉMOUCHENT

Tessalah

MASCARA

Berkane

SIDI-BEL-ABBÈS

Coteaux de Mascara

MAROC

TIARET

Coteaux de Tlemcen

Oujda

TLEMCEN

Monts de Daïa

O. Taria

AÏN-EL-HADJAR

Aïn-Sefra

Laghouia

50 Km.

50 Miles

MER MÉDITERRANÉE

Marseille

BIZERTE
Lac de Bizerte
GOLFE DE TUNIS

MATEUR

Marseille
Napoli

TÉBOURBA
TUNIS
KÉLIBIA

TABARKA

Annaba

ALGÉRIE

BÉJA

O.Medjerda

KHANGUET

THIBAR
MEDJEZ EL BAB
Oe.Hamma
GROMBALIA

JENDOUBA
O. Miliane
ZAGHOUAN

Souk el Arba
TÉBOURSOUK

Le Kef
PONT-DU-FAHS
GOLFE DE HAMMAMET

Maktar

O.Siltana

Maktar
Kairouan
Sousse

TUNISIE

50 Km.

50 Miles

ALGER

Plaine de la Mitidja

Côtes du Zaccar
BEJAÏA

MILIANA
BLIDA
Oued Isser
O. Soumman
Skikda

MÉDÉA
BOUIRA

Coteaux de Médéa

O. Cheliff
AÏN BESSEM

SOUR-EL-GOZLAN

Constantine

O. Mahr Ouassel
Bou-Saâda

Bou-Saâda

ALGÉRIE

THE WINES OF NORTH AMERICA

ROBERT THOMPSON

When considering the wines of the United States of America one must invariably divide them into two categories: those of California and those from other states. This is because Californian wines derive almost exclusively from the European *vitis vinifera* vines, whereas the eastern and northern states, with climate and conditions unsuitable for the growing of European vines, produce wines from native American or hybrid grapes. The *vitis vinifera* grape vines were introduced to Mexico by the Spaniards in the sixteenth century and from there went northwards to California. In 1769 Franciscan missionaries planted the first vines (probably of Spanish origin) in San Diego and in 1824 the first commercial vineyard was started in Los Angeles. Thereafter came a stream of fortune-seeking settlers. Among them were important contributors to Californian viticulture such as the Frenchman Jean Louis Vignes, who introduced French vines in the 1830s and subsequently expanded his vineyards to such an extent that within a generation winegrowing was the principal industry of the Los Angeles area.

In 1851 a Hungarian nobleman, Agoston Haraszthy —now called the father of Californian viticulture—followed Vignes' example and imported over 100,000 cuttings from 300 foreign varieties. With the boom caused by the Gold Rush of 1849 wine consumption rose, as did the number of enthusiasts like Haraszthy. From then onwards the wine industry fluctuated between slumps and outbreaks of phylloxera (between 1870 and 1876) and prosperous periods, with the formation in 1880 of the California State Board of Viticultural Commissioners doing much to stabilize winemaking.

By the end of the nineteenth century the main outlines of the present-day industry had emerged. The coastal districts north and south of San Francisco were concentrating their efforts on table wines, while the warmer regions of the interior were producing dessert wines. But just forty years later American viticultural progress received a severe blow in the form of the Prohibition Law. In 1919 the making of wine was declared unlawful in the United States and so it remained until the Repeal in 1933. Wine was legal, however, for medicinal and sacramental uses and the head of the house could make up to 200 gallons a year for himself and his family's consumption. Within five years of this date California had nearly 800 bonded wineries, the greatest number in its history. Most of them were small and lacked financial backing. Others, alas, were more anxious to make good profits than good wines; not until about 1938 did the market settle down to its present level of some 212 wineries. Regulations were passed to safeguard the industry and, under the guidance of the University of California, it was led to a highly skilled wine technology.

In other states, colonists spent two fruitless centuries attempting to grow imported vines. Only in the 1820s did winegrowers turn to the native grapes. With varieties such as *Isabella*, *Catawba* and *Norton* purely American wines were produced; then in 1852 the first hybrid, *Concord*, was established and thereafter, until the Prohibition Law, hybrids dominated. In fact, the Law was a greater hardship to the eastern states than to California. The native industry never quite regained full stride after the Repeal: of the many thriving states

321

only New York's viticultural concern remains sound and vigorous. Others, such as Ohio, Maryland, New Jersey and Washington, lag behind.

There is, in fact, a continuous struggle between the American winegrowers who advocate the production of native grapes and the growing ranks of those who believe that only French-American hybrids based on European-type and native American parent vines will bring the market level with European competition (from which native American wines, with their distinctive and unusual flavour, have so far been kept). It should be remembered that native American and European wines are extremely dissimilar. If judged on its own particular merits, native American wine has many qualities which could bring it farther into the mainstream of world appreciation, a goal that attempts at imitating French or German wines cannot achieve.

Facts are significant: each year a greater number of connoisseurs add Californian wines to their cellars. And each year the total production rises. In 1952 the figure was 120 million gallons and in 1968 172 million (although dessert wines have lost some ground over the same period). These successes encourage more men to enter the winegrowing scene; so it is that a new name such as Heitz Cellars could be established in 1961 and by 1968 already enjoy a fine reputation.

It is this continuing atmosphere of change that lends much of the excitement to wine in California. One critic said it well: California offers the same sense of discovery that Burgundy must have offered before men know the Clos of Vougeot and of Tart were better than their neighbours. Will the example be followed?

CALIFORNIA

There are nine winegrowing regions in California. Of these, five ring San Francisco Bay; three far larger ones inland occupy the length of the San Joaquin Valley; the ninth lies to the east of Los Angeles.

The five districts near San Francisco are Sonoma-Mendocino (with the sub-districts of the Valley of the Moon and North Sonoma) and Napa to the north, Livermore to the east and Santa Clara-San Benito and Santa Cruz-Monterey to the south. Together they form the North Coast Counties or North Coast Districts. The relatively cold climate of these regions is suited to grapes of European origin: *Cabernet Sauvignon* from Bordeaux, *Pinot Noir* and *Chardonnay* from Burgundy, *Sauvignon Blanc* from Sauternes, *Barbera* from Piedmont, and so forth.

Each of the wine types is likely to be grown in each of the five districts, and with success: most wineries produce eight to twelve different wines, although perhaps two or three afford especial pride. To the uninitiated the fact that more than one wine comes from a single cellar may seem mystifying. However, after the Prohibition Repeal of 1933 every winery offered a wide selection of wines in order to survive the competition and this practice has continued. In addition, the climate of western America is so diverse and changes so subtly within each region (a reliable summer sun can be tempered from one mile to the next by cool, frequently foggy ocean breezes) that growers mostly own small, widely-scattered vineyards in order to take full advantage of the natural diversity of climate and soil.

The San Joaquin Valley districts are Lodi, Modesto and Fresno. Traditionally winemakers in these uniformly hotter and more spacious parts have concentrated on sweet grapes such as *Palomino*, the *Tinta* varieties of Portugal and several grapes of the *Muscat* family. But in order to keep up with the increasing demand for table wines (and counteract the falling dessert wine figures) growers are gradually turning to table wines to boost the limited capacity of the North Coast Counties. New agricultural techniques and grape types developed by research centres and at the University of California at Davis have helped with this.

The ninth region, Cucamonga, is named after a crossroads in the plain east of Los Angeles, and under the hot sun grapes producing a light, sweet wine are cultivated.

In California wines are named by three methods. The first group, known as "generics", covers the names brought over with the vines by immigrant settlers in the late nineteenth century; some of these names are still in use today, like CHABLIS and SHERRY. Then, since the late 1940s, there has been a growing tendency to call wines after their predominating grape variety, for example, CHARDONNAY and PALOMINO, and these are collectively termed "varietals". Thirdly, some wineries use proprietary names of their own coinage.

WHITE WINES

Several varietal wines offer themselves as light, fresh-flavoured types best drunk young with subtly flavoured poultry or shellfish: EMERALD RIESLING, GEWÜRZTRAMINER, GREEN HUNGARIAN, GREY RIESLING, JOHANNISBERG or WHITE RIESLING and SYLVANER. Of these six wines, only occasional bottlings of JOHANNISBERG RIESLING and GEWÜRZTRAMINER are expected to age; each has shown ability to remain fresh for five years, sound for ten. In California, JOHANNISBERG RIESLING makes a richly fruity, even robust wine.

322

323 Previous page:

The fertile hills of California have proved excellent for the growing of the grape, and a steadily increasing number of wineries are establishing a high reputation for their products.

The first commercial wineries were founded in the Napa Valley, California in 1861. The Beringer Brothers' winery, top, was started in 1876, and is still operated by the family. Inglenook, above, was in business in 1879, and was sold in 1963 by a descendant of the founder. Weinberger, left, seems to have vanished from the bottle labels—but as the estate combined a ranch as well, perhaps this side triumphed.

324

A second group of fuller-bodied varietal white wines includes CHARDONNAY (or PINOT CHARDONNAY), CHENIN BLANC, SEMILLON and SAUVIGNON BLANC, of which CHARDONNAY and SAUVIGNON BLANC command the greatest interest. The former, at its richest in California, evokes associations with ripe, sun-warmed fruit, apples or peaches. It has a lush, velvet smoothness that recommends it as an accompaniment to the buttery Maine lobster. A Napa Valley or Sonoma bottling from a favourable vintage will gain with age for up to six or seven years. SAUVIGNON BLANC just as intensely flavoured as CHARDONNAY, but it is less full and more austere. It ranks among the best of Californian wines as a companion to Pacific Ocean fish.

Californian vintners offer a roughly parallel series of white generics. Rhines are light and sweet; SAUTERNE (the final "s" of the French spelling is usually omitted) can be either sweet or dry, and have a more intensely fruity character than the Rhines. CHABLIS and MOUNTAIN WHITE are dry and the most intensely flavoured of the generics. Nearly all are offered as *vins de consommation* and are priced accordingly. Some come as press or blend wines from North Coast County cellars, but the great majority are made in the San Joaquin Valley.

RED WINES

The lighter and fruitier of Californian varietal red wines include: GAMAY, GRIGNOLINO, PINOT ST. GEORGE, RUBY CABERNET and ZINFANDEL. California has no wine quite so frivolous as French Beaujolais; its light reds have to be considered more vinous than that. But they are fresh and appealing, eminently suited to informal meals, or to summertime when a light chilling enhances them. RUBY CABERNET deserves special note. It is a University of California hybrid, descended from *Cabernet Sauvignon* on one side and *Carignane* on the other, designed to produce distinctive red wines in warm districts. *Zinfandel* (a grape unique to California) is incredibly adaptable. It makes relatively good wines in each of the five climate zones of California, and in each of the nine geographic districts; its best showing, however, is in Napa and Sonoma, where it produces a highly distinctive red wine capable of ageing for ten years and often described as raspberry-like.

The more robust varietal reds of California are BARBERA, CABERNET SAUVIGNON, PETITE SIRAH and PINOT NOIR. PINOT NOIRS have a highly characteristic flavour. The failing—frequent but not inevitable—is a lack of that velvety smoothness associated with this grape in Burgundy. Most California PINOT NOIRS peak within five years, a few have needed ten years and some have required twenty. CABERNET SAUVIGNON, on the other hand, can almost always be expected to age twenty years with some grace. A spate of cool years since 1960 has even led to the wine from this grape being aged longer in barrels in California than it is in Bordeaux. The CABERNET SAUVIGNON is highly tannic, strongly marked by the instantly recognizable flavour of its grape, yet readily able to draw nuances through ageing.

Of California's generic reds BURGUNDYS are the most popular at present and are usually dry with pronounced fruitiness. MOUNTAIN REDS are an equable alternate, CHIANTIS are quite tart and VINO ROSSOS are sweeter.

ROSÉS

The great majority of Californian rosés are generics, although a few are made as varietals. The grape giving the best results is the GRENACHE, although the GRIGNOLINO, CABERNET SAUVIGNON, ZINFANDEL and GAMAY have been used successfully for rosé wines.

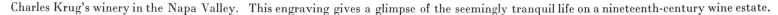

Charles Krug's winery in the Napa Valley. This engraving gives a glimpse of the seemingly tranquil life on a nineteenth-century wine estate.

ESTATE BOTTLED 4

Buena Vista 2

HARASZTHY ZINFANDEL 1

ESTATE GROWN AND BOTTLED BY
HARASZTHY CELLARS 3
BUENA VISTA VINEYARDS, SONOMA, CALIF

ALCOHOL 12½% BY VOLUME 5 2

HARASZTHY ZINFANDEL
1. Name of the wine and of the grapevine. The grapevine was imported into California from Europe around the middle of the nineteenth century by Count Agoston Haraszthy. The exact place of origin has never been definitely established. The grape gives a fragrant and fruity red wine characteristic of California. – 2. Name of the vineyard. – 3. Address and registered name of the vineyard. – 4. Indication of place of original bottling. – 5. Statement of alcohol content.

CABERNET SAUVIGNON
1. Name of the wine and of the grapevine. This grape, the same as that which gives Bordeaux claret, was imported into California. It gives a red wine of a beautiful deep ruby colour and with a most agreeable flavour. – 2. Name of the vineyard. – 3. Geographical origin of the wine and registered name of the vineyard. – 4. Indication of place of original bottling. – 5. Statement of alcohol content.

Beaulieu Vineyard

BV
ESTATE BOTTLED

NAPA VALLEY

CABERNET SAUVIGNON 4

3

1

PRODUCED & BOTTLED BY BEAULIEU VINEYARD
AT RUTHERFORD, NAPA COUNTY, CALIFORNIA 3

ALCOHOL 12.5% BY VOLUME 5

Vineyards Established 1852 4

ALMADÉN 2

California Mountain 1
PINOT NOIR

A distinguished, authentic Pinot Noir, velvety and fine,
made entirely from grapes of this illustrious Burgundian variety,
grown in Mountain Vineyards at Paicines, California 2

PRODUCED AND BOTTLED BY
Almadén Vineyards, Los Gatos, California 3
Alcohol 12½% by volume   0-67 5

PINOT NOIR
1. Name of the wine and of the grapevine. The grape is the same as that grown in Burgundy and which gives the famous red wines. – 2. Name of the vineyard and of the region. – 3. Name and address of the vineyards. – 4. Date of the foundation of the vineyard. – 5. Statement of alcohol content.

PINOT CHARDONNAY

1. Name of the wine and of the grapevine. This grape is very widespread in Champagne and Burgundy and gives a white wine resembling the dry white wine of Champagne that is much appreciated today. – 2. Name of the region. – 3. Name of the proprietor. – 4. Vintage date. – 5. Statement of alcohol content.

GEWÜRZ TRAMINER

1. Name of the wine and of the grapevine. This grape, which gives a white wine with a spicy scent and flavour, was imported from Alsace. – 2. Name of the region. – 3. Name of the proprietor. – 4. Date of the foundation of the vineyard. – 5. Statement of alcohol content.

SAUTERNE

1. Name of the wine. The name does not indicate the grapevine but the type of wine, which is a sweet white variety similar to French Sauternes. This wine can be made from grapes coming from several different regions of California. – 2. Name of the wine-merchant. – 3. Statement of alcohol content.

DINNER WINES

VARIETALS

Named for the grapes from which they are made.

White Wines

Serve chilled with fish, shellfish or poultry.
Light, crisp white wines, pale golden, or slightly green-gold in colour. Most are pleasantly dry. Some may have a hint of sweetness.

Johannisberg Riesling – Grey Riesling – Traminer – Sylvaner

Rich, fuller-flavoured wines. These are usually dry wines, pale to light golden in colour. Some may have a hint of sweetness.*

Pinot Chardonnay – Folle Blanche – Pinot Blanc – Dry Semillon – *Chemin Blanc

Medium to pronounced sweetness in these wines. They can be enjoyed most with dessert, fruit, fruit salad, and sweet food.

Semillon – Sauvignon Blanc

Rosé Wines

Serve chilled with ham, pork, veal, lamb, poultry.
These are light, fruity wines, sometimes dry, sometimes slightly sweet*, with a cheerful pink colour, ranging in tone from deep rose to a pale, orange tinted hue.

*Grenache Rosé – Gamay Rosé – Grignolino Rosé

Red Wines

Serve at cool room temperature with steaks, roasts, game, spaghetti, cheeses, stews, casseroles.
Fresh, fruity, red wines, dry and aromatic, light to medium in body.

Zinfandel – Ruby Cabernet

Rich, red wines with distinctive flavour and appealing ruby colour, medium to full in body.

Pinot Noir – Cabernet Sauvignon – Barbera

APPETIZER AND DESSERT WINES

Appetizer Wines

Aperitif or appetizer wines are usually dry and are drunk before meals or with the soup course. Chill them, or serve at room temperature, or pour over ice.

Sherry: *dry:* Solera Cocktail – Pale Dry – Ultra Dry – Dry Watch
medium dry: Solera Golden – Flor Sherry
Vermouth – dry or sweet

Dessert Wines

Pour dessert wines after dinner, either with dessert or later. They are all sweet, rich wines that are particularly good with fruit, nuts, cheese, cake. Serve at room temperature.

Sweet and cream Sherry: Solera Cream – Triple Cream – Rare Cream – Cream Flor
Port: Solera Ruby – Solera Tawny – Vintage Port – Tawny Port – Rare Tawny – Tinta Port

Sauterne and sweet Semillon are also served as dessert wines.

Sparkling Wines

These festive wines are appropriate at any time, with food as by themselves. They range from extremely dry to quite sweet, from pale gold to deep red. Sparkling wines are best well chilled.

Champagne type: Natural: very dry – Brut: dry – Extra dry: with just a hint of sweetness – Dry: medium sweet – Sec: noticeably sweet – Demi-Sec: very sweet

Rosé:	*Muscat:*	*Red:*
Pink Champagne	Sparkling Muscat	Sparkling Burgundy

APERITIF AND DESSERT WINES

California sherries are usually made after the fashion of Madeiras, although some are produced by the traditional flor method and aged and blended in a solera system. Ports are made in much the same way as those of Oporto, but rarely from the same grape.

THE WINEGROWERS OF CALIFORNIA

All told, California has around 212 licensed wineries within its capacious boundaries. The wineries that are of more than passing interest are noted in this section, with some incidental description of the districts in which they are found. Very nearly all of California's cellars welcome visitors, which encourages first-hand exploration in some of the state's handsomest countryside.

NAPA

Viticulture in the Napa Valley centres round the timeless little town of St. Helena toward the northern end of the valley.

A German named Charles Krug founded Napa's first commercial winery at St. Helena in 1861, and was soon followed by others; the valley has remained in the forefront of Californian winemaking since that era. Krug's name continues, although the cellars he built are now owned and operated by the family of the late Cesare Mondavi, who restored the estate after Prohibition. Beringer (1876) continued under its founding family. Beaulieu (1900) was sold to Heublein Inc. in 1969, although it still operates as a separate company. Inglenook (1879) was sold in 1963 by a descendant of the founder, Nybom. The Christian Brothers, although they came to this valley only in 1930, have a history dating back to 1882. Otherwise, the names are much newer: Heitz Cellar (1961), Hanns Kornell (1952), Louis M. Martini (1933, after a start elsewhere in 1923), Mayacamas (1947), Robert Mondavi (1966), Souverain (1953) and Stony Hill (1953). New or old, the cellars in the valley are among the most colourful in California and those who make wine in this valley now have made its name familiar in the world of wine far beyond state or even national borders. Its reputation rests with its red wines, especially the Cabernet Sauvignons.

SONOMA

The Valley of the Moon in Sonoma is a focal point of Californian history. It is here that the first revolt against the Mexican government started California on the way to United States statehood. It continues to bear a marked resemblance to its Spanish beginnings.

Buena Vista, Hanzell and Sebastiani in the Valley and Korbel and Pedroncelli in North Sonoma are responsible for the district's reputation. Journalist Frank Bartholomew restored Buena Vista to operation in 1943, long after Agoston Haraszthy had made it famous in the 1860s and in 1906 left it to fall into oblivion. Korbel dates from the 1880s, Sebastiani from 1905. Hanzell was founded in 1956 to see how close California could come to classic Burgundies, both red and white.

LIVERMORE-ALAMEDA COUNTY

Most of the vines of Livermore belong to two old winegrowing families of California: Karl Wente, a German, came to Livermore in 1883, and James Concannon, indisputably Irish, arrived a year later. Other pioneer vinicultural families of Charles Wetmore and Louis Mel have disappeared. Mel had connections with the Château d'Yquem and obtained cuttings from its vineyards to plant in the similar soil of Livermore. The Wente family acquired Mel's vineyards and have retained a small block of those now-ancient vines.

Urban pressure grows steadily in Livermore but Wente has guarded against the future by planting sizeable new vineyards in an unpopulated part of Monterey County, a hundred miles south.

On the San Francisco Bay side of Alameda County lie the vinegrowing centres of Mission San José and Irvington. Here the red wine is almost as good as the white, and sparkling and Champagne-type wines, aperitifs and dessert wines are also produced.

SAN JOAQUIN VALLEY

To meet the growing demand for table wines, winemakers are taking two approaches. One is the use of newly developed grape varieties and climate-modifying vineyard practices to make dry and in some cases distinctive table wines by traditional vinification and ageing methods. The other is the perfection of techniques for handling enormous volumes of wine for mass appeal on the American market. Most of the traditional wines are made at Lodi, northernmost of the districts, especially by Acampo and East-Side.

At Modesto, the firm of E. & J. Gallo stands unmatched in the making of wines in great volume. Using modern equipment and every new technique, the brothers Ernest and Julio Gallo make table wines to carefully established standards in lots of half a million gallons at a time. Guild, United Vintners and several other wineries have taken to using similar methods. This new trend has not come entirely at the expense of aperitif and dessert wines long associated with the valley: they continue to be made as well or better than

before. At Fresno, a tiny cellar named Ficklin produces an outstanding dessert wine from four of the major grape varieties of the Douro, calling it TINTA PORT. The larger Cresta Blanca has two dry sherry types from *Palomino* grapes. Many of the sweet grapes of the sherry type grown and made into wines here are sold under the labels of North Coast wineries such as Novitiate of Los Gatos in Santa Clara, the Christian Brothers in Napa, Weibel in Alameda County.

SANTA CLARA

Urban pressure has affected the Santa Clara-San Benito district even more dramatically than the Livermore district. In fact, these two counties and the Santa Cruz-Monterey region have been blurred into a single four-county district in which the old Santa Clara wineries are completely dominant.

Almaden and Paul Masson, both descendants of the founder Etienne Thee (1852), have gone separate but similar ways in the post-Prohibition era. Both maintain their original cellars near the city of San José, but are growing elsewhere. Almaden has become the largest winegrowing estate devoted to classic table wine types in the world. Paul Masson has proceeded on a scale only slightly lower at another site a few miles away, at Soledad in Monterey County.

Harvest time on a Californian vineyard. Skilled vintagers come to the wine country each vintage season to select and gather the ripe grapes.

329

CUCAMONGA

Southernmost of California's wine districts is Cucamonga. One of the oldest districts, it is now being
inundated by an eastward-sweeping wave of suburban
residential communities. In spite of its declining size,
the region has nearly 17,000 acres in vineyards, so it
is hoped that it will survive for some years to come.

A full range of wines is produced in this region, from
red table wines and sparkling "Champagnes" to
aperitifs and dessert wines. The hot desert climate is
not conducive to full-bodied wines and the light
Cucamonga growths should be drunk when still young.
Connoisseurs with a modest experience of Californian
vintages can inevitably identify wines from Cucamonga
owing to a *goût de terroir* (a special quality of wine
which is attributable chiefly to soil-type) which tran-
scends all grape varieties and methods of vinification.
It is the only Californian district with so pronounced
an individual characteristic.

OTHER STATES

More than half of the fifty American states have local
wine industries, all but a few of them being planted to
native grapes. Five of the states are of special importance for their winegrowing achievements.

New York State has several winegrowing districts,
but owes its reputation to vintages from vineyards lying
along the Finger Lakes, in the northern reaches of the
state. The five Finger Lakes, each of them long and
extremely narrow, are set in steepsided hills with lower
slopes that favour winegrowing.

Local wineries have an average of seventy flourishing
years behind them, and reason to be optimistic about
a growing audience in the eastern and midwestern
population centres of the United States. The largest

winery, Taylor-Great Western, is large by any standards
with its nine million gallon capacity. Widmers and
Gold Seal are much smaller; Konstantin Frank's is a
tiny cellar, but everybody in New York knows about it.

Traditionally the emphasis among the Finger Lakes
cellars has been on sparkling wines and sherry types.
There are sound reasons for this. The vineyards were
planted to native American grapes, primarily of the
genus *vitis labrusca*, for much of their history. Whenever these grapes are talked about in international wine
circles, it is for their "foxy" taste: the flavour is impart-
ed by a substance called methyl anthranilate, unmis-
takable in table wines, but less obvious in sparkling
wines and oxidized sherry types.

DENSE VINEYARD AREAS
SCATTERED VINEYARDS

In recent years wine companies and growers, notably Taylor (founded 1880), have begun to experiment with hybrids such as *Seibel*, *Seyve-Villard* and so forth, and others, in particular Konstantin Frank, have begun experiments with European *vitis vinifera* varieties. In the case of his *Johannisberg Riesling*, Frank modestly claims to have achieved the perfect *auslese*. Gold Seal (1865) maintains both *vitis vinifera* and hybrid plantings in addition to native grapes; Widmeras (1888) also has experiments underway in both.

The distinctive wines of the district are from vineyards of the American *vitis labrusca* varieties, notably *Concord*, *Niagara*, *Elvira*, *Catawba*, *Delaware* and *Ives*. Usually these are softened by blending with hybrids.

Washington State makes very nearly as much wine as New York State, with many of the same grape varieties. But it has never approached the Finger Lakes wine for quality and has not won a following outside its boundaries. The great majority of vineyards in Washington are near the town of Yakima, a famous region of fruit orchards at the eastern foothills of the Cascade Mountain Range. Some growers are experimenting with such *vitis vinifera* as *Pinot Noir* and *Johannisberg Riesling*, but results to date are either inconclusive or discouraging: the primary difficulty appears to be a short season.

Oregon, between Washington and California, has several small vineyards of *Johannisberg Riesling*, *Traminer* and *Pinot Noir* growing in its Willamette Valley south of Portland. A few growers are attempting to found a new wine region based on the Napa or Sonoma lines. Almost no wines have reached the market after the first few years of experiment, but scientists from the Department of Viticulture and Enology of the University of California regard the beginning as propitious.

In the eastern half of the country, Maryland has won widespread recognition as a wine district through the efforts of one man, journalist and viticulturist Philip Wagner. Wagner has spent two decades experimenting with the French-American hybrids in an attempt to diversify and upgrade wines from the native American districts. Work at his Boordy Vineyards has had substantial effect on the New York winegrowing regions.

Ohio was among the earliest of the colonial American winegrowing states, but now its production is waning steadily. The climate remains favourable for the growing of native grapes, but increasing population is crowding the vineyards along Lake Erie into the neighbourhood of Sandusky. Sparkling wines, especially from the *Delaware* grape, continue to be regarded favourably by many wine drinkers in the midwest and east: MEIER's is the best known.

THE WINES OF CANADA

Of all the wines on the North American continent those from Canada are perhaps the least known. The Canadians have two small and persistent wine districts. The largest, the Niagara Peninsula, Ontario, produces about 90% of Canada's grapes. Here, most of the grapes are native American varieties, but some *vitis vinifera*

vineyards are in bearing. The other district is in British Columbia. Its Okanagan Valley lies directly north of Washington's Yakima district, and produces a range of wines from native grape varieties. The Ontario district is the larger, and its wines are found more widely across Canada than British Columbians.

THE WINES OF MEXICO

Mexico is famous throughout the North American Continent for its beers, and unknown even within its borders for wine. The beers deserve their excellent reputation; the wines, although they are not rated by international standards, deserve slightly greater recognition than they receive.

Winemaking began in Mexico with the Spanish missionaries of the mid-eighteenth century, but its development was retarded by a combination of hot climate and poorly trained viticulturists and enologists. Large-scale plantings of vineyards did not take place until after 1920; even today the total acreage is only 25,000. The largest winegrowing district is Aguascalientes, the

most promising one Ensenada in Baja California. Here, technological skills are advanced, and the wineries are properly equipped.

Mexico's most distinctive wines to date have been sweet fortified ones, especially some of the Muscat types from Ensenada. Because of the hot climate, such wines no doubt will continue to surpass table wines in quality. Some of the latter are agreeable *ordinaires*, priced as such and served in Mexico City as well as in their districts of origin. It does not appear likely, however, that Mexican wines will gain great favour at home in the near future. The competition from beer is too great for the wines to expand beyond their small clientele.

Vineyards of the California valley extended in parallel lines as far as the eye can see. The grapes from these vines contribute to the millions of gallons which flow from California vineyards.

WINES OF CALIFORNIA

Red wines	*Claret types* . .	Cabernet Sauvignon . . .	Almadén, Beaulieu, Inglenook, Charles Krug, Louis Martini, Mirassou, Robert Mondavi, Sebastiani, Souverain
		Zinfandel	Buena Vista, Charles Krug, The Christian Bros., Louis Martini, Mirassou, Robert Mondavi, Pedroncelli
		Ruby Cabernet	East-Side
	Burgundy types.	Pinot Noir	Almadén, Beaulieu, Hanzell, Heitz Cellar, Inglenook, Louis Martini, Paul Masson, Martin Ray, Wente Bros.
	Italian types. .	Barbera	Louis Martini, Sebastiani
		Grignolino	Beringer, Heitz Cellar
		Chianti	Gallo, Italian Swiss Colony
White wines	*Sauternes types* .	Sauvignon Blanc	Almadén, Concannon, Robert Mondavi, Wente Bros.
		Semillon	Concannon, Charles Krug, Louis Martini, Wente Bros.
	Burgundy types.	Pinot Chardonnay . . .	Almadén, Beaulieu, Hanzell, Heitz Cellar, Paul Masson, Mayacamas, Robert Mondavi, Souverain, Stony Hill, Weibel, Wente Bros.
		Pinot Blanc.	Heitz Cellar, Paul Masson, Mirassou, Wente Bros.
		Chenin Blanc	Charles Krug, Souverain
		Folle Blanche	Louis Martini
		Chablis	Beaulieu, The Christian Bros.
	Rhine types . .	Johannisberger Riesling .	Almadén, Beaulieu, Charles Krug, Louis Martini, Souverain
		Grey Riesling	Almadén, Charles Krug, Wente Bros.
		Traminer	Charles Krug, Louis Martini, Mirassou, Stony Hill
		Sylvaner	Buena Vista, Inglenook, Louis Martini
Aperitif and dessert wines .	*Sherry types* . .	dry	Solera Cocktail (Almadén)
			Pale dry (Beaulieu, Louis Martini)
			Ultra Dry (Buena Vista)
			Dry Watch (Cresta Blanca)
		medium dry	Solera Golden (Almadén)
			Flor Sherry (Novitiate of Los Gatos, Weibel)
		Sweet and Cream Sherry .	Solera Cream (Beaulieu)
			Triple Cream (Cresta Blanca)
			Rare Cream (Paul Masson)
			Cream Flor (Weibel)
	Port types . . .	Solera Ruby	Almadén
		Solera Tawny	Almadén
		Vintage Port	Buena Vista
		Tawny Port	Louis Martini
		Rare Tawny	Paul Masson
		Tinta Port	Ficklin
	Champagne types	Champagne	Almadén, Korbel, Hanns Kornell, Paul Masson, Weibel
		Pink Champagne	Almadén, Korbel, Paul Masson, Weibel
		Sparkling Burgundy . . .	Almadén, Korbel, Hanns Kornell, Paul Masson, Weibel
		Sparkling Muscat	Hanns Kornell
Rosé wines		Grenache rosé	Almadén, Beaulieu, Novitiate of Los Gatos
		Gamay rosé	Louis Martini, Robert Mondavi
		Grignolino rosé	Heitz Cellar

WINES OF NEW YORK STATE

Red wines	Burgundy	Delaware	Lake Country Red
	Claret	Isabella	Niagara
White wines	Catawba	Johannisberger Riesling Spätlese	Pinot Chardonnay
	Delaware	Lake Niagara	Rhine Wine
	Gewürztraminer	Muscat Ottonel	White Tokay

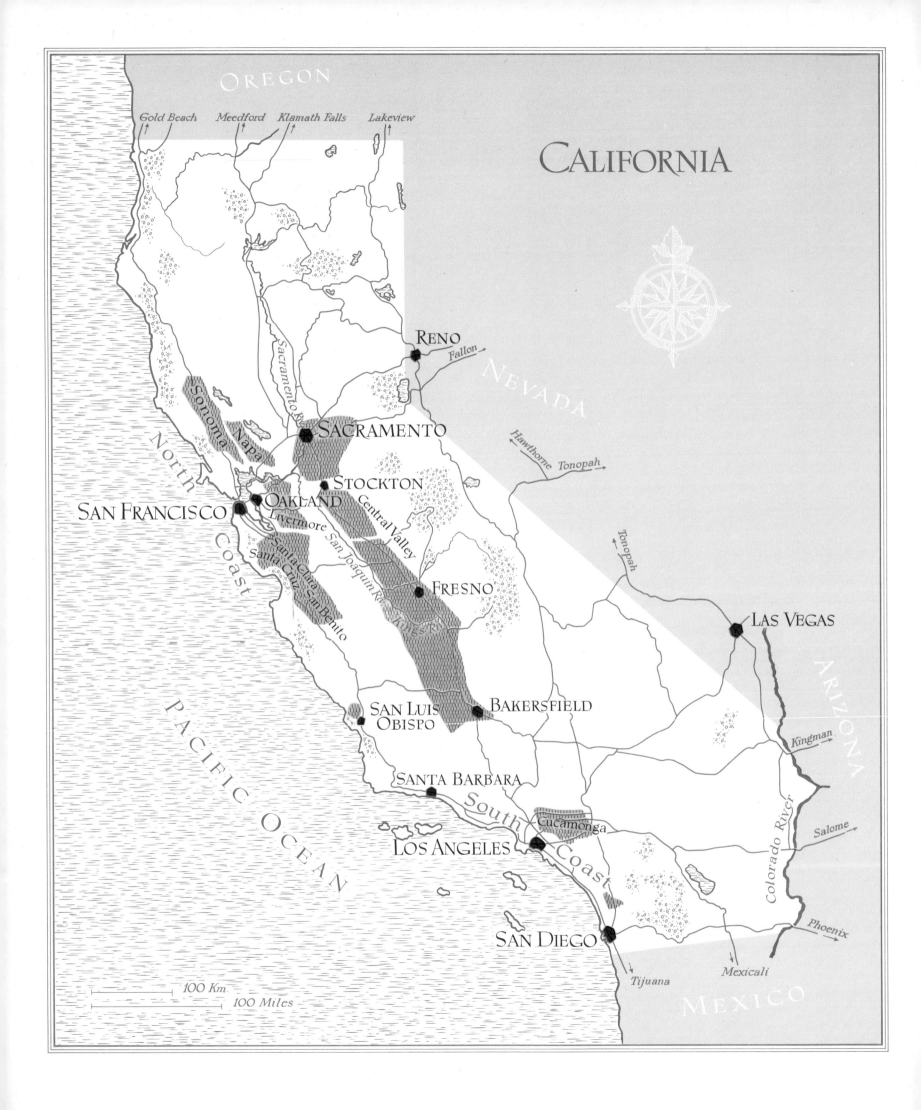

CALIFORNIA

OREGON

Gold Beach   Meedford   Klamath Falls   Lakeview

NEVADA

RENO

Fallon

Hawthorne   Tonopah

Sonoma

Napa

Sacramento River

SACRAMENTO

STOCKTON

OAKLAND

SAN FRANCISCO

Livermore

Santa Clara   San Joaquin River

Santa Cruz   San Benito

Central Valley

Kings R.

FRESNO

Tonopah

LAS VEGAS

ARIZONA

NORTH COAST

PACIFIC OCEAN

SAN LUIS OBISPO

BAKERSFIELD

Kingman

Colorado River

SANTA BARBARA

Salome

Cucamonga

SOUTH COAST

LOS ANGELES

Phoenix

SAN DIEGO

Mexicali

Tijuana

MEXICO

100 Km
100 Miles

THE WINES OF SOUTH AMERICA

DENIS BOUVIER

Within hours of their first landings on the cost of South America, the galleons flying the flags of Spain discharged upon the beaches two very disparate cargoes: barrels of gunpowder for their arms, and barrels of wine for the altar set up in the name of Their Very Catholic Majesties. But the supply of wine soon grew short, and the missionaries who landed with the *conquistadores* found themselves obliged to become winegrowers. In this way wine came to South America.

The aim of the emissaries sent out by Ferdinand of Spain and Manuel the Fortunate of Portugal was to conquer the "Western Indies". The sole purpose of the conquest was to appropriate for themselves the gold and wealth of these new countries which stretched from the Atlantic across the Andes to the "Great Ocean" beyond. But neither the cross, nor the royal standard, nor even the quantities of glass beads they brought could persuade the natives to let invaders plunder the riches of their land. The *conquistadores* then used more summary methods, which the Indians answered in their own way: they tortured their prisoners in original fashion, quenching their thirst by giving them molten gold to drink as a reprisal for the wine which the Franciscan and Jesuit Fathers had forced them to drink with the Host. And what remains today of this immense Empire after it was split up into the separate nations of Chile, Argentina, Brazil and Peru? The gold mines are long since empty, the art treasures shamelessly melted down into bullion; the people, decimated by war and bled dry by taxation, are reduced to poverty. The only living thing remaining

of what the conquerors brought to South America is, here and there, a vineplant, a thriving symbol of eternity.

This vine-plant gave birth to the immense South American vineyard of today, which spreads along the coastline, in the valleys of the Andes right at the foot of the Great Cordillera, and then up on the high plains into the Pampas region and to Uruguay. Wine, which at the heroic time of the *Conquista* was considered to be the perquisite of the new Crusaders, grew to be more appreciated as the Spanish influence came to dominate the people. Viticulture was further intensified when settlers flocked from across the seas; they came from France, Italy and Germany, often bringing with them as their sole possession the love of vineyards and wine as well as the knowledge acquired from centuries of winemaking in Burgundy, the Basque provinces, Tuscany or the banks of the Rhine. Thus viniculture spread through the new land of South America, which previously had only seemed capable of harbouring the sisal plant, or maté, maize and coffee. True, it was first necessary to make the soil suitable for cultivation, for it had been allowed to lie fallow for centuries. Canals were dug to irrigate the land, and experiments made to find the vine-plant best suited to the varied and often capricious climate of the area. Then it was necessary to develop new methods of vinification and culture. Here, the vinegrowers drew on their experiences in the African vineyards.

The South American vineyard has developed well, and it is today of respectable dimensions. The quality of its produce continues to improve, even though the wine it exports (at competitive prices) cannot hope to rival in quality the great wines of Western Europe. These are wines which compare more favourably with those of North Africa.

Not all countries cultivate the vine: Ecuador, Venezuela, Guiana and Paraguay do not. Of those that do, the following are listed in order of importance both as regards the area under cultivation and the production of wine: Argentina, Chile, Brazil, Uruguay, Peru, Bolivia and Columbia. It is interesting to note that until now no South American Government has introduced any official system of classification or control of the proprietary name in South America there is no *appellation d'origine contrôlée*.

ARGENTINA

Argentina, fourth largest wineproducer in the world, is the first in South America. Its wine, however, is grown solely for domestic consumption, not for world markets. How better could an Argentinian accompany the excellent meat of his abundant live-stock than with a bottle of his own wine?

The vine was introduced to Argentina in the sixteenth century, when the Spaniards first conquered the Pampas. Coming down from the high plains and mineral regions of Bolivia, they looked for new treasures in the foothills of the Andes. By comparison with the gold being sought by Don Pedro de Castillo and Juan Jupe, who founded the towers of Mendoza and San Juan, the humble vine planted by the Franciscans and Jesuits did not seem to promise a great future. However, despite the obstacles the kings of Spain brought to the development of viticulture in this part of the American continent, the Cuyo region grew rich in vineyards thanks to the patience and industry of its winegrowers. Alas, as Philip II's coffers grew heavy with rare and precious metals, the Spanish economy, mortally paralysed, came to a standstill.

The first vines planted in the provinces of Mendoza and San Juan would probably not have yielded any grapes unless the fallow soil had been previously irrigated. The Italian immigrants were the first to find a method of using the water which came down in torrents from the Andes and was rich in lime. Thus the vine could be cultivated even in desert-like conditions, and so began the famous "viticultural oases". Later this water brought the deadly phylloxera disease which drastically reduced wine-harvests; but in its turn the water helped, for the same network of irrigation canals which was responsible for spreading the disease later aided the method used to cure it. By plugging and overflowing the canals, it was possible to flood the infected vines and drown out the tiny plant lice that destroyed them.

The South American wine, which at first was produced only for local consumption, gradually began to infiltrate the whole country as new routes were opened up into the interior. In the nineteenth century, considerable progress was made in the field of vinification and viticulture, mainly owing to the influx of European immigrants. Today viticulture in Argentina is flourishing, having developed hand in hand with the demographic growth of the country. The winegrowers could doubtless pay more attention to the quality of their product, which is often the weak point in vinification when practised on too large a scale.

GRAPE VARIETIES. *Criollo* is the first vine-plant cultivated in Argentina. It came, in fact, from Mexico and Peru, but can be considered an indigenous grape. It is probably from this stock that Brother Cedron made the first wine in Argentina 450 years ago. Today it produces white wines. White wines are also made from grapes introduced by French, Italian and Spanish growers, grapes such as the *Pedro Ximenez, Semillon, Pinot Blanc, Malvoisie* and the *Riesling.* Two-thirds of the red wines are made from the *Malbec* grape variety, and the remainder from various other European grape varieties.

VINICULTURAL PROVINCES. In order of importance the chief wineproducing provinces are Mendoza, San Juan and Rio King, which between them provide 96 per cent of Argentina's wine-harvest. Then come the regions of Buenos Aires, Santa Fé, Córdoba, La Rioja, Catamarca, Salta, Jujy and Entrerios.

MENDOZA. This province is by far the most important. It alone produces 70 per cent of Argentina's wine crop: in 1966, the wine-harvest there was 304,304,000 gallons. The area under cultivation is 488,900 acres, or 40 per cent of the entire South American vineyard. There are about 40,000 vintners in this region alone, but 16 per cent of the production is in the hands of only nine large companies. These firms have their own wine-cellars, and a distribution network throughout Argentina. Most of the wines produced here are red, but there is also a small quantity of white and sparkling wines. Very few winegrowers, however, try to produce quality wines; most are only interested in quantity, which they get by mechanizing production. Their well-equipped farms dot the far-flung vineyards which reach far beyond the horizon.

OCEANO PACIFICO

CHILE

Antofagasta

BRAZIL

LA RIOJA

Río Salado

Río Paraná

Río Uruguay

BENTO-GONÇALVES

CAXIAS DO SUL

RIO GRANDE DO SUL

Porto Alegre

JESÚS MARÍA

Córdoba

Santa Fe

Concordia

Salto

SAN JUAN

Pelotas

VILLA DOLORES

Rosario

PAYSANDÚ

Valparaiso

MENDOZA

SAN-NICOLÁS

URUGUAY

SANTIAGO

SAN JOSÉ

FLORIDA

SAN RAFAEL

COLONIA

CANELONES

O'HIGGINS

BUENOS AIRES

MALDONADO

TALCA

Río de la Plata

MONTEVIDEO

LINARES

CONCEPCIÓN

CHILLÁN

ARGENTINA

BÍO-BÍO

Bahía Blanca

OCEANO ATLANTICO

Valdivia

Río Colorado

RIO NEGRO

Río Negro

Osorno

MAPA VITICOLA
AMERICA DEL SUL

Among South American countries Chile produces the wine best known on the export market. Argentina is the largest wineproducer and
after Chile, which holds second place, comes Brazil with an annual yield of about fifteen million gallons, most of which is sold abroad.
Uruguay, although the smallest of the South American states, produces a great deal of wine, most of which is consumed locally.

Everything here is done on a very large scale. The Bodega Giol, in Mendoza, for example, can store about 19,140,000 gallons; and it is merely one of many.

SAN JUAN. Farther along the Great Cordillera, past the province of Mendoza, is San Juan, whose vineyard is one-quarter the size of Mendoza. But acre for acre, its yield is greater: it produces an average of 132,000,000 gallons of wine a year. Here the wine is richer, with more body, although the reason for this might be merely that San Juan is somewhat nearer to the Equator and thus enjoys a warmer climate.

RIO AND OTHER REGIONS. Rio is situated at the southern tip of the viticultural zone of the Republic of Argentina. It produces light red wines, excellent whites and also sparkling wines. These are considered Argentina's best wines. Other wineproducing areas are La Rioja, Salta and Buenos Aires, whose vineyards are being extended. Santiago del Estero is in the process of planting a vineyard.

WINE TYPES. The International Institute of Viti-Viniculture *(El Instituto Internacional de la Viti-vini-cultura)* has classified Argentinian wines into two groups: *comunes* (ordinary wines) and *no comunes* (the better grades). The *comunes* wines, which account for 90 per cent of the total production, are those sold as *vinos de mesa* or table wines. They are mostly red, very full-bodied wines, with an alcohol content ranging from 11º to 12.5º. The whites are ordinary wines with a higher alcohol content. Ordinary wine from the provinces of La Rioja, San Juan, Catamarca, Córdoba, Jujuy and Salta enjoys a form of regional appellation. These are unblended wines *envasado en origen* (bottled by the producer), or mixed with other wines (provided that the other wine used was made from grapes grown on the territory of the corresponding regional vineyard); these are known as *vinos de corte* (blended wines). The third category of wine known as *comunes* is that of special wines labelled *vinos de postre* (dessert wines) or *moscato*. *Vinos de mesa* and *vinos de postre* can be *seco* (dry), *dulce* (sweet) or *abocado* (a mild wine). The *vino de postre abocado* is made by adding a concentrated must to the wine whilst it is fermenting, and is very highly thought of by Argentinians.

The best Argentinian wines are the *vinos no comunes*. They come in four different categories: *finos* (fine wines), *reservas* (wines in reserve), *reservados* (reserved) and *especiales* (special wines). The fine wines are made mainly from the *Semillon*, *Pedro Ximenez*, *Cabernet*, *Barbera*, *Malbec* and *Torrentes* grapes. According to their colour they are known as: *tinto*, *blanco*, *clarete*, *rosado* or *criollo*. The reds are well-balanced, dry, strong and full-bodied wines, with an alcohol content from 12º to 13º. The white wines, whose alcohol content is slightly lower than the red, have a rich bouquet; they are well-balanced and have a very pleasant taste. The rosés are also well-balanced, with an alcohol content of from 12º to 13º. ESCORHUELO, RIO NEGRO and the well-known EL TRAPICHE are some of the best wines of Argentina.

Argentina also produces sparkling wines of the Champagne or Asti type as well as aerated wine, as mediocre here as anywhere else in the world. There are also vermouths and quinine waters.

A few Argentinian wines have adopted foreign names, such as Porto, Jerez, Champagne, Marsala, Médoc and Burgundy. It is interesting to note that although in Argentina there is a strict control on the production and quality of wine, there is none on the brand names.

CHILE

Chilean wines are by far the best in South America, and have established the highest reputation on the continent. However, Chile exports very little wine to the world market: only 1.25 per cent from an annual production of about 99,000,000 gallons. Most of the wines for export are honest table wines, and one must visit Chile, or more particularly the Santiago region, to taste the best the country has to offer.

As elsewhere in South America, the Europeans implanted the *vitis vinifera* in Chile, whose climate proved to be very favourable to the cultivation of the vine. The vineyard was modernized in the nineteenth century by Italian, French and German immigrants. The French techniques in viniculture and vinification were the most successful, hence French methods came to be generally accepted and practised in all the *haciendas* and these techniques are still employed today.

An attempt was made to extend viticulture to the drier and less suitable regions, but irrigation proved to be an inseparable problem. A Chilean, Silvestre Ochagavia, imported and planted French vines, and brought the *Cabernet*, *Sauvignon* and *Pinot* grapes into the central valley in Chile; then, following his example, the Government took measures to encourage the development of viticulture in that area.

Chile has three large viticultural regions. The biggest in area is the southern vineyard. Herein are contained the regions of Linares, the banks of the Maule river, Nuble, Conception and the Bío-Bío valley, where the production is mainly red wines (70 per cent), with a small quantity of white wines (30 per cent). These wines, originating for the most part from humid and cold areas, arc light, with a low alcohol content; they are made from *Malbec, Cabernet, Semillon* and *Riesling* grapes.

The second largest viticultural region—Curico, Talca, Santiago, O'Higgins and Colchaga—has a dry, warm climate, but thanks to irrigation produces excellent wines. Red wines are made from the *Cabernet Franc, Cabernet Sauvignon, Merlot, Malbec* and *Petit Verdot* grapes; the white wines, from the *Semillon* and *Sauvignon* grapes. A few *Pinot Blanc* and *Pinot Noir* grapes can be found here and there, as well as the *País* or *Uva del País*, the national grape, one of the first vines to be planted on Chilean soil.

The third principal vineyard is farther north, near Coquimbo in the Aconcaga valleys and along the banks of the Maipo river, as well as up to the fringes of the Atacama desert. Here the *Muscat* grape flourishes and gives wines of a very high alcohol content: rich and full-bodied, similar to Madeira, ports or sherry. They are often blended with the southern varieties. The climate here in the northern part of the country does not favour viniculture, for it is either too dry or too humid, depending on the season.

Chilean wines are classified into four different categories according to their age. The first category is for ordinary table wines of one year; the second is the *especiales*, which are two-year-old wines; the third, the *reservados*, have been in the bottle for four years, and are often high quality wines; and finally, the *gran vino* wines are recognized as being the best. Their quality is guaranteed by the State, and they are left to mature in barrels for at least six years.

BRAZIL

Brazil is the third largest wineproducer in South America, with vineyards covering 170,500 acres and producing about 33,000,000 gallons. Planted at the time of the Portuguese conquest, the vine came into its own only at the beginning of the last century. It made some progress between the two wars and is still being developed today: within rather less than fifty years, the area under cultivation increased sevenfold. This development was above all the work of Italian immigrants, who knew how to bring the best out of a soil which until then had been neglected. However, as the average Brazilian only drinks about four pints a year, the rest is sold on the international market, where the main customers are the U.S.A., Argentina and Germany.

THE GRAPE VARIETIES. The *Isabella* is the grape most frequently used; it is an American hybrid which produces an ordinary table wine. The other grapes used are the *Duchesse, Merlot, Cabernet, Barbera, Niagara, Folha de Figos, Black July, Siebel* and such varieties as the *Delaware, Jacques Gaillard, Concord, Gothe, Trebbiano,* and *Moscatel.*

WINES. The Brazilian wine industry is controlled by a series of very simple regulations, which merely distinguish between table, dessert and blended wines. These wines can be called by their grape—BARBERA, MOSCATEL, TREBBIANO, MALVASIA, RIESLING and MERLOT—provided they consist of these varieties in an authorized proportion. As a result, one can find good quality ordinary wines, but never great wines. The ordinary table wines are of a red Burgundy or claret type, rosés, or dry, semi-dry and sweet white wines. Good table wines include those of the *Barbera, Cabernet* and *Merlot* grapes, which produce reds; or those of the *Trebbiano, Poverella, Malvasia* and *Riesling* grape which produce whites. Other good wines have their own trade names. Brazil also produces sparkling wines, made in the bottle or in any of several types of closed containers. These *espumante* (effervescent) wines are from the juice of the *Moscatel* and *Malvasia* grapes.

The Rio Grande do Sul represents the biggest viticultural area, for its climate is the most favourable to vine cultivation. Other wineproducing areas are São Paulo, Santa Caterina, Rio de Janeiro and Minas Gerias, with vineyard altitudes varying from 2,100 to 5,400 feet; surely a record.

Caxias do Sul and Bento-Concalves are the main areas of production in Rio Grande do Sul. Having abandoned the *Lambrusca grape,* which produced a very mediocre growth, the winegrowers here turned mainly to the *Concord, Isabella, Tercy* and *Herbemont* grapes, and to hybrids of the *Seibel* grape. The best alternative grapes used to make red wines are the *Sangiovesi, Barbera* and *Cabernet*; while for white wines, there are the *Merlot, Riesling, Malvasia* and *Trebbiano* grapes. The wines produced in this State, especially the reds, are usually of a very high quality.

In the State of São Paulo, the vine is concentrated around the regions of Jundiai and São Roque, but the best wine comes from Pardo, São José do Rio, Serra Negra, Salto de Itu, Ararquara, Campinas and Guararema. These vines are more or less the same varieties as those in the Rio Grande do Sul.

There are other viticultural centres in Brazil, notably Videira in Santa Catarina and Recife in Pernambuco.

URUGUAY

Viniculture was first introduced into Uruguay towards the end of the last century from the Montevideo region. Smallest of all South American States (apart from French and Dutch Guiana), it produces 18,700,000 gallons of wine per annum, which puts it fourth among the viticultural countries on this continent. But wine stocks are insignificant and almost exclusively for domestic consumption. Production just about meets the demand, which is nevertheless eight times greater than in the United States, while production is about one-tenth ! This underlines the importance of viticulture which, despite competition from *maté*, the national drink, almost doubled in the years 1958 to 1963, when it reached almost 27,500,000 gallons. Wine is drunk more and more frequently with meals, especially with lamb roasted on the spit, a choice dish in Uruguay.

A country with a temperate climate and heavy rainfall, Uruguay has several winegrowing regions, mainly in the south. The Canelones region is the most important; there the vines cover more than 24,500 acres, divided into small-holdings. Montevideo follows, with 13,400 acres shared between 1,874 winegrowers; then San José, Colonia, Paysandu, Florida, and Maldonado in order of production. Although there are quite a few vintners—some 7,300 for the whole country—there are also many large co-operatives, or *bodéguéros*, which have their own underground cellars with all the most modern equipment for pressing and vinification. The most common vine in Uruguay is one which is rarely met anywhere else in the world; here it is called *Harriague*. In the Hautes-Pyrénées of France, where it comes from, it is better known as *Tannat*. It gives a good quality red wine. The best wines however, are made from grapes such as *Alicante*, *Carignan*, *Grenache* and *Cinsault*. Other grapes used are *Vidiella*, whose origin is unknown; *Cabernet*, here used to make an ordinary wine; *Barbera* and *Niebbiolo*. Often the quality of the wine is improved through judicious blending. Most white wines are made from *Semillon* and *Pinot Blanc* grapes as well as the American *Isabella*, while some hybrids also produce a very poor quality wine.

Uruguay thus produces the usual variety of wines: *tinto*, *rosado* and *blanco*, of both ordinary and better quality. But there is no methodical classification of wines which would guarantee its quality for the consumer. It seems clear that the wines of the *gran reserva* are better than others, so that an *appellation d'origine* shown on the label might help to distinguish between the local wines and the blended wines. The latter may be blended from a mixture of grapes or with foreign wines. There are also a great many wines which state the name of the grape from which they are made. Finally, Uruguay also produces special wines such a *sherry-quinquina*, dessert wines and sparkling wines.

PERU, BOLIVIA AND COLOMBIA

PERU. Francisco Carabantes, the Spanish conqueror of Peru, introduced the vine there about the middle of the sixteenth century. Peru today has a vineyard of 20,560 acres producing 5,830,000 gallons of wine, making it the fifth wineproducing country on the Latin-American continent. The main wine areas are Lima, Ica, Chincha, Moquegua, Tacana and Lacumba.

The climate here is not at all favourable to the production of great wines and some regions are completely unable to support vine cultivation. The Andes are for the most part too cold and rugged and other regions are too hot and arid for good wine culture.

The white Peruvian wines are, nevertheless, pleasant, light, and have an agreeable bouquet. The red wines, however, are more ordinary, heavy with tannin and of a very poor quality. All the wine in Peru is produced for domestic consumption. Besides wine and *chicha*, a national drink made from sweet maize, some sweet wine such as Madeira or sherry is also drunk. The wines here are usually known by their place of origin: LOCUMBA, MOQUEGUA, CHINCHA, ICA, and so on.

BOLIVIA. The vine was probably brought to Bolivia from varieties originating in the Canaries. Today, the Bolivian vineyard covers some 5,000 acres and produces about 132,000 gallons a year, concentrated in the province of La Paz. There are also an additional 4,000 acres on which table grapes are cultivated. The wines produced are reds or whites, with an alcohol content from 13º to 15º; they are usually heavy. The country also produces some wines similar to sherry.

COLOMBIA. Colombia is the smallest wineproducer in South America, with a mere two thousand or so gallons. The vinicultural conditions here are exceptional owing to the torrid climate of the country, which allows the grape to mature several times a year, thus upsetting the usual wine-harvest cycle. Colombia produces mainly white sherry, port-type wines and light table wines which are decidedly sweet.

THE WINES OF AUSTRALIA

JOHN STANFORD

Modern civilization came late to Australia. In 1788 the establishment of a British colony at Sydney was followed by the planting of European *vitis vinifera* vines at Parramatta in the early 1790s in the garden of the Reverend Samuel Marsden. By 1820, James Busby, working with a grant of money from the new Government, had established commercial vineyards near Newcastle in the Hunter Valley, a hundred miles north of Sydney. This is still one of Australia's premier wine-producing areas.

During the next twenty years vineyards were established around the southern city of Melbourne at Lilydale and Geelong, at Rutherglen and Corowa on the Victoria-New South Wales border, in South Australia near Adelaide, and in Western Australia near Perth. In the next two decades political and religious persecution in Silesia brought settlers to the Barossa Valley who planted vines and founded the settlements of Tanunda, Lyndoch, Nuriootpa, Angaston, Seppeltsfield, Watercale and Clare. In the Swan Valley of Western Australia, vines originally planted for table grapes in the 1820s began to produce wine in the 1880s. The Chaffey brothers came from California in 1887 and established the irrigated vineyards around Mildura on the Murray River in Victoria.

Later development in irrigated districts followed down the Murray into South Australia (Renmark, Berri, Loxton, Waikerie, Nildottie) and upstream along the Victoria border. One most important development was the creation of the Riverina irrigation area around the towns of Griffith, Leeton and Yenda in south-western New South Wales with water from the Murrumbidgee River in 1912.

The climate for vine cultivation in Australia is even, warm during the growing period, with a tendency to too much rather than to too little sunlight, and too little rather than too much rain. Vintage variations are less noticeable than in the colder areas of Europe, but the same grapes are used for the basic wine styles.

Names such as CLARET, BURGUNDY, HOCK, CHABLIS, WHITE BURGUNDY, MOSELLE, CHAMPAGNE, SHERRY, PORT, and MADEIRA indicate wines of very similar style to European counterparts, but with flavours differing with the influence of soil types and warmer ripening conditions. Varietal labels indicating grape varieties and districts are taking over from these traditional wine style names: CABERNET, SAUVIGNON, HERMITAGE, CABERNET SHIRAZ, MALBEC, RIESLING, TRAMINER-RIESLING, SEMILLON, GREAT WESTERN PINOT, COONAWARRA CLARET, HUNTER RIVER DRY RED etc.

Many brand labels indicate skilful blending, usually specified on the label, of wines from different districts with similar style but different flavours. This established technique has been developed by wine families owning vineyards and wineries in similar climatic conditions up to a thousand miles apart. Table wines made in this way have proved their ability to develop and improve for more than twenty years in the bottle.

Australian winemakers are extremely anxious for the quality of their products. Each year a wine fair is held in the principal towns (Melbourne, Sydney, Adelaide, Perth and Brisbane) and an average of 550 samples coming from all the wine districts are judged for awards. Australians wines presented at the fairs in France, Poland and Yugoslavia are very well received.

The volume of production, at around 40 million gallons of base wine per year is small by world standards. Winemaking methods are sound and imaginative. Most winemakers are graduates of the Oenology School at Roseworthy, South Australia or of French, German or American Schools of Oenology. In conjunction with the Australian Wine Research Institute and the Commonwealth Scientific and Industrial Research Organization (C.S.I.R.O.) they have developed their own techniques of cultivation, vine breeding, winemaking methods, chemical research and analysis to suit the conditions imposed by isolation and climate. Wine production is increasing by 10 to 12 per cent per year and is mainly consumed within Australia.

HUNTER VALLEY DISTRICTS. This small but expanding wine region is a hundred to a hundred and fifty miles north of Sydney in New South Wales. The older established area is at Pokolbin, near Cessnock. Recent development has been around Muswellbrook in the Upper Hunter Valley, seventy miles farther north. Production is almost entirely red and white table wines.

Principal plantings: mainly *Shiraz (Hermitage)* and *Semillon* with some *White Hermitage, Mataro, Pinot Noir, Cabernet* and *Traminer.*

Wine styles: soft, round, aromatic Burgundy wines, white and red, with a characteristic district flavour. They develop and mature for long periods in the bottle.

CENTRAL AND NORTH EASTERN VICTORIA. This district was once famous for its gold digging and then, around 1900, it became for a while Australia's largest wineproducing area. But phylloxera destroyed large areas of vines and South Australia then became the producers of 70 per cent of the country's wine.

Principal plantings: *Shiraz, Grenache, Cabernet Sauvignon* (red), *Semillon, White Hermitage, Verdeilho, Muscatel, Marsanne, Riesling* (white).

Wine styles: rich, full-flavoured, sweet dessert wines (Muscat, Madeira, and port styles) and big, full-bodied dry red with some light Riesling and other dry white.

WESTERN VICTORIA. These cool, elevated vineyards situated in the foothills of the Grampian Mountains were established by Swiss settlers in 1853.

Principal plantings: *Shiraz, Cabernet Sauvignon, Malbec, Pinot Meuniere, Mataro, Ouillade, Riesling, Semillon, Chardonnay.*

Wine styles: light, delicate Champagne and Riesling styles, crisp and more robust dry whites from *Semillon* and *Chardonnay,* aromatic dry reds from *Shiraz, Cabernet, Pinot* and *Malbec.*

SOUTH-EASTERN SOUTH AUSTRALIA. This cool, low-lying region 250 miles from Adelaide, near the Victorian border, was originally planted as adjuncts to large pastoral homesteads but later developed as an important district for the production of dry red wines.

Principal plantings: *Shiraz, Cabernet Sauvignon, Riesling.*

Wine types: crisp, full-bodied dry red wines of claret style of high quality.

ADELAIDE AND SOUTHERN VALES. This cool, moist, even-temperature coastal district lies between the suburban foothills near Adelaide, along the south coast of St. Vincent's Gulf to Reynella, McLaren Vale and Langhorne Creek and contains some of the earliest planting established in South Australia (1838).

Principal plantings: *Shiraz, Cabernet Sauvignon, Grenache* (red), *Riesling, Semillon, White Hermitage, White Sauvignon.*

Wine styles: crisp, full-flavoured dry red wines, similar to the French Bordeaux; light, delicate dry white; flor sherry; sweet red (vintage and tawny style ports).

BAROSSA VALLEY - EDEN VALLEY - CLARE. This is one of the largest winegrowing regions of Australia. It ranges from the Clare-Watervale Plateau, eighty miles north of Adelaide, through the main Barossa Valley, around Tanunda, Nuriootpa and Angaston to the high, colder districts of Springton, Eden Valley and Pewsey Vale, forty to fifty miles from Adelaide. It is famous for its Vintage Festival and produces all types of wine.

Principal plantings: *Shiraz, Cabernet, Mataro, Grenache, Malbec, Clare Riesling, Riesling, Semillon, White Hermitage.*

Wines styles: light, fragrant, crisp Rieslings from Clare, Watervale, Eden Valley, Rowland Flat and Angaston. Soft, full-flavoured dry reds from Angaston, Keyneton, Springton, Kalimna, Seppeltsfield and Tanunda. Rich, sweet dessert wines from Tanunda, Lyndoch and Nuriootpa. Sherries and brandy from the main bed of the valley.

SWAN VALLEY. This old winemaking district is between six and twenty miles from Perth, Western Australia. There are many very small makers but only four to five significant companies.

Principal plantings: *Shiraz, Grenache, Cabernet, Malbec, Ouillade.*

Wine styles: because rain seldom falls at all in January and February, during the ripening period for grapes immediately preceding vintage, many wines are full, rich and low-acid Burgundy styles. There is in all the Swan Valley wines, just as in those of the Hunter Valley, a characteristic flavour evident to a greater or lesser degree and determined by the nature of the soil.

MURRAY VALLEY. The Murray River rises in the Australian Alps from rain and snow waters. It runs

342

inland from the eastern seaboard, through the dry plains along the Victoria-New South Wales border into South Australia. Near Waikerie, 150 miles north of Adelaide, it swings south and joins the Southern Ocean about sixty miles south of Adelaide—a total distance of 1,609 miles. Irrigated vineyards are spaced along the whole of its length. The largest winegrowing centres are: Mildura, Robinvale, Renmark, Berri, Loxton, Waikerie-Cadell, Nildottie and Langhorne Creek.

A large proportion of Australian brandy originates in this extended area. Base wines are made mainly from *Sultana*, *Waltham Cross* and *Doradillo* grapes. Here also originate many of the sweet dessert wines made from *Muscat* and similar varieties, which form the blending base of the white dessert and sweet sherry styles for Australian, English and Canadian markets. The same vineyards and wineries produce high quality flor sherry,

base wines and light, soft dry and sweet table wines (hock, Moselle, Sauterne styles) and a growing output of rosé and light, dry red table wines.

In many districts, particularly Cadell, Nildottie, Langhorne Creek, Mildura and Loxton, new plantings of recent years have been in premium wine varieties—*Cabernet*, *Shiraz*, *Riesling*, *Semillon*, etc.

RIVERINA DISTRICT. This vineyard was founded in 1912 when water was reticulated sixty miles overland from Narrandera to water a dry basin of rich, heavy soil around the towns of Griffith, Yenda and Leeton.

The area produces fruit of all types, but almost all the vines are winemaking varieties. Fourteen wineries process these grapes for dry red, dry and sweet white table wines, sherries, sweet dessert wines and brandy. Controlled irrigation techniques developed and used in this area have produced table wines of high quality.

THE WINES OF NEW ZEALAND

New Zealand's two islands lie across the moist trade winds between 35º and 41º south latitude. The South Island has a few experimental vineyards—at Otago and Nelson—but is too cold for commercial planting. On the other hand the North Island climate, which varies between the extreme of sub-tropical forest and volcanic activity in the far north and the cold south, supports the wine industry. In the northern districts of Henderson and Kumeu (near Auckland), the Te Kauwhata Viticultural Research Station and the Coromandel Peninsula, and southward at Hawkes Bay, are the two main areas where the majority of New Zealand's vines grow. There is only slightly more sunlight than in the cooler Australian districts, but the rainfall is much higher—in some areas over fifty inches per year.

Two famous figures in the founding of Australian vineyards, James Busby and the Reverend Samuel Marsden, settled in the far north at the Bay of Islands in the early 1830s. When the seat of Administration was moved farther south to Auckland, these vineyards died out and were never replanted.

Around 1835 priests of the Marist Order planted vineyards at Hawkes Bay. Henderson and Hawkes Bay are now the two most important producing districts, each with about five to six hundred acres planted. The smaller districts of Thames and Te Kauwhata will probably expand with the current increasing demand for wine in New Zealand.

The art of winemaking had not noticeably progressed until the late 1950s. Recent investment by the Australian companies of Penfolds, McWilliams and Seppelts has lent impetus to the New Zealand wine pioneers.

The winemaking region of Henderson is situated on the edge of the city of Auckland and was formed by a few large families of vintners and a larger number of Yugoslav and Dalmatian settlers who have established small wineries for the production of fortified wines.

White wines can be made to a good quality standard from the European varieties *Müller-Thurgau* (*Riesling-Sylvaner* hybrid) and some *Chardonnay* and *Chasselas*. *Palomino* grows well and is used for dry sherries.

Red wines are light and thin. The best styles come from the *Pinotage* (*Pinot-Hermitage* hybrid), *Cabernet Sauvignon*, and one of the better hybrids, *Seibel 5437*, which has good colour but less flavour.

The Mission Vineyard of the Marist Order is the oldest, but its wines do not reach the open market. McWilliams, Glenvale and Vidal are the main producers. The vineyards are near Napier, extending to Hastings through the Taradale-Greenmeadows districts.

Grape varieties similar to those of the Henderson district are used, mainly *Müller-Thurgau* for white wines with some *Cabernet* and *Pinotage* for red. *Seibel 5437* is the best of several varieties of red hybrids used.

The addition of cane sugar to the must is an accepted winemaking principle owing to the short ripening period and low natural sugar content at normal maturity.

The New Zealand wine industry is still small, but it is expanding. The wine consumed by the population of 2 ½ million has trebled in fifteen years to about 2 million gallons. In its early years nearly all its wines were sweet, fortified dessert wines and sherries. However, the recent increases have been largely to table wines, the best of which are light, crisp, dry whites.

TABLE OF WINE QUALITIES
BY REGIONS AND YEARS, TAKING INTO ACCOUNT THE EVOLUTION OF THE WINES
compiled by La Compagnie des Courtiers-Gourmets Piqueurs de Vins de Paris

YEARS	Red Bordeaux	White Bordeaux	Red Burgundy	White Burgundy	Côtes du Rhône	Alsace	Pouilly-s./Loire Sancerre	Anjou Touraine
1924	★	•••	••	••	••			••
1926	•••	•••	••••	•••	•••			•
1928	★	•••	•••	••••	••			••••
1929	••••	••••	★	••••	••••			••
1934	••••	•••	••••	•••	•••			•••
1937	••	★	••••	••••	••••			••••
1943	••	•••	••••	••••	••••			•••
1945	••••	••••	•••	•••	••••	(STOCKS EXHAUSTED)	(STOCKS EXHAUSTED)	
1947	••••	••••	••••	•••	•••			★
1948	•••	•••	••	••	•			•••
1949	••	•••	••••	•••	••••			••
1950	•••	•••	•	•••	•••			••
1952	••	•••	•••	•••	••••			••
1953	••••	•••	•••	•••	••			•••
1955	••••	••••	•••	•••	•••			
1957	••	•••	••••	•••	•••			•••
1958	••	••	•	••	••			••
1959	••••	•••	•••	•••	••			•••
1960	••	••		•	••			••
1961	★	••••	••••	•••	••••	••••	•••	•••
1962	•••	•••	•••	•••	•••	•••	••••	•••
1964	••••	•••	••••	•••	••	••••	•••	••
1965	not classified, some very honest wines							
1966	••••	•••	•••	•••	•••	••••	•••	•••
1967	•••	••	•••	•••	••	••••	••	••
1968	Not exceptional – Some very honest wine							
1969	Very promising in some areas – Young wine had strong bouquet							

• Medium Year   •• Good Year   ••• Very Good Year   •••• Great Year   ★ Exceptional Year

CHAMPAGNE
Vintage: vary according to brands; notable years 1958, 1959, 1961, 1962 and 1964. – Non-vintage: blend of different vintages.

These appreciations are on an average basis, the exception confirming the rule.

THE WINES
OF CHAMPAGNE

JEAN ARNABOLDI

It may be said, without fear of contradiction, that Champagne is one of the most celebrated wines in the world. But if man in his wisdom has raised it to such eminence, he must also admit that its origins have been lost in the mists of time. It is perhaps not an exaggeration to speak of predestination. For when the inland sea which in pre-history covered the Champagne region disappeared, it left in its place a chalky subsoil which was gradually covered by a layer of fertile soil wherein plants might prosper. Recent discoveries made near Sézanne have shown that the vine must have existed there as far back as the tertiary period. Fossilized leaves which were excavated have been judged to be very close to the *vitis rotunda folia*, also known as the *plant américain*. What an extraordinary coincidence this proved to be was seen thousands of years later, when this very same grape was to save the Champagne vineyard from the devastations of phylloxera.

The first real facts about Champagne wine to emerge from history date from the Roman conquest, for when the legions reached the banks of the Marne, they found a flourishing viticulture already in existence. Bringing fresh knowledge and new methods, these legions were to contribute to the development of the vine here as they had previously done in the other provinces of Gaul. The Romans already knew arboriculture as it was then practised in Italy, but they were quick to appreciate the advantages of the methods used by the Gauls. On the other hand, they introduced a new concept, the idea of stock selection. They even imported from Narbonne a quick-growing variety of vine. The reputation of

Champagne wines travelled quickly to Rome, as Pliny himself bears witness: "Other wines from Gaul which have been recommended as fit for the King's table are those from the land of Rheims, known as Ay."

The decree passed by Domitian in A.D. 92 was to prove almost fatal to the future expansion of the vineyards of Gaul and in particular to those around Champagne. The Emperor decreed that all the vines were to be pulled out. Fortunately for posterity, his orders were not everywhere obeyed. It is clear, of course, that occupation troops must live off local produce, and that an army has greater need of cereals and dairy produce than of liquids whose consumption does not always favour military discipline or heroic behaviour. Perhaps other, more worldly commercial reasons crept in too, for the wines of Gaul competed with those of the Mediterranean shores. Be that as it may, the fact remains that for two hundred years the vine had to be cultivated in secret, until that day when another, better-inspired emperor, Probus, raised the ban, and, furthermore, required his troops to help in the reconstruction of the vineyards, a task which the Gauls themselves undertook with much enthusiasm. From Rheims down south to Chalons, the work was quickly done, and memories of Domitian were forgotten.

The advent and spread of Christianity had a marked influence on viticulture, for the monks were obliged to procure locally the wine they used to celebrate Mass. Monasteries also served as inns where travellers sought food, shelter and a welcoming table. The quality of Champagne was noteworthy from this period.

The soil of Champagne has delivered up many proofs of the importance of its vineyard: earthenware jars, coins imprinted with symbols taken from the vine, and even glasses whose elongated shape foreshadows the flute-shaped Champagne glasses of today.

In the fifth and sixth centuries, Champagne became part of the history of France and perhaps even of Heaven, for Clovis was crowned King of France at Rheims by St. Remi, the apostle to the Franks. The chronicles of the time recount the miracles the good saint accomplished: how he caused wine to flow from a barrel of water, and how he gave Clovis, when the latter was warring with Alaric, "a flask filled with holy wine, and recommended him to continue the war for as long as the flask supplied wine for him and others of his train to whom he wished to offer it. The King as well as several of his officers drank the wine, but the jug remained full." From a more practical point of view, the testament of St. Remi is an irrefutable document which portrays faithfully the economic situation and morals of his time. For example, it relates how wine is often offered by the winegrowers as a gift to the king or to the archbishopric of Rheims. Other chronicles speak of the growing expansion of the Champagne vineyard, and enlighten us as to the quality of its wines and how they were used. In those days, Champagne was a still wine *de qualité, pur et fruité* (fine, pure and fruity), excellent for the sick. The decorations and sculptures on monuments, notably those of Rheims Cathedral and Ay Church, have been inspired directly by the wine and depict some part of the life of those who have given their lives to viniculture.

Flodoard, in his history of the church of Rheims, tells us that the wine harvest of 929 was completed by the month of August, which shows that in those days the grapes ripened much earlier. In the eleventh century, Pope Urban II, who had been at one time Canon of Rheims, preached in favour of the Second Crusade at Châtillon-sur-Marne, where a huge statue perpetuates his memory. A kind of redistribution of land took place then, when the Lords leaving for the Holy Land entrusted their property to the Church. During their absence, which sometimes became permanent, the monks reorganized and nationalized viniculture, and it is in fact from this period onwards that their influence on the destiny of the Champagne wines became decisive.

Later invasions and battles only served to increase the fame of these wines. It is said that the Emperor of Germany, Wenceslas, when he met the King of France, Charles VI at Rheims in 1398, indulged in such libations that he was ready to sign "whatsoever was desired".

The consecration of the King of France at Rheims heightened the prestige of the wines of Champagne still further. On February 13th, 1575, for the first time, Champagne was the only wine to be served on the occasion of the coronation of Henry III. Its power of seduction seemed so great that emperors and monarchs, Charles V, François I, Henry VIII and a Pope, Jean de Medicis who later became Leon, all had to own a house in Ay. Henry IV was pleased to think of himself as "Sire of Ay" and valued very highly this *vin de Dieu*, light, fruity, and sacred to boot.

Favoured by kings, Champagne soon captured the Court. Poets sang its praises. Winegrowers multiplied their efforts to satisfy the demand and noticed that for some obscure reason, the wine from time to time would become effervescent. But they were never able to fathom the mystery. Louis XIV was a great lover of the wine of Ay, but even more fervent admirers were the Marechal de Bois-Dauphin, the Marquis Charles de Saint-Evremond and the Count of Olonne, who would drink no other wine with their meals. In 1672, St. Evremond wrote to Count Olonne: "Don't spare yourself any cost to have the wine of Champagne, be you so far as two hundred leagues from Paris. No other province can produce such excellent wines for all seasons as Champagne. It offers us the wines of Ay, Avenet and Auville until the spring; and Tessy, Sillery and Verzenay for the rest of the year. Were you to ask me which of these wines I prefer, without having recourse to tastes in fashion which introduce false delicacies, I would tell you that the good wine of Ay is the most natural of all wines. It is by far the healthiest, and is purged of any objectionable tang of the soil. The peach flavour, which characterizes it, gives one a most exquisite feeling."

This analysis and this delicacy of palate shows that already in those times Champagne had attained a position of eminence. It is said that St. Evremond, having fallen into disgrace with the king in 1661, had to flee to Holland, and later to England where he introduced the Court of Charles II to the delicacies of the table and to fine wine. He easily convinced the court, which soon gave Champagne the place of honour.

At this point in time, one should look more closely into the details of the production of Champagne wines and more particularly into a fundamental change that came about, and which can be said to have ensured their place in history, forever distinctive from other wines. These already famous wines have until this time been still—or almost-still—wines. The black grapes, placed in vats for only a short time or even not vatted at all, produced a grey wine, and were dominated by the red wines, even though it was not possible to conserve the latter for more than a short time and their transportation was somewhat hazardous. In the middle of the seventeenth century (1640 or

Dom Perignon, a Benedictine monk from the Abbey of Hautvillers, had the brilliant idea of blending the produce of different vineyards in the Champagne region so as to obtain a stock whose quality would be superior to any of the individual elements from which it was composed. José Frappa has painted him here, old and blind, tasting grapes with the sensitivity and knowledge that enabled him to distinguish each of the varieties brought in the baskets. There never was a man, said one of his contemporaries, more gifted than he in the secrets of wine-making. Although Dom Perignon died over two centuries ago his name is still honoured and will ever be associated with Champagne.

1660, the date is disputed) the Champagne winegrowers increased their efforts to "produce wines of a finer quality than anywhere else in the kingdom". They succeeded in making pale wines which, in some years, produced in the bottle a certain effervescence which was most agreeable and enhanced their bouquet. This effervescence seemed to occur more often in white wines made from *Pinot* grapes, when the must was fermented separately from the marc, and thus the idea evolved to let this fermentation take place in the bottle. The *vin de Dieu* became *vin Diable* or *saute-bouchon* without,

however, losing any of its original qualities or appeal. On the contrary, it has stood the test of time and change, as history has shown.

Dom Perignon was its man of destiny. It is common knowledge that though the wine's merits are acknowledged, its originator is sometimes disputed. It seems a shame to demolish idols, the more so as every inventor always owes something to his predecessors.

Born in the same year as Louis XIV, Dom Perignon (1638-1715) was also to die in the same year. Brought up in a bourgeois family from St. Menehould, he took

347

his vows in the Benedictine Order and entered the Royal Abbey of Saint-Vanne at Verdun, where he distinguished himself by his great knowledge and devout charity. In 1668 he became cellarer of the Benedictine Abbey at Hautvillers, in the diocese of Rheims. His duties were to supervise the supplies of food and other goods, to check the sources of revenue, the running expenses and generally to keep the accounts. The cellars were therefore also in his care. The village of Hautvillers lies on slopes above the Marne valley, and its situation is therefore particularly favourable for the cultivation of the vine. The domain belonging to the Abbey was quite considerable and several other vineyards were adjacent to it. For these reasons, Dom Perignon concentrated his intelligence on winemaking, in which capacity he was well served by his extraordinary gifts as a wine-taster. His first great idea was to bring together the vines in such a way that by intermarrying they would benefit from each other's better qualities, harmoniously, without any one dominating the others. He had such a delicate palate that by tasting a grape he was able to tell which variety it came from. He decided which grapes to use early in the year, and this procedure came to be acknowledged as essential to the production of sparkling wines. Dom Perignon was also the first in Champagne to seal bottles with cork, which soon replaced the old wooden pegs.

He organized wine production and studied the phenomenon of the rise of foam in the bottle by the rule-of-thumb means at his disposal. No one really knows, however, whether he obtained fermentation in the bottle as a result of the natural sugar content in the wine, that is to say not yet transformed into alcohol, or if he was the first to add a suitable amount of cane sugar.

His body lies at rest in the church at Hautvillers and this epitaph is engraved on his tombstone. "Here lies Dom Perignon, for 47 years cellarer of this Monastery who, after administering the property of our community with a care and dignity that merits praise, blessed with many virtues, the greatest of which was his paternal love for the poor, died in the 77th year of his life, in 1715." His name is remembered to this day.

Henceforth all the humble force of the Benedictine brothers was bent towards the making of Champagne. From this time on, the foam process was "controlled", the wine gained in popularity, and the beginning of the eighteenth century witnessed a great increase in demand. The still wines were neglected for the benefit of the sparkling wines. At the Court, the Marquis of Sillery, well known for his good taste, was an ardent protagonist of the new sparkling wine. The Regent was also convinced of the excellence of Champagne, as were later Louis XV and Louis XVI, though somewhat less flamboyantly. Madame de Pompadour paid it the

highest of feminine compliments by declaring "it is the only wine that makes a woman more beautiful after drinking", and the Comtesse de Parabère was accused of drinking like a *lansquenet* (a German mercenary soldier)! In 1739 the city of Paris gave a brilliant ball at which 1,800 bottles of Champagne wine were drunk.

At about this time wine-merchants set up the first wine-shops in Champagne, some of which still exist today. Their wine cellars were built on the chalky soil which favours the preservation of wine, but there remained two problems which had to be solved: the study of the fermentation process and the breakage of bottles. The latter was solved before the former by an apothecary from Châlons known as François and whose name merits eternal fame. The breakage of bottles affected some 40 per cent of the production, but François learned through his research work to control excessive fermentation by fixing the correct sugar dosage. At the same time, the glass-works made great progress in the quality of their glass. Between the two, the distressing problem of breakage was very considerably decreased. In 1858, Maumené, a professor at Rheims, seems to have been the first to study the action of the yeasts which influence fermentation, but it was not until Pasteur's work in this field became known that Champagne was produced scientifically.

Since then, the history of Champagne has been one of victory and success, if still sometimes acquired the hard way, through a disease of the wine or folly of man. The new techniques and the progress achieved, allied to the tenacity, the skill and the knowledge of the wine-growers and wine-merchants of the Champagne area, found their just recompense in a constant expansion of demand throughout the world.

THE CHAMPAGNE VINEYARD

The Champagne country, whose origins are founded on the same chalky subsoil as the Ele de France, a region which carries through to the Ardennes, forms the eastern part of the Parisian basin. Its landscapes have the same peacefulness, the same harmony born of gently undulating plains, dipping sometimes towards shallow valleys. The slopes dominate by a few hundred feet the rivers whose waters flow peacefully on, and their average altitude is never more than 600 feet.

Its geological make-up and its geographical position have always given the Champagne a singular identity. At the time of the *Ancien Régime*, the region covered 6,177,500 acres, or almost one-twentieth of the whole of France. Under the Revolution, it was divided into four separate *départements*—Aube, Marne, Haute-Marne, Ardennes—while the remainder of its land was given to Yonne and Aisne.

Its subsoil consists of a chalky sediment from which, in thicker or thinner layers, calcareous, clay and flint sands detach themselves.

The viticultural zone was clearly defined by the law of July 22nd, 1927, which marked it out in accordance with its natural boundaries: only those vineyards which came within its confines have the right to the appellation CHAMPAGNE.

The viticultural area is not all in one block. It covers 86,485 acres, which were planted to the wine in their entirety by the last century. The invasion of phylloxera, however, destroyed a great number of the vines; at the present time, 44,500 acres are fully productive. They are divided up in the following manner: 38,500 acres in Marne, 4,000 in Aube and 2,000 in Aisne. This whole represents slightly more than one-hundredth of the entire area given over to viticulture in France.

There are four distinct zones within the Champagne vineyard: the Montagne de Rheims, the Vallée de la Marne, the Côte des Blancs and the vineyards of Aube. The first three are situated in the districts of Rheims and Epernay, and constitute the most important vineyards, the very heart of the Champagne region. It is they that produce the most illustrious growths. The vines, planted in rows along the sides of the slopes, form a ribbon about 75 miles long, but whose width varies from only about 300 yards in some parts to little more than a mile.

Apart from still wines which have their own very specific *appellation d'origine*, Champagne wines do not mention their vineyard of origin in the general classification, for Champagne is, by its very nature, a combination of musts from several varieties of grapes. The particular growth referred to here is therefore called a *cru de raisin*.

THE MONTAGNE DE REIMS. The Montagne de Reims forms the southern side of the Vesle valley, whilst its eastern tip joins up with the Marne valley, which it dominates at Epernay. The Great Growths of the main Champagne vineyard were classified according to very old usage. Verzenay, Mailly, Sillery and Beaumont-sur-Visle are the Great Growths of Montagne de Reims, which is situated to the north at the very edge of Rheims forest. Ludes, Chigny-les-Roses, Rilly-la-Montagne, Villers-Marmery, Verzy, Villers-Allerand and Trépail are some of the best growths.

To the south of the town, Petite Montagne also has some good growths worth mentioning, such as Ville-Dommange, Ecueil, Sacy, Pargny-sur-Saulx, Jouy-lès-Reims.

THE MARNE VALLEY. The slopes of the Marne valley stretch the length of the river between Tours-sur-Marne and Dormans, extending towards Château-Thierry and beyond to Aisne. Its leading vineyard is Ay, framed by Mareuil-sur-Ay and Dizy, followed in a less elevated rank in the classification of vineyards by Cumières and Hautvillers, the region in which Dom Perignon earned his fame.

On the right bank of the river, the vineyards of Damery, Venteuil, Châtillon-sur-Marne, Vandières, Verneuil and Vincelles deserve mention. For quite a different reason, however, the name of the little hamlet of Tréloup is linked with the history of the Champagne area, for it was here that the first sign of phylloxera was seen in 1890. On the left bank, the valley of Cubry, which ends at Epernay, offers a number of interesting varieties made from the *Pinot Fin* grape, in the vineyards of Epernay and Pierry. Other localities such as Moussy, Vinay and Saint-Martin-d'Ablois grow the *Pinot Meunier* grape, which produces wines noted for their fruitiness. Other well-known vineyards are those in the regions of Mardeuil, Boursault, Leuvrigny, Festigny, Troissy and Dormans.

THE CÔTE DES BLANCS AND OTHER VINEYARDS. The Côte des Blancs is situated directly to the south of the Marne. Its great names ring melodiously in the minds of all connoisseurs of Champagne: Cramant, Avize, Oger and Le-Mesnil-sur-Oger. Chouilly, at the junction of two zones, also recalls happy memories, and its vineyards produce very fine quality white grapes, of which the *Chardonnay* is king.

The Côte des Blancs stretches south to the outskirts of Petit Morin, where it gains an extra slope of black and white grapes, considered to be some of its best. The Petit Morin valley is flanked by several vineyards growing the *Meunier* grape, which produces very fruity wines.

These zones, here rapidly reviewed, make up practically the whole of the Champagne area. There is, however, one other zone of a transitional nature whose geological characteristics are no longer quite as well-defined, but which nevertheless produces wine still entitled to be known by the same appellation. From amongst its vineyards, one can mention these of Côte de Château-Thierry, the Sézanne region and those in the vicinity of Vitry-le-François.

Between the region of Sézanne and the Aube vineyard there is quite a large gap, as it is not until Bar-sur-Aube and Bar-sur-Seine that one finds slopes which form a part of the same viticultural zone.

THE SOIL. The soil, as already indicated, has a chalky subsoil—an essential element. The great vineyards are usually planted halfway up the slopes on a fine layer of loose earth left over from slopes of the tertiary period, rich in chalk of the Senonian stratum, a single block of which can be more than 600 feet thick.

The chalky subsoil assures perfect drainage, stabilizes the infiltration of water and so maintains the ideal amount of humidity. Moreover, this geological composition offers another great advantage; it retains the heat from the sun and emits it again in a regular and constant manner. Finally, the light, which plays a very important role in the ripening of the grapes, is stronger here than the climate would lead one to believe, owing to the reflected whiteness of the chalky soil.

THE CLIMATE. The climate of the Champagne area is practically identical to that of the Parisian basin. Usually it is moderate, and the winters are seldom severe. In spring the weather is uncertain but mild, the summers are hot and the autumns are often good, all of which is of great importance to vine culture. The winds blowing from the sea soften the continental climate characteristics, which at their harshest are often too harsh for the vine, and the average annual temperature is about 50° F.

The wine, moreover, benefits from the surrounding forests and groves, which not only shield it from harsh weather but also provide a most desirable humidity. The altitude at which the vineyard is planted, from about 500 to 600 feet, also serves to protect it to a certain extent from spring frosts and cold early morning mists, which are naturally much worse in the valleys below. The vintner has learned to protect himself from these natural enemies of viticulture, and the modern methods at his disposal have enabled him practically to eliminate their often disastrous effects. This, of course, is equally applicable to hail.

GRAPE VARIETIES. Very strict legal provisions define which grapes may be used to produce Champagne. The varieties permitted are the *Pinot Noir* and the *Pinot Meunier*, both black grapes, and the *Chardonnay*, a white grape. Apart from these, the law permits the use of a few local stocks such as the *Petit Meslier* and the *Arbanne*; these, however, are slowly becoming extinct. It should be noted that following the invasion of phylloxera, the indigenous long-rooted plants were naturally replaced by grafted stock.

This law has but sanctioned centuries-old methods of vinification which winegrowers had practised, by confirming the perfect harmony of these plants with the soil and the climate. The influence of these grapes on the quality of the wine is, needless to say, considerable. Each brings its own quality, and the dosage, the inter-marriage, the perfect harmonizing of all these qualities give to Champagne its essential character. Its delicate quality, its bouquet and its mellow warmth are derived from the various grapes, and the different proportions in which they are used decided by the dictates of sensitive palates. This forms a highly complicated and delicate process which will be examined in more detail, although it can be said here that no explanation can take the place of human experience.

The *Pinot Noir* grape (with its varieties) predominates in Champagne (it is also used, more than any others, to produce the great red wines of Burgundy). It makes a wine with a full bouquet, generous, powerful and robust. It produces a white wine by a process which we will study later.

The *Pinot Meunier* is a variety of the *Pinot Noir* grape. More hardy, it plays an important role in second quality Champagnes. The *Chardonnay*, which is a white grape, is found mainly on the Côte des Blancs. When blended with other grapes, it gives forth its essential finesse and elegance.

All these grapes have certain common characteristics: they are precocious, vigorous, quick to mature, produce very sweet musts rich in sugar and have unrivalled finesse and bouquet.

After the phylloxera invasion, all the stocks were grafted to the *American Plant*. It is well known that it is the graft which imparts its character to the stock, from which it derives new strength to enable it to resist any future attacks of the pest.

A vine lives for about thirty years, and only begins to produce fruit four years after it has been planted. The density in the Champagne vineyards reaches a closely-packed and regular thickness of 3,000 to 4,000 plants per acre, the yield (usually about 6,500 pounds per acre) is kept down in order to maintain the quality. This legal requirement is administered by a body called the Institut National des Appellations d'Origine (I.N.A.O.), which sees to it that the law is strictly carried out.

The pruning of the vine is also rigidly regulated by law: all the vines of Champagne must be pruned short, according to the accepted methods of the systems of "Royat", "Chablis", "Guyot" or "Vallée de la Marne".

A WINE-HARVEST TO CONQUER THE WORLD

After a long year of labour, care, anxiety, and hope, harvest-time arrives at last. This penultimate act of the great annual spectacle is performed with extraordinary care and concern, especially in the Champagne region. One might even venture to say that nowhere else in the world are the grapes picked with so much attention paid to each and every detail.

The fruit will have blossomed some hundred days before the date of picking is officially proclaimed by Prefectorial order. Laboratories have carried out tests to establish the exact sugar and acid content of the grapes now attaining their full maturity in the gentle rays of a mid-September sun. Work begins, and it is clear that local labour is not sufficient. The winegrowers get help from all the regions of France, especially miners from the North and from Lorraine. From one

The sumptuous "Oyster Dinner" painted by Jean-François de Troy (1679-1752) also renders homage to champagne. Some of the guests watch the cork blown high in the air, while others appreciatively sip the sparkling wine.

year to the next the growers try to find the "flying squads" of temporary workers who are already familiar with the delicate work of fruit picking and well versed in the habits of the Champagne winegrowers. Split up into small groups called *hordes* or *hordons*, they work methodically and conscientiously, their bright clothes forming multi-coloured patches which bob and weave among the tightly packed green vines. The wine-harvesters receive free board and lodging. Their wages are fixed by the joint committee of the C.I.V.C. according to their age and qualifications. This is to distinguish the pickers (aged from 12, 13, 14 years and up), the carriers of small baskets, the unloaders of big baskets, the general labourers, the group leaders—all these people making up the "foreign" workers.

Then come the press-men, who are also classified by jobs: hand press, hydraulic press, hand dryer, hydraulic dryer and so on. Every army, even a peaceful one, requires a rear-echelon staff, and the kitchen staff must be added too. The grape pickers, men, women and children, pick the clusters from the root of vines with great care, using shears, make a preliminary sorting of the grapes (if necessary); and they place the grape-bunches in small baskets, each of which holds about eleven pounds.

Then it is the turn of the carriers. They collect the baskets and pour their contents on to large wicker-work hurdles under the watchful eye of the "sorters", who are responsible for a final careful sorting. It is necessary to take out the green grapes or those not sufficiently ripe, as otherwise they would reduce the alcohol content of the wine, as well as the bad and overripe grapes which would spoil the quality of the wine. This work is very burdensome, and some argue as to its necessity. The Champagne winegrowers certainly believe in it.

Those grapes considered good enough for vinification are *placed*—not poured—in large wicker-work baskets, quaintly named *mannequins*, or in similar receptacles, often made of plastic, which can hold some 110 to 180 pounds, and which are then placed with great care by the carriers in vehicles with springs—a peculiarity of this region for a long time—which are driven very carefully to the press-house, with care to avoid bumps that might damage the grapes.

The vine-presses are in *vendangeoirs* which belong either to wine-merchants, local co-operatives, vineyard-owners or to wine-brokers. Except in the case of the *récoltant-manipulant*, the work of the vineyard is now completed. This is a special characteristic of viticultural Champagne. The grapes are weighed and then paid for, according to the price fixed each year by the C.I.V.C., after bargaining between winegrowers and wine-merchants. The sale is completed when the buyer has the grapes poured into the wine-press.

PRESSING THE GRAPES. The grapes are pressed as soon as possible. Champagne vintners use special presses, low and squat, so the must can flow out quickly without dissolving the colouring matter from the stalks, and without any risk of the flavour being spoiled by the wood. Some 9,000 pounds of grapes are placed on the floor of the press. The CHAMPAGNE appellation is given only to those wines whose must has been obtained by pressing not more than a hectolitre of juice per 150 kilos of grapes or about 20 gallons from 300 pounds. For this reason, the limit is fixed at 2,666 litres of must per marc which makes 13 barrels of 45 gallons each.

Then the first pressing takes place, or better, the first *serre* (squeeze). Usually electrically-controlled, the *plancher* (ceiling) held by a *mouton* (stock) is lowered on to the grapes, with a pressure attaining as much as 40 tons per square metre.

The must filters through the mass of grapes being pressed and flows through a spout with a filter into a 220-gallon vat called a *bélon*. The operation is repeated. The grapes must be pressed in one and a half hours, or two hours at the most.

The first ten barrels or 450 gallons are the cuvée from which the great Champagnes will be made. The next three pressings are known as *tailles* (cuts), so-called because it is necessary to cut up the compressed marc with a spade before it is squeezed again. One thus has a first and second pressing of poorer quality.

The must remains for only a short time in the graduated vats, of oak or cement, in which it was first collected. It is very quickly transferred to other types of vats known as *débourbage* (settling) vats where it stays for 10 to 12 hours, time enough for it to settle out all the foreign bodies it still contains: stones, skin and any other impurities.

When the wine has fully settled, the must is drawn off in barrels which hold 45 gallons each and is labelled according to origin. This operation is often carried out with mobile vats. Whatever the method, the wine is then transferred to the cellars where the delicate process of vinification commences.

VINIFICATION. Champagne is the product of two successive fermentations, whose essential elements are yeasts. These micro-organisms appear on the skin of the grape just before it ripens, and they are what changes the must into wine.

THE FIRST FERMENTATION. The first fermentation is also known by the evocative name of *bouillage* (boiling). It takes place either in oaken barrels, or in vats made of glazed cement, enamelled steel or stainless steel. The ambient temperature is maintained at 20° or 22°C., and the must seethes. For several days, fermentation is tumultuous, then its violence slackens and calm follows. Three weeks pass before the first clarifying racking takes place. The wine is next left cold in order to let its deposits settle and the liquid become limpid clear. Then it is drawn off for the second time.

Formerly, Christmas would find the cellar doors wide open to the chill air. Alas, the poetry has gone, giving way to sheer efficiency, and today, in many cellars, modern air-conditioning plants turn this part of the vinification process into an example of precision which is at the same time a guarantee of quality and consistency. For it is now that preparations for making Champagne differ from those for other wines.

LA CUVÉE. This operation is also known as *cuvée de tirage* (draught cuvée), and both its preparation and its carrying out require a careful combination of talent and technical know-how.

At the first racking or drawing-off, usually wines from the same growth are assembled in order to produce a homogeneous vatful which can then be used for later blending operations.

Right from the beginning of the year, specialists from each house taste the harvested wines, for they will be obliged to produce a wine, whatever the variations of that particular harvest may have been, which carries on the qualities and is faithful to the character that has made it known. It is therefore only after the second racking that the different growths are blended.

The vintner is now faced with two possibilities. If he wishes to produce a *millésime* (a wine showing the year of manufacture) it is clear that only wines of the same year may be blended. If he does not wish to produce a *millésime*, the shortcomings in the vintage of a particular year may be compensated for by adding wines from previous years which have been specially kept for this purpose. Needless to say, a successful blending requires several trials before the formula is applied to whole casks. The essential characteristics one must bear in mind in order to achieve an ideal result are: vinosity (flavour and strength), bouquet, aroma, elegance, delicacy, spirit and conservation ability. The latter characteristic will have been confirmed by a complex analysis.

The different wines are mixed in huge casks or in vats equipped with mixers which permit a perfect blending. Traditionally, Champagne is made from a blend of both black and white grapes. There are some varieties, however, made from white grapes alone: these are known as *Blanc de Blancs*. There is also a rosé Champagne, usually made by adding to the original mixture red wine from the Champagne vineyards, although sometimes the rosé Champagne is prepared as a rosé from the time it first goes to the press.

By the beginning of March, the exact composition of the *cuvée* must be ready, so that the producer can proceed with clarifying by filtering or by thinning down.

RACKING. At this stage, the wine in the vat is a still wine, but with the coming of spring, when it is racked, its whole destiny will change. To get the wine into the condition to become frothy, it is now transferred into special clearing vats, at the same time adding natural ferments and a liqueur. This liqueur is in fact a solution of pure cane sugar dissolved in wine. The wine is then stirred so that all the ingredients are well blended.

If one is trying to produce a *crémant* type of Champagne, one adds a smaller quantity of the sweet solution to the wine. The next step is to draw off the wine into bottles, where the mysterious transformation will take place. What seems to happen is that the sugar solution changes into alcohol and carbonic acid gas, which provokes the effervescence. Imprisoned within the bottle, which is now firmly corked and wired, the carbonic acid gas remains dissolved in the liquid and only starts to bubble when the bottle is uncorked.

THE SECOND FERMENTATION. This is the slow continuation of the process just outlined above. Taken immediately into cellars dug out of the chalk subsoil, the bottles are laid carefully on special wooden battens. They are constantly under close surveillance, as there is still a risk of bottle-breakage, despite the great improvements made in glass manufacture: the pressure of the gas can sometimes rise to 5 or 6 atmospheres. The corks also might be faulty and let some wine leak.

When the second fermentation is completed, the wine is clear, with all the deposits at the neck of the bottle, and its alcohol content is 12°. It is now necessary to remove the deposit and extract the sediment-coated cork.

REMUAGE, OR SETTLING THE DEPOSIT. The bottles are stacked *sur pointe* (with the cork pointing downwards) in wooden frames designed in such a way that the bottle can be inclined in different positions whilst the deposit is working its way down on to the cork. Every day, skilled cellarists give the bottle a sharp turn whilst also shaking it. At the same time, they rotate it one-eighth of a turn to the right or to the left, according to a guide mark painted at the bottom of the bottle, while the frames are tilted a little more downward. This process needs not only a dexterous hand but a rapid one; a good worker can *passer* 30,000 bottles a day.

Finally, the deposit will have all collected at the neck of the bottle, which reaches a vertical position in from six weeks to three months. By then, all the bottles are in the same position.

DEGORGEMENT, OR REMOVAL OF THE CORK. It is now necessary to remove the deposit whilst at the same time allowing the minimum amount of gas and wine to escape. Disgorging, which is entrusted only to experts, is a manoeuvre which used to depend on great speed to avoid spillage. Today, this delicate operation is more and more frequently being carried out by freezing the

RESERVE CUVÉE

CHAMPAGNE

Perrier-Jouët & C°

Epernay (France)

Finest EXTRA *Quality*
BRUT

N. M. 3.624.332   CONTENTS 26 FLUID OZ.   PRODUCE OF FRANCE

1

2

3

BRUT

FOURNISSEUR DE LA COUR DE
SA MAJESTÉ LE ROI DE SUÈDE

Champagne

MERCIER

MAISON FONDÉE EN 1858

Epernay
FRANCE

N. M. 3.339302.   PRODUCE OF FRANCE   PRINTED IN FRANCE

2

1

3

G. H. MUMM & C°.

Sté VINICOLE DE CHAMPAGNE SUCCrs

REIMS.

FRANCE

G.H.MUMM & C°
· REIMS ·

DOUBLE CORDON.

CHAMPAGNE SEC
PRODUCE OF FRANCE

·D·R· 30.0.08   N. M. 3.921.422

1

2

3

PERRIER-JOUET

1. Trade name "Champagne Perrier-Jouet". – 2. Type of Champagne: *Extra Brut.* This indicates that no liqueur was added to this wine, which is therefore a very dry Champagne. Bottles marked "Finest Quality" and "Reserve cuvée" mean that the *négociant-manipulant* attributes particular importance to this type of Champagne. In other words, the quality of this Champagne may be judged by the reputation of its *négociant-manipulant* or by one's own experience. – 3. In the reference N.M. 3.624.332, the letters N.M. indicate that this is a vintage of first importance produced by a *négociant-manipulant*. The letters M.A. would signify a wine of secondary quality. The number that follows is the index number of the vintage on the register of the *Comité Interprofessionnel du Vin de Champagne* (C.I.V.C.).

MERCIER

1. Trade name: "Champagne Mercier". – 2. Type of Champagne: *Brut.* This indicates that only a small amount (about 1.5 per cent) of liqueur was added to the wine, or possibly none at all. – 3. The initials N.M. indicate that this is a primary vintage wine produced by a *négociant-manipulant*.

MUMM DOUBLE CORDON

1. Trade name: "Double Cordon de G. H. Mumm", commonly known as "Mumm Double Cordon". – 2. Type of Champagne: *Sec.* This indicates that between 2.5 per cent and 5 per cent of liqueur was added to the wine. This Champagne is therefore not as dry as the *Brut* and *Extra-Brut* Champagnes. – 3. The initials N.M. indicate that this is a primary vintage wine produced by a *négociant-manipulant*.

TAITTINGER

1. Trade name: "Champagne Taittinger". – 2. Type of Champagne: *Demi-sec.* This is a wine to which between 5 per cent and 8 per cent of liqueur has been added. It is therefore a slightly sweet wine. – 3. Here the initials N.M. again indicate a primary vintage wine produced by a *négociant-manipulant.*

1 **TAITTINGER**

ANCIENNE MAISON FOURNEAUX, FOREST ET SUCC ᴿˢ

Fondée en 1734

REIMS

2 CHAMPAGNE   DEMI-SEC

3   IOR.30.0108   N. M. 3.924.392   PRODUCE OF FRANCE

CLICQUOT-PONSARDIN

1. Trade name: "Champagne Veuve Clicquot Ponsardin". – 2. Type of Champagne: *Brut* 1962. This is a *Brut* vintage Champagne. Only the very best years are indicated on Champagne labels. – 3. This is also a primary vintage Champagne produced by a *négociant-manipulant.*

DOM PÉRIGNON

1. Trade name: "Dom Pérignon". This is one of the rare occasions where the name of the wine itself has replaced the name of the *négociant-manipulant.* Dom Pérignon is always a vintage *(millésimé)* Champagne, but conversely not every harvest produces a Dom Pérignon. It is always made from the juice of the first pressings of selected grapes, using white grapes only; it is therefore a *Blanc de Blancs.* – 2. Name of the *négociant-manipulant.* – 3. Primary vintage wine of a *négociant-manipulant.*

neck of the bottle. The necks of the bottles are inserted in a brine freezing solution at a temperature of minus 20°; very rapidly, ice forms near the cork, trapping the impurities. When the cork is removed, the ice is immediately blown out, along with a small quantity of froth and wine. The bottle is then examined, and a dosage, liqueur consisting of pure cane sugar dissolved in old and high-class Champagne, is added to make up the lost wine. The strength of the liqueur depends on the type of Champagne desired: *brut, sec* (dry), *demi-sec* (semi-dry) or *doux* (sweet). *Extra-brut* means that the Champagne has no sugar content at all.

CORKING. After such a lengthy and delicate operation, it is understandable that corking is very important. The bottles must be hermetically sealed so only the finest quality cork is chosen for this purpose. The cork is 1 ¾ to 2 ¼ inches long and 1 ¼ to 1 ½ inches wide, and must, by law, have certain information printed on it. Once the cork is in place, a metal capsule is put over it and the whole is encircled by a wire-mesh, so that the pressure of gas in the bottle does not blow the cork out again. The bottles are then put back in the cool cellars to age, some for as long as six or seven years, before they set out to conquer the world.

RANGE OF CHAMPAGNE WINES

Champagne, as has been seen, is obtained by blending wines from three different grapes: the *Pinot Noir* and the *Pinot Meunier*, both black grapes, and the *Chardonnay*, a white grape. Many people are surprised to learn that this wine, so pure and clear, is made to a large extent from black grapes.

As in other vineyards, grapes from the same stocks do not necessarily have the same flavour or qualities, since these are influenced by the soil and place where they are grown. A connoisseur can easily tell the difference between the varieties. But with Champagne it is more difficult to distinguish the range of wines and their varieties because of the grape marriages which initiated the fame of Champagne and contributed so much to its glory. The different firms possess their own particular characteristics, and long experience is needed to distinguish between them.

The soil and a favourable location are so important and make for such a difference in the final variety of the grapes that certain coefficients have been granted to the producing regions, by commune and according to the quality of their produce. It is true that these basic coefficients are liable to change every year, depending on the results of the wine-harvests.

The coefficients range from 77 per cent to 100 per cent; those of 100 per cent are traditionally known as "*grands crus*", while those of 90 to 99 per cent are

entitled "*premiers crus*". These titles are rarely carried on the label, because the guarantee of quality is, in most cases, given by the great names of the firms who absorb 80 per cent of the production. The opposite is true for most other wines, which normally are only too pleased to be able to announce "grand cru".

Before examining the various types of Champagne, it is useful to recall the legal protection of the *appellation d'origine contrôlée*, which benefits producers and consumers alike.

Only the following is recognized as Champagne:

1. wine produced from vines planted from authorized stocks, within the limits of the viticultural Champagne region, pruned to the required height, of a limited yield per acre;

2. wine of an assured quality guaranteed by a limited yield in must and by a minimum alcohol content;

3. wine prepared in accordance with the natural procedure known as *méthode champenoise*, in premises within the Champagne region where only wines from this region may be stored;

4. wine stored in bottles prior to shipping for at least one year (but for three years after the harvesting, in the case of wines with a *millésime*).

These principles, which have been progressively sanctioned by French law, are applied and controlled, to avoid any fraud, by the C.I.V.C. in the name of the public authority, vinegrowers and wine-merchants.

After the final stage, the dosing of the wine, the various types of Champagne can be classified as follows:

Brut without mention of year. This is a wine that is usually light and lively, very suitable as an aperitif as it prepares both the mind and the palate.

Brut millésimé. This is a very good wine which comes from a good vintage year, since only wines of the same year may be blended together in order to produce a first-grade bottle. In some years it might even be a collector's bottle. This type of wine is often more full-bodied and more generous; it deserves to be savoured with particular care. To mention a few of the old vintage wines very difficult to find nowadays: 1928, 1933, 1934, 1937, 1943, 1945, 1949 and 1953. Their merits vary, but one should be wary of those which have been aged too long. Here again, one might ask: should Champagne be drunk young or old? Several things must be considered. First, although the carbonic acid gas in the Champagne gives it a certain resistance to bacteria and assures its conservation, it does not mean that the wine is impervious to everything and can remain in optimum condition forever. It is as much alive as any other wine and must receive the same attention and care. It ages and may change. After ten years or so, it may take on a slight colour and begin to maderize; this will continue with the years. It is then said to have become a *renarde* (a vixen). It remains drinkable, of course, but its essential qualities fade, just as a beautiful flower fades. Moreover, the pressure of the gas decreases and little by little the wine loses its life. There is no point, therefore—except as an experiment and perhaps in the case of a particularly good vintage year—in keeping Champagne for a long time. It is put on the market at the time in its life when it is suitable for comsumption; this is one of the rules which control the quality of Champagne.

Dry and semi-dry Champagne. The present trend is towards the *brut* or extra dry variety, and the sweeter type of Champagne, possessing perhaps a little less character, is certainly much less in demand today. These are wines which are very pleasant with desserts; they must, however, be served at a cooler temperature than the others.

Rosé. This remains an amusing exception, but does not lack attraction nor admirers. A very fruity wine with an excellent colour, it is coming more and more into favour and the big firms have no hesitation in offering it. Its bouquet varies according to the way it has been made. Some are produced by adding a small amount of red wine from Champagne; others—and this is preferable—are produced as a rosé from the start. It cannot compete with great classical Champagnes.

It should be added that the shippers also prepare wines for specific foreign markets, to meet specific preferences of their clients. The fruitiness and sweetness of these vary according to their destination.

There remain two other effervescent wines of Champagne which should be mentioned, both of which are very pleasant to drink:

The *crémant*, whose gas content is lower than that of Champagne. This is done by reducing the amount of liqueur added to the wine before the second fermentation. These lithe, light, fruity wines go down very well, but they can never match their superiors. They have, nevertheless, their own place in the Champagne family.

The *Blanc de Blancs* is made solely from white grapes, using the *Chardonnay* variety. It is a very elegant, light wine, with a particularly fine bouquet.

Finally, the Champagne region also produces non-effervescent, so-called "still wines".

THE STILL WINES OF CHAMPAGNE

The still white wines of Champagne are an excellent introduction to a better knowledge of Champagne. There is a *Blanc de Blancs* which has not been *champagnisé* (given a Champagne sparkle), and also a *Blanc de Noirs*, this latter a much more full-bodied wine. The big firms market it. It offers the dominant characteristics of the Champagne vineyards, with its own particular spirit, colour and charm. The still red wines are simple and excellent, but somewhat fragile. Their flavour and strength remind one of the wines of Burgundy, whilst their tannin content recalls those of Bordeaux. The best known among them is the incomparable Bouzy, but Cumières, Ambonnay, Verzenay, Sillery, Mailly, Saint-Thierry also have excellent wines. The appearance of a red wine from Champagne on the table is always greeted with surprise and interest. These amazing red wines have a very special fruity flavour, while their mischievousness is more apparent than real. They are great wines produced with care and should not be drunk at room temperature; they are at their best when cooled. In great vintage years, they are very full-bodied and may be kept for a long time. There is a limit, however: wine of the year 1959, for example, is of a very different order, far removed from the lightheartedness of other years. These red wines at a certain age would seem to become almost too robust and to lose much of their original appeal.

Bouzy is marketed independently of the large Champagne producers by the individual growers since it is not a wine requiring the skilled blending of the sparkling Champagnes.

THE MARKETING OF CHAMPAGNE

The grape has ripened, the Champagne is born. Now it must be marketed—and it has long been known that the people of Champagne are as prudent as they are smart. The whole structure of commercialization and marketing in the Champagne area is as special as the wines. The marketing structure includes:

– *Négociants-manipulants* who themselves vinify the wines from their own vines, or from the must which they buy from individual vinegrowers. They blend and marry, bottle and market the wine themselves.

– *Négociants non manipulants:* companies or individuals marketing Champagne but not making it.

– *Récoltants-manipulants:* vintners who produce and then market their own wine.

– *Co-opératives de manipulation* who press, vinify and blend wines brought to them by member growers. The co-operatives also market the wine themselves.

In the English-speaking countries these terms are rarely met since almost all Champagne is exported by the *grande marque* houses such as Moët et Chandon, Heidsick, G.H. Mumm and Veuve Clicquot, who belong to the first category, the *négociants-manipulants*.

Certain indications must figure on Champagne labels in order to protect the consumer against possible fraud:

N.M. for a first-quality Champagne belonging to a *négociant-manipulant*.

M.A. (B.O.B.—buyer's own brand—in English) for a lesser Champagne belonging to a *négociant-manipulant* or a *négociant non manipulant* and which he can market under his own chosen name, changing his supplier but not his label should he so wish.

C.M. for a brand from a *récoltant-manipulant*.

R.M. for a brand from a *co-operative-manipulante*.

Another requirement for Champagne labels is for the number accorded to the product by the C.I.V.C. to be indicated after the category initials.

An extraordinary network of cellars dug out of the limestone rock twists and turns its way through the subsoil of Champagne. Some of these chalk cellars can be traced back to Gallo-Roman times, but their continued development required—and still requires—continual maintenance. Today, there are about 125 miles of underground tunnels, sheltering millions of bottles, at a constant temperature of 10º to 11º. Some cellars are up to 45 yards deep, and many of the large Champagne firms feel it a duty, as well as a pleasure, to show people around them. Without these cellars, their wine could not be what it is. In 1970, a total of 102,224,090 bottles left the cellars of Champagne, an increase of 8.77 per cent over the sales for 1966.

This increase, moreover, reflects a steady growth. Only one year, 1958, had sales figures showing a sharp decline, as seen in the statistics kept since 1955. In fifteen years, from 1955 to 1970, the number of bottles to leave the cellars rose from 37,706,826 to more than 102 million per annum. During the same period, the increase in sales was higher for *récoltants-manipulants* than for merchants. The latter nevertheless hold their own and sold 75,509,933 bottles in 1970 as against the 26,714,157 bottles sold in the same year by the *récoltants-manipulants*.

The increase in the sales by the growers can be explained by the fact that they can step up production as much as they wish, while the wine-merchants must set a limit to their trade ambitions. Being directly responsible for their own production, the growers can increase direct sales to clients. The wine-merchants, on the other hand, must rely on purchases from vine-yards and on the state of the grape market, the latter being directly influenced by the vintage. The wine-merchant must constantly bear in mind that the vines he owns directly meet only one-fifth of his needs; he thus has to buy the remaining four-fifths. The amount of capital he must invest may be judged by the fact that in 1971 a kilogramme (about 2 lb.) of grapes was selling for around 5.41 French francs.

Sales abroad are increasing, which is attracting great interest. Nevertheless, the domestic French market remains far and away the most important: 71,169,802 bottles sold there as against 31,054,288 for export. In 1967, the twelve main markets, in decreasing order of importance, were: Great Britain, Italy, United States, Belgium, Germany, Switzerland, Venezuela, Canada, Holland, Sweden, Denmark, Germany-NATO.

WHAT ONE SHOULD KNOW IN ORDER TO BUY WELL. When buying Champagne, first of all, look carefully at the label on the bottle that is the object of your heart's desire, unless it is a particularly well-known name in which you know you can have full confidence. There is practically no fraud in Champagne, but that is not to say that all Champagnes are equally good.

The word "Champagne", as well perhaps as the *millésime* or year of production, should be written either on the main label or on the neck of the bottle, in clearly legible letters. This information is also printed on the side of the cork, which is of course inside the bottle's neck. Note next the signs just describe in detail, bearing in mind the different categories of merchants in the Champagne trade, the C.I.V.C. index number and the initials indicating the category.

Most people know a good wine-merchant whom they feel they can trust. But never allow him to sell a bottle which has been on display, for it has naturally suffered from this. The bottle must be brought up from the cellar, or at least from a bottle-rack in which it was lying flat, for the cork must always be moistened.

There is no point in building up large stocks of Champagne, and in any case, everything depends of course on how much one consumes. One should set up a Champagne cellar with various types of bottles, going from the ordinary to the best vintage Champagne, and including full-bodied vintage Champagne.

The following selection is given as an example:

Fresh wines: Laurent-Perrier, Lanson, Piper Heidsieck, Mercier, Canard Duchêne, Jeanmaire, etc.

Better-balanced wines with more character: Mumm, Perrier-Jouet, Pommery, Ruinart, Taittinger, etc.

Older and stronger wines: Bollinger, Krug, Pal Roger, Veuve Clicquot, Roederer, etc.

It must be stressed that this list is given purely as an indication, not as a recommendation for buying.

THE PRESTIGE WINES. In recent years, a number of the large firms have tended to establish *cuvées spéciales*, or very special selections of Champagnes. This has been done in a move to meet the requirements for an even higher quality, which would satisfy the taste of the most demanding of connoisseurs, and also from a desire to establish still more solidly the renown of their names. These wines are usually presented with a luxurious refinement, albeit inspired by the simple and seductive shapes of old flasks which thus find a new youth. These are growths of great character. Some of the most famous are: Dom Perignon, by Moët et Chandon, which started this trend; the Cuvée Grand Siècle by Laurent-Perrier; the Comtes de Champagne by Taittinger; the Florens Louis by Piper-Heidsieck; the Cuvée Charles VII by Canard Duchêne; the Cuvée Elysée by Jeanmaire; the Cuvée de l'Empereur by Mercier, and the Roederer sold in crystal bottles. Bollinger presented a 1961 vintage Champagne, which was not uncorked until 1971, as the top-quality product of their firm.

Still on the subject of bottles, one can use the opportunity to detail their great variety. Their names are: split (half-pint), pint (1/10 gallon), quart (1/5 gallon), magnum (2 quarts), jeroboam (4 quarts), rehoboam (6 quarts), methuselah (8 quarts), salmanasar (12 quarts), balthazar (16 quarts) and nebuchadnezzar (20 quarts).

It should be said at once that the bottles with resounding biblical names, from magnum on, are only show pieces, derived from folklore. On the other hand, for some inexplicable reason, Champagne in magnums is always first-rate. This also applies to any other first quality wine.

As a general rule, it is a good idea to furnish one's cellar with bottles of various sizes, suitable for different occasions, bearing in mind that one bottle is usually adequate to serve six or seven guests, unless they are real lovers and connoisseurs of Champagne. The half-pint bottles, or "splits" should be avoided, as they are rather too small to warrant cellar-space.

CHAMPAGNE AND SPARKLING WINES

Champagne is so very special that, of all the effervescent wines, it is the only one not to be known as a "sparkling wine" or mousseux. Here, usage and time have gone against etymology. Yet the term "sparkling wine" is applied to all wines which, after a second artificial fermentation, froth when poured into a glass. Depending on the amount of froth, they are called perlants (pearly), pétillants (effervescent), or mousseux (sparkling). Crémant is reserved for Champagne.

Sparkling wines are made in three different ways: the rural or natural method; the méthode champenoise, and the method known as cuve close.

THE RURAL OR NATURAL METHOD. The wine is vinified by its natural fermentation without anything being added to it. It is its natural sugar, which has not been turned into alcohol during the first fermentation, which activates the second fermentation. The wine having been bottled after the first fermentation, a second fermentation now takes place in the bottle which

gives the wine its effervescence. Modern processes of analysis and vinification enable the vintner to control the effervescence throughout the whole procedure, and thus to produce at his pleasure either a pearly or an effervescent wine.

This method is used in France, especially in Gaillac, Limoux (Blanquette) and in Die, whose yellowish-gold Clairette is reputed.

"Methode Champenoise". This method has been described already in detail, but the main principles are recalled here.

The first fermentation, aptly called "tumultuous", in former times took place in wooden casks. Nowadays, through modern progress, it usually takes place in vats. The process becomes calmer after three weeks, and up to that point, vinification is more or less the same as in all vineyards. The preparation of the cuvée (contents of the vat), however, is characteristic of Champagne, for in this region the blending of grapes is far more subtle than anywhere else. Racking follows, then the natural ferments, plus a liqueur made from a mixture of older wine and sugar, bring about the conditions that lead the wine's becoming frothy in the bottle during the second fermentation.

It is in fact this second, very precisely controlled fermentation which brings that fine quality to the wine, for its sparkle and froth must be enduring as well as light. The work of the vintners is not ended when the bottles are cellared, for there remain all those intricate steps which are peculiar to the Champagne vineyards and the méthode champenoise: remuage (moving the deposit towards the cork), uncorking or dégorgement (removing the cork with its wad of sediment), dosage (addition of more liqueur) and so on.

THE "CUVE CLOSE" METHOD. This differs from the two previous ones in that the second fermentation does not take place in bottles but in enormous vats. The wine is inferior when produced by this method and is certainly no substitute for the méthode champenoise. French law forbids Champagne made in cuve close to be sold as an A.O.C. wine.

These methods are the only ones used in France, and are followed more or less closely, in other countries producing sparkling wines. In Italy, for example, Asti Spumante is made by the méthode champenoise up to a certain stage of its development; that is, until the second fermentation in the bottle has taken place. To avoid the remuage and the operation of uncorking, the wines are transferred from the bottles into enormous closed vats where they are clarified and filtered.

Finally, and purely for the record, sparkling wine can also by produced simply by adding carbonic acid gas. It need hardly be said that such wines are of a very inferior quality.

LIFE IN THE CHAMPAGNE REGION

Life in the Champagne region follows the rhythm of the work in the vineyards. Although the history of the province is particularly rich in facts and fables, its folklore today has fallen into disuse. One must not be too harsh in blaming the people of Champagne; rather, it should be recognized that the nature of their soil and climate is less propitious to popular festivities than that of the large vineyards to the south. This is the land, moreover, that has been rocked and torn by cruel wars over the centuries, tragedies which have contributed to the disappearance of pleasant customs and joyous occasions which are very difficult to keep up when the heart has gone out of them.

On the other hand, one should not conclude that the vinegrowers of Champagne are a sad people. Everywhere that wine is to be found, the people are warmhearted and generous.

In former days, when the winegrower poured the grapes into the vat or wooden barrel, he never failed to pronounce a revered formula which expressed all hopes: *Saint Martin, bon vin* ("Saint Martin, make the wine good"). Having thus satisfied his religious beliefs, he did not hesitate to turn to other practices in which piety had no part! A case of "better safe than sorry", no doubt. To take care of superstitions, he also placed a steel knife between the wood of the barrel and the first metal ring.

The Feast of St. Vincent is celebrated on January 22nd here as in all vineyards. Once the simple religious ceremonies have been concluded, including blessing the vines, a propitiatory bottle of good wine is enjoyed.

On the patron saint's day, as well as at all other festivities, whether religious or secular, the sole joy comes from the wine, and the festival of Mardi Gras or *Feux de la Saint-Jean*, in summer, with their maypoles, dances and chorus-singing, are now of the past. The hard work at harvest time does not prevent the workers from enjoying themselves, but workers brought in from other places to help in the harvest are not the ones to bring back the habits and customs of long ago.

If the *Vigneronne* is no longer danced around the wine-press, the last day of harvesting is still celebrated by the *Cochelet*. This consists mainly of a sumptuous meal, with plenty of Champagne, followed by a local ball and *farandole* dances born from the imaginations of the participants.

Modern times have also killed off the friendly *cavées*, or cellar parties, when each vinegrower brought a log to help keep the fire going and joined in the hearty singing before sharing the *queugnots* (a type of biscuit), united with all his friends under the sign of the vine.

THE COMMANDERY OF THE CHAMPAGNE SLOPES. As in other wine regions, an influential brotherhood has pledged itself to spread the fame of Champagne wines. Its origins date back to the seventeenth century when the founders, the Count of Olonne, the Marquis of Saint-Evremond and the Marquis of Mortemart, practising what they preached, formed a group of famed epicures. In those days they were called les *marquis friands* ("the sweet-toothed marquises"), but the irreverant found them another title wherein could be detected some envy: *les fins débauchés* ("the first-class rakes"). In fact, they shared a common love for a good life and had a predilection for the wines of Champagne, which surely absolves them from any sin. Years passed, and it was only after the war that the brotherhood was brought back from its deep sleep by a winegrower from Champillon, Roger Gaucher, and François Taittinger.

The brotherhood is headed by a Commander (at present, Georges Prade, former vice-president of the Municipal Council of Paris) who is helped by a *Conseil Magistral*. The most prominent members of this Council are the *Capitaine Chambellan* (Captain Chamberlain), the *Connétable Premier officier* (High Constable First Officer), the *Grand Chancelier* (Great Chancellor), the *Gardien de la Constitution* (Guardian of the Constitution), and others of lesser mark.

The objectives of the brotherhood are to propagate the noble wine, to defend its prestige and its quality, and to battle relentlessly against malpractice and fraud.

Caps on their heads and swords at their sides, the high dignitaries often go from place to place, organizing or attending important national and international occasions. They insist strictly on remaining an independent group, and though in close contact and on excellent terms with the firms and wine-merchants, they will not accept any protection, nor admit any exclusive rights.

The brotherhood, which today has more than 4,000 members, holds its chapters in the cellars of the most illustrious houses of Rheims and Epernay. It turns out in the vineyards to celebrate St. Vincent's Day, the feast of the patron saint of vinegrowers.

SPARKLING WINES THROUGHOUT THE WORLD

Sparkling wines are produced in nearly all the large viticultural regions in the world, and can be either white, red or rosé, with a very wide range of quality.

THE SPARKLING WINES OF FRANCE

France is the largest producer of sparkling wines in the world, including Champagne: in 1960, 110 million bottles were produced, of which 50 million were Champagne. In 1970, Champagne alone accounted for 102 million bottles.

Burgundy and Bordelais also produce sparkling wines of the *appellation contrôlée* category, but which cannot pretend to compete with the celebrated growths of the Champagne region. The Rhône basin produces the following sparkling wines: ARBOIS MOUSSEUX, L'ETOILE MOUSSEUX or CÔTES DU JURA MOUSSEUX; and farther south there are the sparkling wines of SAVOIE AYSE (Ayse is the name of the growth), the SEYSSEL MOUSSEUX, the SAINT-PERAY MOUSSEUX and the CLAIRETTE DE DIE MOUSSEUX which carry an A.O.C. In the Loire valley, almost every viticultural region has its own sparkling wine: MONT-LOUIS MOUSSEUX, VOUVRAY MOUSSEUX, TOURAINE MOUSSEUX, SAUMUR MOUSSEUX, ANJOU MOUSSEUX, all of which are popular. BLANQUETTE DE LIMOUX and GAILLAC MOUSSEUX, produced in the south-west, deserve more than passing mention.

All French sparkling wines are obliged by law to state on their labels how they have been made, whether by the *méthode champenoise*, *vin mousseux produit en cuve close*, or *vin mousseux gazéifié*.

THE SPARKLING WINES OF GERMANY

After France, Germany is the next largest producer of sparkling wines. They are known either as *Sekt* or *Schaumwein*, the latter being generally inferior to the *Sekt*. The wines sell at a wide range of prices; the best *Sekt* can cost up to ten times more than an ordinary *Schaumwein*. Most German sparkling wines are not made from German but from imported wines, and purchases of foreign wines can sometimes reach as high as three-quarters of the whole German production of sparkling wines. In 1967, only 23.4 per cent of the country's sparkling wines were of German origin.

There are two types of sparkling wine: "Riesling", which retains the fruity bouquet and the original flavour of the grape, and "Champagne" which is more like a traditional aperitif or dessert wine. Both types have the usual range of tastes, varying from the driest to the sweetest, with the same terms being used as those of Champagne. The law obliges the producer to specify on the label in which country the wine was first bottled. Thus a label which says *Französischer Schaumwein* indicates that it is a French sparkling wine, produced in France, while a label *Deutscher Schaumwein* signifies that the wine was prepared and bottled in Germany. However, the origin of the wine used might be German or foreign. The German equivalent for the French *vin mousseux gazéifié* is *mit Zusatz von Kohlensäure*, indicating that CO_2 has been injected. In order to avoid any misunderstandings, one should note that labels with the name *Beeren-Schaumwein* have nothing in common with labels such as *Trockenbeerenauslese* or *Beerenauslese*; "Beeren-Schaumwein" or "Obst-Schaumwein" simply means "sparkling wine made from currants," or "sparkling wine made from fruit". These are therefore not sparkling wines, but aerated fruit juices.

Most producers of German sparkling wines are in the central viticultural region of Hesse in the Rhineland or the Palatinate. The largest producer, Henkell, is at Wiesbaden. Some of the best and oldest producers are Söhnlein at Wiesbaden-Schierstein, Mattheus Müller (MM) at Eltville, Kupferberg at Mainz, Kessler at Esslingen, Burgeff at Hochheim, and Deinhard at Koblenz. Some German sparkling wines carry the name of their growths and a year. The consumption of sparkling wines has greatly increased in the last few years, rising from 50 million bottles in 1956 to 144.2 million bottles in 1965.

THE SPARKLING WINES OF THE SOVIET UNION

The Russians seem to have a partiality for sparkling wines: in 1965, they produced 50 million bottles. The SOWJETSKOJE SCHAMPANSKOJE is produced by a second fermentation either in the bottle in *cuve close* or in double vats. If it is kept for three years before being marketed, the qualification "old" is added. This sparkling wine, when made from red wines, is known as "Soviet Red Champagne". However, if it is made with red wines from Tzymlyansk, it is distinguished by the label ZYMLJANSKSJE. A wine which is artificially injected with carbonic acid gas is known as "aerated wine", and must be so described on the label. The Soviet sparkling wines offer the whole range of varieties, from *brut* to sweet wines with a 10 per cent to 10.5 per cent sugar content. The best Soviet Champagnes are probably KAFFIA in the Crimea, and that produced by Abraou Dursso in the Kouban valley.

Champagne's famous vineyard of Côte d'Hautvillers basks on its Marne valley hillside (above). Here, in harvest time, *porteurs* carry the grapes in small baskets (left) from the vines to the sorters. Time is precious, and the grape-pickers—most of them seasonal workers—eat their midday meal on the spot, among the vines (below).

Once selected, the best grapes are placed in baskets called *mannequins* containing from 150 to 180 pounds of grapes. The *débardeurs* (unloaders) then transport them to the wine-press in horse-drawn carts (right).

The foreman of the vineyard (above) keeps a beady eye on all stages of the harvest, from picking to the presses. In all their various handlings, it is vital that the grapes should never be crushed or even bruised.

Deep in the cellar, a skilled workman performs the delicate task of *remuage*—a slight shake and a twist to every bottle so that the sediment will gradually work its way down and settle near the cork (below).

THE SPARKLING WINES
OF THE UNITED STATES OF AMERICA

The United States produces various types of sparkling wines. There is the wine commonly known in that country as Champagne: it is a light, sparkling wine whose second fermentation takes place in glass containers holding not more than one gallon (about 3.8 litres), and whose appearance and taste tends to resemble true Champagne as closely as possible. French Champagne producers have always fought against the use of the name of their province and of their product by the producers of American sparkling wines. A certain amount of control does, however, exist, since by Californian law the word "Californian" or "American" must appear on the label as well as a statement defining the vinification method used and the place of production.

There is also the "sparkling grape wine" which is made by the *cuve close* method. If this wine has a Champagne-like taste, it is then called "sparkling wine—Champagne type". "Crackling wine" is an effervescent wine, and "carbonated wine" is an aerated sparkling wine. The total United States production of sparkling wine is about 70 million bottles in 1970.

There is not room in these few brief comments on American sparkling wines to permit a fair judgement of their quality. Here, as in many other regions, all the different varieties in all the various prices ranges may be found. The connoisseur of Champagne is, however, always surprised to find the name "Champagne" on the bottles of certain American sparkling wines which are very highly priced and have quite a different taste from true Champagne. In New York State many sparkling wines are made from native grape varieties such as *Catawba*, *Delaware*, *Elvira* and *Isabella* and have often to be blended with Californian wines to reduce the penetrating foxy taste of the eastern grapes. In California the best Champagne-type wines are produced from the *Pinot Noir* and *Pinot Chardonnay* grapes. The *Semillon*, *Sauvignon Blanc*, *White Riesling*, *Pinot Blanc* and *Folle Blanche* also give good results. The Californian Champagnes go through the same *dosage* process as do their French models and have the dry to sweet range, although a really dry Champagne is not often found in this country. The best sparkling wines are produced by F. Korbel and Brothers, Hanns Kornell Cellars, and Almadén Vineyards in California, and Great Western Producers and Gold Seal Vineyards in New York State.

The American connoisseurs of true Champagne are quite numerous: in 1970, 4,509,626 bottles of Champagne were imported into that country.

THE SPARKLING WINES
OF OTHER COUNTRIES

Sparkling wine is called *spumante* in Italy, *espumoso* in Spain and *espumante* in Portugal. Italy has only a small variety of sparkling wines: ASTI SPUMANTE is very well known even outside of Italy's frontiers, but there are also its cousins BARBERA D'ASTI SPUMANTE, GRIGNOLINO D'ASTI SPUMANTE and MOSCATO D'ASTI SPUMANTE. ASTI SPUMANTE is made by the *méthode champenoise* from a muscat wine. It is a sweet wine but the bubbles prevent the sweetness from being disagreeable and if served very cold this drink is even refreshing. The sweetness is not produced by the addition of sugar or by over-ripening of the grapes but from the natural sweetness of the grape itself. In Lombardy, MOSCATO DI CASTEGGIO SPUMANTE is also drunk, and PROSECCO DI CONEGLIANO SPUMENTE in Venetia; both of these wines, however, are less well known than the ASTI.

Spain's centre of production of sparkling wines is San Sandurni de Noya, near Villafranca del Panadès. These wines are clear with a bouquet which savours of honey. Spanish wines are made quite often by the classic Champagne method and the phonetic equivalent, Xampan, often appears on the labels. One of the Catalonian Champagne-type wines once lost a High Court case in London and thenceforth Spanish sparkling wines were not allowed to be sold in England as Spanish Champagnes. The fact that the defendant firm was not one that used the traditional *méthode champenoise* did not help their case. Besides the *méthode champenoise* two other processes are used to make wine sparkle in Spain. One is the *cuve close* method and the other is the regrettable carbonizing method which turns many still wines into unpalatable drinks of the fizzy lemonade order. There are only about forty firms that make a sparkling wine by the *méthode champenoise* and these are the only ones that are entitled to call themselves *cavas*. Many of these *cavas* welcome the casual visitor and are pleased to explain the complicated process used to make their sparkling wines. The visitor may be invited to taste the produce, which he can enjoy in the knowledge that it has been made the right way.

In Portugal, sparkling wines are made in the regions of Bairrada and Lamego, and are often named after the viticultural company which produced them.

Other countries, such as Argentina, Brazil, Israel, South Africa, Switzerland and Uruguay produce some sparkling wines by one or the other of the established methods. Throughout the world, at all latitudes, sparkling wine is a drink for festive occasions, synonymous with happiness, gaiety and joy.

LA CHAMPAGNE

10 Km.

10 Miles

THE WAYS
OF WINE AND MAN

WINE AND HEALTH
A DOCTOR'S GUIDE

GÉRARD DEBUIGNE

Wine has been for a very long time considered as one of the basic elements of human nourishment. In fact, Olivier de Serres, the French agronomist, was only confirming an already widely held opinion when he wrote, in his famous *Théâtre de l'Agriculture* published in 1600: "After bread comes wine, the second nutriment given by the Creator to sustain life and the first to be famed for its excellence." Long before him, the famous words in Ecclesiastes (ix, 7), "Go thy way, eat thy bread with joy, and drink thy wine with a merry heart" proved that even a thousand years before the dawn of Christianity wine was held to be as essential an item of human sustenance as bread.

All this apart, water was actually considered unhealthy to drink during the seventeenth and eighteenth centuries. Sydenham, the English doctor who discovered laudanum, claimed that the poor people who drank water managed to remain in good health only because their organisms were adapted to wretched conditions. Buffon, the French naturalist, expressed a similar opinion when he declared: "Pure water is not sufficient to keep up the strength of working men." From time immemorial, man has sought more in his food than the mere satisfaction of a physical need. He has always looked also for a combination of physical and spiritual gratifications, a means to combat worry and fatigue and a mild and pleasant stimulant.

In addition to its hygienic and dietetic properties, wine is the only source of nourishment that ideally fulfils this inherent desire of the human species. No other earth-grown product occupies its singular place

of honour; none other speaks more eloquently to our hearts, tastes, memories and dreams. Neither grain, which makes the allegorical "daily bread" a nourishing reality for millions, nor rice, which forms the staple diet of an entire continent, nor coffee, nor tea, both much-loved in some countries, can replace it.

This is why wine, whose history is inseparable from that of mankind and even civilization itself, will undoubtedly always retain its special, privileged place in our minds and on our tables.

THE PROPERTIES OF WINE

Wine's qualities are invaluable, innumerable, irreplaceable. It goes without saying, however, that in order to benefit from wine's wonderful virtues, the maximum daily quantities advocated by authorities on the subject, and confirmed by laboratory experiments, should not be exceeded.

Professor Trémolières provided a good guide during the last European Congress on alcoholism: "For healthy adults whose diet is sufficient and well-balanced, the organism can normally oxidise a maximum of one litre of wine in the case of men, and three-quarters of a litre in the case of women. If these measures are exceeded, and if one of the above conditions is not met, as for example in cases of insufficient nourishment, the alcohol is oxidized by toxic processes, and thereby produces a pernicious effect." To which it may be added that, providing reasonable care is taken to distribute the daily intake over the two main meals, wine will not inebriate but contribute its tonic and beneficial properties to the diet of the consumer.

It is worth pointing out that the amount of wine consumed by the average, healthy individual usually falls quite naturally within the specified limits. Alcoholism, so long regarded as a deadly passion and a vice, is increasingly coming to be considered in medical pathology as an illness. The theory of the "alcoholic disease", championed by Jellinek, was introduced into French medical circles around 1956. According to this theory, alcoholism is a "physical compulsion complicated by a mental obsession", its victims being those who suffer from a particular kind of emotional disorder. Only specific types of people, therefore, become alcoholics and there is no reason whatever to stigmatize wine, nor to spoil the pleasure of worthy, decent folk who drink it in moderation by instilling in them a fear that they may become alcoholics.

It is moreover a surprising but accepted fact that the ravages of alcoholism are most marked in those unfortunate regions where no vines are grown. This is not to say that hearty wine drinkers are exempt from the consequences of over-indulgence. But it is primarily those who, already suffering from various nervous or emotional derangements, habitually swallow aperitifs, cocktails, manufactured spirits or anything, good or bad, containing alcohol who are most prone to alcoholism and who have to be treated in the psychiatric wards of hospitals, and rarely those congenial and reasonable imbibers of good wine.

The Nutritional Value of Wine

Since wine is almost 90 per cent water, it is an old and gleeful joke that "any wine drinker is an unwitting drinker of water". Be that as it may, wine also contains many other valuable elements making it a real liquid food with incomparable qualities. But although the most advanced methods of quantitative analysis have succeeded in determining the various proportions of the different constituents of wine, they have yet to reveal the mysterious ingredient which gives wine its reputation of a symbolic and sacred sustenance. The sense of well-being and pleasant euphoria that pervades body and soul while downing a good wine can hardly be expressed in milligrams of one element or another.

We must therefore content ourselves with what information wine itself chooses to divulge as to its own properties and ingredients which, in any case, vary from one wine to another, depending on the kind of soil, the species of grape, the year of harvesting, the length of time the wine has been bottled and, above all, the care and attention it receives during the time it is growing to maturity.

Wine's Calorific Value

This depends on two factors: alcoholic strength and sugar content. Even ignoring all its other ingredients and assuming that wine is merely a dilution of alcohol in water, it would still be a food or, at the very least, a dietary supplement.

As the research carried out by Atwater in 1902 has proved, alcohol is immediately utilized by the body —unlike sugar, fats and amino acids—and it thereby supplements to a certain extent the other energizing foods. However, the work of Schaeffer, Le Breton and Dontcheff has shown that wine can only supply 50 per cent of the body's basic requirements, in other words 600 to 800 calories.

But it cannot be stressed enough that the ten cubic centimetres of alcohol contained in one litre of wine have no relation to the same quantity of alcohol absorbed neat. Wine is not merely and simply a solution of one per cent ethylic alcohol! Intimately blended with a multitude of other living elements, alcohol, an inert substance, enhances the entire complex of wine with its valuable qualities.

The number of calories contained in a litre of wine varies between 600 and 1,000, with an average of 600 to 700 in the case of red wine. Sweet, soft white wines of the Sauternes type with their high sugar content contain more calories than dry white wines. Naturally sweet wines and dessert wines, rich in both sugar and alcohol, contain the most calories of all. In countries enjoying a high standard of living, the calorie content of a wine may seem of trifling importance, and most people are more concerned with reducing an already excessive general intake. Nevertheless, where the source of this body fuel is wine, it certainly seems to possess quite remarkable powers to generate well-being, enthusiasm and intellectual activity.

Vitamins

Wine supplies the body with all the vitamins in the grape. Even on the basis of its wealth of vitamins, wine can be described without exaggeration as a "living drink".

Wine contains the following vitamins:

Vitamin C. This has well-known effects on general physical tone, physical fitness, resistance to cold and fatigue. Athletes need two to three times as much Vitamin C as persons with sedentary occupations.

Vitamin P (or C_2). In association with Vitamin C, this vitamin increases physical resistance and has a very definite effect in certain cases of debility with low blood pressure. Lavollay and Sevestre attribute wine's tonic effect to its Vitamin P content.

369

Vitamin B_2 or riboflavine. Considered by some to be of nutritive value, this vitamin is active in the metabolism of the glucides, proteins, irons, vitamins A, B_1, PP and the adrenocorticotrophic hormones.

Vitamin B_3 or PP. This is a powerful stimulant of the cell functions. Andross has demonstrated that productivity increased when substantial amounts of this vitamin were included in the diet of a group of workmen.

Mineral Salts and Trace Elements

Without certain minerals, the human system cannot survive. Sulphur, phosphorus, chlorine, sodium, potassium, magnesium, calcium and iron are all essential to life. The system can assimilate these substances only in the form of organic salts, in other words combined with vegetable or animal matter. It cannot assimilate them in their natural state or in the form of mineral salts, except for a few substances such as kitchen salt. In wine, the mineral salts are incorporated with other substances and can be assimilated readily. Although total deficiency in mineral salts is rare, relative deficiency is quite common and wine therefore constitutes a far from negligible source of these valuable substances.

BIOCHEMICAL EFFECTS OF WINE ON THE SYSTEM

If only on account of the calories, vitamins and mineral salts which it supplies in a highly palatable and easily assimilated form, wine can be considered one of the most valuable foods. Yet these are only a few of the virtues which were proved by our ancestors' instinctive physical need.

Wine Aids Digestion

St. Paul needed no converting to this virtue. He exhorted Timothy: "Stop drinking only water. Take a little wine for your stomach's sake and for your frequent discomforts." Even at that time it was recognized that wine's natural acidity increased the secretions of saliva. Wine thus makes an excellent aperitif, the first few sips preparing the organs for digestion. Furthermore, it is the only good, natural and healthy aperitif which does not "whet the appetite the way that the wrong key opens a lock, by breaking it," as a famous doctor once wittily remarked.

The secretion of gastric juices is also stimulated and increased. Furthermore, wine also contains enzymes similar to those present in the digestive juices, thus facilitating the work of tired or deficient stomachs. Its tannin stimulates the fibres of the entire alimentary canal. The regular use of good wine also stimulates intestinal secretions and thus helps to combat the constipation with which so many people nowadays seem to be plagued.

But, first and foremost, wine has been found to greatly facilitate the digestion of proteins contained in meat, fish, oysters and cheese. Genevois even went so far as to say that it was the only drink which, because of its ionic acidity and low osmotic pressure, allowed proteins to be easily digested. With today's increased standard of living, the modern diet is particularly rich in proteins of animal origin, formerly luxuries in which only the well-to-do could regularly indulge. Wine, combining excellently with these proteins, achieves a perfect gastronomic harmony and subsequently facilitates their digestion. Thus the well-planned marriage of meats, fish, shellfish or cheese with an eligible wine is not only an epicurean refinement but a sensible and scientifically proven aid to healthy digestion.

Wine as an Antiseptic

The bactericidal power of wine has long been recognized. Even the Sumerians used balms and ointments with a wine base, and our forbears instinctively reached for wine to cleanse and asepticize wounds. The bactericidal action of wine is due not only to the alcohol it contains but also to its acids, tannin, sulphurous acid and ethers.

It has been proved that one cubic centimetre of white wine, mixed with one cubic centimetre of culture medium, kills 99 per cent of the colon bacilli and the bacilli of cholera and typhoid. So it is not surprising that armies were sometimes issued with wine during epidemics of dysentery, as we learn from the *Journal* written by a certain Percy during the Prussian campaign in 1807: "The dysentery is improving. The army is only slightly the worse for it now. Wine is being distributed to the troops: it is the best preventative."

Similarly, the custom of sprinkling oysters or other shellfish with white wine not only adds to their delectability but is a prudent health precaution into the bargain. The wine that children can be seen drinking in restaurants in Europe, albeit well diluted, also serves, at least in part, a hygienic purpose.

The Antitoxic Properties of Wine

Wine has proved an effective therapeutic agent in the prevention of infectious and feverish diseases and in certain toxic-infections such as influenza. Despite the ever-widening range of modern medicines, a glass of good mulled wine is still a sovereign remedy for incipient flu' and one that it would be foolish to relegate to the store of "old wives' tales". The antitoxic action of wine has even prevented certain cases of alkaloid poisoning, such as sparteine and strychnine.

In the same way, marinading and cooking game in wine has shown itself to be a wise precaution. Obviously, wine is primarily used to tenderize rather tough meat and to bring out its flavour. But in the case of beasts or fowl whose bodies may have accumulated a considerable amount of toxins, due to fatigue, or whose wounds may be unclean, wine safeguards against possible food poisoning.

The Anti-Allergic Properties of Wine

These have been demonstrated by Weissenbach who advises crushing strawberries in red wine fifteen minutes before serving, to safeguard against the risk of an allergic reaction to which some people are prone.

WINE AND MODERN MAN

Naturally, wine is no longer the indispensable nutriment of those days when nourishment was very much less rich and varied than today. Nevertheless, it still plays a useful role and remains an ideal drink.

Not only does wine provide stimulating sensations to jaded palates, it also gives our frequently abused systems the necessary tonic to resist the stresses of modern life. Wine meets a pressing contemporary need: to keep the mind alert and the body in top physical condition. The vitamins it contains happen to be those best suited to combat the fatigue and weariness of a world and age increasingly dominated by the rhythm of machines.

Tannin contributes still further to the bracing properties of wine. Red wines, richer in tannin, are more tonic than white and have a more marked stimulant effect. Red wine is therefore preferable to white when energy flags and the organism has need of a fillip. The habit of drinking a "stirrup-cup" before vaulting into the saddle, so popular in times past, proves the value of this tonic to mind and muscles, the cheering qualities of a stimulant so ideally suited to sustain the horseman on his tiring rides. As long as it is taken in moderate quantities, wine never produces depressing after-effects, the penalty of so many modern drugs.

But although it is an ideal tonic, wine is also the best and healthiest promoter of relaxed well-being. More than ever before, modern man needs "tranquillizers" to help him shoulder his cares, resolve the problems that beset him and cope with the discouraging aura of anxiety about him. Wine promotes optimism and *joie de vivre* and even produces a marked mental improvement in cases of anxiety.

Natural, harmless and nearly as old as the world itself, good wine in reasonable quantities is infinitely better than all the "pep pills" with their dangerous artificial happiness. The sense of well-being that comes from good food and wine naturally and spontaneously produces the state of relaxation with which modern man is so obsessed but which our ancestors had much less need to seek. Furthermore, this method calls for no tiresome procedures, no special equipment —all that is needed is a wine list!

Finally, the infectious euphoria created by good wine gives human relations a friendliness and gaiety which are often all too lacking in the modern world. In an age when worries, overwork and jangled irritation beset the world with strangers and enemies, a quiet glass of wine between friends helps to restore those forgotten qualities of comradeship and human warmth.

WINE AND SPORTSMAN

Sport = no alcohol. This is the unequivocal equation advocated by sportsmen and their trainers who believe in rigorous self-denial and who even go so far as to include wine in their uncompromising verdict. However, the latest studies on the subject, far from extolling the special diets formerly in fashion, agree that the ideal diet for an athlete is quite simply the ideal, healthy and well-balanced diet of an ordinary man engaged in a strenuous physical occupation. Spirit-based or manufactured aperitifs and liqueurs, except for special occasions, should indeed be excluded from the athlete's menu and forbidden during training, but to condemn wine would be a sad exaggeration.

Wine, which Pasteur described as "the healthiest and most hygienic of drinks" has shown itself to be ideal for sportsmen, even more so than for those with sedentary occupations.

All drinks other than wine have various disadvantages. Fruit juices, especially those of citrus fruits, are not always well tolerated. Although pleasant enough to drink between meals, they hardly make good gastronomic partners with a well-cooked meal. Beer dulls the mind, burdens the stomach and produces unwelcome belching and flatulence. Cider can provoke gastric troubles and has an irritant, laxative effect on the intestine. Too much coffee or tea lead to insomnia and excitability, and athletes are already quite nervous enough. Milk, usually badly tolerated by most adults, is a food not a drink. Continual consumption of waters with a high mineral or soda content is not recommended for athletes. What else remains, save slightly aerated mineral water or plain tap water?

More than anyone else, the sportsman, dependent on top physical and mental condition to put out his best effort, needs wine, a valuable mixture which stimulates cell functions and whose beneficial and soothing properties can hardly be denied.

Particularly during training, and when the sport in question involves considerable muscular effort, the athlete is advised to adopt a diet very rich in proteins, such as meats, fish, eggs and cheese. Wine, it will be remembered, is a powerful aid to the digestion of these substances. Its vitamins help to counter muscular and nervous fatigue and keep the athlete in good shape.

The mineral salts contained in wine help to prevent deficiencies which may seriously upset the delicate balance of the athlete's physical form. Iron is an essential element in training, increasing the volume of blood and aiding in its aeration. Similarly, sulphur is needed to eliminate the toxins produced by fatigue from intensive training. Both sulphur and iron are found in wine.

Finally, the tonic and calming properties of wine are most beneficial to the general morale of the athlete, whose strict discipline, often fanatically intensive training and obsession with optimum performances often result in a delicate and even precarious mental state. In these conditions, it is in the athlete's interest to drink a reasonable amount of wine. When he is exerting considerable muscular effort, his pulmonary activity speeds up and he can eliminate alcohol more easily than persons leading a sedentary life.

In fact, authorities on sport are by no means against a reasonable consumption of good wine. Doctor Mathieu, medical adviser to Olympic teams, declares: "For a normal subject, if the quantity of wine does not exceed half a litre a meal, or one litre a day, the alcohol is entirely burned up by the organism and wine then becomes an excellent nutritional drink." Boigey, whose work on exercise as a form of therapy is now universally recognized, considers that "natural wine is the most commendable of alcoholic drinks. It contains a wonderful range of useful and well-balanced substances which nothing else can replace."

Doctor Encausse, medical officer of the High Commission for Youth and Sport in France, advocates that consumption of wine should be limited to three-quarters of a litre per day for a healthy adult weighing approximately 150 pounds, wisely concluding that the medical profession should recommend temperance rather than abstinence.

Nevertheless, allowing for a certain flexibility of interpretation, not all wines can be recommended for athletic activities. This applies to robust or fortified wines, rich in bouquet and highly coloured. Burgundies and wines from the Côtes du Rhône should, alas, be reserved for Sundays and holidays and forgotten during training. The same applies to white wine which has the unfortunate reputation, especially among mountain guides, of going straight to the legs. However, the athlete still has an entire range of light, attractive red and rosé wines to choose from. He needs no commiseration.

WINE AND YOUTH

Obviously, nobody would think of giving a young child undiluted wine. However, in the traditional Italian family, children do drink very limited quantities of wine at the table, wine being considered as an integral part of the Italian meal. And it is interesting to note that Italy has a lower rate of alcoholism *per capita*, for example, than the United States.

In France, too, well-diluted wine is served with school meals and this is, in fact, far healthier than the fizzy drinks so liberally dispensed to their offspring by English and American parents.

During adolescence, a small quantity of good, undiluted wine, drunk with meals, can do no harm. It should be remembered that many tonics recommended for "the awkward age" have a wine base, yet nobody worries about the dangers of alcoholism in prescribing them. A healthy respect for wine, moderation in its use and discernment for its quality, instilled at an early age, will do much to prevent livers and mental processes from being damaged in later life by the imbibing of dubious or indifferent mixed drinks based on spirits.

WINE AND THE ELDERLY

The virtues of wine for older people are well known. The Médoc, famous as a wineproducing and winedrinking region, is justly proud of its record for the longevity of its inhabitants.

Diminishing digestive secretions often result in old people having poor appetites. Lack of nourishment and vitamin deficiency may result, aggravated by additional factors such as ill-fitting dentures, sometimes mistaken dietary fads or, quite simply, a restricted budget. Good wine, being easily assimilated and pleasant to drink, stimulates old people's appetites and facilitates digestion. Its stimulant and tonic properties are valuable at an age when there is increasing debility. Especially in the case of dessert wines or naturally sweet wines, it also contributes valuable calories and comforting warmth to the system. Attention should also be drawn to the fact that there are many good but quite modestly priced wines. Despite all the care taken in its production, wine is still fairly reasonable in price when compared to the other alcoholic drinks on the market.

WINE AND ILLNESS

Old Hippocrates, the Father of Medecine, who lived from 460 to 377 B.C., taught that "wine is wonderfully suitable for man if, in sickness as in health, it is administered in proper and fair measure".

As long ago as the Carolingian era, the ordinary diet that the sick and elderly received in the monasteries included strengthening and savoury wine soups. In later history, Joan of Arc was also said to be very partial to them.

The bactericidal and antitoxic properties of wine that make it an excellent agent in the prevention of infection have already been mentioned. And Nature, generously providing man with the remedies for the ills she herself inflicts, has foreseen all eventualities by providing different wines for different ailments.

Thus naturally sweet or dessert wines, those delicacies of the vine, are particularly recommended for convalescents, the emaciated and those suffering from debility. On the other hand, diabetics should on no account be given these wines because their diet does not permit food with a high sugar content.

Light, dry white wines, pleasantly sharp and with their low sugar and alcohol content, stimulate the appetite and digestive processes. They are eminently suitable for dyspeptic subjects. They are also recommended in cases of obesity, their calorific value being very modest and their diuretic properties well known: the white wines of Savoy sustain the morale of those heroes who submit to the cure at Bride-les-Bains.

Sparkling wines are recommended for some kinds of dyspepsia, their carbonic acid being an effective remedy for vomiting. Champagne is the prerogative of convalescents, raising the morale as well as helping the system to recover. It is a wonderful "steadier" after a shock and is even useful in cases of low blood pressure.

Wines light in body and alcoholic strength, whatever their colour, are suitable for all invalids and should be chosen for everyday use. Full-bodied wines with rich bouquets should be kept in the cellar to celebrate the time of recovery.

The last word on the subject could very well be left to Sir Alexander Fleming, who once so wisely remarked: "Penicillin may cure human beings, but it is wine that makes them happy."

DOCTOR'S ORDERS

Wines that may be drunk—and those that may not be—by persons sufferings from certain bodily disorders:

Ailment	Wines Permitted	Wines Prohibited
Hyperchlorhydria (excess hydrochloric acid in the gastric juices)	Light red wines in small quantities.	Full-bodied red wines, very dry white wines, young and acid wines (beware of white and rosé wines in general), dessert wines.
Hypochlorhydria (inadequate secretion of hydrochloric acid in the stomach)	Light red wines or slightly acid dry white wines of low alcoholic content, young wines, Muscadet, Crépy, Fendant, Champagne, Beaujolais.	Wines of high alcoholic strength, dessert wines.
Various gastric disorders	Light red wines in small quantities, old Médoc.	White and rosé wines, sparkling and semi-sparkling wines.
Ulcers	No wine.	All wines.
Between attacks	No limitation.	None.
Intestinal troubles	All red wines when not acute.	White wines, sparkling wines and those of high alcoholic content, Burgundy, Côtes-du-Rhône. Never drink iced wines.
Constipation	All light wines, white, red or rosé.	Wines of high alcoholic strength, Burgundies, Côtes-du-Rhône.
Serious hepatic deficiencies (alcoholism, precirrhosis, cirrhosis resulting from hepatitis and jaundice)	No alcoholic drinks whatever, not even diluted wine.	
Vesicular lithiasis (biliary dyskinesia, abdominal migraine)	Red or white wine diluted with water (no more than $\frac{1}{4}$ litre per day).	Neat wine, dessert wines.

Hypercholesterolemy (excess cholesterol) and arteriosclerosis	All wines but in limited quantities.	
Cardiac deficiency	All wines allowed: white, red, rosé, dry or sweet.	Avoid very full-bodied wines of high alcoholic strength.
Hepatobiliary disease (biliary lithiasis, family cholemia)	Light wine, particularly red, in small quantities or preferably diluted with water, very little white wine.	Full-bodied, fortified wines rich in mineral extracts, dessert wines, Champagne and sparkling wines, iced wines.
High blood pressure (salt-free and soda-free diets)	Use wine and spirits for flavouring in cooking.	Limit the quantity in cases of inadequate blood circulation.
Renal deficiency (acute nephritis and Bright's disease)	All wines but in small quantities.	
Bladder stones	White, red and rosé wines, dry or sweet.	Avoid Bordeaux rich in mineral extracts, Burgundies and full-bodied wines.
Nutritional disorders (arthritis, gout, uric lithiasis, excess of uric acid in the blood, isolated albuminuria)	Young or old red Bordeaux in limited quantities, very little light white wine, local wines of low alcoholic strength.	Burgundies, Côtes-du-Rhône, Saint-Emilion, Champagnes and sparkling wines, ports, Madeira, dessert wines, all full-bodied, highly coloured, noble wines.
Obesity (crash diet)	No wine.	All wines are forbidden, the food intake being insufficient and unbalanced, the alcohol will be oxidized in the body by toxic processes. In addition, wine would add undesirable extra calories.
Obesity (continuous treatment)	Very dry white wines, young and of low alcohol content, Muscadet, Savoy and Alsace wines, light Bordeaux, local red and rosé wines. ¼ to ½ litre per day at the maximum. Remember that the calories contained in wine should be counted in the daily calorie allowance.	Sweet white wines, full-bodied and strong wines, naturally sweet and dessert wines.
Diabetes	Very dry white wine, extra-dry Champagne, red wines of low alcohol content.	Liqueur-like white wines, white Bordeaux, Vouvray, wines of high alcoholic content, Burgundy, Saint-Emilion, dessert wines, naturally sweet wines and fortified French and other wines (muscat, port, Malaga, Madeira and Samos).
Dermatitis	Dry, young and light wines, local red and rosé wines of low alcoholic content.	Full-bodied wines of high alcoholic content, sweet white wines, naturally sweet and liqueur wines.
Emaciation	Sweet white wines, wines made from grapes with "noble rot", dessert wines, naturally sweet and liqueur wines. Médoc, generous Burgundy, Côtes-du-Rhône, old Cahors; a little at frequent intervals through the day, drunk with meals.	Drink as little as possible while eating. Attractive, light wines should thus be avoided.
Convalescence	Champagne, sweet white wines, wines made from grapes with "noble rot", Médoc, old red Burgundy, high-class white Burgundy.	
Low blood pressure	Champagne, full-bodied and aromatic red wines, high-class white wines from Burgundy.	
Nervous breakdown	Champagne, red wines rich in tannin, Bourgueil, Madiran, old Médoc.	Wines with high alcoholic content. Avoid white wines.
Pregnancy	Dry white wines, red Bordeaux (particularly Médoc), Champagne and sparkling wines.	Absolutely no strong wines whatever, particularly fortified wines such as sherry and vermouth.

Should children drink wine?

It is certainly not advisable to give children alcoholic drinks. As far as wines are concerned, heavy or fortified wines should be particularly avoided. At the end of the meal, children may safely be given a little young or light wine, diluted with four times its volume of water, the quantity of wine depending on the child's age. As a rough guide, children between 5 and 7 years could be given a quarter to half a wineglassful, those between 7 and 10 half a glassful, 10 to 12 year olds two-thirds to three-quarters of a glass, while from the age of thirteen onwards a child can quite safely be given a full glass of wine.

YOUR OWN CELLAR

BERNARD GRENOUILLEAU

The first essentials for a good wine cellar are constant temperature, darkness and adequate ventilation. The temperature should be about 11º C., or 52º F. The cellar should be neither too dry nor too humid; ideally it should be cut out of rock or vaulted in mortared stone and always facing north. In certain wineproducing regions, as elsewhere, houses are naturally built with underground cellars. These days, however, in the provinces as well as in metropolitan areas, those who have a good, large cellar under the house can consider themselves as very fortunate.

If the cellar already meets these basic requirements, all that remains is to equip and arrange it to the best possible advantage. If, on the other hand, it is over-dry or over-humid, these disadvantages can be partly remedied by modern materials. An effective and traditional touch is achieved by spreading river-bed sand over the floor and watering it when the weather becomes too hot. If the cellar is equipped with air-shafts or other means of ventilation these should always be kept closed during periods of extreme cold or heat. Condensation should be guarded against as variations in temperature can result in streaming walls and dripping ceilings. Any cellar should be as free as possible from vibrations, something not always easy to achieve for those who live in the city.

Naturally, the cellar must be clean, tidy and well kept and perishables should be prohibited. This can be a delicate problem when the housewife sees this attractive, clean, cool place which is so ideal for storing things. Nevertheless, no fruit or vegetables which might decay should be allowed in the cellar, nor any old clothes, papers and the like as, with time, they can give off a musty smell which is likely eventually to permeate and spoil the wine.

THE APARTMENT CELLAR

From the traditional interpretation of the word, a cellar in an apartment seems a paradox. Yet with a reasonable amount of skill and imagination, what could be called an "apartment cellar" can be easily arranged. Even in a smallish flat, a closet or wall cupboard can serve, providing this is sufficiently far away from the kitchen or a heat source of any kind. If needs be, one can use the recess of a blocked-up door. Ventilation is necessary but this is quite simply achieved with wire mesh at the top and bottom and a lining of fibre glass, necessary for good thermal insulation. Obviously a small cellar of the kind in question cannot contain a large stock of wine, but it should easily hold between fifty and a hundred bottles. If these are choice wines, that is a fair number and also represents a substantial cash investment.

Whatever the size, shape or location of the cellar, once it is ready it is just a matter of filling it. Racks for bottles can be of wood, cement, brick or iron, depending on individual tastes and means. If small barrels of wine are to be stored, then stands of wood, stone or cement must be installed.

	Red			White
California	Pinot Noir	Chianti	Zinfandel	Riesling
Burgundy	Côte de Nuit/1961	Côte de Beaune/1964	Beaujolais/1970	Chablis/1967
Bordeaux	Médoc	Graves	St. Emilion	Sauternes
Assorted	Barolo/Italy	Carmel/Israël	Dôle/Switzerland	Tokay/Hungary

In a real cellar intended to hold several hundred bottles the most rational method is to have one compartment for each wine. There are many ways of arranging the bottles; by region and by *cru*, the reds on the left (diagram); chronologically, the oldest on the left; for lovers of wines of a particular region, one compartment to the wine of each sub-region; in adjoining compartments wines from regions or countries with nothing in common. The important thing is to have an orderly and logical system that facilitates periodic sampling and stock-taking and the replenishing of stocks when necessary. The name and vintage of the wine should be specified on each compartment.

Arranging a stock of fine wines is not necessarily a complicated undertaking. Here are a few suggestions, although there are many other equally good solutions: *(left to right, top)* racks placed one on top of the other; lengths of clay piping; wooden or plastic packing cases; *(bottom)* a gaily painted box divided diagonally; a ready-made bottle holder (available on the market); a converted set of small, deep shelves.

Not surprisingly, the most difficult part of setting up a private cellar is knowing what wine to buy and this, precisely, is the most difficult advice to give. It depends primarily on how much money is available, but also, of course, on personal tastes and preferences and whether or not a wineproducing region is near at hand. In this chapter, some general guidelines will be given as to how cost, personal preference and availability may best be combined.

For private individuals, buying in barrels is recommended only for local wines. For those fortunate enough to have access to such wines, it is often a very good idea to buy a barrel, or even a hogshead, depending on the size of the family and the amount of entertaining that is done. Before ordering wine in barrel, it is most important to find out whether it is ready for bottling or if it requires special attention beforehand. Such a wine will probably be a standard type and the attention needed very simple and straightforward. The most important thing is for the wine to be allowed time to settle. If it has not previously been treated, it is perhaps even advisable to clarify it. There is no need for professional filtering equipment or procedures. The old method of clarifying with white of egg is perfectly adequate and is still practised by reputable wineries producing high-class wines. For a cask containing approximately 50 gallons, two or three egg whites are whisked with a pinch of coarse salt, using an earthenware—but never a metal—bowl. The mixture is then poured into the cask through the bung-hole in the top, stirred with a special whisk or a clean stick and left to settle for a few days. The albumin draws all impurities down to the bottom of the cask. If it is a sound and well-constituted wine, it can be bottled several days later, after ensuring that the tap is placed high enough off the bottom of the barrel so that only perfectly clear wine pours out. If it is considered preferable to siphon the wine out with a rubber tube, a stick should be attached whose end projects about an inch below the end of the tube, so that the tube will not touch the bottom.

If the wine is stored in the cask for any length of time, the cask should be lying down on its stand with the bung on the top; otherwise, when the level of the wine drops, it will be necessary to ullage it frequently to ensure a good wine when bottled. Normally, the cask is not kept in this way until the wine is at least a year old. Should ullage prove absolutely necessary, the traditional method can be used. This consists of putting enough carefully washed and dried pebbles into the liquid to bring the surface of the wine flush with the bung-hole. Obviously, if the wine is very young it must be racked periodically to draw off the clear wine from the lees, but this requires special kinds of vessels. It should be borne in mind that casks are very difficult to keep in good condition. An empty cask quickly spoils and filling it later can be disastrous.

Bottles should be very carefully washed so that not the slightest trace of smell can be transferred to the wine. They must be drained thoroughly on a proper rack, protected from dust. As for corks it is a mistake to economise, particularly in the case of wines which will be kept for a considerable time. For ordinary wines to be drunk in the course of the year, or the following one at the latest, conical corks are available which can be inserted by hand. However, whether conical or any other shape, they must be of good quality. Nothing is more disagreeable than to find that a good wine has been spoilt by a bad cork. Corks should be dipped in boiling water, seasoned in wine or, better still, moistened with a neutral alcohol of the brandy spirit type.

Once the bottles are filled and corked it only remains to lay them carefully in their racks. In some countries, when the bottles are to be kept for a long time, they are buried in sand, temperamental white wines being buried standing up.

As for sealing the wine, it is better to use sealing wax rather than the familiar metal foil for bottles which are to be stored for a long time. Apart from its efficiency, this lends the bottle a good seal, if the pun may be excused, with a touch of old-fashioned charm and craftsmanship. The wax is melted with a spoonful of oil in any kind of small, deep pot, over a gentle heat just sufficient to keep the sealing wax liquid. The necks of the bottles should first be carefully wiped free of any moisture to prevent cracking, then dipped into the wax and removed with a quick turn.

For those people who insist on foil caps, these can actually be applied without a machine, but there is a knack to it. A piece of string should be attached to a hook or some point on the wall, the other end being held in one hand. The capsule is firmly pressed on to the neck of the bottle and the string is then looped round it. The string is pulled as tight as possible and the neck of the bottle twirled up and down the entire length of the string. With a bit of practice the caps are firmly fixed in place.

Bottling and maturing wine is not recommended for amateurs. If a good, clear, filtered local wine can be found and they wish to bottle it themselves, this can be an amusing pastime providing they have enough patience and time. It can also be an economic proposition as bulk wine costs less. But whether the wine is in cask or bottle it is well worth while purchasing it at least several months before drinking.

Even with the humblest of cellars, the average wine-lover should take good care to have at least 50 bottles of *vin ordinaire* in stock for everyday use, and to replenish his supplies before they run really low. This practice makes it easier for purchaser and merchant alike to maintain the same quality. It is a wise and well-known French saying that "it is always a pleasure to change bread, but never the wine". The quantity of 50 bottles only serves as an example for those with limited cellar space, although even the amateur aspires to greater things. Apart from all the pleasure and satisfaction derived from owning a private cellar, laying down a stock of choice wines can also be a financial investment, inasmuch as prices increase as wines age. There is ample proof of this in the astronomical prices fetched by bottles auctioned from private cellars.

A cellar of fine wines with any pretension to being well-stocked should contain, on the average, a thousand bottles covering a variety of wines. The following suggestions give some idea of how the stock would be divided up.

– 25 to 50 bottles of Champagne, to be renewed at least every two years. 50 bottles of SAUTERNES or vintage sweet wines, bought during a good year and laid down for future use.

– 200 bottles, at least, of good red Bordeaux such as MÉDOC, GRAVES, SAINT-EMILION, as many as possible of good vintages, which should be replaced from time to time so that stocks are never exhausted.

– 200 bottles of red and white Burgundy for drinking within three, four or five years.

– 50 bottles of special aperitif or dessert wines such as port, Madeira, SAMOS, BANYULS, MALVASIA, MARSALA and MAVRODAPHNI.

– 100 bottles of assorted whites from such districts as the Rhine and Moselle, from Hungary, Alsace, Switzerland, Italy and Central Europe, including CHABLIS, POUILLY, MUSCADET, GRAVES, HUELVA.

The remainder, about a third of the total, can be made up from miscellaneous or informal red wines, suitable for drinking at any time of day and not necessarily with meals. They will almost certainly include Beaujolais, except for the best vintages which should be laid down for future use; CÔTES-DU-RHÔNE, rosé wines from Provence and elsewhere in France, notably Anjou, fruity red wines from Spain, VALPOLICELLA from Italy, and so on.

This fulfils the basic requirement for a good cellar stock: a good selection of important French wines for drinking with special meals; a range of aperitif and dessert wines; a range of local or unusual foreign wines, depending on the owner's taste; young, delicate white wines of any origin and a good light table wine with a low alcohol content and a clean, fresh taste.

SUGGESTIONS FOR A CELLAR OF MODERATE SIZE

The proportion of white wines to red is obviously a matter of personal preference. Perhaps a good balance would be 12 different kinds of red wine and 10 different white wines, allowing for twelve bottles of each as the minimum. The suggestions below merely provide a guide to constituting a well-balanced cellar, a theme for endless, individual variations.

CHOICE OF WHITE WINES

4 dry white wines to serve with fish and seafood and, occasionally, to drink as an aperitif.

2 medium-dry, mellow white wines for rice dishes, various entrées and vegetable dishes.

2 sweet wines to accompany desserts.

2 Champagnes or, failing this, 2 first-class sparkling wines.

Dry white wines

Germany:	Riesling from the Moselle, Rheingau or Palatinate. These should be tasted before ordering.
Alsace:	Riesling, Pinot Gris, Tokay.

CHOICE OF RED WINES

2 light red wines to serve with roast fowl, veal and lamb.

4 full-bodied red wines to accompany red meat, roast meat of any kind and cheese.

6 good vintage red wines kept in reserve for special occasions and banquets.

Light red wines

Burgundy:	Beaujolais.
Côtes du Rhône:	Châteauneuf-du-Pape, Crozes, Hermitage.

WHITE WINES

Italy:	Orvieto, Vino del garda, Frascati, Vernaccia, Est ! Est !! Est !!!, Trevigiani, Garganega di Ganbellara.
Loire:	Sancerre, Anjou, Muscadet.
Portugal:	Vinho verde (branco).
Savoy:	Roussette de Savoie.
Switzerland:	Neuchâtel, Dorin, Fendant.
Yugoslavia:	Smederevka, Zilavka.
U.S.A.:	Chablis, Riesling and Sylvaner from California.

All these wines should be gradually restocked at the rate they are consumed. On the average they can only be kept for four years.

Mellow or medium-dry white wines

Alsace:	Gewürztraminer.
Germany:	Riesling Spätlese from the Moselle or Rhine, also Sylvaner Spätlese from Franconia and the Rheinhesse.
Bordeaux:	Graves de Vayres, Premières Côtes de Bordeaux, Saint-Foy, Saint-Macaire.
Touraine:	Vouvray.
Italy:	Castelli Romani, Frascati, Orvieto, Verdicchio with the mention *abbocato* or *semi-seccho*.
Switzerland:	Malvoisie, Petite Arvine.
Austria:	Riesling, Zierfandler and Rotgipfler "Spätlese".
Hungary:	Badacsonyi Kéknyelu, Badacsonyi Szurkebarat.

These wines should be gradually restocked at the rate they are consumed. They will not keep in prime condition longer than an average of four years.

Sweet white wines and dessert wines

Bordeaux:	Sauternes, Cérons, Loupiac, Barsac, Montbazillac.
Anjou:	Vouvray.
Hungary:	Tokay aszu (3 to 6 puttonyos).
Spain:	Malaga or Priorato extra rancio, sweet sherry.
Italy:	Cinqueterre (sweet), Malvasia di Lipari, Moscato, Vino santo, Caluso passito.
Greece:	Mavrodaphni, Samos.
Portugal:	Port.
Germany:	Moselle or Rhine wines with the mention "Trockenbeerenauslese".
Yugoslavia:	Spalato prosecco, Stolacer Ausbruch.
Roumania:	Cotnari Grase, Murfatlar-Muskat.
America:	Tokay from California.

These wines can usually keep for five years or more and some of them for about ten years. Their condition can best be judged by periodic tasting.

Champagnes

Champagne brut, dry or demi-sec.

A high-class sparkling wine can replace Champagne if preferred. Champagne can usually be kept for four to five years.

RED WINES

Bordeaux:	Light Médoc or Graves.
Italy:	Chianti, Bardolino, Barbusco, Grignolino Valpolicella.
Spain:	Priorato tinto.
Portugal:	Vinho verde (tinto).
Switzerland:	Salvagnin.
Austria:	Blauburgunder (Pinot Noir).
Germany:	Spätburgunder (Pinot Noir).
California:	Zinfandel.
Bulgaria:	Kramolin.

There is no reason why really good local wines, if available, should not replace the wines in the above list. As in the case of medium-dry or dry white wines, these should gradually be replaced as stocks are depleted. On average, these wines should be drunk within five years.

Full-bodied red wines

Burgundy:	From known regional vineyards or *Premiers Crus* from the Côtes de Nuits and Côtes de Beaune.
Côtes du Rhône:	Hermitage, Côte Rôtie.
Switzerland:	Dôle from the Valais.
Italy:	Barbera, Nebbiolo, Reciotto, Veronese, Falerno.
Bordeaux:	From the best vineyards in the Médoc, Saint-Emilion and Pomerol.
Algeria:	Wines from Médéa and Tlemcen.
Spain:	The best Rioja (Rioja Imperial, Rioja Marquès de Riscal), Vina Pomal.
Chile:	Wines from Curico and Talca.
Portugal:	Dao or Colares wines.
Yugoslavia:	Plavac.
Hungary:	Egri Bikaver.

These wines can be kept six to eight years; certain Bordeaux and Burgundies keep even longer. Only tasting can determine the condition and maturity of the wine.

Great red wines

This list is limited to wines from the best vineyards. They are generally quite costly but have the advantage of keeping longer.

Burgundy:	Chambertin or one of the other great wines from the Gevrey-Chambertin region; Bonnes Mares (Côte de Nuits); Corton (Côte de Beaune); Musigny; Clos-de-Vougeot; Romanée Conti or one of the other great wines from Vosné-Romanée.
Bordeaux:	Château Margaux or one of the great classified wines from Margaux; Château Lafitte or one of the great classified wines from Pauillac; Château Montrose or one of the great classified wines from Saint-Estèphe; Château Ausone or another superior Saint-Emilion; Château Haut-Brion or another superior red Graves.
Italy:	Barolo, Vino Nobile de Montepulciano.
Austria:	Oggauer Blaufränkisch Alte Reserve.
Germany:	Ihringer Blankenhornsberg.

The great red wines can be kept for over ten years but, apart from very exceptional wines, not longer than fifteen. The best vintages should be chosen, bearing in mind that these vary from one wineproducing region to another.

SAMPLE CELLAR STOCKS

1. Those who like vin rosé should choose from the following list

Germany: Assmannhäuser Höllenberg, Durbacher Schlossberg Weissherbst Auslese, Ihringer Jesuitengarten, Burgunder Weissherbst Auslese.
Austria: Schloss Kirchberg.
France: Tavel (rosé), Sancerre (rosé), Cabernet d'Anjou, Brégançon (Provence).
Italy: Chiareto del Garda, Cagarino, Ravello.
Switzerland: Œil-de-Perdrix (Neuchâtel).

All these wines should be drunk young as they rarely keep longer than three years.

2. For those who like Pinot

Here is a selection of wines made from the famous Pinot grape which is cultivated throughout Europe as well as in South Africa and California.

a) Pinot Noir (Blauburgunder, Spätburgunder)

Germany: Oberingelheimer Sonnenberg Spätburgunder (Rheinhesse), Ihringer Winklerberg (Baden), Assmannshäuser Höllenberg (Rheingau).
Switzerland: Dôle (Valais), Duc de Rohan Pinot Noir (Bündner Herrschaft), Auvernier Pinot Noir (Neuchâtel).
France: All the red Burgundies from Côte de Nuits and Côte de Beaune (see lists on pages 90-91).
Italy: Pinot Nero (Trentino).
Roumania: Dealne Mare.
Yugoslavia: Burgundac crni.
California: Pinot Noir or Red Pinot.

b) Pinot Gris (Ruländer in Germany and Austria), Tokay in Alsace and eastern Switzerland, Szürkebarat in Hungary, Malvoisie in Valais.

Germany: Durbacher Herrenberg (Baden), Bickensohler Steinfelsen (Kaiserstuhl).
Austria: Ruster Ruländer (Burgenland).
Switzerland: Malvoisie (Valais), Malauser Tokajer (Grisons).
Italy: Pinot grigio (Trentino).
Hungary: Badacsonyi Szürkebarat (Lake Balaton).
Yugoslavia: Ljutomer Rulendac sivi (Slovenia).

c) Pinot Blanc (Weisser Burgunder in Germany) or Pinot Chardonnay.

Germany: Blankenhornsberger Weissburgunder (Kaiserstuhl), Ihringer Winklerberg (Ihringen).
Austria: Undhof Wieden Weissburgunder (Wachau), Kloster-Cabinet Weissburgunder (Klosterneuburg).
France: Montrachet, Meursault, Chablis and Pouilly-Fuissé.
Italy: Pinot bianco (Trentin).
Yugoslavia: Collio, Burgundac Bijeli (Slovenia).
South Africa: White Pinot.

3. A cellar for Riesling enthusiasts

Germany: Rüdesheimer Schlossberg (Rheingau), Wehlener Sonnenuhr (Moselle), Diedesheimer Leinhöhle (Rheinpfalz), Oppenheimer Sackträger (Rheinhesse), Durbacher Schlossberg (Baden).
Austria: Kremser Kögl, Dürnsteiner Hollerin.
Switzerland: Goût du Conseil (Valais).
France: Riesling d'Alsace.
California: Johannisberg-Riesling.
South Africa: Paarl-Riesling.
Chile: Coquinto-Riesling.
Australia: Quelltaler Hock.

4. A cellar for those specializing in rare or unusual wines

Each wineproducing area has its specialities whose fame sometimes never crosses local boundaries. Travellers and gourmets often appreciate these rarities, choosing them according to the countries they visit and the discoveries made.

Some of these delightful and little-known wines are listed below as a starting point for those who will doubtless add discoveries of their own.

Germany: Wines with the mention "Trockenbeerenauslese" or "Eiswein", Durbacher Herrenberg (Baden), Assmannshäuser Höllenberg Rotwein Edelbeerenauslese (Rheingau).
Austria: Ruster Ausbruch (Burgenland): very sweet.
Switzerland: Réze (*vin de glacier*, Valais), Malanser Completer (Grisons), Païen (Traminer de Visperterminen, Valais).
France: Château-Chalon (young wine from the Jura). Romanée (the rarest of the great red wines from Burgundy, only 2,500 litres produced each year). White Musigny (the rarest of the great white wines from Burgundy, only 800 litres produced each year).
Italy: Falerno (red), the wine extolled by Horace. Cinqueterre (white), praised by Pliny, Petrarch and D'Annunzio. Marsala vergini.
Spain: A wine from Los Moriles (sherry type with a nutty flavour).
Portugal: An authentic vintage port of 1921, 1927, 1931, 1935, 1943, 1945 or 1947.
Cyprus: Commandaria (a sweet wine).

5. Other Suggestions

Some people favour specializing in wines from a certain geographical region. A cellar can be stocked with Rhône wines, ranging from the Canton of Valais to the Côtes du Rhône, or Rhine wines coming from the Swiss Canton of Grisons to the Rheingau. Some people concentrate on wines from Italy, as they are readily available in most places. Further suggestions are given in the second part of this book.

Apart from a conventional basic stock, it is a good idea to lay in a few bottles of some wine that is relatively unknown locally. It makes a good conversation piece as well as a pleasant change for visitors to have something different from the well-known bottles seen every day in the main street windows or the supermarket.

TASTING WINE

Without some kind of basic plan and a few tips from the experts it is difficult to envisage stocking up a cellar, however humble the outlay may be. Beginners should not let themselves be daunted by the prospect for, although in terms of commercial investment the buying price will not grow very quickly, the pleasure of drinking a wine which has been bought and nurtured until it is ready and fully matured is beyond price.

Despite the work of oenologists and the studies of renowned scientists on the inherent properties of wines, particularly great wines, and notwithstanding the results of intensive research by eminent biologists and even mathematicians, wine still retains a good part of its mystery and wine-tasting has not yet been elevated to the level of a science or even a technique. It is still essentially an art.

Nonetheless, the professional wine-taster is guided by certain established and accepted rules and codes. He is ethically bound to subdue his own personal tastes and preferences and endeavour to be as objective as is humanly possible, for his is the duty of pronouncing judgements which could have far-reaching consequences, and for which he will be held personally and professionally responsible. Such strict measures of quality and criticism are the only means by which a norm or standard can be made acceptable to producers and tasters alike.

All the considerations taken into account by the professional, exaggerated as they may appear to the uninitiated, are distilled here into simple, practical hints. The professional aids to wine selection are interesting to know but not absolutely necessary to someone who merely wishes to discover a good wine to his liking. This chapter only aims to guide the amateur through the maze of intricate but infinitely evocative and pleasurable paths that lead to familiarity with wine. As Boileau, Provost of Paris in the thirteenth century, observed, "He who knows not how to drink knows nothing."

TOUCH AND HEARING

It has been argued that the effects of touch and hearing are due more to imagination than anything else, although the pleasant feeling of a fine crystal glass or a silver goblet held between the fingers, and the sound of its delicate ring in the half-light of an echoing cellar, undoubtedly enhance the drinker's pleasure. Actually, touch does in fact play a very real part in the appreciation of wine. It is neither pretentious nor exaggerated to talk of "tactile tasting" in describing the

sensations perceived by the various parts of the mouth which are capable of judging the wine's consistency, its fluidity or viscosity, both valuable clues to quality described as the "architectural relief of wine". And as a certain Monsieur Orizet, well known for his appreciation of the elixirs of the grape and of his own eloquence, once remarked "To what else but our sensations of touch can we attribute our reactions when we describe a wine as harsh, round, supple, tender, thin or velvety?" In a more modest way, hearing also contributes to determining the quality of wine, if only in detecting latent fermentation by holding the glass up to the ear.

SIGHT TEST

The first gesture the wine-taster makes is to raise his filled glass to the light of day. This inspection yields valuable insight into the quality of the wine.

White wine, which should be bottled young and not have been exposed to coloration from a prolonged sojourn in wood, should appear clear and gleam with a whiteness tinted slightly green. There are exceptions to the rule, of course, such as the yellow wines from Arbois and the pale amber of Sauternes. It is also recognized that all the great white wines assume a delicate golden hue over the years. As far as young wines are concerned, an indefinite or murky colour always denotes the presence of some disease or defect while a yellowish tint betrays oxidization, resulting in a sweet, pervasive flavour which only very few people consider as a virtue. But the taster should not attach too much importance to clarity alone: a non-filtered wine can still be of excellent quality.

Sight as well as hearing can detect the tiny gas bubbles which, if they cloud the wine to any appreciable extent, are probably due to a second fermentation. On the other hand, there are some naturally slightly sparkling wines, known as such, whose mild effervescence does not affect their clarity. Many Swiss white wines have this slight effervescence, often depending on how long they have been bottled, as do some of the wines from France and neighbouring countries. Agreeable though it may be, this sparkle can sometimes conceal a certain mediocrity. In the case of red wines, it is rarer and less highly esteemed, although it certainly gives some wines, such as the delicious Valpolicella, a very special charm.

As far as rosé is concerned, the appearance of the wine is very important. From the rose-pink Tavel to the pale red of Côtes de Toul, the colour range is infinite, the more so because with the growing fashion for this wine, many vineyards are now beginning to produce rosé. It should not be too pale in colour as this is both unattractive and often indicates dubious production methods.

None of these observations applies to very new wines which are naturally clouded by a large quantity of lees. Even at this stage, however, a great deal can be learned by visual examination. Moreover, any healthy wine will clear rapidly if allowed to do so.

As far as red wines are concerned, visual inspection is very important and provides valuable hints to quality, age and even origin. The depth of colour, dependent on the species of grape and the length of time the grapes were left to ferment, decreases with time. But whether it be muted, as in the case of Beaujolais, or deep ruby as in Châteauneuf-du-Pape, or even richer in colour for a young Bordeaux, the colour should be pure and true. A good bright red, tending towards cherry-red, usually denotes good quality. Tints of purplish blue, on the other hand, can be a sign of hybrid or mixed wine. The "robe" of a red wine, to use the experts' term for colour, is of the greatest significance. Visual examination also enables the trained eye to detect various diseases, such as casse, and even to differentiate between the various kinds of the disease—brown, blue, ferrous and so on. An experienced taster will be able to diagnose the grease disease, which makes wine oily and ropy, or the *tourne* which betrays its presence by silky ripples when the liquid is agitated. Especially in the case of red wines, a sight test also gives a good indication of whether or not a wine is mature or on the decline.

A GOOD NOSE

"A good nose for wine" should not always be interpreted as a derogatory expression. One of the classic gestures of the wine-taster is to swirl the wine around the glass before raising it to his nostrils. There is good reason for this ritual. The wine, gently swirling, spreads a thin coating of liquid over the upper walls of the glass so that a greater surface of the wine is exposed to the air, resulting in maximum evaporation of the odoriferous substances. This procedure is of paramount importance for, as everyone knows, a wine's "bouquet" determines its character.

At this stage, great powers of discernment and a good memory are required by the taster to recall the characteristics of all the wines he has ever tasted before and all the aromas that have ever been encountered by his nasal passages. It is by smell that he can recognize native tangs and the approximate region of the vineyard, the aroma being closely linked to the type of grape planted in a specific soil.

The primary aroma of a must before aromatic fermentation is essentially a product of the type of grape: it is particularly distinctive, for instance, in the juice from muscat grapes. After fermentation is complete, good new wines exude a multitude of scents constituting the secondary aromas, some flowery, some fruity. These fragrances of iris, violet, rose, lime, blackcurrant, apple, cherry, strawberry and raspberry have led to the designation of new wines as "fruity". Subsequently, through the slow and mysterious alchemy that nature brings to bear, first in the casks and later in the bottle, the wine gradually becomes transformed, the primary and secondary perfumes dwindling, becoming less identifiable, and mingling at last into the final "bouquet", more discreetly floral in character and exuding a whole new range of aromas whose synthesis enables the connoisseur to recognize the wine, its origin and its year. In this final bouquet, which lingers on until the wine begins to deteriorate, the wine-lover will recall many familiar odours such as coffee, Russian leather, amber, truffles and even fowl droppings, as described by vinegrowers of the Médoc.

It is sometimes as well to reserve judgement on those wines which seem to flatter the palate at the first sip but which may, like new-found friends, reveal a lack of sincerity on deeper acquaintance. Most of the great wines only slowly and gradually divulge their true characters as the bottle empties, which explains why producers of red Graves used to declare that their wines should only be judged after the third glass. Although perhaps exaggerated, this sentiment was the sincere distillation of long years of experience.

THE TASTE

Tasting is actually the last and most important stage in judging a wine. The most logical one of all, indeed, since wine is intended to be consumed. After the wine-taster has examined the wine and explored its aromas, he sips and rolls the wine around his mouth.

Strictly speaking, the tongue plays the leading rôle in tasting, but the tongue can only distinguish between the four basic tastes, namely acidity, bitterness, saltiness and sweetness, all other nuances of tastes being but variations of these primary four. Schools of wine-tasting test their trainees' natural aptitudes by presenting them with these four basic tastes.

Bitterness is detected at the back of the tongue; saltiness and sweetness by the tongue's tip and sides. Acidity is recognized by the centre and the sides of the tongue. Simultaneously, fragrance and the subtleties of flavour are discerned by the olfactory cells and swell the harmonic symphony of sensations experienced by the taster who should, by now, be ready to pronounce judgement. If he is a well-trained expert, he will be able to determine the alcoholic strength of the wine, define the amount of reducing sugars, the total acidity and the volatile acidity, if this is present to any marked degree, with only a small margin of error. He should be able to express his opinion as to the wine's quality although subjective factors will inevitably colour his judgement, however objective he may strive to be.

Many are the tales extolling the extraordinary tasting powers of certain palates. Paul Mounet, member of the Comédie-Française, brother of Mounet-Sully and a native of Bergerac, the Dordogne town famed for its wine and truffles, was said to be capable of telling the age and vineyard of any great wine even when blindfolded. It is a pity to debunk such stories but this one is scarcely credible. The worthy gentleman may well have successfully performed such a feat once, or even on several occasions, but the wines in question were very likely those of a distinctive type and ones with which Mounet was already reasonably familiar. Furthermore, probably only one or two wines were submitted to him at any one time, thus husbanding the sensitivity of his palate.

Correct and unerring recognition of the origin and year of a wine is really only possible on a local or, at the most, a regional scale by an inhabitant of the region. Obviously a wineproducer in Beaujolais, accustomed to sampling all the different local wines each season, is able to recognize wines from the various vineyards in his area and even to distinguish between those of individual producers which, although made from the same type of grape, can differ to a considerable extent. Although identification of new wines is relatively simple, the process becomes very much more difficult in the case of fully matured ones.

In any case, as a certain Monsieur de la Palice once so rightly remarked, a wine must be tasted to be known. And who can possibly have tasted every wine? Hence the necessity for the professional taster to specialize in only various types of wines.

PRACTICAL ADVICE

A few words are in order concerning the physical and material circumstances surrounding the ritual of tasting. It has been established beyond doubt that the taster's state of health, the time of day and even the general ambiance will all affect his reactions. His state of health is particularly important and even so slight an indisposition as a cold can seriously impair the judgement. In my early days, I remember that I would often seek the advice of an old wine merchant whose sureness of palate I had always admired. After several years it seemed to me that the old man's judgements

were less accurate, until one day we found ourselves in complete contradiction on certain points. Extremely awed by the old gentleman and not daring to contradict him outright, I solicited the opinions of his acquaintances and learned that for some time he had had diabetes, undoubtedly the cause of his failing acumen.

The best time for tasting is usually at the end of the morning, just before the midday meal, when most people begin to feel the first stirrings of appetite. The mental state as well as the general surroundings are of great importance. Some interesting experiments have been made on the effects of external influences such as light, temperature and even ambient noise and it has been found that the same taster can experience different reactions depending on the colour of the light, the temperature of the room and whether tasting took place in silence or to the accompaniment of music.

As far as the amateur is concerned, the essential requirement for serious tasting is total concentration and any noise should be discouraged. Tasting should take place in daylight or, if this is not possible, the light should be white and non-fluorescent. In a cellar, the clarity and brilliance of the wine is best judged by candlelight. If the wine-lover is seriously interested in determining the wine's quality for future reference, he should abstain from eating all those tempting titbits such as cheese, nuts and canapés which are habitually offered round on such occasions. The least of all evils is a small piece of dry bread.

The importance of the type of glass cannot be overestimated. It should preferably be of crystal with a very fine rim, barrel-shaped or in the form of a chalice. The washing of the glasses is a very important factor and one that gives rise to many difficulties. The increasing habit of putting everything into dishwashing machines which use detergents can result in a pervasive taste clinging to the glass which can fundamentally affect the taste of the wine. Certain tasters insist on their glasses being rinsed in distilled water while professionals always carry their own silver tasting cup, although this is definitely less acceptable than a fine crystal glass, especially for white wines.

Wine should not be tasted in an over-heated or a very cold room. The ideal temperature is between 20° and 22° centigrade (around 68° to 70° F.). Naturally, any manufactured or natural perfumes must be avoided and even vases of flowers should be abandoned on the day of the tasting. A strongly flavoured toothpaste or tobacco smoke can be ruinous.

Tasting may be a complicated art but it is also much more pleasant and rewarding than is generally thought. As Paul Claudel, French diplomat and writer, so eloquently proclaimed, "... wine is the professor of taste, the liberator of the spirit, and the light of intelligence..."

GLOSSARY OF WINE-TASTING TERMS

Acid	excessively sharp taste
Aromatic	smooth, subtle and pleasant aroma, usually "grapey"
Astringent ...	excessive tannin, harsh on the palate
Attractive	light, fresh, easy to drink
Austere	under-developed; often applicable to bouquet of a fine wine expected to develop
Bitter	flavour sometimes met in the aftertaste; usually a sign of ill health in the wine
Body	the weight of a wine in the mouth
Bouquet	scent or smell of good wine; often characteristic
Clean	fresh, unalloyed taste
Complete	well-built and balanced, fragrant and agreeable
Corked	tasting of cork, unpleasantly musty
Dainty	fresh and fruity
Delicate	of good quality; just short of distinguished
Distinguished	of the highest quality in all respects
Dumb	under-developed as yet
Fading	deteriorating in quality but still drinkable
Fiery	goes to the head quickly, often a sign of too much alcohol for true balance
Fine	elegant, distinguished, with a delicate bouquet
Firm	rather hard and pungent but well-built
Flabby	unattractive, lacking in body and natural acidity
Flat	dull, lifeless, insipid flavour
Fleshy	full-bodied, rich with good general consistency
Fresh	having the fruitiness and qualities of young wine
Fruity	mellow, fragrant; fleshy quality derived from, but not generally tasting of, ripe grapes
Full	rich, fleshy, well-knit with a clean taste
Generous	strong, robust, invigorating, full of flavour
Goût de terroir	a characteristic earthy taste of wine from specific vineyards
Green	young, sharp and acid (not vinegary)
Hard	excessive tannin, lacking in smoothness and fruit
Harsh	rough, astringent, catches the tongue
Heady ...:..	fiery and aromatic, high alcohol content
Heavy	unctuous and full-bodied, containing much "extract"
Light	pale in colour, moderate strength, well-balanced
Lively	vigorous, acid, pleasantly pungent effect on nose and palate
Long	descriptive of a great wine, well-sustained flavour and aroma
Madérisé	having acquired the yellowish-brown tint and smoky, burnt taste of Madeira, due to heat and oxygen
Massive	full-bodied, powerful, spirited, rich
Mellow	soft and smooth, mature
Noble	with the distinctive characteristics of its origin
Nose	term applied to a wine with a fine bouquet
Ordinary	undistinguished, of indefinite origin
Perfumed ...	powerfully scented
Rich	silky, smooth, well rounded
Robust	rich, full, good consistency and alcoholic strength
Round	full-bodied, well balanced and mellow
Sharp	slightly over acid with a tartness that stings the palate
Short	ephemeral taste, lacking in persistence
Sinuous	lively, fresh, vigorous, promising to mature well
Sound	a healthy wine with good lasting qualities
Sweet	very sugary, full, noticeable glycerine quality but pleasant in taste
Thin	lacking in body and strength (usually wines from poor years)
Unbalanced ..	lack of harmony between physical constituents and aesthetic elements
Velvety	fine, full, silky and particularly soft in texture
Vinous	full-bodied, good alcoholic strength, plenty of grip, fruit and strength of character
Well-knit	balanced, robust and harmonious in all respects
Young	raw, harsh and under-developed (not a fault)

USEFUL TERMS FOR DESCRIBING WINE

	Qualities	Defects
General Character	Robust, well-built, rich, full, fleshy, velvety, clean, well-knit, dainty, rugged.	Thin, harsh, ill-balanced, acid, sour, austere, short, mediocre.
Colour	Sumptuous, ruby, amber-coloured, clear, lively, brilliant.	Faded, cloudy, over-strong.
Flavour and Strength	Lively, sinuous, noble, massive, full, heady, stout, robust.	Flabby, flat, light, cold.
Sugar Content	Dry, sweet, mellow, liqueurish.	Ill-balanced, flat, raw, rugged, insipid.
Bouquet	Fruity, fine, flowery, scented.	Short, dull, corked, fading.

FOR DRINKING

PIERRE ANDRIEU

The drinking glass appears only relatively late in the history of mankind. It was certainly known by the Egyptians and Phoenicians; the glass-works of Sidon and Alexandria were famous. The origin of glass itself is obscure. A French authority on the subject, J. Girardin, once wrote, "Chance played a considerable rôle in the invention of glass. However, it is difficult to believe the writings of Pliny the Elder in this connection. According to him, the Phoenician soda merchants, having landed on the banks of the River Balus, there prepared their meals. For lack of anything better, they used slabs of natron with which to steady the cooking pots. But during the cooking process the slabs melted and the sand underneath was turned into glass. Obviously, considering the high temperatures required, glass as we know it today could never have been produced in the circumstances reported by Pliny."

Whatever its origins, the Persians were already using glass receptacles during the reign of Alexander the Great, and archaeologists have discovered ancient Egyptian flasks containing evidence of their use for wine. It was probably around 1800 B.C. that the Phoenicians started to make the glassware that graced Roman tables during the reign of Nero, and in the first century A.D. glass-works were established in Gaul and Spain. Egypt, especially the region around Alexandria, supplied most of the very expensive and sometimes coloured crystal glass during this period. It is very surprising to discover in ancient writings that these crystal glasses and goblets did not break when they were dropped. François Carnot, a noted glass expert, has drawn attention to the fact that these were probably the first blow-moulded glass articles. "They were very slowly cooled in the mould," he wrote, "thereby producing a toughened glass." Manufacture developed rapidly and, all over the territory occupied during the Roman Conquest, small cups, flasks and other glass vessels are found interred in graves with the ashes of their owners.

Apart from the jewel-encrusted goblets or wine cups in gold and silver, served at the palace tables of emperors and kings, the first tableware made for a prosperous clientele was in copper. The designs on the Greek and Roman vessels were admirably wrought and featured heads of contemporary gods such as Bacchus, vine leaves, bunches of grapes and similar appropriate designs in relief.

On the other hand, the metal specimens remaining from the pre-Roman era in Gaul, such as bronze and pottery vessels, are much simpler in design although their shape is not without elegance. At Celtic feasts, beer, mead or wine were served in horns. Wild ox horns, often richly ornamented with gold and silver trimmings, were particularly favoured and continued in use throughout the Merovingian era; they are even mentioned up to the fifteenth century. Another somewhat macabre drinking vessel was made from a human skull, either, so the historians claim, that of an enemy killed in battle or of some ancestor. It was considered a great honour for a guest to be invited to drink from a skull, and in order to qualify for such a privilege he had to have killed an enemy in battle.

Glass-making was already flourishing in Roman times, as may be seen from this carafe, goblet and drinking glass, all vessels made for wine.

For less ceremonial, family gatherings, earthenware cups or bowls were used, each guest serving himself by dipping his cup into an earthenware pot placed on the table or on the ground, a custom not far removed from our punch bowl.

From King Dagobert's solid gold wine cup to the gilded silver ostrich egg facsimile belonging to Charles V, many bizarre, opulent or unusual drinking vessels were created according to the fashion of the day or to satisfy the whims and wit of those who ordered these personal expressions of their eccentricities.

Among these memorable historic vessels was the richly decorated goblet encrusted with diamonds belonging to Good King René of Anjou. It held three pints, a fair draught of wine in any age. As curios or merely specimens of extremely fine craftsmanship, these examples of early glass now fetch very high prices as collectors' pieces on the world's markets, on those rare occasions when they change hands.

During the Middle Ages, glass drinking vessels, oddly enough, disappeared for several centuries from some regions, becoming so rare that two guests often shared

Roman wine receptacles were very varied as may be seen from these exhibits in the Mouton-Rothschild Museum in the Bordeaux region of France. In the background, on the right, a Syro-roman "bubble" flagon; on the left, a Turkish jug (fifteenth to sixteenth century) and, below it, a Persian earthenware bottle (twelfth to thirteenth century). In the foreground are two examples of twelfth-century Persian pottery.

one glass. At this period, the window-glass makers, producers of a coarse green glass, occasionally turned out a few small goblets with inverted conical bases, but these were rather rare. The outside surfaces carried ornamental tracery and arabesque patterns, decoration achieved by sticking coarse glass threads on to the first blown shape.

Glassware certainly proliferated during the Renaissance, when the craft attained its peak under the Italian influence. Glass-makers established themselves over all the wooded regions of France such as Normandy, Lorraine, Nevers, Orleans, Poitou, Dauphiné and Provence. Although recognized as Guilds of Gentlemen, they were inclined to be nomadic, moving on when their local fuel supply of wood or bracken ran out. From the sixteenth century onwards, they often intermarried with glass-making families from Murano and Altare brought from Italy by the French nobility. The glass they made differed markedly from region to region. Amber glass came from Provence; a bluish variety from the Margeride region, marbled in appearance and lined with white, pale blue or dark red enamel; and rose-coloured glasses from Burgundy and Nevers, although these unfortunately often "threw out their salt and spoilt the wine". From each place came glasses of different shape, colour and design with simple or elaborate decoration in jewels or multi-coloured enamels. "Bell-shaped goblets" and the hanaps made in the forests of Chamborant around 1340 by a certain Guionet are no longer to be found, and rare indeed are examples of pre-Renaissance glassware.

Renewed interest in the use of glass drinking vessels stemmed from the Arabs and, to a great degree, the glass-makers of Damascus who produced very fine enamelled glasses from the thirteenth to the fifteenth century. Contrary to the generally accepted belief, the Venetians copied the delightfully designed glasses which their seafarers brought from the far coasts. Famous as shrewd merchants and shippers, the burghers of Venice traded in this glassware and established the celebrated Venetian glass industry. They had greater success than their counterparts in other countries, since they were able to improve on the original production methods. They were also more skilled in applying gold, and their enamelling was more delicate. The Venetian pearl-workers, accustomed to working with minute pearls, wielded the sticks of enamel with a light and delicate touch. The beautiful Venetian goblets or decanters are superb works of art and were reserved for the tables of sovereigns and high dignitaries.

Two specimens of seventeenth-century glasses from the Lower Rhine. The one on the right is reminiscent of the *Römer* in general shape and by the superposition of two elements, in this example a cone on a cylinder, moulded separately. The drinking vessel on the left is made of green glass in the form of a small barrel.

By the sixteenth century the Venetians' skill in making glass had progressed to the point of producing white glass so pure and clear that it was called "crystalline" or "Venetian crystal". During the same period they manufactured a more ordinary "fern glass", so called because of the engraved design on its sides. It is only fair to mention that the famous works of Murano were founded by Greek workers who took refuge in Venice, after the fall of Constantinople.

These ordinary glasses were not always highly esteemed and pedlars, heedless of possible breakages, hawked their wares through town and countryside, the streets echoing to the refrain,

> Lovely glasses, pretty glasses,
> Beer glasses, a penny a pair.

In the sixteenth century the influence of the Venetian glass-makers spread to Holland. Here, as in most other countries, the glass-works were installed by natives from the City of the Doges. In Holland, already recognized as the home of the diamond cutter, glassware was decorated with fine engravings of arms and other heraldry, cut into the glass with a diamond point. During the eighteenth century some of these engravers perfected a new type of stippling.

Silver drinking mugs were very practical when travelling, hunting or eating out of doors, a whole set easily nesting one inside the other. These were German cups personalized with engravings of the owners' names and with various decorative motifs.

These two elegant glasses are made in a shape which was popular throughout Germany in the eighteenth century. Their fine engraving and delicate lines are in striking contrast to the glasses on the facing page. Admirable though they are as collection items, all the drinking vessels shown on these pages are ill suited to modern requirements.

389

From the sixteenth century on, the Venetians were past masters in the art of glass-making, enamelling and relief ornamentation. The oval drinking cup, above, in engraved agate dates from the late sixteenth century. Emeralds set in enamelled gold and silver give it a regal air. The seventeenth-century Venetian flute glasses (left) are worthy of any collector's pride—or envy.

The two nautilus cups on the facing page bear witness to the consummate artistry of German goldsmiths and silversmiths in the seventeenth century. Splendid show pieces as they may be, they are scarcely suitable as vessels for drinking wine.

Across the Channel, glasses were designed with a very heavy cap-shaped base, but the stem became finer as time went on. Small bubbles of air were sometimes purposely trapped inside the crystal, resulting in an original effect in the play of light. Some of the glasses were also ornamented with filigree work. Towards the end of the seventeenth century the English discovered their own special type of crystal by adding barium of lead to the glass. Compared to Venetian glass, crystal produced in Britain was heavy, but fickle fashion, perennial follower of the newly created or novel, developed a taste for the heavy, pure glass, with dire effects on the Venetian glass-making industry. The English shipped their glass to Holland for engraving, not by the diamond method but with a small wheel, a technique demanding considerable solidity in the glass.

Jacobean engraved glasses, glasses for religious ceremonies and those used on board sailing vessels were particularly conspicuous because of their short stem and their solid, heavy base.

In Silesia, as in Bohemia, crystal with a potash base was generally used, while engraving was replaced by mouldings on the outside of glasses which were lavishly ornamented in gold and often delicately etched. Occasionally landscapes were painted in black, and all over Germany examples of enamelled glassware, not without artistic merit, could be found. In Bohemia the method of tinting glass with purple by means of gold salts was discovered and these glasses were often further enhanced by designs interwoven with purple and gold.

At the invitation of Catherine the Great, the Silesian glass-makers set up a factory near Moscow, bringing

Passglas: to reduce the measures of wine staked during card games, these glasses were divided into sections, each corresponding to one game.

The numerous fiefs that split Germany during the seventeenth century gave rise to endless disputes over inheritances. On these emblazoned glasses, the feudal lord asserted his properties, his territorial claims and even the territory he hoped to acquire.

392

The best glasses are those that allow the maximum development and appreciation of the wine's qualities. A clear white tulip glass is ideal for most wines. It should be slightly larger for red Burgundies than for red Bordeaux and in general rather larger for red wines than for whites. For sparkling wines some prefer the *flûte* but for Champagne the tulip glass is better. The wines of Alsace and Anjou are drunk from traditionally shaped glasses set on high stems, white Swiss wines from glass tumblers and the wines of the German Rhineland from the *Römer*.

with them experience and skill acquired in Bohemia, which could again be traced back to the Venetians.

Spanish glass was not unnaturally first influenced by that from the Arab countries resulting in glassware with garish, ill-assorted colours. Venetian craftsmen subsequently transformed the yellow Spanish glass by giving it a delicate crackle finish and enlarging the coloured scrolls favoured by their predecessors.

During the sixteenth century, Venetian glass-makers installed their first works at Antwerp, in Flanders. Early in the seventeenth century they opened another in the Principality of Liége. These yellowish glasses were usually tall, decorated with masks and blue beaded designs. The enamelled varieties always bore the distinctive sign of a lily of the valley.

Although Louis XIV owned five magnificent goblets in rock crystal, this noble material fell from favour during the eighteenth century and was replaced on royal and lordly tables by Bohemian glass which was also produced in France. At Tourlaville in the region of Cherbourg, at Saint-Louis, Montcenis, Baccarat and Sèvres, still renowned today for its fine table-ware, crystal-works sprang up and thrived. Cafés and *bistros* had also to be supplied and so bar or counter glasses for serving spirits were produced — "trick" glasses, really, as their shape and thickness gave the impression of holding much more than they actually did.

The well-known "hock" glasses with their graceful long stems surmounted by a bulbous cup, the *Römer* as they are called in German, were manufactured at Cologne. Here, the other typical glasses were also made with scrolls and enamelled serpents' heads.

Bavarian enamelled glasses were well suited to the renowned capacity of their users. They provided ample space for portraying the full Imperial Eagle as well as the armorial bearings of all the states under the Emperor. In celebration of the Augsburg peace treaty, glasses were designed bearing the portraits of the French, German and Swedish monarchs, Catholics on one side of the glass and Protestants on the other, all receiving the Lord's blessing and embrace. All such occasions gave rise to commemorative glassware and the family arms or those of the great dynasties were often used to decorate these expansive surfaces.

No discussion of European glassware is complete without mention of Saint-Louis crystal. Reported in print as long ago as 1673, the Saint-Louis glass-works were in existence under the name of Münsthal as far back as 1586. During the Thirty Years' War they were destroyed, then reborn as the "Royal Glass Works of Saint-Louis" when Lorraine came once more under French rule. "The Company of Crystal Makers of Saint-Louis", as it has been known since 1829, is the birthplace of the first crystal in France.

BOTTLES AND DECANTERS

Wine bottles are taken so much for granted today that scarcely a thought is given to their history. Actually, the custom of storing wine in glass bottles only goes back to the fifteenth century.

Glass vessels were certainly known earlier, as far back as Alexandria, Athens and Rome, but they were usually reserved for perfumes. If glass was employed at all to hold wine the vessels had an intermediate use — similar to that of our decanters — and brought the wine from wherever it was stored for serving.

Before glass bottles came into general use, ceramic or metal pots and jugs of varying artistic merit were provided by the potters or metal workers, and archaeologists have uncovered proof of their existence in Gallo-Roman time. A silver pot dating back to the first century B.C., glass goblets and bottles together with medals and coins bearing the effigy of the Emperor Trajan, a wine cup in red clay with the words *Reims Feliciter* and dating from the second or third century, a clay carafe, the lower part of its handle ornamented with a bunch of grapes, have all been excavated in the province of Champagne.

In homes in Gaul, servants brought wine to the table in earthenware or silver receptacles which resembled cooking pots. Each guest helped himself in turn with a small cup called a *cyathe*.

Froissart, the French chronicler, records that when the Earl of Douglas carried the heart of the King of Scotland to the Holy Sepulchure in 1328, there was little else in his baggage save gold bottles—though posterity is not informed as to the contents of these opulent flasks. Two silver bottles are listed in the inventory of the personal belongings of Charles V after his death. In the Louvre Museum in Paris are two beautiful gilt silver bottles bearing the arms of Henry III, exquisite in their simplicity of form and decoration, their general shape seemingly inspired by the gourd. Even King John of England used bottles in 1360, as shown by the following entry in a list of the royal expenses: "To Jehan Petit Fay, the sum of sixty sous minted at Tours for four leather bottles in which to carry water and wine for the said Sire when he is going to the country." When travelling, wine was also carried in metal flasks, usually made in silver.

In many ways, the silversmith made a considerable contribution to the development of the common wine bottle's illustrious ancestors. During the ninth century their powerful guild was granted a charter by King Charles the Bald. Previous to this, silver work appears to have been almost entirely confined to the monastery workshops. Fourteenth-century records show that

glass receptacles were beginning to compete for favour with those in precious metals. The last will and testament of a certain Jehanne of Burgundy in 1352 mentions "two small bottles in glass mounted with silver".

From the sixteenth century onwards, glass receptacles began to appear in well-to-do homes and the word "bottle" began to assume the bacchic implications which it has enjoyed ever since. Pierre de l'Estoile, in his "Diary of a Parisian Bourgeois", dubbed the Cardinal of Guise "Cardinal of the Bottles", remarking that ". . . he loved them so dearly and hardly concerned himself with anything but the delights of the kitchen of which he had so much greater knowledge and understanding than affairs of Church and State." It is better to gloss over the unhappy end of this epicurean prelate whose afflictions were so prolonged as to allow him ample time to reflect on his self-indulgent past and to be scourged with pain.

During this period, glass-making was the only manual craft to which a gentleman could turn his hand without any loss of dignity. In the glass-works, strange to relate, only the nobility had the right to blow bottles. When the glass was melted, the nobleman took the iron blow-pipe and started the operation. Savary, a duke, general and high functionary under the First Empire, noted "It behoves only a gentleman glass-maker to blow glass." This tradition can be traced back to the fourteenth century and there is evidence to prove that even the haughty Louis XIV blew glass on December 19th, 1655.

In the province of Anjou, mounted travellers used a kind of leather bottle, placed beside them on the saddle, containing a small quantity of wine for the journey. This receptacle was called a *boutille*, an early form of the French word *bouteille*. Changes in pronunciation and spelling during the gradual but wider adoption of the English language in the British Isles gave rise to that comforting form of the well-worn word, bottle. While the bottle was emerging as a form of practical packaging, most farmers and agricultural workers used earthenware receptacles or those made from other forms of fired clay. These shapes, too, were probably inspired by the gourd. Others carried their wine ration in small barrels of the same materials, decorated with pastoral or allegorical scenes.

It was only around the fifteenth century that the bottle began to assume a more elegant and practical shape, similar to that of today; but glass bottles had not yet supplanted those in metal or leather used until then. Silver bottles, engraved with the arms of the owner, were still being made in the sixteenth century.

Towards the seventeenth century, glass containers came into everyday use. They were called flagons, carafes, decanters, flasks and so on, the word *bouteille* being strictly reserved for receptacles containing wine. Although other forms of containers abounded, bearing heraldic devices or decorative emblems, in the wine cellar and the church the bottle reigned supreme. Such bottles were designed with a broad base and, in order to minimize the effect of sediment on the contents, the bottom of the bottle was recessed inwardly, a device that had already been employed by goldsmiths and silversmiths in the Middle Ages.

Until the end of the eighteenth century, goblets and drinking glasses did not form part of the table setting, but remained on the sideboard together with whatever contained the wine. It was customary to signal to a servant who filled the glass, brought it to the table on a small tray, waited while it was drunk and then returned

Despite the gradual appearance of glass, earthenware containers for wine have never altogether disappeared. Light wine regains the freshness of the cellar when reposing in the hollow of a cool earthenware pitcher. Shapes have altered little since ancient times. In the centre can be seen a small Roman jug dating from the third century. On the right, a rustic German pot, turned on a wheel at the beginning of the sixteenth century.

Imported or produced locally by the Romans between the years A.D. 50 and 75, this flagon was discovered in a cemetery at Barnwell in Great Britain. It was the custom in those days to bury familiar objects in the grave with the deceased. On a moulded base, the craftsman has fashioned the neck and body, blown from a single piece. Then a ball of molten glass was stuck to the body and drawn up to form a handle. The spiral decorations were applied later.

The family of Champagne bottles shown below has many members. The smallest, the split (7 oz), corresponds to a quarter of a standard bottle; the pint (14 oz) corresponds to half a standard bottle, a standard bottle (third from right) containing a quart (1 pt 11 oz) of Champagne. Next comes the magnum (2 quarts), the jeroboam (4 quarts), the rehoboam (16 quarts) and the mighty nebuchadnezzar (20 quarts). Champagne is always better from the standard or magnum bottle than from one of the smaller sizes. The bottle should be placed in an ice-bucket an hour before serving but not in the freezing compartment of the refrigerator since wine cooled too abruptly will lose its flavour. The cork should be removed gently and gradually so that the only sound one hears is a light sigh, and the wine poured into a glass shaped like a tulip or a rugby ball.

The bottles shown above belong to several different families. Starting from the left there is the Burgundy shape (bottle and half-bottle) and then the Bordeaux shape (bottle and half-bottle). A bottle contains 1 pint 9 ounces of red or white wine, a half-bottle 13 ounces. The bulging, straw-covered *fiasco* originates from Central Italy and has a capacity of about 3 ½ pints. Although usually associated with Chianti, this bottle is also used for the white wines of Orvieto. The Boxbeutel, a flat, oval bottle used in Franconia in Germany and Styria in Austria, is best-known abroad as the container for the pale green-gold coloured Steinwein.

The half-litre bottle on the left of this pair has a long neck and prominent shoulders; it is used exclusively for the Hungarian Tokay. Most other Hungarian export wine is sold in the slender bottle shown on the right, a shape now widely used but principally identified with the wines of the Moselle and the Rhine, its areas of origin. Standard Rhine and Moselle bottles have a capacity of 1 pint 5 ounces.

it to the sideboard. In surroundings of great luxury, two servants performed this service, standing on the left of the diner, one holding the glass while the other filled it from a decanter of carafe. The unconventional Marquis de Rouillac, who died in 1662, was the first member of high society to have the idea of dismissing the servants and eating in peace. Few dared to imitate him, so bottles and glasses did not cross the hallowed gap between sideboard and dining table until about 1760.

In the region of Montreuil-Bellay in Anjou, a certain number of highly interesting old bottles have been collected, such as a seventeenth-century half-bottle, called a *fillette*, and others dating from the same period in dark glass, varying in capacity and irregular in shape with the shoulder sometimes wider than the base. There are also some amusing specimens such as the "priest's bottle". These ecclesiastical gentlemen were entitled to levy a tithe in kind on the year's wine harvest, and with this in mind of course took good care to select bottles of generous cubic capacity.

In the eighteenth century, bottle shapes began to assume more slender, graceful lines, similar to those we recognize and accept today. About this time, too, French crystal began to face serious competition from England, the popularity of whose lead-glass was fast spreading, and French glass-makers were obliged to turn their production over to other products, including bottles and flagons. Owners of estates ordered their heraldic arms to be emblazoned on bottles especially blown for them, and various vintners, notably those from Liége, had their coats-of-arms represented on the bottles coming from their own cellars. By 1775, the fame of the glass-works in Ingrandes-sur-Loire, in the province of Anjou, was widespread. Its bottles were exported as far afield as America and the Indies.

In the seventeenth century it had already been discovered that the inverted conical recess in the bottom of the bottle facilitated precipitation of the sediment which forms after bottling. Being heavier than the liquid, it remained at the lowest level with little risk

At the beginning of the eighteenth century, flagons still lacked grace and slenderness. The silhouette of the English bottle on the right is still similar to that of the twelfth century. The shape of the Dutch bottle (left) was much seen at the end of the seventeenth century.

Up until the last century, merchants did not always supply the exact quantity of wine for which they charged and the buyer was often tricked by the shape of the bottle. Certainly, the "weights and measures" system of those days was rather rudimentary.

of it contaminating the wine if care is taken in handling the bottle. The bottle's neck gradually tapered up, to a certain point, leaving very little surface exposed to the air and thus helping to prevent evaporation. So the evolution of the bottle's shape was not arbitrary, but determined by good sense and experience.

In the extremely rare *Treatise on the Cultivation of Vines and the Art of Making Wine*, many notes are found relating to bottles, whose shape varied from country to country. "In England," it is noted, "the neck is short and flattened out, the body practically the same width all the way down. In France, its capacity varies, thus encouraging knavery. Some bottles have a very elongated neck, short body and deeply recessed base. All these bottles are more or less in the shape of a pear. It would be desirable that the regulations drawn up for Champagne were enforced throughout France; one would thus be sure of the quantity of wine one orders, for the buyer often sees

only the shape of the bottle and is misled as to its contents. For example, the ordinary bottle does not even hold three-quarters of a pint whereas, according to the law of equity, it should contain a pint. Therefore the buyer is always cheated to a greater or lesser extent, as he cannot be in Champagne."

During the eighteenth century the bottle came into general use. While Louis XV was on the throne, one thousand one hundred and four bottles, large and small, with or without coats-of-arms, were counted at the house of Mlle Desmares, evidence that the bottle had, at last, been granted the "freedom of the city" on the tables of the world, in the homes of rich and poor alike.

During the greater part of the nineteenth century, the shrewder wine merchants turned topical events and personalities to good account by having special bottles designed in unexpected shapes. Among the more popular were a cockerel, an umbrella, a grenadier, the Eiffel Tower, a pipe, a lantern, a dwarf holding a pistol,

The bottles of times past were heavier yet more fragile than the containers of today and perhaps even more handsome and attractive.

the heads of eminent French politicans such as Gambetta and General Boulanger and a beatified Joan of Arc.

The famous Belgian wine connoisseur, Maurice des Ombiaux, however, seemed to care little what shape the bottle might be when he wrote, "I like to see a bottle of Médoc or Pauillac with its stamped cork, a dusty bottle of old Vougeot over which several generations of spiders have spun their gossamer, or the bottle covered with tide-marks from the winter's floods. But, also, I like to contemplate the ruby of a St. Emilion, the purplish-brown of a Nuits, the sea-green of a Pouilly, the corn yellow of a Sauternes, the gold of a Meursault or the straw yellow of an Arbois through the faceted crystal of a decanter. What greater pleasure for the eyes can there be than the tints which Bacchus has bestowed on his nectars?"

LABELS

In the first century, during the time when Gaius Petronius was proconsul in Bethany, wine was kept in two-handled jugs called amphoras. Corks being as yet unknown, the neck was closed with a plaster stopper or a plug of oil-soaked cloth. But even these primitive amphoras bore a mention not only of the vineyard but also of the consul in office at the time of filling.

So far, extensive research has failed to reveal any examples of labels, even handwritten ones, prior to the eighteenth century. The earliest specimens were very plain. Bereft of coats of arms or any kind of decorative design, they were simply bordered with a thin line, often drawn with pen and ruler, and stated their contents with matter-of-fact succinctness: "Vins Mousseux—1741—Claude Moët" or "Rozé—Claude et J.-R. Moët—Epernay", or "Vins vieux—1743—Claude Moët —Epernay", nothing more enlightening than that.

Later in the eighteenth century, the form of the label became more elaborate. A certain Commander Quenaidit supplies the following description: "Generally in the shape of a vertical rectangle, or trapezoid with the shorter side at the base, some with the tops rounded to a lesser or greater degree. They were very ordinary and nondescript with floral borders, like most chemists' labels of the same era. This type is still used to label samples of wine, the year and the name of the vineyard being written in the centre by hand."

The art of labelling reached its prime in the nineteenth century. Such was the proliferation of rich and luxurious symbols that they have been described as "the orchestration of a triumphant hymn to the glory of the vineyards of the world". Up until the twentieth century, liqueur labels of the same period reflected changing tastes and fashions, whereas wine labels never busied themselves, one might say, with such trivia, loftily contenting themselves, with very few exceptions, to indicating the year, the vineyard and its owner, and occasionally the wine's name.

A full study of wine labels is an immense undertaking requiring far greater space than is available here and so those used on Champagne bottles over the ages must serve as representatives of the gradual evolution.

Researchers are universally grateful to an anonymous municipal employee, long since unmindful of such earthly things, who collected Champagne labels in his youth, sticking them into an old school exercise book. Together with other collections, the fruits of his youthful zeal give us a good idea of the type of labels in use during the first half on the nineteenth century. The earliest appears to date from about 1820 and carries the name of the Chanoine brothers who decorated this label according to contemporary taste with silver lettering on a black ground. Shortly afterwards, Moët and Chandon followed suit with a similar design featuring blue lettering on white. Although this was designed for their Ay rosé wine by the painter J.-B. Isabey, it was to be the forerunner of their famous *carte bleue*. All these labels were lithographed. Early in the nineteenth century, Moët and Chandon also used a shield-shaped label which was later redesigned for their famous 1928 vintage.

In certain wineproducing areas, where vineyards were owned by individuals rather than syndicates, little attempt was made for a very long time to distinguish the produce of one vineyard from another, hence those labels so uniform and alike in appearance.

Towards 1835, the sparkling wines from Champagne were decked with labels having a coloured ground with a white or gold ornamental border composed of parallel hatchings which gradually developed into ornamental foliage, garlands and Renaissance-style fleurons. In Rheims, around 1830, the first labels for Pommery and Greno appeared. These were extremely simple, featuring only the name in black on a white ground. Roederer bordered their labels with vine leaves while Clicquot-Ponsardin favoured beautiful ornamental script. Some wineproducers believed in small labels, such as those used by Ruinart Père et Fils for their sparkling Œil de Perdrix or that chosen by Jacquesson & Fils for the sparkling Ay at about the same time. Apart from surmounting their name with a crown they seemed to think their wine needed no further introduction.

Most wine merchants at this time considered that the function of the label was merely to indicate the nature of the contents. In consequence, labels simply and unceremoniously read: "Sparkling Burgundy", "Volnay", "Vosne", "Beaune", "Romanée" with the renowned Chambertin which was spelt as "Chambetin".

This assortment of labels from the last century demonstrate how little importance producer and merchant alike attached to the appearance of the bottle, even in the case of great wines. Granted the public of those days was probably less enlightened, easier to please and placed greater trust in their suppliers. The label of Château d'Yssan, the oldest of the three, is very reticent as to the origin of its contents. The Margaux label is slightly more forthcoming, although the description is still vague. The label below suggests that the innkeeper was the only guarantor for the wine.

The name Meursault was boxed in with vine leaves or occasionally appeared, like those of Volnay and Pommard (spelt at that time with only one "m"), below a small oval picture showing the imposing gateway to a château in Burgundy.

With the Second Empire came a great variety of decorative labels, but copper-plate engraving and lithography were often abandoned in favour of rather carelessly produced glossy lithographs in colour.

Since the laws and other special legislation concerning *appellations d'origine* came into force in the 1930s the wording on most labels has been strictly controlled. However, this by no means prevented printers and designers from giving free rein to their imagination; landscapes, scenes from the grape harvest, costumes or symbolic emblems resulted in a colourful fresco, gay as the bubbles in wine, blending pictorial skills and the needs of sales promotion. Some printers specializing in labels produced what can legitimately be considered works of art. Perhaps this progress in label design was responsible for the expression that a bottle was *bien habillée*, or "well-dressed".

In Burgundy, various viticulturists and wine merchants now vie with one another to produce labels in the old-fashioned style, while taking advantage of modern techniques. In the region around Bordeaux the great number of vineyards has given rise to a plethora of labels, most of which have "the château" represented in varying degrees of importance. Some are excellent, others still content themselves with the old conventional style.

Baron Philippe de Rothschild is to be commended for his initiative in approaching the greatest artists of the day to design labels for his famous vintages. Artists like Jean Cocteau (1947), Marie Laurencin (1948), Dignimont (1949), Vertès (1951), Leonor Fini (1952), Carzou (1954), Georges Braque (1955), Salvador Dali (1958), Jacques Villon (1960) and Georges Mathieu (1961) contributed to the value of the Rothschild vintages. The labels on wines from Alsace, Provence, Roussillon, the Côtes du Rhône, the Jura and the province of Béarn also deserve honourable mentions while those from Champagne maintain a lordly grandeur. The label serves as a visiting card for the bottle's contents. It is both an advertisement and a pedigree, an indication of status, and an invitation to better acquaintance. It should attract yet impress, reflect the quality within and provide a visual foretaste of the gastronomic delights that lie in store. But, above all, it must be in keeping with the type of wine inside. It would scarcely be appropriate for a modest red wine to bear the glowing label of a vintage port, nor would a costly Chambertin be fittingly attired with the rough-and-ready label of a *vin ordinaire* to wash down a simple snack.

Labels also reflect national characteristics. The Swiss dress their bottles with typical reserve and delicacy. In France, character varies from one region to another. Alsace labels are restrained in colour, Champagne labels shine with gold, a splash of colours lights up those from Provence and Roussillon. Pouilly-Fumé, Muscadet and wines from the Loire reflect the clear sky above their homes and are circumspect in their attire. The labels of Côtes-du-Rhône shimmer with the sunshine of their birthplace, while Burgundies and Bordeaux maintain a non-committal dignity.

Spanish labels with their bright colours and bold lettering display a flamboyant nobility and Moorish richness. Rich as the wine from Oporto and sparkling as the "green wines" of their country, the Portuguese labels are as illuminated as old manuscripts. They feature saints and holy figures on stained glass windows, conquistadores portrayed in flame, blood-red and gold, as if to remind one of the accumulated riches in the treasure houses of Villanova de Gaya.

Italy surrounds its vermouths and chiantis in bright but less subtle colours. Sometimes its labels are unexpectedly quiet and subdued but this is more the exception than the rule. Those from Naples and Piedmont, Venice and Florence exude an extrovert, meridional flavour. Luxembourg labels are similar to those from Alsace and share, with the Rhine wines, the soft tints of their local skies.

Around the world, similar relationships exist between each country, its national characteristics, its wine and its labels to which, one hopes, artists will continue to contribute all their skills and imagination. They need have no fear of belittling their reputation.

WINE AND FOOD

FLAVIEN MONOD

Few housewives who pride themselves in the appearance of their home will leave it without flowers, however modest the bouquet. For very similar reasons, the master of the house will see to the proper care and stocking of his wine cellar. In both cases, it is knowledge and skill in selecting that makes the difference between an ordinary home and one brightened by a touch of colour and harmony—and the reward is the pleasure of sharing one of the joys of life.

A man's home may be his castle, as is frequently heard in Britain, but a house anywhere is a meeting place where friends and relations gather. The inside as well as the outside aspect reflects the taste of those who live there, reveals their personalities and shows to what extent they have acquired the art of living. A quick glance at the books on the shelves or the wines on the racks in the cellar can divulge many secrets. One meal may not reveal all, but it will serve to show whether the guest is made the object of special attention, with spontaneous gaiety and warmth, or whether he is merely the object of dutiful obligation.

Quite often, a posy of wild flowers or, as on the European Continent, a bunch of dried aromatic herbs is more appreciated than a sumptuous basket of flowers arranged by strange, impersonal hands, or an overflowing store-bought cornucopia. Better often the warm, lively embrace of unsophisticated family repartee and sincere cordiality than the strained conventional social conversations. In the same way, a friendly little wine with its clean, simple taste and fresh colour in a humble bottle is sometimes better received than a famous vintage, heavily labelled and pretentious, decorated with the arms of some distant nobility.

THE DAILY TABLE WINE

How would you choose an "everyday" wine to drink with the family or share with an intimate friend? What is "a wine for everyday"? And what kind of wine is suitable for drinking with meals, every day, and to offer occasionally to those friends who don't need to be impressed with a showy label? Such a wine should quench the thirst, be light enough to drink deeply from brimming glasses and have a consistently reliable quality. Above all, it should be friendly and unpretentious. There is no need here to flatter a creation from the kitchen, or raise a meal to olympian heights; but at the same time, the wine should not quarrel with a dish. It should be accommodating, jovial, sympathetic and, above all, without after effects. Therefore it will not suffice to choose just any little *vin rosé* or red wine for this purpose without prior trial or testimonial. That innocent pink blush often conceals unpleasant surprises: drowsiness, heavy heads, and confused thoughts.

A light wine does not always mean a mediocre wine, just as simplicity does not always mean foolishness. A wine without frills can be a good companion to a quick meal. It can help work go smoothly, inspire goodwill and a genial disposition, all important qualities in our age of frenzied activity.

For everyday wines, we shall consider only light young red wines here. White wines and those of famous vintages are for other occasions. Naturally, personal taste plays its part here as in everything else. Anyone who lives in a wine-producing region does not have far to look for suitable, often even excellent wines.

Nor should hybrid wines be spurned. If they are chosen carefully they can reveal many attractive qualities. As a rough guide to local taste an Italian would probably opt for a light wine from Piedmont, the Spaniard for one from Galicia, while the favourite with a Portuguese would be a Colares.

SOME SUGGESTIONS

From the wines of France, one would choose a light Médoc, Pomerol, a Beaujolais of the current year, a Côtes du Ventoux, a Châtillon en Diois, a Bourgueil or a Chinon. From Italy, Chianti or Valpolicella would fit the bill. From Spain, the choice would be one of the light reds of Galicia. If you know where to find a Swiss wine you cannot do better than ask for a Salvagnin.

FEASTS, FRIENDS AND FAMILY

Wine is the best of friends on any occasion. All over the world, the gathering of friends and family around the table on Sundays is synonymous with relaxation of body and freedom of the spirit. A family table is a friendly table and its preparation is inspired more by love, affection and friendship than by respect for form or etiquette. And to choose a wine for friends and relatives is one of those truly unselfish pleasures; pleasurable in itself, it gives pleasure to others.

In discussing the choice of wines, a few words on food are necessary. The passing years have happily eroded the habit of confusing quantity with quality, which often left guests so overstuffed as to be apoplectic and weak at the knees. A well-planned meal with a properly chosen wine should leave the wits clear and the shanks firm. Consider, for instance, a meal of hors-d'œuvres, a light entrée, a meat dish, vegetables, cheese and dessert. If the main dish is rich and heavy—a meat with a rich cream sauce, or game—then one of the other courses can be left out. Some people may also appreciate a light salad, and there is no need to fear the truism that salad does not go well with wine—this is the moment to serve a glass of fresh (but not iced) water. It is refreshing to the palate and makes a "taste interval" between the main wine and the wine served with the cheese. The dessert does not have to be a heavy dish but can be a pastry or, possibly, fresh fruit.

A simply chosen menu will influence the choice of wines. On the other hand, a very good way of choosing a menu is to plan it around some well-known wine which has reached its full and glorious maturity and thus becomes the focal point for the whole meal. The main dish is decided upon first and from this point one can go backwards and forwards through the menu. The wine can be from Burgundy, Bordeaux, Tuscany, Douro, Rioja or of even more exotic origins such as the Romanian Kadarka, the Yugoslavian Plavac, Naonassa from Greece or one of many others from all over the old and new worlds.

The most generally accepted and popular choice for the main wine is a red and if this be so then the main course should be red meat, a meat with rich sauce or a fowl. But this does not mean that a classic dry white wine cannot be served beforehand as a piquant overture. The tried and true belief that such a wine goes with such-and-such a dish still holds good. A more comprehensive guide to compatible wines and dishes can be found on pages 431-32.

FAMILY REUNIONS

Family reunions usually fall into two main classifications; those with religious overtones and those which are simply social get-togethers. In the Anglo-Saxon world families naturally gravitate together at Christmas, for New Year celebrations, wedding anniversaries, birthdays and on other traditional occasions, but in Continental Europe families meet on any pretext, even if only to enjoy a good old unrestrained gossip. Wedding breakfasts and lunches, the receptions which follow, christenings and similar celebrations are traditionally formal, restrained and discreet. Although they should not be the occasion for gastronomic over-indulgence, the food may nevertheless be excellent and the wines of top quality. In such solemn circumstances the wines should be limited to three, a white wine and two reds. The classic rule still applies: progression in strength and richness throughout the meal.

Many changes can be rung on these three basic choices. If, for example, all the wines are to be from Burgundy then a dry white and two reds, the second being of greater body, can be chosen. All the wines can be from Bordeaux or from one cellar, in which case the host's pocket and knowledge guide his choice.

MENU BASED ON BURGUNDY

Concentrating on Côtes de Beaune

White . . . Meursault, Montrachet
First red . . Pommard, Savigny
Second red . Pernand-Vergelesse, Aloxe-Corton

Concentrating on Côtes de Nuits

White . . . Clos Vougeot Blanc
First red . . Chambolle-Musigny, Fixin
Second red . Romanée-Conti, Clos-Vougeot

MENU BASED ON BORDEAUX

White . . . DRY GRAVES
First red . . MÉDOC, POMEROL
Second red . PAUILLAC, ST-ESTÈPHE, ST-EMILION

A MENU FROM YOUR OWN CELLAR

Balancing three wines from your own stock depends on the size and variety of your cellar. At times like these one wishes one had been more courageous by investing in a few more bottles! But one should not be afraid to mix the vintages. There is no reason why a Swiss or German white cannot be followed by, say, a red Italian and then a Portuguese or Spanish red.

For special occasions when an unexpected meal with wine is required (and these can occur quite frequently), the meal may well be preceded by a good *brut* Champagne; but, it must be repeated, this should be served before the meal. In exceptional circumstances, Champagne could possibly be drunk before the coffee, but to serve it immediately afterwards would be bad taste and one of the few existing deadly sins left in this permissive age.

FORMAL DINNERS OR RECEPTIONS

Wine can make or break a formal dinner. Without its noble presence the whole affair would be much less memorable or spectacular. Its inherent prestige, the way it is handled, the care with which it is chosen, sets the seal on the dignity and the importance of the occasion. The most valuable wines play their regal part in a setting of good taste, impeccable manners and a relaxed if formal atmosphere. The house is a stage set to impress the guests and establish the mood. Serving plates, dishes, and glasses, silver and linen are all proudly on view. The food has been chosen and cooked with patience and care and now the guests have assembled. When they have had time enough to make or renew aquaintanceships they proceed to their places at the table. The memory of the pre-dinner drinks fades from the fickle mind as the first wine makes its impressive entrance.

Bottles, opened beforehand, are brought from a cool store; the reds that have been breathing in the *chambré* atmosphere are brought to the fore. The term *chambré* can, as a reminder, bear some explanation here. It was adopted by our forbears and is somewhat of an anachronism today. Inside the thick stone walls of ancient and unheated houses, dining-rooms were much cooler in olden times. Today, with very rare exceptions, no wine can bear the temperature of a room where men may be wearing tropical weight suits or women can sit comfortably in topless evening or dinner dresses. It is as unthinkable to put a lump of ice into a glass of white wine as it is to serve an over-warm red wine.

It is taken for granted that most of the guests, if not experts, will be at least reasonably knowledgeable about wine. Their comments or even criticisms will not be judged out of place. Pertinent remarks will be appreciated by the host who will gladly reveal the wine's origin and pedigree as far as he knows it.

Professional tasting terms should be used with caution and accuracy. The technical vocabulary should simplify conversation and not complicate it. One can say, for example, that a great red wine has a beautiful colour, a strong bouquet of well-blended aromas, that it leaves a clean taste on the palate, that it is long with a lingering flavour. Never say that it is well-dressed (that means the label), that it has an agreeable perfume or a delicious taste. Say, if you must, that it has body and bouquet and that it will age well. Best of all, say that it has been selected by a true connoisseur and that little as you profess to know about the subject, you can appreciate its qualities. Everyone will then marvel at your modesty!

Returning to the first bottle on the menu, a white wine makes a good introduction to most meals. The quality must be carefully taken into account observing the golden rule which demands that no wine must ever make the palate regret the wine which precedes it. Thus the triumphant entry of a great white wine should not make the first red wine that follows it appear too modest in comparison. Wine, in all its nobility, has an inborn courtesy and should never intrude or attract attention to itself. A dinner should never be allowed to turn into a tiresome wine-tasting; there is a time and place for both. Like a well-mannered friend the wine's presence should not compete with, but should complement the subtle tastes produced in the kitchen, or even ennoble them.

When four wines complement a meal they should progress from lightest to fullest in body, from humblest to noblest, from youngest to most mature, from first to last or, in other words, from better to better.

WHEN FRIENDS DROP BY

There is no doubt that the very appearance of a bottle of wine creates an atmosphere of relaxation. It creates a level on which people of like tastes can meet and informally pass the time. If the weatherman permits, then eating and drinking in the open air, having a picnic or a barbecue adds to the informality. Here all pretence is abandoned and a simple friendly meal is as enjoyable as something cooked with great care after many hours of preparation. Wine can even be served at a sausage party, preferably with the Vienna variety, as the grease on fried or grilled sausages does not combine well with wine.

Wines on these occasions should be able to stand up to unwonted extremes of temperature. There is no reason why such a party cannot be held with snow on the ground providing there is shelter from the wind. If one lives near or by a vineyard it is only a matter of buying what the local producers drink themselves in the same circumstances. These wines only need to be attractive, lively, gay, young and pleasant. Light whites, light reds, authentic *vin rosé* but not *pelure d'oignon*, fruity or "flinty" wines, dry white wines are good choices. Highly alcoholic wines should be avoided.

Popular wines for drinking in this open atmosphere are French white wines from the Loire or those from the Swiss canton of Vaud, the light SYLVANERS and the REISLINGS from Alsace, or wines from the Rhine and Moselle districts. A *rosé* from Provence in France might be chosen, as would the pinkish wines of the Balearic Islands, the MAVROD from Bulgaria, or the CVICEK from Slovenia. There are innumerable reds of almost every nationality to choose from. They should be light in colour, fruity, and clean on the palate. They can come from places as far apart as Beaujolais and Austria, Périgod and California, where SANTA ROSA is a good example. Slightly sparkling natural wines are ideal at such times, whether they come from Anjou, Saumar, Touraine, Seyssel or Neuchâtel. The RIESLING ITALICA or LAMBRUSCO would be excellent.

Modern technology has come to the aid of the wine-lover: the portable ice-box or insulated container should be used whenever possible to carry the wines and to store them while they are being served. The wine warms up only too quickly in glasses held between the fingers, or in the sun. Of course, if you can lay hands on one, a small cask is a worthy centre-piece for any meal in the open, even if covered with old wet sacks soaked in brine to keep it cool or nestling on a bed of crushed ice. There is nothing like the sensation of drawing off a glass of wine from a wooden barrel.

WINE IN RESTAURANTS

A business lunch or a restaurant meal with friends is an important part of the eating-out habits of the modern male. For business lunches, most people want to order a contradiction in terms; a good meal, a light meal, and a quick meal. Accordingly, the special delights of the kitchen must sometimes be sacrificed. To make up for this, the wine may be carefully selected. The golden rule is, the simpler the better. Work in the afternoon prohibits the choice of wines that are too rich. Most wine waiters now appreciate this and

have a good light wine which does not tend to put a client or an associate to sleep over his desk during the afternoon. Such after-effects are inclined to make the guest think twice before accepting another invitation.

It is just as well, however, to know how to read the wine list and not only the right-hand column! Those "little white wines" which "go down just like milk" can sometimes have a treacherous delayed action, whilst light red wines, for instance those with a high tannin content, are often more open and less insidious.

Dining with friends or entertaining a guest who is just passing through is quite a different matter. There is usually more time, and the whole night following for the constitution to recover. In these circumstances that favourite showplace of a restaurant or popular country inn can be just as important as the local architecture or the natural scenic beauty. Fewer limitations are imposed and a wide choice of carefully selected wines can show the guest he is not only welcome but appreciated. Of course, knowing the guest's tastes beforehand makes everything simpler. Knowing the restaurant and its cellar is a great help, too, as it is not always the most expensive or most well-known shipper's or château label which is best suited to the guest's palate or the host's pocket.

TALKING OVER WINE

When a friend drops in for a gossip, to put the world to rights or just to renew old aquaintance, wine can be a splendid change from the old, tired, spirit-based concoction of the cocktail era. As a matter of fact, some hosts, especially when dining out or even at business lunches, have taken to seating their guests at the table instead of standing by the bar, and serving them a light wine instead of an aperitif. The wine blends better with whatever is to follow and is less of a shock to the system than a potent iced mixture.

With a private cellar, following the habit of the continental European, it is a delightful practice to invite visitors to make their own choice of wine guided by a few words of expertise. The welcome offering of a bottle of wine, too, is always a compliment to the caller who brings it. For the casual visitor, the wine should be chosen from its personal history, such as one brought back from an interesting journey, or a particularly good year which is maturing in a bin; but whatever it is, it should be something special.

To talk over a bottle of wine is an experience. Conversation flows, stimulated by the quiet genie in the bottle which relaxes the mind and soothes the way to near-forgotten conversational delights. Choose wines that bring mental pictures of grapes harvested in distant places. Serve wines that have been bought for the cellar and not yet tasted. A new wine on a strange palate is a good opening for conversation.

This is the time to find out if the year fulfils its expected promise. These are the times to try the wines from Israel or Turkey, from Yugoslavia and Hungary. Their names sing an invitation to taste; TEKIGRAD, BOZCAADA, MÜREFTE, ELAZIG, and KOKINELLI from Cyprus, KOONAWARA from Southern Australia, STELLENBOSCH from South Africa, and EL TRAPICHE from the Argentine. It is the time when you can test out your guests' knowledge, their recognition of the wine regions, and their tastes for future occasions. You might even imbue them with your own enthusiasm for this fascinating subject, wine.

CHEESE AND WINE

It is well known that the taste of wine is at its most glorious with cheese. There are so many cheeses and so many wines that it would require an encyclopedic work to marry them all. However, there is a general rule that certain cheeses go with certain wines, just as with other dishes, and classic partners are cited in this chapter, well-established after long aquaintance. Roquefort with a great red wine? Most certainly, but there are esoteric connoisseurs who sing the praises of Roquefort combined with MONTBAZILLAC. Who is to say? There is ample choice and the field is open for all tastes. Here is a general guide to the marriage of wines and cheeses:

Great, strong, robust and well-knit red wines from all regions: Danish blue, Gorgonzola, Roquefort, and Stilton.

Red wines of high to medium strength from all regions: Brie and Camembert.

Red wines of medium body and bouquet from Dalmatia, Médoc, Morgon, The Palatinate, and Tuscany: Maroilles, Livarot and Munster.

White wines and robust red wines from Bordeaux, Burgundy, Andalusia, Piedmont and Tunisia: Cheddar and Gruyère.

White wines, rosés, dry or fruity red wines from Beaujolais, Galicia, the Loire, Umbria, Savoy and Serbia: Cantal, Gouda, Hervé and Port-Salut.

Light and dry wines, local wines from the cheese-producing regions: goat cheese and dry cheese made from ewes' milk.

Apart from these, there are those cream and curd cheeses like Petits-Suisse which are served sprinkled with salt or sugar. Sweetened cheeses come to the table as desserts or with salads. White wines, rosé or light red wines on the dry side should be drunk with such world-famous cheese dishes as *fondue* or *raclette*.

There is little complication with cheese soufflés as the wine is chosen to suit the cheese on which the dish is based. Cheese savouries, most common on the Anglo-Saxon table and usually eaten at the end of the meal, can be accompanied by a sherry or a dry port.

The main wine served with the meat or game, can equally well accompany the cheese, bearing in mind that it should not interfere with the good order of the hierarchy of the wines as the meal progresses.

SWEETS, DESSERTS AND WINES

As a general rule, wines are not desirable with sweet dishes. There are exceptions which are listed here, and they should be studied to complete a knowledge of wines and food. Under no circumstances should wine be served with aciduous fruits or any desserts containing chocolate in any form. Although this law should really not be transgressed, a little cheating is forgivable in some cases and authorities on the subject reluctantly admit there may be something to be said for the following combinations:

Soft and sweet wines: ALICANTE, BARSAC, LACHRYMA CHRISTI, MOSCATI DI PANTELLERIA, MARSALA ALEATICO, SAUTERNES, VINO SANTA.

Slightly sparkling sweet wines: ASTI SPUMANTE, BLANQUETTE DE LIMOUX, medium-dry CHAMPAGNE, CLAIRETTE DE DIE, may be drunk with cakes, biscuits, petits fours and tarts.

Red wines of medium body with a fruity bouquet with strawberries, raspberries and peaches.

Sweet, unfortified wines: FRONTIGNAN, MALVOISIE, MAVRODAPHI DE PATRAS, MOSCATEL with pastries without much cream.

It is not always possible to prevent someone from finishing their wine with the dessert, but with careful management the meal can be arranged so that the glass can be finished earlier. A good way around the problem is to provide a cool, but not iced, glass of fresh water and then, immediately after the sweet course, serve a dessert wine when the palate has been cleared. Frequently, those delicious dessert wines are forgotten: the good ports, Madeiras, Malaga and oloroso sherry, while the taste of a great MONTBAZILLAC is a pleasure and an experience not to be missed.

WINE IN FOOD

Countless recipes prescribe wine in making a sauce or for including in the cooking, as in casseroles or marinades. If a cheap *vin ordinaire* is not obtainable it always seems a pity to raid the cellar, but the accepted rule demands that the wine used in the cooking should be the same as that served on the table. However, here too a little cheating is permissible, and normally, a Riesling, a cheap Burgundy or a simple Côtes du Rhône will do well enough.

Old menus have more value as comparative history than as practical hints for the modern kitchen. Many explanations have been put forward for the continued decrease in the quantity of food consumed by guests at table. It may not be necessary but perhaps just as well to point out that in the days of the great banquets guests were only helped to a choice of the fifty or so courses served and were not obliged to eat their way through them all. However, it must be understood that social class structures were totally different from those of today and such menus were only served in baronial castles, in the palaces of royalty and the clergy, and the mansions of the rich leisured classes whose pleasures were mainly active and out of doors and entailed quite a lot of physical exercise and expenditure of energy.

Modern society has produced different pressures and the demands of work and hygiene have developed a more balanced, simplified and cleaner diet gradually to replace the gluttonies of yesteryear. However, it is to be hoped that our modern physical condition still allows us to do justice to the menu of a banquet.

ANCIENT MENUS

In the year 1656, a certain Madame la Chancelière invited Louis XIV to dinner at her château at Pont-chartrain. The first course was composed of twenty-four dishes, including sixteen warm hors-d'œuvre, and eight rich soups. This was followed by eight plates bearing the meat that had been cooked in the soup and sixteen dishes of lean meat. The third course was made up of eight platters of roasts and sixteen dishes of vegetables prepared in the meat gravy. The fourth course offered the choice of eight pies, cold meat or fish and sixteen kinds of salads with oil, cream and butter. Last of all, twenty-four different pastries, twenty-four dishes of fresh fruit, twenty-four dishes of sweetmeats, preserves and sweet sauces. In all, 168 dishes or prepared plates were served, without counting the different desserts.

In this account by Prosper Montagné no mention is made of the wines served with the dinner. It does, however, give an indication of the abundance of the food served at the time of the Sun King, who was himself reputed to have an extraordinarily large appetite. The following menu, served to three great nineteenth-century figures, is nearer our subject and less shocking to our modern tastes:

Menu for the dinner of the "Three Emperors"
served to Alexander II, the Czar
and the King of Prussia at the Café Anglais, Paris,
June 7, 1867

Soups
Imperatrice, Fontanges

Removes
Soufflé à la Reine
Sole filets à la vénitienne
Turbot steaks au gratin
Saddle of mutton

Entrées
Poulets à la portugaise
Hot quail pie
Lobster à la parisienne
Champagne sorbet

Roasts
Duck à la rouennaise
Canapés of bunting

Desserts
Aubergines à l'espagnole
Asparagus
Cassolettes princesse
Bombe glacée

Wines
MADEIRA, RETURN FROM INDIA 1846
XÉRÈS 1821
CHÂTEAU YQUEM 1847
CHAMBERTIN 1846
CHÂTEAU MARGAUX 1847
CHÂTEAU LATOUR 1847
CHÂTEAU LAFITE 1848

In this example the wines are mentioned, but the question arises as to what dish was served with which wine. Was the Château Yquem served with the soufflé, the buntings or the *bombe glacée*? One can guess or, better still, try them out. In the next menu there are still no details but the combinations are easier to guess.

Banquet held in the honour of
Emile Loubet, President of the French Republic,
on his return from Russia,

May 27, 1902, at the invitation of
the Conseil général du Nord, at Dunkirk.

Hors-d'œuvre à la Russe

Dunkirk salmon à la Flamande

Filet de Bœuf à la Parisienne

Jellied duck

Poularde du Mans à l'Estragon

Salade Jean-Bart

Suprêmes de Pêches and Greengage plums
à la Montmorency

Desserts

Wines

Barsac

Médoc

Château Gruaud-Larose

Montebello Frappé

Liqueurs

☆

GREAT MENUS OF TODAY

WITH BURGUNDY

A meal based on Burgundy wines alone can combine all possible and imaginable variations. The choice of food can, as previously suggested, be guided by the wines. The Montrachet goes just as well with another fish entrée, while the Côte de Beaune wines, because of their good colour and reputation, marry well with strongly flavoured meats.

Salmon mousse
Chevalier-Montrachet
Ham à la Villandry
Savigny-lès-Beaune
Fowl stuffed with truffles
Timbales Agnès Sorel
Mimosa Salad
Richebourg
Sabayon au Madère
Madeira

For an official or intimate dinner it is sometimes preferable to order according to the established gastronomic rules. A first-class and reputable restaurant can always provide a small separate room with service,

WITH BORDEAUX

The great white wines of Bordeaux are not very well known but similar wines can be found outside France and have been mentioned in this book. In the following menu salmon mousse has been included for Bordeaux as well as, previously, for Burgundy. As for drinking a soft and sweet wine with *foie gras*, just try it and you will be convinced that it is an excellent combination.

Salmon mousse
Côtes-de-Blaye
Crawfish tails au gratin
Sainte-Croix-du-Mont sec
Saddle of lamb
Château Lafite
Parfait au foie gras
Crêpes fourrées
Château Yquem

and will supply all the needs from its kitchens and cellars. A good head waiter will be able to guide you in creating a symphony of wine and food which will enchant the guests so do not hesitate to consult him.

MENU WITH CHAMPAGNE

Champagne wines are either liked or disliked—it is as simple as that. If they are enjoyed then there is no further comment to be made and the following dishes are well-married to the wine.

Jellied filets of sole
AVIZE
Truffles in pastry
CRAMANT
Pheasant à la Bohémienne
MAREUIL-SUR-AY
Cardons à la moelle
Salade Aïda
BOUZY
Biscuit glacé Lyrique
MAILLY-CHAMPAGNE

MENUS WITH DIFFERENT WINES

Before dinner: CHAMPAGNE BRUT
Foie gras en croûte
CHAMPAGNE NATURE
Soufflé de truites Beauvilliers
ENTRE-DEUX-MERS-HAUT-BENAUGE
Prague Ham à la Chablisienne
POMMARD
Nest of Quails
Pommes Bonne-femme
Salades Béatrix
NUITS-SAINT-GEORGES
Nut cake
CHÂTEAU-CHALON

Médaillons de jambon Polignac
BLANC DE L'ETOILE
Crawfish tails à la mode du couvent de Chorin
MEURSAULT
Poulet de grain Jaqueline garniture Marie-Louise
Salade Orloff
POMEROL
Charlotte Royale
QUART-DE-CHAUME

Lobster and coconut salad
MÂCON BLANC
Timbale Sully
MARGAUX
Filets de bœuf Wellington
Samade Rachel
CHAMBOLLE-MUSIGNY
Diplomate chaud
VIN DE PAILLE

Langouste en Bellevue
PALETTE
Selle de chevreuil Grand Veneur
Timbales Maréchale
Salade Belle Hélène
GEVREY-CHAMBERTIN
Croûte à l'ananas
PINEAU DES CHARENTES

Unfortunately, not many people nowadays have the time, the means or the inclination to set off on a purely gastronomic journey. However, it may just be possible to arrange a business trip, a cultural or educational tour even a relaxing holiday which takes in places famous for their blend of cellar and kitchen, whether they be towns, provinces or countries.

The itineraries suggested here are based on personal experiences and include some memorable possibilities. The choice of localities has been dictated more by the wines than food. If French provinces predominate,

this is because France is the mother of wines, and there are many different regions which have their own typical vintages. All in all the names represent an imaginary journey across the Continent of Europe and a sampling of regional delicacies and specialities encountered all too rarely elsewhere.

Many of these specialities and wines, listed alphabetically to spare regional and national jealousies, are not widely known or acclaimed. Simple and exquisite, each dish is accompanied by a special wine and they are minor poems in casseroles and carafes.

ALSACE	Tokay from Alsace	White	Braised ham and apple crumble
	Gewürztraminer	White	Pheasant *à la Strasbourg*
ANJOU	Champigny	Red	*Bouilleture* (fish stewed in red wine and herbs)
AUSTRIA	Prälatenwein	White	Quetsche plums with almonds in pastry
AUVERGNE	Chanturgue	Red	Besse-en-Chandesse *coq au vin*
BEARN	Irouléguy	Red	Wild goat with mushrooms
BERRY	Chateaumeillant	Red	Pancakes with pork cracklings
BORDEAUX	Pomerol or Lalande de Pomerol	Red	Lamprey *à la bordelaise*
BOURBONNAIS	Saint-Pourçain	Red	*Truffat* (potato pie)
BURGUNDY	Passe-tout-grain	Red	Pigeon stew
	Beaujolais	Red	*Pot-au-feu* or *Boeuf-gros-sel*
BRITTANY	Muscadet	White	Rabbit cooked in Muscadet wine
BUGEY	Charveyron	Red	Bernardine ragout of woodcock
CORSICA	Sciaccarello	Red	*Coppa, figatello, lonzo* (cold meat specialities)
DAUPHINÉ	Jarjayes	White	*Poulet roussille*
FRANCHE-COMTÉ	Hypocras	Red	Baume-les-Dames quince cheese
GASCONY	Madiran	Red	*Sanguète de poulet*
GERMANY	Schloss Böckelsheimer Kupfergrube	White	Goose breasts grilled over vine shoots, sautéed potatoes and cranberry sauce
ITALY	Rocca-di-papa	White	Mozzarella in carrozza (toasted cheese and ham sandwich)
	Chianti	Red	Beefsteak *alla Fiorentina*
	Vino Nobile di Montepulciano	Red	*Osso buco*
LANGUEDOC	Minervois	Red	Mourtayrol (boiled beef, chicken and ham with saffron)
LORRAINE	Gris de Pagny-sur-Moselle	White	Boulay frogs *au gratin*
LYONS	Beaujolais of the year	Red	Stuffed veal
ORLEANS	Cour Cheverny	White	Montargis mushrooms on toast
PÉRIGORD	Côtes de Duras	Red	Goat's cheese
PORTUGAL	Moscatel de Setubal	White	*Doce d'ovos* (dessert made from egg yolks)
PROVENCE	Taradeau	White	Snails *à la suçarelle*
SAVOY	Princess-Rocheray	Red	Pork cooked in wine with a cream sauce
SPAIN	Ribeiro	White	Octopus stewed in its own ink
SWITZERLAND	Dézaley	White	Liver sausage
	Abbaye de Mont	White	Filet of perch

LIST OF COLOUR MAPS

CHABLIS   Chablis grands crus, Chablis, Petit-Chablis   79

CÔTE DE NUITS   Fixin, Gevrey-Chambertin, Morey-Saint-Denis, Chambolle-Musigny, Vougeot, Vosne-Romanée, Nuits-Saint-Georges   80

CÔTE DE BEAUNE   Aloxe-Corton, Pernand-Vergelesses, Savigny-lès-Beaune, Beaune, Pommard, Volnay, Monthélie, Auxey-Duresses, Meursault, Puligny-Montrachet, Chassagne-Montrachet, Saint-Aubin, Santenay, Ladoix, Chorey-lès-Beaune, Blagny   82

COMMUNE OF GEVREY-CHAMBERTIN   Chambertin, Chambertin-Clos-de-Bèze, Charmes-Chambertin, Griotte-Chambertin, Latricières-Chambertin, Mazis-Chambertin, Ruchottes-Chambertin, Chapelle-Chambertin   84

MERCUREY, MACONNÂIS   85

BEAUJOLAIS   Juliénas, Saint-Amour, Chenas, Moulin-à-Vent, Fleurie, Chiroubles, Brouilly et Côte de Brouilly   86

CÔTES DU RHÔNE   Côte-Rôtie, Condrieu, Château-Grillet, Crozes-Hermitage, Hermitage, Saint-Joseph, Cornas, Saint-Péray, Côtes-du-Rhône   109

SWISS RHÔNE, BANKS OF LAKE LEMAN AND SAVOY   110

CÔTES DU RHÔNE   Châteauneuf-du-Pape, Tavel, Lirac   112

LOIRE REGION   Coteaux de la Loire, Coteaux du Layon, Coteaux de l'Aubance, Saumur, Coteaux de Saumur, Anjou   127

LOIRE REGION   Coteaux de Touraine, Saint-Nicolas de Bourgueil, Bourgueil, Montlouis, Jasnières, Coteaux du Loir   128

BORDEAUX   Médoc, Graves, Cérons, Barsac, Sauternes   168

BORDEAUX   Premières-Côtes-de-Bordeaux, Loupiac, Sainte-Croix-du-Mont, Entre-Deux-Mers, Sainte-Foy-Bordeaux, Graves-de-Vayres, Côtes-de-Bordeaux-Saint-Macaire   169

BORDEAUX   Saint-Emilion, Pomerol, Fronsac, Blaye, Bourg, Néac   170

RIOJA REGION   191

JEREZ-SHERRY REGION   192

DOURO REGION   214

CENTRAL ITALY   239

NORTHERN ITALY   240

SOUTHERN AND INSULAR ITALY   241

SWISS RHINE AND BANKS OF LAKES NEUCHÂTEL AND BIEL   278

ALSACE   280

THE PALATINATE, RHEINHESSE, NAHE   281

RHEINGAU   282

MOSELLE, SARRE, RUWER   284

AUSTRIA   295

TOKAY REGION   296

GREECE   303

SOUTH AFRICA   317

MOROCCO – ALGERIA – TUNISIA   318

CALIFORNIA   334

CHAMPAGNE   365

WINE MUSEUMS

GERMANY

Weinbaumuseum
MEERSBURG/LAKE CONSTANCE

Historisches Museum der Pfalz
mit Weinmuseum
Gr. Pfaffengasse 7
SPEYER

Museum für die Geschichte des Weines
RÜDESHEIM

GREAT BRITAIN

Harvey's Winemuseum
BRISTOL

AUSTRIA

Museum der Stadt Krems
Theaterplatz 9
KREMS AN DER DONAU

SPAIN

Museo del Vino
Plaza Jaime Iº
VILAFRANCA DEL PANADÉS

FRANCE

Musée du Vin
ANGERS

Musée du Vin
Hôtel des Ducs de Bourgogne
BEAUNE

Château d'Entrecasteaux
Ile de Bendor (off Bandol)

Maison du Vin
1, cours du 30-Juillet
BORDEAUX (GIRONDE)

Musée du Vin
CÉRONS (GIRONDE)

Musée du Vin de Champagne
ÉPERNAY

Château-Lascombes
MARGAUX (GIRONDE)

Musée Rothschild
Domaine Mouton-Rothschild
par PAUILLAC (GIRONDE)

Musée d'Espelosin
ROCHECORDON (I.-et-L.)

Musée de la Mission Haut-Brion
TALENCE (GIRONDE)

ITALY

Museo del Vino
Castello Ringberg
CALDERO (BOLZANO)

Musée du Vin Martini
PESSIONE (TURIN)

SWITZERLAND

Musée de l'Areuse
BOUDRY/NE

PHOTOGRAPHIC ACKNOWLEDGEMENTS

Graphische Sammlung Albertina, Vienna, p. 11. Archives départementales, Dijon: Yves Debraine, Lausanne, p. 45. Archives Nationales, Paris: Patrick Guilbert, Saint-Brice, p. 131. Archives photographiques, Paris, p. 224. Badisches Landesmuseum, Karlsruhe: Willi Moegle, Leinfelden-Oberaichen, p. 395 centre. Bavaria-Verlag, Munich: Ruth Hallensleben, p. 34 at right. Bibliothèque de l'Arsenal, Paris: Patrick Guilbert, Saint-Brice, p. 20. Bibliothèque cantonale et universitaire, Lausanne, p. 22, 24, 26 top, 27 top; Scope, Lausanne, p. 95. Bibliothèque du Muséum d'Histoire naturelle, Paris: Patrick Guilbert, Saint-Brice, p. 17. Bibliothèque Nationale, Cabinet des Estampes, Paris: Patrick Guilbert, Saint-Brice, p. 23, 30. British Museum, London, p. 388, 392 at left, 395 at left. Companhia Geral da Agricultura das Vinhas do Alto Douro, Vila Nova de Gaia, p. 203. Confrérie des Chevaliers du Tastevin, Nuits-Saint-Georges, p. 31 centre. J. Decker, Saumur, p. 117, 118. Edita, Lausanne, p. 92 top, 223, 249. Ami Guichard, Lausanne, p. 146. Historisches Museum, Basle, p. 32. Historisches Museum der Pfalz, Speyer, p. 15 at right. Instituto do Vinho do Porto, Porto, p. 197, 206. Juliusspital Keller, Würzburg: Gundermann, Würzburg, p. 34 bottom right. Kunsthistorisches Museum, Vienna: Erwin Meyer, Vienna, p. 287. Kunstmuseum, Düsseldorf, p. 265, 392 at right; Walter Klein, Düsseldorf, p. 389 at left; Carlfred Halbach, Mettmann, p. 389 at right; Willi Moegle, Leinfelden-Oberaichen, p. 395 at right. Luftverkehr Strähle, Schorndorf, p. 262, 266. Pierre Mackiéwicz, Aix-en-Provence, p. 57, 61, 65, 66, 74, 154 top left, 362 top, 363 bottom left. Mainfränkisches Museum, Würzburg: Alfred Burkholz, Würzburg, p. 31 at right. The Mansell Collection, London, p. 13. Gaston Marchou, Cambes: National Foto Persbureau, Amsterdam, p. 154 bottom right. Martini & Rossi, Turin, p. 15 at left. Moët & Chandon, Epernay: Yves Debraine, Lausanne, p. 347, 400. Musée des Beaux-Arts, Orléans: Yves Debraine, Lausanne, p. 229. Musée Condé, Chantilly: Giraudon, Paris, p. 26 bottom, 27 bottom. Musée du Louvre, Cabinet des Dessins, Paris: Patrick Guilbert, Saint-Brice, p. 14. Musée de Mouton-Rothschild, Pauillac: Pierre Berdoy, Morainvilliers, p. 387, 391. Museo Nacional del Prado, Madrid: Edita, Lausanne, p. 191. Museo Nazionale, Naples: Scala, Florence, p. 298. Museum für die Geschichte des Weines, Rüdesheim: Ami Guichard, Lausanne, p. 399. National Gallery of Art, Washington, p. 35. Oriental Institute, University of Chicago, p. 10. Österreichisches Museum für Volkskunde, Vienna: Ritter, Vienna, p. 34 at right. Österreichische Nationalbibliothek, Vienna, p. 25, 36. Charles Page, Vevey, p. 92 bottom, 145. Perestrello's Photographos Ltda., Funchal, p. 210. Abbé Perrodin, Conliège, p. 31 at left. Photo Giraudon, Paris, p. 351. Römisch-Germanisches Museum, Cologne: Willi Moegle, Leinfelden-Oberaichen, p. 386. O. Ruppen, Sion, p. 91. Roger Schall, Paris, p. 73, 154 top right, 362 bottom right and left, 363 top left, at right. Schweizerisches Landesmuseum, Zurich, p. 33, 34 top left. Victoria and Albert Museum, London, p. 398, 402. Wallraff-Richartz-Museum, Cologne: Heinz Doppelfeld, Cologne-Ehrenfeld, p. 232. Weinbaumuseum, Krems: K. Gartler, Krems, p. 37, 401. Wine Institute, San Francisco, p. 323, 324, 325, 326, 327, 329, 332. Dr. Wolff & Tritschler, Offenburg, p. 257. Württembergische Landesbibliothek, Stuttgart: Hermann Schnepf, Stuttgart, p. 18-19. Zähringer Museum, Baden-Baden: Willi Moegle, p. 390.

ACKNOWLEDGEMENTS

The Publisher extends his warmest thanks to the Curators of Museums and libraries, the Directors and Administrators of official organizations or private societies and the Collectors who have helped in the preparation of this work. Special thanks are due to:

Israelian Embassy, Bern; Pierre Androuët, Paris; Piero Antinori, Florence; François des Aulnoyes, Centre National de Coordination, Paris; Dr von Bassermann-Jordan'sches Weingut, Deidesheim; Ferdinando de Bianchi, Madeira Wine Association Ltd., Funchal; Bouchard Père & Fils, Beaune; Louis Philippe Bovard, Office de propagande pour les vins vaudois, Lausanne; Carlos Cavero Beyart, Presidente del Sindicato Nacional de la Vid, Madrid; Champagne Mercier, Epernay; Champagne Perrier-Jouët, Epernay; Champagne Taittinger, Reims; Jacques Chevignard, Grand Chambellan de la Confrérie des Chevaliers du Tastevin, Nuits-Saint-Georges; Cockburn Smithes & Co. Lda, Vila Nova de Gaia; Comité Interprofessionnel du Vin d'Alsace, Colmar; Comité Interprofessionnel des Vins à Appellation Contrôlée de Touraine, Tours; Companhia Geral da Agricultura das Vinhas do Alto Douro "Real Companhia Velha", Vila Nova de Gaia; Confrérie Saint-Etienne d'Alsace, Colmar; Confrérie des Vignerons de Saint Vincent, Mâcon; Confrérie des Vignerons Vevey; Conseil Interprofessionnel des Vins d'Anjou et de Saumur, Angers; Consejo Regulador de la Denominación de Origen Jerez, Jerez de la Frontera; Consejo Regulador de la Denominación de Origen Panadés, Vilafranca del Panadés; Consejo Regulador de la Denominación de Origen Rioja, Logroño; Il Corriere Vinicolo, Rome; J. M. Courteau, Conseil Interprofessionnel du Vin de Bordeaux, Bordeaux; J. Dargent, Comité Interprofessionnel du Vin de Champagne, Epernay; Kemalettin Demirer, Turkish Embassy, Bern; Manuel Cotta Dias, Junta Nacional lo Vinho, Lisbon; Pedro Domecq S.A., Jerez; Joseph Drouhin, Beaune; H. Duboscq, Saint-Estèphe; J. Faiveley, Nuits-Saint-Georges; F.A.O., Rome; Héritiers Fourcaud-Laussac, Saint-Emilion; P. Fridas, sous-directeur Office International de la Vigne et du Vin, Paris; Pierre Galet, Ecole Nationale Supérieure Agronomique de Montpellier, Montpellier; Garvey S.A., Jerez Gonzalez, Byass & Co. Ltd., Jerez; Dr Heger, Ihringen; Juliusspital-Weingut, Würzburg; A. S. Hogg, Peter Dominic Limited, London; Dr. Harry Kühnel, Archivdirektor, Krems a.d. Donau; Restaurant Ledoyen, Paris; Henri Leyvraz, Station fédérale d'essais agricoles, section de viticulture, Lausanne/Pully; Madame Edmond Loubat, Pomerol; Henri Maire, Arbois; Manuel & Cie S.A., Lausanne; Dr A. Miederbacher, Unione Italiani Vini, Milan; Moët & Chandon, Epernay; Jean Mommessin, Mâcon; Monimpex, Budapest; G. H. Mumm & Co., Reims; New Zealand High Commission, London; H.F.M. Palmer, Adelaide; Dr Adolf Paulus, Museum für die Geschichte des Weines, Rüdesheim; Americo Pedrosa Piros de Lima, Instituto do Vinho do Porto, Porto; Porcelaine Limoges-Unic, Paris; R. Protin, Directeur de l'Office International de la Vigne et du Vin, Paris; Joh. Jos. Prüm, Wehlen; C. Quittanson, Inspecteur Divisionnaire du Service de la Répression des Fraudes et du Contrôle de la Qualité, Ministère de l'Agriculture, Dijon; Real Companhia Vinicola do Norte de Portugal, Vila Nova de Gaia; Représentation Commerciale de l'U.R.S.S. en Suisse, Bern; Gilbert Rohrer, Lausanne; Roth & Sauter, Lausanne; Baron Philippe de Rothschild, Mouton-Rothschild; Fritz Salomon, Präsident des Österreichischen Weininstituts, Vienna; Sandeman Bros. & Co., Jerez; José Augusto dos Santos, Casa de Portugal, Paris; Francisco Sanz Carnero, Dirección General de Agricultura, Madrid; Antonio Carlos Sarmento de Vasconcellos, Instituto do Vinho do Porto, Porto; Dr Karl Schultz, Konservator, Historisches Museum der Pfalz, Speyer; Antonio José da Silva Vinhos, S.A.R.L., Vila Nova de Gaia; Jean-Louis Simon, Station fédérale d'essais agricoles, section de viticulture, Lausanne/Pully; Société Civile du Domaine de la Romanée-Conti, Vosne-Romanée; Société Vinicole Perroy S.A., Epesses; Société des Domaines Woltner, Bordeaux; Staatliche Lehr- und Versuchsanstalt für Wein- und Obstbau, Weinsberg; Staatsweingut, Weinbaulehranstalt, Bad Kreuznach; Syndicat régional des Vins de Savoie, Chambéry; Szende László, Orszagos Borminösitö Intézet, Budapest; J. Thorin, Pontanevaux; E. Tomov, Embassy of the Republic of Bulgaria, Bern; Johann Traxler, Österreichisches Weininstitut, Vienna; Verwaltung der Staatsweingüter im Rheingau, Eltville; Veuve Clicquot-Ponsardin, Reims; Wente Bros., Livermore, California; Fred Wick, Vevey; Dr Robert Wildhaber, Basel; Williams & Humbert Ltd., Jerez; Terence McInnes, The Wine Institute, San Francisco; Leo Wunderle, Lucerne; Zoilo Ruiz-Mateos S.A., Jerez.

The colour maps were drawn by Robert Flach, from documents and information provided by:

Pierre Forgeot, Beaune; Office International de la Vigne et du Vin, Paris; Office de propagande pour les vins vaudois, Lausanne; Fédération des Vins de Savoie, Chambéry; Comité Interprofessionnel des Vins des Côtes du Rhône, Avignon; Comité Interprofessionnel des Vins à Appellation Contrôlée de Touraine, Tours; Conseil Interprofessionnel des Vins d'Anjou et de Saumur, Angers; Conseil Interprofessionnel des Vins de Bordeaux; Comité Interprofessionnel du Vin d'Alsace, Colmar; Consejo Regulador de la Denominación de Origen Jerez, Jerez de la Frontera; Consejo Regulador de la Denominación de Origen Rioja, Logroño; Dirección General de Agricultura, Madrid; Instituto do Vinho do Porto, Porto; Verkehrsverein Rüdesheim; Österreichisches Weininstitut, Vienna; Wine Institute, San Francisco; Comité Interprofessionnel du Vin de Champagne, Epernay.

The English translation is by Michael and Angela Kelly, Pully, Switzerland and Peter Dewhirst, I.T.E.S., Geneva.

INDEX OF WINES

Ag=Algeria   Arg=Argentina   Aus=Australia   A=Austria   Bz=Brazil   Bg=Bulgaria   Cal=California   C=Cyprus   Cs=Czechoslovakia   E=Egypt
F=France   Gy=Germany   G=Greece   H=Hungary   Is=Israel   I=Italy   N.Y.=New York   P=Portugal   R=Roumania   S.A.=South Africa   Sp=Spain
Sw=Switzerland   Tu=Tunisia   T=Turkey   Yg=Yugoslavia

Sur les Abbayes (Sw), 106
L'Abbaye de Bonlieu (F), 161
Abbaye de Mont Ville de Lausanne (Sw), 106, 411
Abbeureben (Gy), 269
Abelha (P), 213
Äbleten (Sw), 247
Abolengo (Sp), 189
Abraham (Sp), 190
Abtsleite (Gy), 274
Abtsweingarten (Gy), 254, 269
Abtei (Gy), 275
Abtsberg (Gy), 265, 269, 274, 275
Del Abuelo (Sp), 189
El Abuelo (Sp), 190
Abymes (F), 107
Ackerbergen (Gy), 277
Acordo Finest Old Tawny Port (P), 213
Adabag (T), 299, 302
Adler (Gy), 275
Adom Atic (Is), 300, 301
Advat White (Is), 300
Afames (C), 299, 302
Affentaler (Gy), 255
Afonso III (P), 200
Aglianico (I), 238
– del Vulture (I), 234, 238
Agritinsberg (Gy), 266, 275
Agrylos (G), 301
Agustinito (Sp), 189
Aigle (Sw), 105, 247
– Royal (Sw), 105
Les Aigrots (F), 63, 77
Les Aiguillons (F), 125
L'Aillerie (F), 123
Aïn Bessem-Bouira (Ag), 309, 315
– El Hadjar (Ag), 315
Airen (Lairén) (Sp), 188
Albana di Romagna (I), 237
Albariño (Sp), 187
Aleatico di Porto-Ferraio (I), 227, 233, 237
– di Puglia (I), 232, 238
– viterbese (I), 230, 237
Alfonso (Sp), 189
Algar (Sp), 189
Aliança (P), 212
Aligoté-Ay-Danil (U.S.S.R.), 292, 294
Allonnes (F), 126
Almeirim (P), 200
Almirante (Sp), 189
Aloque (Sp), 178
Aloxe-Corton (F), 49, 61, 77, 78, 404
Alphen Dry White (S.A.), 314, 315
– Red (S.A.), 316
– Selected Riesling (S.A.), 314, 315
– Special Old Vintage (S.A.), 315
Alsterweiler Kapellenberg (Gy), 272
Altärchen (Gy), 265, 275
Altenberg (Gy), 266, 269, 270, 271, 272, 273, 274, 275
Altenburg (Gy), 272
Altenwald (Gy), 275
Alter Knabe-Saint Laurent (A), 293
Althälde (Gy), 271
Altlay (Gy), 276

Altstätter Forst (Sw), 268
– Rebhaldner Blauburgunder (Sw), 268
Alvaro (Sp), 189
Alvear Montilla (Sp), 188
Amaliensteimer (S.A.), 316
Amarella (S.A.), 316
Ambelakia (G), 298
Amboise (F), 119
Ambrosia (Sp), 190
Ameisenberg (Gy), 276
Amella (I), 228
Amigne (Sw), 93, 105
Amigny (F), 123
Aminei (I), 234
Amontillado (Sp), 48, 189
– S.S.S. (Sp), 189
Amour de Dieu (F), 107
Les Amoureuses (F), 49, 58
Amselfelder Spätburgunder (Yg), 292
Anadia (P), 200
Ancenis (F), 126
Ancien Manoir de La Valette (F), 167
Andard (F), 126
Les Angles (F), 77
Anguis (F), 152
Anhaux (F), 152
Anjou (F), 121, 122
– Mousseux (F), 361
Ankelspfad (Gy), 277
Annaberg (Gy), 269, 272, 275
Annung (Gy), 271
Ansinoe (C), 299
Anticuario (Sp), 189
Antika (G), 298
Antinori (I), 237, 240
Antoniusberg (Gy), 276
Antoniusbrunnen (Gy), 276
Anweg (Gy), 276
Aperitive (P), 213
Aphrodite (C), 299, 302
Apitiv (Sp), 189
Apotheke (Gy), 265, 275
Appenhalde (Sw), 247
Apremont (F), 107
Aqueria (F), 107
Arad (Is), 301
L'Arbalète (Sw), 106
Arbia (I), 227, 237
Arbois (F), 97, 107
– Mousseux (F), 361
Arboisset (F), 107
Arcadia (G), 301
Archanès (G), 301
Les Arches (F), 108
Arealva (P), 212
Arenenberg Domaine (Sw), 247, 268
Aux Argilats (F), 76
Les Argillats (F), 76
Les Argillières (F), 77
Argonauta Dry White (P), 213
L'Argonette (F), 126
Les Argouges (F), 124
Les Argoulets (Sw), 106
Aris (Sp), 189
Arlesheimer Blauburgunder (Sw), 268
– Schlossberg Gutedel (Sw), 268

Armada (Sp), 190
L'Arnesque (F), 107
Arsinoe (C), 302
Artimino (I), 227, 237
Les Arvelets (F), 56, 76, 77
Arvine (Sw), 105
Ashdod (Is), 301
Askalon Blanc 1963 (Is), 301
– Rouge 1965 (Is), 301
Aspen (Gy), 272
Asprinio (I), 233, 238
Assénovgrad Mavroud (Bg), 294
Assis Brasil (P), 212
Assmannshäuser Berg (Gy), 274
Astasberg (Gy), 275
Asti spumante (I), 221, 232, 236, 359, 364, 407
Atalaya (Sp), 189
Ataulfo (Sp), 189
Atlantic (P), 213
Atlantida (Sp), 190
Attila Felsen (Gy), 269
Auberg (Gy), 273
Les Aubuis (F), 125
Auerberg (Gy), 271
Auflangen (Gy), 259, 273
Augenscheiner (Gy), 275
Augustinerberg (Gy), 269
Aureo (Sp), 188
Les Aussy (F), 77
Autecour (Sw), 106
Autumn Leaves (Sp), 189
Auvernier (Sw), 269
Auxey-Duresses (F), 63, 77
Les Avaux (F), 63, 77
Avdat Red (Is), 301
– White (Is), 300, 301
Aveberg (Gy), 277
Avoine (F), 125
Azay-le-Rideau (F), 119, 123

Babenberg (Gy), 274
Baccastieler-Beerli Sevelen (Sw), 268
Bach (Gy), 274
Backhaus (Gy), 274, 275
Backofen (Gy), 277
Back's Claret (Light-bodied) (S.A.), 316
Badacsonyi Kéknyelü (H), 288, 293
– Szürkebarát (H), 288, 293
Badenberg (Gy), 269
Badener Lumpentürl-Neuburger (A), 293
Badstube (Gy), 275
Bagneux (F), 126
Baiken (Gy), 264, 274
Bailen (Sp), 189
Balatonfüredi (H), 293
Balbino (I), 234, 238
Balgach Beerli Blauburgunder (Sw), 268
Balgacher Buggler (Sw), 246, 268
– Riesling-Sylvaner (Sw), 268
Balgarshe Slantse (Bg), 291
La Ballena (Sp), 189
Banatski rizling (Yg), 294
Banda Azul (Sp), 187

Banda Roja (Sp), 187
Banderolle (Sw), 106
Bandol (F), 108
Bangert (Gy), 273
Bank Riesling (Gy), 276
Banquete (Sp), 189
Banyuls (F), 104, 378
Barbacarlo dell'Oltrepo pavese (I), 221, 236
Barbadillo (Sp), 189
Barbaresco (I), 220, 236
Barbaros (T), 302
Barbe d'Asne (F), 107
Barbera (Bz), 339
– (Cal), 325, 333
– d'Alba (I), 220, 236
– d'Asti (I), 220, 236
– d'Asti Spumante (I), 364
– del Monferrato (I), 236
Bardolino (I), 222, 236
Barletta (I), 238
La Barnuine (F), 107
Barolo (I), 219, 220, 236
Baron (Sp), 190
Baroness Cocktail (Sp), 189
Barratin (F), 107
La Barre or Clos-de-la-Barre (F), 77
Les Barres (F), 124
Barros (P), 212
Barsac (F), 156, 407, 409
Les Bas-des-Duresses (F), 77
Le Bas-des-Teurons (F), 77
Basseron (F), 108
Bas-Serres (F), 107
Basses-Mourettes (F), 77
Les Basses-Vergelesses (F), 77
Basses Vergelesses (F), 77
Les Batailleries (F), 124
Bâtard-Montrachet (F), 64, 78
Les Battereaux (F), 125
Les Baudes (F), 58, 76
Baugeois (F), 126
Bauregard (F), 125
Bausch (Gy), 273
Bayon (F), 167
B. C. 200 (Sp), 189
Beaujolais (F), 49, 70, 71, 78, 411
– supérieur (F), 70, 71, 78
Beaujolais-Villages (F), 70, 71, 78
Beaulieu-sur-Layon (F), 126
Beaumes (F), 107
Beaumes-de-Venise (F), 101
Beaumont (F), 123
Les Beaux-Monts (F), 76
Beaumont-en-Veron (F), 125
Beaune (F), 49, 63, 77
Beaupuy (F), 125
Beauregard (Sw), 106
– (F), 77, 123
Les Beauregards (F), 123
Beau Renard (F), 107
Beaurepaire (F), 77
Beau-Soleil (Sw), 106
Beauvais (F), 125
Beau Velours (Sw), 105
Aux Beaux-Bruns (F), 58, 76
Les Bédines (F), 107

Les Beduaux (F), 123
Beerlesberg (Gy), 271
Beerliwein (Sw), 246
Bel-Air (F), 76, 124, 125
Belan (Yg), 294
Bellarosa (Sw), 106
Belle Provinciale (Sw), 105
Bellet (F), 108
Belletaz (Sw), 106
Les Belletins (F), 123
Belle Valaisanne (Sw), 105
Bellevue (F), 107
Bellingham Almeida (S.A.), 315
– Late Vintage (S.A.), 315
– Premier Grand Cru (S.A.), 314, 315
– Riesling (S.A.), 315
– Rosé (S.A.), 315
– Selected Steinwein (S.A.), 314, 315
– Shiraz (S.A.), 314, 315
– Vintage Johannisberger (S.A.), 314, 315
Belz (Gy), 273
Benais (F), 125
Ben-Ami 1965 (Is), 301
Bender (Gy), 256, 272
Béni Melek (Ag), 308
Benito (Sp), 189, 190
Benkener Blauburgunder (Sw), 268
Berg (Gy), 269, 270, 271, 272, 273, 275, 276
Bergantin (Sp), 189
Berg-Bildstock (Gy), 274
Berg-Bronnen (Gy), 274
Berg Burgweg (Gy), 274
Bergel (Gy), 272
Bergerac (F), 152
Berggarten (Gy), 276
Berghalde (Gy), 272
Berghäusle (Gy), 271
Bergpächter (Gy), 275
Berg Ramstein (Gy), 274
– Roseneck (Gy), 274
– Rottland (Gy), 274
– Schlossberg (Gy), 274
Bernecker Blauburgunder (Sw), 268
Bernecker Rosenberger (Sw), 246, 268
Bernhell (Gy), 276
Bernstein (Gy), 276
Bergstrassenwein (Gy), 255
La Béroche (Sw), 269
Berson (F), 167
La Bertaude (F), 107
Les Berthiers (F), 123
Bertholod (Sw), 106
Bertinoro (I), 226, 237
Les Bertins (F), 77
Bertola (Sp), 189
Bertola Cream (Sp), 190
Bertrams Biscuit Sherry (S.A.), 316
Bertrams Oloroso Sherry (S,A.), 316
Les Bessadières (F), 125
Les Bessards (F), 107
Besselicher Klostermauer (Gy), 277
– lange Zeilen (Gy), 277
Besteurein (Gy), 269
Betis (Sp), 189
Bettelhaus (Gy), 272
Beulsberg (Gy), 276
Bex (Sw), 105, 106
Beyaz (T), 299, 302
La Beylesse (F), 107
Bianchello del Metauro (I), 228, 237
Bianchi dei Colli Friulani (I), 237
– del Collio Goriziano (I), 237
– vergini dell'Arestino (I), 227, 237
Bianco d'Avellino (I), 238
– dei Colli Berici (I), 236
– dei Colli Euganei (I), 236
– dell'Elba (I), 237
– di Alcamo (I), 238
– di Breganze (I), 236

Bianco di Gambellara (I), 236
Bickert (Gy), 275
Bienenberg (Gy), 274
Bienengarten (Gy), 272, 275, 277
Bien-Venu (Sw), 106
Bienvenues-Bâtard-Montrachet (F), 64, 78
Biergarten (Gy), 269
La Bigote (F), 107
Biguet (F), 107
Bildchen (Gy), 275
Bildstöckl (Gy), 256
Bill (Gy), 276
Binyamina Blanc (Is), 301
– Red (Is), 301
– Rosé (Is), 300, 301
Biousse (F), 107
Birkenberg (Gy), 273
Birmenstorfer Klevner (Sw), 268
Bischofsberg (Gy), 263, 274
Bischofsteiner (Gy), 276
Bischofstube (Gy), 276
Bisser (Bg), 294
Bistum (Gy), 275
Bitsch (Gy), 275
Bittigrain (Gy), 269
Bitzenberg (Gy), 269
Bizay (F), 125
Blaches (F), 107
Black Tom (Sp), 189
Blaise d'arbres (F), 107
Blanc Fumé de Pouilly (F), 114
Les Blanches-Fleurs (F), 77
La Blanchonne (F), 108
Blankenhornsberger (Gy), 269
Blanquette de Limoux (F), 103, 359, 361, 407
Les Blaquières (F), 107
Blassinges (Sw), 105
Blauburgunder (A), 293
– Beerli Munötler (Sw), 268
– Burg Schiterberger (Sw), 268
– Klingnauer Kloster Sion (Sw), 268
– Oberembach (Sw), 268
– Schlossberg Villigen (Sw), 268
– Schloss Goldenberg (Sw), 268
– Schlosshof Berg am Irchel (Sw), 268
Blauer Berg (Gy), 270
Blauer Burgunder Spätlese (A), 293
Blaufränkisch (A), 293
Blaufränkisch Spätlesen (A), 293
Blaye (F), 151, 167
Blaye-Plassac (F), 167
Blazquez (Sp), 189, 190
Bleidenberg (Gy), 189
Blindstöckle (Gy), 269
Les Blonnaises (Sw), 106
Blücherschanze (Gy), 272
Blüchertaler (Gy), 277
Blumberger Late Harvest (S.A.), 315
Boal (P), 211, 212
Boa Vista (P), 213
Bobadilla (Sp), 190
Boca (I), 220, 236
Bocksberg (Gy), 276
Bockstein (Gy), 266, 275
Bodenheim (S.A.), 316
Bodental (Gy), 274, 276
Böhlig (Gy), 256, 272
Bohren (Gy), 274
Boilauzon (F), 107
Boisdauphin (F), 107
Bois de Boursan (F), 107
Bois de la Vieille (F), 107
Bois-Fleury (F), 123
Boisgibaud (F), 123
Bois Guyon (F), 124
Bois Senescau (F), 107
Bois-Soleil (F), 124
Les Bois Turmeaux (F), 124
Bolliattaz (Sw), 106

Bollwerk (Gy), 277
Bombita (Sp), 189
Bömisberg (Gy), 269
Bommes (F), 156
Bonardo amabile (I), 221, 236
La Bonatière (F), 123
Bone Dry (Sp), 189
Les Bonnes-Mares (F), 58, 76
Les Bonnevières (F), 108
Bonnezeaux (F), 122, 126
Bonvillars (Sw), 249
Bopparder Hamm (Gy), 276, 277
Bordeaux (F), 135, 136, 144, 150, 151, 152
Bordeaux Clairet (F), 136
Bordeaux Supérieur (F), 135, 136, 144
Bordo Ay-Danil (U.S.S.R.), 292, 294
Bordon (Sp), 187
Borgogna (I), 222
Borlido (P), 212
La Borne (Sw), 106
Bornhofertal (Gy), 277
Les Borniques (F), 58, 76
Les Bosquets (F), 107
Bösselsberg-Wanne (Gy), 269
Les Bossières (F), 123
Botaina (Sp), 189
El Botanico (Sp), 189
Botticino (I), 236
Bouchemaine (F), 126
Boucher (F), 107
Les Bouchères (F), 78
Les Boucherottes (F), 63, 77
Bouchot (F), 123
Le Bouchot-du-Bas (F), 123
Le Bouchot-du-Haut (F), 123
Les Bouchots (F), 76
Le Boucou (F), 107
Aux Boudots (F), 76
La Boudriotte (F), 77, 78
Bouquet Royal (Sw), 106
Bourg (F), 123, 167
Bourgogne (F), 49, 55, 56, 76, 77, 78
– aligoté (F), 49, 55, 78
– Blanc (F), 69, 78
– grand ordinaire (F), 49, 55, 76, 77, 78
– Hautes Côtes de Nuits (F), 76
– Marsannay (F), 76
– ordinaire (F), 76, 77, 78
– Passe-tout-grain (F), 49, 76, 77, 78
Bourgueil (F), 119, 125, 404
Les Bourguignons (F), 107
Bourret (F), 107
Bousse-d'Or (F), 77
Aux Bousselots (F), 76
Boutefeu (Sw), 106
La Boutière (F), 77
Bouton-d'Or (Sw), 106
Bouvettes (F), 107
Boux d'Epesses (Sw), 106
Bouzigues (F), 107
Bouzy (F), 355
Bozcaada (C), 407
Bözer Riesling-Sylvaner (Sw), 268
Brachetto d'Acqui (I), 221, 236
Brain-sur-Allones (F), 126
Brain-sur-l'Authion (F), 126
Braise d'Enfer (Sw), 106
Branco Extra Seco (P), 213
Brandenberg (Gy), 275
Bratenöfchen (Gy), 275
Brauneberg (Gy), 275, 276
Braune Kupp (Gy), 266, 275
Braunfels (Gy), 275
Bravade (Sw), 106
Brehmich (Gy), 271
Breten (Gy), 271
Breitscheid und Rechtel (Gy), 276
La Bressande (F), 78
Les Bressandes (F), 63, 77

Brestenberger Klevner (Sw), 247, 268
Le Bret (F), 107
Les Bretterins (F), 77
– dit La Chapelle (F), 77
Brézé (F), 125
Brigné (F), 126
Brig's Port White Dry (P), 213
Brillante (Sp), 187
Brindamour (Sw), 105
Brioli (I), 227
Brissac (F), 126
La Brocarde (F), 108
Brolio (I), 237
Bromberg (Gy), 271
Bronnen (Gy), 263
Les Brosses (F), 123, 124
Brotwasser (Gy), 255, 268
Les Brouillards (F), 77
Brouilly (F), 71, 72, 78
Brückstück (Gy), 277
Brückenstück (Gy), 276
Brückes (Gy), 259, 273
Bruderberg Na Oes (S.A.), 316
– Selected Cabernet (S.A.), 316
Brudesberg (Gy), 258, 273
Bruderschaft (Gy), 275
Brühl (Gy), 272, 273
Aux Brûlés (F), 76
Les Brûlées (F), 124
Brûlefer (Sw), 105
Les Bruneau (F), 124
Brunello di Montalcino (I), 227, 237
Bruniers (F), 123
Am Brünnchen (Gy), 277
Les Brusquières (F), 107
Brüssele (Gy), 270
Les Brussoles (F), 77, 78
Bubenhalde (Gy), 270
Bucelas (P), 199, 212
– Velho (P), 212
Buchberg (Gy), 269
Buchberger (Sw), 246, 268
Buchbrenner Berg (Gy), 274
Buchenberg (Sw), 246
Büchsenberg (Gy), 269
Bühl (Gy), 269
Bühlertal (Gy), 254
Buissonnet (F), 107
Buleria (Sp), 189
Burg (Gy), 271
Burgberg (Gy), 269, 270, 271, 273, 275, 276, 277
Bürgel (Gy), 273
Burgenberg (Gy), 275
Bürgengarten (Gy), 272
Bürgerslay (Gy), 275
Burggarten (Gy), 272
Burggraben (Gy), 274
Burghalde (Gy), 270
Burg Katz (Gy), 277
Burglay (Gy), 275
Burgrave (Sw), 105
Burgstall (Gy), 271
Burgundac crni (Yg), 294
Burgundy (Aus), 341
– (Cal), 325, 333
Burgweg (Gy), 263, 272, 273, 274
Burgwengert (Gy), 275
Burg Wildecker (Gy), 270
Burignon (Sw), 105
Bürkele (Gy), 269
Busard (Sw), 106
Busslay (Gy), 265, 275
Buttafuoco dell'Oltrepo pavese (I), 221, 236
Butte de Saumoussay (F), 125
Büttenberg (Gy), 276
Buzbag (T), 276, 302

Cabane Saint-Jean (F), 107
Cabanette (F), 107

Cabernet (Aus), 341
– (Bg), 291
– (I), 225, 236
– (S.A.), 341
– Abraou (U.S.S.R.), 292, 294
– d'Anjou (F), 126
– friulano (I), 237
– Livadia (U.S.S.R.), 292, 294
– de Saumur (F), 126
– Sauvignon (Cal), 325, 329, 333
– Shiraz (Aus), 341
– delle Venezie (I), 222, 236
Cabrières (F), 103, 107, 108
La Cacharde (F), 107
Cacique (Sp), 189
Le Cadet Bon (F), 163
La Caille (Sw), 106
Les Caillerets (F), 67, 78
Le Cailleret (F), 78
En Cailleret (F), 77
Caillerets-Dessus (F), 77
Les Cailles (F), 76
Cairanne (F), 100, 107
Calamin (Sw), 106
Caldaro (I), 222
Calouères (F), 76
Caluso Passito (I), 221, 236
Camborio (Sp), 189
Campero (Sp), 189
Campey (F), 107
Campidano di Cagliari (I), 238, 242
Canchales (Sp), 187
Cange (F), 123
Canneto (I), 221, 236
Cannonau del Campidano (I), 238
Cannstatter Berg (Gy), 270
– Steinhalde (Gy), 270
– Wolfersberg (Gy), 270
– Zuckerle (Gy), 270
Cansaud (F), 107
Canto (Sp), 189
Cap Bon (Tu), 315
La Capilla (Sp), 189
Capinella (S.A.), 316
Capitan (Sp), 189
La Capitana (Sp), 189
La Capite (Sw), 106
Capri (I), 233, 238
Le Car (F), 108
En Caradeux (F), 77
Carcavelos (P), 198, 199
Carcavelos-Quinta da Bela Vista (P), 212
Carcenies (F), 107
Cardenal Cisneros (Sp), 190
Carelle-Dessous (F), 77
Carelle-sous-la-Chapelle (F), 77
Carema (I), 220, 236
Caricia (Sp), 189
Cariñena (Sp), 175, 187
Cariño (Sp), 188
Carito (P), 213
Carla (Sp), 190
Carlonet Cabernet (S.A.), 314, 315
Carlsheim 8 (S.A.), 314, 315
Carlton House (Sp), 190
Carmela (Sp), 190
Carmel Hock (Is), 300, 301
Carmelita (Sp), 189
Carmignano (I), 227, 237
Carola (Sp), 189
Carta Blanca (Sp), 189
Cartago (Brown), (Sp), 190
Carta Real (Sp), 189
Cartaxo (P), 200
La Carte (F), 124
Carthage (Tu), 315
Dei Castelli (I), 229, 230
Cartujo (Sp), 189

Carvalho, Ribeiro & Ferreira (P), 212
Casalinho (P), 212
Casanovas (Sp), 189, 190
Casino Dry White (P), 213
Le Cas-Rougeot (F), 77
Le Cassereau (F), 124
Les Cassiers (F), 123
Castel Acquaro (I), 238
Castelas (F), 107
Castel Danielis (G), 301
– del Monte (I), 231, 238
Castelo Port (S.A.), 316
Castel San Giorgio (I), 231, 237
Castillo de las Arenas (Sp), 187
– de Tiebas (Sp), 187
– Ygay (Sp), 187
– Ygay Reserva (Sp), 187
El Catador (Sp), 189
Catawba (N. Y.), 333
Cave de Fischer (Sw), 106
– des Allours (Sw), 105
– du Prieuré (Sw), 106
Caves de l'Hôpital (Sw), 105
Caves des Hospices cantonaux (Sw), 105
Cazetiers (F), 76
Cesanese (I), 230, 237
Cesanese del Piglio (I), 230, 237
Celebration (Sp), 190
Cellatica (I), 236
Les Celliers (F), 126
Cencibel (Sp), 188
Century Port (P), 213
Les Cent-Vignes (F), 77
Cerasuolo di Abruzzo (I), 231, 237
– di Vittoria (I), 234, 238
La Cerise (F), 107
Cerisier (F), 107
Cérons (F), 141, 156
El Cesar (Sp), 189
Chabiots (F), 76
Chablais (Sw), 94, 105, 106
Chablis (F), 55, 72, 76, 292, 378
Chablis (Aus), 341
Chablis (Cal), 322, 325, 333
Chablis-Beauroy (F), 55, 76
Chablis-Blanchots (F), 55, 76
Chablis-Bougros (F), 55, 76
Chablis-Côte de Léchet (F), 55, 76
Chablis-Forêts (F), 55, 76
Chablis-Fourchaume (F), 55, 76
Chablis Grand cru (F), 49
Chablis-Grenouilles (F), 55, 76
Chablis-Les-Clos (F), 55, 76
Chablis-Mélinots (F), 55, 76
Chablis-Montmains (F), 55
Chablis-Mont de Milieu (F), 55, 76
Chablis-Montée de Tonnerre (F), 55, 76
Chablis Premier Cru (F), 49
Chablis-Preuses (F), 55, 76
Chablis-Vaillons (F), 55, 76
Chablis-Valmur (F), 55, 76
Chablis-Vaucoupin (F), 55, 76
Chablis-Vaudésir (F), 55, 76
Chablis-Vaugiraud (F), 55, 76
Chablis-Vaugros (F), 55, 76
Les Chabœufs (F), 76
Chacé (F), 126
Chäfer-Steiner Blaurock (Sw), 268
Chafeune (F), 107
Les Chaffots (F), 76
Aux Chaignots (F), 76
Les Chaillots (F), 77
En la Chaîne-Carteau (F), 76
Les Chalumeaux (F), 78
Chambelan (Sp), 189
Chambergo (Sp), 189
Chambertin (F), 49, 57, 59, 76, 408
Chambertin-Clos-de-Bèze (F), 56, 76

Chambolle-Musigny (F), 58, 60, 76, 404, 410
Chambraste (F), 123
Chambre-tout (F), 108
Le Champ (F), 126
Champagne (Aus), 341
Champagne (Cal), 333
Champagne (F), 349, 352
En Champans (F), 77
Le Champ-Canet (F), 78
Champ Chardon (F), 125
Champ-Clou (F), 78
Champeaux (F), 76
Champigny (F), 411
Champigny-le-Sec (F), 126
Champs-Pimont (F), 77
Champitonnois dit « Petite Chapelle » (F), 76
Champlot (F), 77
Champonnets (F), 76
Champréveyres de la Ville (Sw), 269
Les Champs-Fulliot (F), 77
Les Champs-Gain (F), 77, 78
Aux Champs-Perdrix (F), 76
Champtin (F), 123
Chançay (F), 124
La Chanière (F), 77
Chanlin (F), 77
Les Chanlins-Bas (F), 77
Le Chant des Resses (Sw), 105
Chanteauvieux (Sw), 105
La Chanteleuserie (F), 125
Chanteperdrix (Sw), 106
Le Chantey (Sw), 105
Chanturgue (F), 411
Chapelle-Chambertin (F), 57, 76
La Chapelle-Heulin (F), 126
Chapelle de Salquenen (Sw), 105
Les Chapelles (F), 124
Les Chapelles (Sw), 105
Chapitre (F), 78
Les Chaponnières (F), 77
Chapotannaz (Sw), 106
Chapouin (F), 107
Charantelle (S.A.), 315
Charbonnières (F), 107
Chardonnay (Cal), 322
Les Charmes (F), 58, 76
Aux Charmes (F), 76
Charmes-Chambertin (F), 49, 57, 76
Les Charmes-Dessus (F), 49, 78
Les Charmes-Dessous (F), 49, 78
Es-Charmots (F), 77
Charmus de la Cure (Sw), 105
Les Charnières (F), 77
Les Charrières (F), 76
La Chartreuse (F), 107
Charveyron (F), 411
Chassagne or Cailleret (F), 64, 67, 78
Chassagne-Montrachet (F), 64, 77, 78
Les Chassaignes (F), 123
Chasselas, Alsace (F), 252
– Genève (Sw), 105, 106
Chasse-Peines, (Sw), 269
Chatagnéréaz (Sw), 106
Château l'Abbé-Gorsse-de-Gorsse (F), 159
– Agassac (F), 158
– de l'Aiguillette (F), 159
– Les Alberts (F), 167
– Alphen (S.A.), 316
– Andron-Blanquet (F), 158
– l'Angélus (F), 163
– Angludet (F), 158
– d'Anice (F), 157
– Archambaud (F), 157
– d'Arche (F), 156, 159
– d'Arche-Lassalle (F), 160
– d'Arche-Pugneau (F), 156
– d'Arche-Vimeney (F), 156
– d'Arcins (F), 159

Château d'Armajan-des-Ormes (F), 156
– les Armuseries (F), 124
– Arnaud-Jouan (F), 161
– Arnauton (F), 167
– d'Arricaud (F), 158
– l'Arrosée (F), 163
– des Arrouches (F), 162
– d'Arsac (F), 159
– Ausone (F), 163
– d'Auvernier (Sw), 269
– Badette (F), 163
– Baladoz (F), 164
– Baleau (F), 163
– Balestard-la-Tonnelle (F), 163
– Balestey (F), 157
– Balogues (F), 159
– Barakan (F), 161
– de Barbe (F), 167
– Barbet (F), 167
– La Barde (F), 164, 167
– Barde-Haut (F), 164
– Bardins (F), 157
– Baret (F), 157
– Barrabaque (F), 166
– Barrère (F), 160
– Barreyre (F), 159
– Barrieux (F), 167
– Barthez (F), 157
– Les Basiliques (F), 164
– Bas-Pommarède (F), 157
– Bassaler Castanède (F), 161
– des Basses-Rivières (F), 124
– La Bastienne (F), 164
– Bastor-Lamontagne (F), 156
– Batailley (F), 158
– Batsères (F), 158
– Les Bavolliers (F), 167
– Bayard (F), 164
– de Béard (F), 164
– de Beauchêne (F), 157
– Beauchêne (former Clos Mazeyres) (F), 165
– Beauduc (F), 162
– Beaufresque (F), 162
– Beaulac (F), 156, 157
– Beaulé (F), 162
– de Beaulieu (F), 161
– Beaulieu (F), 157, 158
– Beau-Mazerat (F), 163
– Beaumont (F), 159
– de Beaupuy (F), 160
– Beauregard (F), 165
– de Beauregard (F), 107
– Beauséjour (F), 162, 163, 164, 165
– Beausite (F), 158
– Beau-Site Monprimblanc (F), 161
– Beauval (F), 162
– La Bécade (F), 159
– du Bedat (F), 162
– La Bégorce (F), 159
– Bel-Air (F), 157, 160, 161, 162, 163
– de Bel-Air (F), 166
– Belair (F), 165
– Bel-Air Haut-Montguillon (F), 165
– Bel-Air Lagrave (F), 159
– Bel-Air, Marquis d'Aligre (F), 158
– Bel-Air-Ouy (F), 164
– Belgrave (F), 158
– Belle-Brise (F), 165
– de Bellefontaine (F), 162
– Bellefontaine (F), 158
– Bellefont-Belcier (F), 164
– Bellegarde (F), 161
– Bellegrave (F), 159
– Belle-Isle-Mondotte (F), 164
– Bellerive (F), 159
– Belleroque (F), 167
– Belle-Rose (F), 159
– Belles-Plantes (F), 163

Château Bellevue (F), 161, 163, 164, 165, 167
– Belloy (F), 166
– Belon (F), 157
– Bel-Orme (F), 159
– de Benauge (F), 162
– Bergat (F), 163
– de Bergerie (F), 162
– Berliquet (F), 163
– Bernard-Raymond (F), 157
– Berthenon (F), 167
– Berthou (F), 167
– La Bertonnière (F), 167
– Bertranon (F), 160
– des Bessanes (F), 157
– Beychevelle (F), 158
– de la Bézine (F), 161
– Bézineau (F), 163
– Biac (F), 160
– Bibian-Darriet (F), 159
– La Bichaude (F), 164
– Binyamina (Is), 294
– Birot (F), 161
– de Blagnac (F), 162
– La Blancherie (F), 157
– de Blissa (F), 167
– Bodet (F), 166
– Boiresse (F), 157
– Boisset (F), 167
– Boisson (F), 161
– du Bonnat (F), 157
– Bonneau (F), 159
– Bonnet (F), 162
– Bord-Ramonet (F), 163
– Le Boscq (F), 158
– La Bouade (F), 156
– Bouchoc (F), 160
– du Boulay (F), 123
– Le Bourdieu (F), 159
– Bourgneuf-Vayron (F), 165
– Bourseau (F), 166
– Bouscaut (F), 157
– du Bousquet (F), 167
– La Bouygue (F), 164
– Bouyot (F), 156
– Boyd-Cantenac (F), 158
– Bragard (F), 163
– Branaire-Ducru (F), 158
– Brane-Cantenac (F), 158
– Brassens-Guiteronde (F), 156
– de La Brède (F), 157
– Brémontier (F), 161
– Brethous (F), 161
– du Breuil (F), 126
– Le Breuil (F), 159
– Breuil (F), 167
– Brigaille (F), 161
– La Brousse (F), 167
– Broustet (F), 156
– Brun (F), 164
– Brun-Mazeyres (F), 165
– de Budos (F), 158
– du Burg (F), 162
– du Burk (F), 162
– de Bursinel (Sw), 106
– Bussac (F), 162
– La Cabane (F), 167
– La Cabanne (F), 165
– Cabannieux (F), 157
– Cadet-Fonroque (F), 163
– Cadet-Piola (F), 163
– Cadet-Soutard (F), 163
– Caïla (F), 161
– de Caillavet (F), 161
– Caillou (F), 156
– Le Caillou (F), 165
– Calon (F), 165
  Calon-Ségur (F), 158
– de Camarsac (F), 162
– Cambes-Kermovan (F), 167
– Camensac (F), 158

Château Cameron (F), 156
– Camperos (F), 156
– Campet (F), 161
– Canon (F), 163, 166
– Canon-Bourret (F), 166
– Canon de Brem (F), 166
– Canon Chaigneau (F), 166
– Canon-La-Gaffelière (F), 163
– Canon-Lange (F), 166
– Cantau (F), 157
– Cantebau-Couhins (F), 157
– Cantegril (F), 156
– Canteloup (F), 159, 161
– Cantemerle (F), 158, 167
– Cantenac (F), 163
– Cantenac-Brown (F), 158
– Canterane (F), 164
– de Cantereau (F), 165
– Capbern (F), 158
– Capet (F), 164
– Capet-Bégaud (F), 166
– Capet-Guillier (F), 164
– Cap-de-Haut (F), 159
– Cap de Mourlin (F), 163
– de la Capelle (F), 164
– Carbonnieux (F), 157
– Carcanieux-les-Graves (F), 159
– Cardinal-Villemaurine (F), 163
– La Cardonne (F), 159
– de Carignan (F), 161
– Carillon (F), 165
– de Carles (F), 156, 167
– Caronne-Ste-Gemme (F), 158
– Cartau (F), 163
– La Carte (F), 163
– du Cartillon (F), 159
– Cassagne (F), 166
– Cassevert (F), 163
– Le Castelot (F), 164
– du Casterat (F), 159
– La Caussade (F), 160
– du Cauze (F), 164
– Cauzin (F), 163
– La Cave (F), 167
– Cayre (F), 161
– Cazeau (F), 162
– Cazeaux (F), 167
– Cazès (F), 157
– de Cérons et de Calvimont (F), 156
– Certan-Demay (F), 165
– Certan-Marzelle (F), 165
– La Chabanne (F), 161
– Chaigneau-Guillon (F), 166
– Chaillou (F), 167
– Chalon (F), 107
– Chambert (F), 159
– Champion (F), 163
– de Chanze (F), 126
– Chante-l'Oiseau (F), 158, 161
– La Chapelle-de-Lescours (F), 164
– La Chapelle-Lariveau (F), 166
– Chapelle-Madeleine (F), 163
– de Chardonne (Sw), 105
– Charmail (F), 159
– des Charmettes (F), 158
– Charron (F), 167
– Chasselauds (F), 167
– Chasse-Spleen (F), 158
  Châtain (F), 166
– Châteauneuf (F), 162
– de Châtelard (Sw), 105
– Le Châtelet (F), 162
– du Châtelet (F), 163, 165
– Châtelet-Moléonne (F), 163
– Les Chaumes (F), 166, 167
– Chauvin (F), 160, 163
– Chaviran (F), 157
– de Chelivette (F), 161
– Chelivette (F), 162
– du Chêne-Liège (F), 165
– Chêne-Vert (F), 157

Château Chêne-Vieux (F), 165
– Cheval-Blanc (F), 163
– Cheval-Noir (F), 163
– Chevrol-Bel-Air (F), 166
– Cissac (F), 159
– Citran (F), 158
– Clauzet (F), 159
– Clerc-Milon (F), 158
– Climens (F), 156
– Clinet (F), 165
– du Clocher (F), 163
– Clos d'Amières (F), 167
– Clos de l'Oratoire (F), 164
– La Closerie (F), 158
– La Closerie Grand Poujeaux (F), 159
– La Clotte (F), 163, 165
– La Clotte et Cazalis (F), 156
– La Clotte-Grande-Côte (F), 163
– La Cluzière (F), 163
– des Combes-Canon (F), 166
– de Come (F), 159
– de la Commanderie (F), 166
– La Commanderie (F), 165
– Comte (F), 166
– Le Cone Moreau (F), 167
– Le Cone Sebilleau (F), 167
– Le Cone Taillasson (F), 167
– Conseillante (F), 165
– Constantia (S.A.), 316
– Copis (F), 160
– Corbin (F), 163, 164
– Corbin-Michotte (F), 163
– Corconnac (F), 159
– Cordeliers (F), 160
– Cormey (F), 163
– Cormey-Figeac (F), 163
– Cos-d'Estournel (F), 158
– Cos-Labory (F), 158
– Costeriou (F), 161
– Côte-Belle (F), 161
– Côte Bernateau (F), 164
– Cottière (F), 167
– Coucy (F), 164
– Le Coudeau (F), 167
– Coudert (F), 164
– Coufran (F), 159
– Couhins (F), 157
– Coullac (F), 160
– de Courauneau (F), 162
– La Couronne (F), 158
– du Courreau (F), 161
– de Courtade (F), 161
– Courtade Dubuc (F), 161
– de Courteillac (F), 162
– La Couspaude (F), 163
– Coustet (F), 156
– Coustolle (F), 166
– Coutelin-Merville (F), 159
– Coutet (F), 159, 163
– Le Couvent (F), 163
– Crabitey (F), 157
– de Crans (Sw), 106
– Cravignac (F), 163
– Le Crock (F), 158
– La Croix (F), 161, 165
– La Croix-Chantecaille (F), 163
– Croix-de-Blanchon (F), 165
– Croix-de-Chantecaille (F), 163
– La Croix-Landon (F), 159
– de la Croix (Millorit) (F), 167
– La Croix-Saint-André (F), 166
– La Croix-Saint-Georges (F), 165
– La Croix-Saint-Jean (F), 166
– Croizet-Bages (F), 158
– Croque-Michotte (F), 163
– du Cros (F), 160
– Croûte-Charlus (F), 167
– Croûte-Mallard (F), 167
– Crusquet (F), 167

Château Cruzeau (F), 164
– Les Cruzelles (F), 166
– Le Cugat (F), 162
– La Cure (F), 167
– Curé-Bon-la-Madelaine (F), 163
– de Cypressat (F), 161
– la Dame-Blanche (F), 159
– Damluc (F), 161
– Dassault (F), 163
– Daugay (F), 163
– La Dauphine (F), 167
– Dauphiné-Rondillon (F), 163
– Les Dauphins (F), 162
– Dauzac (F), 158
– de Dauzay (F), 125
– Desmirail (F), 158
– Despeyrères (F), 157
– Dillon (F), 159
– Doisy (F), 156
– Doisy-Daene (F), 156
– Doisy-Védrines (F), 156
– du Domaine de Descazeaux (F), 167
– Domeyne (F), 159
– La Dominique (F), 163
– de Doms (F), 157
– Donissan (F), 159
– Doumayne (F), 164
– Drouilleau-Belles-Graves (F), 166
– Ducasse (F), 156
– Ducru-Beaucaillou (F), 158
– Dudon (F), 156
– Duhart-Milon (F), 158
– de Duillier (Sw), 106
– Dupeyrat (F), 167
– Duplessis (F), 161
– Duplessis-Fabre (F), 159
– Duplessis Hauchecorne (F), 159
– Durand (F), 165
– Durfort-Vivens (F), 158
– Dutoya (F), 160
– Dutruch-Grand-Poujeaux (F), 158
– de l'Eglise (F), 160
– de l'Emigré (F), 157
– l'Enclos (F), 165
– Enclos Haut-Mazeyres (F), 165
– d'Epire (F), 126
– l'Ermitage (F), 159, 161
– de l'Escaley (F), 160
– de l'Espérance (F), 157
– de l'Espinglet (F), 161
– de l'Etoile (F), 124
– Etoile-Pourret (F), 163
– L'Evangile (F), 165
– Eyquem (F), 167
– Faget (F), 159
– La Fagnouse (F), 164
– de Faleyrens (F), 164
– Falfas (F), 167
– Fantin (F), 162
– de Fargues (F), 156
– Faubernet (F), 160
– Fauchey (F), 161
– Faugas (F), 161
– Favols (F), 161
– Fayard (F), 160
– Fayau (F), 161
– Fellonneau (F), 159
– Ferran (F), 157
– Ferrand (F), 165
– de Ferrand (F), 164
– Ferrande (F), 157
– La Ferrière (F), 165
– Ferrière (F), 158
– Feytit-Clinet (F), 165
– de Fieuzal (F), 157
– Figeac (F), 163
– Filhot (F), 156
– La Fleur-Canon (F), 166
– La Fleur-Mérissac (F), 163
– La Fleur-Milon (F), 159
– La Fleur-Perruchon (F), 165

Château La Fleur-Petrus (F), 166
- La Fleur-Pourret (F), 163
- La Fleur-Saint-Bonnet (F), 159
- La Fleur-Vachon (F), 163
- Fleury (F), 156
- Fombrauge (F), 164
- Fonbadet (F), 159
- Fonchereau (F), 162
- Fongaban-Bellevue (F), 163
- Fongravey (F), 159
- Fonpetite (F), 159
- Fonpiqueyre (F), 159
- Fonplégade (F), 163
- Fonrazade (F), 163
- Fonréaud (F), 159
- Fonroque (F), 163
- La Fontaine (F), 167
- Fontebride (F), 156
- Fontesteau (F), 159
- de Fontmurée (F), 164
- Fort-de-Vauban (F), 159
- Formont (F), 162
- Foucla (F), 157
- Fougeailles (F), 166
- des Fougères (F), 157
- Fourcas-Dupré (F), 159
- Fourcas-Hosten (F), 159
- Fourney (F), 164
- de France (F), 157
- Franc-Mayne (F), 163
- Franc-Patarabet (F), 163
- Franc-Pourret (F), 163
- La Fresnaye (F), 126
- Le Gabachot (F), 166
- Gaby (F), 166
- Gachet (F), 166
- Gadeau (F), 167
- La Gaffelière (F), 163
- Gagnard (F), 167
- Gaillard (F), 77, 125
- Galan (F), 159
- Gallais-Bellevue (F), 159
- La Ganne (F), 166
- du Gard (F), 161
- La Garde (F), 167
- Le Gardera (F), 160
- La Garde Roland (F), 167
- Garde-Rose (F), 164
- La Garosse (F), 159
- Garraud (F), 166
- de Garreau (F), 161
- Gassies (F), 161
- Gaubert (F), 164
- Gaudrelle (F), 124
- Gaussens (F), 160
- Le Gay (F), 166
- Gay-Moulin (F), 164
- de Gayon (F), 158
- Gazin (F), 157, 165
- du Gazin (F), 166
- Génisson (F), 161
- Gigault (F), 167
- Gilette (F), 156
- La Girouette (F), 167
- Giscours (F), 158
- du Glana (F), 158
- de Glérolles (Sw), 105
- Gloria (F), 159
- Godeau (F), 164
- de Goélane (F), 162
- Gombaude-Guillot et Grandes Vignes Clinet réunis (F), 165
- La Gommerie (F), 163
- Gontier (F), 167
- La Gorce (F), 160
- Gordat (F), 167
- Gouprie (F), 165
- Gourran (F), 160
- La Grâce-Dieu (F), 163
- Grand-Barrail-Lamarzelle-Figeac (F), 163

Château Grand Bourdieu (F), 157
- de Grand Branet (F), 161
- Grand Carretey (F), 156
- Grandchamp (F), 165
- Grand Chemin (F), 157
- Grand-Clapeau (F), 159
- Grand Corbin Despagne (F), 163
- Le Grand-Corbin-Pécresse (F), 163
- Grandis (F), 159
- Grand-Duroc-Milon (F), 159
- Les Grandes Murailles (F), 163
- Grand-Jour (F), 161, 167
- Grand-Mayne (F), 163
- Grand-Mayne Guy-né-Marc (F), 156
- Grand Mirande (F), 163
- Grand-Monteil (F), 162
- de Grand-Mouëys (F), 161
- Grand-Ormeau (F), 166
- Grand-Pey-Lescours (F), 164
- du Grand-Peyrot (F), 160
- Grand-Pontet (F), 163
- du Grand Puch (F), 162
- Grand-Puy-Ducasse (F), 158
- Grand-Puy-Lacoste (F), 158
- Grand-Renouil (F), 166
- Grand-Saint-Julien (F), 159
- Grand-Village-Capbern (F), 159
- Grangey (F), 164
- Granins (F), 159
- Grate-Cap (F), 165
- du Grava (F), 161
- Gravas (F), 156
- de la Grave (F), 167
- de la Gravère (F), 158
- des Graves (F), 157
- La Grave-Trigant-de-Boisset (F), 166
- Gravelines-Semens (F), 161
- de Graveyrion (F), 157
- La Gravière (F), 160, 166
- La Gravière-Couerbe (F), 159
- Les Gravières (F), 157
- La Graville (F), 160
- Gressier-Grand-Poujeaux (F), 159
- Gréteau (F), 161
- Grillet (F), 98, 107
- Grillon (F), 156
- de Grissac (F), 167
- La Grolet (F), 167
- Gros (F), 164
- Gros-Moulin (F), 167
- Gruaud-Laroze-Sarget (F), 158, 409
- du Gua (F), 162
- Guadet-Le-Franc-Grâce-Dieu (F), 163
- Guadet-Saint-Julien (F), 163
- Gueyrosse (F), 164
- Gueyrot (F), 163
- Guibaud (F), 165
- Guibot-la-Fourvieille (F), 165
- Guienne (F), 167
- Guillaumet (F), 162
- Guillaumot (F), 157
- Guillemot (F), 164
- Guillonnet (F), 167
- Guillot (F), 165
- Guillou (F), 165
- Guimbalet (F), 156
- Guiraud (F), 156, 167
- Guiteronde (F), 156
- La Gurgue (F), 159
- Hallet (F), 156
- Hanteillan (F), 159
- L'Haouilley (F), 156
- La Hargue (F), 167
- d'Hauretz (F), 162
- Haut-Bages-Libéral (F), 158
- Haut Bages Monpelou (F), 159

Château Haut-Bailly (F), 157
- Haut-Ballet (F), 166
- Haut-Bardin (F), 160
- Haut-Batailley (F), 158
- Haut-Bergeron (F), 156
- Haut-Bernon (F), 165
- Haut-Berthonneau (F), 163
- Haut-Bommes (F), 156
- Haut-Bourdat (F), 157
- Haut-Brana (F), 157
- Haut-Breton (F), 159
- Haut-Brignon (F), 161
- Haut-Brion (F), 157
- Haut-Cabat (F), 167
- Haut-Cadet (F), 163
- du Haut-Carmail (F), 159
- Haut-Carré (F), 157
- Haut-Chaigneau (F), 166
- du Haut-Gravat (F), 167
- Les Hautes-Graves (F), 164
- Haute-Nauve (F), 164
- Haut-Fonrazade (F), 163
- Haut-Goujon (F), 164
- Haut-Grâce-Dieu (F), 163
- Haut-Grand-Faurie (F), 163
- Haut-Gravier (F), 157
- Haut-La-Huntasse (F), 157
- Haut-Laroque (F), 161
- Haut-Larose (F), 165
- Haut-La Rose (F), 163
- Haut-Marbuzet (F), 158
- Haut-Mayne (F), 156
- Haut-Mazerat (F), 163
- Haut-Nouchet (F), 157
- Haut-Padarnac (F), 159
- Haut-Piquat (F), 165
- Haut-Plaisance (F), 164
- Haut-Plantey (F), 164
- Haut-Plateau (F), 165
- Haut-Pontet (F), 163
- Haut-Pourret (F), 163
- du Haut-Rat (F), 157
- du Haut-Rocher (F), 164
- Haut-Sarpe (F), 163, 164
- Haut-Segotte (F), 163
- Haut-Simard (F), 163
- Haut-Troquard (F), 165
- de Haux (F), 160
- La Haye (F), 159
- Le Hère (F), 156
- Hermitage-Mazerat (F), 163
- Houissant (F), 158
- Le Huzet (F), 157
- d'Intrans (F), 161
- d'Issan (F), 158
- Jacquemeau (F), 163
- Jacques-Blanc (F), 164
- Jacques-le-Haut (F), 156
- Janisson (F), 161
- Jany (F), 156
- du Jardin-Saint-Julien (F), 163
- du Jardin-Villemaurine (F), 163
- des Jaubertes (F), 158
- Jauque-Blanc (F), 163
- Jean-Blanc (F), 164
- Jeandeman (F), 167
- Jean-Faure (F), 163
- Jeanganne-Préfontaine (F), 161
- Jean-Gervais (F), 157
- Jean Lamat (F), 160
- Jean de Mayne (F), 163
- Jean-Voisin (F), 163
- Jonka (F), 156
- Jourdan (F), 161
- du Juge (F), 160, 161
- Junayme (F), 166
- Jura-Plaisance (F), 164
- Justa (F), 161
- Kirwan (F), 158
- Labatisse (F), 159
- Labatut (F), 161, 162

Château de Labégorce (F), 159
- Labégorce-Zédé (F), 159
- Laborde (F), 166
- Labory (F), 160
- Lacroix (F), 166
- Lacroix-de-Gay (F), 165
- Ladouys (F), 159
- Lafargue (F), 157
- Lafaurie (F), 166
- Lafaurie-Peyraguey (F), 156
- Lafite-Canteloup (F), 159
- Lafite-Rothschild (F), 158
- Lafitte (F), 161, 162
- Laffitte-Carcasset (F), 159
- Lafleur (F), 164, 165
- Lafleur-Lambaret (F), 166
- Lafon (F), 156, 159
- Lafon-Rochet (F), 158
- Lafont (F), 156, 167
- Lafuë (F), 160
- Lagarde (F), 157
- Lagarette (F), 161
- Lagareyre (F), 160
- Lagarosse (F), 160
- Lagrange (F), 158, 166, 167
- Lagrange Marquis de Luppe (F), 167
- Lagraula (F), 162
- Lagueloup (F), 158
- La Lagune (F), 158
- Lalanette (F), 157
- Lalibarde (F), 167
- Lamarche-Candelayre (F), 166
- Lamarque (F), 159
- Lamartre (F), 164
- Lamothe (F), 156, 157, 160, 167
- Lamothe-Bergeron (F), 159
- Lamothe-Bouscaut (F), 157
- Lamothe de Haux (F), 161
- Lamourette (F), 156
- Lamouroux (F), 156
- Lande de Gravet (F), 164
- Landeron (F), 162
- Lanère (F), 156
- Lanessan (F), 158, 159
- de Langalerie (F), 162
- Langlade (F), 165
- Langoa (F), 158
- Langoiran (F), 160
- Laniotte (F), 163
- de la Lanterne (F), 124
- Lanusse-Couloumet (F), 160
- Lapelletrie (F), 164
- Lapeloue (F), 156
- Lapeyreyre (F), 160
- Lapeyruche (F), 160
- Laplagnotte-Bellevue (F), 163
- Laporte (F), 163
- Larchevesque (F), 166
- Larcis-Ducasse (F), 163, 164
- Lardiley (F), 161
- Lardit (F), 161
- Laribotte (F), 156
- Lariveau (F), 156
- Larmande (F), 163
- Laroche (F), 160
- Laroque (F), 164
- Larose (F), 161
- Larose-Perganson (F), 159
- Larose-Trintaudon (F), 159
- Laroze (F), 163
- Larquet (F), 164
- Larrieu-Terrefort (F), 159
- Larrivaux (F), 159
- Larrivet-Haut-Brion (F), 157
- Larronde-Desormes (F), 159
- Lascombes (F), 158
- Lassalle (F), 159, 161, 167
- Lassègue (F), 164
- Latour (F), 158, 161, 408
- Latour-L'Aspic (F), 159

Château Latour Feugas (F), 161
– Latour de Marbuzet (F), 159
– Latour à Pomerol et Grandes Vignes réunies (F), 166
– Latrézotte (F), 156
– Laujac (F), 159
– Laurétan (F), 160
– des Laurets (F), 165
– Laurette (F), 160
– Laureusanne (F), 167
– Lavergne (F), 162
– Laville Haut-Brion (F), 157
– Lavinot-la-Chapelle (F), 166
– Lavison (F), 161
– Léon (F), 161
– Lespault (F), 157
– Les Lesques (F), 159
– Lhospital (F), 158
– La Ligassonne (F), 160
– Lion-Perruchon (F), 165
– Liot (F), 156
– Libertas (S.A.), 313, 316
– Liversan (F), 159
– Livran (F), 159
– Lognac (F), 157
– Loubens (F), 160
– Loudenne (F), 159
– Loustauvieil (F), 160
– La Louvière (F), 157
– Louys (F), 125
– Lynch-Bages (F), 158
– Lynch-Moussas (F), 158
– Lescadre (F), 167
– Lescart (F), 162
– de Lescours (F), 164
– de Lesparre (F), 162
– Lestage (F), 159, 162, 165
– Lestage-Darquier (F), 159
– Lestange (F), 161
– Léoville-Barton (F), 158
– Léoville-Lascases (F), 158
– Léoville-Poyféré (F), 158
– Lestrilles (F), 162
– Lezongard (F), 161
– de Lisse (F), 164
– de Loupiac-Gaudiet (F), 160
– Lucques Bessan (F), 160
– Ludeman (F), 158
– Ludon-Pomiès-Agassac (F), 159
– de Luins (Sw), 106
– de Lussac (F), 165
– Lusseau (F), 157
– de Lyde (F), 160
– du Lyonnat (F), 165
– Luziès (F), 156
– Macay (F), 167
– Mac-Carthy (F), 159
– Mac-Carthy-Moula (F), 159
– Machorre (F), 160
– de Maco (F), 167
– Macquin (F), 165
– La Madeleine (F), 163
– Madelis (F), 158
– de Madère (F), 157
– Magdelaine (F), 163
– Magence (F), 158
– Mageot (F), 161
– Magnan (F), 164
– Magnan-La-Gaffelière (F), 164
– des Mailles (F), 160
– Maison-Blanche (F), 164
– Maison blanche (Sw), 105
– Malagar (F), 161
– Malagin (F), 165
– Malartic-Lagravière (F), 157
– Malécot (F), 159
– Malescasse (F), 159
– Malescot-Saint Exupéry (F), 158
– de Malgarni et Coutreau (F), 167
– Malherbes (F), 161
– Malineau (F), 164

Château de Malle (F), 156
– Malleprat (F), 157
– Malleret (F), 157, 159
– Malromé (F), 160
– Mamin (F), 158
– Mangot (F), 164
– Le Manoir (F), 163
– Maran (F), 161
– de Marbuzet (F), 158
– Marcelin-Laffitte (F), 161
– La Marche-Canon (F), 166
– Les Marcottes (F), 160
– Margaux (F), 138, 158, 408
– Margès-Dusseau (F), 160
– de Marsan (F), 161
– de Martillac (F), 160
– La Marzelle (F), 163
– Maillard (F), 161
– Malbec (F), 161
– Marquis-d'Alesme-Becker (F), 158
– Marquis-de-Therme (F), 158
– Marrin (F), 164
– Marsac-Séguineau (F), 159
– Marsens (Sw), 106
– Martin (F), 164
– Martinens (F), 159
– Martinet (F), 164
– Martinon (F), 162
– Martouret (F), 162
– Massereau (F), 156
– Massereau-Lapachere (F), 156
– Materre (F), 161
– Mathalin (F), 156
– Matras (F), 164
– Matras-Côte-Daugay (F), 164
– Maucamps (F), 159
– Maurac (F), 159
– Mauras (F), 156
– Maurens (F), 164
– Mauros (F), 162
– Maussé (F), 166
– Mauvezin-La-Gommerie (F), 163
– Mayence (F), 167
– du Mayne (F), 156, 165
– Mayne-Binet (F), 156
– Le Mayne Boye (F), 167
– Le Mayne Gozin (F), 167
– Mayne-Viel (F), 167
– Mazarin (F), 160
– Mazerat (F), 164
– Mazeris (F), 166
– Mazeris-Bellevue (F), 166
– La Mazerolle (F), 162
– Mazerolles (F), 167
– Mazeyres (F), 166
– Médouc (F), 160
– Médrac (F), 159
– du Méjean (F), 157
– Menate (F), 156
– Le Menaudat (F), 167
– Menauta (F), 156
– Mendoce (F), 167
– Meneau (F), 162
– des Menuts (F), 164
– Mercier (F), 156
– Méric (F), 157
– Le Mesnil (F), 160
– Meyney (F), 158
– Mille-Secousses (F), 167
– Millet (F), 158
– Miraflorès (F), 161
– Le Mirail (F), 158
– Le Mission-Haut-Brion (F), 157
– Les Moines (F), 167
– des Moines (F), 164, 166
– Monbousquet (F), 164
– Monbran (F), 166
– Moncets (F), 166
  de Mongeneau (F), 126
– Monconseil (F), 167
– Monis (S.A.), 316

Château Monlot-Capet (F), 164
– Monregard La Croix (F), 166
– de Mont (Sw), 106
– Montaigne (F), 161
– Montaiguillon (F), 164
– Mont-Belair (F), 164
– Montbrison (F), 159
– Montbrun (F), 159
– Mont-Célestin (F), 161
– Montcontour (F), 124
– de Montgouverne (F), 124
– Monthil (F), 159
– Montjoie (F), 156
– Montjon-Le-Gravier (F), 161
– Monteils (F), 156
– Montlabert (F), 164
– de Montlau (F), 162
– Montonoir (F), 161
– Montrose (F), 158
– Mony (F), 161
– La Morère (F), 159
– Morin (F), 159
– La Mothe (F), 162
– Mouchac (F), 162
– Mouchet-Montagne (F), 164
– La Mouleyre (F), 160
– Moulin (F), 158
– Moulin à Vent (F), 159
– Moulin-à-Vent (F), 166
– Moulin-Blanc (F), 164, 166
– Moulin du Cadet (F), 163
– La Mouline (F), 161
– Moulin-Pey-la-Brie (F), 166
– Moulin-Riche (F), 158
– Moulin-Rose (F), 159
– Moulin-Rouge (F), 159
– Moulinet (F), 166
– Moura (F), 156
– Moulis (F), 159
– Mouton-Baron-Philippe (F), 158
– Mouton-Blanc (F), 164
– Mouton-Mazeyres (F), 166
– Mouton-Rothschild (F), 158
– Le Mugron (F), 167
– de Musset (F), 165, 166
– de Myrat (F), 156
– Nairac (F), 156
– de Naujan (F), 162
– La Navarre (F), 161
– Négrit (F), 164
– Nenin (F), 166
– La Nère (F), 160
– Nicole (F), 166
– Nodoz (F), 167
– du Nozet (F), 123
– Olivier (F), 157
– d'Ories (F), 162
– Les Ormes de Pez (F), 159
– Les Ormes-Sorbet (F), 159
– d'Ouche (F), 124
– Pabeau (F), 159
– Pageot-Couloumet (F), 160
– Pailhas (F), 164
– Paillet (F), 161
– Paillon-Claverie (F), 156
– Le Palat (F), 164
– Palmer (F), 158
– Panet (F), 164, 166
– Le Pape (F), 157
– Pape-Clément (F), 157
– La Papeterie (F), 164
– Parabelle (F), 162
– Paradis (F), 164
– Pardaillan (F), 167
– de Parempuyre (F), 159
– Pascot (F), 161
– de la Passonne (F), 161
– Patache-d'Aux (F), 159
– Patris (F), 164
– Patrouilleau (F), 162
– Paveil-de-Luze (F), 159

Château Pavie (F), 163
– Pavie-Decesse (F), 163
– du Pavillon (F), 160
– du Pavillon-Haut-Gros Bonnct (F), 166
– du Payre (F), 161
– Péchon (F), 156
– Péconnet (F), 161
– Pédesclaux (F), 158
– Peironnin (F), 161
– Peller (F), 161
– Peneau (F), 161
– Péran (F), 158
– Pernaud (F), 156
– La Perotte (F), 167
– Perrayne (F), 160
– Perrein (F), 167
– Perreyre (F), 167
– Perron (F), 166
– Pessan (F), 158
– Pessille (F), 158
– Les Petits-Arnauds (F), 167
– Petit-Bocage (F), 166
– Petit-Clos (F), 165
– Petit-Cormey (F), 164
– Petit-Faurie-de-Soutard (F), 163
– Petit-Faurie-Trocard (F), 164
– Petit-Figeac (F), 164
– Petit-Mayne (F), 156
– Petit-Refuge (F), 165
– Petit-Trou (F), 167
– Petit-Village (F), 166
– Petrus (F), 166
– Peybrune (F), 167
– du Peychaud (F), 162
– Peychaud (F), 167
– Peydebayle (F), 158
– Peygenestou (F), 164
– Pey-Labrit (F), 166
– Peyrabon (F), 159
– Peyrat (F), 161
– du Peyrat (F), 161
– Peyraud (F), 164
– Peyroutas (F), 164
– Peyruchet (F), 160
– de Pez (F), 159
– Phélan-Ségur (F), 158
– Piada (F), 156
– Pibran (F), 159
– Pic (F), 160
– Picard (F), 159
– Pichelèvre (F), 166
– La Picherie (F), 164
– Pichon-Longueville (F), 158
– Pichon-Longueville-Lalande (F), 158
– du Pick (F), 156
– Pierrot-Plaisance (F), 165
– du Pin (F), 161
– Pindefleurs (F), 164
– Pinet (F), 167
– Pinet La Roquette (F), 167
– du Pingoy (F), 158
– Piot (F), 156
– Pipeau (F), 164
– Pipeau-Ménichot (F), 164
– Pique-Caillou (F), 157, 161
– Piron (F), 157, 165
– Plaisance (F), 165
– de Plassans (F), 160
– de Pleytegeat (F), 156
– Plince (F), 166
– La Pointe (F), 166
– du Point-de-Vue (F), 161
– Poitou-Lussac (F), 165
– Pomard (F), 167
– Pomeys (F), 159
– Pomirol le Pin (F), 161
– Pommarède (F), 160
– Pommarède de Haut (F), 157
– Pomys (F), 159

Château Pontac (F), 160
- Pontac-Gasparini (F), 162
- Pontac-Lynch (F), 159
- Pontac-Monplaisir (F), 157
- Pontet (F), 164
- Pontet-Canet (F), 158
- Pontet-Clauzure (F), 164
- Pontet-Fontlabert (F), 164
- de Pontus (F), 167
- Le Portail Rouge (F), 160
- Portarrieu (F), 156
- de Portets (F), 158
- Potensac (F), 159
- Pouget (F), 158
- Poujeaux (F), 159
- Pouly (F), 161
- Poumey (F), 157
- de La Prade (F), 157
- Prieuré-Lichine (F), 158
- Poyanne (F), 167
- de Pranzac (F), 161
- Pressac (F), 160, 164
- de Pressac (F), 162
- Le Prieuré La Croix (F), 166
- Le Prieuré Saint-Emilion (F), 163
- La Prioulette (F), 161
- Le Privera (F), 159
- Prost (F), 156
- La Providence (F), 159, 160, 166
- de Puisseguin (F), 165
- Puy-Bardens (F), 161
- Puy Beney (F), 167
- Puy Beney Lafitte (F), 167
- Puy-Blanquet (F), 164
- Puygenestou (F), 164
- Puygueraud (F), 160
- Quantin (F), 162
- Quentin (F), 164
- des Queyrats (F), 158
- Quercy (F), 164
- Queyreau-de-Haut (F), 167
- Quinault (F), 164
- Quinsac (F), 162
- Rabaud-Promis (F), 156
- Rabaud-Sigalas (F), 156
- Raboul (F), 158
- Rambaud (F), 162
- La Rame (F), 160
- Ramondon (F), 161
- Ramonet (F), 162
- Rausan-Ségla (F), 158
- du Raux (F), 159
- Rauzan-Gassies (F), 158
- Rauzé (F), 161
- Rauzé-Sybil (F), 161
- Raymond (F), 162
- Raymond-Lafon (F), 156
- Rayne-Vigneau (F), 156
- Rebeymont (F), 167
- Rebeymond-Lalibarde (F), 167
- Rebouquet (F), 167
- Régent (F), 164
- de Reignac (F), 162
- des Remparts (F), 161
- Renon (F), 160
- Renouil-Franquet (F), 159
- de Respide (F), 158
- Respide (F), 158
- Reysson (F), 159
- Ricadet (F), 167
- Les Ricards (F), 167
- de Ricaud (F), 160
- des Richards (F), 167
- Richon Red (Is), 294
- Rider (F), 167
- Rieussec (F), 156
- La Rigaudière (F), 161
- La Ripaille (F), 125
- Ripeau (F), 163
- Rivasseau (F), 162
- Robert-Franquet (F), 159

Château du Roc (F), 156
- Le Roc (F), 159
- du Roc de Boissac (F), 165
- La Roche (F), 157, 162
- du Rocher (F), 164
- Rocher-Corbin (F), 165
- des Rochers (F), 156
- des Roches (F), 160
- De Rol (F), 163
- Rol-de-Fombrauge (F), 164
- Rolland (F), 156, 159
- Romer (F), 156
- Romefort (F), 159
- La Ronde (F), 160
- de Rondillon (F), 160
- La Roque (F), 161
- de Roques (F), 162
- Roquegrave (F), 159
- Roqueys (F), 161
- La Rose (F), 163
- La Rose-Anseillan (F), 159
- Rosemont (F), 159
- La Rose Pourret (F), 163
- La Rose-Rol (F), 163
- Rose-Sainte-Croix (F), 159
- Roubric (F), 161
- Rouchonne-Vignonet (F), 164
- Roudier (F), 161
- Rouge Port-Aubin (F), 159
- Rouget (F), 166
- Roulet (F), 166
- Roumieu (F), 156
- Rousselle (F), 167
- Rousset (F), 167
- Roustin (F), 160
- Roustit (F), 160
- Le Roux (S.A.), 316
- Royland (F), 164
- Ruat-Petit-Poujeaux (F), 159
- du Sable (F), 164
- Saint-Amand (F), 156
- Saint-André (F), 166
- Saint-André-Corbin (F), 165
- Sainte-Barbe (F), 162
- Saint-Bonnet (F), 159
- St-Christoly (F), 159
- Saint-Christophe (F), 164
- Saint-Georges (F), 164, 165
- Saint-Georges Cap-d'Or (F), 165
- Saint-Georges-Côtes-Pavie (F), 163
- Saint-Germain (F), 161
- Saint-Jacques-Calon (F), 165
- Saint-Jérôme (F), 157
- Saint-Julien (F), 164
- Saint-Louis (F), 165
- Saint-Marc (F), 156
- Saint-Martial (F), 164
- de Saint-Pey (F), 164
- Saint-Pierre (F), 158, 164, 166
- Saint-Robert (F), 156
- Saint-Roch (F), 159
- Saint-Sève (F), 161
- de Sales (F), 166
- La Salette (F), 157
- de la Salle (F), 162
- Samion (F), 165
- Samson (F), 166
- de Sancerre (F), 123
- Sansonnet (F), 163
- Saransot-Dupré (F), 159
- Sarpe-Grand-Jacques (F), 164
- Sarpe Pelletan (F), 164
- Saugeron (F), 167
- Sauvage (F), 160
- Segonzac (F), 167
- Seguin (F), 162
- Ségur (F), 159
- Semeillan Balleu-Faulat (F), 159
- Semeillan-Mazeau (F), 159
- Senailhac (F), 162
- Sénéjac (F), 159

Château Sentour (F), 160
- Sergant (F), 166
- La Serre (F), 160, 163
- du Seuil (F), 157
- Siaurac (F), 166
- Simard (F), 164
- Simon (F), 156
- Simon Carrety (F), 156
- Siran (F), 159
- Smith Haut-Lafitte (F), 157
- Sociondo (F), 167
- La Solitude (F), 157
- Souchet-Piquat (F), 165
- Soutard (F), 163
- Soutard-Cadet (F), 164
- Suau (F), 156, 161
- Sudrat-Boussaton (F), 166
- de Suduiraut (F), 156
- Sylvain (F), 156
- du Tailhas (F), 166
- du Taillan (F), 159
- Taillefer (F), 166
- Talbot (F), 158
- Tanesse (F), 160
- Tarey (F), 160
- Le Tarey (F), 160
- du Tasta (F), 161
- Tasta (F), 167
- Tasta-Guillier (F), 167
- Taveney (F), 165
- Tapiau (F), 161
- de Taste (F), 167
- de Tastes (F), 160
- La Taure Sainte-Luce (F), 167
- Tayac (F), 167
- Tayac et Siamois (F), 159
- Templiers (F), 166
- Terfort (F), 160
- Terrasson (F), 160
- Terrefort (F), 160
- Terrien (F), 165
- Le Tertre (F), 158
- de Teste (F), 161
- du Testeron (F), 159
- Tertre-Daugay (F), 163
- Tertre du Renard (F), 161
- La Tête-du-Cerf (F), 164
- Teyssier (F), 165
- de Teysson (F), 166
- de Thau (F), 167
- de Thauvenay (F), 123
- Thôme-Brousterot (F), 167
- Tiffray-Guadey (F), 165
- du Tillac (F), 162
- des Tilleuls (F), 158
- Tinan (F), 157
- de Touilla (F), 156
- de Toumalin (F), 166
- Toumalin-Jonquet (F), 166
- Toumillon (F), 158
- La Tour (F), 162
- des Tours (F), 165
- La Tour d'Anseillan (F), 159
- de La Tour Beaupoil (F), 162
- La Tour Beau-Site (F), 167
- La Tour-Bicheau (F), 158
- La Tour-Blanche (F), 156, 159
- La Tour-de-By (F), 159
- La Tour-Calon (F), 164
- La Tour-Canon (F), 166
- La Tour-Carnet (F), 158
- La Tour-Corniaud (F), 164
- des Tourelles (F), 161
- La Tour-Figeac (F), 163
- La Tour-Fonrazade (F), 163
- La Tour Gayet (F), 167
- La Tour-de-Grenet (F), 165
- La Tour-Gueyraud (F), 161
- La Tour-Haut-Brion (F), 157
- La Tour Marcillanet (F), 159
- La-Tour-Martillac (F), 157

Château La Tour Maudan (F), 160
- La Tour-Milon (F), 159
- La Tour du Mirail (F), 159
- La Tour-de-Mons (F), 159
- La Tour-Montagne (F), 164
- La Tour-Paquillon (F), 164
- La Tour du Pas-Saint-Georges (F), 165
- La Tour-du-Pin-Figeac (F), 163
- La Tour-Pourret (F), 164
- La Tour-Puymirand (F), 162
- La Tourte (F), 158
- La Tour-du-Roc (F), 159
- La Tour-St-Bonnet (F), 159
- La Tour-St-Christophe (F), 164
- La Tour Saint-Joseph (F), 159
- La Tour-Saint-Pierre (F), 164
- La Tour-de-Ségur (F), 165
- La Tour-Seguy (F), 167
- La Tour-des-Termes (F), 159
- Tournefeuille (F), 166
- Tourteau (F), 165
- Tourteau-Chollet (F), 158
- de Toutigeac (F), 162
- Trapeau (F), 164
- Trianon (F), 164
- Trimoulet (F), 163
- Tristan (F), 166
- des Trois-Croix (F), 167
- « Trois-Moulins » (F), 159
- des Trois Moulins (F), 163
- Tronquoy-Lalande (F), 159
- Troplong-Mondot (F), 163
- Troquard (F), 165
- Trotanoy (F), 166
- Trottevieille (F), 163
- Truquet (F), 164
- Les Tuileries-de-Bayard (F), 165
- de Tuquet (F), 157
- de Tustal (F), 162
- Tustoc (F), 158
- Vachon (F), 164
- La Valade (F), 167
- du Vallier (F), 160
- Valmer (F), 124
- de Valois (F), 166
- Verdignan (F), 159
- du Verger (F), 160
- des Vergnes (F), 162
- du Vert (F), 162
- de Veyres (F), 156
- de Viaud (F), 166
- Victoria (F), 159
- de Vidasse-Pessac (F), 162
- Videau (F), 161
- de la Vieille-Cloche (F), 164
- Vieille-France (F), 158
- Vieille-Maison (F), 165
- Vieux-Ceps (F), 164
- Vieux-Certan (F), 166
- Les Vieux-Chênes (F), 165
- Vieux-Grand-Faurie (F), 164
- Vieux-Guillou (F), 165
- du Vieux-Guinot (F), 164
- Le Vieux-Logis (F), 165
- Vieux-Moulin (F), 159
- du Vieux-Moulin (F), 160
- Vieux-Moulin-du-Cadet (F), 164
- Vieux-Pourret (F), 164
- Vieux-Sarpe (F), 164
- Villebout (F), 164
- Villefranche (F), 156
- Villegeorge (F), 158
- Ville-Georges (F), 158
- Villemaurine (F), 163
- Villotte (F), 162
- Vincent (F), 166, 167
- de Vincy (Sw), 106
- de Vinzel (Sw), 106
- La Violette (F), 166
- de Virelade (F), 158

Château Le Virou (F), 167
 – Vrai-Canon-Bodet-La-Tour (F), 166
 – Vrai-Canon-Bouché (F), 166
 – Vray-Canon-Boyer (F), 166
 – La-Vraye-Croix-de-Gay (F), 166
 – Yon-Figeac (F), 164
 – La Yotte (F), 160
 – d'Yquem (F), 64, 142, 156, 408, 409
 – Yveline (F), 166
 – Yvon-Figeac (F), 163
Châteaux Sociando-Mallet et Pontoise-Cabarrus (F), 159
Châteauneuf (F), 88
Châteauneuf-du-Pape (F), 98, 100, 107
Châtelard (Sw), 106
Les Chatelots (F), 58, 76
La Chatenière (F), 77
Châtillon-en-Diois (F), 108, 404
La Chatillone (F), 108
Chatillons (F), 123
Chaudefonds (F), 126
La Chaume (F), 107
Les Chaumes (F), 76
Chavagnes (F), 126
Les Chavaroches (F), 108
Chavignol (F), 123
Les Chavoches (F), 123
Cheilly (F), 67, 77, 78
Chemakha (U.S.S.R.), 294
Chemarin (F), 123
Chemin de Châteauneuf (F), 107
 – de Fer (Sw), 106
 – de Sorgues (F), 107
Chenas (F), 72, 78
Chenaux (Sw), 106
Chêne (Sw), 105
Le Chêne (F), 107
Chêne Marchand (F), 123
Les Chenevery (F), 76
Les Chenevottes (F), 77, 78
Chenin Blanc (Cal), 325, 333
Cherbaudes (F), 76
Chéri (F), 107
Cheste (Sp), 177
Les Chétives-Maisons (F), 123
Aux Cheusots (F), 56, 76
La Chevalière (F), 108
Chevalier-Montrachet (F), 64, 78, 409
Les Chevillots (F), 123
En Chevret (F), 77
Chevrette (F), 125
Chianti (Cal), 325, 333, 411
 – (I), 226, 237, 404
 – Bianco (I), 227
 – Classico (I), 226, 227, 237
 – Colli Aretini (I), 226, 237
 – Colli Fiorentini (I), 200, 237
 – Colli Senesi (I), 226, 237
 – Colline Pisane (I), 226, 237
 – Montalbano (I), 226, 237
 – Rufino (I), 226, 237
 – Vecchio (I), 227
Chiaretto del Garda (I), 236
Chignin (F), 107
Chincha (Peru), 340
Chinon (F), 119, 125, 404
Chip Dry (P), 213
Chipka (Bg), 294
Chiquilla (Sp), 189
Chiroubles (F), 71, 72, 78
Choco (P), 213
Chopet (F), 124
Chorey-lès-Beaune (F), 62, 77, 78
Chorherrenhalde (Sw), 247
Les Chouacheux (F), 77
Chouzé-sur-Loire (F), 125
Christenlay (Gy), 275
Churer Costamser Beerli (Sw), 268

Churer Süssdruck Lürlibader (Sw), 268
Churer Tokayer aus dem Lochert (Sw), 268
El Cid (Sp), 189
Les Cigales (Sw), 105
Cinqueterre (I), 222, 236
Cinqueterre passito (I), 236
Cintra Grand Corona (P), 213
Cirial (Sp), 188
Cirò di Calabria (I), 234, 238
Cirò di Sardegna (I), 238
Clairette de Die (F), 108, 407
Clairette de Die Mousseux (F), 359, 361
Clairette du Languedoc (F), 103
La Clape (F), 103, 108
Claret (Aus), 341
Claret (F), 140
Claret (N. Y.), 333
Clarita (Sp), 189
Clasica (Sp), 189
Clastidium (I), 221, 236
 – di Casteggio (I), 236
Clavoillons (F), 78
Les Clefs d'Or (Sw), 106
Clemensberg (Gy), 275
Clevner Schipfgut (Sw), 247
Clevner Sternhalden Stäfa (Sw), 247, 268
Climat-du-Val called Clos-du-Val (F), 77
Clipper (P), 213
Le Clos (F), 107, 124
Clos de l'Abbaye (Sw), 106
 – des Abbayes (Sw), 106
 – des Abbesses (Sw), 106
 – de l'Alleau (F), 124
 – d'Anzou (F), 124
 – de l'Archerie (F), 124
 – des Argillières (F), 76
 – des Arnaud (F), 166
 – de l'Augmendaz (Sw), 106
 – des Augustins (F), 124
 – Avocat (F), 157
 – de l'Avocat (F), 157
 – Badon (F), 163
 – Baguelin (F), 124
 – de Balavaud (Sw), 105
 – Barail (F), 156
 – La Barde (F), 164
 – des Barguins (F), 124
 – Mon-Baril (F), 124
 – de la Barre (F), 77, 123, 124
 – du Bas Lançon (F), 157
 – des Batonnières (F), 124
 – Baudoin (F), 124
 – des Bayels (Sw), 106
 – de Beauregard (Sw), 105
 – de Beauregard (F), 124
 – Beauregard (F), 165
 – Bel-Air (F), 124
 – Belle-Vue (F), 160
 – Bellevue (F), 167
 – des Berneyses (Sw), 105
 – des Bidaudières (F), 124
 – de la Bienboire (F), 125
 – Blanchon (F), 165
 – de Blottières (F), 125
 – du Bois d'Ouche (F), 124
 – du Bois-Rideau (F), 124
 – de la Bordette (F), 164
 – Le Bouchet (F), 124
 – du Boudeur (F), 161
 – de la Bourdonnerie (F), 124
 – du Bourg (F), 124
 – Bourgelat (F), 157
 – de la Bretonnière (F), 124
 – de la Brianderie (F), 124
 – des Brûlées (Sw), 106
 – La Burthe (F), 161

Clos Cantalot (F), 158
 – Cantemerle (F), 157
 – des Capucins (F), 161
 – des Carmes (F), 125
 – du Castel (F), 166
 – Cazebonne (F), 158
 – de Chaillemont (F), 124
 – de Chamaley (Sw), 106
 – Champon-Ségur (F), 160
 – sur la Chapelle (Sw), 105
 – de Charmigny (F), 124
 – de la Chasse-Royale (F), 124
 – du Châtain (F), 166
 – du Château (Sw), 105, 106
 – du Château de Bursins (Sw), 106
 – du Châtelard (Sw), 105, 106
 – Châtonneyre (Sw), 105
 – Chauvin (F), 124
 – de la Chenalettaz (Sw), 105
 – Chenevières (Sw), 269
 – du Clocher (F), 165
 – du Cloitre (Sw), 105
 – des Cloîtres (Sw), 106
 – des Corvées (F), 76
 – de la Cour (Sw), 106
 – des Curiades (Sw), 106
 – de la Dame (Sw), 106
 – Dezarneauld (F), 161
 – de Dominge (F), 162
 – de la Donery (Sw), 106
 – de la Donzelle (Sw), 106
 – Dubois (F), 124
 – des Echelettes (Sw), 106
 – de l'Ecole (F), 156
 – l'Eglise (F), 165
 – de l'Eglise (F), 166
 – l'Eglise-Clinet (F), 165
 – de l'Epaisse (F), 125
 – de l'Epée (F), 123
 – de l'Ermite (Sw), 106
 – l'Etoile (F), 166
 – de la Forêt (F), 124
 – des Forêts (F), 76
 – de Fougerai (F), 124
 – Fourtet (F), 163
 – Franc (F), 124
 – de la Frelonnerie (F), 123
 – Froidefond (F), 164
 – de Gaimont (F), 124
 – des Galonnes (F), 125
 – de la George (Sw), 105, 106
 – des Geslets (F), 125
 – des Girardières (F), 124
 – de Giron (F), 160
 – de Gourgues (F), 161
 – du Grand-Bonneau (F), 161
 – du Grand-Châtelet (F), 163
 – des Grandes Vignes (F), 76
 – des Gues d'Amant (F), 124
 – de la Haie-Martel (F), 124
 – de la Hallotière (F), 124
 – Haut-Cailleau (F), 166
 – Haut Cavujon (F), 166
 – Haut-Forcade (F), 161
 – Haut-Peyraguey (F), 156
 – Haut-Pourret (F), 163
 – des Hautes Graves (F), 165
 – Hure (F), 124
 – Jean (F), 160
 – Jean-Voisin (F), 163
 – du Langon (F), 125
 – Lariveau (F), 166
 – Léhoul (F), 158
 – des Lions (F), 124
 – des Longs-Reages (F), 124
 – Louloumet (F), 158
 – La Lucassière (F), 124
 – du Lyonnat (F), 165
 – La Madeleine (F), 163
 – des Madères (F), 124

Clos La Magine (F), 158
 – de la Maréchale (F), 76
 – Marie (F), 125
 – de Marigny (F), 124
 – Mariout (E), 300, 302
 – Marteau (F), 124
 – du Martheray (Sw), 106
 – La Marzelle (F), 163
 – Matamir (E), 300, 302
 – Mauguin (F), 124
 – Mazeyres (F), 166
 – des Menuts (F), 164
 – de la Meslerie (F), 124
 – des Messieurs (F), 123
 – de Millanges (F), 161
 – des Moines (Sw), 106
 – des Moines (F), 164, 166
 – du Monastère du Broussey (F), 161
 – le Mont (F), 124
 – des Morains (F), 125
 – de Mosny (F), 123
 – du Moulin (F), 159
 – du Moulin-à-Vent (F), 158
 – des Moulins à Vent (F), 157
 – des Mousquetaires (Sw), 105
 – des Murs (F), 125
 – Napoléon (F), 56
 – Nardon (F), 166
 – Naudin (F), 124
 – Nodot (F), 167
 – de Nouis (F), 124
 – de l'Oie-qui-casse (F), 125
 – de l'Olivier (F), 124
 – des Panissières (Sw), 106
 – du Pape (F), 156, 157
 – du Papillon (F), 126
 – du Paradis (Sw), 105, 106
 – du Parc (F), 125
 – de la Patrie (F), 126
 – des Pentes (F), 124
 – des Pères (F), 125
 – de la Perrière (F), 59, 76
 – du Petit-Mont (F), 124
 – du Philosophe (Sw), 106
 – du Piat (F), 167
 – Picard (F), 162
 – Picon-Cravignac (F), 164
 – Pierre-Jean (F), 161
 – Pilate (F), 126
 – du Pin (F), 125
 – du Pineau (F), 126
 – des Plantaz (Sw), 105
 – de la Platerie (F), 125
 – de Pouvray (F), 124
 – des Princes (F), 156
 – Queron (F), 125
 – Renard (F), 123
 – René (F), 124
 – des Rennauds (Sw), 105
 – de Ricouet (F), 161
 – Roc-Etoile (F), 124
 – de la Roche (F), 76, 124, 126
 – du Rocher (Sw), 105
 – de la Rochère (F), 124
 – des Roches (F), 124, 157
 – des Roches (Sw), 106
 – du Roi (F), 56, 63, 77, 166
 – des Rotissants (F), 125
 – de Rougemont (F), 124
 – du Rousillon (Sw), 106
 – du Roy (F), 106, 156
 – Saint-Come (F), 124
 – Saint-Cricq (F), 161
 – Saint-Emilion (F), 164
 – Saint-Georges (F), 124
 – Saint-Hilaire (F), 125
 – Saint-Marc (F), 76
 – Saint-Martin (F), 163
 – Saint-Mathurin (F), 124
 – de Sainte-Catherine (F), 126
 – des Saints-Pères (F), 125

Clos de Sarpe (F), 164
– des Sarrazins (F), 164
– du Saut-du-Loup (F), 125
– de Seillas (F), 167
– de Sens (F), 124
– des Sous-Monthaux (Sw), 269
– des Surins (F), 124
– de la Taisserie (F), 124
– du Tauzin (F), 157
– des Templiers (F), 166
– de Terrefort (F), 162
– des Tertres (F), 126
– Thenot (F), 124
– des Thierrières (F), 124
– de la Torrillère (F), 125
– Toulifaut (F), 124, 166
– Toumalin (F), 166
– des Treilles (F), 125
– des Truits (Sw), 106
– d'Uza (F), 158
– Valentin (F), 164
– de Val-Roche (F), 124
– de Vau (F), 124
– Vaufuget (F), 124
– du Vendôme (F), 125
– de Venise (F), 124
– les Verneries (F), 124
– de Verteuil (F), 160
– de la Vieille-Forge (F), 166
– du Vigneau (F), 125
– le Vigneau (F), 124
– de Vilmier (F), 124
– de la Vineuvaz (Sw), 105
Clos-Blanc (F), 76, 77
Le Clos Blanc (F), 59
Clos-Bussières (F), 76
Le Clos du Chapitre (F), 56, 76
Les Clos et Claperonne (F), 108
Le Clos-des-Chênes (F), 77
Clos de la Commaraine (F), 77
Le Clos-des-Ducs (F), 77
Clos-des-Fourneaux (F), 68, 78
Les Clos du Château de Brézé (F), 125
Le Clos-Gauthey (F), 77
Clos-Marcilly (F), 68, 78
Le Clos-Micot (F), 77
Le Clos-des-Mouches (F), 63, 77
Le Clos-de-la-Mousse (F), 77
Le Clos-des-Ormes (F), 76
Clos Prieur (F), 76
Le Clos des Réas (F), 76
Le Clos-des-Rois (F), 77
Clos-du-Roy (F), 68, 78
Clos-St-Denis (F), 58, 76
Clos-St-Jean (F), 77, 78, 162
Le Clos-Sorbès (F), 76
Clos-de-Tart (F), 58, 76
Clos-des-Tavannes (F), 77
Le Clos Vaufoinard (F), 124
Clos-du-Verger (F), 77
Clos-de-Vougeot (F), 49, 58, 59, 76, 404
Clos-Voyens or Les Voyens (F), 68, 78
Les Closeaux (F), 76, 125
Aux Clous (F), 77
Cloux (F), 78
Club (Sp), 189
Cob-Nut (Brown) (Sp), 190
Cochero (Sp), 189
Cocktail Port (P), 213
Le Cognet (F), 108
Les Coinches (F), 123
Colares (F), 198, 199
Colares M.J.C. (P), 212
– V.S. (P), 212
Colli Albani (I), 230, 237
– Fuganei (I), 232
– Lanuvini (I), 237
– Trevigiani (I), 236
La Colline (F), 125

Colline des Planzettes Sierre (Sw), 105
Le Colombier (F), 107
Colombis (F), 107
Colonna (I), 237
Le Combard (F), 108
Les Combes (F), 77, 107
Combes d'Arnavel (F), 107
Combe de Calon (F), 108
Les Combes-Dessus (F), 77
Combe d'Enfer (Sw), 105
Combes Masques (F), 107
Combes-aux-Moines (F), 76
Combette (F), 107
Les Combettes (F), 67, 78
Aux Combottes (F), 76
Les Combottes (F), 58, 76
Comeyre (F), 107
Commandaria (C), 299, 302
La Comme (F), 77
Commendador (P), 213
Los Compadres (Sp), 189
Companhia Velha (P), 212
Comtes de Champagne (F), 359
La Comtesse (F), 123
Conca (I), 238
Concourson (F), 126
La Condesa (Sp), 189
Condrieu (F), 98, 107
Consanto (S.A.), 316
Consejero (Sp), 190
Constantia Berg (S.A.), 316
– Riesling (S.A.), 315
– Valley Stein (S.A.), 316
Les Contamines (Sw), 106
La Contrie (F), 125
Coonawarra Claret (Aus), 341
Coquinero (Sp), 189
Les Corbeaux (F), 76
Corbières (F), 103, 108
– du Roussillon (F), 108
– Supérieures du Roussillon (F), 108
Cori (I), 230, 237
– Bianco (I), 230
– Rosso (I), 231
Cornançay (F), 123
Cornas (F), 98, 99
Corona (Sp), 187
Coronata (I), 236
Coronation (Sp), 190
Coronel (Sp), 189
Corps des Loups (F), 108
Cortaillod (Sw), 269
Cortese (I), 220
Cortese dell'Oltrepo pavese (I), 236
Cortese di Gavi (I), 236
Corton (F), 49, 61, 62, 77
Corton-Charlemagne (F), 49, 62, 78
Les Corvées-Paget (F), 76
Corveta (P), 212
Corvo (I), 234
Corvo di Casteldaccia (I), 238
Costantiaberg (S.A.), 314
Coste Claude (F), 107
Coste-Froide (F), 107
Costières du Gard (F), 103, 108
Coteau de l'Ange (F), 107
– de Bannon (F), 123
– de Beaumont (F), 124
– Caillard (F), 107
– de Chançay (F), 124
– Chatrie (F), 124
– de Gilly (Sw), 106
– des Girarmes (F), 123
– J.-Jouffroy (F), 124
– de Lully (Sw), 106
– de la Rochère (F), 124
– de Saint-Jean (F), 107
– de Vaux (F), 124
– de Venise (F), 124
Coteaux d'Aix-en-Provence (F), 108
– de l'Aubance (F), 122, 126

Coteaux des Baux (F), 108
– des Brosses (F), 124
– de Crépy (F), 96, 107
– du Haut-Léman (Sw), 105
– de Khanguet (Tu), 315
– du Languedoc (F), 103, 108
– du Layon (F), 122, 126
– des Loges (F), 123
– du Loir (F), 119, 122, 126
– de la Loire (F), 122, 126
– de Mascara (Ag), 309, 315
– de Médéa (Ag), 309, 315
– de la Méjanelle (F), 108
– de M'Silah (Ag), 315
– de Pierrevert (F), 108
– de Saint-Christol (F), 108
– de Saumur (F), 125
– de Sonnay (F), 125
– de Tlemcen (Ag), 315
– du Tricastin (F), 108
– de Verargues (F), 108
La Côte (F), 107, 123
Côtes-d'Agly (F), 104
La Côte Baudnin (F), 108
Côte de Beaune (F), 72, 77, 78
Côtes de Beaune-Villages (F), 49, 60, 62, 67, 77
Côtes de Bergerac (F), 152
Côtes-de-Blaye (F), 150
Côtes de Bordeaux-Saint-Macaire (F), 144
Côte de Brouilly (F), 71, 78
Côtes de Buzet (F), 151
Côtes de Canon-Fronsac (F), 146
Côtes-de-Castillon (F), 150
Côtes de Courseboux (Sw), 106
Côte Dorée (Sw), 105
Côtes de Duras (F), 411
Côtes de Fronsac (F), 147
Côtes-de-Haut-Roussillon (F), 104
Côte Mignon-Lagaffelière (F), 164
Côtes de Montravel (F), 152
Côte de Nuits (F), 56, 60, 76
Côte de Nuits-Villages (F), 56, 60, 76
Côtes du Rhône (F), 88, 97, 98, 100, 103, 107, 309, 378
Côte-du-Rhône Chusclans (F), 107
Côte Rôtie (F), 76, 88, 98, 108
Côtes de Saussignac (F), 152
Côte de la Vallée (F), 123
La Côte-de-Verdigny (F), 123
Côtes de Courseboux (Sw), 106
Côtes-du-Jura (F), 97, 107
Côtes du Lubéron (F), 108
Côtes de Pallens (Sw), 105
Côtes-de-Provence (F), 101, 102, 108
Côtes de Ventoux (F), 108, 404
Côte de Verschiez (Sw), 105, 106
Côtes du Zaccar (Ag), 315
Les Côtelins (F), 123
Les Côtières (F), 123
Cotnar (R), 290, 294
Les Couagnons (F), 123
Aux Coucherias (F), 77
Coucoulet (F), 107
Les Coudebraults (F), 123
Coudiol (F), 107
La Coudraie (F), 124
Le Coulaire (F), 107
La Coulée de Serrant (F), 126
Les Coulets (F), 107
Coup de l'Etrier (Sw), 106
Cour Cheverny (F), 411
La Coutière (F), 77
Les Coutures (F), 125
Couvent-des-Jacobins (F), 163
Craipillot (F), 76
Aux Cras (F), 77
Les Cras (F), 58, 59, 76, 78
Crasto
La Crau (F), 107

Cravailleu et Alexandre (F), 107
Cravant-les-Coteaux (F), 125
Cray (F), 123
Cream Flor (Cal), 333
– Sherry (Sp), 190
– 201 (Sp), 190
Crépy (F), 88
Cressier (Sw), 269
Cressier La Rochette (Sw), 269
Le Crêt (F), 108
Crêt-brûlé (Sw), 106
Crêt-dessous (Sw), 106
Crêta Plan (Sw), 105
Crête de l'Enfer (Sw), 105
Creux-de-la-Net (F), 77
Les Crilles (F), 123
Criots-Bâtard-Montrachet (F), 63, 78
Le Cristia (F), 107
Cristina (Sp), 190
Crochet (Sw), 106
La Croix (F), 107
La Croix-de-Bois (F), 107, 124
La Croix de Jamot (F), 107
La Croix-Marie (F), 125
Les Croix-Noires (F), 77
Croix-de-Vaux (F), 124
Crosex-Grillé (Sw), 105
Les Croulards (F), 125
La Croze (F), 107
La Crozette (F), 107
Crozes-Hermitage (F), 98, 107
Cru des Arroucats (F), 160
– de Baylen (F), 158
– Baylibelle (F), 160
– Bel-Air (F), 156
– Belair (F), 165
– Bergeron (F), 156
– du Bérot (F), 158
– de Bichon (F), 157
– Boisson (F), 157
– du Bourdieu (F), 161
– Le Bourdieu (F), 157
– des Bourguillards (Sw), 269
– de Brazé (F), 157
– du Brouillaou (F), 157
– des Brunetières (F), 125
– des Cabanes (F), 157
– Cantegrit (F), 161
– Casi-Devant (F), 166
– Chacha (F), 157
– des Chair d'Ane (Sw), 269
– Cleyrac (F), 157
– Combes-Canon (F), 166
– du Couloumet (F), 160
– de Couloumet-Les Boupeyres (F), 160
– Cravaillas (F), 157
– Dauphin (F), 157
– d'Eyquem (F), 157
– Fillau (F), 156
– du Freyron (F), 157
– des Gravanys (Sw), 269
– La Gravette (F), 161
– de La Gravière du Tich (F), 160
– Gros-Bonnet (F), 166
– Haut-Belloc (F), 157
– Haut-Boutoc (F), 157
– Haut-Mayne (F), 157
– du Haut-Roudey (F), 161
– d'Hauterive (Sw), 269
– de l'Hermitage (F), 158
– Hournalas (F), 156
– Larrouquey (F), 156, 157
– Lassalle (F), 159
– de Lionne (F), 157
– La Liste (F), 157
– Mâdérot (F), 157
– des Magens (F), 157
– de Magneau (F), 157
– Majans (F), 157

Cru Maucouade (F), 157
– Le Mayne (F), 157
– des Merloses (Sw), 269
– Menaut-Larrouquey (F), 157
– de Méric (F), 157
– du Merle (F), 160
– de Montallier-Lambrot (F), 160
– Mothes (F), 156
– du Moulin (F), 157
– du Moulin-à-Vent (F), 157, 166
– des Moulins à Vent (F), 157
– Navarot (F), 157
– de Nazareth (F), 161
– de La Nouvelle-Eglise (F), 000
– Peyraguey (F), 156
– de Du Peyrat (F), 157
– Peyrouquet (F), 164
– de Peyroutène (F), 156
– Peytoupin (F), 161
– de Pineau (F), 157
– La Pinesse (F), 156
– des Ptolémées (E), 300, 302
– Rigal (F), 160
– Ségur-Fillon-Isle-d'Arès (F), 159
– Terrefort (F), 160
– La Tour-Ballet (F), 166
– Troquart (F), 164
– de Vigneyre (F), 161
– de la Ville (Sw), 269
– Vincent (F), 167
– Voltaire (F), 157
Cruet Montmelian (F), 107
Crus Ferbos-Lalanette (F), 157
– des Grands-Chênes (F), 157
Çubuk (T), 300
Cuesta Alta (Sp), 189
Culée de Senant (F), 122
Culemborg Perlé (S.A.), 316
– Rose (S.A.), 316
– Selected Riesling (S.A.), 315
– Selected Stein (S.A.), 316
Cure d'Attalens (Sw), 105
Les Curiades (Sw), 106
Curzille (Sw), 106
Cuvée Charles VII (F), 359
– Elysée (F), 359
– de l'Empereur (F), 359
– Grand Siècle (F), 359
Cvčiek (Yg), 294, 406
Cyprus (C), 302
Cyriakusberg (Gy), 274

Dachsberg (Gy), 263, 271, 274
Dachsteiger (Gy), 271
Daley Villette (Sw), 106
Dalgar (Sp), 190
Dalva's Dry White Port (P), 213
Dalva's Port (P), 213
Aux Damodes (F), 76
Le Damoiseau (Sw), 106
Dampierre (F), 125, 126
Damsberg (Gy), 273
Danúbio (P), 212
Dão (P), 198, 199
– Cabido (P), 212
– Caves Aliança (P), 212
– Caves Império (P), 212
– Grão Vasco (P), 212
– Monástico (P), 212
– Real Vinicola (P), 212
– Sóvida (P), 212
– U.C.B. (P), 212
– Vale da Fonte (P), 212
Daubenpflänzer (Gy), 273
Daubhaus (Gy), 273, 274, 276
Daufenberg (Gy), 277
D.C. Vintage Port (S.A.), 316
Dealul Mare (R), 294
Debröi Hárslevelü (H), 288, 293
Dechaney (Gy), 274
Decker (Gy), 263

D. Fernando Extra Dry White (P), 213
Delaware (N.Y.), 333
Delheim Cabernet-Sauvignon (S.A.), 314, 316
– Late-Harvest « Spatzendreck » (S.A.), 314, 315
– Pinotage (S.A.), 314, 316
– Riesling (S.A.), 315
– Selected Riesling (S.A.), 315
– Selected Stein Goldspatz (S.A.), 315
– White-French (S.A.), 315
Deliciosa (Sp), 189
Dell (Gy), 276
Dellchen (Gy), 273
Demestica (G), 298, 301
Deportivo (Sp), 189, 190
Les Deronières (F), 124
Derrière-la-Grange (F), 58, 76
Derrière-Saint-Jean (F), 77
Descarado (Sp), 190
Déseret (F), 107
Deutelsberg (Gy), 264, 274
Deutschherrenhöpfchen (Gy), 275
Devès d'Estouard (F), 107
Devon Cream Sherry (S.A.), 316
Devonvale Port (S.A.), 316
– Solera Dry « Flor » (S.A.), 316
Dézaley de la Ville (Sw), 106, 411
Dezberg (Gy), 271
Dezize (F), 67, 77, 78
D.G.Flor Nº 2 (S.A.), 316
D.G. Olorose (S.A.), 316
Dhronhofberger (Gy), 275
Diamante (Sp), 187
Diamond Jubilee (Sp), 190
Dickerstein (Gy), 263
Les Didiers (F), 76
Dieblensberg (Gy), 271
Diestro (Sp), 189, 190
Diestro (Brown) (Sp), 190
Dimiat (Bg), 290
Dingač (Yg), 291, 294
Diogenes (Sp), 188
Les Diognères (F), 107
Les Diognères et Torras (F), 107
Diosig (R), 294
Dique (Sp), 189
Directorial (P), 213
Directors Reserve (P), 213
Diren (T), 302
Disibodenberg (Gy), 273
Dohr (Gy), 266, 275
Doktor (Gy), 275
Doktor und Graben (Gy), 265, 275
Dolceacqua (I), 222
Dolcetto delle Langhe e d'Ovada (I), 220, 236
Dôle (Sw), 93, 105
– de Balavaud (Sw), 105
– de Chamoson (Sw), 105
– d'Epesses (Sw), 106
– du Mont (Sw), 105
Dôle-Pinot noir (Sw), 105
Dôle-Pinot noir sur Plan d'Uvrier (Sw), 105
Dôle Ravanay (Sw), 105
– von Salgesch (La Chapelle) (Sw), 105
– de Salquenen (Sw), 105
Doluca (T), 302
Dom (Gy), 272
Domaine d'Armaing (F), 160
– de l'Auberidière (F), 124
– des Augiers (F), 167
– de Badon-Patarabet (F), 163
– de Balestard (F), 162
– de Barbe-Maurin (F), 160
– de La Barde (F), 165
– du Barque (F), 157
– de la Bastide (F), 161

Domaine de la Bâtie (Sw), 106
– de Beaudron (F), 165
– de Beaulieu (F), 160
– de Bel-Air (F), 167
– de Belle-Croix (F), 160
– de Bellevue (F), 160
– de Bernadon (F), 161
– de La Bertrande (F), 161
– de la Bigaire (Sw), 106
– des Biscarets (F), 161
– de Bonne (F), 167
– du Boucaud (F), 167
– de Bouche (F), 167
– de Bourgalade (F), 161
– de Boustit (F), 161
– de Bouteilley (F), 161
– du Broussey (F), 161
– de Brufanno (F), 162
– de Bujan (F), 167
– de Cabirol (F), 162
– de Caillou (F), 157
– de Calamiac (F), 162
– de Calbet (F), 157
– du Calvaire (F), 164
– de Camelon (F), 161
– de Cardonne (F), 161
– des Carmes (F), 162
– de Carsin (F), 161
– de Castagnaou (F), 157
– de Castagnon (F), 161
– de Castebelle-des-Praud (F), 162
– de Cazelon (F), 165
– du Chai (F), 167
– de Chalet-de-Germignan (F), 159
– de Chambleau P.H. Burgat (Sw), 269
– de Champréveyres (Sw), 269
– de Chante-Grive-Badon (F), 163
– des Charmettes (F), 160
– de Chasse-Pierre (F), 160
– de Chastelet (F), 161
– du Château de Valeyres (Sw), 269
– du Châtelet (F), 163
– du Chay (F), 160
– de Chevalier (F), 157
– de Cholet (F), 161
– de Christoly (F), 167
– de La Clotte (F), 165
– de Cluseau (F), 161
– de la Commune (Sw), 105, 106
– des Conseillants (F), 161
– Le Cossu (F), 157
– de la Côte Rôtie (F), 160
– de Côte-Rôtie-Lamothe (F), 160
– de Courbon (F), 158
– du Courlat (F), 165
– du Coy (F), 156
– Crassat-Gramman (F), 160
– de la Croix (F), 167
– Croix-de-Mission (F), 165
– de La Cure (F), 161
– du Daley (Sw), 106
– de l'Eglise (F), 165
– de Faizeau (F), 165
– de Fauchey (F), 162
– de Fermis (F), 162
– du Ferron (F), 162
– du Fihl (F), 161
– de Flous (F), 160
– de Fonbonne (F), 167
– de Fongrane (F), 162
– de Fontmurée (F), 165
– de la Forêt (F), 156
– de la Frairie (F), 161
– de Freyron (F), 157
– de la Gaborie (F), 162
– La Gaffelière (F), 163
– de Gallier (F), 157
– de la Gaucherie (F), 125
– de Gillet (F), 165
– de La Girafe (F), 157

Domaine de la Girolatte (F), 162
– de Glayse (F), 162
– des Gluchets (F), 158
– de Gouas (F), 162
– du Gourdin (F), 160
– de Goursin (F), 162
– du Grand-Canteloup (F), 162
– de Grand-Chemin (F), 167
– du Grand-Faurie (F), 163
– de Grand-Maison (F), 157
– du Grand-Parc (F), 161
– des Grands-Champs (F), 165
– de la Grangeotte (F), 162
– de Graulet (F), 167
– de Grava (F), 161
– de La Grave (F), 162
– de Gravette (F), 157
– de Grimon (F), 165
– de Guerrit (F), 167
– de Guinot (F), 160
– du Haurin (F), 161
– du Haut-Bruly (F), 164
– Haut-Patarabet (F), 163
– de Haut-Pignon (F), 165
– Haut-Pommerol (F), 165
– de Haut-Veyrac (F), 163, 164
– de Hautes-Graves (F), 161
– du Houre (F), 162
– de Jacob (F), 160
– du Jau (F), 157
– de Jaussan (F), 157
– de Joffre (F), 161
– de Labatut (F), 165
– de Lagaloche (F), 160
– de Lagrange (F), 161, 165
– de Lalibarde (F), 167
– de Lamarque (F), 161
– Lambert (F), 161
– de Lamothe-Vigneau, Château des Remparts (F), 156
– de Landreau (F), 162
– de Lasalle (F), 157
– de Lescure (F), 161
– de Lhoste (F), 161
– de Luc (F), 161
– de Maisonneuve (F), 165
– de Malendure (F), 160
– de la Maroutine (F), 161
– de la Marquise (F), 161
– du Mas des Chaux (Sw), 269
– Le Mayne (F), 162
– de Mayne (F), 162
– de Melin (F), 160
– de Menjou (F), 157
– de Mespley (F), 161
– de Meyssau (F), 162
– de Miqueu-Bel-Air (F), 160
– de Mondain (F), 162
– de Morange (F), 160
– du Moulin de Ballan (F), 161
– des Moulins à Vent (F), 156
– de Moutons (F), 160
– de Nicot (F), 162
– du Noble (F), 160
– de Noriou-Lalibarde (F), 167
– d'Ogoz (Sw), 105
– d'Ordonnat (F), 158
– de Pardaillan (F), 161
– de Pasquet (F), 160, 162
– de Paty (F), 167
– Pavie-Macquin (F), 163
– de Pédebert (F), 162
– Petit-Val (F), 164
– de La Peyrère (F), 157
– de Peyrines (F), 162
– de Peyror (F), 157
– du Pin (F), 160, 161
– Le Pin (F), 162
– des Places (F), 158
– de Poncet (F), 161
– de Potiron (F), 161

425

Domaine de Prentigarde (F), 161
– de Prouzet (F), 157
– de Rambaud (F), 165
– de Rey (F), 163
– de Riencourt (Sw), 106
– de Rivereau (F), 167
– de la Rivière (F), 162
– de Roby (F), 160
– du Rocher (F), 160
– de Roquebrune (F), 161
– de la Rouergue (F), 162
– de Rouquette (F), 160
– de Roustit (F), 160
– de Saint-Cricq (F), 161
– de Sainte-Anne (F), 161
– de la Salle (F), 164
– du Salut, Château Huradin (F), 157
– de Sansaric (F), 157
– de Sarraux-Dessous (Sw), 106
– des Sorbiers (F), 160
– de Souba (F), 156
– de Talusson (F), 162
– de Terrefort (F), 162
– de Teychon (F), 158
– du Tich (F), 160
– de Toumilot (F), 158
– des 3 Etoiles (Sw), 106
– de Troubat (F), 162
– de Turon-Lanere (F), 160
– de Viaud (F), 167
– de Videau (F), 158
– de la Vieille (F), 165
– de Vignolles (F), 162
– de Vincent (F), 167
– de Yon (F), 164
De nos Domaines (Sw), 105
Domberg (Gy), 276
Domdechaney (Gy), 263, 274
The Dome (Sp), 190
Domherrenberg (Gy), 275
La Dominode (F), 77
Domley (Gy), 277
Dom Perignon (F), 359
Domprobst (Gy), 265, 275
Dom Scharzhofberger (Gy), 275
Domtal (Gy), 273
Domtaler (Gy), 277
Don Algar (Sp), 189
– Gonzalo (Sp), 189
– José (Sp), 190
– Nuño (Sp), 189
– Quijote (Sp), 189
Donski (U.S.S.R.), 292
Don Zoïlo «Cream» (Sp), 190
– Zoïlo «Dry» (Sp), 189
– Zoïlo «Medium» (Sp), 189
Doña Juana (Sp), 189
Doosberg (Gy), 263, 274
Dopp (Gy), 256
Dorfberg (Gy), 271
Dorin (Sw), 93, 94, 105
Doron (Is), 301
Sous-le-Dos-d'Ane (F), 78
Döttinger Clevner Auslese (Sw), 268
– Süssdruck (Sw), 268
Double Century (Sp), 189
Dounavska Perla (Bg), 291
Douro Favaios (P), 212
– Velho (P), 213
Dow's Boardroom Port (P), 213
– Dry White Aperitif Port (P), 213
Drachenley (Gy), 277
Drachenstein (Gy), 274
Drâgâsani (R), 294
Drain (F), 126
Dreispitz (Gy), 256
Dry Don (Sp), 189
– Finish White Port (P), 213
– Grand Solera (Sp), 188
– Old Port (P), 213

Dryor (P), 212
Dry Pale (Sp), 189
– Port (P), 213
– Sack (Sp), 189
– Tang (P), 213
– Tua (P), 213
– Watch (Cal), 333
– White Port (P), 213
D.S. (Sp), 189
Ducal (Sp), 189
Ducha (Sp), 190
Duff Gordon (Sp), 189
Duque (Sp), 189
El Duque (Sp), 189
Duque de Bragança (P), 213
Duquesa (Sp), 190
Duresse (F), 77
Les Duresses (F), 77
Dürnsteiner Himmelsstiege (A), 293
– Hollerin (A), 287, 293
– Liebenberg (A), 287, 288, 293
– Muskat-Ottonel (A), 293
Durtal (Loire, F), 126
Duvet (F), 107
D. Velhissimo (P), 213

Ebenbreit (Gy), 273
Eberfürst (Gy), 271
Echezeaux (F), 59, 76
Eck (Gy), 276
Eckartsberg (Gy), 269
Eckberg (Gy), 269
Ecloseaux (F), 78
Eco (Sp), 189
A l'Ecu (F), 77
Les Ecusseaux (F), 77
Edelberg (Gy), 275
Edelmann (Gy), 263, 274
Edelzwicker (F), 252, 269
Der edle Twanner Chroshalde (Sw), 269
Eglisauer Blauburgunder (Sw), 268
– Riesling-Sylvaner (Sw), 268
– Stadtberger Beerli (Sw), 268
– Tokayer (Sw), 268
Egri Bikavér (H), 288, 293
– Leanyka (H), 288
Ehrenberg (Gy), 271, 276
Eich (Gy), 275
Eichberg (Gy), 254, 269
Eichen (Gy), 269
Eichenlaub (Gy), 269
Eichert (Gy), 269
Eichholz (Sw), 246
Eichquell (Gy), 270
1827/Eighteen hundred and twenty-seven (Sp), 190
1870/Eighteen hundred and seventy (Sp), 190
1874/Eighteen hundred and seventy-four (Sp), 190
Eilfingerberg (Gy), 271
Ein Guedi (Is), 301
– Red (Is), 301
– Red Wine (Is), 301
– White (Is), 301
Eiserweg (Gy), 263
Eiswein (Gy), 263
Elba (I), 227, 237
Elazig (C), 407
Elfinger Blauburgunder Schlotterboden (Sw), 268
Elisenberg (Gy), 275
Eloro (I), 234, 238
Elsberg (Gy), 277
Elsfeld (Gy), 263
Elster (Gy), 272
Eltzerberg (Gy), 275
Elzoberg (Gy), 275
Embleyres (Sw), 106
Emerald Riesling (Cal), 322

Emir (P), 212
Emperor (P), 213
Enclos de Soutard (F), 164
Engass (Gy), 275
Engehell (Gy), 276
Engelmannsberg (Gy), 263
Engelsberg (Gy), 258, 273, 274
Engelsgrube (Gy), 265, 275
Engweg (Gy), 271
Ennetbadener Beerli (Sw), 268
Enselberg (Gy), 269
Entre-Deux-Mers (F), 144
Enzhälde (Gy), 270
Les Epenots (F), 77
Les Epenottes (F), 77
Epesses (Sw), 94, 106
L'Epinay (F), 124
Erbaluce di Caluso (I), 220, 236
Ergots (F), 76
Erkenbrecht (Gy), 272
Erlach Chasselas Lamperten (Sw), 269
Erlenhalde (Gy), 269
Ermitage (Sw), 93, 105
Ermitage «Cuvée réservée» (Sw), 105
Ermitage Vétroz (Sw), 105
Erntebringer (Gy), 274
Erzgrube (Gy), 273
Escogido (Sp), 189
Les Escondures (F), 107
Escorhuelo (Arg), 338
Escuadrilla (Sp), 189
Eselsberg (Gy), 270, 271, 274
Eselshaut (Gy), 272
España (Sp), 189
La Especial (Sp), 189
La Espuela (Sp), 189
Les Esqueiron (F), 107
Est! Est!! Est!!! (I), 230, 237
Estournelles (F), 76
Estremadura Lezirão (P), 212
– Silveira (P), 212
Etiqueta Blanca (Sp), 187
Etna (I), 234, 238
Etna rosato (I), 238
L'Etoile (F), 107
– Mousseux (F), 361
Etoile de Sierre (Sw), 105
Etournailles (Sw), 105
Euchariusberg (Gy), 275
Eulenberg (Gy), 271
Eulengrube (Gy), 259, 273
Eulenlay (Gy), 275
Euxinograd (Bg), 294
Eva (Sp), 189, 190
Evangelio (Sp), 190
Evel (P), 212
L'Evêque (Sw), 106
Les Evois (F), 125
Evora (Sp), 190
Ewig Bach (Gy), 276
– Leben (Gy), 274
Extra Dry White (P), 213
Eyrans (F), 167

Fächer (Gy), 277
Fächern (Gy), 276
Fachtel (Gy), 274
Les Faconnières (F), 76
Faena (Sp), 189
Fahrberg (Gy), 277
Fahrsfels (Gy), 275
Fairyland (Gy), 276
Faisca (P), 199, 200
Fajardo (Sp), 189
Falerno (I), 217, 219, 233, 237, 238
Falkenberg (Gy), 265, 275
Falkensteiner (Gy), 266, 275
Falkly (Gy), 275
Falset Garnacha Priorato (Sp), 187
Famolens (Sw), 106

Fandango (Sp), 189
Fara (I), 220
Farguerol (F), 107
Faro (I), 234, 238
Faugères (F), 103, 108
Fauterie (F), 107
Faverges (Sw), 105
Favorito (Sp), 189
Faye-sur-Layon (F), 126
Le Feau (F), 124
Féchy (Sw), 94, 106
Feigenberg (Gy), 277
Feinerde (Gy), 272
Felicita (Sp), 190
Fels (Gy), 272, 273
Felsen (Gy), 271
In den Felsen (Gy), 273
Felsenberg (Gy), 272, 273
Felsengarten (Gy), 270
Felsenleiste (Gy), 274
Felsenrot (Gy), 274
Felsensteyer (Gy), 273
Fenchelberg (Gy), 258, 273
Fendant (Sw), 93, 105
– du Ravin (Sw), 105
Fenecio (Sp), 189
Fensel (Gy), 277
Feria Sherry (Sp), 189
Feteasca de Tirnave (R), 290
Fettgarten (Gy), 275
Fetysk (U.S.S.R.), 292
Feuer (Gy), 271
Feuerbacher Lehmberg (Gy), 270
Feuerberg (Gy), 269, 272, 273, 275
Feuerlay (Gy), 276
Les Fèves (F), 63, 77
Fiano (I), 233
Les Fichots (F), 77
54/Fifty-four Port (P), 213
Le Figuier (F), 123
Filisberg (Gy), 275
Fina (Sp), 189
Findling (Gy), 273
Fine Port (P), 213
– Royal Choice (P), 213
Finest (Sp), 189
Finito (Sp), 189
Fino F.M. (Sp), 189
– Ideal (Sp), 189
– Zuleta (Sp), 189
Le Fin de la Pierraz (Sw), 105
Fischer (Gy), 274
Fischerpfad (Gy), 273
Fitou (F), 103, 108
Fixin (F), 56, 76, 404
Flamenco (Sp), 189
Los Flamencos (Sp), 190
Flanzer (Gy), 269
Fläschenhall (Gy), 258, 273
Fleckinger (Gy), 272
La Fleur du Gazin (F), 166
Fleurie (F), 71, 72, 78
Les Fleuries (F), 123
Flockenberg (Gy), 273
Flor de Jerez (Sp), 190
Flor de Montilla (Sp), 188
Florens Louis (P), 359
Florian (Gy), 272
Florido (Sp), 189
Flor Sherry (Cal), 333
Floss (Gy), 258, 273
Flur (Gy), 276
Flurlinger Tokayer (Sw), 268
Fohrenberg (Gy), 254, 269
Les Folatières (F), 67, 78
La Folie (F), 124
Folle blanche (Cal), 333
La Follière (F), 124
Les Fondis (F), 125
La Font du Loup (F), 107
La Font de Michelle (F), 107

426

La Fontainerie (F), 124
La Fonteny (F), 76
Fonte Segale (I), 228
Fontgent (F), 108
Forcine (F), 125
Les Fornets (Sw), 105
Forst (Gy), 272, 273
Forstberg (Gy), 270, 277
Forstwein (Sw), 246
Les Forteresses (Sw), 105
La Fortisse (F), 107
La Fosse (F), 78
Les Fosses (Sw), 105
Fougerolles (F), 125
Les Fouinières (F), 124
Four à Chaux (F), 107
Aux Fourneaux (F), 77
Les Fournières (F), 77
Fourniers (F), 107
Fours (F), 167
Les Fousselottes (F), 58, 76
Fracia (I), 221
Los Fraïles (Sp), 188
Francarmin (Sw), 269
Franciacorta (I), 236
Francœur (Sw), 269
Frangy (F), 96, 107
Frankenhöll (Gy), 276
Frankenlay (Gy), 275
Frankenthal (Gy), 274
Frankovka (Yg), 294
Franquizons (F), 107
Franzhauser Kabinett-Neuburger (A),
  293
Frappato di Vittoria (I), 234, 238
Frascati (I), 230, 237
Frauenberg (Gy), 275
Freccia Rossa di Casteggio (I), 236
Frecciarossa di Casteggio (I), 221,
  236
Freisa (I), 220
– d'Asti (I), 236
– di Chieri (I), 236
– di Chieri e d'Asti (I), 236
Les Fremières (F), 76
Les Fremiers (F), 77
Fremiets (F), 77
Frenz (Gy), 274
Freudenberg (Gy), 271
Freudenberger Beerli (Sw), 268
Freudentaler Berg (Gy), 269
Freundstück (Gy), 272
Fricambault (F), 123
Les Frionnes (F), 77
Fritzenhölle (Gy), 273
La Frizonne (F), 108
Frohnberg (Gy), 272
Frohwingert (Gy), 276
Les Froichots (F), 76
Fronhof (Gy), 256, 272
Fronklinge (Gy), 270
Fronsac (F), 147, 166, 167
Frontignan (F), 105, 199, 407
Fron-Weingarten (Gy), 276
Frühlingsplätzchen (Gy), 273
Frühmesse (Gy), 273
Fruska Gora (Yg), 292
Fruta (Sp), 190
Fuchsberg (Gy), 274
Fuchsloch (Gy), 258, 273
Fuchsmantel (Gy), 256, 272
Les Fuées (F), 76
Furmint (Cs), 293
Furor divina Costiera (I), 256
Fürstenberg (Gy), 273, 274, 276

Gabarnac (F), 143
Gabelstich (Gy), 273
Chez Gaboulet (F), 108
Gächlinger (Sw), 268
Gaditano (Sp), 189

Gaeiras (P), 200
Les Gagères (F), 108
Gaillac (F), 152
– Mousseux (F), 361
– Premières Côtes (F), 152
– Perlé (F), 152
La Gaillardière (F), 124
Gaisengrund (Gy), 271
Gaispfad (Gy), 265
Galarza (Sp), 189
Galgenpfad (Gy), 274
Les Galimardes (F), 107
La Galippe (F), 125
El Gallo (Sp), 189
La Gallotière (F), 125
Les Galuches (F), 125
Gamay (Sw), 96, 106
– de Gondebaud (Sw), 106
Gamay-Lully (Sw), 106
– rosé (Cal), 325, 329, 333
Sur Gamay (F), 77
Gamay Pinot (Sw), 106
La Gamone (F), 107
Gamza (Bg), 291
Gamza of Novosseltzi (Bg), 294
– of Pavlikeni (Bg), 294
– of Soukhindol (Bg), 294
Ganghalde (Gy), 269
Garbosa (Sp), 189
La Garde (F), 108
La Gardière (F), 125
La Gardine (F), 107
La Gardiole (F), 107
La Garenne (F), 78, 107
Garganega di Gambellare (I), 225
Les Gargouilles (F), 123
Gärkammer (Gy), 276
Garnacha (Sp), 188, 199
Les Garollières or Jarollières (F), 77
Les Garrigues (F), 107
Gartenley (Gy), 277
Gattinara (I), 220, 236
Les Gaudichots (F), 76
Le Géant (F), 107
Geheu (Gy), 272
Gehrn (Gy), 264, 274
Geierslay (Gy), 265, 275
Geigersberg (Gy), 270
Geisberg (Gy), 266, 275
Geisböhl (Gy), 272
Geissberg (Gy), 276
Geisseberg (Gy), 276
Geisspfad (Gy), 275
Les Gémeaux (F), 76
La Genestière et Fourcadure (F), 107
En Genêt (F), 77
En Genévaz (Sw), 106
Les Genévrières (F), 76
Les Genévrières-Dessus (F), 78
Les Genévrières-Dessous (F), 78
Gentileza (Sp), 190
Gerania (G), 301
Les Germines (F), 108
Gertrudenberg (Gy), 277
Gerümpel (Gy), 256, 272
Gevrey-Chambertin (F), 49, 56, 57, 60,
  76, 410
Gewürztraminer, Alsace (F), 244, 251,
  252, 269
– (Cal), 322, 325
– (N.Y.), 333
Geyersberg (Gy), 273
Geyerskopf (Gy), 275
Gezellen Liebfraumilch (S.A.), 316
Ghemme (I), 220, 236
Gickelsberg (Gy), 273
La Gidonnière (F), 123
Giebelhölle (Gy), 277
Gies (Gy), 277
Gietel (Gy), 276
Gigliano (I), 232, 238

Gigondas (F), 100, 107
Girandole (Sw), 105
Les Girarmes (F), 123
Giro (I), 242
La Giroflarie (F), 108
Givry (F), 68, 78
Glanzer Berg (A), 293
Glasten (Gy), 276
Glöck (Gy), 258, 273
Glockenberg (Gy), 273
Glockenzehnt (Gy), 272
Gloire du Rhône (Sw), 105
Gloria (Sp), 189
Glorioso reserva (Sp), 187
Glottertäler (Gy), 254
Glückenhälde (Gy), 271
Goetheberg (Gy), 277
Goguenne (F), 124
Goldatzel (Gy), 274
Goldbächel (Gy), 256, 272
Goldberg (Gy), 271, 272, 273, 274,
  275
Goldemund (Gy), 276
Golden Bonwin (S.A.), 316
– Cream (Is), 301
– Crown White Extra Dry (P), 213
– Mantilla (S.A.), 316
Goldkaul (Gy), 276
Goldknöpferl-Rotgipfler (A), 293
Goldkupp (Gy), 275
Goldlay (Gy), 275, 276
Goldschmied (Gy), 272
Goldwand (Sw), 247
Goldtröpfchen (Gy), 265, 275
Goldwändler (Sw), 268
Goldwingert (Gy), 275
La Goleta (Sp), 190
Les Gonnordes (F), 126
Gonzales (Sp), 190
– Byass Dry (S.A.), 316
– Byass Medium (S.A.), 316
– Byass Sweet (S.A.), 316
Görlay (Gy), 275
Görn (Gy), 269
Goron (Sw), 93
Gotas de Ouro (seco) (P), 213
Götighofer (Sw), 268
Gottesacker (Gy), 269, 272
Gottesfuss (Gy), 273
Gotteshilfe (Gy), 273
Götzenberg (Gy), 270
Götzenfels (Gy), 273
Les Goulots (Gy), 76
Goût du Conseil « Mont d'Or » (Sw),
  105
La Goutte-d'Or (F), 78
Goutte d'or (Sw), 269
Les Gouttierreries (F), 78
Government House Port (S.A.), 316
La Goya (Sp), 189
Graben (Gy), 275
Grabensgrund (Gy), 271
Grafenberg (Gy), 270, 271, 277
Gräfenberg (Gy), 264, 271, 274, 275
Gragnano (I), 233, 238
Grain (Gy), 272
Grainhübel (Gy), 256, 272
Gran Fruta (Sp), 190
Gran Señor (Sp), 189
Grand Baillif (Sw), 105
Grand Bathes (F), 124
Le Grand Bouchot (F), 123
Grand Bouquet (Sw), 105
Grandchamp (Sw), 106
Grand-Champ (F), 107
Le Grand Chaumoux (F), 123
Grand chemin de Sorgues (F), 107
Le Grand Collet (F), 107
Le Grand Coteau (F), 124
Grand Devès (F), 107
Grand Echeneau (F), 124

Grand enclos du Château de Cérons (F),
  156
Grand Mousseux (S.A.), 314
Grand Pierre (F), 107
Le Grand Plantier (F), 107
Le Grand Puizac (F), 123
Le Grand-Schiner Chapeau Rouge (Sw),
  105
– Le Père du Valais (Sw), 105
– Prince de l'Eglise (Sw), 105
– Saint Empire (Sw), 105
Grand Vigne (Sw), 105
Les Grands-Champs (F), 77, 125
Grands-Echezeaux (F), 59, 76
Les Grands Galiguières (F), 107
Aux Grands-Liards (F), 77
Le Grand Taillé (F), 108
La Grande Côte (F), 123
Grande Natal (P), 212
Grande Plantée et la Garelle (F), 108
La Grand'Rue (F), 76
Les Grandes-Lolières (F), 77
Les Grandes Ouches (F), 125
Les Grandes Places (F), 108
Grandes-Ruchottes (F), 78
Grandes Serres (F), 107
Grandélite (P), 212
Grandjó (P), 212
Grape Cream (Sp), 190
Graševina (Yg), 294
Grasparossa (I), 237
Grassnitzberg (A), 287, 293
La Gratitude (S.A.), 313, 315
Grauberg (Gy), 275
Grauer Stein (Gy), 273
Aux Gravains (F), 77
Graver Stein (Gy), 258, 378, 404
Graves (F), 138, 140, 141
– de Bordeaux (F), 141, 378
– de Vayres (F), 144
Les Gravières (F), 77
Les Gravoches (F), 123
Great Western Pinto (Aus), 341
Greco di Gerace (I), 238
– di Todi (I), 228, 237
– di Tufo (I), 233, 238
Green Hungarian (Cal), 322
Les Greffieux (F), 107
Greiner (Gy), 270
Greisenmund (Gy), 274
Grenache Rosé (Cal), 329, 333
La Grenade (F), 107
Le Grès (F), 107
Grésigny (F), 78
La Gresille (F), 125
Les Gresilles (F), 125
Greta (Sp), 189
Les Grèves (F), 49, 63, 77
Sur-les-Grèves (F), 77
Grey Riesling (Cal), 322, 333
Gries (Gy), 273
Grignolino (Cal), 325, 329, 333
– (I), 220
– d'Asti (I), 236
– d'Asti Spumante (I), 364
La Grillette (Sw), 269
Le Grillon (Sw), 105
Grinzing (A), 286
Griotte Chambertin (F), 57, 76
Gris de Pagny-sur-Moselle (F), 411
Grk (Yg), 294
Gropello (I), 221
Les Groseilles (F), 76
Les Gros des Vignes (F), 107
Gross (Gy), 272
Grossenberg (Gy), 276
Grosswingert (Gy), 275
Grosse Roche et la Balayat (F), 108
Grosser Herrgott (Gy), 275
La Grotte (F), 124
Les Groux (F), 123

427

Grub (Gy), 276
Grube (Gy), 276
Grub-Höge (Gy), 269
Les Gruenchers (F), 58, 76
Grumello (I), 221, 236
Grunberger Stein (S.A.), 314, 315
Grüner Veltliner (A), 293
Grünmädchen (S.A.), 313
Guadalupe (Sp), 189
Guapito (Sp), 189
Guatturnio dei Colli Piacentini (I), 226, 237
Guckinsland (Gy), 272
La Gueniettaz (Sw), 106
Chez Gueraud (F), 108
Les Guérets (F), 77
La Guérite (Sw), 105
Guerrero (Sp), 189
Aux Guettes (F), 77
Guigasse (F), 107
Grignolino rosé (Cal), 333
La Guillambaule (F), 108
Les Guimonières (F), 126
Guldenmorgen (Gy), 273
Gumben (Gy), 273
Gumpoldskirchner Golknöpfel (A), 293
 – Grimmling (A), 293
 – Rasslerin (A), 293
 – Sonnberg (A), 287, 293
 – Spiegel (A), 287, 293
 – Stocknarrn (A), 293
 – Wiegel (A), 287
 – Zierfandler (A), 293
Günterslay (Gy), 265, 275
Gurdjurni (U.S.S.R.), 294
Gutental (Gy), 273
Gutes Domtal (Gy), 273
Guthenberg (Gy), 274
Guthenthal (Gy), 274
Güzelbag (T), 300
Güzel Marmara (T), 300

Haag (Gy), 270
Haardt (Gy), 271
Les Habrards (F), 107
Hadar (Is), 301
Häder (Gy), 270
Hägelich (Gy), 270
Hagenrain (Gy), 271
Hahlen (Gy), 269
Hahn (Gy), 276
Hahnen (Gy), 272
Hahnenberg (Gy), 266
Hahnenböhl (Gy), 256, 272
La Haie-Martel (F), 125
Haigern (Gy), 270
Halde (Gy), 270, 271
Halenberg (Gy), 273
Helkididi (G), 301
Hallauer Beerli Graf von Spiegelberg (Sw), 268
 – Blauburgunder (Sw), 247, 268
 – Süssdruck vom Schälleweg (Sw), 268
Halsbach (Gy), 275
Halsberg (Gy), 275
Hambach (Gy), 276
Hambuch (Gy), 276
Hameau-de-Blagny (F), 78
Hamm (Gy), 274, 276, 277
Hammerstein (Gy), 266
Hangestein (Gy), 276
Haniob (Gy), 277
Hansenberg (Gy), 274
Harchlevelu (Cs), 293
Hardilliers (F), 124
Hardtberg (Gy), 276
Hardthell (Gy), 276
Harfe (Gy), 274

Harmony (Sp), 189, 190
Les Harrassons (F), 125
Hartberger Löffelbach (A), 287, 293
 – Ring (A), 287, 293
In und ober der Hartel (Gy), 276
Harvey's Dry Sherry (Cal), 316
 – Extra Dry (S.A.), 316
 – Full Cream Sherry (S.A.), 316
Harzberg (Gy), 270
Haselberg (Gy), 269
Hasen (Gy), 272
Hasenbiss (Gy), 273
Hasenflöz (Gy), 276
Hasenläufer (Gy), 265, 275
Hasensprung (Gy), 263, 274, 275
Hasenweg (Gy), 273
Hassel (Gy), 263, 274
Hauptmann (Gy), 263
Les Haurières (F), 123
Hauser (Gy), 269
Haut-Benauge (F), 143
Haut-Brion (F), 141
Haut-Comtat (F), 108
Haut-Cousse (F), 124
Haut-Dahra (Ag), 315
Le Haut-Lieu (F), 124
Haut-Médoc (F), 138
Haut-Montravel (F), 152
Les Hauts-Bois (F), 124
Les Hauts-Champs (F), 125
Les Hauts Doix (F), 58, 76
Les Hauts-Jarrons (F), 77
Les Hauts-Marconnets (F), 77
Les Hauts-Pruliers (F), 76
Haute-Cour (Sw), 106
Hebros (Bg), 294
Hechacq (F), 152
Hedelfinger Linsenberg (Gy), 270
Hegnach (Gy), 271
Heiderstein (Gy), 277
Heilgraben (Gy), 277
Heiligenbaum (Gy), 258, 273
Heiligenberg (Gy), 272, 274
Heiligenhaus (Gy), 275
Heiligenhäuschen (Gy), 275
Heiligensteiner Sauvignon (A), 277
Heiligenstock (Gy), 274
Heiligkreuz (Gy), 272
Heimberg (Gy), 271, 273
Heislay (Gy), 275
Vom heissen Stein (Gy), 275
Heisterberg (Gy), 277
Heitersbrünnchen (Gy), 273
Held (Gy), 275, 276
Hellersberg (Gy), 274
Hellholz (Gy), 272
Hellpfad (Gy), 263
Helmestal (Gy), 277
Hémona (Bg), 294
Hendelberg (Gy), 264, 274, 275
Hengstberg (Gy), 213, 273
Henkenberg (Gy), 254, 269
Heppenstein (Gy), 275
Herberg (Gy), 274
Herbweg (Gy), 264
Les Héridaines (F), 123
Hermannsberg (Gy), 259, 273
Hermannshöhle (Gy), 259, 273
L'Hermineau (F), 124
Hermitage (Aus), 341
 – (F), 88, 98, 99, 107
 – (Sw), 105
L'Hermite (F), 107
Hernan Cortés (Sp), 189
Herrenberg (Gy), 256, 265, 266, 269, 272, 273, 274, 275, 276
Herrengarten (Gy), 272
Herrenletten (Gy), 272
Herrenmorgen (Gy), 272
Herrenweiher (Gy), 273
Herrgott (Gy), 275

Herrgottsacker (Gy), 256, 272
Herrlesberg (Gy), 270
Herrschaftsberg (Gy), 274
Herschelberg (Gy), 277
Les Hervelets (F), 56, 76
Herzen (Gy), 269
Herzenhöll (Gy), 277
Herzfeld (Gy), 272
Herzgrüble (Gy), 270
Herzlay (Gy), 275
Herzog (Gy), 272
Hessern (Gy), 277
Hetz (Gy), 276
Heyerberg (Gy), 271
Hidalgo (Sp), 189
Hiesgen (Gy), 276
Hietzert (Gy), 277
High Nemea (G), 298
 – Priorato (Sp), 187
Hilda (Sp), 189
Himmelburg (Gy), 269
Himmelchen (Gy), 276
Himmelreich (Gy), 265, 270, 271, 272, 275
Himmelsberg (Gy), 274
Himmelsleiter (Gy), 269
Himmeltal (Gy), 273
Hindenburglay (Gy), 276
Hinkelstein (Gy), 273, 274
Hinterberg (Gy), 275
Hinterer Berg (Gy), 270, 271
Hintere Reste (Gy), 277
Hinterfels (Gy), 273
Hinterhaus (Gy), 274
Hinterkirch (Gy), 263, 274
Hipping (Gy), 258, 273
His Eminence's Choice (P), 213
Hitz (Gy), 273, 274
Hitzlay (Gy), 276
Hitzpfad (Gy), 272
Hoch (Gy), 273
Hochbenn (Gy), 256, 272
Hochberg (Gy), 269
Hochbrudersegg (A), 293
Hoch Chapf Eichberg (Sw), 268
Hochenmorgen (Gy), 256
Hochgewann (Gy), 272
Hochheimer (S.A.), 313
Hochkittenberg (A), 293
Hochmess (Gy), 256, 272
Hochstadt (Gy), 254, 269, 277
Hock (Aus), 341
Hock of Askalon (Is), 301
Hock Patron (Is), 301
Hofberg (Gy), 265
Hofstück (Gy), 256, 272, 273
Hohburg (Gy), 259, 274
Hoheburg (Gy), 256, 272
Hohe Lay (Gy), 277
Hoheleite (Gy), 273
Hoheneck (Gy), 270
Hohenlay (Gy), 274
Hohenlinde (Gy), 274
Hohenmorgen (Gy), 272
Hohenrain (Gy), 263, 274
Hohenstock (Gy), 277
Hoher Berg (Gy), 271
Hoher Decker (Gy), 263
Hohlbaum (Gy), 272
Hohlweid (Gy), 275
Hohnart (Gy), 273
Höll (Gy), 273
Hölle (Gy), 263, 273, 274, 277
Höllenberg (Gy), 263, 274
Höllenpfad (Gy), 273
Holzenberg (Gy), 270
Hömberg (Gy), 275
Homberg (Gy), 274, 275
L'Homme (F), 107
Hongrie (F), 107
Honigberg (Gy), 274

Honigsack (Gy), 272
Honigsäckel (Gy), 256, 272
Hôpital Pourtalès (Sw), 269
Hörecker (Gy), 266, 275
Horn (Gy), 272, 273
Hospices Cantonaux (Sw), 105
Hötlay (Gy), 275
Hubertusberg (Gy), 265, 266, 275, 276
Hubertushofberg (Gy), 275
Hubertuslay (Gy), 275
Huelva (Sp), 378
Huguenot Riesling (S.A.), 315
Hühnerberg (Gy), 275, 277
Huillé (F), 126
Huismes (F), 125
Humagne (Sw), 93, 105
 – Vétroz (Sw), 105
Hummelsberg (Gy), 271
Hundertmorgen (Gy), 272
Hundsberg (Gy), 270, 271
Hundsrück (Gy), 272
Hunnenstein (Gy), 276
Hunter River Dry Red (Aus), 341
Hurlevent (Sw), 105
Husi (R), 294
Les Hussières (F), 123
Hütte (Gy), 266, 275
Hüttenberg (Gy), 269, 273
Hüttwiler Stadtschryber (Sw), 268
Huxlay (Gy), 275
Hypocras (F), 411

Ica (Peru), 340
Idig (Gy), 256, 272
Ile-des-Vergelesses (F), 77
Imperial (Sp), 187, 189
Imperial (P), 213
Imperial Crown (P), 213
Imperial Tawny Doce (P), 213
La Ina (Sp), 189
Independence Wine (Is), 300, 301
Infanta (Sp), 190
La Infanta (Sp), 189
Inferno (I), 221, 236
Ingrandes (F), 126
Ingrandes-de-Touraine (F), 125
Innere Leiste (Gy), 274
Inocente (Sp), 189
Irouleguy (F), 151, 411
Isabel (P), 212
Isabella (N.Y.), 333
Ischia (I), 233, 238
Issartel (F), 107
Issarts (F), 76
Izmir (T), 300
La Jaca Andaluza (Sp), 189

Jagenstiel (Gy), 277
La Jamasse (F), 107
Janville (F), 108
Jaquinotte (F), 107
Jarana (Sp), 189
Jardin (Sp), 189
Jarjayes (F), 411
La Jarnoterie (F), 125
Les Jarrons (F), 77
Jasnières (F), 119, 123
Les Jasnières (F), 123
Jauna (Sp), 189
J.C. le Roux Mont Pellier (S.A.), 315
Jeninser Chüechler Beerliwein, 295
La Jennelotte (F), 78
Jerez (Sp), 180, 189
Jesuitengarten (Gy), 263, 266, 272, 274, 275, 276
Jesuitenstein (Gy), 274
Jesusberg (Gy), 275
Jeu du Roy (Sw), 105
Jirane (F), 107
J.M. da Fonseca (P), 212
Johannesberg (Gy), 273

428

Johannes Strunk (Sw), 105
Johannisberg (Gy), 273, 274, 275
– (S.A.), 314
– (Sw), 93, 94, 96, 105
– Balavaud (Sw), 105
– de Chamoson (Sw), 105
Johannisberger Riesling (Cal), 322, 325, 333
– Riesling Spätlese (N.Y.), 333
Johannisbrünnchen (Gy), 265, 275
Johanniskirchel (Gy), 272
Johannislay (Gy), 275
John Peter (Sp), 189
Joli Cœur (Sw), 106
– Site (Sw), 106
Josephberg (Gy), 269
Josephshöfer (Gy), 275
La Joubardière (F), 124
Les Jouets (F), 126
Les Journaries (F), 108
Juffer (Gy), 265, 275
Juigné-sur-Loire (F), 126
Juliénas (F), 72, 78
Julius Echterberg (Gy), 259, 274
Jumilla (Sp), 178, 188
Jumilla-Monastrell (Sp), 178
Jungfer (Gy), 264, 274
Jungfernberg (Gy), 266
Jungherrn Müller-Thurgau (A), 293
Junkerberg (Gy), 275
Junkersberg (Gy), 275
Jurançon (F), 153

Kadarka (R), 290, 291
– "Roses Valley" (Bg), 294
Kafels (Gy), 273
Käferhalde (Gy), 269
Im Käfersberg (Gy), 269
Käfersberger (Gy), 269
Kaffia (U.S.S.R.), 361
Kahlenberg (Gy), 273
– Traminer (A), 293
Kahlig (Gy), 274
Kaiserberg (Gy), 272, 277
Kaisersteinfels (Gy), 274
Kalb (Gy), 259, 274
Kalbrech (Gy), 275
Kalbspflicht (Gy), 263, 274
Kalchrainer Blauburgunder (Sw), 268
– Tokayer (Sw), 268
Kalebag (T), 299, 302
Kalkgrube (Gy), 272
Kalkofen (Gy), 272
Kallmuth (Gy), 274
Kalmont (Gy), 275
Kalouger (Bg), 294
Kammer (Gy), 259, 274, 275
Kandel (Gy), 275
Im Kanzler (Gy), 277
Kapelle (Gy), 272, 273
Kapellberg (Gy), 270
Kapellenberg (Gy), 269, 270, 271, 273, 274, 275, 277
Kapertchen (Gy), 275
Kappelrodeck (Gy), 254
Kardinalsberg (Gy), 265, 275
Karlsberg (Gy), 271, 275
Karlskopf (Gy), 276
Karrenweg (Gy), 277
Karroo Sherry (S.A.), 316
Karstel (Gy), 277
Karthäuser Hofberg (Gy), 266, 275, 276
Käsberg (Gy), 270
Käselberg (Gy), 269
Käsleberg (Gy), 269
Kastanienbusch (Gy), 272
Katharinenberg (Gy), 276
Katterloch (Gy), 273
Katzenbeisser (Gy), 270

Katzenhauer (Gy), 272
Katzenkopf (Gy), 273
Katzenloch (Gy), 274
Katzenöhrle (Gy), 270
Kaufmannsberg (Gy), 275
Käulgen (Gy), 266, 276
Kautzenberg-Stübchen (Gy), 259, 273
Kauzenberg (Gy), 273
Kavalier-Zierfandler (A), 293
Kavčina (Žametna črnica) (Yg), 294
Kay (Gy), 293
Kebelberg (Gy), 276
Kehle (Gy), 271
Kehr (Gy), 258, 273
Kehrenberg (Gy), 273
Kehrweg (Gy), 273
Kélibia (Tu), 307, 315
Kellerberg (Gy), 263, 273, 277
Kelterberg (Gy), 275
Kelterweinberg (Gy), 270
Kerler (Gy), 276
Kernagel (Gy), 266, 276
Kerzenstück (Gy), 274
Kessler (Gy), 269
Kieselberg (Gy), 256, 272
Kiesling (Gy), 276
King Alfonso (Sp), 189
King Minos (G), 301
Kinzgen-Lot (Gy), 269
Kirchberg (Gy), 254, 259, 269, 271, 273, 275
Kirchenberg (Gy), 277
Kirchenpfad (Gy), 274, 275
Kirchenstück (Gy), 263, 272, 273, 274, 275
Kirchenweinberg (Gy), 270
Kirchgarten (Gy), 272, 274
Kirchgraben (Gy), 275
Kirchköppel (Gy), 277
Kirchlay (Gy), 275
Kirchrech (Gy), 275
Kirchspiel (Gy), 274
Kirchweg (Gy), 271
Kirchscheck (Gy), 273
Kirchenacker (Gy), 274
Kirschgarten (Gy), 270
Kirschheck (Gy), 271
Klaus (Gy), 263
Klauser Berg (Gy), 263
Kläuserweg (Gy), 274
Klevner Villiger Steinbrüchler Beerliwein (Sw), 268
Klinge (Gy), 270
Klingelberg (Gy), 269
Klingenberg (Gy), 270
Klingle (Gy), 270
Klöcher Berg (A), 286, 293
Kloosterberg (S.A.), 316
Kloovendal (S.A.), 316
Klopplay (Gy), 276
Kloster (Gy), 275
Klosterberg (Gy), 254, 256, 270, 271, 273, 274, 275, 276
Klostercabinet (A), 293
Kloster Fürstental (Gy), 276
Klostergarten (Gy), 272, 275, 276
Klosterlay (Gy), 274, 275
Klosterley (Gy), 276
Klosterneuburger Rheinriesling (A), 293
Klümbchen (Gy), 274
Knappengraben (Gy), 272
Knüppelberg (Gy), 276
Köbelberg (A), 287, 293
Kobnert (Gy), 272
Kocherberg (Gy), 271
Köchersberg (Gy), 270
Kochlay (Gy), 276
Kochsberg (Gy), 274
Kohlenberg (Gy), 269, 276

Kohlgrube (Gy), 276
Kokkineli (C), 299, 302, 407
Kolben (Gy), 277
Kölscheberg (Gy), 276
Königin-Viktoria-Berg (Gy), 274
Königsberg (Gy), 270, 273, 275
Königsfels (Gy), 273
Königslay (Gy), 275
Königsstuhl (Gy), 275
Königswein Zierfandler (A), 293
Königswingert (Gy), 272
König Wenzel (Gy), 277
Koonawara (Aus), 407
Kopf (Gy), 270
Im Köpfle (Gy), 269
Koppelstein (Gy), 277
Kosakenberg (Gy), 263, 274
Krähenschnabel (Gy), 274
Kramolin (Bg), 291, 294
Kranich (Gy), 256, 272
Kranzberg (Gy), 258, 273
Kränzler (Gy), 272
Krappenfelsen (Gy), 270
Kraski Teran (Yg), 294
Kratošija (Yg), 294
Kräuterberg (Gy), 276
Kräuterhaus (Gy), 265, 275
Kreidkeller (Gy), 272
Kremser Kremsleiten (A), 287, 293
– Kögl (A), 287, 293
– Pfaffenberg (A), 293
– Wachtberg (A), 287, 293
Kreuz (Gy), 258, 272, 273, 275
Kreuzberg (Gy), 273, 274, 277
Kreuzhalde-Staig (Gy), 269
Kreuzkugel (Gy), 273
Kreuzweingarten-Spätlese (A), 293
Kreuzwingert (Gy), 273
Kriegacker (Gy), 269
Kriegsberg (Gy), 270
Kripp (Gy), 276
Krone (Gy), 266, 274, 276
Kronenberg (Gy), 259, 273, 275, 276
Kronsberg (Gy), 259, 274
Krötenbrunnen (Gy), 258, 273
Krötenpfuhl (Gy), 259, 273
Krumbchen (Gy), 263
Küchenmeister (Gy), 273
Kuckstein (Gy), 277
Kuckucksberg (Gy), 275, 276
Kuckuckslay (Gy), 275
Kugel (Gy), 273
Kuhstall (Gy), 276
Kulüp (T), 302
– Beyaz (T), 302
Kupferberger Auslese (S.A.), 315
Kupfergrube (Gy), 259, 273
Kupferhalde (Gy), 271
Kupp (Gy), 266, 275, 276
Kurdamir (U.S.S.R.), 294
Kützenberg (Gy), 277

Laboye (F), 107
Le Lac (F), 107
Lacre Gualda (Sp), 187
– Violeta (Sp), 187
Lacrima di Castrovillari (I), 238
Lacrima Christi (P), 213
Lacrima Christi del Vesuvio (I), 233, 238
Lacrimae Christi (Sp), 179, 188, 407
Ladoix (F), 60, 77, 78
Lagarino rosato (I), 236
Lago di Caldaro (I), 236
Lagos (P), 212
Lagrein (I), 222, 236
Laiere (Gy), 269
Lake Country Red (N.Y.), 333
Lake Niagara (N.Y.), 333

Lalande de Pomerol (F), 146, 166, 411
Lalanette-Ferbos (F), 156
Lambrusco Maestri (I), 226
– grasparossa di Castelvetro (I), 226, 237
– di Montericco (I), 226
– Salamino di S. Croce (I), 226, 237
– di Sorbara (I), 237
Lämmerberg (Gy), 274
Lämmler (Gy), 270
Lança 2 Coroas (P), 213
Lancement (F), 108
Lancers (P), 199
La Landonne (F), 108
Landskroner Berg (Gy), 276
Langenacker (Gy), 272
Langenberg (Gy), 273, 274
Langenböhl (Gy), 256, 272
Langenmorgen (Gy), 256, 272
Langenstück (Gy), 274
Langgarten (Gy), 276
Langhälde (Gy), 271
Lanzerac Cabernet (S.A.), 315
– Grünmädchen (S.A.), 315
– Pinotage (S.A.), 315
– Riesenschön (S.A.), 315
– Rose (S.A.), 315
Larchevesque (Sw), 105
Lare (F), 123
Laroche (Gy), 273
Les Larrets or «Clos-des-Lambrays» (F), 76
Lasenberg (Gy), 275
Latricières-Chambertin (F), 57, 76
Lattenberg (Sw), 247
Laubenheim (Gy), 258
Laudamusberg (Gy), 265, 275
Laudun (F), 107
Lauerbaum (Gy), 276
Laura (Sp), 190
Laurel (Sp), 190
Laurentiusberg (Gy), 265, 273, 275, 277
Laurentiuslay (Gy), 275
Laurenziusberg (Gy), 277
Lauterberg (Gy), 275
Lavaut (F), 76
Sur Lavelle (F), 77
Les Lavières (F), 77
Lavilledieu (F), 151
Les Lavrottes (F), 76
Lay (Gy), 263, 265, 273, 275, 276
Layenberg (Gy), 275
Layenkaul (Gy), 276
Léanyka (H), 293
Lefkas (G), 301
Lefouvier (F), 108
Legionario (Sp), 190
Lehn (Gy), 274
Leidhecke (Gy), 273
Leinburg (Gy), 271
Leinhöle (Gy), 256, 272
Leiste (Gy), 259, 262, 274
Leistenberg (Gy), 273
Leitzberg (Gy), 272
Lenchen (Gy), 263, 274
Lenzhalde (Gy), 270
Lerchenberg (Gy), 270
Lerchenbühl (Gy), 271
Lerdenberg (Gy), 269
Lessona (I), 220, 236
Letterlay (Gy), 275
Leyfelsen (Gy), 277
Les Lézardes (F), 108
Lézigné (F), 126
Libertas (S.A.), 316
Lichtenberg (Gy), 270
Lickerstein (Gy), 263
La Lidia (Sp), 189
Liebedell (Gy), 277

Liebenberg (Gy), 273
Liebensteiner (Gy), 277
Liebental (Gy), 274
Lieberstein (S.A.), 313
Liebfrauborg (S.A.), 316
Liebfrauenberg (Gy), 272
Liebfrauenmilch (Gy), 258
Liebfrauenstift (Gy), 273
Liestaler Blauburgunder (Sw), 268
Ligerzer (Sw), 269
Ligerzer Kirchwein (Sw), 269
Les Lignes (F), 125
Les Lignys (F), 123
Ligré (F), 125
Liguria (I), 222
Lilienpfad (Gy), 275
Le Limas (F), 107
Limberg, (Gy), 269
Limburg (Gy), 272
Lindenberg (Gy), 269
Lindhälder (Gy), 270
Lindleinsberg (Gy), 274
Lindos of Rhodes (G), 301
Linsenberg (Gy), 270
Linsenbusch (Gy), 272
Linsenstück (Gy), 272
La Lionne (F), 107
Lipouvina (Cs), 293
Lirac (F), 98, 100, 103, 107
Liré (F), 126
Loch (Gy), 274
Locorotondo (I), 232
Locumba (Peru), 340
La Loge (F), 124
– aux Moines (F), 123
Löhningen (Sw), 268
Löhninger Clevner-Beerli (Sw), 268
Löhr (Gy), 273
Loibener Kaiserwein (A), 287, 293
Lombards Liebfraumilch (S.A.), 316
Longenburgerberg (Gy), 277
Long Life (Sp), 190
Les Longues Vignes (F), 123
Lord Sherry (Sp), 189
Loredo (Sp), 189
Loreley-Edel (Gy), 277
Lorenzberg (Gy), 276
Loud Guidia (Bg), 294
Loupiac (F), 143
Löwenberg (Gy), 275
Löwenhell (Gy), 276
Lozucco (I), 242
Lubac (F), 107
Lückerstein (Gy), 274
Lugana (I), 221, 236
Luginsland (Gy), 256, 272
Luins (Sw), 94, 106
Lully (Sw), 106
Lump (Gy), 259, 273
Luomilla (Cs), 290
Luque (Sp), 189, 190
Les Lurets (F), 77
Lussac-Saint-Emilion (F), 146, 165
Lussault (F), 123

Macarena (Sp), 189
Les Macherelles (F), 77, 78
Mâcon (F), 49, 69, 78, 250, 410
– supérieur (F), 69, 78
Mâcon-villages (F), 69, 78
Macvin (F), 97
Madeira (Aus), 341
– (Sp), 212, 242, 408, 409
La Madeleine (F), 126
Madère de Napoléon (P), 211
Madiran (F), 152, 411
Magdalenenkreuz (Gy), 274
Maienfelder Blauburgunder Kuoni-Wii (Sw), 268
– Schloss Salenegg, 295

Mainhölle (Gy), 274
Mainzerweg (Gy), 273
Maison Blanche (F), 107
– (Sw), 106
– Brûlée (F), 76
La Maladière (F), 77
Malaga (Sp), 179, 188, 242
– Red (S.A.), 316
Malanser Beerli Weisstorkel (Sw), 268
– Blauburgunder (Sw), 268
– Blauburgunder Fuchsen (Sw), 268
– Blauburgunder Rüfiser (Sw), 268
– Completer (Sw), 268
– Rüfiwingert (Sw), 268
– Tokayer (Sw), 268
Malbec (Aus), 341
Aux Malconsorts (F), 76
Malessert (Sw), 106
Malgazon (F), 107
Malmsey (P), 211, 212
La Maltroie (F), 77, 78
Malvasia (Bz), 339
– (I), 225, 242
– (P), 211
– (S.A.), 316
– (Sp), 188, 199, 378
– di Bosa (I), 238
– di Casorso (I), 236
– di Cosenza (I), 238
– di Grotta-ferrata (I), 237
– di Lipari (I), 238, 242
– di Lucania (I), 238
– de Sitges (Sp), 176
– Spumante (I), 221
– del Vulture (I), 238
Malvazija (Yg), 294
Malvoisie (Sw), 93, 105, 407
– de la Fiancée (Sw), 105
– mi-flétrie (Sw), 105
– Pinot gris (Sw), 105
Mamberg (Gy), 269
Mamertino (I), 217, 234, 238
Manadis (U.S.S.R.), 294
Mancha (Sp), 177
Mandacher Riesling-Sylvaner (Sw), 268
Mandelacker (Gy), 272
Mandelberg (Gy), 272
Mandelgarten (Gy), 272
Mandelgewann (Gy), 272
Mandelgraben (Gy), 275
Mandelpfad (Gy), 272
Mandelring (Gy), 272
Mandelstein (Gy), 276
Mangualde (P), 198
Manissy (F), 107
Mannberg (Gy), 263, 274, 277
Mantecoso (Sp), 189
Mantineia (G), 298, 301
Manzanares (Sp), 177
Manzanilla (Sp), 183, 186, 189
Les Maranges (F), 77, 78
Maraština (Yg), 294
Marbacher (Sw), 246
Marcale (F), 107
Marcelin (Sw), 106
Marco (G), 301
Marcobrunn (Gy), 274
Les Marconnets (F), 63, 77
La Maréchaude (F), 77
Les Maréchaudes (F), 77
Marestel (F), 96, 107
Marfil (Sp), 187
Margaux (F), 138, 410
Margotey (F), 78
Marienberg (Gy), 276
Mariengarten (Gy), 272
Marienholz (Gy), 276
Marienpichter (Gy), 275

Marignan (F), 96, 107
Marin (F), 96, 107
Marinero (Sp), 189
Les Marines (F), 107
Marino (I), 230, 237
Markobrunn (Gy), 263
Mari-Paz (Sp), 189
Marismeño (Sp), 189
Marissou (F), 78
Marjolaine (Sw), 105
Marmara Incisi (T), 302
Marmorberg (Gy), 277
Les Marnais (F), 123
Marquês de Pombal (P), 213
Marques Riscal (Sp), 187
Marron (F), 107
Marsala (I), 234, 238, 242, 378
– Aleatico (I), 407
– vergine (I), 238
Marsberg (Gy), 274
Marschall (Gy), 274
La Martellière (F), 125
Martial (Sp), 189
– (Brown) (Sp), 190
– Golden (Sp), 190
Martigné-Briand (F), 126
Le Martinet (F), 125
Martinet (F), 107
Martinskirch (Gy), 274
Martinsley (Gy), 277
Marzemino (I), 222, 236
– d'Isera (I), 236
Mascara (Ag), 309, 315
Martinafranca Locorotondo (I), 232, 238
Les Mascarrons (F), 107
Matador (Sp), 189
– (Brown) (Sp), 190
– Cream (Sp), 190
– Pale Dry (Sp), 189
Mateus (P), 200
Matrassa (U.S.S.R.), 294
Mättenziel (Gy), 269
Mattersons Fine Dry (S.A.), 316
Les Mauchamps (F), 76
Maucoil (F), 107
Mauer (Gy), 274
Auf der Mauer (Gy), 277
Mauerberg (Gy), 254, 269
Mäuerchen (Gy), 263, 272, 274
Mauerseugen (Gy), 270
Maury (F), 104
Mauseberg (Gy), 275
Mäusehöhle (Gy), 256, 272
Mäusekammer (Gy), 271
Maustal (Gy), 274
Mavrodaphne (G), 298, 301, 378, 407
Mavroud of Assenovgrad (Bg), 291, 406
Maximin Grünhäuser Bruderberg (Gy), 266, 276
– Herrenberg (Gy), 276
Maximiner Herrenberg (Gy), 275
A Mayne d'Imbert (F), 157
Mayoral (Sp), 190
Mazermino d'Isera (I), 236
Mazis-Chambertin (F), 57, 76
Les Mazots (Sw), 105
Le Méal (F), 107
Médéa (Ag), 309
Medieval Port (P), 213
La Médinette (Sw), 106
Medium Golden (Sp), 189
Médoc (F), 136, 137, 141, 378, 404, 405, 409
Meerspinne (Gy), 256, 272
Mehrhölzchen (Gy), 274
Meilener Räuschling (Sw), 268
Meisenberg (Gy), 276
Les Meix (F), 77
Les Meix-Bas (F), 56, 76

Le Meix-Bataille (F), 77
Meix-Caillet (F), 78
Meix-Rentiers (F), 76
Méjanelle (F), 103
Les Mejeans (F), 107
Melnik (Bg), 291, 294
Meloso (Sp), 190
Melser Beerli Ritterweg (Sw), 268
Menesteo (Sp), 189
Ménetou-Salon (F), 115, 123
La Merced (Sp), 190
Mercedes (Sp), 190
Mercurey (F), 68, 78
Merih (T), 302
Merito (Sp), 189, 190
Merlot (Bz), 339
– (I), 225, 236
– (Sw), 105
– di Aprilia (I), 230, 237
– friulano (I), 237
– delle Venezie (I), 222, 236
Mertesdorfer (Gy), 276
Merveilles de Roches (Sw), 105
Mesland (F), 119
Messerschmitt (Gy), 269
Messias (P), 212
Metropol (Sp), 187
Mettinger Lerchenberg (Gy), 270
– Schenkenberg (Gy), 270
Meursault (F), 64, 67, 78, 404, 410
Meursault-Blagny or Blagny (F), 77, 78
Mezières (F), 123
M.G.L. (Sp), 190
Mialet (F), 124
Micalet (Sp), 189
Michaelsberg (Gy), 271
Michelmark (Gy), 274
Michelsberg (Gy), 256, 272, 273, 275
Mi-Flétri (S.A.), 313
La Mignotte (F), 77
Mikwe Israel (Is), 300, 301
– Blanc (Is), 301
– Israel-Dessert (Is), 301
Miliana (Ag), 315
Les Millandes (F), 76
Millésime (Sw), 105
La Milletière (F), 123
Millonario (Sp), 190
Minervois (F), 103, 108, 411
Minière-Château (F), 125
Miranda (S.A.), 316
Miranda (Sp), 189
Mireval (F), 103
Le Miroir (F), 126
Misket of Karlovo (Bg), 290
– of Songurlaré (Bg), 291, 294
– of Vratza (Bg), 294
Les Mitans (F), 77
Mittelberg (Gy), 274, 276
Mittelhöll (Gy), 276
Mittelholle (Gy), 263
Mittelpfad (Gy), 277
Mois de Mai (F), 107
Molavillé (F), 124
Molenburg Stein (S.A.), 316
Molenburg Riesling (S.A.), 315
Molenhof Stein (S.A.), 316
Molino (Sp), 190
Le Mollar (F), 108
Mollenbrunnen (Gy), 273
Les Mollières (F), 123
Monaco (F), 124
Monart (Gy), 273
El Monasterio (Sp), 190
Monbazillac (F), 151, 152, 250, 407
Mönchberg (Gy), 273, 276
Mönchenberg (Gy), 277
Mönchhanach (Gy), 263, 274
Mönchpfad (Gy), 273, 274

Mönchsberg (Gy), 271
Mönchshalde (Gy), 270
Mönchwingert (Gy), 276
Monica di Sardegna (I), 238, 242
Monis Barbola (S.A.), 316
– Cardinal Port (S.A.), 316
– Dry Cream Sherry (S.A.), 316
– Marsala (S.A.), 314, 316
– Moscato (S.A.), 316
– Palido Sherry (S.A.), 316
– Steinheimer (S.A.), 316
Monopole (Sp), 187
Mon Pichet (Sw), 106
Monsteiner (Sw), 246
Mont (Sw), 94
Les Montachins (F), 123
Montado (Sp), 190
Montagne-St-Emilion (F), 146, 164, 165
Montagny (F), 68
– (Sw), 106
Montana (Sp), 189
Montbenay (Sw), 106
Mont-Crochet (Sw), 106
Monte-Carlo (I), 227, 237
– Bianco (I), 227
Montecastelli (I), 228
Montecompatri (I), 237
Monte Crasto (P), 212
Monte-Haro (Sp), 187
Monte Jupp (Gy), 277
Montenapoleone (I), 221
Monteneubel (Gy), 275
Montepulciano di Abruzzo (I), 231, 237
Monte Real (Sp), 187
Monte Serves (P), 212
Montée-Rouge (F), 77
Monterminod (F), 107
Montezardes et Trinquevedel (F), 107
Monthélie (F), 63, 77
Monthoux (F), 96, 107
Montibeux (Sw), 105
Montilla Albero (Sp), 178
Montjean (F), 126
Montlouis (F), 119, 123
Mont-Louis Mousseux (F), 361
Montmain (F), 108
Montolivet (F), 107
Mont d'Or (Sw), 105
Mont-Palais (F), 78
Mont Pertuis (F), 107
Montpeyroux (F), 103, 108
Mont Redon (F), 107
Montrobert (F), 125
Mont Rouge (Is), 301
Montsoreau (F), 125
Mont de Viès (F), 107
Les Monts-Damnés (F), 123
Monts-Luisants (F), 76
Monts du Thessalah (Ag), 315
La Montoise (Sw), 106
Montrachet (F), 49, 64, 78, 404, 409
Montravel (F), 152
Les Montrevenots (F), 77
Montuclas (F), 108
Mooiuitsig Fine Old Port (S.A.), 316
– Red Muscadel Liqueur Wine (S.A.), 316
– White Muscadel (S.A.), 316
– Wynkekders (S.A.), 314
Moquegua (Peru), 340
Les Morandières (F), 124
Morchberg (Gy), 274
Morey-Saint-Denis (F), 58, 60, 76
Morgenbach (Gy), 276
Morgeot (F), 77, 78
Morges (Sw), 94
Morgon (F), 71, 72, 78
Móri Ezerjó (H), 288, 293
Moriles Albero (Sp), 178

Moriles extra san Joaquin (Sp), 187
Morillon (A), 293
Morilos Marsala (S.A.), 316
Mortaga (P), 198
Le Mortier (F), 124
Moscatel (Sp), 178, 179, 186, 188, 407
– (Bz), 339
– Delicioso (Sp), 188
– de Setúbal (P), 199, 200, 411
– de Setúbal-Setúbal superior (P), 212
– de Setúbal-Setúbal Roxo (P), 212
Moscatello di Montalcina (I), 237
Moscato d'Asti (I), 221, 236
– d'Asti Spumante (I), 364
– atesino (I), 236
– del Campidano (I), 238, 242
– di Casteggio (I), 236
– di Casteggio Spumante (I), 364
– di Cosenza (I), 238
– dell'Elba (I), 227, 237
– di Noto (I), 238
– Passito di Pantelleria (I), 238, 407
– del Salento (I), 232, 238
– di Salento (Salento liquoroso) (I), 232, 238
– di Siracusa (I), 238, 242
– di Tempio (I), 238
– di Terracina (I), 237
– di Trani (I), 232, 238
– trentino (I), 236
– del Vulture (I), 238
– Lo Zucco (I), 238
Moselle (Aus), 341
Moselweisser-Hamm (Gy), 277
Mostaganem-Dahra (Ag), 315
Mottalciata (I), 220
Moulesne (F), 78
Le Moulin (F), 108
Le Moulin-Avensan (F), 159
Au Moulin des Graves (F), 161
Moulin de la Pitance (F), 167
Moulin-à-vent (F), 72, 78, 107
Moulis (F), 138
Mountain White (Cal), 325
– Red (Cal), 325
Le Mourre de Gaud (F), 107
– des Perdrix (F), 107
– de Vidal (F), 107
Mousquetaires (Sw), 106
La Moussière (F), 123
Les Moutonnes (F), 108
Mouzillon (F), 126
Mückenhaus (Gy), 272
Müdersgass (Gy), 277
Mühläcker (Gy), 273
Mühlbächer (Gy), 270
Mühlberg (Gy), 270, 273, 274, 276, 277
Mühle (Gy), 256, 276
Mühlenberg (Gy), 269, 273, 276
Mühlenstein (Gy), 277
Mühle und Geheu (Gy), 256
Mühlhäuser Berg (Gy), 270
– Wolfersberg (Gy), 270
Mühlheimer (Gy), 275
Mühlstein (Gy), 263
Mukuzani (U.S.S.R.), 292, 294
La Mule (F), 123
Müller-Thurgau (A), 293
– Beerenauslese (A), 293
Mulley-Hofsberg (Gy), 275
Les Mullonnières (F), 126
Münchslay (Gy), 275
Münich (Gy), 275
Münichsberg (Gy), 276
Munot (Sw), 247
Munötler Tokayer (Sw), 268
Münsterberg (Gy), 269
Münzlay (Gy), 275
Les Murailles (Sw), 105

Muratie Bordeaux (S.A.), 314
– Cabernet Sauvignon (S.A.), 314, 316
– Claret (S.A.), 316
– Port (S.A.), 316
– Riesling (S.A.), 315
– Pinot noir-Gamay (S.A.), 314, 316
– Stein (S.A.), 315
Mürefte (C), 407
Les Murets (F), 107
Les Murettes (Sw), 105
Murfatlar (R), 290, 294
Aux Murgers (F), 76
Les Murgers-des-Dents-de-Chien (F), 77
Murs (F), 126
Murs-Erigné (F), 126
Murtelas (P), 212
La Muscadelle (F), 124
Muscadet (F), 122, 411
– des Coteaux de la Loire (F), 113, 126, 378
– de Sèvre-et-Maine (F), 126
Muscadine (S.A.), 314, 316
Muscat (Sw), 93
– Achaïa of Patras (G), 301
– Alsace (F), 251, 252, 269
– Alupka (U.S.S.R.), 292
– of Cyprus (C), 302
– of Kélibia (Tu), 315
– Kuchuk-Lambat (U.S.S.R.), 292
– of Limnos (G), 301
– Livadia (U.S.S.R.), 292
– de Lunel (F), 103
Muscat-Massandra (U.S.S.R.), 292
– Ottonel (N.Y.), 333
Muscat de Radès (Tu), 307, 315
– of Rhodes (G), 301
– Rion of Patras (G), 298, 301
Muscat of Samos (G), 298, 299, 301
– Supérieur (Is), 301
Muscat de Thibar (Tu), 307, 315
Muscat de Tunisie (Tu), 307
Muscatel-19º (Is), 300, 301
Muscel (R), 294
Musenhang (Gy), 256, 272
Musigny (F), 49, 58, 63, 76
Musikantenbuckel (Gy), 272
Muskateller (A), 293
Muskat of Lunel (Cs), 293
– Ottonel (A), 293
– Ottonel (Yg), 294
– ruza (Yg), 294
– Sylvaner (A), 293
– Traminer (A), 293
– Ztly (Cs), 293
Mütterle (Gy), 272
Myshako Riesling (U.S.S.R.), 294
Mzvane (U.S.S.R.), 294

Nacktarsch (Gy), 275
Nadenkopf (Gy), 277
Nadussa (G), 298, 301
Nägelförst (Gy), 254
Nährnberg (Gy), 270
Napureouli (U.S.S.R.), 292, 294
Narbag (T), 302
Les Narbantons (F), 77
Narrenkappe (Gy), 259, 273
Nasco (I), 238, 242
Nauheimer (S.A.), 316
Navarra (Sp), 175
Navigator (Sp), 190
El Navio (Sp), 189
Néac (F), 147, 166
Nebbiolo d'Alba (I), 219, 236
– di Retorbido (I), 221, 236
– Piemontese (I), 219, 236
Neckarhalde (Gy), 270
Neckarhälde (Gy), 270
Nectar (Sp), 190

Nederburg Cabernet (S.A.), 316
– Hochheimer (S.A.), 315
– Late Harvest (S.A.), 315
– Riesling (S.A.), 315
– Rose (S.A.), 315
– Rosé Sec (S.A.), 315
– Selected Cabernet (S.A.), 315
– Selected Riesling (S.A.), 315
– Stein (S.A.), 315
– Sylvaner (S.A.), 315
Negri of Purkar (U.S.S.R.), 292
– Nemea (G), 298, 301
La Nerthe (F), 107
Neto Costa (P), 212
Netteler (Sw), 247
Neuberg (Gy), 272, 273, 274, 275
Neuburger (A), 293
Neuburg Spät- und Auslesen (A), 293
Neuchâtel (Sw), 248
Neuchâtel-Château d'Auvernier (Sw), 248
Neuchâtel-Cortaillod (Sw), 248
Neuchâtel-Hôpital de Pourtalès (Sw), 248
Neuchâtel-Saint-Blaise (Sw), 248
Neueberg (Gy), 273
Neue Weinsteige (Gy), 270
La Neurie (F), 124
La Neuveville Œil-de-Perdrix (Sw), 269
Neuwingert (Gy), 276
Nève (F), 108
Niagara (N.Y.), 333
Nicoresti (R), 294
Niederberg (Gy), 265, 275, 277
Niederflur (Gy), 274
Niedernberg (Gy), 270
Niedersagen (Gy), 276
Niederspray (Gy), 276
Nierstein (Gy), 258
Niesgen (Gy), 266, 276
Nila (Sp), 189
Nill (Gy), 256, 272
Nina (Sp), 190
Ninos (Sp), 190
Nipozzano (I), 227, 237
Nobile di Montepulciano (I), 227, 228
La Noblaie (F), 125
Noblejas (Sp), 178, 188
Les Noëls (F), 126
Les Noirots (F), 76
Noizay (F), 124
Nonnenberg (Gy), 265, 270, 271, 275
Nonnengarten (Gy), 256
Nonnenhölle (Gy), 274
Nonnenlay (Gy), 275
Notre-Dame-d'Alençon (F), 126
Noval 20 Anos (P), 213
Novembre (Sw), 105
La Novia (Sp), 190
Novosseltzi Gámzá (Bg), 294
Noyer-de-Cens (F), 124
N.P.U. (Sp), 189
Nuits-Saint-Georges (F), 60, 76, 410
Nº 10 R.F. (Sp), 190
Nº 28 (Sp), 190
Nuragus (I), 238, 242
Nussbaumer (Sw), 268
Nussberg (Gy), 275
Nussberger Schwarze Katz (A), 293
Nussbien (Gy), 256, 272
Nussbrunnen (Gy), 263, 274
Nussdorf (A), 286
Nussriegel (Gy), 272
Nutty Solera (Sp), 190
Nychteri (G), 298

Oberau (Gy), 277
Oberberg (Gy), 263, 274, 277
Ober-Kirchtal (Gy), 269
Oberrain (Gy), 269

Oberrimsingen (Gy), 269
Obere Weinsteige (Gy), 270
Obersberg (Gy), 275, 277
Oberstnest (P), 272
Obertürkheimer Ailenberg (Gy), 270
– Kirchberg (Gy), 270
Obstberg (Gy), 275
Ocaña (Sp), 188
Ochavico (Sp), 190
Œil-de-Perdrix (Sw), 105, 106, 248, 269
Œil-de-Perdrix-Chantemerle (Sw), 106
Œil-de-Perdrix-Clos du Terraillex (Sw), 106
Oelsberg (Gy), 276
Oggauer Ambrosi (A), 293
– Blaufränkisch (A), 293
Ohlenberg (Gy), 276, 277
Ohliger Berg (Gy), 273
Ohligsberg (Gy), 275
Ojo de Gallo (Sp), 190
Ölberg (Gy), 258, 272, 273
Old Dry Classic (Sp), 189
Old Lodge (P), 213
Old Master Amontillado (S.A.), 316
Oliena (I), 238, 242
Olivar (Sp), 189
Olivet (F), 107
Olk (Gy), 275
Olorosa Angelita (Sp), 189
Oloroso Alvear (Sp), 188
Ölsberg (Gy), 276
Olterberg (Gy), 277
Oñana (Sp), 189
Opol dalmatinski (Yg), 294
Oppenheim (Gy), 258
Orbel (Gy), 258, 273
Original Golser Welschriesling (A), 293
– Gumpoldskirchner Rheinriesling (A), 293
– Joiser Ruländer (A), 293
Orleans (Gy), 274
– 1886 (Sp), 190
Orlenberg (Gy), 272
En l'Orme (F), 77
En l'Ormeau (F), 77
Oro Viejo (Sp), 187
– Solera 1902 (Sp), 188
Orrantia (Sp), 190
Orvieto (I), 216, 237
Osborne (Sp), 189, 190
Oscaña (Sp), 188
Oschelkopf (Gy), 272
Osterberg (Gy), 272
Osterfinger (Sw), 268
Osterfinger-Beerli Badreben (Sw), 268
Osterfinger Blauburgunder (Sw), 268
Osterhölle (Gy), 273
Osterlämmchen (Gy), 275
Ostuni (I), 232, 238
Othello (C), 299, 302
Ottenberger Witscheinberg (A), 287, 293
Ovaille (Sw), 94, 105
L'Ovaille (Sw), 105

Paares (Gy), 263
Paarl Valley Old Riesling (S.A.), 315
Padre Lerchundi (Sp), 190
Païen (Sw), 105
Pain-Perdu (F), 124
Pajarete 1908 (Sp), 188
Los Palcos (Sp), 188
Pale dry (Cal), 333
Palestor (F), 107
Palette (F), 108, 410
Palinteau (F), 107
Le Pallet (F), 126

Pallini (G), 298, 301
Palma (Sp), 189
Palmela-Clarete (P), 212
Palmela superior (P), 212
Palomino (Cal), 322
– (Sp), 190
Pamid (Bg), 291, 294
Pando (Sp), 189
La Panesa (Sp), 189
Panzoult (F), 125
Papirusa (Sp), 189
Pappenscheren (Gy), 277
Paradies (Gy), 271, 274, 275
Paradiesgarten (Gy), 272
Le Paradis (F), 123, 125
Le Parc (F), 107
Pardillo (Sp), 188
Pares (Gy), 258, 273
Parnay (F), 125, 126
Paros (G), 301
Les Parrans (F), 107
Parsac-Saint-Emilion (F), 146, 165
Le Parsan (F), 152
Particular (P), 213
Le Passe-Temps (F), 77
Passe-tout-Grain (F), 411
Pastorenberg (Gy), 273
Pateaud (F), 107
Paterberg (Gy), 273
El Patio (Sp), 189
Patouillet (F), 107
Pattig-Heyerberg (Gy), 277
Pâtureaux (F), 124
Les Patus (F), 107
Pauillac (F), 136, 138, 405
En Pauland (F), 77
Paulinsberg (Gy), 276
Paulinshofberger (Gy), 275
Paulinushofberg (Gy), 265
Paulsberg (Gy), 272
Pavillon Cadet (F), 163
Le Pavillon Rouge (F), 108
Pavon (Sp), 189
Pavlikeni Gamza (Bg), 294
Payaso (Sp), 190
Payen (Sw), 93
Pazo (Sp), 187
Pechstein (Gy), 256, 272
Pedro Dry (Sp), 189
Pedro Ximenez FP (Sp), 181, 186, 188
Péléat (F), 107
Peligno (I), 237
Pelivet (F), 125
Pellaro (I), 238
Pellet (Gy), 274
Pelous (F), 107
Pemartin (Sp), 189, 190
Periquita (P), 212
La Perle (Sw), 106
Perle du Mandement (Sw), 106
Perle Rose (Sw), 106
Pernand-Vergelesses (F), 62, 77, 78, 404
Perrets-de-Fou-Joint (F), 124
Perrets de Minuze (F), 124
Perrier (F), 107
La Perrière (F), 56, 76, 123
Les Perrières (F), 77
Aux Perrières (F), 78
Les Perrières-Dessous (F), 78
Les Perrières-Dessus (F), 78
Perrière-Noblet (F), 76
Pertuisots (F), 77
Pertuizet (Sw), 106
Petenera (Sp), 189
Petersberg (Gy), 273
Petersbühl (Gy), 270
Petershöhle (Gy), 272
Petershorn (Gy), 275
Petit Chablis (F), 49, 55
Petit Clos de Brouard (F), 166
Petit Crépy (F), 96, 107

Petit-Mont (F), 125
Le Petit Soumard (F), 123
Le Petit Vignoble (Sw), 105
Les Petits-Epenots (F), 77
Petits-Godeaux (F), 77
Aux Petits-Liards (F), 77
Les Petits-Monts (F), 76
Les Petits-Vougeot (F), 59, 76
Petite Arvine de Chamoson (Sw), 93, 105
Petite Bastide (F), 107
Petite Combe (Sw), 105
La Petite Crau (F), 107
Petites Bastes (F), 124
Les Petites-Lolières (F), 77
Petite Sirah (Cal), 325
Petites Serres (F), 107
Petrus (Gy), 275
Petrusberg (Gy), 275
Pettental (Gy), 258, 273
Les Petures (F), 77, 78
Peu-de-Cartes (F), 124
Les Peuilles (F), 125
Les Peuillets (F), 77
Peza (G), 301
Les Pézerolles (F), 77
Pfaffenberg (Gy), 270, 272, 273, 274, 275
Pfaffenklinge (Gy), 270
Pfaffenpfad (Gy), 274
Pfaffenweg (Gy), 273
Pfaffenwein (Gy), 271
Pfaffenwies (Gy), 274
Pfalzgraben (Gy), 275
Pfalzgrafenstein (Gy), 277
Pfarrberg (Gy), 269
Pfarrwingert (Gy), 273
Pfefferberg (Gy), 275
Pflanzenberg (Gy), 276
Pfauenhalde (Sw), 246
Pfingstweide (Gy), 273
Pfülben (Gy), 259, 274
Phälat (Gy), 265
La Philebernière (F), 125
Les Picasses (F), 125
Piceno (I), 228
Les Pichaudières (F), 124
Mon Pichet (Sw), 106
Pichter (Gy), 275, 276
La Piconera (Sp), 189
Pico Plata (Sp), 190
Picpoul de Pinet (F), 103, 108
Pic Saint-Loup (F), 103, 108
La Pièce-sous-le-Bois (F), 78
Pied-de-Bau (F), 107
Pied-Redon (F), 107
Piedra (Sp), 189
Piegeoulet (F), 107
Les Pielons (F), 107
Les Pierrailles (Sw), 106
Pierre-à-Feu (F), 107
Pierrafeu (Sw), 105
La Pierre-Gauderie (F), 126
Pierre Noire (Sw), 105
Les Pierres (F), 78
La Pierelle (F), 107
Pignan (F), 107
Pilgerpfad (Gy), 273
Pilion (G), 301
Pillot (F), 78
Le Pin (F), 125
Pinchenas (F), 107
Les Pineaux (F), 125
Pink (Is), 301
Pink Champagne (Cal), 333
Pinnerberg (Gy), 274
Pinot (Sw), 94, 106
– (I), 222, 225, 236
– (U.S.S.R.), 292
– blanc (Cal), 333
– Blanc (I), 225

Pinot blanc-clevner, Alsace (F), 251, 252, 269
– Chardonnay (Cal), 325, 333
– Chardonnay (N.Y.) 333
Pinot-Chardonnay (Sw), 94
Pinot-Chardonnay-Mâcon (F), 78
Pinot-Gamay (Sw), 106
– sous l'Auvent (Sw), 106
– Burignon (Sw), 106
– Montorgueil (Sw), 106
– Roche rouge (Sw), 106
– Saint-Saphorin printanier (Sw), 106
Pinot gris (I), 222, 225
– gris (Sw), 93, 269
– noir (Cal), 325, 333
– noir (I), 222, 225
– noir (Sw), 96, 105, 269
– noir, la Béroche (Sw), 269
– noir de Chamoson (Sw), 105
– noir Clos du Satyre (Sw), 106
– noir Clos du Terraillex (Sw), 269
– noir Coin des Serpents (Sw), 106
– noir Cru des Chanez (Sw), 269
– noir Cuvée du Docteur (Sw), 106
– noir Grand Brocard (Sw), 106
– noir Grand-Croix (Sw), 106
– noir Lully (Sw), 106
– noir Monseigneur (Sw), 106
– noir le Notable (Sw), 106
– noir de Salquenen (Sw), 105
– noir Sept Murs (Sw), 106
– noir du Valais (Sw), 105
– noir Vin des Croisés (Sw), 269
– Saint George (Cal), 325
Pinotage (S.A.), 313, 314
Les Pins-Les-Sablons (F), 125
Pinta (Sp), 189
Pintray (F), 123
La Pirée (F), 124
Pirgovo (Bg), 294
Piriquita (P), 199
Pittermännchen (Gy), 273
Pittersberg (Gy), 273
Les Pitures-Dessus (F), 77
Pizarro (Sp), 189
Les Plagnes (F), 107
Plaine de Vallongue (F), 107
Plaisance (F), 126
Plan d'Essert (Sw), 105
Sur Plan d'Uvrier (Sw), 105
Plans et Palus (F), 107
Planète (Sw), 105
Les Plantes (F), 58, 76, 123
Les Plantes-de-Marangues (F), 77
La Plantier (F), 107
La Platière (F), 77
Plattenberg (Gy), 275
Plattenstück (Gy), 277
Plauelrain (Gy), 269
Plavac (Yg), 294
Pochola (Sp), 189
Pointe-d'Angles (F), 77
Le Pointu (F), 107
Poissenot (F), 76
Polca (Sp), 190
Polcevera (I), 236
Pollino (I), 234, 238
Pomerol (F), 144, 147, 165, 166, 404, 405, 410, 411
Pomino (I), 227
Pommard (F), 63, 77, 404, 409
La Pommeraye (F), 126
La Pommière (F), 108
Pomoria (Bg), 294
Pomoria Dimiat (Bg), 294
Porath Atic (Is), 301
Les Porets (F), 76
Poria (Is), 301
Le Portail (F), 124
Portaser Blauburgunder (Sw), 246, 268

432

La Porte du Clos (F), 123
Les Portes Rouges (Sw), 105
Port (Aus), 341
Port (P), 201, 203, 204, 207, 208, 213
Port (U.S.S.R.), 292
Port Dry White Estoril (P), 213
Portet (F), 152
Port-Guyet (F), 125
Porto Antonat Tawny (P), 213
– Aperitivo (P), 213
– Clube (P), 213
– Cruz (P), 213
– Fino (P), 213
– Imperial Dry White (P), 213
– Nogueira Genuio (P), 213
– Triunfal (White Dry Port) (P), 213
– V V (P), 213
Le Poruzot (F), 78
Le Poruzot-Dessous (F), 78
Le Poruzot-Dessus (F), 78
Pošip (Yg), 294
La Possonnière (F), 126
Posten (Gy), 276
Postup (Yg), 291, 294
Pöttelsdorfer Bismarckwein (A), 293
Pouilly-Fuissé (F), 69, 78, 114, 378
Pouilly Fumé (F), 114, 115, 123
Pouilly-Loché (F), 69, 78
Pouilly-sur-Loire (F), 114, 123
Pouilly-Vinzelles (F), 69, 78
Les Poulettes (F), 76
Poupine (F), 124
La Poussie (F), 123
Les Poutures (F), 77
Les Pradels (F), 107
Prälat (Gy), 275
Prälatenwein (Aus), 411
Préau (F), 78
Predilecto (Sp), 189
Le Préféré (Sw), 105
Preferido (Sp), 189
Premières côtes de Bordeaux (F),
  143
Les Prés (F), 107
Preslav Dimiat (Bg), 294
Près Roc (Sw), 105
Prestige Selected Riesling (S.A.), 315
– Stellenblanche (S.A.), 315
Prieuré (F), 107
Primero (Sp), 189
Primitivo di Gioia e Manduria (I), 238
Prince Henry (P), 213
Princesse-Rocheray (F), 411
Principe (Sp), 189
– Real (P), 212
Priorato extra Rancio Solera 1918 (Sp),
  187
– Reserva especial (Sp), 187
Probstberg (Gy), 271, 275
Probstei (Gy), 273
Probsteiberg (Gy), 276
Procer (Sp), 190
Les Procès (F), 76
Prokupac (Yg), 294
Promesa (Sp), 190
Proppelstein (Gy), 272
Prosecco di Conegliano (I), 236
– di Conegliano Spumante (I), 364
Prosek (Yg), 292
La Provence (S.A.), 316
Province Red (S.A.), 316
Provitaro (I), 238
Les Pruliers (F), 76
Les Prunelles (F), 108
Les Pucelles (F), 67, 78
Puisseguin-Saint-Emilion (F), 146,
  165
Pulchen (Gy), 275
Puligny-Montrachet (F), 64, 77, 78
Pulvermächer (Gy), 270
Pusterla (I), 222, 236

Putier (F), 107
Aux Putiers (F), 107
Pützbach (Gy), 276

Quakaya yildizi (T), 302
Quarts de Chaume (F), 122, 126, 410
Quatourze (F), 103, 108
Les Quatre-Ferrures (F), 125
Quincé (F), 126
Quincy (F), 115, 123
Quinta (Sp), 189
– do Bom Retiro (P), 213
– do Junco (P), 213
– das Quartas (P), 213
– do Seminário (P), 212
Quisquilla (Sp), 189

Rabenack (Gy), 277
Rablay (F), 126
Raboso di Piave (I), 225
– Veronese (I), 225
Raboursay (F), 78
Raclot (F), 78
Radès (Tu), 307, 315
Les Raguenières (F), 125
Raifersley (Gy), 276
Rainha Santa Dry White (P), 213
– 840 (P), 213
Rainwater (P), 212
Raisin d'Or (Sw), 105
Ranberg (Gy), 271
Randersacker (Gy), 262
Ranzenberg (Gy), 271
Raposeira (P), 212
Räppel (Gy), 272
Rapsani (G), 298
Rare Cream (Cal), 333
– Tawny (Cal), 333
Ras-Cassa (F), 107
Rasteau (F), 101, 107
Rathausberg (Gy), 275
Ratsherr (Gy), 273
Räucherberg (Gy), 274
Rauchloch (Gy), 263, 274
Raul (Gy), 275
Rausch (Gy), 276
Räuschling Küsnacht (Sw), 268
Ravanay (Sw), 105
Ravello (I), 233, 238
Ravenley (Gy), 276
Ravensburg (Gy), 274
Rawyre (Sw), 105
Le Rayas (F), 107
Rayito (Sp), 189
La Raza (Sp), 190
Real (Sp), 190
Real Tesoro (Sp), 190
Rebsteiner Süssdruck Blauburgunder
  (Sw), 246, 268
Rebtal (Gy), 269
Rebula (Yg), 294
Rechbächel (Gy), 256, 272
Rechi (Sp), 189
Recioto della Valpolicella (I), 225,
  236
– Veronese (I), 225, 236
Redoble (Sp), 189
Redrescuts (F), 77
La Refene (F), 77
Les Referts (F), 78
Refoschi (I), 225, 237
Refošk (Yg), 294
Regina (Sp), 189
Regio (Sp), 190
La Regrippière (F), 126
Rehbach (Gy), 258, 273
Reichshalde (Gy), 271
Les Reignots (F), 76
Reigny (F), 123
Reisekahr (Gy), 258, 273
Reiss (Gy), 272

Reiterpfad (Gy), 272
Relagnes (F), 107
Reliquia (Sp), 190
En Rémilly (F), 77
Renard (Sw), 106
La Renarde (F), 78
La Renardière (F), 124
Rennpfad (Gy), 256, 272
Repos de Saint-Martin (F), 125
La République (Sw), 106
Reserva Sogrape (P), 212
– Yago (Sp), 187
Ma Réserve (Sw), 106
Réserve du Procureur (Sw), 105
– de Tous-Vents (Sw), 105
– du Vidame (Sw), 105
La Résidence Alto Rouge (S.A.), 316
– Theuniskraal (S.A.), 315
Restigné (F), 125
Retsina (G), 298, 299
Retz (Gy), 276
Reugne called La Chapelle (F), 77
Reuilly (F), 115, 123
Reuschberg (Gy), 274
Reveirores (F), 107
Reverencia (Sp), 190
Les Reversées (F), 77
Les Revès (F), 107
Revinor (P), 213
Revisec Extra Seco (P), 213
Rèze (Sw), 105
Rheinberg (Gy), 276
Rheinblick (Gy), 273
Rheinbrohler Ley (Gy), 277
Rheingarten (Gy), 274
Rheinhell (Gy), 263, 276
Rheinheller (Gy), 277
Rheinnieder (Gy), 277
Rhine Wine (N.Y.), 333
Rhodes Kair (G), 301
La Rhone (S.A.), 316
Rhoneblut (Sw), 105
Ribeiro (Sp), 187, 411
Rhonegold (Sw), 105
Ribolla Giallo (I), 225
Richebourg (F), 59, 76, 409
La Richemonne (F), 76
Rickelsberg (Gy), 275
Riedenberg (Gy), 270
Riesenberg (Gy), 269
Riesenschon (S.A.), 313
Rieser (Gy), 271
Riesling (Bz), 339
– (Aus), 341
– Alsace (F), 244, 252, 269, 406
– (H), 288
– (S.A.), 312, 313
– (Sw), 105
– Abraou (U.S.S.R.), 294
– Alkadar (U.S.S.R.), 294
– of Anape (U.S.S.R.), 294
– of Dealul-Mare (R), 290
– Italico (I), 225, 406
– of Liaskovetz (Bg), 294
– Massandra (U.S.S.R.), 292, 294
– dell'Oltrepo pavese (I), 236
– renano (I), 222, 236
– of the Roses Valley (Bg), 294
Rieslingberg (Gy), 277
Riesling-Sylvaner (Sw), 94, 95, 106
Riesling-Sylvaner Berg am Irchel (Sw),
  268
– Meilen (Sw), 268
– Satigny (Sw), 106
– Schloss Heidegg (Sw), 268
– Stäfner (Sw), 268
– Sternenhalde (Sw), 268
– Weiningen (Sw), 268
– Würenlingen (Sw), 268
Rimonet (F), 123
Ring (Gy), 273

Ringmauer (Gy), 276
Rinsol (Sp), 187
Rioja (Sp), 174, 187
Rioja Claretes (Sp), 174
La Riondaz (Sw), 105
La Riotte (F), 76
Les Riottes (F), 77
Rio Negro (Arg), 338
Rio Viejo (Sp), 190
Ripaille (F), 96, 107
Ritsch (Gy), 275
Ritterberg (Gy), 272
Ritter von Dalberg (Gy), 272
Ritterpfad (Gy), 275
Rittersprung (Gy), 269
Rivaz (Sw), 94, 105
Les Riverettes (Sw), 105
Rivero (Sp), 189
Rivesaltes (F), 104
Rives du Bisse (Sw), 105
Riviera del Garda (I), 236
Rivière (F), 125
Roaix (F), 107
Robardelle (F), 77
Rocailles (Sw), 105
Rocca-di-papa (I), 411
Roc Crispin et Malaven (F), 107
Roc Noir (Sw), 105
Les Rochains (F), 108
La Roche-de-Cestres (F), 124
La Roche-Clermault (F), 125
Roche-Honneur (F), 125
La Roche-aux-Moines (F), 122, 126
Roche Ronde (Sw), 105
Roches Brûlées (Sw), 105
Rochecorbon (F), 124
Rochefort-sur-Loire (F), 126
Rochegude (F), 107
La Rochelle (F), 125
Rochette (F), 107, 125
Les Rochons (F), 123
Rochusberg (Gy), 258, 273
Röckenberg (Gy), 271
Les Rocoules (F), 107
Rödchen (Gy), 274
Rodenstein (Gy), 258, 273
Rodo (P), 213
Roggenberg (Gy), 269
Rohrackerer Edenberg (Gy), 270
Rohrsteig (Gy), 271
Rolandsberg (Gy), 256
Romane (Sw), 105
La Romanée (F), 59, 76, 77, 78
Romanée-Conti (F), 59, 76, 404
Romanée-St-Vivant (F), 59, 76
Romagnac (F), 107
Romate (Sp), 190
Romeira (P), 212
Römerberg (Gy), 276, 277
Römerblut (Sw), 105
Römerheg (Gy), 277
Römerpfad (Gy), 275
Römerstrasse (Gy), 272
Ronce (F), 125
Ronceret (F), 77
La Roncière (F), 76
Rondell (Gy), 273
Roodezand Sherry (S.A.), 316
Roquefort (F), 124
La Roquette (F), 107
Rosa (Sp), 189
Les Rosaies (F), 125
Rosala (S.A.), 316
Rose of Carmel (Is), 301
Rose Reine (Sw), 106
Rosé d'Anjou (F), 126
– of Cabernet (F), 120
– de Chusclan (F), 103
– d'Eros (Sw), 105
Rosenbaum (Gy), 273
Rosé of Groslot (F), 120

433

Rosenberg (Gy), 259, 271, 274, 275, 277
Rosenberg (Sw), 246
Rosenbuhl (Gy), 272
Roseneck (Gy), 263
Rosengärtchen (Gy) 265, 275
Rosengarten (Gy), 271, 272, 273, 274, 277
Rosenhang (Gy), 275
Rosenheck (Gy), 273
Rosenhügel (Gy), 277
Rosenkranz (Gy), 254, 269
Rosental (Gy), 276
Les Rosettes (F), 125
Rosier (F), 108
Rossberg (Gy), 270, 274
Rossel (Gy), 259, 273
Rossenberg (Gy), 277
Rossese di Dolceacqua (I), 236
Rossi del Colli Friulani (I), 237
Rossi del Collio Goriziano (I), 237
Rossillion (Sw), 105
Rosso dei Colli veronesi (I), 236
– delle Colline Lucchesi (I), 237
– Conero (I), 228, 237
– Piceno (I), 237
Rosstal (Gy), 273, 274
Im Rot (Gy), 269
Rotenberg (Gy), 273
Rotenberger Hinterer Berg (Gy), 270
– Schlossberg (Gy), 270
Rotenburg (Gy), 274, 275
Rotenfels (Gy), 259
Roter Berg (Gy), 270
Roterd (Gy), 265, 275
Roterde (Gy), 273
Rotgipfler Spät- und Auslesen (A), 293
Auf Roth (Gy), 277
Rothenack (Gy), 277
Rothenberg (Gy), 263, 273, 274, 276
Rother-Pfad (Gy), 277
Rötherweg (Gy), 274
Rotkirch (Gy), 275
Rotlay (Gy), 275
Rotmauer (Gy), 276
Rottenberg (Gy), 258
Röttgen (Gy), 274, 276, 277
Rottland (Gy), 263
Rougemont (S.A.), 314, 316
La Roulerie (F), 126
Roumiguières (F), 107
Roussard (Sw), 106
Roussette (F), 96, 107
Roussillon dels Aspres (F), 108
Les Rouvrettes (F), 77
Rouzilles (F), 125
Royal (Sp), 187, 190
– (Brown) (Sp), 190
– Delicate (P), 213
– Diamond (P), 213
– Double (Sp), 190
– Esmeralda (P), 213
– Port N° 1 (P), 213
– Port N° 3 (P), 213
Rozenberg (Gy), 270
Ruby Bonwin (S.A.), 316
– Cabernet (Cal), 325, 333
Les Ruchots (F), 76
Ruchottes-Chambertin (F), 57, 76
Rüdesheimerberg (Gy), 263
Rudolffinger Beerli Blauburgunder (Sw), 268
Rue Baffert (F), 124
Rue-de-Chaux (F), 76
Les Rueyres (Sw), 105
Les Rugiens-Bas (F), 49, 77
Les Rugiens-Hauts (F), 49, 77
Ruines de Crussol (F), 107
Ruith (Gy), 271
Ruländer (A), 293

Ruländer (I), 222, 236
Rully (F), 68, 78
Russhalde (Gy), 269
Rust-Limberger (A), 286, 293
De Rust Riesling (S.A.), 315
– Stein (S.A.), 315
Rustenburg (S.A.), 316
Ruster Ausbruch (A), 293
– Baumgarten (A), 286, 293
– Blauburgunder (A), 293
– G'märk (A), 286, 293
– Greiner (A), 286, 293
– Mittelkräften (A), 286, 293
– Muskateller (A), 293
– Ruländer (A), 293
– Satz (A), 286, 293
– Turner (A), 286, 293
– Vogelsang (A), 293
Ruthe (Gy), 271
Rütiberger (Sw), 268
Rutzenhalden (Gy), 269
Ruzica (Yg), 294
Rynilla (S.A.), 316

Saarstein (Gy), 276
Sables-St-Emilion (F), 146, 164
Sabloire du Grand Moine (F), 166
Les Sablonnettes (F), 126
Sackträger (Gy), 273
Sacrantino di Montefalco (I), 228, 237
Sadova (R), 290
La Saillanderie (F), 126
Saillans (F), 167
Saint-Amour (F), 72, 78, 106
St-Amour (Sw), 106
Saint-Aubin (F), 67, 77, 78
Saint-Aubin-de-Luigné (F), 126
Saint-Barthélemy (F), 126
Saint-Chinian (F), 103, 108
Saint-Christol (F), 103
Sainte-Croix-du-Mont (F), 143
Saint Cyprien (Tu), 307, 315
Saint-Cyr (F), 125
Saint-Drézéry (F), 103, 108
Saint-Emilion (F), 141, 146, 147, 153, 163, 378, 405
Saint-Etienne-de-Baigorry (F), 151
Saint-Fiacre-sur-Maine (F), 126
Sainte-Foy-Bordeaux (F), 146
Saint-Georges (F), 107
Les Saint-Georges (F), 76
Saint-Georges-d'Orques (F), 103, 108
Saint-Géréon (F), 126
Saint-Herblon (F), 126
Saint-Jacques (F), 126
Saint-Jean (F), 125
Saint-Jean-des-Mauvrets (F), 126
Saint-Jean-de-la-Porte (F), 107
Saint-Joseph (F), 98, 99, 107
Saint-Julieu (F), 138
Saint-Lambert-du-Lattay (F), 126
Saint-Laurent (A), 293
Saint-Laurent-Ausstich (A), 293
Saint-Louand (F), 125
Saint-Martin (F), 123, 167
St-Martin (Sw), 106
Saint-Martin-le-Beau (F), 123
Saint-Maurice-sur-Eygues (F), 107
Saint-Nicolas-de-Bourgueil (F), 125
Saint-Pourçain (F), 411
Saint-Romain (F), 64, 77, 78
Saint-Saturnin (F), 103, 108
Saint-Saturnin-sur-Loire (F), 126
St-Théodule (Sw), 105
Ste-Anne (Sw), 105
St-Augustine (S.A.), 316
Sainte-Fleurie (F), 107
Sainte-Melaine-sur-Aubance (F), 126
Saint-Péray (F), 98, 99, 100, 107
– Mousseux (F), 100
Sainte-Radegonde (F), 124

Saint-Saphorin (Sw), 94, 105
Saintes-Vierges (F), 107
Salgesch (Sw), 105
Salinera (Sp), 189
La Salpêtrerie (F), 125
Salvador (Sp), 189
Salvagnin (Sw), 93, 94, 106, 404
– du Baril (Sw), 106
– des Caves de l'Hôpital (Sw), 106
– Cep d'Or (Sw), 106
– Chapeau Rouge (Sw), 106
– Château de Saint-Saphorin (Sw), 106
– Chevron rouge (Sw), 106
– Clos du Manoir (Sw), 269
– Commune de Morges (Sw), 106
– Coteaux du Haut-Léman (Sw), 106
– Croix du Val (Sw), 106
– Domaine de Valmont (Sw), 106
– Eminence (Sw), 106
– Forban (Sw), 106
– Grain rouge (Sw), 106
– Grand Nef (Sw), 269
– de l'Hôpital des Bourgeois de Fribourg (Sw), 106
– Licorne (Sw), 106
– Mille pierres (Sw), 106
– Piganot (Sw), 106
Salzberg (Gy), 271
Salzbornberg (Gy), 276
Samonac (F), 167
Samos (G), 301, 378
Sampigny-lès-Maranges (F), 67, 77, 78
San Patricio (Sp), 189
San Pedro (Sp), 190
San Rafael (Sp), 190
Sancerre (F), 114, 115, 123
Sancho (Sp), 189, 190
Sand (Gy), 272, 274
Sandberg (Gy), 271
Sangiovese di Aprilia (I), 230
Sandgrub (Gy), 264, 274
Sandmorgen (Gy), 270
Sang (Gy), 276
Sang de l'Enfer (Sw), 105
Sängerei (Gy), 265, 275
Sangiovese di Romagna (I), 237
Sangue di Giuda dell'Oltrepo pavese (I), 221
– di Giuda Oltrepo pavese (I), 236
St-Alban (Gy), 258, 273
St-Estèphe (F), 138, 139, 405
St. Irminer (Gy), 275
St. Jost (Gy), 276
St. Kiliansberg (Gy), 258, 273
St. Martin (Gy), 273
St. Michael (Gy), 275
St. Michelsberg (Gy), 272
St. Nikolaus (Gy), 274
St. Oswald (Gy), 276
Sansevero (I), 232, 238
Santa Comba (P), 198
Santa Cruz (Sp), 189
Santa Helena (G), 298, 301
Santa Laoura (G), 298, 301
Santa Maddalena (I), 222, 236
Santa Rosa (P), 198
Santenay (F), 67, 77
Les Santenots (F), 77
Les Santenots-Blancs (F), 78
Les Santenots-du-Milieu (F), 78
Santo Stefano di Cerignola (I), 231, 238
Santyis Old Ruby Vintage Port (S.A.), 316
Saperavi Massandra (U.S.S.R.), 292, 294
Les Sapettes (F), 107
Sarganser Langstrich Blauburgunder (Sw), 268

Sarica-Niculitel (R), 294
Sarraux (Sw), 106
Le Sarrazin (Sw), 105
Sassay (F), 125
Sassella (I), 221, 236
Sauloch (Gy), 273
Les Saumades (F), 107
Saumagen (Gy), 256, 272
Saumoussay (F), 126
Saumur (F), 120, 122, 125, 126
– Mousseux (F), 361
Sausaler Welschriesling (A), 293
Les Sausilles (F), 77
Saute-aux-Loups (F), 125
Sauterne (Cal), 325
Sauternes (F), 143, 156, 199, 378, 407
Sauternes-Barsac (F), 141, 142
Sauvignon (A), 293, 341
– (I), 225
– blanc (Cal), 325, 333
Sauvines (F), 107
Sauzelles (F), 124
Savennières (F), 122, 126
Savigny-lès-Beaune (F), 62, 77, 404, 408
Savoie Ayse (F), 361
Sayen (Gy), 276
Sazbornberg (Gy), 276
Schädert (Gy), 277
Schafenstein (Gy), 274, 275
Schäferberg (Gy), 274
Schafiser (Sw), 248, 269
– Bois de Dieu (Sw), 269
– Engel (Sw), 269
– Pinot noir (Sw), 269
– Schlössliwy (Sw), 269
– Stägli-Wy (Sw), 269
Schafsteige (Gy), 271
Schalksberg (Gy), 259, 274
Schalkstein (Gy), 270
Scharfenstein (Gy), 274
Scharlach (Gy), 274
Scharlachberg (Gy), 273
Scharzberg (Gy), 266, 275
Scharzberger (Gy), 275
Scharzhofberger (Gy), 266, 275
Schäwer (Gy), 272
Scheibenbuck (Gy), 269
Scheiderberg (Gy), 275
Schemelsberg (Gy), 271
Schenkelböhl (Gy), 256, 272
Schenkenberg (Gy), 270
Scheuelberg (Gy), 271
Scheuerberg (Gy), 270
Schiava (I), 221
Schiedberg (Gy), 271
Schieferley (Gy), 276
Schieferstein (Gy), 276
Schiesslay (Gy), 275
Schilcher (A), 293
Schild (Gy), 256, 272, 273
Schillerwein (Gy), 255
Schinznacher Riesling-Sylvaner (Sw), 247, 268
– Rütiberger (Sw), 268
Schippen (Gy), 276
Schlangengraben (Gy), 275
Schlichten (Gy), 269
Schlierbach (Gy), 271
Schloss (Gy), 274
Schlossberg (A), 293
– (Gy), 254, 258, 263, 265, 269, 270, 271, 272, 273, 274, 275, 276, 277
– Erlach Gutedel (Sw), 269
Schlossberger Erlach Blauburgunder (Sw), 269
Schloss Böckelsheimer Kupfergrube (Gy), 411
Schloss Freudenberg (Sw), 268
– Heidegg Clevner (Sw), 268

434

Schloss Johannisberg (Gy), 263, 274
- Leyer (Gy), 273
- Marienlay (Gy), 276
- Saalecker (Gy), 274
- Saarfelser (Gy), 276
Schlossgarten (Gy), 269, 272
Schlossteige (Gy), 272
Schlossweinberge (Gy), 271
Schloss Werdenberg (Sw), 246
Schmalberg (Gy), 273
Schmecker (Cy), 271
Schmiedberg (Gy), 270
Schmiedenbrünnle (Gy), 269
Schmitt (Gy), 273
Schnappenberg (Gy), 273
Schneckenhof (Gy), 271
Schnepfenflug (Gy), 256, 272
Schöllkopf (Gy), 272
Schönberg (Gy), 274, 275
Schönbühl (Gy), 270
Schönhell (Gy), 264, 274
Schoongezicht (S.A.), 314, 315
- Frontignac (S.A.), 314
- Rustenberg (S.A.), 314
Schreckenberg (Gy), 272
Schreiberlay (Gy), 277
Schützenberger Rotkelch (A), 293
Schützenhaus (Gy), 274, 277
Schützenhöll (Gy), 273
Schützenhütte (Gy), 273
Schwalbenwinkel (Gy), 274
Schwalkaul (Gy), 277
Schwanen (Gy), 275
Schwanleite (Gy), 273
Schwarzberg (Gy), 275
Schwarze Katz (Gy), 275
Schwarzenberg (Gy), 274
Schwarzenstein (Gy), 274
Schwarzerde (Gy), 272
Schwarzer Herrgott (Gy), 272
Schwarzlay (Gy), 275
Schwarzloch (Gy), 269
Schwätzerchen (Gy), 273
Sciaccarello (F), 411
Sciacchetra (I), 222
Secco Branco (P), 213
Sedgwick's Medium Cream (S.A.), 316
Seeberg (Gy), 271
Seewein (Gy), 254
Segarcea Cabernet (R), 290
Séguret (F), 107
Selected Riesling (S.A.), 313
Seligmacher (Gy), 272, 274
La Semellerie (F), 125
Sémillon (Aus), 341
- (Cal), 325, 333
- Oreanda (U.S.S.R.), 292, 294
Seneca (Sp), 187
Senex (P), 213
Sur-le-Sentier-de-Clou (F), 77
Les Sentiers (F), 76
Sercial (P), 211, 212
Aux Serpentières (F), 77
Serradayres (P), 212
Les Serres (F), 107
Les Seurey (F), 77
Les Sévenières (F), 108
Seyssel (F), 96, 107
- Mousseux (F), 361
Sfurzat (I), 221
Sherry Joselito (Sp), 190
- (Aus), 341
- (Cal), 322
- (Sp), 180, 181, 183, 186, 189
Shippers (P), 213
Shiraz (S.A.), 314
Sibillenstein (Gy), 273
Siblingen Eisenhalder (Sw), 268
Les Sicots (F), 123
Sidi-Tabet (Tu), 315
Siebenköpfchen (Gy), 275

Siebenmorgen (Gy), 274
Siebering (A), 286
Siegelsberg (Gy), 263, 274
El Siglo (Sp), 187
Siglo de Oro (Sp), 189
Les Signaux (F), 107
Silberberg (A), 293
- (Gy), 258, 273, 274, 275, 276
Im Silberlöchle (Gy), 269
Silbern (Gy), 269
Silbernagel (Gy), 277
Silvanac (Yg), 294
Simonsberg (Gy), 275
Sinnenberg (Gy), 276
Sirena (Sp), 189
Les Sisies (F), 77
Sizzano (I), 220, 236
Slantchev Birag (Bg), 291
Slavianka (Bg), 291, 294
Smederevka (Yg), 292, 294
Soave (I), 222, 225, 236
Solar (P), 212
Solariego 1807 (Sp), 190
Soldado (Brown) (Sp), 190
Solear (Sp), 189
Soleil de Sierre (Sw), 105
Solera (P), 212
- (Sp), 188
- 1842 (Sp), 190
- 1847 (Brown) (Sp), 190
- 1865 (Sp), 190
- 1906 (Sp), 188
- Cocktail (Cal), 333
- Cream (Cal), 333
- E (Sp), 190
- Florido (Sp), 190
- Golden (Cal), 333
- Granada (Sp), 190
- Misa V.O.B.S. (Sp), 190
- P. J. (Sp), 190
- Ruby (Cal), 333
- Superior (Sp), 190
- Tawny (Cal), 333
- Tizon (Sp), 190
- Victoria Regina (Sp), 190
Solignon (Sw), 105
Solito (Sp), 189
Solopaca (I), 238
Sommerberg (Gy), 270, 271, 275, 277
Sommerhalde (Gy), 270
Sommerheil (Gy), 274
Sommerseite (Gy), 272
Sondersberg (Gy), 276
Songurlare Misket (Bg), 291, 294
In der Sonne (Gy), 189
Sonnenberg (Gy), 247, 254, 258, 263, 266, 269, 270, 271, 272, 273, 274, 275, 276, 277
Sonnenborn (Gy), 273
Sonnenbühl (Gy), 270
Sonnenburger (Sw), 246
Sonneneck (Gy), 272
Sonnenkönig (A), 293
Sonnenlay (Gy), 275, 277
Sonnenring (Gy), 276
Sonnenschein (Gy), 272
Im Sonnenschein (Gy), 269
Sonnenseite (Gy), 275
Sonnenstuhl (Gy), 274
Sonnenteil (Gy), 275
Sonnenuhr (Gy), 265, 275
Sonntagsberg (Gy), 271
Soonecker Schlossberg (Gy), 276
Soosser Blauer Burgunder (A), 293
Sooser Blauer Portugieser (A), 293
Soproni Kékfrankos (H), 293
Sorbara (I), 226
Les Sorbès (F), 76
Sorrent (Gy), 275
Soukhindol Gamza (Bg), 294
Soulignasses (F), 107

Sous-le-Bois (F), 123
Sous-le-Puits (F), 78
Souza Port Dry White (P), 213
Souzay (F), 125, 126
Sowjetskoje Schampanskoge (U.S.S.R.), 359
Spanish Red Wine (Sp), 188
Sparkling Burgundy (Cal), 333
- Muscat (Cal), 333
Spätlese (S.A.), 312
Spätrot-Rotgipfler (A), 293
Spatzendreck (S.A.), 314
Special Pale Dry (P), 213
- Reserve (P), 213
- White Dry (P), 213
Spiegel (Gy), 271
Spiegelberg (Gy), 273
Spielberg (Gy), 256, 259, 272, 274, 276
Spielbühl (Gy), 271
Spiessberg (Gy), 272
Spiral (P), 212
Spitzenberg (Gy), 273
Spumante di S. Maria della Versa (I), 236
Staaden (Gy), 275
Staat (Gy), 276
Stablay (Gy), 275
Stahlbühl (Gy), 270
Staig (Gy), 271
Stammheimer Beerli Blauburgunder (Sw), 268
- Blauburgunder (Sw), 268
Starkenberg (Gy), 272
Staufenberg (Gy), 269, 270
Steeger Mühlberg (Gy), 276
Stefansberg (Gy), 275
Stefanslay (Gy), 275
Steffensberg (Gy), 275
Stehleberg (Gy), 277
Steig (Gy), 258, 270, 273
Steil (Gy), 274
Stein (Gy), 259, 262, 263, 269, 274
- (S.A.), 312, 314
Im Stein (Gy), 274
Steinacker (Gy), 271, 272
Steinbach (A), 293
Steinbach (Gy), 274
Steinbacher (Gy), 275
Steinbachhöfer (Gy), 271
Steinberg (Gy), 264, 269, 270, 272, 273
Steinbuck (Gy), 254, 269
Steinbühl (Gy), 272
Steinchen (Gy), 274
Steiner (Sw), 268
- Goldberg (A), 287, 293
- Pfaffenberg (A), 293
- Schreck (A), 293
- Veltliner 1959 (A), 288
Steinern (Gy), 269
Steinern Kreuz (Gy), 274
Steinfelsen (Gy), 254, 269
Steingerg (Gy), 274
Steingrube (Gy), 269, 271
Steingrubenberg (Gy), 269
- Steinhalde (Gy), 271
Steininger (Gy), 276
Steinmächer (Gy), 274
Steinmauer (Gy), 275
Steinmorgen (Gy), 274
Steinritz (Gy), 274
Steinstück (Gy), 274
Steinweg (Gy), 273
Steinwein (Gy), 259
Stellenbosch (S.A.), 407
Stellenrood (S.A.), 315
Stellenvale Cabernet (light-bodied) (S.A.), 316
- Estate Riesling (S.A.), 316
- Hochheimer (S.A.), 316

Stellenvale Marsala (S.A.), 316
- Selected Riesling (S.A.), 315
- Selected Stellenblanche (S.A.), 315
Im Stenner (Gy), 277
Sternberg (Gy), 277
Sternenhalde (Sw), 247
Stiehlweg (Gy), 274
Stiel (Gy), 277
Stiftsberg (Gy), 270
Stiftsgarten (Gy), 273
Stöckach (Gy), 270
Stolzenberg (Gy), 275
Streng (Gy), 273
Strohberg (Gy), 277
Stumpfenort (Gy), 263
Subotical (Yg), 292
Les Suchots (F), 76
Südlay (Gy), 276
Sülzenberg (Gy), 277
Sulzgriesser Rosenholz (Gy), 270
Sulztal (A), 293
Sumoll (Sp), 188
Super Old (P), 213
Superior (Sp), 190
Superior Alto Douro Dry White (P), 213
Superior Old Marsala (I), 242
Super Marfil reserva (Sp), 187
Suser (Gy), 255
Süssdruck Bündner Rheinwein (Sw), 268
- Duc de Rohan (Sw), 268
Sylvaner (Cal), 322, 333
- Alsace (F), 244, 251, 252, 269, 406
- (Sw), 96
- Edelzwicker, Alsace (F), 269
- Nederburg (S.A.), 313
- verde (I), 222, 236

Taboa (P), 198
Tabourneau (F), 124
La Tâche (F), 59, 76
Tafelheim (S.A.), 315
Tafelstein (Gy), 273
Taille-Pieds (F), 77
Les Talmettes (F), 77
Tambora (Sp), 190
Tannenberg (Gy), 274
Taradeau (F), 411
Tarnovo (Bg), 294
Tarragona (Sp), 176, 188
- Campo (Sp), 176
- Clasico (Sp), 176
Tarragona-Tawny (Sp), 188
Tartegnin (Sw), 94, 106
Tasheimer Goldtröpfchen (S.A.), 313, 316
Tassenberg (S.A.), 313
Taubenberg (Gy), 263, 274, 276
Taubengarten (Gy), 271, 275
La Taupine (F), 77
Taurasi (I), 233, 238
Tavel (F), 98, 100, 103, 107
Tavelet et les Oliviers (F), 107
Tawny Port (Cal), 333
- Superior (P), 213
Tayler's Full Cream Sherry (S.A.), 316
- Mmooth Medium Sherry (S.A.), 316
- Pale Dry Sherry (S.A.), 316
- Rich Brown Sherry (S.A.), 316
Tchirpan (Bg), 294
Tébourba (Tu), 315
Tekel Gaziantep (T), 300
- Kalebac Ankara (T), 300
- Misbag Izmir (T), 300
- Ürgüp (T), 302
Tekez Misbag Izmir (T), 302
Tekigrad (C), 407
Tempelberg (Gy), 277
Tercia (Sp), 188

Tercios (Sp), 190
Terlano (I), 222, 236
Termeno (I), 236
Terne (F), 124
Terodelgo (I), 222, 236
Les Terranges (F), 123
Terrano (I), 225
Les Terrasses (Sw), 105
Terre à Boire (Sw), 106
Terre-Ferme (F), 107
Terres-Blanches (F), 107
Teufelskeller (Gy), 259, 274
Les Teurons (F), 63, 77
Theuniskraal (S.A.), 313, 315
Thibar (Tu), 307, 315
Thierlay (Gy), 275
Thioulet (F), 107
Aux Thorey (F), 76
Thorins (F), 72
Le Thou (F), 123
Thouarcé (F), 126
Le Thoureil (F), 126
Thramon de Gron (F), 108
Thüngersheim (Gy), 262
Tielandry ou Clos-Landry (F), 77
Tiergarten (Gy), 272
Tigné (F), 126
Tinta Port (Cal), 330, 333
Tinto Basto (Sp), 188
Tio Diego (Sp), 189
– Guillermo (Sp), 189
– Mateo (Sp), 189
– Pepe (Sp), 189
Tierlei (Gy), 275
Tirnave Peari (R), 290
Tito Jaime (Sp), 189
Tocai Friulano (I), 225, 236
– di San Martino della Battaglia (I), 236
Tocayo (Sp), 189
Tokay (Cs), 290
Tokaji Aszu (3-5 puttonos) (H), 225, 289, 293
– Eszencia (H), 289
– Furmint (H), 289, 293
– Maslas (H), 289
– Szamorodni (H), 289, 293
Tokay (U.S.S.R.), 292
– d'Alsace (F), 251, 252, 269, 411
– (H), 288, 289
Tokayer Eigenbau (Sw), 268
– Hoch Chapf Eichberg (Sw), 268
– Schlossberg Villingen (Sw), 268
– Weiningen (Sw), 268
Toneless (Sp), 190
To-Night (Sp), 190
Topaz Ein Guedi (Is), 301
Top Dry (P), 213
– Honours (P), 213
La Toppe-au-Vert (F), 77
Torgiano (I), 237
La Tornale (Sw), 105
Torre Breva (Sp), 189
Torre Giulia di Cerignola (I), 238
Torrecera (Sp), 190
Tortemains (F), 124
La Touche (F), 126
De la Tour (Sw), 106
Sur la Tour (Sw), 105
Touraine (F), 119
– Mousseux (F), 361
Tour de Pierre (Sw), 269
Tourtousse (F), 107
Les Toussaints (F), 63, 77
Trafalgar Solera 1805 (Sp), 190
Trakya (T), 299, 302
Traminac (Yg), 294
Traminer (I), 222, 223, 236
– (Cal), 333
– Riesling (Aus), 341

El Trapiche (Arg), 338, 407
Trasadinger (Sw), 268
Traubengarten (Gy), 269
Trebbiano (Bz), 339
– di Abruzzo (I), 231, 237
– di Aprilia (I), 230, 237
– di Romagna (I), 237
Treize Vents (Sw), 106
Trémazières (Sw), 105
La Tremblaie (F), 124
Treppchen (Gy), 265, 275, 276
Tres Cortados (Sp), 190
Tres Palmas (Sp), 189
El Tresillo (Sp), 189
Les Tresquous (F), 107
Treuenfels (Gy), 273
Les Triottes (F), 108
Triple Cream (Cal), 333
Triunfo (Sp), 190
Trottberg (Gy), 269
Trotzenberg (Gy), 276
Le Truchet (F), 108
Trutzberg (Gy), 276
Tschugger (Sw), 269
– Pinot noir (Sw), 269
Tsinandali (U.S.S.R.), 292, 294
Tudor Medium Cream Sherry (S.A.), 316
Les Tuileries (F), 152
Tulbagher (S.A.), 315
Tulita (Sp), 189
Tummetchen (Gy), 274
Les Turcos (F), 152
Turmberg (Gy), 264
Turmgut (Sw), 247
Turquant (F), 125
La Turque (F), 108
El Tutor (Sp), 190
Twanner (Sw), 248, 269
– Auslese Johanniter (Sw), 269
– Blauburgunder (Sw), 269
– Closer (Sw), 269
– Engelwein (Sw), 269
– Engelwein pinot gris (Sw), 269
– Kapfgut Clos des Merles (Sw), 269
– Kapfgut Sous la Roche (Sw), 269
– Steinächt (Sw), 269
Twee Jongegezellen Liebfraumilch (S.A.), 313, 315
– Riesling (S.A.), 313, 315
Riesling «39» (S.A.), 313, 315
– Rose (S.A.), 316
– Spätlese (S.A.), 312, 315
– Stein (S.A.), 313, 315
– Stein Superior (S.A.), 313, 315
Tzymliansk (U.S.S.R.), 292

Übigberg (Gy), 276
Uhlbacher Götzenberg (Gy), 270
– Haldenberg (Gy), 270
– Steingrube (Gy), 270
Uhlen (Gy), 274, 277
Ulananeck (Gy), 277
Ultra (Sp), 189
– dry (Cal), 333
– Tawny (P), 213
Undhof Goldberg (A), 293
– Wieden Spät- und Auslese Grüne Veltliner (A), 293
– Wieden-Weissburgunder (A), 293
Ungeheuer (Gy), 272
Ungsberg (Gy), 275
Unkeler-Berg (Gy), 277
Unterberg (Gy), 274, 275
Unterloibener Burgstall (A), 287, 293
– Rotenberg (A), 293
Unterrain (Gy), 269
Untertürkheimer Altenberg (Gy), 270
– Blick (Gy), 270
– Diethof (Gy), 270
– Goldberg (Gy), 270

Untertürkheimer Hetzen (Gy), 270
– Mönchsberg (Gy), 270
– Semlis (Gy), 270
Urbelt (Gy), 275
Urlay (Gy), 275
Utiel-Requena (Sp), 177
La Uvita (Sp), 189
Uvrier (Sw), 105

Vacqueras (F), 106, 107
Valais Rouge (S.A.), 316
Valdepeñas (Sp), 177, 188
Valderrama (Sp), 190
Valdespino (Sp), 190
Valdobbiadene (I), 236
Valea lui Mihai (R), 294
– Târnavelor (R), 294
Valencia (Sp), 177
Valgella (I), 221, 236
Vallée Coquette (F), 124
Les Vallerots (F), 76
Vallet (F), 126
Valori (F), 107
Les Valozières (F), 77
Valpantena (I), 222, 236
Valpolicella (I), 222, 225, 236, 378, 404
Valréas (F), 107
Valrosé (S.A.), 316
Varela (Sp), 189, 190
Les Varennes (F), 123
Varna (Bg), 294
Varogne (F), 107
Varrains (F), 126
Vasconcellos (P), 213
Le Vau-Breton (F), 125
Vau et Clos (F), 107
Vau-Louis (F), 124
Vauchrétien (F), 126
Les Vaucrains (F), 49, 76
Vaucroze (F), 107
Voucroze et Vacquières (F), 107
Vaudieu (F), 107
La Vaussière (F), 107
La Vaute (F), 107
Vauvry (F), 78
Vaux-Barres (F), 124
La Vauzelle (F), 125
Veaux (F), 124
Velho Seco (P), 213
Velletri (I), 237
Veltliner 1959 (A), 288
La Venance (F), 107
Vendémiaire (Sw), 105
Venerable (Sp), 190
Les Verboisières (F), 123
Les Vercots (F), 77
Verdelho (P), 211, 212
Verdes (G), 301
Verdicchio dei Castelli di Jesi (I), 228, 237
– di Matelica (I), 228, 237
Verduzzo (I), 225, 236
Aux Vergelesses (F), 77
Les Vergers (F), 77, 78
Vergomars (F), 107
Vermentino (I), 222, 236, 242
– di Gallura (I), 238
Vernaccia di Oristano (I), 227, 238, 242
– di San Gimignano (I), 227, 237
– di Sardegna (I), 227, 238
– di Serrapetrona (I), 228, 237
Vernon (F), 107
Vernou-sur-Brenne (F), 124
Les Véroilles (F), 76
En Verseuil (F), 77
Very Dry, Old (P), 213
– White Port (P), 213
Very Old Superior (P), 213
Very Superior Old Port (P), 213

Vesargues (F), 103
Vespaiola (I), 225
Vestides (F), 107
Vesuvio (I), 238
La Viallière (F), 108
La Viborne (Sw), 106
Les Vicairies (F), 123
Vicosa Generoso Priorato (Sp), 187
Victória (P), 213
Victoria (Sp), 189
Viejo M.M.M. (Sp), 189
Vieux Cellier (Sw), 105
Vieux Château Chevrol (F), 166
– Cloquet (F), 166
– Goujon (F), 165
Vieux Collège (Sw), 105
Vieux Salquenen (Sw), 105
Vieux Sierre (Sw), 105
Vieux Sion (Sw), 105
Vieux Villa (Sw), 105
Vieux Coteaux (Sw), 106
Vieux Murs (Sw), 106
Vieux Plants (Sw), 105
Les Vignes-Chatton (F), 123
Les Vignes-Franches (F), 63, 77
Les Vignes de Ménetou (F), 123
Vignes-Morier (F), 124
Les Vignes-Rondes (F), 77
Aux Vignes-Rondes (F), 76
Villa (I), 221
Villa Bianca (S.A.), 314, 315
Le Village (F), 107
Village Saint-Jacques called «Le Clos Saint Jacques» (F), 76
Village-de-Volnay (F), 77
Villalin (F), 123
Villamarta (Sp), 189
Villa Rose (S.A.), 314, 316
La Villatte (F), 125
Villaudric (F), 151
Ville de Lausanne (Sw), 106
Vin des Chanoines (Sw), 105
– des Chevaliers (Sw), 105
– de l'Empereur (Sw), 105
– du Glacier (Sw), 93, 105
– de Haut-Pays (F), 151
Supérieur de Tunisie (Tu), 307
Rosé of Askalon (Is), 301
Viña AB (Sp), 189
– Albina Vieja reserva (Sp), 187
– Ardanza (Sp), 187
– del Carmen (Sp), 189
– del Cuco (Sp), 189
– Ercoyen (Sp), 187
– Isabel (Sp), 190
– Monty (Sp), 187
– Paceta (Sp), 187
– del Perdon (Sp), 187
– Pomal (Sp), 187
– Real (Sp), 187
– Sole (Sp), 187
– Tondonia (Sp), 187
– Vial (Sp), 187
– Vinlo (Sp), 188
– Zaco (Sp), 187
– Zaconia (Sp), 187
Vinhos Verdes (P), 199, 200
Vinho Verde Agulha (P), 212
– Alvarinho-Cepa Velha (P), 212
– Amarante (P), 212
– Aveleda - 1 R (P), 212
– C. Mendes (P), 212
– Casa do Landeiro (P), 212
– Casal Garcia (P), 212
– Casal Miranda (P), 212
– Casal de Pejeiros (P), 212
– Casal da Seara (P), 212
– Casalinho (P), 212
– Deu-la-Deu (P), 212
– Folgazão (P), 212
– Lafões (P), 212

Vinho Lagosta (P), 212
– Moura Basto (P), 212
– Quinta da Aveleda (P), 212
– Quinta do Tamariz (P), 212
– Reserva da Aveleda (P), 212
– São Gonçalo (P), 212
– Sico (P), 212
– Valverde (P), 212
– Verdeal (P), 212
Vino nobile di Montepulciano (I), 237, 411
– Rosso (Cal), 325
– Santo (G), 407
– Santo of Santorin (G), 298, 301
– Santo toscano (I), 237
Viño del Virrey (Sp), 189
Vinsobles (F), 107
Vintage Port (Cal), 333
Vintners (Sp), 190
– (Brown) (Sp), 190
– Choice (P), 189, 212, 213
Vinzel (Sw), 94, 106
La Viria (F), 108
Visan (F), 107
Viseu (P), 198
Vitoria (Sp), 190
Viva la Pepa (Sp), 189
Vlakkenberg (S.A.), 316
Vlei Sherry (S.A.), 316
Vlottenheim Estates of Vlottenberg (S.A.), 314
Vlottenheimer Honigberg (S.A.), 314, 316
– Riesling Kabinet (S.A.), 314, 315
– Schlossberg (S.A.), 314, 315
– Selected Riesling (S.A.), 315
– Sylvaner (S.A.), 314, 315
Vogelberg (Gy), 275
Vögelein (Gy), 273
Vogelsang (Gy), 270, 271, 272, 273, 274, 275, 276
Vögelsgärten (Gy), 273
Vogler (Gy), 269
Volnay (F), 63, 77
Volnay-Caillerets (F), 63
Volson (S.A.), 316
Vom Heissen Stein (Gy), 275
Vorderberg (Gy), 277

Vordere Reste (Gy), 277
Vorderer Berg (Gy), 270, 271
Vorderer Winklerberg (Gy), 269
Vöslauer Rotwein (A), 287, 293
Vosne-Romanée (F), 60, 76
Votrys (Gy), 301
Vougeot (F), 59, 76
Vouvray (F), 119, 124
– Mousseux (F), 361
Vranac (Yg), 294
Vredenburg (S.A.), 316
Vrsac (Yg), 292
Vugava (Yg), 294

Wachauer 1959 (A), 288
Wachhügel (Gy), 273
Wahrheit (Gy), 276
Wahrsager (Gy), 275
Waldulm (Gy), 254
Walenstadt Beerli Felixer am Oelberg (Sw), 268
Walkenberg (Gy), 274, 277
Walshöhle (Gy), 256
Wanne (Gy), 270
Warnenski Dimiat (Bg), 291
Warr's Nimrod Port (P), 213
Wartberg (Gy), 270
Wasserros (Gy), 265, 274
Weierbach (Gy), 275
Weilberg (Gy), 272
Weingarten (Gy), 269
Weingrube (Gy), 275
Weinhalde (Gy), 271
Weinhex (Gy), 277
Weiniger Klevner (Sw), 268
Weininger Räuschling (Sw), 268
Weinkammer (Gy), 275
Weinsack (Gy), 273
Weinsteige (Gy), 271
Weissburgunder (I), 222
Weissenberg (Gy), 277
Weissenkirchner Achleiten (A), 293
– Klaus (A), 293
Weissenstein (Gy), 275
Weisser Burgunder (A), 293
Weisser Storch Ruster Welschriesling (A), 293

Weissherbst (Gy), 255
Welbersberg (Gy), 275
Welschriesling-Spätlesen (A), 293
Wertspitz (Gy), 275
Westrum (Gy), 258, 273
Wettinger Herrenberg Blauburgunder (Sw), 268
– Kläfner (Sw), 268
– Scharten (Sw), 268
Wetzstein (Gy), 270
White Burgundy (Aus), 341
White Leipzig (S.A.), 315
White Tokay (N.Y.), 333
Wiener Nussberg (A), 286, 293
Wiesberg (Gy), 273
Wiesborn (Gy), 276
Wieshell (Gy), 265, 274
Wilberg (Sw), 246
Wilchinger Beerli (Sw), 268
Wildenberg (Gy), 271
Wildsau (Gy), 274
Wilfenberg (Gy), 271
Wilm (Gy), 273
Wingertsheck (Gy), 276
Wingertsstätte (Gy), 273
Winklerberg (Gy), 254, 269
Winterhock Stein (S.A.), 316
A Winter's Tale (Sp), 189
Wisdom (Sp), 190
– & Warter (Sp), 189
Wisdom's Choice (Sp), 190
– Cream (Sp), 190
Wisselbrunn (Gy), 263, 274
Wittel (Gy), 269
Witzenberg (S.A.), 314, 315
– Grand (S.A.), 315
– Grand Rose (S.A.), 316
– Spätlese (S.A.), 316
Wohlfahrtsberg (Gy), 271
Wohnweg (Gy), 273
Wölflein (Gy), 274
Wolfsberg (Gy), 275, 276
Wolfsdarm (Gy), 272
Wolfshöhle (Gy), 276
Wolkenstein (Gy), 270
Wölm (Gy), 273
Worrenberger Blauburgunder Rebhüsli (Sw), 268

Wülfen (Gy), 265
Wunnenstein (Gy), 270
Würgehöll (Gy), 276
Wurmberg (Gy), 270
Würzberg (Gy), 276
Würzburger Helenenberg (Gy), 276
– Marienberg (Gy), 276
Würzgarten (Gy), 265, 274, 275

Yakut Damcasi (T), 302
Yepes (Sp), 188
Ymettos (G), 301
Yvorne (Sw), 94, 105

Zagarese (I), 238
Zapfenberg (Gy), 276
Zechpeter (Gy), 272
Zeilberg (Gy), 271
Zeininger Clevner (Sw), 268
– Riesling-Sylvaner (Sw), 268
Zellerberg (Gy), 275
Zeller Schwarzer Herrgott (Gy), 256
Ziegler (Gy), 272
Ziehberg (Gy), 276
Zierfandler (A), 293
– Ried Kramer (A), 293
Zierfandler-Rotgipfler Sonnberg (A), 293
Žilavka (Yg), 292, 294
Zinfandel (Cal), 325, 329, 333
Zitsa (G), 298, 301
Zöbinger Muskat-Ottonel (A), 293
Zollhaus (Gy), 263, 274
Zonnebloem Cabernet (S.A.), 263, 315
Zonnebloem Late Harvest (S.A.), 313, 315
Zonneheimer (S.A.), 313
Lo Zucco (I), 238
Zuckerberg (Gy), 273, 275
Zuleta (Sp), 190
Zupa (Yg), 292
Zumilla (Sp), 187
Zymljansksje (U.S.S.R.), 361
Zweifelberg (Gy), 271
Zwicker, Alsace (F), 251, 252, 268

This book is published under the direction of
AMI GUICHARD

Editorial responsibility and supervision by
JOSEPH JOBÉ
in collaboration with Percy Knauth and Valerie Green

Production under the direction of
CHARLES RIESEN

Printed by Presses Centrales Lausanne S.A.

Binding by Maurice Busenhart, Lausanne

Printed in Switzerland